LLOYD'S NAUTICAL YEAR BOOK

1990

Lloyd's of London Press

LLOYD'S NAUTICAL YEAR BOOK

Editor
Harry Arnold

Editorial Assistant
Pam Wood

Advertisement Manager
Anita Sparrow

Advertisement Production
Steve Robson

Publisher
Alan Condron

The History of Lloyd's Nautical Year Book

Hints to Captains of the Mercantile Marine   1885
One edition only

The Seaman's Almanac   1892
First edition of a regular annual publication

Lloyd's Calendar   1899
First name change

Lloyd's Calendar and Nautical Year Book   1978
First year in which Nautical Year Book was incorporated into the title

Lloyd's Nautical Year Book and Calendar   1979
First year in which this became the principal title

Lloyd's Nautical Year Book   1980
First year in which this title was used alone

First year in enlarged, Royal Octavo, format   1987

3

Published by
Lloyd's of London Press Ltd.,
Sheepen Place
Colchester, Essex CO3 3LP,
England.
Telephone 0206-772277.
Telex 987321 LLOYDS G.
Facsimile 0206-46273.

Far East (Excluding Japan) —
Lloyd's of London Press (Far East) Ltd.,
Room 1101, Hollywood Centre, Hollywood Road, Hong Kong.
Telephone 5-8543222. Telex 66224 LLPFE HX.
Facsimile 5-8541538.

Germany —
Lloyd's of London Press GmbH,
59 Ehrenbergstrasse,
2000 Hamburg 50, West Germany.
Telephone 40-389723. Telex 212951 GHCO D.
Facsimile 40-386883.

U.S.A. and Canada —
Lloyd's of London Press, Inc.,
611 Broadway, Suite 523,
New York, N.Y., 10012 U.S.A.
Telephone 212-529 9500. Telex 7105812659 LLP PUB INC.
Facsimile 212-529 9826.

Typeset by Facsimile Graphics Limited,
5 Queen Street, Coggeshall, Essex CO6 1UF, England.
Printed and bound in Great Britain by William Clowes Limited, Beccles and London.

The Council of Lloyd's do not guarantee the accuracy of the information contained in Lloyd's Nautical Year Book, nor do,they accept responsibility for any errors or omissions or their consequences. Views expressed in this Year Book are not necessarily those of the Council of Lloyd's or the Publishers.

British Library Cataloguing in Publication Data

Lloyd's Nautical Year Book. — 1990 —
1. Shipping — Serials
387.5'05

ISBN 1-85044-250-9
ISSN 0952-5394

PREFACE

In this, the 1990 edition of Lloyd's Nautical Year Book, we have continued to strengthen the publication as an invaluable annual reference to developments and trends in all aspects of ship management and those professions associated with the effective operation of the shipping industry.

Looking ahead to the 1990's, new articles have been included in this edition on Financing Shipping and the Future of the LNG Trades. The position of Lloyd's of London is discussed by Mr. Murray Lawrence, the Chairman of Lloyd's. Additional space has been allocated to the constantly changing shipbuilding industry, and the developments that are taking place in ship propulsion.

As would be expected by our readers, the four key sections of the Year book which cover "The Shipping Industry, Lloyd's and Insurance, Legal and International Regulations and General Information", have been fully revised and updated to provide a comprehensive source on a vast range of subjects.

Now sold in over 70 countries worldwide, Lloyd's Nautical Year Book is moving and will continue to move to supply the reference material that an ever changing market is asking for. As always, we will welcome your suggestions for consideration for future editions.

Alan Condron
Publisher

6

CONTENTS

The Shipping Industry

Lloyd's and Insurance

Legal/International Regulations

General Information

ALPHABETICAL INDEX

Telephone 071 or 081 for Londo

From 6th May 1990, the London 01 dialling code will change to 071 (for inner London) and 081 (for outer London).

To find out the new code for a London phone or fax number (eg 01-**434** 0000), simply look up its first three digits in the table below. Against **434**, for example, you will see 071. That means 01-**434** 0000 will become 071-**434** 0000. Similarly, the table shows 01-**666** 0000 will change to 081-**666** 0000.

If the first three digits of the number you want are not in the table, please call Directory Enquiries.

First 3 digits of the number	The new code	First 3 digits of the number	The new code	First 3 digits of the number
403	071	452	081	495
404	071	453	081	496
405	071	455	081	497
406	071	456	081	498
407	071	458	081	499
408	071	459	081	500
409	071	460	081	501
420	081	461	081	502
421	081	462	081	504
422	081	463	081	505
423	081	464	081	506
424	081	466	081	507
426	081	467	081	508
427	081	468	081	509
428	081	469	081	511
429	081	470	081	512
430	071	471	081	513
431	071	472	081	514
432	071	473	071	515
433	071	474	071	517
434	071	475	081	518
435	071	476	071	519
436	071	478	081	520
437	071	480	071	521
438	071	481	071	523
439	071	482	071	524
440	081	483	071	526
441	081	484	071	527
442	081	485	071	529
443	081	486	071	530
444	081	487	071	531
445	081	488	071	532
446	081	489	071	533
447	081	490	071	534
448	081	491	071	536
449	081	492	071	537
450	081	493	071	538
451	081	494	071	539

First 3 digits of the number	The new code	First 3 digits of the number	The new code	First 3 digits of the number	The new code	First 3 digits of the number	The new code	First 3 digits of the number	The new code	First 3 digits of the number	The new code
200	081	235	071	266	071	301	081	337	081	371	071
202	081	236	071	267	071	302	081	339	081	372	071
203	081	237	071	268	071	303	081	340	081	373	071
204	081	238	071	269	071	304	081	341	081	374	071
205	081	239	071	270	071	305	081	342	081	375	071
206	081	240	071	271	071	308	081	343	081	376	071
207	081	241	071	272	071	309	081	345	081	377	071
208	081	242	071	273	071	310	081	346	081	378	071
209	081	243	071	274	071	311	081	347	081	379	071
210	071	244	071	276	071	312	081	348	081	380	071
214	071	245	071	277	071	313	081	349	081	381	071
215	071	246	071	278	071	314	081	350	071	382	071
217	071	247	071	279	071	316	081	351	071	383	071
218	071	248	071	280	071	317	081	352	071	384	071
219	071	249	071	281	071	318	081	353	071	385	071
220	071	250	071	283	071	319	081	354	071	386	071
221	071	251	071	284	071	320	071	355	071	387	071
222	071	252	071	286	071	321	071	356	071	388	071
223	071	253	071	287	071	322	071	357	071	389	071
224	071	254	071	288	071	323	071	358	071	390	081
225	071	255	071	289	071	324	071	359	071	391	081
226	071	256	071	290	081	325	071	360	081	392	081
227	071	257	071	291	081	326	071	361	081	393	081
228	071	258	071	293	081	327	071	363	081	394	081
229	071	259	071	294	081	328	071	364	081	397	081
230	071	260	071	295	081	329	071	365	081	398	081
231	071	261	071	297	081	330	081	366	081	399	081
232	071	262	071	298	081	332	081	367	081	400	071
233	071	263	071	299	081	335	081	368	081	401	071
234	071	265	071	300	081	336	081	370	071	402	071

First 3 digits of the number	The new code	First 3 digits of the number	The new code	First 3 digits of the number	The new code	First 3 digits of the number	The new code	First 3 digits of the number	The new code	First 3 digits of the number	The new code	First 3 digits of the number	The new code	First 3 digits of the number	The new code	First 3 digits of the number	The new code
40	081	584	071	635	071	679	081	732	071	783	081	839	071	889	081	946	081
41	081	585	071	636	071	680	081	733	071	785	081	840	081	890	081	947	081
42	081	586	071	637	071	681	081	734	071	786	081	841	081	891	081	948	081
43	081	587	071	638	071	682	081	735	071	788	081	842	081	892	081	949	081
44	081	588	071	639	071	683	081	736	071	789	081	843	081	893	081	950	081
45	081	589	071	640	081	684	081	737	071	790	071	844	081	894	081	951	081
46	081	590	081	641	081	685	081	738	071	791	071	845	081	897	081	952	081
47	081	591	081	642	081	686	081	739	071	792	071	846	081	898	081	953	081
49	081	592	081	643	081	687	081	740	081	793	071	847	081	900	081	954	081
50	081	593	081	644	081	688	081	741	081	794	071	848	081	902	081	958	081
51	081	594	081	645	081	689	081	742	081	796	071	850	081	903	081	959	081
52	081	595	081	646	081	690	081	743	081	798	071	851	081	904	081	960	081
53	081	597	081	647	081	691	081	744	081	799	071	852	081	905	081	961	081
54	081	598	081	648	081	692	081	745	081	800	081	853	081	906	081	963	081
55	081	599	081	650	081	693	081	746	081	801	081	854	081	907	081	964	081
56	081	600	071	651	081	694	081	747	081	802	081	855	081	908	081	965	081
58	081	601	071	653	081	695	081	748	081	803	081	856	081	909	081	968	081
59	081	602	071	654	081	697	081	749	081	804	081	857	081	920	071	969	081
60	081	603	071	655	081	698	081	750	081	805	081	858	081	921	071	974	081
61	081	604	071	656	081	699	081	751	081	806	081	859	081	922	071	976	071
62	081	605	071	657	081	700	071	752	081	807	081	861	081	923	071	977	081
63	081	606	071	658	081	701	071	754	081	808	081	863	081	924	071	978	071
64	081	607	071	659	081	702	071	755	081	809	081	864	081	925	071	979	081
66	081	608	071	660	081	703	071	756	081	811	081	866	081	927	071	980	081
67	081	609	071	661	081	704	071	758	081	818	071	868	081	928	071	981	081
68	081	618	071	663	081	706	071	759	081	819	071	869	081	929	071	983	081
69	081	620	071	664	081	707	071	760	081	820	071	870	081	930	071	984	081
70	081	621	071	665	081	708	071	761	081	821	071	871	081	931	071	985	081
71	081	622	071	666	081	709	071	763	081	822	071	874	081	932	071	986	081
72	081	623	071	667	081	720	071	764	081	823	071	875	081	933	071	987	071
73	081	624	071	668	081	721	071	766	081	824	071	876	081	934	071	988	081
74	081	625	071	669	081	722	071	767	081	826	071	877	081	935	071	989	081
75	081	626	071	670	081	723	071	768	081	828	071	878	081	936	071	991	081
76	081	627	071	671	081	724	071	769	081	829	071	879	081	937	071	992	081
77	081	628	071	672	081	725	071	770	081	831	071	881	081	938	071	993	081
78	081	629	071	673	081	726	071	771	081	832	071	882	081	939	071	994	081
79	081	630	071	674	081	727	071	773	081	833	071	883	081	940	081	995	081
80	071	631	071	675	081	728	071	776	081	834	071	884	081	941	081	997	081
81	071	632	071	676	081	729	071	777	081	835	071	885	081	942	081	998	081
82	071	633	071	677	081	730	071	778	081	836	071	886	081	943	081		
83	071	634	071	678	081	731	071	780	081	837	071	888	081	944	081		

British
TELECOM

USE THE NEW CODES FROM 6TH MAY 1990

THE SHIPPING INDUSTRY

ATLANTIC TOWING LIMITED
Saint John, New Brunswick, Canada

The Tugs *Irving Miami* (foreground) and *Irving Cedar* with a combined bollard pull in excess of 170 Tons, towing the 720 ft. Panamax Dry Dock into Halifax Harbour, Nova Scotia.

For the winter season, the ice breaking tug *Irving Cedar* (70 Tons Bollard Pull, Ice Class 1A) usually stationed near the Cabot Strait and Lower St. Lawrence and is available for towing, ice breaking and escort duties.

Atlantic Towing has a fleet of tugs available for harbour, coastal and deep sea towing, ranging up to 10,000 ihp (100 Tons Bollard Pull) and additional marine equipment such as deck barges to 3,500 dwt, and petroleum product barges, including Bunker "C" and Asphalt to 10,000 tons capacity.

300 Union Street, PO Box 5777, Saint John, E2L 4M3,
Office: (506) 648-2750, Dispatch 24hr: (506) 648-2790, Fax: (506) 632-0116, Telex: 014-47518.

THE SHIPPING INDUSTRY YEAR

As told through the pages of Lloyd's List International.
by David Burrell

Much can happen in a year although it is such a short time span. When first thinking back over the past twelve months it appeared little had happened, such is the limitation of human memory. However leafing through Lloyd's List and picking the major changes and trends clearly illustrates how events are moving. Although many have been pessimistic the year has seen steady movement in the right direction with improved outlook for shipowners and builders, especially if viewed in the context of a longer time span.

The August 1988 ceasefire in the Gulf War between Iran and Iraq must take its place as the most important event of the period. The eight years of conflict had not only brought both countries to their knees but also had major influence on shipping in the area, especially the tanker trades. So many ships have ben lost and damaged by belligerent action with, regretably, loss of over 400 lives among seamen. Tension was high to the last, especially following the shooting down of an Iranian Airbus by the USS *Vincennes* early in July. Peace in the Gulf has been credited with the price rise noted for general cargo vessels.

Ownership Changes

In Britain the contraction of the national flag fleet continued. Following British & Commonwealth's withdrawal from shipowning a further break with the past came when Blue Funnel (Ocean Transport & Trading plc) completed a policy of selling off their shipping interests that effectively signalled their final withdrawal from deep-sea shipping. Having already sold Straits Steamship, then their interest in OCL to P&O, they parted with their 32% share of Barber Blue Sea to Wilh Wilhemlmsen (the two ships employed going with the service) and in late February 1989 announced the sale, with no ships, of their West African interest (Elder Dempster Lines, Palm Line and Guinea Gulf Line) to the French Delmas Vieljeux group. Ocean's shipping interests, after these sales and disposal of their 50% interest in John Kelly Ltd to Powel Duffryn in March 1989, is now limited to the oil supply vessels of O.I.L. and Cory Towage.

The position of shipowners in the British economy has changed beyond all recognition in little more than thirty years. From the mid 1960s their withdrawal from both the tramping and dry bulk sectors has been followed by a decline in the tanker market due to the rise in oil prices and consequent overtonnaging. At the same time entry into the Common Market saw the importance of routes to the Commonwealth wane and European trade grow, to the benefit of ferry and short sea operators. As a result in 1986 British owners foreign currency earnings of £3.23 billion had to be offset against £4.3 billion paid to foreign owners, leaving a net deficit of £1.1 billion. In an endeavour to reverse the trend the Business Expansion Scheme introduced incentives to encourage investment in shipping, resulting in several new undertakings associated with established owners. New names include Bromley Shipping, Edinburgh Tankers, Altnacraig Shipping and, from the Everard stable, Short Sea Europe.

Elsewhere ownership changes were also to be noted. In Sweden Bilspedition moved in rapid steps from nothing to being the country's largest shipowner. A truly impressive entry into shipowning! Having taken control of Cool Carriers, the world's largest reefer operation, in January 1988 they followed in August by purchasing a 72% holding in Transatlantic and finally in December "iced the cake" with the forest products carrier Gorthon Lines. Within a year three purchases took Bilspedition from being a land carrier to control of some one hundred ships. Will next year see them developing wider European ambitions?

Other major changes of ownership will be noted when we turn our mind to the cruise industry. In Britain the sale of Houlder Offshore by the Tung Group continued to feature from time to time. In the sale of non-core assets following the near collapse of the Group Houlder Offshore was in the process of sale to China Merchants Holdings and then on to the French Foralso-Foramer Group. This sale collapsed and at the time of writing the result of bids from Stena Offshore, The Mosvold Group and Exmar are awaited. The summer of 1988 also saw the disappearance of Dart and Manchester Liners from the North Atlantic. Part of Tung's Orient Overseas Container Line since the takeover of Furness Withy in 1980 it was a logical step to incorporate them into the skein of OOCL routes.

In Brazil the sale of Lloyd Brasileiro, with mounting losses, was proposed but suspended following remedial action. However, in New Zealand the nationally owned New Zealand Shipping Coporation was placed on the market. Interest was reported from Lloyd Triestino, Australian National Line, Associated Container Transportation and P&O Containers. Finally the bid chosen in 1989 was that submitted by ACT.

Brief reports reminded us of the problems in past years. In Hong Kong the Wah Kwong restructuring began to show results. Further east in Japan Sanko continued the climb back from their 1985 collapse while in Denmark DFDS continued their recovery from the edge of bankruptcy five years ago.

An interesting development has been the sale by Burmah Oil of a half interest in their Indonesia to Japan LNG trade to Mitsui-OSK Lines. Another oil company transaction has been the withdrawal of Marathon Petroleum from shipowning. They retained one vessel on a sale and charter back basis. Four of their ships went as a block to Bergvall & Hudner, New York, one of the modern style managers who have floated three equity funds totalling $130 million in the last three years for investment in shipping. For future implementation Sealink secured an option to purchase the SNCF ferries when the French company withdrew to concentrate on the Channel Tunnel.

Containership — Future Overtonnaging

A build up of orders for container ships caused the spectre of an overtonnaging crisis to loom for a few years hence, as 60% of the cellular fleet has been built since 1980. Many large "post-Panamax" vessels were to be noted in the list of ordered or planned vessels, demand for which is expected to accelerate into the 1990s. Projections for the next decade, and the quest for economy of scale, suggest 85 ships of between 3,000 and 4,000 TEU and 34 of over 4,000 TEU will enter service whilst talk has been of designs up to 6,000 TEU. Malcolm McLean, whose twelve 4,400 TEU fleet caused the collapse of United States Lines, appears to have anticipated this trend a few years too early.

At the head of the list Evergreen confirmed an order for eleven (originally, and possibly yet to be, double that number) GU type 4,000 TEU ships to run on their round-the-world service with the 23 smaller (27000-3400 TEU) vessels currently employed. The ACE consortium doubled their capacity on the Europe to Far East run, totally retonnaging with eight 3,200 TEU ships. Strong growth and extra tonnage on this route poses a threat to stability and the conference. Other orders or plans

American President Lines J9-class containership *President Eisenhower*

Norwegian cruise liner *Sovereign of the Seas*

included Hapag-Lloyd for five 4,400 TEU to be built by Samsung to replace five smaller 2,900 TEU in TRIO service and Nedlloyd's fifteen ship $750 milion project (five each 3,000 TEU, 3,800 TEU and 4,600 TEU for 1991—4 delivery).

In February 1989 the list of likely orders stood at nearly 140 ships of approaching 400,000 TEU. One commentator stated "There is no way the world's trade routes will be able to sustain this volume of tonnage over the next few years without scrapping". With the age pattern of ships scrapping on any scale appears unlikely. The scene is likely to be further confused as the sizes of containers proliferate from the ISO 20 and 40 foot to include 48, 49 and 53 ft standards.

The Elusive Search for Economy

The search for economy and competitiveness continued. The strike of P&O ferry crews at Dover continued, albeit with decreasing media interest, while quietly their ferry fleet returned to service under the new crewing arrangements. The Government commenced to prepare for the abolition of the Dock Labour Scheme, with predictable union response. Established in 1947 at 84 ports with 79,000 dockers the changing world has seen the number shrink to just more than 9,000 men. Removal of this archaic anomoly will enable some British ports to become competitive in the European port industry and recover some of their past glory.

Owners continued to move ships to offshore registers, Stephenson Clarke planned the transfer of 14 ships to the Isle of Man, as did also T & J Harrison with the last of their British flag ships. The transfer of their fleet to Denholm management saw yet another British owner complete their withdrawal from ship operations. Blue Star employed another method, the sale of *Southland Star* and *Wellington Star* to Fiji and lease back with Fijian crews replacing British.

The popular offshore registers continued to proliferate and grow in size. On its first anniversary the Norwegian International Register was able to announce the transfer of over 250 ships in the year. Poland mooted a second register for Western Europe, other European countries floating second registers included West Germany and Denmark, while Portugal introduced Madeira and, further afield, Macao. The Gambia also entered the lists and Belgium turned to Luxembourg for offshore registry of its fleets. With the growing strength of the Common Market it will be interesting to see how long before a European flag and registry is established.

Shipbuilding

No clear single pattern could be seen, optimism in certain areas was balanced by problems elsewhere. The world order book in the autumn of 1988 with nearly 24 million tons was the highest for two years. Of this total South Korea accounted for 27% and Japan a further 24%, although there was still pressure to reduce capacity in those countries. Forecasts optimistically expect orders to double as demand for tonnage soars after 1995. The country to benefit most could be China where output has doubled from 1981 to 1987 (1.92 million tons) and is expected to increase to 4 million tons in the next decade.

The single headline of greatest consequence must be the take over of Sulzer Diesel by MAN-B&W. Adding the Swiss builder of low speed marine engines to the combined German-Danish group creates a virtual world monopoly in the supply of such machinery as between them, they control, directly or through licencing arrangments, 90% of the market.

In the United States Matson's interest in ordering a new lift on-lift off/bulk/ro-ro vessel for their service to Hawaii heralded the prospect of a return to merchant shipbuilding, the last American order having been the three SeaLand ships in 1987 for the Alaska route.

The first half of 1988 had seen a doubling of Japan's foreign order book, while in March 1988 the domestic order list at 33 ships had tripled. However, Ishikawajima-Harima Heavy Industries and Sumitomo, both Sulzer licences, merged their engine building facilities as Diesel United. Japan engine builders reduced their capacity by 19%. At the same time Mitsubishi Heavy Industries announced a rationalisation programme to reduce jobs by 1,900 by September 1989. For the first time the number of shipyard workers fell below 20,000, in seven major yards. In April 1985 the number was 41,580, by April 1988 it had fallen to 18,390.

South Korea's pursuit of orders at the expense of profit led to financial troubles at both Daewoo and Korea Shipbuilding. Rescue operations saw the Hanjim Group set to take over Korea Shipbuilding at Pusan. Other builders endeavoured to overcome the problem of low fixed prices by re-negotiating contracts, not always with success.

European Shipbuilding

The European scene had one interesting problem. The Lenin Yard at Gdansk was scheduled to close, then reprieved. This was followed by the appointment of a liquidator, with closure mooted for the end of 1990, and major restructuring plans. The outcome of such a situation in a socialist climate will be watched with interest. In France the Normed Group, formed in 1982 by the merger of three builders, slowly wound down after their June 1986 receivership with the La Seyne yard taken over as an extension to the Toulon Naval Base and La Ciotat closing. Further north Finland's three shipbuilders considered a merger which came to nothing. After decades of good business and continuous Russian orders the loss of these left a cold wind blowing through the yards. Italian builders reported 18 domestic orders, a welcome injection after political wrangling had caused a two year blight of orders.

The year has witnessed the final phase of the privatisation of British Shipbuilders. In August 1988 the Govan yard passed to Kvaerner Industrier of Norway and the three berths have been reduced to two prior to laying the keels of two gas carriers in the summer of 1989. The most traumatic scene was North East Shipbuilders at Sunderland where the fraught Danish "Superflex" ferry order was finally cancelled, the last one launched in December 1988, and fifteen left in yard hands. During the course of the year it was possible to sell these vessels to interested parties in Denmark and Norway. Bids included one from Alex Copson with plans to build a series of waste disposal "bucket boats", not welcomed in today's environmental atmosphere. Their phantom Cuban order for ten ships continued to refuse to take on a more solid character. With the final closure of North East Shipbuilders this left Kvaerner's Govan yard as the only British building of large merchant ships. Clarke Kincaid's engine works finally went to a management buyout, who later acquired Ferguson's Port Glasgow yard as well.

Harland & Wolff, Belfast, although no part of British Shipbuilders, were also listed for transfer to the private sector. Possible bidders included Ravi Tikkoo with his "Ultimate Dream" cruise ship project — the number of bids for various yards linked to orders led to the flippant comment "Build a ship — take a shipyard free". So far the "Ultimate Dream" has failed to become anything more than a dream as Government subsidy on the scale requested ($200 million) was not forthcoming as it had been in 1970 for the Tikkoo tankers Globtik London and Globtik Tokyo. Various British and foreign bidders were reported, ultimately a management bid back by a 45% participation from Fred Olsen of Norway surfaced as the winners with transfer set for

September 1989.

An interesting trend was the continued planning of passenger carrying cellular container or ro-ro ships, the modern equivalent of the old cargo-passenger liner. Ivaran Lines' *Americana*, running on their service from the United States to South America with nearly 90 passengers and 1120 containers has been followed by orders for between two and five others. This lead has also been followed by the Grimaldi Group's *Republica di Genova* and *Republica di Amalfi* built by Fincantieri. Modern ro-ro container carriers of 37,000 gt they have accommodation for 54 passengers on the Grimaldi/Cobefret service from Europe to West Africa and Grimaldi's Brazilian run.

The interest in speed seems slowly to be reviving after the period of high oil prices had thrown economy into the premier position. Japanese Government funds were allocated to finance the prototype of a 45-knot fast cargoship to carry 250 containers. Designed round a 112 metre semi-submerged hull with a displacement of 14,000 tons the idea is to cross the Pacific in 100 hours.

Laid up vessels

The recommissioning of laid up tonnage has steadiily, if not spectacularly, eroded the number and tonnage of idle ships. In October 1988 the tonnage out of commission fell below ten million for the first time in fifteeen years and in December it was noted that the total had fallen every month for the previous seventeen months. Compare this with the 1983 peak of 100 million tons laid up, including 83 million in the form of 537 tankers. Such low figures have not been seen since before the oil price rises of 1973. Numerical the bulk of laid up tonnage is older general cargo vessels with a few bulkers (in the summer of 1988 there were about two dozen bulkers laid up of some 880,000 dwt). In January 1989 tankers included six VLCC and two ULCC, which compares with 148 and 62 six years ago.

With the end of the Gulf War the future of the ships employed on the Gulf Shuttle could impinge on the recommissioning record as nearly 11 million tons (42 ships) were in use bringing oil down the Gulf plus 3.75 million tons (12 ships) as storage vessels. Their return to lay up was delayed by the need to rebuild the Kharg Island and other war damaged facilities. The rising demand for tonnage also gave hope that further employment would emerge as they were slowly released from their Gulf duties.

Shipbreaking

With the increasing buoyancy in the marine market the numbers sold for demolition has shown a spectacular fall. When figures for 1988 were finally compiled they were 65% down on the previous year, making 1988 the lowest since the mid 1970s. The total of 370 ships of 6.1 million tons (deadweight) included 55 tankers of 3.175 million tons and 53 bulkers of 1.514 million tons. In May 1989 the demoliton trade was simply described as at a standstill, with totals expected to end the year at half those for 1988.

In June 1988 the 206,000 dwt *Stilikon* was sold to Taiwan breakers, the first VLCC of the year. This compares with one a week only a few years ago — in 1985 Taiwan broke up 18 million tons of tankers. The future role of Taiwan in the breaking trade was placed in doubt as the Kaohsiung port authorities gave notice to vacate two thirds of the 36 demoliton berths to make way for extension to the container port. As in shipbuilding the role of mainland China looks set to grow as the market changes radically. It may well be that as the clearing of the Shatt Al Arab releases many war damaged ships they will find their way east to China.

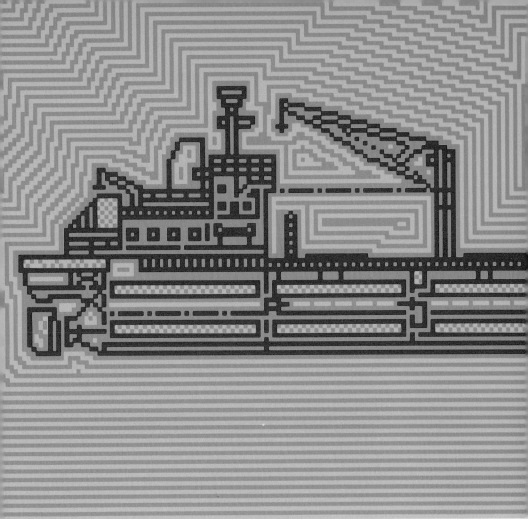

About being technically competitive.

Our marketing managers are well known, and we hope appreciated, by shipowners all over the world. But even the best marketing man cannot succeed in this harsh and competitive shipbuilding business if he is not backed, among others, by the most appropriate technology.

Did you know that the five 140,000 dwt. tankers under construction include superoptimized hydrodynamic shapes leading to large reductions in installed power over conventional systems?

Did you know that Astilleros is building nine freezers for Del Monte that consume only 124.5 gr bhp/h and can burn fuel up to 6000 Redwood No. 1 at 100°F?

Did you know that, through engine room automation, automatic manoeuvring (AUT-PORT notation) and control systems including CRT's for monitoring all spaces, some of our constructions may be operated by between 10% and 22% less crew than in conventional constructions?

While some yards complain about lack of orders, our yards are growing steadily in newbuildings.

Astilleros continues to make a genuine contribution to the expansion of Spain, the fastest growing economy in Europe...Marketing? Technical excellence?

The answer is Astilleros. Check on us.

ASTILLEROS ESPAÑOLES

For further information: Astilleros Españoles, S.A.
Padilla, 17
28006 Madrid
Tel. (341) 435 78 40
Telex. 27648 ASTIL-E
Fax: (341) 276 29 56

The Shipbuilders of Spain

Marine casualties

The casualty record for 1988 is dealt with by Norman Hooke elsewhere in this Year Book. Meanwhile after eight years the report on the loss of *Derbyshire* was finally published; with a conclusion "overwhelmed by forces of nature" the reaction of crew relatives was predictable. Later, in the aftermath of the *Herald of Free Enterprise* tragedy seven Sealink P&O ferries were identified as failing to meet the stability tests carried out on all pre-1980 build vessels.

While the loss of vessels like *Derbyshire* and *Berge Istra* is widely publicised the risk of going to sea was quantified when the 26,000 dwt bulker *Singa Sea* disappeared in July 1988 after leaving Bunbury with mineral sand for Rotterdam. A month later six survivors from her Philippino crew of 27 were picked up by *Standard Virtue* 200 miles west of Fremantle. Examination of the loss records indicates over 160 bulkers have been lost since 1980, an average of one every two months. With many of these large bridge aft vessels masters at the stern are unaware of happenings at the bow, where slamming can cause extensive damage before anyone is aware of it.

The first installation of Lloyd's Register's "black box" on the Wescol managed container ship *Gulf Spirit* was reported — I wonder how long it will be before data from such a source figures in a court of inquiry for the first time.

October 1988 saw the Philippine based Sulpico Lines lose their ferry *Dona Marilyn* in typhoon Ruby. With over 500 passengers and crew only 185 survivors were reported. Fresh from the sinking of *Dona Paz* the previous December when over 4,000 were lost this fresh publicity was of an unwelcome nature. However it served to highlight the loss of over 5,000 lives in Philippine ferry disasters in recent years, including five of the worst disasters of the 1980s. In addition to the *Dona Paz* and *Dona Marilyn* these include the *Dona Cassandra* in 1983 and *Venus* in 1984. Another serious tragedy in 1988 was the Indonesian *Bintang Madura* when over 200 lives were lost. On 21 October 1988 what could have been a catastrophe happened at Piraeus when the Epirotiki Lines cruise vessel *Jupiter* was sunk in collision with the Italian car carrier *Adige*.

The dangerous nature of many commodities carried by ship has been highlighted by losses such as *Anna Broere*, a chemical tanker sunk in the North Sea in collison with *Atlantic Compass*. There were fears of environmental pollution and damage before she was raised in pieces by Smit Tak and sold to Belgian owners for rebuilding. This was followed in March 1989 by the sinking of the *Perintis* northwest of Guernsey. Amongst her cargo was a container containing six tons of lindane which was lost overboard as she sank. A month later four of the five crew of *Belgrave* were killed by fumes from her apparently innocent cargo of scrap. Another nightmare on a horrendous scale started on 23 March 1989 when the tanker *Exxon Valdez* grounded in Alaska's Prince William Sound after loading at Valdez. Despite efforts to contain the consequent pollution the damage both to the environment and fishing industries was extensive. Alongside this the declaration of the car carrier *Reijin* as a total loss was minor — Smit Tak and Bugsier were commissioned to remove this 58,000 ton vessel lost on her maiden voyage.

Under the heading of marine casualties it might be appropriate to refer to the disposal of toxic waste. This ever growing world problem has been tackled at times by shipping and dumping the material in Third World or other innocent destinations. Publicity is curbing this practice and led to the *Karin B* travelling round Europe like a pariah until her cargo was returned to Italy, whence she had originally loaded it. Later four toxic waste ships, *Isola Turchese*, *Mare Equatoriale*, *Isola Blu* and *Isola Celeste* were arrested at Manfredonia where they were loading waste from the Government controlled Enichem for shipment to Sardinia.

General view of the Harland & Wolff shipbuilding, engineering and ship repair complex at Queen's Island. Belfast

Piracy

Although, often little is reported, the scale of piracy and terrorism at sea can be gauged from occasional reports, like the holding of the German tug *Fairplay IX* by Philippine pirates and the seizure of the master of the Singapore flag containership *Hai Hui* from his vessel east of Singapore. Possibly better known are incidents such as the attack on the Greek ferry *City of Poros* at Piraeus when eight were killed and the recapture of the Maldivian *Progress Light* by Indian troops after an attempted coup in the Maldive Islands.

The disappearance of the *Bona Vista No 1* in September 1988 with a cargo of steel and pvc valued at $3.5 million, while on passage from Kaohsiung to China, reminds us of the continued deviation of ships and theft of their cargo. In the past Lebanon has been one of the most publicised destinations but today the Far East appears to have a highly organised racket with at least eleven ships with cargo valued at some $2 million each disappearing since the summer of 1987. It is believed that some of these are phantom ships which change name and identity regularly to enable them to repeat the fraud by picking up cargo from more innocent victims.

The Cruise Industry

Beginning in 1987 the cruise companies went through eighteen months of intense ordering. The result was a January 1988 order book of 28 vessels representing investment of $2.7 billion. With such an order book and the threat of overcapacity some form of rationalisation looked on the cards.

The "dark horse" throughout this period was P&O who were not amongst those placing orders. They played their hand in the summer of 1988 with the announcement of a $210 million deal to take over Sitmar Cruises from the Vlasov Group. Adding a fleet of four operating plus three building to P&O's own Princess Cruises produced the world's largest cruise group. Their fleet of ten ships with 9,770 berths placed Royal Caribbean Cruise Lines with eight ships and 9,000 berths second, with Carnival Cruise Lines, Kloster Cruises, Holland America Line and Cunard Cruises following in that order.

The new *status quo* was to have little time before being ruffled again. Within a month Carnival Cruise Lines bid $260 million for Gotaas Larsen's cruise interests promised to usurp the premier role. Larsen's one-third share in Royal Caribbean Cruise Line and 51% of Admiral Cruises (or a 36% share following the planned merger of Royal and Admiral) promises Carnival the chance to influence a fleet twice the size of P&O and a market share of 25% by 1991. Additionally Carnival's "Tiffany Project" for three 45,000 ton vessels added to their future potential. It came as no surprise to read of Carnival's next move, to increase their Royal Admiral holding to 70% by buying a second major partner, I.M. Skaugen, and some minority stakes for $567 million. At this stage the third major partner, Anders Wilhelmsen, exercised an option to retain control. Within a few months Wilhelmsen was able to complete the financial package, with investment from Hyatt Hotels and others, and withdrew Royal Admiral from Carnival's hands. At the same time Royal Admiral announced plans to build two sisters to *Sovereign of the Seas* at Chantiers de l'Atlantique for 1991 delivery, although one was later amended to a possible smaller vessel. Their cost, $300 million each, compares with *Sovereign of the Seas* priced at $180 million when ordered in 1985.

Rather overshadowed by the big league Holland America Line followed their takeover of Home Lines by absorbing Wind Star Sail Cruises in the autumn of 1988, adding the three 148 berth sailing cruise ships *Wind Star*, *Wind Song* and *Wind Spirit* to their own fleet of *Rotterdam*, *Nieuw Amsterdam*, *Noordam* and *Westerdam* (ex *Homeric*). They followed this with an order for two 1,876 berth ships to Bremer

Vulkan at $270 million each. Then, on the rebound from their failed Royal Admiral bid, Carnival Cruise Lines ended 1988 by completing a $625 million takeover of Holland America Line to move into the top slot as the largest operator with over 14,000 berths. One casualty of this was the Bremer Vulkan order which was cancelled in the face of Carnival's already heavy commitment to new tonnage.

The league table when the dust settled indicated the four main cruise operators would control over half the world capacity, estimated to be 105,000 berths at the end of 1991. The list is —

1 - Carnival/Holland America	13,000 berths plus	9,630 building
2 - P&O/Sitmar	9,770	4,670
3 - Royal Admiral	9,000	1,600
4 - Kloster (Norwegian Cruise/ Royal Viking)	8,400	750
Total	40,170	16,650

Expansion has been followed by rationalisation; the only major name in the business which has failed to play has been Cunard Cruises who have concentrated on serving the customer; but what plans may they have for the coming year? In May 1989 they were noted as considering building three new cruise ships. P&O are also worth watching, will they build a sister t the 1984 built *Royal Princess* or utilise the newbuildings taken over with Sitmar? They also have the ageing *Canberra* dating from 1962. Approaching 30 years of age her replacement by one means or another must be uppermost in P&O's research projects.

Amongst the smaller cruise operators it is interesting to note the growing Japanese presence. In 1989 Showa Line commissioned the 120 passenger, 5,200 gt *Oceanic Grace*, while Mitsui O.S.K. Lines took delivery of the 600 berth, 23,500 gt *Fuji Maru* and ordered a sister from Mitsubishi for 1990 delivery. Mitsubishi also had in hand the larger 960 berth, 49,000 gt *Crystal Harmony* for 1990 delivery to N.Y.K.'s Los Angeles based Crystal Cruises.

Various novel designs for the 1990s flitted on and off stage, as elusive as ever. These included Kloster Cruises *Phoenix World City* being discussed with a consortium of German builders. With a price tag reported at $1 billion she was presented as a 380 metre, 250,000 gt giant accommodating 5,600 passengers and 1,800 crew. A marina built into the afterbody would accommodate four 400 passenger tenders and make her independent of shore support at ports of call. Smaller, at 160,000 gt, was Ravi Tikkoo's *Ultimate Dream*, priced at half the *Phoenix* estimate. Also equipped with two 400 passenger tenders, her name has been linked with the privatisation of Harland & Wolff. With either of these dreams see the light of day? A wide variety of influences will play vital roles in this. The financial package that can be put together to finance construction, the level of any state subsidy — as has been mentioned earlier under the shipbuilding heading with Tikkoo seeking a $200 million subsidy to build his *Ultimate Dream* at Belfast — and the perceived state of the cruise market in the coming decade with the many newbuildings coming into service and the level of customer demand. Placing these all in perspective is the juggling match to be undertaken by the interested parties.

Looking back, then, over the past year to the early summer of 1988 can leave us quietly optimistic. Many major changes have taken place, the general trend has been to the benefit of shipowners and the political climate would appear to suggest that this trend can continue for some time to come.

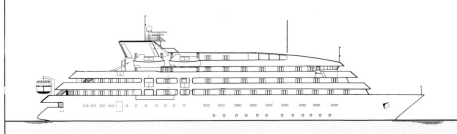

SHIPPING — AN INDUSTRY WITH A NEW LEASE ON LIFE

by Dr Helmut Sohmen

Chairman, World-Wide Shipping Agency Ltd.; Chairman, Hong Kong Shipowners Association; ex
President, Baltic and International Maritime Council (BIMCO)

The message I would like to place at the beginning of these remarks is that international shipping in all its variety and global reach is really *one* industry, where individual decisions *can*, and in fact very quickly *do* determine the collective well-being of all participants. So while we as shipowners often pride ourselves on our individualism and risk preference, we should remember that the very factors that make this highly mobile, competitive and international business so exciting also makes it both very transparent and very cohesive. Modern technology, facilitating better communications will make this even more so, but a few more comments on that later.

The conclusions we should draw from this situation are threefold:

Firstly, commercial decisions by the market participants are normally subject to both early imitation and positive feed-back and can quickly establish market trends even though by themselves they are not generally able to have a direct or immediate influence on market behaviour.

Secondly, the industry should recognise its unity through more rational representation than we have today.

Thirdly, national governments as well as supra-national bodies must accept that they should not deal with the shipping industy in a fragmented or piece-meal fashion — or look at shipping only in terms of national aspirations, in specific geographic or socio-economic contexts, or on a scale of purely local priorities. Much too often in the last decade has the wider industry become the object of political tugs-of-war which have tended to result in an encroachment on the traditional freedom of the seas and in government interference in commercial decision-making.

Governments do not, by and large, improve economy and efficiency by intervening, even in circumstances where there is need for regulatory intercession which ultimately has to be accepted. Often that need is not there or not proven and the distortions to the normal interplay of market forces becomes that much greater, without corresponding benefits.

The industry unquestionably supports the endeavours to improve operational and safety standards, and has — despite the major financial sacrifices required at a particularly difficult time for shipowners — accepted the measures proposed to combat environmental pollution. The work of the International Maritime Organization (IMO) has generally been lauded as pragmatic, non-partisan, and largely effective — albeit at times excessive. The industry rightly asks why UNCTAD, for example, has to get involved in charter party drafting work, or why the Code of Conduct for Liner Conferences should, by supranational dictum, be extended to the carriage of goods in bulk. Or why shipowners still often cannot hire the best-qualified personnel for their ships but must give preference to nationals of the flag state.

Easy prey

Because of their visibility, and the siimple way in which their ships can be found and legally attached wherever they sail, shipowners are easy prey for national governments pursuing specific policies, and not just those that are revenue-inspired like the infamous U.S. Tax Reform Act. Shipowners are frequently becoming the "fall guys" for governments in their quest to achieve goals in other spheres. It seems to me that the standard of diligence expected of shipowners is being raised all the time through a constant increase in the degree of legal liability that is being imposed by legislation, by court decisions, or by international conventions. Let me only mention a few recent examples, such as the U.S. Drug Abuse Act of 1986 (where the shipowner is mandated to exercise "the highest degree of care and diligence" to prevent drug smuggling on his vessels, in order to be able to avoid large fines or the seizure of his ship), the concerted push for the adoption of the Hamburg Rules (which would shift liability for cargo claims substantially onto shipowners and destroy a rational regime of sharing that has built up over many decades), heavy sanctions in pollution cases based on claims that are often nothing more than legal blackmail, the greater responsibility demanded by underwriters for the reporting on ship conditions and the timeliness of Classification Society surveys to maintain effective insurance cover, or the liability for personal injury cases, no matter how stretched the casual connection with the ship. I believe the industry needs to defend itself strongly against *unjustified* or outright *spurious* attempts (and I use these words with purpose) to force it to pay for events over which it has little or no control simply to satisfy various, sometimes contradictory, national or international aspirations. That many of the substantive issues must necessarily be accepted and supported also by the shipping community is *not* the point; I merely wish to argue that shipowners should not have to carry a disproportionate financial burden to the rest of society just because they and their assets are easier or more prominent targets.

Dawn of a new era

At the end of a period of profound misery and the dawn of a new era for the shipping world, it may be useful to briefly take stock of our current situation and see where difficulties may lie during the next few years. Clearly we should avoid creating another set of circumstances like the one in the 1970's which gave rise to the fundamental imbalance between tonnage supply and demand. I am not at all sure that the lessons learned during the years of depresison will be remembered for very long. It is as fundamental a part of human nature to forget pain quickly as it is to repeat mistakes. Indeed, the liquidation of many old-established shipping enterprises during the past 14 years, the further internationalisation of shipping through a move away from the traditional maritime nations, the upheavals in the oil industry, and the more intensive involvement (often very involuntary) of financial institutions in the business, have produced a new generation of shipping people for whom a good market is a relative novelty, the long-term employment of ships a curiosity, and ships themselves just like any other portfolio of investments to be traded at frequent intervals as market prices dictate. These new shipping people see the separation of ownership and management of ships more and more as the norm rather than the exception. They are confronted with novel financing techniques, although in reality many of them nothing more than variations on the old themes but with trendy new terminology. There are also new legal arrangements to dress up shipping ownership and the employment of ships.

It is indisputable that there is a discernible trend in shipping towards professional management acting as a very separate and distinct class from beneficial owners who more often than not consist of an annonymous group of investors not interested in ships *per se* but only in whatever income, capital gains, or tax advantages they can produce. This is not necessrily a bad thing. Shipping just hapens to be moving finally into the modern age in following the developments of those other industries where the necessary total capital commitments have become of a size that are beyond the capacity of most individuals, and where the resultant need for a pooling of financial resources has led to a larger number of stakeholders and the consequential

Which cargo would you load first?

NYK's proprietary vanning software gives the right answer right away.

NYK's Optimum Vanning System graphically produces the most efficient vanning plans for various cargo sizes and weights in the containers of your choice. So you'll always know the perfect sequence for ideal loading.

NYK clients can achieve close to 100% loading efficiency. And can expect to cut their shipping costs by 5%. And vanning time by about 80%. Container quantities are exact and the best package sizes can be precisely determined. Significant savings in time and money are assured.

The Optimum Vanning System is only one of NYK's many advanced services providing truly better answers for our clients.

Point-to-point total global services.

NYK LINE
NIPPON YUSEN KAISHA

■ **Head Office:** Tokyo, Japan Tel. (03) 284-5151 ■ **London Branch:** Tel. (01) 283-2099 ■ **Res. Reps.:** Hamburg: Tel. (40) 3593148 Düsseldorf: Tel. (0211) 370803 **Oslo:** Tel. (033) 2-3000 **Paris:** Tel. (01) 4285-1900 **Milan:** Tel. (2) 864416 **Athens & Middle East:** Tel. (1) 452-3646 ■ **Agents:** London: Van Ommeren UK Limited, Tel. (01) 594-7191 **Hamburg:** Van Ommeren Hamburg GmbH, Tel. (40) 35 930 **Rotterdam:** Van Ommeren Rotterdam B.V., Tel. (010) 464-9111 **Le Havre:** Worms Services Maritimes, Tel. 35-535300 **Milan:** Agenzia Marittima Clivio S.R.L. Tel. (2) 8057941 ■ **Overseas Affiliates** •NYK International PLC.: Tel. (01) 929-2925 •NYK Bulkship (Europe) Ltd.: Tel. (01) 495-5252

development of managers to look after their collective interests. The benefits are obvious: ownership is reduced to a formalisitic legal and accounting relationship that is unencumbered by any emotional attachment to the assets themselves which were either the hallmark or the downfall, depending on how you look at it, of the traditional shipowner. Professional corporate management is now normally being watched carefully and regularly for its ability to deliver good results. The old-fashioned shipowner only had to wrestle with his own conscience, and with the displeasure of his creditors *only* when things went terribly wrong — by which time it was of course already too late! There is something to be said for the gut feeling of the legendary shipping tycoon who is flexible and makes strong and fast decisions just by following instincts. But as we all know, more is at stake today, and the shipping world, like all other commercial endeavours, has become a lot more complex, substantially increasing the chances for error and demanding a wider level of technical knowledge and competence.

However, there is another side to the coin. Normally a strong sense of caution is present when gambling with one's very own money. That caution is not perhaps so readily apparent when it happens to be somebody else's dollars. And the relentless pressure to "produce" good corporate results and managerial "coups" at frequent intervals, a feature especially noticeable among publicly-listed companies under the constant scrutiny of share analysts, can also translate into the taking of greater risks, into accelerated expansion and higher gearing. It removes the final responsibility for ships and their personnel as operating entities at least one step, and leaves financiers with the dilemma whether to ultimately rely on the beneficial owners or the managers for their assessment of the credit risk. A large number of new entrants into the industry with easy access to capital but less know-how of the pitfalls of shipping may also result in more pronounced market cycles. Certainly the more rapid transfer of vessel ownership over a given time will not necessarily improve ship conditions or find consistent operating standards. Still, I believe the growth of shipmanagement services will continue, encouraged also by the move on a broader scale to flags-of-convenience situations and the now very significantly higher vessel replacement costs.

In contrast to some other shipping commentators, I am not particularly worried about the availability of capital to rejuvenate the world fleet in the next decade. Where a good case can be made for new investments, the necessary funds *will* be generated even if we are talking potentially in many billions of U.S. dollars. As we have seen not so long ago, with often very unhappy consequences, capital has been available even where there has been *no* case or only a *bad* case for the purchase of vessels, both old and new. I am afraid that many of the new financial promoters today who prophesise financing bottlenecks do so only to get investors, including shipowners to subscribe to their imaginative schemes. These schemes usually have high up-front costs with no risk for the promoters; the market and operating risks are left with the shipping managers.

Let us be realistic. While many governments have by now learned the political penalties of direct subsidisation, indirect subsidies to shipping continue on a broad front. Stock market activity is expanding around the world, and long-term credit is also procurable even in the absence of any period employment for vessels. Money is not a constraint and collectively we should be grateful for high newbuilding prices for keeping the potential of new tonnage supply in check; otherwise I fear we would already see the beginning of a rush into new construction now that market sentiment and outlook has changed very much for the better.

The River Thames

The Busy River

London — Britain's largest central cargo port, handling some 49 million tonnes of cargo annually.

London — best connected UK port.

London — where Road, Rail and River combine to give you a distribution service unsurpassed by any other UK port.

London — where experience and service has counted for over 2,000 years.

PLA

London's Highway to Prosperity – Now and into the Future

Contact: Business Development Department, Port of London Authority, Europe House, World Trade Centre, London E1 9AA
Tel: 01-481 8484   Telefax: 01-481 2458   Telex: 995562

Shortage of skilled and experienced manpower

What worries me more are two other constraints faced by the industry today, and for which the long depression is the direct cause. they are the shortage of skilled seafaring manpower, and the dearth of experienced technical personnel in the shipbuilding and shiprepairing industries. Both are becoming increasingly more difficult to overcome, as living standards rise and a career at sea is no longer a desirable goal, while the struggle for sheer survival by the shipyards and the maritime supply industry in recent times has meant the laying-off, retraining, or re-assignment of tens of thousands of qualified workers in the various countries. Many will not wish to nor can come back, new recruits of course take time for training. When one considers the popular assumption that many shipowners will try to extend the life of their existing vessels by a few more years to avoid paying the high newbuilding costs, when one calculates the time required to put all the large ships through third Special Surveys — and of course more are coming up to that event — or when one thinks of all the ageing tonnage which requires more frequent repairs, one should not necessarily rejoice over the fact that so many shipyards have shrunk or gone completely out of business. Competition especially for repair berths will likely be fierce in the next few years, and put a great deal of pressure on the yards, the sub-contracting industry, and the Classification Societies. More technical shortcuts will be taken and act as additional generators of operational hazards to the lack of qualified personnel. Technical after-sale services have not exactly been for some time already what one would have wished for or was used to. P. & I. claims have risen substantially since last year, always a good indicator for falling standards of safety and operation, although clearly one year is not a long enough period to jump to firm conclusions.

In Hong Kong we have worried for some time about insufficient student numbers in our marine engineering and nautical courses, about lower productivity, about fading loyalties, about the sheer overall lack of officers and crews with relevant experience and sufficient years of service. It is not, I believe, just a matter of remuneration and service conditions but the result of a wide-spread disenchantment with work in the maritime industries. It is a global problem which calls for co-ordinated international action but of which we still see very little. Although great strides have been made in facilitiating the reduction of complements aboard ships, we will likely be facing a people squeeze before too long, particularly, so if the market upturn continues and does ultimately again lead to a net increase in overall world tonange figures. This I believe is an area where governments are duty-bound to establish and support more educational facilities, this is where the maritime subsidies should go first and foremost. The best market conditions and the most sophisticated assets will not allow us to exploit the commercial opportunities if we are short of the bodies to do it with.

THE NEW CHALLENGES FOR MARITIME INDUSTRIES 1989

In this extract from the Chartered Institute of Transport Reginald Grout Memorial Lecture Mr. J. G. Davis, C.B.E., F.C.I.T., Chairman of the IMIF and the Marine Society considers the problems of manpower resources now facing the industries.

On the eve of what could be an era of strengthening and recovery, the alarm bells are ringing for the worsening manpower situation. The dread word "demography", which until recently was not in common usage outside the academic arena has suddenly and ominously become fashionable. You would think that at some stage we actually counted the numbers of children we were having, but it seems, throughout the western world, we have not been having enough children to ensure our industrial future. Worried men from ICI and General Accident have been getting up and saying that in five years time there just won't be sufficient school leavers in East Anglia and Western Yorkshire to fill even their situations vacant. Their Lordships of the Admiralty and senior persons in the War Department to say nothing of the Police are having serious conversations about the possibilities of recruiting able seawomen and the moral problems of having ladies in control of battlefield nuclear weapons or WPCs with guns respectively.

Where this demographic time bomb now ticking away leaves the marine industries, I scarcely like to even consider. The industry for many years suffered from a chronic over capacity of people particularly seafarers and has lived off the fat of this for a decade; now the workforce is becoming old and already there is a serious shortage of junior officers developing. It gives me no particular pleasure to note that for the past two years The Marine Society (of which I am the Chairman) has made strenuous efforts to alert industry and governments to the need to regenerate maritime training in this country. It was as much a reflection of our conviction that the crisis would come sooner than later that we have commissioned our two small training ships to try and give some practical expression of our concern. It may be a small enough gesture, but it is costing us an annual expenditure bill of more than half a million pounds. We feel that it is well justified in that it is giving youngsters some flavour of life at sea and of what shipping is about. It is this "sea-consciousness" and the need to promote this which should be concerning us all in maritime transport.

Should we really be concerning ourselves with this problem? After all much of the UK controlled fleet is now happily flagged out and is being operated by crews from the developing world. Why may not this tendency be permitted to continue, to give employment to the third world at a price we can enjoy paying? We now have international open registers, bareboat charter arrangements are being more widely employed and perhaps the day of the truly international or EEC flag may be not that far away. What, some argue, is wrong with that if it provides the cheapest possible transport?

I think the trend has considerable disbenefits and it is facile to ignore such matters as a spread of international maritime crime, the exploitation of labour from the poorer parts of the world and the very real problem of the sub-standard ship. If you look further at the consequences of these problems you find the shipping industry groaning under the weight of legislation brought in as a reaction to sub-standard operations. Port State Control, I have to admit was and remains one of the enthusiasms of IMIF, and it is a powerful weapon against the sub-standard, but it is as well to remember that it has become necessary only because contracting governments to IMO Conventions have proved unable properly to administer the standards of ships flying their flags: they have frequently found themselves in this situation because they have lacked the people trained and qualified to provide a competent marine administration.

Pride in one's Company

Once we start down the road of permitting the greater part of the British controlled merchant fleet to be operated abroad by non-Britons we enter a new world of considerable vulnerability. Don't think for a minute that I am suggesting that British seafarers are necessarily the *best* seafarers, because there has been far too much of that sort of talk about and as well as being manifestly untrue, it does nobody any good. If you still think along these antedeluvian lines may I suggest that you examine rather more carefully the sort of company ethos, and the capability of the crews that work for operators like Captain Chang's Evergreen Lines.

So when I hark back to the days of some of the great British shipping companies, and the excellence of their operations, I am not suggesting we should be nostalgic for the rigid hierarchies, the silver service and the duplication of services for officers and ratings. What I would like to see is a return to the pride in one's company that was evident in some of the best managed British concerns — the ethos of teamwork and a knowledge that only the best is good enough. Indeed those maxims that clearly galvanise the fifteen-man ship teams that operate the Evergreen ships.

We should, I am suggesting, look much closely at our human resources and how they can be developed. We have concentrated so hard on our hardware over the past decade of desperate cost cutting that we have tended to neglect our humans. There is a direct connection between the health of the industry and the intelligent, well paid and motivated people it must attract if it is to have a meaningful future. If, as I have suggested, transport may be on the threshold of a better life, with more realisitc rewards for its services you can only sustain this recovery by offering excellence. One can do a lot with equipment, and money, but one cannot achieve real excellence, and make capital investment worthwhile without well motivated people.

Somethimes I think that we cannot see the wood for the trees. I was closely associated with passenger ships during much of my time with P&O and today as Chairman of DFDS Limited I still keep a close eye on this field. If as a member of the public you go aboard a passenger ship one can tell in a trice whether a crew is well motivated. I still recall with sadness seeing a dirty Red Ensign wound uncaringly around the ensign staff with halyard broken and flying in the wind of a British super-ferry on my way to the Continent, and seeing it in exactly the same state on my way back fourteen days later. That same vessel had stickers all over the crew accommodation windows proclaiming "Keep the Red Duster flying". Of course on a passenger ship the enthusiasm of the crew can make an immediate impact upon the financial health of that particular ship, but even with a cargo ship it does not take too long before a scruffy and inept crew produces damage, insurance claims and other costs. Why do we not sufficiently recognise this? If, as seems likely, ships are to get ever more expensive to build, surely it becomes even more important to staff them with efficient and skilled crews, who are above all, well motivated. Surely the United Kingdom cannot completely surrender this role?

"I have seen the future, and it works" said Lincoln Steffens after a visit to post revolution Moscow, and he was wrong too! Do you remember all those amazing futuristic pictures of what cities would be like in the year 2000 produced by people like Corbusier — of tower block and curving concrete, of flyovers and people movers and perspex tubes. Maybe you thought, as I always did when looking at these visions by architects that the human perspective was entirely missing.

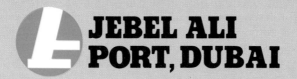

The human element

Is the maritime future really going to be a five man operated deep sea ship, automated to their eyebrows with a small group of people whom you could only describe as social misfits marooned in a sort of floating lighthouse and doing nothing more than peering at the outer manifestations of a computer controlled machine and wondering what they are doing there? If you are looking for a story that will keep you awake at night I can commend to you one of the last years winners of the College of the Sea short story competition. Fashioned in the style of Poe, with fusions of Kafka, he told the story of a single watchkeeper on a huge car carrier driving through thick fog, subsequently discovering, when he was not relieved that he was the only person on the ship! Is this the future and how can we humanise it?

Surely there must be some sort of shipborne organisation that will depend not upon an uneasy and uncomfortable cultural mismatch of the cheapest possible combination of European master and third world crew, all of them hired as casual labour for the duration of the voyage. Where is the company ethos in this? Where is the motivation for excellence? And where, pray, is the next generation of European master going to get his experience if only senior officers can get a job?

Is the shipping industry, and transport efficiency really best served by small groups of exhausted people operating hard-run ships as close to the legal limits as is possible? Did we go through fifteen years of recession for that? Is it progress that will produce the single watchkeeper on his automated bridge, a lonely man or woman watching clocks, punching his deadman's button to demonstrate his physical wakefulness and praying for the voyage to end so that normal service can be resumed.

If we are to ever get that share of school leavers and intelligent entrants to the industry of tomorrow, we must address these very human problems. We have been, I suggest rather too obsessed by instrumentation and automation and we have failed to grasp the connection between de-skilling and automatic operation.

Before spending a fortune on automatic navigation systems, on electronic charts, on closed circuit TV systems, on all the developments that will go to make up the ships of the future, it is as well to consider the effect it will have on the seafarers, the users of the hardware. If you are investing in this hardware to enable you to employ morons in the full expectation you will be able to find nobody more intelligent, then you should perhaps say so. One ought perhaps to be aware that much of the equipment which one is being sold by an enthusiastic marine equipment industry has not really been tested for user friendliness and may well be resented as absurd and demeaning by those it seems designed to help. It's a delicate balance between Luddism and a sensible appreciation of skill, but perhaps it is something we should appreciate more if we are to persuade intelligent people to join our companies.

Somehow, real responsibility, real reward and a sense of enjoyment must be put back into the industry. Maybe this will come as a function of recovery in the industry, but it won't come by itself.

Well trained seafarers

I have laboured at some length on the need for seafaring to be kept as an attractive occupation for a number of reasons. First as Chairman of the Marine Society, in close touch with thinking seafarers through the College of the Sea, and with a close interest in our founder Jonas Hanway's aim to provide sufficient seafarers for Britain's maritime needs I am bound to have these concerns.

If the United Kingdom is to have a "core fleet", then it cannot rely on foreign expertise to run it. Although ships' crews are not very numerous, it is essential if ships are to be properly run, that seafarers are well trained. There is a point of view, which is by no means confined to Britain that suggests actual "hands on" experience of

SHIP & YACHT
REGISTRATION
UNDER THE
MALTA
FLAG

WE have registered well over 4 million tons under the Malta Flag.

WE have been providing professional assistance to satisfied clients for over 12 years.

WE are now the leaders in the formation and maintenance of offshore companies.

GM INTERNATIONAL SERVICES LTD
A MEMBER OF THE ECONOMICARD WORLDWIDE GROUP
146/1, St. Lucia Street, Valletta, Malta.
Tel: 226043, 607785, 221294
Telex: 1462 ECOCRD MW 1725 ECOCRD MW Fax: 220101

41

operating ships is not really necessary to understand the business. That it is perfectly possible to sit in an office in London and adminster a fleet operated entirely by foreign operatives. It will be sufficient, say the proponents of such ideas, for the ship managers to concern themselves with the financial and commercial aspects of fleet management leaving the hired hands to sort out the nuts and bolts. British seafarers, I'm afraid are seen by these enthusiasts as almost irrelevant, with the cheaper, Far Eastern and third world varieties very much in favour.

It is a comfortable notion, but I am not entirely sure that those who suggest it really believe it. Perhaps they are really just rationalising to compensate for the perceived difficulty of obtaining, or affording European seafarers. The fact that such a scenario currently exists does not mean that it will be possible to operate in this way in five, or ten years time. At present the shipping centres of the industrialised countries have a residue of well-trained former seafarers as technical directors, superintendents, fleet managers ready to hand. The fact that these experts operate with ships under every conceivable flag is really not important. What is important is the fact that they are part of the nation's maritime infrastructure. When they have sailed away to well-earned retirement, where is the next generation coming from?

Maritime expertise and experience

We make much of the supposed maritime expertise of the City of London, and indeed it is fully justified. In this city a ship operator can find all he needs to operate a great fleet of ships and make money with them. He can finance their building, he can find experts who will class them, design them and supervise their construciton. He will find here the insurance and P&I requirements, and he will find expert shipbrokers to fill them with cargo. There are liner conferences and owner's associations, there are maritime lawyers of fabled reputation and all manner of surveyors, superintendents and technical experts.

Throughout this great warp of expertise and maritime fabric you will find interwoven a continuous thread of actual marine experience. Lord Mayors of London, lawyers, arbiters, underwriters and brokers, bankers and administrators are all to be found in this city with actual marine experience and an intimate knowledge of the sea. If you break this thread, because you have ceased to train seafarers, you eventually end up having only an abstract idea of how ships are operated. Take away the maritime expertise and the vital infrastructure becomes vulnerable to attack from clever people in Piraeus and Hong Kong who would dearly love to transport London's maritime primacy to warmer climes.

At present, because of our residue of maritime experts, the UK still, despite her much reduced owned and controlled fleet, manages to command considerable respect in maritime circles. We can still take a lead in international safety through a strong and expert presence at the International Maritime Organization and a host of other important organisations. But if we have lost our fleet and our expertise, how then will we be able to cope?

Which is why The Marine Society and Trinity House and a number of private and concerned interests are trying very hard to train seafarers again, through offering scholarships, trying hard to at least maintain a nucleus of newcomers into the industry. It is good to see that the UK government and the shipping industry between them are now stepping up recruitment, although it is still far below the numbers needed to man even a modest "core fleet". It is good to hear that the Secretary of State for Transport himself has said that young entrants to the Merchant Navy can be assured of good prospects and swift promotion. It is worth remembering that maritime skills take a long time to acquire and there is still no real substitute for actual experience.

There seems no doubt that there is a link between the size of the "core fleet" and the health of the maritime infrastructure, although it is not easy to quantify.

At what stage does the shrinking fleet start to affect the availability of shore side expertise? Here it is important to introduce a further complication in the fact that very few seafarers actually go to sea for the whole of their working lives. Seven years was always quoted as the average, although in times with poor employment prospects ashore people tend to stay longer. But substantial numbers of former seafarers, as I have hinted, do work ashore in marine related jobs, as part of an unofficial career pattern that shipowners, I am glad to say, are now acknowledging.

There is, I suggest, a good case for smoothing the career path from ship to shore, because seafarers make excellent employees. They are used to responsibility, they are intelligent and practical, they are loyal and very hardworking. Perhaps their training ought to give more credence to this seafarers' "afterlife", and that besides the arts of navigation and seamanship, management and finance ought to figure in their studies rather more. Suitably trained, such people would be a valuable human resources for a vital maritime industry in the future. I am delighted that the Council of the Maritime Society has decided to fund a most useful study by the British Maritime Charitable Foundation into the link between ship and shore industry and in particular the critical levels below which the infrastructure becomes irretrievably damaged by a shrinking fleet. Good information will be certain to come out of this.

Let us remember too that maritime expertise is to be found outside the realms of the ordinary "commercial" merchant navy. The oceans of the world beckon, and there is such a lot to discover about them. If we are ever going to manage the resources of the ocean then we must seek to understand it and here too there is a great challenge facing us. I'm afraid that there are other countries which are also taking their oceanic responsibilities very seriously indeed. The Soviet Union, with a hundred naval research ships and about the same number of civilian manned oceanographic and

fisheries research ships is not running such a fleet for the good of its collective souls or idle curiosity. The United States and Japan also have large oceanographic research fleets, both of them utterly convinced that knowledge is power and knowledge about the deep ocean will confer the power to exploit it.

There are other maritime challenges awaiting us. The maritime and coastal environment needs careful management and this presupposes considerable expertise. It may be quite a long way from transport, but many of the same skills will be needed in any job where an understanding and respect for the elements is a prerequisite.

Optimistic outlook

My final point is also I hope both challenging and optimistic, because there is, as I have suggested considerable room for optimism. It is that we should, after so many years of retrenchment, start now to build for our maritime future.

By that I certainly am not suggesting we should be rushing around the world's shipyards demanding new tonnage on tick, and I have already suggested that such a course would preclude recovery. What I believe we should be doing is laying down the foundations for recovery. We should be husbanding our human resources, consolidating our research programmes so that we are building and designing the right kind of ship for the future.

This is important, for there is plenty of evidence that suggests that the world we are moving towards will not merely be the same old cycle that much further on. There have been important structural changes that have taken place in the world in recent years which will greatly affect the type and numbers of ships we design. Many cargoes are becoming miniaturised and require less volume. Production bases are moving between continents and that requires fewer tonne miles, although this is doubtless compensated by the extraordinary amount of to-ing and fro-ing in the component and distribution fields. There are pipelines to consider, new oilfields coming on stream, old cargoes which are completely disappearing to be replaced by others which need very different types of transport. There are channel tunnels and inter-continental double-stacked railway trains to worry about and shippers must go quite mad trying to decide between all water, landbridge, air-sea or air cargo shipping a box of clockwork toys from Tokyo to Minnesota.

So it is a different world we are planning for, and that, if anything should make us even more careful about rocking the boat of recovery by incautious over-investment. Which really completes our circle, with the thread coming inescapably back to the old injunction about our optimism being founded on the premise that there will not be a return to the bad old days of easy terms and overbuilding.

Eight years ago I myself had the privilege of being your President of the Chartered Institute of Transport and the theme I chose for my year in office was the absolute necessity of transport being better rewarded for its efforts. In shipping this has taken a long time, but I believe that because surpluses are under control, better rewards are indeed just around the corner. And from this, all else will flow. A better reward will engender improved standards and a return to rather more excellence in transport. It will mean a better marine transport system run by better people who are able instead of living hand to mouth as they have been forced to do for the past fifteen years, are thinking up better systems still for the future.

"Not to understand what happened before you were born is to be a child all your life". — *Cicero.*

SHIP MANAGEMENT

by David Tinsley
Technical Editor, Lloyd's List

Independent ship management is the tool that has helped bring about some of the major structural changes in shipping in the past decade. Professional ship managers form a distinct, and increasingly influential segment of the shipping industry. Yet it has taken some time for recognition to be forthcoming from all parts of the industry that ship management is a science, practised by experts in specific fields or across a whole range of disciplines.

Some of the major shipowning organisations, notably those maintaining containership fleets, have demonstrated tremendous resilience through the leanest years of the 1980s, fine-tuning their operating skills to a remarkable degree. However the increased activity and sophistication of the high-grade 'outside' management undertakings, where the precepts of service and accountability underpin every aspect of their business, has had perhaps the greatest impact on the restructural process.

Although firms such as Denholm Ship Management have been providing comprehensive management services for many years, the sector really came into its own during the depths of the shipping recession. With the intensification of competition in the international market, the inability of shipowners in the traditional maritime countries to secure what they regarded as a more realistic and less stringent wage and fringe benefit structure,coupled with penal tax rates in many of those countries, encouraged the shift of tonnage to more co-operative administrations and cost effective managers.

Large numbers of shipowners have made far-reaching cuts in their own establishment levels, assigning responsibility for manning and technical operations to the specialist concerns which have proliferated in the last 10-15 years. The scope and prowess of the management companies has grown commensurately with the shipowners' desire to concentrate resources on the mainstream function of gainfully employing the vessels and generating cargo.

The true 'globalisation' of the industry in the past few years, through the greatly accelerated trend in Europe towards the adoption of government-approved international and offshore registers, and the flexibility which this process has offered in terms of sourcing of seafarers, has provided considerable new opportunities for the outside management sector.

The lessons learned from reputable ship managers able to offer a cost edge over in-house management by dint of greater efficiency and smaller overheads have been etched deeply on the industry as a whole. Tight budgetary control, scrutiny of every aspect of costs, and lean administrations can be expected to prevail irrespective of the extent of recovery in the shipping market.

For many shipowning principals, cost pruning is no longer the main motive in seeking offshore, third-party ship management. Economies of scale, business locations offering a freer operating and fiscal environment, and an entirely service-orientated staff, are appreciated by owners who have decided — notwithstanding an upturn in market fortunes — to keep their central organisation small and to focus on the commercial essence of their business.

Moreover, newcomers to shipping such as the increasingly numerous investment companies, generally have no interest in setting-up in-house operating divisions, and are looking to the gamut of consultancy and technical services being provided at a competitive rate rather than at specific areas of cost savings.

Vessel performance

Parallel to the close budgetary control which has to be exercised in the interest of cost efficiency, a primary task of professional ship management is to secure optimised vessel performance. Implicit in this is the requirement to meet overall objectives without sacrificing levels of safety or the maintained asset value of the ship. With the considerable increases in newbuilding prices and secondhand values over the past three years, the responsibilities associated with ship husbandry have grown enormously.

It is not only symptomatic of the competition within the sector, but also of the client market's characteristic frugality, that the entrusting of assets with a substantially increased trading and resale value has not reflected in the levels of management fees. Some of the leading operators in the field claim that, in real terms, fees are lower than they were in 1979.

Although margins have always been relatively small in outside management, the sector has tended to flourish when the shipping market has been in poor shape. With a sustained improvement in trading conditions, managers face the prospect of a leaner period. Owner's determination to rebuild profitability, coupled with the upward pressures on costs that will inevitably be exerted by shortages of trained, seagoing personnel and by the demand:supply situation as concerns worldwide shiprepair capacity, will impact upon bottom-line earnings in the ship husbandry sector.

The onus will thus be on ship management companies to respond to the inflationary pressures without running the risk of becoming uncompetitive. The fact that the number of firms offering management services stands at an all-time high looks set to sharpen the competition ever more. It could be that this situation will lead to sector rationalisation, through company takeovers or — perhaps more likely — through more joint ventures.

Group of Five

The formation of a working group by five of the leading ship management companies has provided a much-needed focus for key issues confronting this vibrant sector of the shipping industry. Moreover, the initiative of Denholm Ship Management, Barber International, Wescol International Marine Services (Wallem Shipmanagement), Hanseatic Shipping Company and Columbia Shipmanagement in providing a means for dialogue, and a medium for contact with international and national organisations, attests to the present-day stature of the outside management sector.

While concern has been expressed in some quarters at the 'muscle' which the so-called Group of Five could potentially exert, or the defensive position which it could adopt in the interests of the specific companies involved, the grouping has stimulated some welcome debate about the future course of ship management.

According to the founders, the objective has been to establish a working party to evaluate and promote new methods of improving training, safety, operational standards and ethics within the management field. Between them, the five companies control upwards of 900 vessels. Individually, these concerns have considerable clout with insurers, suppliers, labour unions, and shipyards. All five are part of large groups, with interests to a varying extent in other areas of maritime services and in shipowning itself.

Formalisation of the association into some kind of trade body has been rejected by the parties involved, the majority view being that an informal working group is better able to remain flexible and to react speedily to events of mutual concern. Moreover, it has been decided that the group should remain a team of five, and that requests for admission by other ship managers should be declined. It is this exclusivity which has attracted adverse comment from other sectors of the service industry.

Cadet intake

As Jim Davis discusses in his article "The New Challenges for Maritime Industries 1989" elsewhere in this book, one result of the protracted period of austerity and restructure in shipping has been the tremendous fall-off in the number of cadets taken on by West European owners. This, coupled with demographic trends in Europe, has caused alarm in the industry at a time of market recovery. A shortfall in skilled sea-going personnel, is already having an impact. Longer-term, there is a very real prospect of a shortage of qualified seafarers to fill key posts ashore. The ports industry, and shipowners themselves, have every reason to be as concerned as the management companies over this development.

Not suprisingly, the 'Group of Five' has identified recruitment and training as one of the key issues to be addressed. A representative of the five-company working party has already suggested that specific training facilities be made available in the countries from where crews predominantly originate, with governments carrying the costs, in view of the invisible earnings generated by seafarers for the respective economies. Another proposal put forward by the same industry figure was that training structures be changed to take into account the requirements of shoreside management positions in addition to those of the particular sea-going disciplines.

Some of the smaller management companies, however, are sceptical about the usefulness of the working group. They also feel that the types of owners who employ the services of the more modestly sized, third-party undertakings may be concerned at collaboration between five of the largest management fleets.

Economies of scale

Scale economies underpin the competitiveness of the larger companies, which are able to pass unit cost savings down the line to the client. One of the factors which has been instrumental in weakening the position of many shipowning organisations in the last 10-15 years, i.e. high establishment costs resulting from a large central administration, has to be guarded against. Fragmenting the organisational structure through the creation of a network of offices in different parts of the world, and through the allocation of groups of ships to individual fleet managers and/or operating teams, may thus be seen not only as a means of enhancing service to the individual customer, but also as a way of ensuring internal efficiency.

Expectations as to quality of service have risen in all market sectors, and the 'closeness' or otherwise of the ship manager to the client has a direct bearing on perceived standards of service. Thus the larger, professional undertakings have to structure their operations in such a way that individual owners get personal treatment while benefiting from the scale economies offered by a large fleet operation. Furthermore, the smaller and medium-sized managers have to ensure that expansion does not jeopardise service quality.

Monte Carlo-headquartered V ships — which extended its international network through the opening of a new office in Southampton in early 1989 — has developed the idea of management teams based in regional offices. Rather than splitting staff in the conventional manner into specialist groups, such as technical, purchasing and accounting departments, multi-disciplinary teams have been formed and assigned to relatively small groups of vessels.

A typical six-person team comprises a fleet manager, a marine superintendent, an engineering superintendent, a fleet administration assistant, a purchasing clerk and an accountant. In this way, individual members of staff have a far greater feel for

specified vessels and for the owners' needs. As a result, the company can offer a better overall level of flexibility and service quality.

V ships considers that with this structure, and with a network of subsidiaries in key areas, business growth can be fostered without sacrificing the quality of service and attention accorded clients on an individual basis.

The larger fleets have strengthened their market position during the period under review, with the six, numerically-strongest companies accounting for some 20-25% of outside-managed vessels worldwide. Some observers feel that this trend will continue, but that gains in market share will be at the expense of the medium-sized companies. The inference is that as the large concerns become larger, there will be a continuing market for the small outfits.

With the marked appreciation in ship values, investment companies have become increasingly active, providing an important source of business for the specialists in technical and operational services. However, like the financial institutions who during the market trough accounted for such a large part of the professional ship managers' business, the asset traders and speculators generate work that is predominantly short-term in nature, so contributing to the increasingly high turnover rates in managed fleets.

Portuguese link

Expansion-minded Barber International has forged new links during the past year, including a joint venture operation in Portugal. Providing the Norwegian group with a foothold in one of the EEC's lowest labour cost areas, while affording State-owned tanker company Soponata an opportunity to widen its field of operations, the partnership is initially concentrating on manning. It is hoped that the Portuguese joint-stock enterprise will eventually develop into a full management operation. Barber and Soponata have had a working relationship since 1987, when a manning agreement was signed covering the supply of Portuguese seamen to the Norwegian group.

Portuguese seafarers command lower wage levels than most in Western Europe, and their international competitiveness has been further enhanced by the creation this year of the Madeira register. Unlike other European offshore registers, the Portuguese-administered island does not require a shipping company to establish a local presence in order to qualify for registration. Although 50% of the crew have to be Portuguese nationals, they are exempt from income tax and social security payments if the ship is engaged in international trade. Moreover, it is possible for an owner to secure an exemption from the mixed-manning stipulation if the vessel is operating outside the European area, or if it is not possible to recruit Portuguese seamen.

While Barber continued its expansionary policy on foreign shores, Wescol International Marine Services — the Hill Samuel-owned shipping division which includes Wallem Shipmanagement — made a move into the Norwegian market. This resulted in the formation during May of a joint venture management company representing the interests of Wescol and Sandefjord-based owner Jorgen Jahre. As the newly-styled Wescol Norway undertaking is aimed mainly at owners using the Norwegian International Ship Register (NIS), the development brings the London-based group into direct competition with Barber International — one of the leading lights behind the creation of NIS.

Wescol Norway, domiciled in Jorgen Jahre's home town, began operations with 12 vessels under management, adding several more to its fleet during the summer. Before the break into the Norwegian sector, Wescol/Wallem's sphere of management influence already equated to something in excess of 200 vessels.

In mid 1989, Wescol was involved in discussions to take over two US service

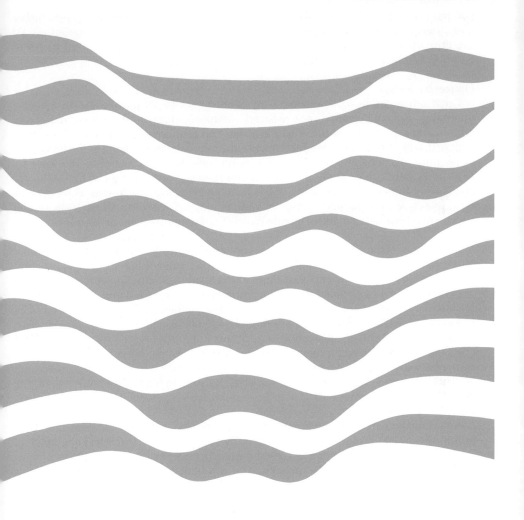

V. Ships
27, Bld. d'Italie
P.O. Box 39
MC 98007 Monaco Cedex
Phone: 33 (93) 15 10 10
Telex: 479 495
Fax: 33 (93) 30 54 02

V. Ships (Bombay)
c/o IMS Ship Management
Private Limited
401, Regent Chambers,
Nariman Point
Bombay 400 021, India
Phone: 91 (22) 230 395
Telex: 011 4893
Fax: 91 (22) 221 579

V. Ships (Italy)
Via B. Bosco, 33/35/37
16121 Genoa
Italy
Phone: 39 (10) 565663
594681
564018
Fax: 39 (10) 564031

V. Ships (UK)
Gate House,
1, Farringdon Street
London, EC4M 7NS
United Kingdom
Phone: 44 (1) 489 0088
Telex: 886266
Fax: 44 (1) 489 0529

V. Ships (USA)
Meadows Office Complex
201 Route 17 North
Rutherford, N.J. 07070
U.S.A.
Phone: 1 (201) 896-9700
Telex: 232453
Fax: 1 (201) 896-8401

V. Ships (Norway)
Kirkeveien 64
P.O. Box 5207 Maj
0302 Oslo 3
Norway
Phone: 47 (2) 46 12 05
Telex: 76955
Fax: 47 (2) 46 31 21

V. Ships (UK)
30 Channel Way
Ocean Village
Southampton SO1 1TG
United Kingdom
Phone: 44 (703) 634 477
Telex: 477501
Fax: 44 (703) 634 319

companies, in a bid to establish the group name in a market where Denholm, Barber and other prominent companies already have active ship management operations. At the time of writing, neither of the projected two deals — with a potential worth of $12m — had been formalised.

Optitech concept

Great advances have been made in recent years in terms of ship design and operating systems geared to reduced manning levels. At the same time, administrations in most of the West European and Scandinavian countries have been supportive of owners in their efforts to cut running costs, by agreeing to the formation of offshore registers, and by concentrating on 'safe' levels of manning on a case by case basis rather than applying rigid manning scales irrespective of the technical standard of the vessel and quality of her management. The single watchkeeper trials now under way or contemplated in various countries are an illustration of the sustained efforts being made to ensure European competitiveness in the international market.

One of the leading ship management concerns, the 150-ship Barber International enterprise, argues that the minimum-manned, state-of-the-art vessel is still uncompetitive with a low-cost flag ship having a substantially bigger complement.

In early 1989, it was stated that the manning costs alone for a vessel crewed by 13 Norwegian nationals could typically be twice those entailed with a complement of 24 Indian seafarers, amounting to an additional $400,000-worth of expenditure per year. Actual cost differentials are even greater, it was contended, given the higher capital costs entailed in equipping the national-flag vessel with the latest technology and in fitting her out with the highest standard of accommodation.

The Norwegian-headquartered group is of the view that advanced tonnage of this type will remain uncompetitive with less sophisticated vessels under low-cost flags for the next 10-20 years.

As a consequence, the organisation has developed a design concept based on optimum — not minimum — low-cost manning, and on a practical blend of advanced and unsophisticated technology. Called Optitech, this has been devised for a 'non-domiciled' crew of some 20-24 persons, and is reliant on vessel designs which offer the right combination of high reliability and productivity on the one hand, and straightforward and robust equipment on the other, in order to minimise the sum of capital and operating costs. In offering a cost-competitive alternative to high-tech tonnage, Barber claims that purpose-designed Optitech vessels will be superior to current low-cost flag ships by dint of their better productivity and cost-efficiency.

Barber has already applied the Optitech approach to several different types of vessel and claims that these offer savings in capital costs of $1m-$3m relative to advanced ships, in addition to substantial reductions in running costs.

The major stumbling block with Optitech, considers the Norwegian management specialist, is getting shipowners, builders and marine equipment companies to swtich from the current high-tech/low manning way of thinking, to providing efficient, reliable and robust equipment and ship designs adapted to an ample, but lower-cost crew.

55

FINANCING SHIPPING IN THE 1990s

by Paul Slater,
President, First International Financial Corporation

Since the very beginnings of seaborne commercial transportation, shipping has been an avaricious consumer of capital and today, the industry is more capital-intensive than ever. Uniquely, however, its revenue base is entirely dependent on the demand for transport of raw materials and finished goods between the world's various land masses and around their shorelines. It is a truly offshore industry, dependent for its very existence on the vagaries of numerous onshore economies.

This, together with the predominantly private ownership structure has meant that international shipping has found difficulty in establishing itself in the world's capital markets ashore. Today, following more than a decade of almost universally unprofitable operation, it faces the daunting question of how an industry, seriously deficient in equity and with a banking popularity second only to the Third World, can raise the capital required to replace its ageing assets.

Twelve months or so ago it was estimated that more than $12 billion would be needed each year from 1990 onwards for fleet replacement. At about the same time, Det norske Veritas put the figure above $15 billion; since then newbuilding prices have risen sharply. With VLCC prices in the Far East now exceeding $80 million and bulk carrier and containership prices showing similar percentage increases, the capital requirements for fleet replacement look closer to $20 billion per annum. The shipping industry must expand its financial horizons if it is to meet this massive capital requirement during the next decade.

One of the negative developments of the last ten years has been the trend towards short-term decision making, largely forced on the industry by the very need to survive. The level of freight rates has given cargo owners and shippers a unique opportunity to take advantage of the over-tonnaged market by keeping their chartering commitments short. Price, not quality or security of service, has been the all-important criterion.

The shipping industry and its customers must now undertake a dramatic reappraisal of their approach to transportation so that they may solve the severe problem of raising capital. 1988 saw a flurry of equity offerings mainly sold over the counter in the United States. These offerings were all based on buying various numbers of secondhand ships, many over-age, with the investors encouraged to believe that significant profits could be achieved in the short term from selling these ships in a rising secondhand market.

Meanwhile, the managers and promoters — some of whom sold the ships to these newly created companies — take exorbitant managment fees from the companies, take no risks themselves, and leave the shareholders with all the downside risks. This type of capital raising will continue to preserve shipping's image as a risky speculative industry, run by unscrupulous enterpreneurs, in which profits may only be made by selling the operational assets into hopefully rising markets.

Change of image required

International shipping needs to change its public image radically — in particular, its approach to capital markets. Ships are, after all, at the very heart of world trade; they provide the only means by which the vast majority of raw materials and finished products move between the nations of the world. Few industries can offer investors the long-term certainty that the shipping industry does; the certainty that there is no forseeable alternative to ships for moving large quantities of raw materials and finished goods across the oceans of the world. Thus, properly capitalised and professionally managed shipping companies have a unique opportunity for long-term growth and profitability from maintaining and operating large diversified fleets of cargo ships capable of operating competitively in many different sectors of the market.

Shipping has always been an intensely private industry which is still largely controlled by numerous private companies and individuals around the world. There are probably fewer than 20 public shipping companies quoted on the world's stock exchanges, and some 25,000 private companies which altogether own more than 75,000 ships sailing the world's oceans.

The industry's limited access to public capital is a direct result of its private ownership which has led in the past to excessive reliance on bank debt which by its very nature has been short to medium term in length and mostly at floating interest rates. The last ten years of heavily depressed freight rates have highlighted the weaknesses of asset financing based primarily on ships' values with too little equity and excessive debt. This has resulted in substantial bankruptcies in the shipping capitals of the world, most of which could have been avoided by more carefully structured financing at the outset.

Leasing companies

During the last 15 years there has been a movement by the end-users of ships away from direct ship-ownership themselves. Instead they have increasingly passed on the onus of acquisition and the risks of operation to shipowners who rely on revenues from shippers and raw materials buyers and sellers to fund the cost of acquiring and operating their ships. Thus shipping companies are effectively operating leasing companies which may, in some instances, even lease out their ships on a bareboat basis.

However, the similarity between shipowners and leasing companies ends on the funding side of the balance sheet, and it is in this area that the opportunity for tomorrow lies. It could be argued that leasing has always played a vital role in the financing of shipping — ownership and operation of ships invariably lies in different hands. The main operating contracts of the shipping industry are essentially forms of leases. The timecharter is an operating lease while the bareboat charter is a non-operating or financial lease. The contracts are so commonplace in the industry that few shipowners or operators would recognise the leasing similarity and few equipment leased companies include ships in their portfolios of assets. Today, some 75% of commercial aircraft are leased compared with less than 20% of commercial ships.

The end-users of sea transport, in addition to reducing the numbers of owned ships, have been able to take their pick of chartered ships and pay unrealistically low rates for their use. Furthermore, there has been no need to hedge against rising freight costs by adopting a strategy whereby charter commitments are spread in a portfolio of medium and long term arrangements. Instead, the charterers have continued to think short-term.

Unless a new approach is adopted, users of ships may well face substantial increases in transport costs from the early nineties onwards. Freight rates have already risen dramatically in many sectors; newbuilding costs are up by as much as 40%; some of the earliest available berths at yards in the Far East are for late 1991 delivery; secondhand prices in all sectors have risen sharply.

Emergence from depression

Shipping has probably never had a better opportunity to raise equity capital than now. The industry is undoubtedly emerging from a prolonged depression, it has an enormous need for equity and debt financing and it is looking at capital markets awash with funds seeking new opportunities for the future.

Future capital requirements can be satisfied by consolidation of some existing shipowners and the establishment of financial shipowners or leasing companies who fund themselves in the major capital markets using a variety of financial techniques. The issuing of securitised debt instruments, long term bonds, and shorter term floating rate notes, combined with a strong equity base will enable the ships to be offered on attractive medium and long term leases to their users, while the actual operations can be carried out by professional ship managers. These longer arrangements could lead to the establishment of risk reward partnerships between owners and charterers, enabling banks to sell the mortgage-backed securities to long-term financial institutions.

These securities would be priced more according to the credit-standing of the charterer than the owner and, if packaged properly, could allow for the substitution of ships of different sizes to accommodate changes in trading patterns. Thus, contracts of affreightment and flexible timecharters could form the basis for a whole new structure of ship financing.

The offshore nature of commercial shipping, whereby ships are registered in a wide variety of offshore financial centres and tax havens, should provide a catalyst for such arrangements. There are many valid commercial reasons for ships to be operated under flags or registrations other than those of the major developed nations, not least of which are the high labour costs and restrictive practices of many maritime unions.

Until recently, the country of the operating flag required that the shipowning company also be registered in that country, together with all mortgage and security documentation. This had a negative influence on investors and financiers in the major capital centres, particularly insurance companies and pension funds whose foreign lending is restricted by statute.

Recent developments among some of the largest offshore registries have sought to encompass the bareboat or transfer registry concept. This has significant potential for the future of ship leasing in that it enables the ownership to remain in one jurisdiction while the ship is operated under a more economically convenient flag. While the experienced lessor may argue that this is common practice in cross-border leasing of other assets — even commercial aircraft — it is still in its infancy in the shipping industry.

Partnerships exist in many European countries through which ship leasing is conducted primarily to generate tax depreciation for the high-income individuals in the partnership. A certain amount of ship leasing has also been carried out by Japanese leasing companies primarily to assist in the export of new ships from Japan or to assist Japanese trading companies. However, these combined activities account for less than 20% of all commercial ships. The opportunity is therefore considerable for leasing to provide the bridge between the capital markets, and the commercial markets in which the ships operate.

While many shipowners have acted as quasi leasing companies, they have done so without adequate capital resources, and with inappropriate financing techniques. Many have gambled and still do, on residual or secondhand values to cover the shortfall on inadequate income streams. The active secondhand market, together with the ability to recover 10-15% of original cost from scrapping ships at the end of their working lives, should be viewed only as an added financial incentive to the lessor, not as a reliable fall-back position.

THE NATIONAL BANK
EVERYBODY'S BANK

Welcome to the world of **the largest Greek Bank,** the National Bank of Greece.

Ranking among the **100 largest banks** in the world. For 147 years now it is pioneering in every aspect of banking activity; building the world of tomorrow.

The contributions it has made to our society, its prestige, its competent workforce, coupled with the sense of security it offers while retaining its human touch despite its size, have won the trust and confidence of some **6,000,000 Greek** customers.

Operating a network of 500 branches at home and 55 abroad and maintaining close co-operation with thousands of correspondent banks around the world make for a strong National Bank of Greece presence on the national and international scene.

Today, on the threshold of the 21st century, National Bank of Greece is poised to best apply the latest technological developments in banking and to **spearhead efforts to promote the economic development of our country.** National Bank of Greece is not just a strong banking organization, it is **everybody's Bank.**

NATIONAL BANK OF GREECE

National bank of Greece is among the 100 largest banks in the world

The future

The failure of so many shipping companies in recent years, combined with the immediate need to start replacing a rapidly ageing fleet is likely to cause a capital crisis in the early nineties which could have a serious impact on transportation costs of both raw materials and finished goods. These economic pressures will cause ship users to re-examine their transportation policies, which for the last decade have focused on maximising advantage from ship oversupply.

A new era is about to dawn. Users of ships — be they oil majors, steel companies, power utilities, car manufacturers or food distributors — will need to protect their freight costs by re-entering the shipping industry, and thereby providing freight contracts of a longer term nature. This, in turn, will enable potential investors to evaluate the financial risks of shipping from the quality of the revenue streams with less reliance on the volatility of ship values.

SHIP FINANCE

by Peter Stokes, Maritime Consultants Ltd

Anyone looking for a textbook case of the damage which can be done to an industry's investment and credit standing by the adoption of an inappropriate capital structure coulddo no better than to study the history of shipping during the past twenty years. Essentially, it is a story of excess and waste leading to retribution. The plain fact is that, when given access to substantial amounts of capital in the late 1960s and early 1970s, the shipping industry demonstrated an alarming lack of discipline, prudence and simple common sense. The effects of its excesses have been dramatic and long-lasting.

Efforts are now being made to rebuild the capital resources of the industry in preparation for the large-scale asset replacement programme which will be required in the coming decade. So far, however, these efforts consist principally of the creation of special-purpose investment vehicles intended to finance the speculative purchase of second-hand vessels. Attraction of long-term capital to finance new ships has so far proved an intractable problem. This is hardly surprising. After all, how can an industry which has made such a comprehensive mess of its affairs in the past hope to regain the confidence of long-term lenders and investors? Does it even deserve to do so?

Fundamental principles

In addressing these questions, it may be helpful to start with a few fundamental principles. First, one should not fall into the trap of condemning debt as bad simply because it was misused by the shipping industry in the past and is perhaps being misused by a sizeable part of corporate America in the present. Nor should one assume that equity financing is *per se* the best and most wholesome type of financing. A corporation which never borrows will almost certainly produce a below average return for its shareholders. A corporation which borrows unwisely may well end up destroying its equity. Somewhere in between will lie the correct capital structure for a given corporation in a given industry.

Second, the assessment of an appropriate level of debt in a corporate capital structure should not be based entirely on the book value — or indeed the current market value — of the corporation's assets or equity. To quote the latest edition of Graham & Dodd's "Security Analysis": "There is no assurance that earnings will be commensurate with the book investment. . . .Thus the primary criterion of sound borrowing is not necessarily the balance sheet, but may be primarily the income account over a number of past years and a business-like appraisal of the hazards of the future." (Graham and Dodd's "Security Analysis", Fifth Edition, published by McGraw-Hill Book Company 1988.) The cautious phraseology is significant. This is a far cry from the current obsession with the optimistic cash flow projections as a justification for inherently risky leveraged buy-out structures.

Third, except where there is a long-term, predictable stream of earnings — as, for example, in the case of an LNG carrier chartered to Japanese utility for 20 years — the characteristics of shipping income are not such as to justify high proportions of debt to total capital. The average debt-total capital ratio of major, mature U.S. industries between 1982 and 1985 was around 25%. There is no reason to suppose that the shipping industry can sustain a degree of leverage any greater than this in the absence of any bankable long-term contractual income.

This implies a formidable requirement for equity — whether from retained earnings or newly subscribed capital - if the billions of dollars worth of capital expenditure to be undertaken in the 1990s is to be soundly financed. Simply stating this rather obvious fact, however, is hardly an argument for the professional investment community to begin meeting the industry's needs. Institutions have been burned too often before to be sanguine about shipping's prospects now, and they have good reason to be sceptical about the ability of shipping company managements to exercise prudent financial control.

In such circumstances the issue of capital structure assumes particularly critical importance, and the only way to justify a capital structure is by reference to the average rate and degree of volatility of return on capital which can reasonably be projected.

Let us take the tanker sector as an example. A hypothetical shipowner who established a tanker fleet by ordering, say, four VLCCs in 1969 would have invested approximately US$80 million. Over the subsequent 10 years he would have seen the annual average timecharter equivalent income per vessel of his fleet move within a range of US$62,000 a day in 1970 and US$1,300 a day in 1975.

Assuming that the ships were depreciated by equal instalments over 15 years and — for the sake of simplicity — that there was no reinvestment of net profits, the return on capital would have been highly impressive in 1970-73 before dropping to virtually nothing in 1974 and becoming negative thereafter. The average return on capital for the 10 years was around 8%, but it is difficult to draw any practical conclusions from this fact because of the extreme volatility of the income progression during the period under review.

Indeed, one of the trickiest problems in making any kind of reasoned case for a tanker investment is establishing a "normal" historical period as a basis for future projections. Was the 1970-73 period, during which VLCC timecharter equivalent rates averaged US$40,000 a day, "normal"? Were the long depression years, with rates generally well below US$10,000 a day and often below US$5,000 per day, entirely "abnormal".

Suffice it to say that the contracting of a VLCC newbuilding at a price in excess of US$70 million today implies the expectation of average timecharter equivalent rates back at the US$40,000 a day level of the early 1970s. Simply to cover the cost of 25% debt financing over 10 years, operating costs and depreciation over 15 years would require income of around US$26,000 a day. Interestingly, the fourth quarter of 1988 was the first time since the early 1970s boom that VLCC rates have reached this level. That may be significant, but it hardly provides much of a statistical basis for projecting this as a reasonable minimum income figure for the early 1990s.

Until or unless a pattern of greater stability develops in tanker freight rates, which can only occur if there is a return to longterm employment contracts with major charterers, the importance of keeping leverage within very tight limits will be paramount. Probably the ratio of 25% debt to total capital is as good a guideline as any.

Finance problems

While the tanker sector is admittedly an extreme case — no other shipping sector has been subject to such massive excesses of supply and declines in demand — it is not unrepresentative of the problems associated with the sound financing of the industry. In shipping generally, the absence of long-term assured income streams and the unpredictability of second-hand values demand an equity ratio far above those which have been the norm for many years.

The closed-end asset funds which have been the subject of public offerings and private placements over the past two years have generally recognised this fact by incorporating strict limits on gearing and the reinvestment of cash flow. They have not begun, however, to address the fundamental issue of constructing shipping investment projects on the basis of long-term revenues rather than asset value speculation and optimistic cash flow expectations. Only in this way can the high equity requirement in a prudent capital structure be reduced in favour of long-term fixed interest debt.

In the past 20 years, shipping has failed to earn a consistent return on capital comparable with that of most mature industries. Consistency is indeed the quality which shipping earnings most noticeably lack, and unless projects can be developed which are able to corrrect this defect, it will be hard to convince institutional investors that shipping securities are really of investment grade.

The structuring of shipping investment propostions will therefore make limited progress until cargo interests can be persuaded to "underwrite" a basic level of earnings and cashflow sufficient to provide the sort of regular returns which investors have a right to expect. Shipping has suffered from being dependent on a derived demand over which it has no control, and yet is a capital-intensive industry which needs to generate substantial reserves for the financing of fleet renewal, let alone expansion. Cargo shippers have been able to congratulate themselves for so long on the cheapness of freight that they appear to have forgotten that there is an economic cost associated with safe and efficient marine transportation. The difficulty so far has been to create an awareness of this fact among major shippers and to involve them directly in the financing of the shipping industry.

There have been some signs recently that charterers are becoming increasingly aware of the need to assist in the mobilising of capital for an orderly fleet replacement programme — particularly in the tanker sector but also in other segments of the fleet. As long as the level of the spot charter market is considered the determinant of rates which should be paid for the long-term employment of new ships, however, little progress will be made.

In the meantime, the New York investment banks which have been attracted to shipping as a recovery sector continue to concentrate on the marketing of high-yield funds for the purchase of ageing second-hand ships, while Norwegian investors in K/S partnerships have shown a preference for the rapid turnover of their investments in the bulk market conditions of the past two years, thereby generating very high internal rates of return.

It is widely assumed among shipowners, bankers and shipping investors that steadily rising newbuilding prices will ensure continuing firmness of second-hand ship values, irrespective of seasonal and cyclical fluctuations in the freight market. So far, that opinion has been borne out by market behaviour. Banks which had been obliged to make substantial provisions against their ship loans in the early and mid-1980s have been able to write back large amounts in the past couple of years, thereby swelling their reported profits and encouraging a more positive attitude towards shipping business.

While the unrestrained competition seen in the ship finance market during previous periods of optimism has so far been avoided, there is no doubt that the resources available for ship loans are being materially augmented. Sumitomo Bank has established a specialist ship finance department in London, and the German ship mortgage banks are undergoing a realignment of shareholders which will leave Dresdner Bank and Commerzbank controlling a merged Deutsche Schiffahrtsbank and Deutsche Schiffsbeleihungsbank and Deutsche Bank acquiring Schiffshypothekenbank zu Luebeck. For a change, perhaps it will be the European and Japanese banks setting the pace in the ship finance market rather than the Americans.

Despite a relative measure of restraint up to now by most lending banks, the second-hand market has shown clear signs of over-heating, and it is possible that some of the financing structures arranged during the enthusiasm of late 1988 may be found wanting if cash flows falter in 1989 and 1990. Seasoned professionals would regard that as no bad thing. There has been more than enough short-term speculative investment in shipping and far too little attention paid to the creation of coherent and consistently profitable transportation businesses. Unless this situation is corrected in the next five years, the capital structure of the shipping industry will remain unbalanced and acutely vulnerable to adverse supply and demand influences.

PORTS SET FOR BOX GROWTH

A review of the latest and planned developments by Clive Woodbridge

Container traffic volumes at the world's major ports seem set for a sustained period of growth. International trade is increasing at a steady rate, and this is the most important factor behind optimistic projections, but there is still conversion of break-bulk trades to the box, and this too is leading to higher container throughput levels. A recent study, published by CSR Consultants of the UK*, for example, has forecast that container throughputs at world ports will increase from a level of 64.1 million TEU in 1987 to 73.4 million TEU by 1990, a 15% increase over a four year period. By the year 2000, the same study predicts that container traffic will have risen further to 11.06 million TEU, a 73% jump.

Of course, not all ports will share equally in this increasing container business, and it is likely that those in the strategic Pacific Rim centres will see the greatest rise in box handlings. By comparison, many ports on the US North Atlantic Coast, as well as in Europe, will experience more modest rates of growth.

In all areas, though, there will be an extremely competitive container port environment, as terminals bid for traffic which will be concentrated in the hands of a smaller, more powerful group of lines and consortia, who in turn will be looking to rationalise their ports of call. At the same time, the pressure on ports to invest in infrastructure and latest generation handling equipment, will grow sharply.

This creates a difficult set of circumstances for container ports, in the sense that the tendency for lines to establish regional 'load centres' must introduce an element of uncertainty, as some ports must inevitably lose out by this process, just as others will gain. Yet investment requirements for those bidding for traffic will increase. The CSR Consultants' report significantly comments that, "Only a small number of front rank container ports and terminals world wide possess the volume throughput bases and superior inland linkage necessary to justify the sizeable requisite investment." In other words, there is a danger that some of the massive port investment projects now underway will prove to be expensive 'white elephants'.

Four ports, Hong Kong, Singapore, Kaohsiung and Rotterdam stand out for their recent growth record, and seem likely to assert their positions as dominant load centres. All four handled over 3 million TEU in 1988, while Hong Kong managed to top the 4 million TEU mark.

In fact, throughput at Hong Kong's Kwai Chung container terminals totalled 4,033,000 TEU, nearly 17% up on the 1987 figure. A further growth in excess of 10% is anticipated for this year, suggesting that the port will exceed 5 million TEU in 1990.

To cope with this staggering volume of container traffic, major infrastructural improvements are underway. The Terminal 6 facility came on stream in mid-1988 and should be fully operational by the end of this year. Last year, terminal operator, HIT, won the right to the new Terminal 7, which should be ready by 1991.

The explosion of container traffic at Hong Kong means that even these new terminals are unlikely to be sufficient to meet the ports needs into the 21st century. Consequently, a major study is in progress to determine where to put Terminals 8 and 9, now that all space at Kwai Chung has been exhausted. A decision on this is expected to be made in the next few months.

Singapore, Hong Kong's nearest rival, handled some 3.4. million TEU in 1988, a massive 27.5% leap from 1987 throughput. Here too space constraints are making themselves felt, and the Port of Singapore Authority has started to build a new container complex on the offshore island of Pulau Brani. When this is finished it will have five container berths and three feedership berths.

The first of these berths, and the causeway linking the island to the mainland, should be ready by 1991.

Development in Taiwan

Taiwan's Kaohsiung port consolidated its position as the third largest container centre in the Far East, handling some 3.08 million TEU, a 12% increase on the previous year. It, too, is investing heavily in additional facilities, to cater for future trade increases.

This work centres on the new Terminal 4 development on Chi-Chin island. In March this year a $100 million two-berth facility for Sea-Land was opened, following the completion of two other berths, leased to Evergreen and K Line. Three additional berths at Terminal 4 are due to come on stream by the end of 1990.

Another massive container terminal development is already being planned by the Kaohsiung Harbour Bureau. The Harbour 5 complex will be built on a 100 acre site which until recently was used for shipbreaking purposes.

Work could well start on this project later in 1989, to meet projected increases in traffic in the 1990s. Up to 8 additional berths are to be constructed as part of Harbour 5, increasing the port's capacity by a further 1.5 million TEU.

Although Japan does not have one single port in the 3 million TEU+ league, it has three ports, Kobe, Yokohama and Tokyo, in the World Top 20 container ports, based on TEU throughput. Between them, these three handled over 4.7 million TEU last year, and collectively Japanese ports handle more containers, in TEU, than any other country in the world, with the exception of the United States.

Currently, several hundred million dollars are being invested to expand these ports. Perhaps the most striking of these projects is the Rokko Island development at Kobe, phase one of which is due for completion in 1990. Five container berths are already in operation here, with two more scheduled to come on stream by the end of the year.

Work has, in fact, recently started on Phase Two of the Rokko Port Island project, and land reclamation is expected to be finished in the mid-1990s. Current plans include five new container berths.

It has also recently been announced that K Line is to build a new container terminal on 50,000 square metres of land next to the RC-3 Rokko Island terminal, after acquiring the land from the municipal government of Kobe.

In Tokyo, construction work has now started on a second berth at the Aomi Terminal. This will be a 350m long facility, equipped with two ship to shore container gantries. It is expected to be completed in 1991.

The port of Yokohama also has significant plans for development. In the short term, two berths totalling 650m are being built at the Daikoku Piers. These should be ready by the end of 1989.

In addition, however, it is expected that work will start this year on the new container facilities which are to be built at South Honmoku Piers. Comprising four berths, each 350m long, with a depth of 14m alongside, the terminal should be completed by 1991.

European growth

Although container throughputs in Northern Europe are not expected to match those of the main Far East facilities for dynamic growth over the next few years, a major surge in the development of container terminal facilities is currently underway.

By far the biggest container port in Europe, Rotterdam's container throughput rose

to 3.29 million TEU from 2.81 million in 1987, when industrial disputes hit the port. A further 12-15% increase is projected for 1989.

Several major projects are in progress at Rotterdam, including the construction of three distribution centres, or "Distriparks". On the quayside, Phase 1 of Unitcentre's Pier 6 complex has recently been completed, bringing into service 445m of quay, with two new container gantry cranes. A second phase, involving a further 400m of quay space, will be ready for use by the end of 1989.

Elsewhere, the largest terminal operator in Rotterdam, ECT, is to build additional facilities on the Maasvlakte, as part of its deal to keep Sea-Land, and these will be completed in 1993, while Bell Lines is investing heavily to expand its Rozenburg terminal.

The rival port of Antwerp is also pressing ahead with the major new Scheldt container terminal, which will offer lines modern facilities outside of the lock gates, and so faster turnround times. Work on the terminal, which will be operated by Hessenatie, is on schedule, and is expected to be operational by April 1990.

The Belgian port of Zeebrugge is also mounting a serious challenge for box business, and has said that work on a new three berth container terminal in the outer port will start later this year. The extension of the Ocean Containerterminal Zeebrugge facility is already in progress.

U.K. east coast

In the UK, container terminal development activity is concentrated almost exclusively on the east coast. Most notably, the Port of Felixstowe is spending around £50 million to extend its Trinity container terminal by some 315m, adding three new quayside container cranes and 10 rubber tyred gantry cranes. Trinity II, which is needed to handle the rapidly increasing volume of container traffic through the port, is scheduled to start operations later this year, and to be completed by early 1990.

When Trinity II comes on stream it will be faced with a new competitor, in the form of Thames Estuary Terminals, a subsidiary of Highland Participants, which is building a £80 million 'superport' on the Isle of Grain. Phase 1 of the container terminal development is due to be operational by the end of this year. With an initial capacity of 150,000 TEU a year, the Isle of Grain terminal will eventually be capable of handling up to 350,000 TEU annually, or some 10% of total UK box traffic.

A largely unknown factor on the east coast is Sea Containers' intentions for the port of Harwich; the company has plans, and permission, for a container terminal at Bathside Bay.

West Germany and France

No major new facilities are planned in West Germany, although there is still considerable spending on port infrastructure. In Hamburg, for example, terminal operator HHLA is adding a new 210m long berth on the Burchardkai, and two new 'beyond Panamax' container cranes are to be installed here in the next year. Extensive work to expand the Eurokai terminal is also in hand.

Meanwhile, Bremer Lagerhaus-Gesellschaft (BLG) is extending the quay at Neustaden in the port of Bremen by 450m, and is buying two new gantry cranes for Bremerhaven.

The French ports of Le Havre and Dunkirk are similarly investing in additional container handling infrastructure. Perhaps the most ambitious is Le Havre's new Rapid turnround Port, which is geared towards attracting transhipment container business. However, the Port of Dunkirk is also to build an additional container berth, by lengthening the quay by some 200m.

THE PORT OF BRISTOL

The Gateway and the Great way to and from Great Britain!

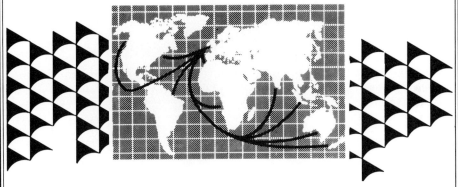

You want your company to be run ship-shape and Bristol fashion. That means the best!

So, when you're talking about importing and exporting, where else could you go for the finest port facilities but Bristol itself?

It's the gateway — and the great way — into and out of Great Britain.

Centuries of experience in world trade, plus the most modern deep-water berths and immediate Motorway outlets to the nation make Bristol your first port of call.

With savings of up to 300 nautical miles on Mediterranean and Atlantic routes, plus swift access to two-thirds of the population of England and Wales within 125 miles of the Port, shipping through Bristol saves time all round.

And that means hard cash to your company.

That's why — whatever the cargo — it pays to ship Bristol fashion.

THE PORT OF BRISTOL
WE'RE PART OF YOUR FUTURE

St. Andrews Road, Avonmouth, Bristol BS11 9DQ.
Tel: (0272) 823681 24 Hrs.
Telex: 44240 PBAAMG. Facsimile: 820698.

73

Risk of overcapacity

All in all, then, there is a great deal of activity, and capital spending, on container terminals in northern Europe. The use of new technology, including highspeed container cranes, will improve performance at these ports, but there must be a danger of serious over capacity in the European container port sector emerging in the early 1990s.

United States and Canada

On the US North Atlantic coast, where container throughputs have been under pressure in recent times, the largest new container terminal development is to be seen in the port of Baltimore, where the Maryland Port Administration (MPA) is pinning its hopes on its $250 million Seagirt container facility, which is to come on stream in stages. Equipped with six high technology cranes on three new berths, Seagirt will be one of the most modern container terminals in the United States.

Associated with this project, the MPA has also constructed an Intermodal Container Transfer Facility (ICTF) close to Seagirt, with a view to facilitating the transfer of containers moving to and from the hinterland. The MPA has signed a 15 year deal with the CSX railroad for the latter to use the ICTF.

Further south, the Georgia Ports Authority (GPA) has two major planning projects in hand to upgrade Savannah's container handling facilities. Firstly, the intention is construct a sixth berth at the Garden City containerport, to be operational in the early 1990s.

In the longer term, however, the GPA's plans for development focus on a 2200 acre site called Mulberry Grove. Eventually, it is envisaged that an integrated container port and intermodal facilities will be built here.

The US South Atlantic port of Charleston handled some 717,000 TEU in 1988, an increase of over 23% on 1987, taking cumulative growth at the port since 1987 to 81.5%. The Wando terminal at Charleston is being expanded, with the addition of 1300ft of berth and 62 acres of container storage space. Completion is expected for late 1989, and should increase capacity at the terminal by some 30%.

A number of sites for a fourth terminal at Charleston are under consideration, and it is expected that plans for a major expansion to take the port into the 1990s will be announced later this year. This project would involve building a further 8 berths on a area of over 800 acres. These berths are unlikely to be ready before 1995, however.

A considerable amount of activity in terms of new infrastructure is to be found on the Canadian East Coast. To press home its position as Canada's leading container port, Montreal is planing to invest around Can$ 60 million in container handling facilities over the next five years, including the possible development of a new container terminal adjacent to the Cast facility. In the longer term, plans are being drawn up for a new terminal on a 150 hectare site on the south of the St Lawrence River.

At Halifax, there are plans to build a third container terminal, following the recent completion of a 50m extension to the Halifax International Container Terminal at a cost of Can $ 5.4 million. Furthermore, in a surprise move, the port of Quebec is to return to container handling after a gap of some 10 years. The port plans to develop a new terminal at Pier 54, adjacent to an existing bulk facility.

Pacific coast expansion

Linked in to the Pacific Rim economic boom, ports on the West Coast would appear to be in a more expansive phase of development. For example, at Long Beach's six container terminals, over 1.5 million TEU were handled in 1988, with the result that the port is now operating close to full capacity.

PORT OF PONTA DELGADA
ST. MICHAEL'S, AZORES

The only bunkering station and port of refuge in the CENTRAL NORTH ATLANTIC OCEAN area, between NORTH AMERICA, BERMUDA or the CARIBBEAN ports and EUROPE directly on the route of the great air and shipping lines.

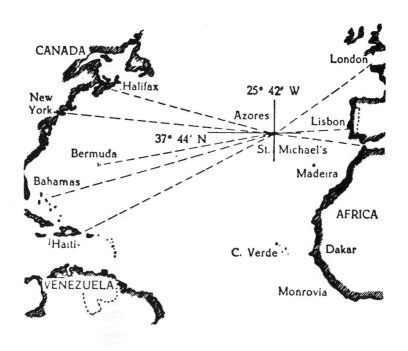

GENERAL FACILITIES

PILOTS — 24-hour service.

REPAIRS — All kinds, Electronic.

TUGS — "São Miguel" (3400 H.P.); "Corpo Santo" (1100 H.P.).

BUNKERS — Supplied by pipeline in all quays (minimum depth L.W. 36ft.).

FRESH WATER — From quays (at 85.00 Esc per ton plus Waterman charge).

SHIP CHANDLERS — Fresh provisions and stores.

PORT OF PONTA DELGADA
ST. MICHAEL'S, AZORES

25° 42' W

ST. MICHAEL'S

37° 44' N

P. Delgada

Its exceptionally favourable position, close to the NORTH ATLANTIC LANE ROUTES, half-way across the line of navigation NORTH AMERICA - GIBRALTAR and CARIBBEAN SEA - EUROPE, makes PONTA DELGADA a most valuable help for ships seeking a good and safe shelter to:

repair damages from bad weather;

repair engine and electronic troubles;

land sick or wounded people needing urgent medical assistance;

bunker fuel oil, diesel oil, gas oil and lubrication oils; take fresh water, fresh provisions and stores.

PILOTAGE RATES

Ships entering for bunkering, provisions, water, repairs or for those on tourist cruises, 50% reduction.

Ships entering to land sick or wounded people, a nominal fee only will be charged for services rendered.

PORT CHARGES

Ships entering to land sick or wounded people and hospital ships *are exempt* from harbour dues.

Enquiries to:

Director of Port, Ponta Delgada
TELEX: 82287 PORTOS P
Harbour Master, Ponta Delgada
TELEX: 82287 PORTOS P

Cables:

Director Porto
   Ponta Delgada
Capitaniamar
   Ponta Delgada

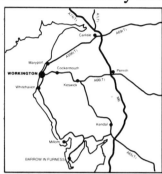

To alleviate this pressure, a $1150 million project to expand Pier J is now in progress, to add two new container terminals and four ship berths, the first of which will be operational within two years. Additional container-related projects at Long Beach include the modification and expansion of the Sea-Land container terminal, and the transformation of Pier C into a container area.

In the next three years, over $ 100 million is being invested in the development of new terminal facilities at the port of Oakland, as part of its bid to compete for increasing levels of container traffic on the West Coast. An important element in its plans is the construction of a new container terminal in the outer harbour on a 38 acre site. The Carnation Terminal, as it is to be called, will be equipped with two ship-to-shore container gantry cranes, and is scheduled to be operational by the end of 1989.

To keep pace with growth in its container tonnage throughput, which last year totalled over 1 million TEU, the port of Seattle opened up its new Terminal 30 container terminal, a facility built at a cost of $39 million, and equipped with two post-panamax container cranes.

During 1989, Seattle will construct its first on-dock rail facility at Terminal 18. The intermodal rail yard, with direct access from both the Burlington Northern and Union Pacific railroads, will be able to accommodate 28 double stack container rail cars at one time.

Investment in other areas

Of course, these container port developments are only a selection of the work in progress, or planned, at the major port centres. There are numerous others at subsidiary ports, particularly in Asia. For example, there is considerable investment being made at ports in Malaysia, Indonesia and Thailand, in an effort to upgrade facilities to cope with growing export volumes. In addition, there are several important projects in China, and in India, where container port development work at Calcutta, Madras and Bombay is in progress.

By comparison, though, there is relatively little investment in container facilities in South America, Africa or the Middle East, as a reflection of the economic problems which these regions have had to face.

As conduits for international trade, ports are vulnerable to movements in the world economy. At the present time, the situation looks good, and this has prompted some of the projects described. There are however a number of imponderables.

The trade deficits of the United States, and now the UK, are matched by the huge surpluses of countries like Japan and West Germany. Unless some steps are taken to reduce this imbalance, protectionist pressures must mount, and this can only be bad for trade.

The impact of the single market in Europe after 1992 is another uncertain influence. If a "Fortress Europe" policy is adopted this too could lead to damaging trade wars between the developed countries.

If there is a major slow-down in world trade in the 1990s, ports may reflect that their optimism in investment in additional facilities for container traffic was mis-placed. If trade continues to grow, the money in many cases will have been well spent.

*"Container Transportation Costs and Profitability 1980/2000" is available, price £390 (UK), or US $ 750, from CSR Consultants, 4 Gainsborough Avenue, St Albans, Hertfordshire, AL1 4NL, England.

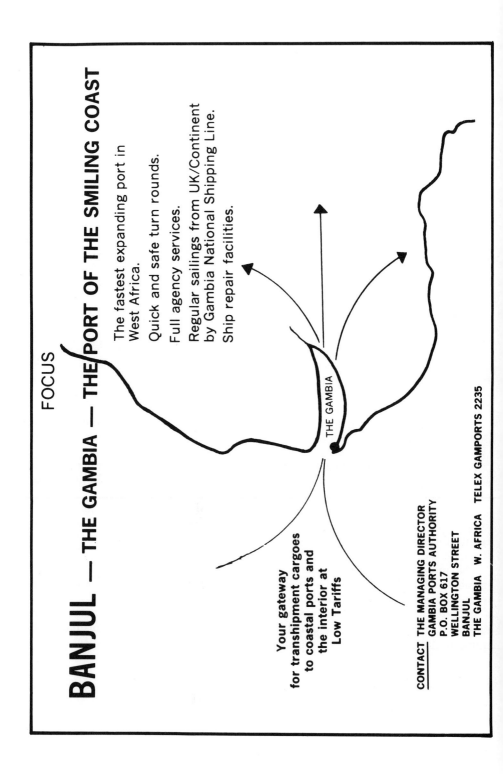

FOCUS

BANJUL — THE GAMBIA — THE PORT OF THE SMILING COAST

The fastest expanding port in West Africa.

Quick and safe turn rounds.

Full agency services.

Regular sailings from UK/Continent by Gambia National Shipping Line.

Ship repair facilities.

THE GAMBIA

Your gateway
for transhipment cargoes
to coastal ports and
the interior at
Low Tariffs

CONTACT THE MANAGING DIRECTOR
GAMBIA PORTS AUTHORITY
P.O. BOX 617
WELLINGTON STREET
BANJUL
THE GAMBIA   W. AFRICA   TELEX GAMPORTS 2235

BEYOND-PANAMAX CONTAINER CRANES BECOMING STANDARD

Clive Woodbridge examines the development of container crane design

The past year has seen the beginning of a new era as far as the design of ship-to-shore container gantry cranes is concerned. Around the world, major throughput ports are commissioning fourth generation cranes, with the capability to handle ships of beyond-Panamax dimensions.

Although only one container operator, American President Line (APL), has so far actually put ships with dimensions such that they cannot sail through the Panama canal into service — its C10 class vessels are now in operation on the Pacific — it is likely that others will follow suit in time. Indeed, Nedlloyd has invited tenders from a number of shipyards for beyond-Panamax ships for delivery in the early 1990s.

Since container cranes can cost around £2.5 million each, they have to be viewed as a long term investment, with a working life of at least 20 years. It may seem a little premature to invest in cranes which are only needed by a handful of ships, but ports have to take the long term view. To do otherwise would run the risk of premature obsolence.

Not surprisingly, the most substantial investment in the new generation cranes has been made by facilities serving APL's C10s in the Pacific Rim. At least 27 post-Panamax container gantry cranes, with outreach capabilities of up to 152ft, are being installed at the ports of Los Angeles, Oakland, Yokohama, Kobe, Hong Kong and Kaohsiung.

The Hong Kong terminal operator, HIT, for example, has ordered seven post-Panamax cranes from Mitsui Engineering and Shipbuilding (MES) for its new Terminal 6 facility. It has followed this up in the past few months by placing a massive US $43 million contract with MES for another nine cranes capable of servicing beyond-Panamax ships for the Terminal 7 facility, which is now under construction.

These latest cranes feature a 41m outreach from the quay wall and a 33m lift above the quay. This will allow them to handle ships with up to 17 rows of containers stacked across the deck, and up to five high. These cranes are expected to be delivered in stages from November 1989 to August 1990.

New cranes for Singapore

It is not just APL-orientated facilities which are opting for the new generation cranes. The Port of Singapore Authority, has ordered 10 Mitsubishi cranes, each with an outreach of 47m and a 34m clear lift above the crane rails. Furthermore, rival US flag containership operator, Sea-Land, is to take delivery of three 'super gantry' cranes for its recently completed Berth 118-119 at the port of Kaohsiung, Taiwan. These are expected to be in operation by September 1989.

Similarly, a sister company of the Danish Maersk Line, Maersk Container Services, has ordered three 50 long ton capacity ship-to-shore cranes from Coast Engineering and Manufacturing Co. (CEMCO). These cranes will all have post-Panamax capability, and are to be installed at the ports of New York/New Jersey, Long Beach and Oakland in the first half of 1990. They will have outreach dimensions of 135ft, 140ft and 150ft respectively, suggesting that the company expects the larger vessels to be deployed on the Pacific trades.

Other US West Coast ports have also arrived at this conclusion, and specified greater outreach cranes for container handling. In addition to Oakland and Los Angeles, which are the US base ports for the APL C10s, the port of Seattle now has a total of six beyond-Panamax cranes, while the port of Portland has commissioned two 145ft outreach cranes from Hyundai of South Korea. The port authority of Long Beach California, says it is "specifically studying the handling and berthing needs of beyond-Panamax vessels in terms of crane modification, crane safety and harbour deepening."

It will be some time before a European port sees containerships of the greater-than-Panamax type on a regular basis. This is not deterring many terminal operators from specifying cranes that can handle such vessels, however.

In West Germany, for instance, the Bremen operator BLG is to take delivery of two cranes built by local manufacturer Vulcan Kocks, each with an outreach of 48m, while in Hamburg, HHLA has ordered a 44m outreach unit from Peiner Noell, with an option for a second, similar crane.

Perhaps one of the biggest investments in greater-than-Panamax cranes has been made by Hessenatie of Antwerp for its new container terminal on the Scheldt. The company has chosen Rotterdam-based Nelcon to manufacture four high-speed ship-to-shore cranes, each featuring a 47.5m outreach and a 50 tonne lift capacity under the spreader.

The UK, too, is being equipped to handle the ships of the future. Southampton Container Terminals has taken delivery of such a crane from Davy Morris, while this company is also building three beyond-Panamax container gantry cranes for the Trinity II container terminal at Felixstowe. The new Isle of Grain container terminal, due to open late in 1990, is to be equipped initially with two high speed cranes currently under manufacture in Italy by Magrini Galileo of Padua. These cranes will be able to handle containers stacked 16 across on the deck of a containership, giving them beyond-Panamax capacity.

Double-trolley systems

As well as the trend towards larger size, to accommodate the latest generation of containerships, there is also a movement towards the use of double-trolley systems, as a way of improving productivity. This idea started with the ECT cranes built by Nelcon for the Delta terminal, and has been adapted by Kone for Virginia International Terminals (VIT) at the port of Norfolk on the US East Coast. There are signs, though, that the idea is catching on.

Many of the cranes installed at terminals handling APL ships, for instance, have incorporated a capability for installing a dual trolley system at some time in the future. These include the Mitsubishi-built units at Oakland and Los Angeles, as well as those built by MES for Kaohsiung.

The Tokyo Port Terminal Corporation has actually specified a dual trolley container gantry crane, from MES. This was due to be delivered around mid-1989, for a terminal operated by Mitsui OSK Line (MOL). This is the first crane of double-trolley type to be ordered by a Japanese port.

On the US East Coast, the Maryland Port Authority is currently in the process of taking delivery of a total of six cranes built by Sumitomo Heavy Industries in South Korea, for the new Seagirt Container Terminal at the port of Baltimore. Of these, two are fitted with a double-trolley system, with the other four designed with a view to retro-fitting such a facility at some time in the future.

On the Seagirt double trolley cranes, the main trolley will be able to operate at speeds up to 700ft/minute, while the second trolley will have a speed of 440ft/minute.

For its two new post-Panamax cranes, BLG has also specified a design that makes it possible to attach a second trolley at a later date should this be required. The port says that this can be achieved without exceeding the corner and wheel loads permissable on the Bremerhaven berth, and the technical requirements for such alterations have

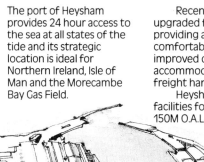

in fact already been prepared. The new quayside cranes being installed at Felixstowe by Davy Morris are similarly being provided with the capability of conversions to dual hoist at a later date.

The benefits of the dual-hoist approach are evident at VIT, where operational experience of Kone's dual-hoist system indicates greatly improved container handling productivity.

Cost savings potential

According to VIT, when handling Panamax class vessels, a stevedoring productivity of almost 40 containers per hour can be achieved, a figure which includes time spent for operational delays. When these do not occur, a level of 50 boxes an hour can be maintained.

Given this improvement in productivity, it is evident that this technology does offer considerable potential for cost saving. Indeed, Kone has estimated that for a shipping line handling 30,000 boxes a year at a terminal, and asusming a low-side productivity of 35 containers an hour, saving of over $1 million a year can be obtained, when compared with single hoist operation.

Another path towards improved performance has been the incorporation of more sophisticated control systems, with digital drives replacing analong devices. As an example, HIT has specified digital drive in its latest 9-crane order. The company says it believes this type of drive offers the best form of control and reliability, and also facilitates eventual incorporation of a data transmission system.

The drive mechanisms on the two new BLG cranes have also been upgraded for greater power and speed. In particular, the recording and control systems for the drive mechanisms, along with those for surveillance, are fully digital, and are micro-processor based.

Further confirming the trend, the Hessenatie order for four cranes from Nelcon, and the Port of Felixstowe's three for the Trinity II terminal specify digital drives.

Increasingly then, the "standard" quayside container crane for the 1990s is taking shape. It will be 'beyond-Panamax', usually with an outreach in excess of 140ft to allow it to lift the 16th container on deck; it will be designed with dual trolley facilities in mind, if not in place; and will feature digital electronic controls, using microprocessors, rather than the more traditional analog or hard Leonard devices. Automation, or semi-automation, is another possiblity, but in reality only a few exceptionally high throughput facilities are likely to be in a position to justify this, for the time being at least.

GAS — THE LNG TRADES IN THE 1990s.

by John Prescott,
Energy Correspondent, Lloyd's List

A review

For the first time in many years a sense of excitement is pervading the maritime gas trades. There are now real prospects that the international gas supply business, which suffered as a result of the oil crises of the 1970s, now has the chance to lay strong foundations for solid growth through the 1990s and the first decade or more of the new millenium.

There is a tangible mood of optimism for both the pipeline and ship bourne trades of natural gas — a contrast to the situation as recently as two years ago, when the world was basking in an unreal world of low oil prices and taking rather a complacent view of future energy needs.

At the same time there has been growing pressure for a complete rethink, if not revisal, of many countries' plans for nuclear power. In one notable case, that of Sweden, a complete ban has been put on building new nuclear power stations and existing nuclear plants are being phased out. Thinking in many industrialised countries is following the same lines, although it is doubtful whether such extreme action will be taken.

While nuclear power carries the cachet of potentially dreadful contamination, oil and coal, the only real alternatives with gas as fuels for large-scale power generation in the industrialised world, are increasingly seen as heavy pollutants of the atmosphere and aiding damage to the earth's ozone layer. Gas, conversely, is viewed increasingly as a clean-burning fuel with much fewer of the harmful emissions associated with oil and coal.

Against this, gas has been perceived as a premium fuel. It is a resource for which it is much more difficult to organise a flexible transport system so that it can be easily traded in varying amounts, for varying terms and across any geographical pattern. This question of gas' inflexible infrastructure is likely to remain with us, regardless of other developments that favour its wider use.

By its nature, natural gas must be transported either by pipe at relatively low pressures, or by tank in its liquefied state. Overland pipelines are comparatively inexpensive to build and maintain and enable a continuous or variable flow of gas. They are permanent structures, though, and thus inflexible for varying sites of source or delivery. Tankers — or more properly liquefied natural gas carriers — do allow gas transport between any number of different sites (although those coastal sites still have to be served by pipeline from the gas source and to the customer's premises) but the ships are expensive to build and operate and shipments are "batched" and non-continuous.

Transport of natural gas by ship is only feasible if the product is first condensed to a state where the maximum volume can be carried in the smallest space. This liquefaction process to produce liquefied natural gas (LNG) is also expensive in both capital plant and in operation, and at the receiving port the liquid must be re-gasified for onward pipeline transmission. These factors alone can negate the advantage to worldwide trading that ships otherwise have over pipelines.

Both transport modes need large capital resources, long gestation, and above all require assured long term contracts. For example, one LNG project now entering the realisation phase with the signing of actual sales contracts, will not deliver first gas until the beginning of 1995 and will absorb $2.5 billion. The 4 million tonnes a year project, based on supplies from Nigeria, has already been in the planning phase for many years.

Disenchantment with other energy sources is leading many industrialised countries to review policies taking account of gas, for the first time in some cases. Among producers, gas has long since ceased to be a wasted resource — its value is now receiving due universal recognition. Apart from in the Far East, this new climate of opinion has largely manifested itself, if at all so far, in additional pipeline sales. The Norwegians, for example, have sold to European customers piped gas which is to come on stream in the mid-1990s from the massive North Sea developments centred on the Troll field.

In the Far East, where energy sources are removed from the large Japanese industrial market and the growing markets of Taiwan and South Korea, geography dictates that gas is transported by sea, and it was this Far East demand that sustained modest growth in the LNG business in the 1980s. It was a period when, until 1988, recession caused by the fuel's poor competitive standing hit the LNG trades virtually everywhere except the Far East.

The position for LNG had worsened to a stage where as recently as the beginning of 1988 12 LNG carriers — among the world's most expensive ships — were laid up with no prospect of employment. Algeria was a focus of much of this downturn, being the major supplier of LNG in the western hemisphere. By 1985, Algeria's customers in the US and Europe were taking less than a third of their contracted volume. The volume not taken was the equivalent of more than nine of the Nigerian projects.

Pricing of LNG is crucial. It was rigid prices for Algerian gas in the early eighties that forced US buyers in particular to pull out of their contracts. A new realism now pervades the market with Algeria settling several long-standing arguments over prices and other supplies showing they are prepared to negotiate realistic prices. Indeed, sensible prices are necessary if producers want to make headway in the

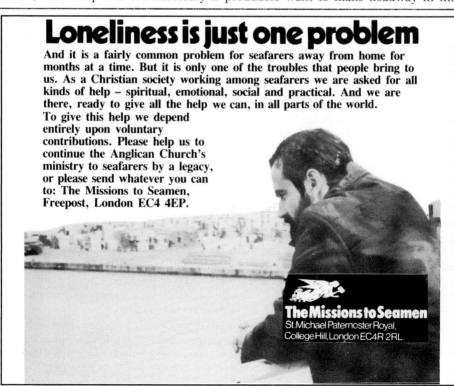

market.

During 1989, Statoil in Norway introduced a novel natural gas pricing formula linked to coal prices for certain Dutch customers, rather than the more common oil-related pricing. Apart from offering a more stable base, a coal-related price shifts the competitive framework so that gas has a more even fight in the market. Other gas buyers are looking for a similarly stable index if they are to commit themselves to major long-term contracts.

Developments in the LNG Trades

After 14 years' planning Australia's North Shelf LNG project has been realised with deliveries of the first cargoes to Japan under a 20 year, 6m tons/year contract. The project costing Aus$9.8 billion is a joint Australian-Japanese development which includes the construction of seven 125,000 cubic metre capacity purpose-built LNG carriers, the first built worldwide for several years. The ships, of which two have still to be ordered from builders, are owned by the various project partners.

With the North West Shelf debut, Australia becomes a major league competitor in the Far East LNG trades. Closest to it, both geographically and in volume terms, is Indonesia, the world's largest LNG exporter. Indonesia's state oil company Pertamina was among the first into the LNG arena in the Far East when deliveries to a group of Japanese companies started in 1977. The 7m tons a year are carried by British operator Burmah using eight US-owned timechartered ships.

Japanese imports from Indonesia doubled by 1984 when fresh fob contracts came into operation, calling for delivery of 6.5m tons of LNG a year. Seven Japanese built, owned and operated ships are employed on this run.

The most recent project between these countries is more modest involving deliveries of just over 2m tons a year. The contract demonstrated that LNG can be brought on stream very quickly. Signed in 1987, it was an incremental, short-term contract for Chubu Electric and with the purchase by Japanese owners of a secondhand ship (P&O's *Pollenger*) deliveries were able to start almost immediately.

Japanese utilities are also the buyers of around 6m tons a year from the Malaysian LNG scheme at Bintulu — a joint Petronas and Shell project. The 20 year contract, the shipping phase of which is covered by five Malaysian ships, expires in 2003. Shell is also involved in the neighbouring Brunei's LNG export project delivering around 4.8m tons a year to a group of three Japanese utilities. Brunei, started in 1972, was one of the world's first large-scale export projects and is among those due for renewal within the next few years. Both Malaysia's and Brunei's are cif contracts.

Abu Dhabi and Alaska are minor suppliers to Japan, delivering about 2m and 1m tons a year respectively under 20 year contracts. Abu Dhabi has the potential, because of a massive gas discovery, to increase sales to this and other buyers, while the Alaskan contract has been renewed for 15 years, plus a five year option.

South Korea and Taiwan are new purchasers on the market. Indonesia's Pertamina began deliveries of 2m tons a year to Korea Gas under a 20 year contract in 1986, and Chinese Petroleum begins buying of 1.5m tons a year from Pertamina next year. CPC's project is of added interest as it will mark the first LNG cross-trade for Japanese owners. A consortium of owners has built the world's largest LNG carrier (136,400 cu m) for the trade.

In Europe and the Mediterranean, the most mature region for LNG shipping, a clutch of projects are in progress based on supplies from Algeria and Libya. A total of about 1.5m tons a year is sold by Libya to national utilities in Italy and Spain, with Algeria's Sonatrach selling more than 12m tons a year to France, Spain and Belgium.

Sonatrach also has also recently supplied a nominal few cargoes across the Atlantic to Distrigas in Boston, Mass., that could be the basis for patching up soured relationships with North American buyers, which were among Sonatrach's biggest customers until deliveries fizzled out three years ago over differences on price.

Outlook for the nineties

The new realism of producers over LNG pricing has already borne fruit. Once infrastructure — liquefaction plant, terminals, ships and the like — is in place and amortised, the natural resource is comparitvely cheap to produce. Long-established producers such as Algeria have realised this and are actively seeking fresh outlets of incremental increases to existing contracts.

The progress gathered pace in 1988 when Algeria's Sontrach signed deals with Greece, Turkey, the UK and the US. Small though these contracts were, they demonstrated that opportunities exist for all types of LNG schemes, especially if indexing of prices over the life of, say, a 20 year contract can be made against coal or some other base that will fluctuate over a relatively narrow range.

The question on many people's minds now is whether a real spot market in LNG will be permitted to establish itself through the emergence of factors such as these and the new view of gas as a clean-burning, efficient form of energy suitable for electricity generation. Contract periods are becoming shorter and contract volumes more flexible, as the three year Pertamina/Chubu Electric deal and the winter peak shaving Sonatrach/British Gas contracts illustrated. Clearly, the big projects will continue — they are needed to underwrite the huge cost of development — but there is a growing need for smaller and less frequent deliveries than buyers commit themselves to under a major scheme, and these deals are already forming the nucleus of a spot market.

The question then is: Should shipowners invest in LNG carriers to supply an emergent spot market? The answer, bearing in mind the $150 million or more price tag of a single large ship, is almost definitely no. A more likely course will be for the

ships coming off long term hire from the major projects during the 1990s to be snapped up for the variable spot or short-term trades.

Already a number of such vessels present themselves as subjects during the next five to ten years. An interesting group is Burmah's eight ships timechartered from the US to perform the Indonesia-Japan contract. The 126,000 cu m ships come off hire under the contract in 1997/8 and yet Burmah (and its new partner in the project, Mitsui) have the ships for a further five years, at the moment without contracted employment.

It seems likely that with this key link to the Japanese market through one of Japan's largest shipowners, the vessels will find employment at the end of their present contract in the Far East trades, where several possibilities will exist in both the Japanese and the cross-traders in the late 1990s. Equally, there will almost certainly be short-term opportunities in the Atlantic basin.

Major project for Nigeria?

The next major project to get underway is almost certain to be Bonny in Nigeria. Among recent developments, are the formation by the partners, Nigerian National Petroleum, Shell, Elf and Agip, of an operating company and the signing of sales agreements with US, West German, Spanish, French and Italian buyers. First deliveries of the project's 4m tons a year are expected at the beginning of 1995.

Shrewd moves by Shell, which is technical adviser to the project, have ensured that Bonny will probably start with the cheapest LNG carriers any major shipping project has yet been able to obtain. Almost before many realised the LNG trade was starting to move again after its early 1980s' setbacks, Shell secured options and commitments on a total of seven unemployed LNG carriers, two of which had never been used. This gambit virtually cleared the market of free tonnage within the space of six to nine months in 1988, while ensuring that Bonny had the five ships it needed, and at unrepeatable prices.

The move also deprived potential competitors of getting a foot on the ladder to cheap ships. At least one — the Norwegian scheme to ship LNG to the US — is regretting its failure to act sooner to secure its shipping needs. For Shell,the possibility of taking a total of seven ships will not only serve the needs of the Bonny project but possibly the expansion of other schemes in which the group is involved, although it emerged in 1988 that an expansion of Malaysian exports from around 6m tons to 10m tons a year in 1992 will be with four newbuildings, rather than secondhand ships. Any expansion of the Brunei project, where Shell is 33% partner, could benefit, or perhaps Shell is looking further ahead to the end of the present Brunei contract in 1993 when the existing 75,000 and 77,000 cu m ships will be 20 years old.

The Middle East is among the best prospects for major LNG schemes in future. At the moment Abu Dhabi exports a modest 2m tons a year to Japan under a contract expiring 1977 but has reserves that, if tapped, could be exploited for further LNG sales. Similarly, Qatar has the world's largest gas field and ambitions under the field's third stage of development to export to the Far East, although this phase is still only a possibility.

In the Pacific basin, Japan has imported Alaskan gas for many years but there are plans to raise a new LNG project based on gas reserves from Prudhoe Bay in the north. Some scepticism has been voiced over the $11 billion scheme which would require 15 large LNG carriers. However, manager Yukon Pacific has denied suggestions that the project would not be viable unless it produced a minimum of 14m tons a year. The company claims that a minimum of seven to eight million tons exported annually to three Far East buyers would make the scheme viable.

Doubt continues over exports of LNG to the US. Several countries have ambitions to either start or expand sales there, especially to the eastern seaboard — Norway, Algeria and Nigeria are the best placed geographically quantitively. Norway is striving to bring in US customers, while Nigeria has achieved this aim and Algeria, after earlier contract failures, is trying to rebuild its US market.

It has not been lost on these producers that LNG need not be exclusively a short or medium distance trade. The occasional cargo has crossed the Pacific and in 1989 Algeria sold LNG to Japan for the first time. The Atlantic rim producers therefore face possible competition in the US market just as they themselves present competition to traditional suppliers to the Far East markets. The phenomenon will be more marked in the short term and spot trades.

The future

Further change in LNG shipping will be seen in the perceived life expectancy of LNG carriers. Though the ships were once built and financed for a 20 year life, many, including the containment system designers defending reputations for good structural integrity and shipowners keen to benefit from trading fully amortised ships, now assert their ships are capable of at least 30 or 35 years' safe operation. It poses an acute question in the coming decade when more than 65% (50 ships) of the world fleet reaches its 20th anniversary.

Large LNG projects with specific long term customers will undoubtedly emerge during this last ten years of the millenium — and some will look for new tonnage to meet political or environmental concerns. Other, perhaps with sharper commercial objectives, will find the lure of older, cheaper tonnage highly alluring. The nascent spot trades will also find such vessels attractive and this, as in the sale of gas itself, will present an interesting new dimension to the LNG trades. It will be a tussle worth watching.

SHIPBUILDING IN AN ERA OF CONSTANT CHANGE

From an address given by Michael Grey of Lloyd's List at the United Nations Economic Commission for Europe Seminar "Shipbuilding 2000" at Baltexpo 88 in Gdansk, Poland.

An age of structural change

There is a tendency for shipbuilders, when faced with the pressures of the world to shrug philosophically and suggest that there is nothing that can be done to change the cyclical evolution of world trade. Their responsibility, they argue, rests only with the need to build ships at the price that ship operators are prepared to pay. If this is quite insufficient to keep the shipyard afloat, it is regrettable, but there is not a lot that can be done about it. If governments can keep the industry in business just a little longer, the progression of the cycle will eventually mean that demand for ships returns.

Similar philosophies govern the actions of ship operators, who never it seems tire of complaining that shipping is a service industry which is by itself completely unable to influence events that keep freight rates and ship demand at a low level. It is always somebody else's fault — the banks or finance houses that supply the credit, the government which offers the guarantees. Everyone, it seems, operates in what might be described as an atomosphere of mutual helplessness. Only history, in the shape of those freight rate and world trade cycles is on our side. Eventually demand will be restored.

It probably will be, albeit briefly, and after terrible carnage in the shipbuilding industry. So the cycle will grind on into the next short period of prosperity that will see far too many ships ordered for a demand which will never ever be as large as is anticipated.

Much of the problem lies in the apparent isolation of the various industrial sectors, in that each part — shipbuilders, government, shippers, bankers and ship operators to name but those we are concerned with operates as a separate entity cocooned against the world outside. For as we emerge from the last recession it is important to realise that the world is greatly changing, that the calculation of supply and demand for shipping services and ships is no longer a matter of simple extrapolation. Nobody involved in long range strategic planning in the marine industry in either public or private sector can ignore these fundamental changes that are taking place. To recognise them is to be taking a positive step towards a longer term recovery.

This paper looks in detail at seven of what I have called *Changes in Structure*. Some will be familiar, others less so, but all profoundly affect the demand for ships and are essential to the shipbuilder's understanding of the changing world. These are: Scale economics; Internationalism; Conservation; Use of alternative materials; Industrial relocation; Product miniaturisation; Value adding at source.

The effects of scale economics

This phenomena I have elected to begin with, for of the seven listed this is really the only one which is described properly in economic textbooks. It is also that which most people will be familiar, as the economies of scale have been applied to virtually every sector of the shipping industry. Virtually every type of ship today is larger than that of the previous generation, from the deep sea container ship now edging above 3,500 TEU to the extraordinary deadweight that creative naval architects manage to cram into a "paragraph" coaster.

There are certain cautions as regards scale economics which we ought to be aware of. The dreadful example of the United States Lines "Super-econships" showed that a line hoping to secure a competitive advantage by pure scale economics can be confounded by outside factors, and that operating costs are only one part of the calculation.

Similarly, the sheer inflexibility of the ultra large ships is a factor that cannot be ignored. Thus it proved very practical, from a technical point of view to build half-million tonne tankers, but the limitations on their use were so great that it became difficult to re-employ them when their original Gulf-Europe or Japan pattern of trade was interrupted. Very fast ships tend to have their economic *raison d'etre* destroyed by quite small variations in the price of fuel, very economical ships which are extremely sophisticated have been found similarly vulnerable when their competitive advantage is reduced by a reduction in operating costs. Scale economics remain crucial but I would suggest that it is the carefully tailored design for a range of options that tends these days to have the edge over the technical *tour de force*.

Internationalism

At first sight, shipbuilders might be led to believe that internationalism in shipping is of only peripheral interest to them. By this we mean the profound structural change that is taking place to the shipping sector in so many parts of the world as it struggles to contain its costs. But it certainly is important to the shipbuilder to know who his potential clients might be, and this is not always immediately apparent in the convolutions of modern ship ownership.

The growth of the international open registers, the spread of bareboat charter arrangements and the complexities of modern ownership which take the ship way beyond the responsibilities of a maritime administration would all appear to be here to stay. It is as well to remember that it is not simple logic, but a defence mechanism against higher costs or taxes or bureaucracy which drives a ship operator to seek refuge under strange and wonderful flags.

There is a downside to maritime internationalism and that includes the spread of maritime fraud, the exploitation of labour from the poorer countries of the world and a sub-standard shipping fleet which existing institutions based on the concept of competent maritime administrations seem to be having great difficulty in eradicating.

There is plenty here to interest shipbuilders, who after all want to know who their potential customers are. If, as seems likely another example of internationalism is to be a growth in the direct involvement of cargo interests — I offer as an example — a steel company in one country securing a ten year's period of ore, complete with purpose built shipping arrangements for the whole period, who should the shipbuilder be trying to sell to? In such an arrangement the shipowner, as we know him, may take only a small part, with the financial package, the technical specification and the choice of shipyard and contract price all being within the brief of one of the principals rather than the ship operator, who will be that and little more. In such circumstances the shipbuilder wishing to market tonnage has to re-learn the rules.

Conservation

It is difficult to emphasise enough the effects of conservation upon the demand for ships, for this is one phenomena which is entirely new and which guarantees that the world which is emerging from the recession is a very different one that went into the slump in 1973. Virtually every user of primary materials and energy is making them go further and too few shipbuilders have been really aware of this profound change on the demand for their products. It is just one example of how the relationship of economic conditions to world trade has altered.

When applied to the most efficient users of energy and other materials, the effects

LISNAVE
QUALITY, COMPETITIVENESS
AND 'ON TIME' REPAIRS

Drydocking Flexibility

South Yard - Margueira

SINCE 1937

Shiprepairing Facilities
(for all kind of vessels)

Unlimited Drydocking Capacity ■
North Yard – Rocha, 4 Drydocks (up to 21 000 D.W.T.)
South Yard – Margueira, 4 Drydocks (up to 1 000 000 D.W.T.)

Blasting and Painting (own equipment) ■
External: 5 000 sqm/day; Internal: 1500 sqm/day

Lifting Means (up to 300 tons) ■
20 Rail Cranes, 10 Mobil Cranes and 2 Floating Cranes

Well Equipped Mechanical, Piping and Plate Shops ■

Highly Skilled Manpower ■

North Yard - Rocha

Other Services

■ **Gasfree Certificates; Cathodic Protection**
(GASLIMPO)
■ **Reconditioning and Repairing of Propellers**
(REPROPEL)
■ **Electrical and Electronic Repairs**
(ENI)
■ **Industrial Cooling; Air Conditioning**
(FRINIL)
■ **Towage and Marine Services**
(REBOCALIS)
■ **Tankcleaning Storage and Bunkering Station**
(BOLIDEN)
■ **Reconditioning of Spare Parts**
(LISNAVE)
■ **Steel Fabrication**
(LISNAVE)

Available in the Port of Lisbon at a Privileged Geographical Situation and Excellent Weather Conditions

⊕LISNAVE
ESTALEIROS NAVAIS DE LISBOA, S.A.

"TELEFAX"
No.276 46 70
LISBON-PORTUGAL

 LISMAR
Marketing Services Ltd.
CREE HOUSE
18-20 CREECHURCH LANE
LONDON EC 3A 5AY – ENGLAND
TELEX: 269739 CMI G
PHONE: 01-623 12 33
FAX: 01-6231200

APARTADO: 2138 – 1103 LISBOA CODEX – PORTUGAL □ TELEX: 18172-12649-16370 LSNAV P □ TELEFS: 2750811, MARGUEIRA YARD; 606171, ROCHA YARD

of conservation processes are staggering. Who, for instance in 1973 would have believed that within a decade Japan would be able to reduce the volume of its imported oil by some 50%. High prices and a knowledge that energy sources were vulnerable and finite have been powerful arguments for conservation, whether we are talking about using energy more efficiently or making expensive raw materials actually go further in the production process. There is a new interest in recycling, and this too is tending to depress the demand for original raw materials.

All of this is already having a profound effect upon the demand for new ships. The changes in primary energy consumption have meant that a resumption of demand for tankers, which might have been anticipated with industrial recovery and an ageing tanker fleet has effectively been postponed. Alternative fuels such as coal, LNG and LPG are being reassessed yet again and there may be changes to demand for ships serving these sectors. The shipbuilder must watch these changes very closely.

The use of alternatives

The demand for new ships is also being greatly affected by the consequences of industry seeking out and using alternative materials in so many of its production processes. It is worth noting, especially if you are concerned with the design of ships for the carriage of iron ore, that a modern car design incorporates up to 40% less steel in its construction that a vehicle of perhaps 20 years ago. Even in the production of that steel, the most efficient users of iron ore have changed their production processes fundamentally. In Japan, for instance, nearly one third of the country's steel production comes from scrap, rather than pig iron and this proportion is growing. There is a tendency for steel industries to concentrate production in the most efficient blast furnaces, on the use of electric furnaces reducing scrap, and on continuous casting processes. In Japan alone, which country has been responsible for at least half the worldwide tonne miles in the iron ore trade and forty per cent in the coking coal trades, this change is of great significance for the shipping and shipbuilding industry.

Then we must consider the effects of alternative methods of transport,such as the long-distance pipelines which are being used with increasing effect as an alternative to the ship for the carriage of oil, gas and even solids transported in slurry form. Although pipelines are often costly and vulnerable, when they directly compete with the ship on a trade route, there is an immediate effect upon the demand for vessels.

If the pipeline is an example of radical new thinking in the transport of raw materials, even more dramatic with a startling effect on the distribution of manufactured goods is the trend towards intermodalism in the liner trades.

Shipbuilders might stifle a yawn when the talk turns to liner trains and inland distribution systems, but they will do so at their peril as the development of intermodal systems is already begining to affect the demand for the coming generation of container ships. It must be remembered that here we are talking about a great wave of replacement tonnage which will be ordered to take over from the first generation of containerships which started deep sea containersation from about 20 years ago. That first generation represented the "container revolution" that was to sweep away break bulk handling methods. The coming generation must be viewed not as the first, as an upgrading in sea transport efficiency, but merely the improved sea link in an intermodal chain. The establishment of efficient land transport systems in the shape of liner trains, good trucking facilities for container transport and as important,the means to swiftly transport goods across land frontiers is causing shipowners to rethink their needs for new containership tonnage. This is a very fast changing world and shipbuilders must stay closely attuned to the changes which better land links will have on the demand for both deep sea and feeder ships.

Industrial relocation

This too has been with us for a long time, although the scale has changed and there can be no doubt that it has an important effect upon the demand for ships and upon the tonne-miles steamed. There are few industries which are unaffected by the process. On one hand we can see the wishes of OPEC countries to build up their downstream activities in the establishment of their own petrochemical industries close to the source of crude oil — a value adding process which I will come to a little later. This has coincided with the need for many of the principal industrial countries to shift many of their manufacturing processes to cheaper locations. Staying with oil, we can see refineries closed down in Europe and the U.S., their products being shifted to new refining centres such as that of Singapore. This is a function of high costs, but it is often a defence mechanism by international corporations seeking to cross tariff barriers. This is amply demonstrated by the dramatic changes taking place in the motor industry and in many other industries producing consumer durables, with component production and even complete product lines being established in countries thousand of miles away from the original corporation's base. It is always difficult to prove whether the chicken came before the egg, but it is arguable that this type of relocation of industry, this internationalism, would not have been possible without the efficiency of modern shipping, which enables the co-ordination of manufacture from all these various sources to take place in an organised manner, without the need to maintain enormous component buffer stocks.

Here it is very difficult for the shipbuilder hoping to benefit from a growth in sea transport of components to accurately gauge what manufacturing industry is actually doing. All we can say is that the whole process has meant that much oil once transported in crude form is now carried in product and chemical tankers and that an awful lot of criss-crossing of components between producer countries goes on. There is probably a sea transport gain and a demand for more ships resulting. Here as this process continues it will be necessary for the shipbuilder to become attuned to the end users demands rather than those of the traditional shipowners.

Product miniaturisation

This important phenomena is already manifesting itself in a reduced demand for the transport of weight and volume, and in the shift of a sizable portion of high value products into the air. It is to be seen everywhere, from the growth in micro-electronics where technology has managed to compress items like computers which once would require hundreds of cubic feet to stow into hand-portable containers, to virtually all manufactured goods, thinner, lighter and more compact. There may be an enormous growth in the value of the goods shipped these days, but they need far less raw material to produce and they have smaller demands upon the volumes within a ship's hold.

Value adding at source

This too is a function of changing technology contributed to by the internationalism of production. However, it is more fundamental than that, representing as it does the ability of so much of the developing world to obtain a better reward from its products, which were once shipped in their raw state, but are now increasingly processed prior to shipment. Possibly one of the best examples of this phenomena is the well-known cargo phosphor rock, once almost exclusively exported in its raw form for processing in developed countries to be re-exported back to the developing world farmers. Today so much of this cargo, which once formed an important tramp trading load is now processed in the producing countries and exported direct as phosphoric acid, thus ensuring a far better reward.

Baltimore Marine Division

Sparrows Point Yard

SHIP REPAIR & CONVERSION

The Sparrows Point Yard is fully equipped to perform all phases of ship repair including steel work, outfit repair, machinery and engine rebuilding, and complete refurbishing and conversions of a wide range of ships. Skilled mechanics in all shipyard trades are readily available to support multi-ship overhauls with around-the-clock work shifts. The yard's capacity is enhanced by its expansive machine shop, the second largest on the east coast.

Multiple levels of repair and conversion projects can be accommodated by the Sparrows Point Yard simultaneously. An impressive variety of shops and facilities are housed in more than 1.2 million square feet. The yard's repair group recognizes the need for providing cost-effective services while maintaining a superior level of quality control.

Baltimore Marine Division's Sparrows Point Yard has more than 70 years of experience in the construction of virtually all types of ships and in the performance of all phases of ship repair and maintenance.

Centrally located on the east coast, the yard can be accessed via the Chesapeake Bay and the C&D Canal. Multiple building sites, advanced automation, skilled tradesmen, and an impressive machine shop are among the facility's many features.

Baltimore Marine Division
Bethlehem Steel Corporation
Sparrows Point Yard
Sparrows Point, MD, USA 21219

Phone: (301) 388-7701   Fax: (301) 388-6687   Telex: 84-7417 (BETHSCO BETM)

All of these seven characteristics of modern shipping are continuing phenomena and while they will be better understood by the year 2000, they will still rank as very important in the calculations of all those concerned with the supply and demand for marine transport. For this, we believe is not something that can be simply calculated from a study of past cyclical trends, extrapolating past circumstances to provide a forecast upon which policies can be based. There is too much in a state of change, and we have only alluded to a small portion of the phenomena which will influence future thinking. There are basic changes taking place in ship ownership which the shipbuilder must be aware of. It has been suggested that the days of the operating shipowner are numbered with so many of his functions being sub-contracted out to specialist agencies. How often these days do you encounter a shipowner who has retained a large technical staff on his payroll. Most of the time he will retain consultants. As a result of this change so much of the onus for technical advancement devolves upon the shipbuilder. It is the shipbuilder who must produce the designs that he will try and sell, which of course increases both his costs and his responsibilities.

In the field of ship finance much is changing with cargo interests taking a much more involved approach, often becoming intimately concerned with the long term financial package around which a shipping contract is based and for which ships will be built. It might be seen as the customers finally controlling the means of transport, and some have suggested that such a process may well lead to a dampening down on the violent peaks and troughs which have characterised the shipping industry over the years. There is a new interest in leasing and much discussion about shipping equipping itself in the same way as the aircraft industry.

As always, much of the demand for ships in the year 2000 will depend upon what can only be described as political factors. You can read a million words of well argued economic and statistically correct studies, proving that there will be an "x" percent growth in Mediterranean cruising over the next five years. Then a gang of terrorists strike on a cruise ship in the Mediterranean and all these calculations go out of the window. You can be completely convinced about the requirements for LNG imports into the United States and even build a great fleet of expensive carriers to service this. Then there is a pricing dispute, a political change in the wind that determines energy policies and you have half a dozen of the world's most expensive ships in long term layup. It is worth remembering that energy policies, the decision to raise or lower tariff walls, questions of protectionism, agricultural policies and international trading accords are all fundamental to the demand for future ships. They are also dependent upon decisions made by people who may have other considerations than economic criteria or even logic!

I am not suggesting that the shipbuilder ever had it easy, but it certainly was not so hard in the old days where he left the thinking to the customer and just built what he asked for. Today the shipbuilder must anticipate demand and design and market accordingly; to do this he must have in mind all of what I have enumerated above, and a lot more beside. He must be aware of the overriding importance of the great political events of our day and their maritime connotations. He must attempt to weigh up the effects of protectionism and liberalism, of national self-sufficiency programmes, of Glasnost and Peristroika, of war and peace in the middle east, of intermodalism and internationalism, of channel tunnels and of farm policies.

Flags flown by the fastest yachts.

⊠M   ◻T   ◨U

Some of the yachts sailing under the colour of MTU: New Horizon L · Acajou
Paraíso · Randa II · Nachite · Three Y's · Shergar · Fox II · Jahala · Gallant Lady
Mes Amis · Alhaja · Lady Saryah · Luwima K · Al Fahedi · Never say Never
Natalina · Kalamoun · Silver Shalis · Lady Alice · Alliance · No lo sé · Avanti · Falco
Southern Cross III · Parts VI · Equinox · Adler · Lady Amfimar · Cricket · Al Menwar
Maria Arabella · Princess Tina · Ron IV · Time · Longitude−0 · Octopussy
Antipodean · Rima · Nourah of Riyadh · Eleen Sara · Chato · Pioneer · Andromeda
Sun Paradise · Alfa Alfa · Renegade · Clear Skies · Joy · Pia · L'Azzura · Top Shida
Masayel · Houssam · Luisamar 5

mtu
Deutsche Aerospace

Motoren- und Turbinen-Union Friedrichshafen GmbH
P.O. Box 2040 · D-7990 Friedrichshafen/W-Germany
Phone (0 75 41) 29-1 · Telex 7 34 280-0 mt d · Fax (0 75 41) 29-22 47

102

NEWBUILDING INVESTMENT

by David Tinsley,
Technical Editor, Lloyd's List

The two major trends in the newbuilding market over the past 12 months have been the marked firming in shipbuilding values and increasing emphasis on design sophistication aimed at improving owners' competitiveness.

For large sectors of the business, notably container shipping and trades in the higher-value neobulks such as forestry products, developments in ship design have been keyed to the growing commercial requirement for rapid freight transit times and reliability of service. Emphasis on operational peformance in this regard is closely allied to 'just-in-time' delivery/production scheduling and reduced stocking levels.

Enormously powerful single-engine installations using the latest slow-running, two-stroke machinery are being specified for the new generation of container vessels. A. P. Moller of Copenhagen took single unit ratings to a new high when it decided on a 64,320 bhp plant — of MAN B&W design — for the most recently ordered examples of its M-class 4,000 TEU newbuildings at the Odense yard in Denmark.

Indeed, the period under review has witnessed a return to higher design service speeds in a number of sectors of the shipping industry after some years of restraint fostered by concern over fuel costs in a difficult trading environment.

It was not that long ago that West European shipbuilders were being exhorted to concentrate wholly on the more specialised and more advanced types of merchant vessel, and to distance themselves from the more populous categories which yards in the Far East could construct on an altogether more competitive basis. Indeed Japan, and latterly South Korea have made tremendous efforts to develop a presence in those higher-value sectors in which the West European builders have hitherto remained influential — to the extent that there is virtually no type of tonnage now which can be regarded as the province of one or other area.

Japanese and Chinese orders

While cruise ship and high-grade ferry construction is still dominated by a relatively small number of West European yards, Japanese endeavours to develop a western Pacific cruise ship industry have resulted in a number of orders for sophisticated passenger vessels being awarded to domestic builders. The entry into service in April 1989 of Showa Line's 5,200 gt *Oceanic Grace* and the Mitsui-OSK Group's 23,500 gt *Fuji Maru* signified an important new chapter in the evolution of both Japanese shipping and shipbuilding.

As contractor for the luxury yacht-cruiser *Oceanic Grace*, NKK Corporation enhanced a reputation which had already been strengthened in 1987 through the delivery of the first Japanese-built cruise ferry for European ownership, in the form of Nedlloyd's 31,500 gt *Norsun*.

Similarly, South Korea — despite the enormous problems faced by the yards in a period of fundamental change in industrial relations and in the costs of production — has demonstrated its determination to build a position in the more advanced fields of merchant vessel construction. Contracts for sophisticated, high capacity container liner vessels for West German and French account have ensued, as has an appreciable volume of business from overseas owners for small and medium size gas carriers.

Many well-informed members of the international shipbuilding community believe that China will in time emerge as the world's major volume producer. While there is little doubt that the Chinese shipbuilding industry, assuming a stable domestic situation, will exert growing influence in the world-wide market during the 1990s, it has adopted something of a stand-off position during the period concerned. The industry has been careful not to over-extend its orderbook at a time of rising prices, given a dependency still on foreign equipment and technology in certain fields.

While much has still to be achieved in terms of productivity, Chinese yards' undoubted cost-competitiveness has succeded in attracting further important export business. More significantly, perhaps, the industry has continued to broaden its technical capabilities. A domestic contract for a 3,000 cu m-capacity LPG carrier formalised in the early part of 1989 was indicative of this. Already, China has brought-in foreign know-how in the LNGC and LPGC fields.

Containership resurgence

The resurgence of interest in containership fleet re-tonnaging and expansion has been one of the highlights of the past 12 months. An enormous volume of enquiry gradually gave rise to firm newbuilding commitments, and West German owners were in the vanguard of these developments.

Hapag-Lloyd's five-ship deal with Samsung, calling for vessels of 4,300 TEU capacity, ranks as one of the greatest affirmations to date of European shipowner confidence in the South Korean shipbuilding industry and in its increasing technological capability. This series of vessels will embody the Schiffsfuhrungszentrale (SFZ) concept of centralised ship control developed by Hapag-Lloyd in conjunction with West German electronics companies in mind of industry moves to single-watchkeeper manning.

Continuing a significant advance on the principles arising from West Germany's successful Schiff der Zukunft programme, the sophisticated SFZ operating system was first encapsulated in the 2,200 TEU *Bonn Express* and *Heidelberg Express*, which were commissioned by the Hamburg-based organisation from HDW at Kiel during the first half of 1989.

The SFZ command/management centre concept will be applied in all Hapag-Lloyd newbuildings between now and the end of the 1990s.

The coming spring will see the entry into service of one of the most remarkable vessel types ever designed for short-sea container operations. The 300 TEU newbuilding ordered by through-transport specialist Bell Lines should trim turnround times at European terminals by 18-28%.

These prospective gains in productivity will arise from a design which dispenses almost entirely with hatch covers and which employs a cargo section that has been developed to optimise 'pick and take' handling methods. An unusually fast service speed capability (in a short-sea context) — 14.5 knots at only 75% main engine output, and sustainable in very poor weather conditions — should also reduce seatime by 20-25%.

Overall, the so-called BCV300 design has been conceived to ensure that Bell Lines can compete in terms of transit times with freight routings via the ferry network and potentially also with services via the Channel Tunnel. Although the UK is the fulcrum of its operations, particular consideration has been given to the trade between Ireland and the Continent.

Three of the 5,000 dwt vessel's four holds are of the open-hatch design developed and patented by Advance Ship Design of North Sydney, Australia. Only No 1 hold — immediately abaft of which is the bridge and accommodation block — is closed by conventional hatch covers.

The open-ship concept — largely obviating the need for cargo lashing and opening and closing of hatch covers — should integrate well into the Bell system, where the ratio of port turnround time to seatime is characteristically high. Moreover, any given ship's cargo is rotating on practically a daily basis, so the hike in productivity and transit time performance should be especially beneficial.

Teraoka Shipyard of Awaji Island, Japan, booked the newbuilding order in May 1989, with a commitment to deliver the ship 12 months thereafter. Bell has options on five further vessels of the design, and the first six months of operations with the prototype will probably determine whether all of these are converted into firm contracts.

Exemptions from carrying hatch covers, and the issuance of a Load Line certificate have only been made possible by exhaustive model testing at the Wuxi Seakeeping Basin in China and by special design provisions, including a high profile and sophisticated pumping arrangements. A 'get-you-home' auxiliary propulsion system is another of the outstanding features of the new ship.

The same considerations of freight transit time, but on an altogether different scale, have led Nedlloyd Lines to look at the open-ship concept as the design basis for up to 15 newbuildings in the 3,000-4,600 TEU range.

At the time of writing, the first stage of the envisaged programme — five cellular vessels of 3,000 TEU — had still to be implemented. The intensity of competition, and a 1991 delivery requirement, saw an unprecedented level of co-operating grouping among yards bidding for the deal in both eastern Asia and western Europe. With the Rotterdam-based organisation planning to apply the same design concept to its prospective five-ship series of Panamax beam 3,800 TEU newbuildings, and to the planned, wider-than-Panamax 4,600 TEU quintet — possibly favouring a single builder or co-operation group — the stakes are very high.

Dispensation with hatch covers and the adoption of a full-height cellular structure would in Nedlloyd's view not only benefit turnround and through-movement times, but would also be in the interests of overall cargo security. The loss of deck-stowed containers in heavy weather is an industry-wide problem, and can be expected to increase with the mounting pressure on vessels and their masters to maintain fast service speeds irrespective of prevailing sea conditions.

Dry cargo sector

The Cape-size bulk carrier sector has generated a modest, but steady flow of newbuilding work. This was spurred by renewed confidence in the dry cargo sector and by consideration of the age profile of bulkers in the 100,000-150,000 tonne category.

By mid 1989, outstanding orders amounted to over 30 vessels in this range, with the vast majority due for delivery from 1990 onwards. All but three of the newbuildings had been contracted in the Far East, with South Korea and Taiwan having maintained a particularly high profile in this field of construction.

Price appreciation in this category has been symptomatic of the whole, with reference levels having climbed from around $28m in the second half of 1987 to $43m less than two years later.

Indications of increasingly tight berth availability and of shipbuilders' new resolve to obtain realistic prices were implicit in certain major projects where work was split between two or more yards. A particular case in point was the London- and Tokyo-based Golden Ocean Group's decision in April to assign orders for three 145,000 dwt bulkers to as many Japanese yards, namely Kawasaki Heavy Industries, NKK Corporation, and Sumitomo Heavy Industries.

At about the same time, Sven Salen of Stockholm considered it expedient to contract two yards — Hyundai and Daewoo — to fulfil a four-ship OBO carrier programme. This latter project, involving a 165,000 dwt design, was of added significance in being the largest order in some years for combination carriers.

Japanese sources have estimated that there are some 200 vessels in the Cape-size category and that 40% of these are 15 years or older. This would seem to allay fears that the current investment programme might result in overtonnaging, while also indicating scope for further, selective ordering.

The dramatic appreciation in newbuilding prices over the past three years has restrained ordering activity in key sectors of the market. VLCCs, for instance, will soon be commanding $75-80m — double the level pertaining in the second half of 1986. Despite the substantial operating cost advantages associated with newbuildings compared with vessels commissioned only 10, let alone 15, years ago, the capital expenditure required can still not generally be justified by the current, albeit improved level of earnings.

The prospect of an increasingly superannuated world fleet and the likelihood of a sustained rise in newbuilding prices — with a slimmer, international shipbuilding industry exerting greater muscle — have provided certain shipowners with the stimuli to invest. Those who have gone ahead with newbuilding projects have been mainly Japanese organisations together with some of the more entrepreneurial interests in the shipping business.

With the South Korean shipbuilding industry in particular holding out for better price levels, Japanese yards have built on their earlier pre-eminence in the VLCC field to secure the bulk of the orders for tankers over 200,000 dwt placed in the past year.

In the opening months of 1989, Hitachi Zosen tied-up business for no less than four 260,000-tonners, all for overseas principals. Two of these ships were booked from the Fred Cheng-headed Golden Ocean Group, and the other two were contracted by John Fredriksen's Seatankers Management. At the same time, Tokyo Tanker — looking to the future needs of the Arabian Gulf trade to Nippon Oil refineries — ordered two 250,000/260,000 dwt vessels from Mitsubishi Heavy Industries and IHI.

Shipowners are increasingly looking to vessel designs which incorporates optimised operating and manning arrangements. Shipbuilders, moreover, faced with cutbacks in their own technical resources as regards both design capacity and personnel, are keen to buy-in 'packages' from specialists in the various fields, such as integrated control and monitoring. This combination of factors has seen the widespread application of integrated bridge systems and rationalised ship operating techniques.

One man bridge operation

A milestone in advanced ship design was the completion towards the end of 1988 of the first vessel with a special Class notation for 24-hour, one-man bridge operation. Although by no means the first vessel to have been conceived with this capability, the 84,000 dwt Burmeister & Wain-built products tanker *Petrobulk Mars* is the first to conform to Det norske Veritas' W1-OC notation (Watch 1 — Ocean area and coastal waters).

This vessel, and subsequent newbuilding completions, notably the Hapag-Lloyd containerships *Bonn Express* and *Heidelberg Express*, take the industry an important stage on towards the ultimate objective of ship design in which all shipboard systems interact with one another so as to optimise operational monitoring.

Although trials are being conducted with vessels developed for 24-hour single watchkeeper manning, this technical capability where it exists cannot as yet be fully exploited until sanctioned by the International Maritime Organization. Current rules permit single watchkeeper operations (on vessels of the requisite technical standard) only during daylight hours.

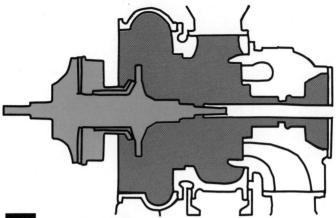

Easy servicing

Even Asea Brown-Boveri turbochargers need servicing but because our turbochargers have always been designed and manufactured with ease-of-service in mind very rarely does servicing present a problem. More important, Asea Brown-Boveri have made obtaining service and spares equally easy. In the U.K. for example, there are three service stations plus region stores plus skilled service engineers in most major ports. Add to this U.K. capability 61 other service stations on five continents and you get some idea of what real turbocharger servicing is all about. Servicing can be easy – when you know how.

ASEA BROWN BOVERI

ABB Turbo Systems Limited,
BBC Turbocharger Division, 5401 Baden,
Switzerland. Tel: 56 754037 Tlx: 82829120 AB CH
ABB Power Limited,
Darby House, Lawn Central, Telford, Shropshire.
TF3 4JB. Tel: 0952 290000

Service Division

TELFORD	**ABERDEEN**	**SUNDERLAND**
Unit G,	Unit 25,	11 Lombard Street,
Stafford Park 12,	Denmore Road,	Hendon,
Telford,	Bridge of Don,	Sunderland,
Shropshire. TF3 3BJ.	Aberdeen,	Tyne & Wear. SR1 2HS
Tel: 0952 290000	Shropshire. AB2 8JW	Tel: 091 567 7807
	Tel: 0224 822692	

Gas carriers

The gas carier sector has produced a good crop of LPGC newbuilding orders right across the cubic capacity range during the period under assessment. At the time of writing, considerable attention was focused on several LNG tanker projects which had moved into advanced stages of planning.

Norwegian LNG Group, the joint-stock company set up by Gotaas-Larsen, A/S Laboremus, I.M. Skaugen and A/S Kosmos, had put in a bid for a methane shipment contract from Statoil. This would call for movements of North Sea gas to the US market via a new liquefication plant on the Norwegian west coast, and would call for the construction of two 120,000 cu m LNG carriers.

Meanwhile, consideration was being given to quotes for two LNGCs to serve the Alaskan trade. Two posisble types — one of 125,000 cu m and one of 91,500 cu m — have been evaluated by Marathon Oil and Phillips as replacements for smaller, 1969-built vessels employed in the Alaska-Tokyo Bay traffic.

The Japanese shipbuilding industry's unparalleled productivity and reputation for contractual performance was underscored in April with the delivery six months ahead of schedule of the first of the 125,000 cu m capacity carriers ordered for the Australian North-West Shelf project.

The fact that the design is based on proven systems for large LNGCs, in terms of cargo containment and propulsive power, helped to reduce lead times, although the rapidity of build achieved by Mitsubishi Heavy Industries' Nagasaki complex was nevertheless outstanding. The steam turbine-powered *Northwest Sanderling* will be followed by the *Northwest Swift* from Nagasaki and by three other sister vessels from Kawasaki Heavy Industries and Mitsui Engineering & Shipbuilding in the course of 1989-91. Contracts for sixth and seventh examples of the class are expected to be placed with Japanese yards during the spring of 1990, against a 1993 delivery requirement.

On the West European scene, the Kvaerner Group's acquisition of British Shipbuilders' technologically-advanced Govan yard on Clydeside was accompanied by orders for two 56,000 cu m LPG carriers.

Privately-owned West German and Italian yards attracted further business for ethylene and LPG carriers in the small and medium-size categories, while Boelwerf secured new orders for its handy-size LPG carrier class under favourable domestic credit arrangements. Financial provisions covering a 34,000 cu m capacity addition to its LPGC work backlog were sanctioned in March. This vessel will transport the range of liquefied petroleum gases as well as anhydrous ammonia and vinyl chloride monomer (VCM), and is based on the design adopted for a trio of 28,000 cu m tankers. The first of the latter, the *Cheshire*, was handed over to Bibby Line of Liverpool in June.

World's Leading Shipbuilder of New Generation LNG Carriers

LNG Carrier "Northwest Sanderling" for the Northwest Shelf Project

▲ MITSUBISHI HEAVY INDUSTRIES, LTD.

Tokyo Head Office	London Office	Nagasaki Works
Shipbuilding & Ocean Development Headquarters	**Mitsubishi Heavy Industries Europe, Ltd**	**Nagasaki Shipyard & Machinery Works**
5-1 Marunouchi 2-chome	Bow Bells House, Bread St	1-1- Akunoura-machi
Chiyoda-ku, Tokyo	(Cheapside) London	Nagasaki
Phone: Tokyo (03)212-3111	EC4M 9BQ, England	Phone: Nagasaki
Cable: HISHIJU TOKYO	Phone: (01) 248 8821	(0958) 61-2111
Telex: J22443	Cable: HISHIJU LONDON EC4	Telex: 752451 MHINGA J
Telefax: Tokyo (03) 216-3021	Telex: 888994 MHI LN G	Telefax: Nagasaki
	Telefax: (01) 248 1329	(0958) 62-8320

110

SHORT-SEA SHIPPING

by David Tinsley,
Technical Editor Lloyd's List

The economic and political goal of a single European Community market by 1 January 1993 is likely to have important implications for intra-European trade by sea, notwithstanding the continuing development of the rail infrastructure on the Continent and the prospect of a fixed link between Britain and France.

The likelihood of increased freight exchange between member states, and of new demands on the type and quality of services provided by ship operators, are already influencing investment policy in this vibrant sector of the shipping industry.

One of the most salient aspects of '1991' from a short-sea shipowner's point of view is the question of liberalisation of cabotage regimes within the EC. Traffic subject to cargo reservation in Europe is reckoned to account for some 200m tonnes annually, with 50m tonnes on the Italian coast alone, and 40m tonnes in Spain.

Countries with an 'open coasts' policy, notably the UK, Ireland, the Netherlands and Belgium, are hoping that a degree of harmonisation in the way that coastal shipping operates in the EC will be achieved in the short-term as a first stage towards the liberalisation of the market.

Owners' appreciation of the needs of industry, coupled with considerations of operating flexibility and running and capital costs, have seen modest sizes of vessel prevail in the past year's investment pattern. Much of the newbuilding activity has involved designs around 4,000 dwt capacity.

One of the single largest developments in this category has been the construction in West Germany of a series of six, gearless, single-hold ships to the account of Finnish operators Godby Shipping and Engship. Led by the 4,000 dwt *Najaden*, the J.J. Sietas-built class has been conceived primarily for the movement of forest products and steel from Finland to West Germany, the Netherlands and UK, with backhaul cargoes of cellulose and other bulks.

Two derivations of this type, moreover, are currently entering service with the Oldendorf owner K.W. Tom Worden. These West German sisters, more pre-disposed towards the container traffic, are each equipped with two low-stowing deck cranes on the port side.

Neobulks

The generators of the intra-European flows of so-called neobulks such as forest products and steel have to be especially discerning in their choice of shipping because of the intensity of competition on the markets for their goods. These demand service reliability and the delivery of finished or semi-finished products in first class condition. The quality and efficiency of handling and transportation thus has a key bearing on the shipper's market standing. Increasingly, with the adoption of 'just in time' principles, it also influences the costs associated with production.

Two 1989 entrants to the Finnish fleet reflect a current trend for designs developed both to ensure delivery of goods in pristine condition and to afford a high degree of shipping flexibility. The 4,100 dwt *Mini Star* and sister vessel *Link Star* combine sto-ro and bulk cargo carrying capabilities. Intended mainly to handle Finnish forest product exports to Continental European and UK markets, the design allows bulk backhaul cargoes to be targeted. The vessel type is a result of technical collaboration between the J.J. Sietas shipyard at Hamburg-Neuenfelde, vessel owner Godby Shipping of Mariehamn and long-term charterer Transfennica.

Palletised or unit cargo can be loaded on the weatherdeck and in a main tweendeck which is completely isolated from the lower hold. The tweendeck's scantlings and the inherent stability of the ship are such that the full design deadweight of bulk raw materials associated with forestry goods manufacture, such as china clay and salt, can be accepted at this intermediate level.

Three modes of access are provided, all systems having been designed and supplied by Macgregor-Navire: horizontally, over a stern ramp/door; vertically, through two full width hatches closed by folding covers; and laterally via a midships sideport. The latter mode includes a starboard-mounted Sideshifter unit featuring two slewing platform lifts, each with a capacity of 12 tonnes, for handling paper reels and pallets at all deck levels.

The modest size of the *Mini Star* and *Link Star* is indicative of the emphasis now on regularity of shipments on a conveyor-like basis, in keeping with reduced provision for carrying stock at both the producer and user ends of the transportation chain. A similar type of vesel was also ordered during the period under review by Ernst Russ of Hamburg.

Economics of inland shipping

One of the most remarkable vessel designs commissioned in 1989 testified to the economics of inland shipping. The hybrid sisters *Shuttle Goteborg* and *Shuttle Karlstad* were put into operation between the northern shore of Lake Vaner and Gothenburg via the Trollhattan Canal.

The 2,150 dwt vessels carry paper and other forestry goods southbound (for transhipment at Gothenburg), returning not only with empty trailers and containers but also with revenue-earning consignments of light oil products in special, underdeck tanks. These sto-ro/lo-lo cargo ships-cum-tankers have been built to the

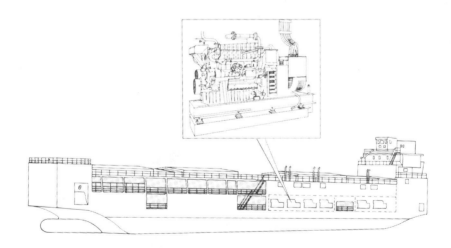

Shuttle Goteborg has its six Volvo Penta TAMD162 diesels skid-mounted for ease of removal

optimum dimensions for passage through the Trollhattan navigation.

Construction of the two ships in the Netherlands was initiated by Rotterdam-based Van Nievelt Goudriaan & Co. on the strength of a long-term shipment contract secured from the Stora Group, one of Sweden's premier forest product shippers. This calls for the southward movement of 350,000 tonnes of goods annually. Cargoes are loaded out of Karlstad, with the VNG subsidiary Seahorse Shipping Lines providing six sailings per week in each direction.

The lower hold area of each ship forms the tankage for 2,240 cu m of refined petroleum products. This is surmounted by a trailer/container deck, designed for Rolux-type cassettes and Mafi-type rolltrailers. Ro-ro access is over the stern, and lo-lo transference is through movable upper shields which afford weather protection to high-value paper, liner board and other products.

A diesel-electric system is employed with six Volvo Penta-powered 325 kw gensets supplying power to thruster motors feeding the twin 1,000 kw KaMeWa rotatable thrusters for main propulsion. The genset modules are arranged at main deck level on the port side. The shuttle carriers are double-skinned throughout so as to reduce the risk of pollution of Lake Vaner, which supplies drinking water to Swedish coastal communities.

UK-based inland-going coaster exponents Union Transport and the BES (Business Expansion Scheme) company Bromley Shipping (whose vessels are under the technical management of UT) initiated a newbuilding programme at the beginning of 1989. Orders were awarded to Cochrane Shipbuilders at Selby, Yorkshire, for the construction of three 3,000 dwt restricted air draught vessels to UT's account, with a fourth of class destined for Bromley Shipping.

Options on a further two units of the 99.9 m-long design for the BES venture were still outstanding at the time of writing. Of the initial four vessels, two were subcontracted to the Damen Group subsidiary Richard Dunston on North Humberside. Delivered price (i.e. exclusive of government intervention funding to the Selby yard) was £3.165m per ship, and subventive assistance also reflected in a 7.5% fixed rate loan covering 80% of the purchase price.

The two companies consider that the 3,000 tonne size — larger than any previous UT-operated vessels — is the optimum to maximise payload while maintaining the upriver navigation capacity which is an important feature of their respective trades.

The newbuilding design offers about 160,000 cu ft of earning capacity in two box-shaped holds, each incorporating a portable steel bulkhead, such that a total of four cargo separations are possible. A fully-laden draught of only 4.2m and a ballast air-draught of 6.35m (compared with 6.5m on UT's preceding class of 2,300-tonners) confers a very high degree of operating flexibility, meeting the criteria for navigation to, for instance, key industrial locations on Belgium's Albert Canal, to upriver points on the Rhine and adjoining waterways, and to restricted coastal and river berths in eastern and northern England.

Newbuildings for Norwegian owners

Norwegian investment in new tonnage fitted for the River Rhine short-sea trade was forthcoming in mid-89, in the shape of a series of 3,500 dwt box-hold singledeckers. Project initiator Paal Wilson Management of Bergen has a long association with the traffic between the Norwegian coast and inland ports on the Rhine, particularly the industrial berths and terminals in the Duisburg area.

The company's quartet of newbuildings, which will be operated under the Cypriot flag, has been assigned to northern Dutch shipbuilders J. Pattje and Scheepswerf Bodewes in a deal reported to be worth in the region of NKr 180m overall. The Dutch yards landed the contract in part because of their ability to meet the very early deliveries required by Paal Wilson as regards the first two ships of the class. The lead

LIBERIA TELECOMMUNICATIONS CORPORATION

P.O. BOX 9039

LYNCH STREET

MONROVIA

LIBERIA

Telephone: 222222

Telex: 44330/44429 LIBTELCO

vessel was due to be handed over before the end of September 1989, with the second 3,500-tonner following within the opening two months of 1990.

The cargo section comprises a single hold of 157,000 cu ft bale/bulk, accessed via two hatches and designed for the economic handling and stowage of a wide range of cargoes including steel products (reflective of the Ruhr region's standing as the 'steel kitchen of Europe'), containers, aluminium products and grain.

Ship-to-shore pallet handling

A particularly notable entrant into the European short-sea fleet during the second half of 1989 was a small, low air draught vessel incorporating its own ship-to-shore pallet handling facility. The 98.55 m-long, West German-owned newbuilding has been designed principally for palletised forest products such as paper reels.

Although her single hold can be accessed in conventional manner through full-width hatches, she incorporates a powerful Sideshifter side loading unit for the efficient working of high value, weather and handling-sensitive goods. The midships port side-mounted loading/unloading system comprises a hydraulic folding shell door and a MacGregor-Navire Sideshifter equipped with two 12-tonne capacity lifting platforms. Limited air draught restrictions for river transits are met by arranging for the extended platform guides to fold down and stow horizontally. The wheelhouse is also height-adjustable.

Commissioned by Drochtersen shipowner Peter Nagel from Cassens Werft at Emden, the innovative newbuilding offers additional flexibility through the subdivision of her single hold by means of two hydraulically-operated, upward-swinging bulkheads.

New series of singledeckers

A leading North European operator of short-sea/coastal vessels, Delfzijl-based Wagenborg Shipping, put a new series of 3,000 dwt box-hold singledeckers into service in 1989. In its various roles as owner, part-owner, bareboat charterer, timecharterer and commercial manager, Wagenborg controls a fleet of nearly 60 vessels up to 6,500 tonne capacity, engaged in European coastwise and intermediate trades. The company occupies an important position in the Baltic forest products traffic, and the new class of gearless 3,000-tonners from the Ferus Smit yard at Foxhol, in the northern Netherlands, has been conceived with this in mind. The box-like nature of the single hold is indicated by a common cube measurement (160,000 cu ft) for both bale and bulk cargo.

Modernisation and expansion of the fleet by up to six 3,000 dwt singledeckers (not all of which are owned by Wagenborg) follows the commissioning in 1988 of four 1,250 dwt box-hold coasters ordered from Ferus Smit by various Dutch interests. This design offers a revenue-earning capacity equating to 65,000 cu ft, and the flexibility to work into the smallest ports and berths which have traditionally been encompassed by Wagenborg.

During the period under review, a Dutch ship management company with strong Scandinvian links implemented a major newbuilding programme involving seven short-sea cargo vessels of between 4,000 and 4,500 dwt. Construction of the entire series has been assigned by Haren-based Sandfirden BV to Scheepswerf Ferus Smit.

The design has been developed in mind of the needs of the Baltic/North Continent trade, given Sandfirden's connections in a management capacity with the Swedish shipowners Thunrederierna and O.F. Ahlmark. All seven vessels will employ a similar hull form and similar main dimensions (including an overall length of about 88 m and a laden draught of 5 m), but there will be three versions in terms of hold cubic measurement. Three of the newbuildings will offer 184,000 cu ft and the four other ships will have either 171,000 or 200,000 cu ft of below-decks cargo space.

As is increasingly the way with new construction assigned to the modestly-sized Dutch shipbuilding companies, a high level of subcontracting is entailed with this project.

Reinvestment by British operators

Two British operators of coastal/short-sea tankers have pressed ahead with fleet reinvestment. The Hays Marine services company Bowker & King (now absorbed by sister company Crescent Shipping) received a pair of 2,675 dwt vessels from Cochrane Shipbuilders substantially ahead of the contractual delivery dates. Further south, Richards (Shipbuilders) laid down two 3,000 dwt clean products carriers for F.T. Everard & Sons.

The 3,050 cu m capacity *Brabourne* and younger sister *Blackrock* were phased into Bowker & King's contract business in British, Irish and near-Continental waters, further raising the profile of a fleet which in recent years has steadily developed from its traditional, estuarial traffic base into the wider short-sea market.

The £3.2m *Brabourne* type has been conceived for the fast turnrounds which are crucial to market competitiveness in this sector of the tanker trade. Each of the 10 cargo tanks is served by its own 100 cu m/hr deepwell pump, such that, depending upon the intake capacity of the terminal ashore, full cargo discharge can be effected within three hours. The design provides for segregation of three types or grades of clean product.

One of the most eye-catching features of the new generation of Bowker & King (viz Crescent) tankers is a fully enclosed, free-fall lifeboat installed right aft in a special stowing/launching frame.

Each of the £4m prospective additions to the Everard fleet, now taking shape at Lowestoft, will provide efficient new capacity to serve existing coastal/short-sea contracts, while providing a worldwide trading flexibility. Hull strengthening to permit loading and discharge while aground at drying berths, coupled with provisions for full cargo outturn in three hours, underline the importance attached to turnround performance.

The moulded hull lines emanate from Skipskonsulent, the Norwegian firm of naval architects, but otherwise the design — based on the contractual owners' specific requirements — is from Richards itself. The East Anglian shipbuilder has maintained a strong design team at a time when many yards have cut back their in-house resources, and this factor influenced the direction of the Everard contract.

DEVELOPMENTS IN PROPULSION

by Dag Pyke

Right from the beginning of shipping up to the present day there has been a constant search to improve the efficiency of ships. Sailing ships sought to take maximum advantage of the wind and this was a question of both hull and sail design. With steam ships it becomes a question of machinery and propulsion efficiency as well as hull design but weather still plays its part. Now that fuel has become a significant cost factor in the operation of ships there is a growing interest in new concepts of propulsion with the belief that the propulsion systems are the one major unexplored area where improvements in efficiency can be gained.

Many of the developments now taking place in propulsion are not just simply to improve efficiency and reduce fuel consumption. There is a strong case being made out for many types of ship operations where improved handling and manoeuvrability can be an advantage, particularly if this saves costs in port operations by not having to employ tugs. On passenger ships noise and vibration can be an important factor and here the propulsion system can be one of the main culprits. Equally important in modern propulsion systems is the question of reliability and here designers often have to balance out the conflicting requirements of mechanical complexity against reliability, bearing in mind that most of the components of the propulsion system are underwater and therefore any failure can have high cost consequences.

Some of the so-called new concepts being looked at today are in fact old ideas which have been dusted off and are being given a fresh look. Throughout history this has often been the case, with the first marine gas turbine being developed back in 1905, but the metals and machining techniques of those days were not up to the high temperatures involved. Similarly systems such as contra-rotating propellers and water jets have a long history of intermittent use in the marine world but only in recent years have these concepts been developed to the point where they start to prove attractive particularly in terms of reliability. Then there are exciting new possibilities such as the linear induction motor which has no moving parts outside the ship, which in the long term must be an attractive proposition but in the short term presents enormous technical hurdles to overcome. This sort of development is probably at the same sort of state as the original gas turbine was 80 years ago, but with the modern pace of development the gap between conceptual design and practical application is closing rapidly.

Many of the developments now taking place in propulsion systems started off life as systems for small craft. This is a reasonable approach bearing in mind that it is much cheaper to experiment on a smaller scale, but now there are several systems which have made the grade and are finding application on larger sizes of vessel. In particular here is the water jet propulsion system which is now available in very high power capacities and is even being considered as a propulsion system for large passenger ships.

Even the humble propeller has developed out of all recognition in recent years as designers have sought to improve the power absorption capabilities. With a conventional propulsion system the propeller is the essential link between the engine and the water and any increase in the efficiency of the propeller improves the amount of power transmitted as thrust and thus gives immediate benefit.

Propeller research is a highly complex subject because of the large number of variables which can be altered in the design of a propeller, but one of the latest developments in this field is the highly skewed propeller which is particularly applicable for use on faster ships both to improve efficiency and reduce noise. The highly skewed propeller was originally developed for high speed craft such as petrol boats but the overlapping blades of this type of design are now being used on passenger ships in particular because of their low noise characteristics and good efficiency.

The controllable pitch propeller has been with us for a long time, but here again improved design particularly with controllable pitch highly skewed propellers is leading to increased efficiency. The big advantage of the CP propeller of course is its ability to match the propeller performance closely to the engine loading, so that the propeller can be optimised for different loading conditions of the ship. Tugs and trawlers are particular examples of ships where the loading on the propulsion system can vary widely but even on cargo ships where a vessel operates at different draft levels the increased complexity of the controllable pitch propeller can be justified in terms of improved performance. The CP propeller also improves the manoeuvrability of the ship allowing speeds very close to zero and also giving an improved astern response in terms of time.

The Grim Wheel

Over the years there has been a number of innovative devices to try and improve propeller efficiency, but the one which seems to be attracting most attention recently is the Grim Wheel. The Grim Wheel was invented by a German engineer and is like a secondary propeller mounted freely behind the main propeller. Part of the blades of the Grim Wheel absorb the thrust generated by the main propeller which causes it to rotate and the Grim Wheel then generates additional thrust. The diameter of the Grim Wheel is some 20% larger than the main propeller and on the latest developments the Wheel is mounted on a bearing on the rudder post rather than mounted on a propeller shaft extension as was tried in earlier applications.

Despite the disastrous application of the Grim Wheel on the liner Queen Elizabeth II, the latest application on a large tanker built in Japan shows that the Wheel adds 7% to the thrust increasing the speed of this 16 knot tanker by 2 knots.

Contra-rotating propellers were first tried 150 years ago and made a reappearance on the Volvo stern drive unit for small craft some 10 years ago. Now two ship installations are under trial one on a large car carrier where fuel savings of up to 15% have been recorded and the other on a small coaster where the contra-rotating propellers are fitted to an Aquamaster azimuthing propulsion unit.

There is no doubting the increased efficiency available with contra-rotating propellers but the main argument against them has always been the increased mechanical complexity because the system requires an inner and outer propeller shaft to feed the two propellers and these two shafts have to be linked by a gear system. With a conventional propeller shaft installation additional power is absorbed by the gear box which connects the two shafts, but in both the Volvo stern drive unit and the Aquamaster unit where the drive is taken down through a vertical shaft and then translated into the horizontal propeller shaft through bevel gearing, driving the two shafts becomes a simple matter of taking the one drive from each side of the bevel gear on the vertical shaft.

Initial trials with these contra-rotating propellers have shown useful results in terms of improved efficiency and so far the reliability has also been good. Whether the higher costs of the installation and the additional complexity can be justified by the fuel savings and higher efficiency is a complex equation to balance and it will probably require another rise in fuel prices to justify wider application of this concept.

The electric propeller concept

A new propeller concept developed by Jastrum is an electric propeller. This propeller works in a nozzle and this nozzle forms the fixed part of an electric motor with electric coils forming and strong magnetic field. The propeller has an outside ring to which strong fixed magnets are attached. This ring runs in close proximity to the nozzle and when current is applied to the nozzle coild, the propeller turns just like an electric motor. The propeller is supported at its centre by bearings but because there are no gears or shafting at the centre, there is less interference with the water flow to the propeller. The main application of such a propeller is to thrusters or to ships such as research vessels and mine-sweepers where a quiet propulsion system is required.

Thrusters have tended to be used for providing additional manoeuvring control for ships which require a high degree of manoeuvrability. Tugs are an obvious answer where thrusters can be used to advantage and the water tractor concept of tug is now widely accepted although there is a growing trend now to move the thrusters from the amidships position to aft in order to give tugs a better seaworthiness capability.

Similar drive systems are also being used in some offshore vessels and producers such as Schottel and Aquamaster have developed sophisticated and reliable thruster units for use in these applications. There is a loss of propulsion efficiency to a certain extent with these units but in specialised applications this is acceptable, as is the higher cost, because of the benefits in manoeuvrability which are gained. Now there is growing interest in the use of these azimuthing propulsion units for cargo ships particularly those operating on short sea routes where there is a lot of harbour manoeuvring involved. The idea of a ship being self-sufficient for its manoeuvring in harbour saves on the cost of tugs and can save time, but the use of thrusters also gives greater flexibility in the engine installation and in the fact that the whole propulsion unit is packaged in one easy to instal unit. Added to this they also combine the steering of the vessel so that no rudders are required and controllable pitch propellers can be easily incorporated. It all adds up to a package which is proving increasingly attractive and the Aquamaster contra-rotating thruster is an example of how these units are being developed for cargo shipping. They are now available to handle power outputs up to 10,000 hp and one of the latest companies to come into this market is the Swedish manufacturer KaMeWa.

Water jet propulsion for high speed vessels

Water jets are another propulsion system which have been with us for a long time, but it is only in the past 10 years that their use has grown. The water jet is in effect a pump unit which sucks in water from underneath the hull and ejects it through the stern to give propulsion thrust. By deflecting the outgoing water jet, steering is obtained and the jet can also be reversed in direction to give astern thrust. The advantages of water jets are that there are no external protrusions under the vessel which can give a shallow draft capacity and reduce the chance of damage, but they also offer a high degree of manoeuvrability and modern day units come close to matching the efficiency of propellers.

Water jets tend to be specified for high speed vessels where their efficiency increases. Current large motor yachts have water jet units absorbing over 10,000 hp and they are particularly useful when a powerful centre engine is matched by two wing engines to give a flexible propulsion package. The application of water jets in smaller sizes covers a wide range of craft. In the larger sizes much of the development has been in the propulsion systems for large, fast motor yachts but now we are seeing patrol boats adopting this type of propulsion system with powerful water jets being fitted to new patrol boats being built for the Finnish Navy. KaMeWa and Riva Calzoni are the two main builders of high power water jet units with the latter now offering water jets with power capabilities up to 25000 kw. Riva Calzoni sees a particular application for water jets in the passenger vessel market and already water jets are widely used on many of the new generation of catamaran passenger boats.

Here one of the main attractions is the turbine like smoothness of the water jet and this benefit could also be extended to large passenger liners where propulsion efficiency has to be balanced against passenger comfort and the water jet could offer a smoothness and lack of vibration not possible with propeller propulsion.

Like many of the other propulsion units systems mentioned, the water jet has benefitted greatly from modern materials and technology to become a highly reliable unit. Another advantage of the water jet is its ability to absorb a wide range of loadings, and example of this being in the trans-Atlantic record breaker Azimut Atlantic Challenger which carried twice its own weight in fuel. Here 8000 hp was connected to twin Riva Calzoni water jets to give efficient propulsion both at the full loaded speed of 29 knots, and the light speed of 50 knots.

The surface piercing propeller

The latest propulsion concept to come out of the high speed boat market is the surface piercing propeller. With this propulsion system which is designed for planing boats, only the bottom blades of the propeller do useful work at high speed. The propeller shaft is designed to emerge from the bottom of the transom so that the hub of the propeller is on the waterline at planing speeds. With only the bottom blades in the water at high speed there is no drag from the propeller shaft or appendages and this gives improved efficiency which has been well demonstrated at speeds up to 100 knots. The surface piercing propeller is probably only viable at speeds over 40 knots at present and tends to be used with fixed shafts, but one concept developed in

America, the Arneson drive has the propeller mounted on a shaft which incorporates a universal joint. The propeller end of the shaft is supported by two hydraulic rams, one vertical and one horizontal, the horizontal ram allowing the shaft to be turned in this plane to give steering using the propeller thrust, and the vertical ram allows the height of the propeller in relation to the water surface to be adjusted.

This Arneson drive concept has been used on some low speed boats but here it is the ability to vary the vertical height of the propeller which can have benefits particularly for craft like landing craft which may have to beach or for craft which have to operate at widely varying draft levels.

Complex drive units

An even more complex drive system being tried out in high performance small craft uses a trimming drive unit rather like the Arneson drive, but also incorporating contra-rotating propellers. This Technodrive unit is probably taking mechanical complexity to the limits but in the quest for efficiency there is a growing acceptance for the need for complex drive units. There is no doubt that with the modern range of propulsion systems and concepts available on the market a drive system is available to match any particular requirement. Careful engineering can ensure reliability of these modern drive systems and modern materials can ensure that they will stand up to using sea water. Of course with the increasing complexity there is also an increase in cost and in some cases these modern propulsion systems come close to matching the cost of the diesel engines which are linked to them. However in the quest for efficiency cost can be a secondary factor, although in the hard commercial world there may be a reluctance to invest on this scale unless there is a proven level of return.

The choice of propulsion systems has never been wider and there is certainly

A screwed five bladed propeller fitted to a research ship to give quieter running and improved efficiency

growing interest in the shipping world in these advanced propulsion systems as they demonstrate their viability. What would appear to be the ulitmate propulsion system is already under development by the Japanese and this is a linear induction motor which simply propels the ship along by electrical reation against the sea water. Here there are no external protrusions from the hull with all the machinery being contained inside the hull and the Japanese are already building a small prototype to explore the idea. Such a concept may already be a long way ahead but the idea of such a propulsion system would be as revolutionary as the switch from sail to steam. There is a lot of development work going on and the only real conclusion which can be reached in the propulsion system market is that there is no shortage of new ideas.

THE FUTURE WITH GPS

by Dag Pyke

Seafarers have dreamed about a system which would offer position fixing with a high degree of reliability and accuracy, 24 hours a day, anywhere in the world. That dream is now nearing reality and the biggest revolution in navigation since the invention of the chronometer is about to take place. The change is likely to be gradual rather than dramatic, but in the long term, the new system will bring about changes which may challenge some of the long-cherished traditions of the sea.

Behind all this change is the Navstar Global Positioning System, GPS for short. It is a satellite based system using the latest in space technology and its introduction marks two significant advances in satellite navigation. Unlike the earlier Transit system, GPS offers continuous position fixing with updates every few seconds. The second advance is the high degree of reliable accuracy.

Before satellite systems were introduced, navigators relied on terrestrial based electronic systems. Omega was worldwide in coverage but low on accuracy, while Loran C and Decca Navigator tended to be local in coverage but with higher accuracy. All were affected by atmospheric conditions, Before GPS, no one system would do the job for ships trading worldwide. Now with one standard system a lot of interesting possibilities are opened up.

The original concept

Before we get too excited about GPS we should remember its somewhat chequered history. It was conceived as a position fixing system for use by the U.S. Department of Defense. The original plan was to put 24 satellites in orbit and fix the position by measuring ranges from the satellites in "sight" at any one time. Economies have forced the satellites to be reduced to 18, which is still enough to give at least four satellites in "sight" anywhere on earth but it cuts down on the number of spares available, so if a satellite fails, coverage could be less than 100%.

Seven trial satellites were launched with the remainder scheduled to be taken up into space by the Space Shuttle. The schedule as originally planned, would have seen the whole system operational by now, but the disaster to Challenger put paid to these plans and the launch of the satellites has been switched to Delta rockets. Even so, the whole project has been put back at least two years and GPS should become fully operational by 1992.

As the satellites are put into orbit, the coverage is gradually being expanded. The trial satellites gave coverage for about six hours a day and by 1990 there should be full worldwide 2-dimensional coverage. This should be sufficient for marine use, the 3-dimensional coverage being required for aircraft and space vehicles.

Technically GPS is moving ahead well despite its initial problems, but now we come to the political aspects. To understand these it must be realised that GPS is a military system and no military organisation wants to give help to its potential enemies. Being based on satellite transmissions which can be received by all, in theory this worldwide system was available to all users with a suitable receiver.

The Transit satellite system was opened up for use by commercial operators long after it was established as a military system, but with GPS the commercial aspect have been thought out from the beginning. Built into the system were two codes with the P code giving access to the full accuracy of the system whilst the C code would offer a downgraded accuracy. This C code would be the one available to commercial users and, of course to any enemies of the United States.

Available to all

The original intention was to charge commercial users for the system. A number of options were proposed, but this idea has now been dropped because it would cost as much to collect fees as would be gained and because of the problems inherent in collecting such fees. So GPS will be freely available to all-comers with a suitable receiver. The accuracy level with the C code is currently set at 100 metres which is adequate for most practical navigation purposes, but the story does not end there.

By using differential techniques, the accuracy of the C code GPS can be upgraded considerably. Differential GPS works by having a receiver established in a position which is known very accurately and measuring the difference between the received position and the known position. There are established as the errors in the system and they are transmitted out to users at sea and automatically applied as corrections to the received position on board.

Differential techniques allow a great deal of the downgraded accuracy to be restored. The P code gives accuracy of between 3 and 5 metres whilst with differential GPS, accuracies of around 10 metres are possible. The accuracy of differential GPS degrades with distance from the base receiver but can be valid up to 1000 miles away. All of which leaves the U.S. Department of Defense with egg on its face, and it looks as though in time a higher level of accuracy will be freely available without having to resort to differential techniques.

The Soviet system

The Russians are also developing their own version of GPS called Glonass, and without the satellite launching problems of the Americans, they could well have their system operational first. The Russians have not been very forthcoming about the commercial availability of their system but they could score a useful political coup by making it available before the U.S. system. However, time is running out for that to happen, but in the present harmony that seems to exist between the two countries it would make a great deal of sense if the two systems could operate in conjunction. By having double the number of satellites available much better reliability and back up could be provided.

The new practical approach to relations between the U.S. and the U.S.S.R. is already demonstrating that both sides recognise the benefits to be gained by a joint approach. The initiative has come from the commercial aircraft industry which saw the new satellite systems as ideal for air navigation, but was concerned about the long delays in getting information through about possible satellite failures. Aircraft wanted a maximum 10 second warning of failure, the Americans were offering about two hours warning with GPS alone. Combine the two systems and the 10 second warning time can be achieved simply because nearly double the number of satellites are available to check the position.

An agreement signed in Paris has set the two parties down the road of co-operating on the integration of the two systems. Just how far this will go is open to speculation but whatever level of integration is finally achieved, it can only lead to improvements in the overall system which in turn will lead to wider use of GPS in more critical situations.

High levels of accuracy

As far as general navigation for shipping is concerned, GPS as proposed is adequate. An accuracy of 100 metres is more or less compatible with existing navigation systems and the consistency of GPS and the worldwide coverage give GPS the advantage. It is in more critical navigation situations that the higher levels of accuracy achieved with differential techniques could give a considerable advantage

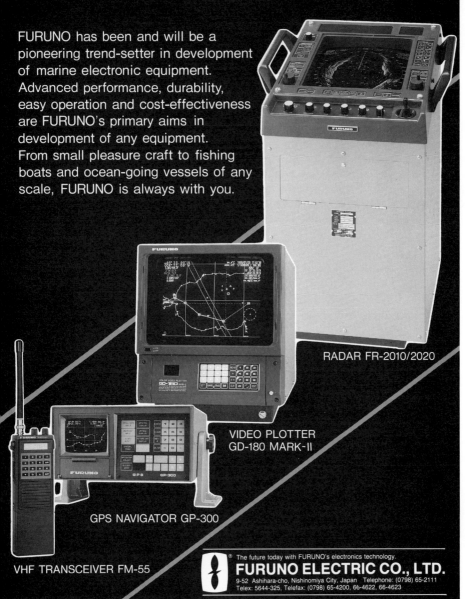

over current methods of navigation.

Because GPS will be equipped with the system and it could eventually become mandatory. This could open up the way to standard systems of harbour navigation particularly if differential systems can be standardised from port to port. With differential accuracy of say 5 metres with a system established to give coverage within a port area and approaches, then a ship would be able to navigate very precisely within that port area.

The navigation would be even more precise bearing in mind that the same position fixing system would be used for harbour surveys and for the positioning of navigation marks. One can envisage a system of the future where the ship, on approaching a harbour, selects the appropriate computer disk for that harbour and feeds it into the on board computer. This is linked to the differential GPS system and the ship controls, allowing the ship to be navigated automatically to its berth.

There could be considerable cost savings because pilots would not be necessary and navigation marks could be done away with. The ship would be much more precisely positioned than with present manual systems and one could assume that a higher level of safety could result. It's easy to see in this situation the need for an early warning system for any satellite failure or malfunction and the aircraft requirements would be adequate.

Redundancy would also have to be built in to any such system, but this can be used to further advantage. Aircraft currently use three position fixing systems and a voting system to ensure that any rogue information or equipment failure is detected at an early stage. A similar system could be adopted on board ship and if one receiver is located at the bow, and one at the stern, then by interpellation of the readings it would be possible to have a precise reading of the ship's heading. Interpellation of the accurate positions could also indicate the ship's speed.

Far reaching effects

All of these developments fly in the face of tradition. It is hard to imagine that the long held tradition of doing without pilots to bring ships into port could be abandoned. It is equally hard to imagine the compass disappearing from the ship's bridge, but these could be the far reaching effects of the introduction of GPS. However, bear in mind that the magnetic compass has been relegated to a standby function and sextants are almost unused on today's ships, so that change is taking place.

Probably the hardest people to convince about changes will be the regulatory authorities. They always adopt a belt and braces approach, allowing the new but still requiring the old. It is going to be hard to convince them about the capabilities of GPS and its Russian counterpart, but by careful design it should not be hard to build adequate reliability into systems.

Power supplies offer the biggest weakness, but battery operated GPS receivers are already on the market. We already rely almost entirely on electronics to indicate when a vessel is in distress these days, so why not place the same reliance on position fixing equipment provided it is engineered properly?

Cost is hardly likely to be a significant factor. The current generation of receivers costs around the £3000 mark. Experts confidently predict that the cost will drop to around a quarter of this figure when the system is fully operational and the market expands. Already manufacturers have such cheap receivers on the drawing board virtually ready for production.

GPS and Glonass combined receivers

The other development which is also on the drawing board is combined GPS and

SIMRAD ED-161
Affordable Navigation.

The SIMRAD ED-161 Navigation Sounder has been proven in years of use throughout the world and it is still an affordable solution to your navigation sounder needs.

Features:

- Meets and exceeds IMO regulations for navigation sounders on merchant vessels.
- The depth alarm can be preset at any depth between 1 and 999 meters.
- Digital indication may be run with the paper stopped.
- A minimum range of 0 to 50 meters and a maximum range of 100 meters.
- 6-inch dry paper.
- 50 kHz operation.
- 350 watt transmitter.

NOTE: Transducer supplied by SIMRAD; steel tank supplied by the shipyard.

SIMRAD, INC.
620 N.W. Bright Street
Seattle, WA 98107 USA

Telephone: (206) 789-6482
Telefax: (206) 789-1766
Telex: 211098

Member of the SIMRAD Subsea Group

Glonass receivers. Even without any changes to either system, such receivers are a viable proposition. However, it is confidently expected that the orbits of the satellites of the two systems will be subtley adjusted to give a better integrated coverage. GPS operates on a spread spectrum transmission to reduce the chance of jamming while Glonass operates on a fixed frequency, but these are not really problems to a modern software based receiver.

Where the two systems differ is that the positions given are based on different geodetic references. GPS is based on the sophisticated World Geodetic System No.4 which is a computer model of the earth's surface. Glonass is based on the Moscow reference, details of which have not been released. One of the first objects of any co-operation would be to match up the two reference systems by computer modelling so that they can be interfaced.

Another problem which will be presented with the introduction of GPS is that it will produce positions which may be more accurate than the chart on which the position is being plotted. In most developed countries the charts have been kept up to date with the available accuracies, but even here discrepancies can occur as land surveys may use a different reference to the sea survey. In more remote parts of the world where the chart positions may have been fixed many years ago by sextant observation, GPS positions could be dangerously at variance.

The various survey authorities are striving desperately to keep up to date with these developments. GPS provides them with a marvellous position fixing tool, but developments are moving ahead faster than they can cope. They are already trying to cope with the implications of electronic chart systems which are a logical system to use in connection with GPS to provide a real time tactical picture of the navigation situation.

The delay in the introduction of GPS has brought about a welcome relief from the pressures of coping with the new system. When GPS finally reaches fruition it will bring about a revolution in navigation, of that there is no doubt. This revolution will be a gradual process of necessity to give all those involved time to adapt to change. In the same way as when radar was introduced there were "radar assisted collisions", so with GPS there will probably by "GPS assisted groundings." These will be caused by a failure to fully understand the system and putting too much reliance on the output. Confidence with the system will only grow with time, particularly if Glonass is integrated, but then navigators will have the tool they have long dreamed about, one which will open new horizons in navigation.

MARINE CASUALTIES

Norman Hooke, of Lloyd's Maritime Information Services and author of "*Modern Shipping Disasters 1963-1987*", looks at the major casualties and settlements of 1988, summarises losses over the last 25 years and gives a statistical review of the Gulf war hostilities between Iraq and Iran.

According to the 1988 annual summary of the monthly casualty returns issued by the Institute of London Underwriters (ILU), which is produced with the assistance of the Casualty Branch, Intelligence Department, Lloyd's of London Press, during that particular year there were 147 vessels of 500 tons gross and over reported to have become either totally lost or to have been declared constructive total losses (CTL), giving a grand total of 775,856 grt. This equates to approximately three normal marine losses per week, with the average tonnage for each vessel being 5,278 grt.

Of this total of 147 vessels, no fewer than 35 flew the Panamanian flag. Except for the 10 total losses each recorded for both Cyprus and the Philippines, no other nationality reached double figures. Flags which in the not too distant past have recorded extremely high annual losses, Greece and Liberia, accounted for just six and two respectively.

The last 25 years

A brief look back at the last 25 years' total loss statistics reveals some interesting facts. During the period from 1964 to 1988, inclusive, a total of 817 vessels over 500 grt flying the flag of Panama are recorded as being lost, while there were 750 Greek flag losses, with Liberia totalling 351. Cyprus registered vessels, which were only listed separately from 1969, account for 275 losses in the 20 years to date. Remember these figures do not include war losses. Because of the way in which the figures were compiled previous to 1969, British and British Commonwealth flag vessels were listed under the same heading. In the five years 1964 to 1968 there were 84 total losses recorded for British and Commonwealth vessels but, in the 20 years from 1969 to 1988, only 78 British flag vessels have been listed as lost.

The Greeks worst three years were 1978, 1979 and 1981 with 74, 72 and 63 losses respectively, while the Panamanians lost 58 in 1982, 56 the following year and 52 each in both 1976 and 1979. The Liberians worst years were 1972 — 27 losses, 1966 — 24 losses, and 1965 and 1968 with 21 each. Cyprus flag vessel losses totalled 25 in 1978, 24 in 1979 and 20 each for both 1974 and 1976. So by complete contrast there were only six Greek vessels lost in 1988 and just two Liberian.

The annual grand total of all vessels over 500 grt reported totally lost due to marine causes during the 25-year period in question rose from 117 in 1964 to a staggering 278 in 1979. Indeed, in the 12 years from 1974 to 1985, inclusive, the figures read at least 188 per year, with nine of those years taking a toll in excess of 200 vessels per annum. According to the figures compiled in the monthly casualty returns the total number of vessels over 500 grt reported to have become totally lost or to have been declared CTL's due to normal causes during this 25-year span is 4,692, with a gross tonnage totalling 28,189,998 tons. This averages out at approximately 188 vessels lost per year. Interestingly in the last five years the number of losses dropped from 214 in 1984 to 139 in 1987, this latter figure being the lowest since 1964. However, in terms of gross tonnage lost, the 139 vessels of 1987 totalled 1,178,973 but 1988's total of 147 vessels lost only equated to 775,856 grt. The worst year for tonnage lost was, again, 1979, with 2,258,221 grt.

The Gulf War

These figures almost pale into comparative insignificance when the Gulf war losses are studied. From figures compiled by Lloyd's Maritime Information Services (LMIS) there were reported to have been 547 acts of hostility on vessels in the Gulf during the period from May, 1981, to August, 1988, during which time merchant vessels came under attack by both Iraqi and Iranian forces in the open Gulf (as opposed to those trapped in the Shatt al Arab waterway in September, 1980). Tonnage attacked equated to 35,352,854 grt. Of these the large total of 144 vessels, 26.4 per cent, — tankers, bulkers, general cargo, tugs and supply vessels — became either totally lost or were declared war constructive total losses due to the severity of the damage sustained by the exploding missiles and subsequent fires, and in a few cases due to striking mines. This total included 38 vessels over 100,000 grt. The grand total gross tonnage reported to have been thus lost during the eight years was 6,943,211, giving an average gross tonnage loss per vessel of 48,217. Added to these figures are the 17 vessels trapped in the Shatt al Arab that were so seriously damaged in cross-river fighting in September and October, 1980, that they were settled as war constructive total losses. These 17 totalled 136,846 grt, giving total Gulf war total losses of 161 vessels of 7,080,057 grt. Of course many of the over 70 other vessels to be trapped in the Shatt, but not seriously damaged, were settled as CTL's due to their owners being deprived of their use for over 12 months. (They were, in fact, trapped for the eight years duration of the war and are still presently anchored in the river, unable to be released due to the severe siltation and accummulated war debris. Only those vessels detained at the Iraqi ports of Umm Qasr and Khor al Zubair, which are approached via the Khor Abdulla to the west of the Shatt entrance, were subsequently released in August and September, 1988.)

For a comparison, according to "Lloyd's War Losses — The Second World War Vol. I", the number of British, Allied and neutral merchant vessels sunk or destroyed by war causes during the six-year period, 3 September, 1939 to 14 August 1945, was 5,411, totalling 21,314,648 grt. Deaths at sea or in port due to enemy action comprising seamen of all nationalities who served in British ships and British seamen who served in foreign-flag ships chartered or requisitioned by H.M. Government from 3 September 1939 was 29,180 in merchant vessels and 814 in fishing vessels, totalling 29,994.

Poor year for insurers

However 1988 was to become one of the worst years on record for maritime casualties in terms of payments of actual insurance settlements because not included in ILU figures are war losses and the enormous offshore industry claims.

While the Gulf war continued unabated until August, when a cease-fire was agreed to by Iraq and Iran, 1988 proved to be one of the worst for attacks on vessels — 97 reported in total. Not only was the world's largest vessel, the 564,739 tons deadweight Liberian steam tanker *Seawise Giant*, declared a war CTL due to the devastating attack made on her by Iraqi warplanes on 14 May while she was berthed at Hormuz Terminal, Larak Island, while acting as a crude oil storage vessel, but the most lives were lost in any one day as a direct result of the Iraqi attacks on the two Iranian flag tankers *Avaj*, 316,379 dwt, and *Sanandaj*, 253,877 dwt, at Kharg Island on 19 March. A total of 22 men died on the former vessel while, on the latter, 26 men perished.

The 14 May raid on vessels berthed at Hormuz Terminal also proved to be the most costly single raid for insurers because not only was the $9m. (£4.76) *Seawise Giant* extensively damaged but the 235,000 dwt Spanish tanker *Barcelona* was also subsequently settled as a war CTL at Pesetas 1,500,000,000 (£7.18) due to the severity of the damage that she, too, sustained when bombed and set on fire. Two other

tankers, the Cyprus flag *Argosy* and the British flagged, Hamilton, Bermuda registered *Burmah Endeavour* were also badly damaged when struck by the Iraq bombs.

Offshore insurers were faced with the huge Enchova Oilfield loss in mid-1988 Enchova, which was Brazil's biggest producing platform, blew-out and caught fire on 23 April when leaking gas exploded and forced the closure of five fields that had an output of 77,000 barrels of oil a day as well as two million cubic metres of gas. There were no injuries when the blow-out occurred but it proved to be a severe set-back to the Brazilian economy as it resulted in the loss of approximately 11 per cent of the country's oil and gas production. It took more than a month to control and resulted in very extensive damage to the platform, which is located in the Campos Basin some 180 miles east of Rio de Janeiro. The Petrobras platform was insured by Instituto de Resseguros do Brasil but a substantial proportion of the risk was placed in the London market. The full insured value was $330m. (£178.38m).

This staggering loss was set to produce the biggest-ever offshore insurance claim but, just a few months later, came the even worse *Piper Alpha* catastrophe in the North Sea on 6 July. Not only were the lives of no fewer than 167 men lost but the platform was insured for just over $800m. (£470.58m.). There was also substantial business interruption cover that took the total payout to over $1bn.

Bad start to the year

Nineteen eighty-eight had started off badly with the grounding of the Cyprus flag motor vessel *Mitera Sotiria*, 8,372 grt, which had an insured value of $1.5m (£819,672). She was on a ballast voyage from Augusta to Bilbao when she was wrecked on 3 January near Corunna after sustaining engine failure in heavy weather. The following day the Faroese fish factory *Sundaberg* was wrecked off Vardo in the far north of Norway. Even though only of 856 grt, she was insured for £2.27m.

An unusual loss occurred on 5 January with the grounding of the Singapore registered motor exhibition vessel *Logos* in the Beagle Channel while on passage from Ushuaia to Puerto Madryn carrying passengers and religious books. However, no lives were lost. A Gulf war casualty, the Cyprus flag tanker *United Venture*, 13,16 grt, was severely damaged by a missile and the resultant fire on 12 January. She had an insured value of $3.5m. (£1.9m.).

No fewer than nine highly-valued Mexican motor fishing vessels sustained extensive storm damage and then sinking off Ensenada on 17 January. Their value ranged from $3.1m. (£1.73m.) to $10.2m. (£5.7m.). The American non-propelled jack-up drill barge *ENSCO III* was another victim of heavy weather, becoming a constructive total loss due to the extent of damage sustained on 27 January when off Jamaica while being towed from Port Arthur to Lake Maracaibo on board a semi submersible pontoon. Her value was $10.5m. (£5.76m.). The first major loss of life in 1988 occurred on 29 January with the deaths of 12 men from the Cyprus registered motor vessel *Rolandia*, 2,723 grt, which sank in the Atlantic in heavy weather while en route from Point Comfort, Texas, to Grangemouth with a cargo of alumina. Her value was £2.86m.

The next loss in excess of £2m. took place on 19 February. With a value of £4.2m. the timber-carrying Panamanian motor vessel *Star Kim*, 4,252 grt, was wrecked off Taiwan while on voyage from Sambas to Gamagori. She subsequently sank but no lives were lost. Three days later the American 4,089 grt non-propelled drilling platform *Keyes 302* capsized and sank in the Gulf of Mexico when one leg "punched through" the seabed. The crew was saved but the platform was a loss at $8.4m (£4.69m.).

After being in service for only about nine months, the Swedish roll-on, roll-of

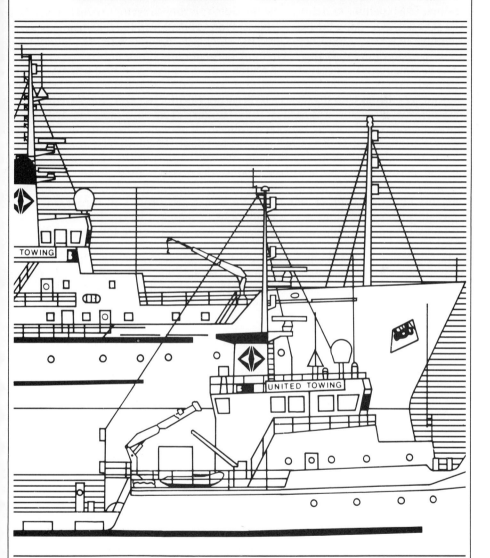

UNITED TOWING

Providing assistance to the shipping and offshore industries worldwide.

A NORTH BRITISH MARITIME GROUP COMPANY

BOSTON HOUSE, ST. ANDREW'S DOCK, HULL, ENGLAND.
TELEPHONE: 0482 224181. TELEX: 597692 (TOWING). FAX: 0482 24669.

motor vessel *Vinca Gorthon*, 18,773 grt, was totally lost on 29 February after she capsized and sank in gale-force winds in the southern North Sea off the Dutch coast while en route from Oskarshamn in Sweden to the River Thames berth of Purfleet, via Antwerp, carrying a cargo of paper and woodpulp. Her 17-man crew was safely lifted off the stricken vessel while she drifted helplessly before finally sinking, coming to rest in 20 metres of water, but lying across an undersea, 50,000 barrels-a-day, oil pipeline. The pipeline, stretching from the Dutch North Sea sector to Amsterdam, had to be shut down, causing the loss of at least Florins 500,000 ($263,000) per day in lost revenue. The wreck of the *Vinca Gorthon*, which was unsured with the Gothenburg-based Swedish Club for $21m. (£11.73m.), subsequently broke in two.

The next major loss occurred on 8 March with the sinking of the 3,940 grt Cyprus registered motor container carrier *Miriam Borchard* in the eastern Mediterranean following a collision with the Cyprus bulk carrier *Eftihia*. Her crew was saved but the container vessel's value was D.Mks 10m. (£3.2m.). Ten days later the 41,922 grt Cyprus flag tanker *Kyrnicos* became another Gulf statistic when attacked by Iraqi aircraft. Seriously damaged by fire, her value was $5m. (£2.86m.). The worst-ever loss of life in the eight-year old Gulf war in one day due to one attack took place 19 March with the devastating missile strikes against the large Iranian tankers *Avaj* and *Sanandaj*, both of which are mentioned above. This resulted in a total of 48 lives being lost. Four days later, 23 March, saw the 18,876 grt Cyrpus bulk carrier *Odysseas H.* sustain such severe damage as a result of being attacked by two Iranian gunboats and being set on fire that she was declared a war constructive total loss at $4.4m. (£2.5m.).

The following day the 3,692 grt Greek roll-on, roll-off motor vessel *Italia Express* capsized and sank at her repair berth at Drapetzona. Her value was $4m. (£2.28m.). This took the Sterling equivalent of all major losses reported during the first quarter to in excess of £80m. ($143m.).

Heavy losses in second quarter

Within the space of four days in April, 1988, just three losses subsequently brought claims totalling $401.5m. (£217m.). On 22 April the 18,251 grt Cyprus flag tanker *Athenian Venture* was found in the western Atlantic in two sections, having been blown apart after explosions and fire on board. She had been on voyage from Amsterdam to New York carrying a cargo of gasoline. There were no survivors from the 25 crew members and four wives on board. Both parts of the *Athenian Venture*, which had a hull and machinery value of $7.5m. (£4m.), subsequently sank.

The *Enchova No 1* blow-out occurred on 24 April leaving insurers to face the massive $330m. (£178.38m.) claim and then, just two days later came the loss of the world's largest car-carrying ship, the newly-built Panamanian flag, Japanese controlled, *Reijin*. This 58,128 grt vessel was on her maiden voyage when she ran aground and capsized off the Portuguese coast. Declared a constructive total loss, her hull and machinery insurance value was $34m. (£19.2m.) but the value of her wrecked 5,466 Toyota cars still on board added another $30m. (£16.9m.) to the loss.

May 14 brought the devastating attack on Hormuz Terminal that saw the *Seawise Giant* and *Barcelona* being declared war constructive total losses at £7.19m. and £4.76m. respectively. Another expensive loss occurred on 20 May when the four-year-old 18,639 grt Panamanian motor bulk carrier *Korean Star* was wrecked on the rocky Western Australian coast near Cape Cuvier during a cyclone. She broke up two days later but no lives were lost. Her hull and machinery insurance value was £8.97m.

Another Gulf war CTL, the 12,251 grt Liberian liquefied petroleum gas tanker *Mundogas Rio* sustained serious fire damage due to being attacked by Iranian gunboats in the Strait of Hormuz on 26 May while en route from Jubail to India carrying an ammonia cargo. This cost war insurance underwriters $7m. (£3.7m.). The

hilippine bulk carrier *Singa Sea* which broke in two off Western Australia in July 1988   *Skyfotos*

reek tanker *Anangel Greatness* which sustained explosion and fire while under
pair at Perama   *Skyfotos*

day following this attack, the 10,526 grt Maltese motor bulk carrier *Don Miguel* wa
also attacked by Iranian gunboats. She, too, was settled as a war CTL at $3m
(£1.59m.) due to the severity of the damage sustained by the resultant fire.

This brought the second quarter's major loss total to an almost unbelievabl
$469m. (£262m.). However, July was just around the corner.

Survival at sea

One of the more amazing stories of survival at sea occurred in July and August c
1988. The Philippine motor bulk carrier *Singa Sea*, 16,244 grt, had loaded a cargo c
mineral sand and copper ore at Geraldton and Bunbury, Western Australia, fc
discharge at Rotterdam. Sailing from Bunbury on 2 July, she reported to her agents b
radio the following day, after which she failed to make scheduled contact on 4 Jul
Searches by sea and air were made but to no avail. Then, on 2 August, after bein
adrift in a lifeboat for 29 days, six surviving members of the crew, suffering fror
exposure and sunburn, were located in the Indian Ocean about 200 miles west c
Perth. Amongst the six was the second officer, Sabas Martius, who subsequentl
advised that the *Singa Sea* broke in two and sank in just five minutes, throwing seve
survivors into the sea. They were able to reach a lifeboat which, miraculously, ha
been torn clear of its davits just as their vessel disappeared beneath the wave:
However, the first officer died of head injuries some 31 hours later and war buried a
sea, making the total number of lives lost 18, mainly Filipinos. According to th
second officer, the *Singa Sea*, when about 300 miles off the Western Australian coas
was battered by three huge waves and then taken up by a mountainous sea onto th
crest of a wave and thrown into the trough, breaking her in two. The loss of the vess
and her valuable cargo was estimated to have cost insurers more than $15m. With he
hull and machinery insured for $6m. (£3.35m.), the cargo was understood to be wort
considerably more than the vessel — $10m. — due to the 13,000 tons of zircon sand o
board. This represented 1.7 per cent of the annual worked consumption of tha
particular commodity and was insured for $8m. The copper ore also being carried ha
a value of $2m.

The *Piper Alpha* diaster, which put all other 1988 tragedies and claims in the shad
as far as loss of life and insurance figures were concered, occurred on 6 July.

August brought three losses ranging from $3.5m. (£2m.) to $5m. (£2.9m
involving the 1,530 grt Taiwanese motor fishing vessel *Yuh Soon*, which sustaine
serious fire and explosion damage on 10 August, the non-propelled dredger *Estalsc
with major bucket line damage on 16 August and the 9,799 grt Bahamas flag moto
vessel *Helix*, which was declared a CTL due to sustaining severe fire damage on 2
August while under repair at Las Palmas.

The next major loss concerned the 41,390 grt Greek motor tanker *Anange
Greatness* which, incredibly, became only the second tanker total loss in some nin
months as a result of normal marine perils (that is, excluding the Gulf War). With
hull and machinery value of $16.25m. (£9.6m.) the *Anangel Greatness* was unde
repair at Perama, Piraeus district, when she was wracked by an explosion and fire on
September. Partially sinking, her hull was seriously cracked on her starboard side. Si
persons lost their lives. The following day the 8,229 grt Norwegian drilling shi
Viking Explorer capsized and sank in the Bekapi field, Makassar Strait, following a
explosion as a result of a gas blow-out during drilling operations. Four crew died. Th
Viking Explorer's value was $6.7m. (£3.96m.). Another expensive offshore industr
loss occurred on 22 September when the $50m. (£29.59m.) 11,693 grt American self
propelled semi-submersible drilling platform *Ocean Odyssey* was seriously damage
by explosions and fire due to a gas blow-out in the Fulmar field, North Sea. She wa
declared a constructive total loss, bringing the third quarter's major losses to a total c
$899,330,800 (£529,018,125).

MODERN SHIPPING DISASTERS 1963–1987 by **Norman Hooke**

A maritime reference book — the one the shipping historian and enthusiast has been waiting for for 20 years.

Modern Shipping Disasters, by *Norman Hooke* continues from where Charles Hocking's classic Dictionary of Disasters at Sea, 1824–1962, left off. It covers the era of the supertanker, a period in which many of the world's most dramatic maritime disasters have taken place; casualties such as the **Torrey Canyon**, the **Amoco Cadiz**, as well as the **Herald of Free Enterprise** and the **Betelgeuse**.

Norman Hooke's meticulously researched book, which covers some 6,000 vessels, includes all merchant and naval losses and constructive total losses over 500 tons between 1963 and 1987. It also accommodates information on smaller vessels down to 100 grt where loss of life was reported to exceed 15. The book also analyses, over the 25 year period, the loss of life due to maritime disasters and the losses sustained in all international conflicts since 1963, including ships trapped in the Suez Canal and the casualties of the Gulf War and the Falklands.

This book is sure to be a valuable source of information to insurers, salvors, divers and treasure seekers as well as historians and ship lovers.

1 85044 211 8	**Hard Cover**	**548 pages**	**April 1989**

Order Form   To: The Book Sales Department, Lloyd's of London Press Ltd,
Sheepen Place, Colchester, Essex CO3 3LP, England.

Please send me:

_____ copy(ies) of Modern Shipping Disasters 1963–1987 £39.95/$80
Please add £2/$3.50 postage and packing per order.

Name _____ Company _____

Address _____

Nature of business _____
☐   Please invoice me (pro forma). Your order will be despatched upon payment of invoice.
☐   I enclose a cheque for

Collision off Piraeus

Amongst the major losses in October was the 27-year-old, 6,306 grt, Greek passenger vessel *Jupiter*, which sank on 21 October off the port of Piraeus following a collision with the Italian motor vehicle carrier *Adige*. The *Jupiter* had just sailed from Piraeus harbour for an eastern Mediterranean cruise carrying mainly British schoolchildren and their teachers. Tragically, two passengers and two children died but, miraculously, 471 children, teachers and their helpers, plus over 110 crew members survived, mainly due to the cruise ship taking about 40 minutes to sink. The *Jupiter* had a hull and machinery value of $9m. (£5.39m.) but there was also a $2.25m. (£1.35m.) increased value policy payable only in the event of a total loss. Some 92 per cent of the hull insurance was placed in London.

The Panamanian motor vessel *Golden Park*, 6,020 grt, was the next major total loss. On voyage from Sandakan to Inchon carrying a cargo of logs, she listed and sank south of Taiwan on 5 November with the loss of five of her crew. She was insured for $3.5m. (£2m.).

In a year in which there were remarkably few major tanker incidents only the third large tanker loss occurred on 10 November when the 65,746 grt Liberian motor tanker *Odyssey* broke in two in very heavy weather conditions in the North Atlantic some 700 miles off the coast of Nova Scotia while on voyage from Sullom Voe, Shetland Islands, to Come by Chance, Newfoundland, carrying a cargo of 132,157 tonnes of North Sea Brent crude oil. The stern section caught fire and sank the same day, while the bow section sank later. All 27 crew, comprising 15 Greek officers and 12 Honduran ratings, were lost. The hull and machinery insurance was placed directly in Italy, while the value of the crude oil was estimated to be around $13m. (£7.4m.).

Five days at the end of November and beginning of December brought four losses in excess of £2m. each. On 27 November the 13,514 grt Moroccan chemical tanker *Ibn Otman* sustained severe fire damage to her engine-room when about 70 miles off New Mangalore, India, having just sailed from the port for Morocco, in ballast. Declared a CTL, she had a hull and machinery value of £8.25m. Two days later came the sinkings of the £2.43m. Singapore registered container carrier *Pumori* during a cyclone in the Bay of Bengal and the highly-valued 472 grt American motor fishing vessel *Deep Sea Producer* in the Bering Strait some 30 miles west of Unimak Island after taking on water. Her hull and machinery insurance value was $5.2m (£2.97m.). Then on 2 December the Turkish ro/ro vessel *Kaptan Sait Ozege*, valued at $6m. (£13.3m.), was extensively damaged by fire while en route from Izmir to Trieste and Venice, carrying vehicles and containers. Abandoned off Corfu she was subsequently reported aground off the Albanian coast. Thirty-seven of her 38-man crew were safely rescued.

Another valuable container carrier sank on 12 December. With a hull and machinery insurance of $3.8m. (£2.1m.), the Panamanian registered *Selina* foundered in heavy seas off the north-east coast of the Philippines but all her crew members were safely rescued. Three days later came a further blow to the offshore industry with the loss of the 1983-built 13,190 American self-elevating drilling platform *Rowan Gorilla I* in the gale-tossed North Atlantic about 550 miles east-south-east of Halifax, Nova Scotia, while being towed from that Canadian port to Great Yarmouth, Norfolk. Her ballast tanks cracked then took in water, resulting in the platform capsizing and sinking. Insured mainly in the London market for $72m. (£39.56m.), marine insurers at Lloyd's and the Institute of London Underwriters faced their fourth huge offshore claim of the year.

Then on 26 December, in, as noted above what was a very quiet year for tanker disasters, came the fourth major tanker loss during the 12 months. The 114,630grt Cyprus registered motor tanker *Boni* had her engine-room and accommodation

gutted by fire off the coast of Sri Lanka while on voyage from Kerteh Terminal, Malaysia and Arun Terminal, Sumatera, to Puerto Rico, carrying a cargo of crude oil and condensate. However, all 39 crew members were safely rescued from the blazing vessel, which had a hull and machinery value of $22m. (£12.1m.). The last quarter of 1988 saw major settlements reach $164.56m. (190.42m.), making the grand total for the year $1,675m. (£961m.).

Heavy loss of life

The highest number of lives lost caused by the loss of a merchant vessel during 1988 took place, once again, in Philippine waters on a Philippine registered ship. Only nine months after the *Dona Paz* catastrophe, the 2,855 grt inter-island passenger/general cargo vessel *Dona Marilyn*, en route from Manila to Tacloban, carrying a reported 431 manifested passengers and 60 crew, capsized and sank in the Visayan Sea in the vicinity of Manocmanoc and Gigantangan Islands, Philippines, on 24 October during the ferocity of typhoon "Ruby". Battered by heavy seas, she sheltered at an islet for an hour before turning back but she was then completely overwhelmed by the elements. Dozens of unlisted passengers were among the survivors, with the owners of the vessel, Sulpicio Lines, admitting that they were aware that at least 511 passengers had been on board. Some survivors put the actual number on board at up to 1,000 but this was rejected by the Sulpicio manager in Cebu. The confirmed death toll was reported to be 150 but at least 248 other passengers and crew members were still listed as missing a week after the tragedy. The number of survivors totalled 263.

The *Exxon Valdez* Disaster

Almost every year brings a maritime disaster that hits theheadlines and stays in the public eye for some time because of the immense media attention given to it. It was the turn of the three-year-old 214,861 tonnes deadweight American registered tanker *Exxon Valdez* in 1989 which, loaded with a cargo of Alaskan crude oil, hit Bligh Reef in Alaska's Prince William Sound on 24 March, spilling nearly 11 million gallons that subsequently fouled hundreds of miles of coastline.

As a result of the extensive pollution that not only destroyed prime fishing areas but was also responsible for the deaths of thousands of sea birds and sea mammals, almost 10,000 square miles of coastline and sea areas were affected, with the clean-up operations having cost some $155m. by 1 June. It was by far the biggest oil spil in United States history.

The *Exxon Valdez* ran aground only 22 miles from Valdez terminal, from where she had just sailed, and only 45 minutes after the Valdez pilot had disembarked, immediately rupturing her tanks to release her lethal cargo. At the subsequent public hearing, the third mate left in command of the vessel, Gregory Cousins, aged 28, testified that attempts to steer her away from the reef were defeated because the *Exxon Valdez* failed to respond to the helm. He had ordered the helmsman to steer 10 degrees to starboard to get the ship back into the normal traffic land but when the instruments failed to show any response he then ordered a 20 degree turn. Finally, with the fully laden vessel heading towards the Bligh Reef dead ahead, he spun the wheel in a last desperate attempt to prevent her from grounding,. Mr Cousins then told the National Transportation Safety Board that he had telephoned the master, Captain Joseph Hazlewood, who had left the bridge to rest in his cabin, to report: "I think we're in serious trouble" as the tanker started a bumpy ride along the reef. Some 10 jolts shuddered through the hull in the space of a minute, following which she came to a dead stop at 0004 hours. Captain Hazelwood immediately returned to the bridge to try to rock the stranded ship free, but she remained stuck hard and fast, her cargo beginning to ooze from the torn tanks.

After the cargo remaining in her tanks had been pumped out into another Exxon tanker, the *Exxon Valdez* was successfully refloated on 5 April, then moved to sheltered water for surveys and preliminary repairs. It was almost three months after the original grounding that a decision was made to have the seriously damaged vessel repaired at the same yard where she had been built in 1986 in San Diego, California, in a nine-month job costing $25m. The 2,000 mile tow by three tugs was estimated to take 20 days.

Claims resulting from the spill were almost certain to exceed the $400m. reinsurance protection of the International Group of Protection and Indemnity clubs. Member clubs reserved for a full claim, which was likely to leave Lloyd's underwriters with a massive bill at a time when claims were already running at a very high level. The *Exxon Valdez* was insured with the Bermuda-based International Tanker Owners' Indemnity Association for pollution liabilities and, with a large number of claims being filed before United States courts in respect of the pollution caused, the likely total cost was put at approximately 11bn. Liabilities in excess of $400m. revert to Exxon, the vessel's owners, under the limited liability arrangements for pollution incidents but Exxon was reported to have an excess of loss insurance policy placed in the London market. Market sources suggested that the *Exxon Valdez* loss, by the time it had been finalised, would exceed the other recent major energy catastrophes such as the Enchova blow-out to rank second only to the Piper Alpha disaster as an energy-related loss.

The Herald of Free Enterprise — Manslaughter charges

In June 1989 the U.K. Director of Public Prosecutions issued manslaughter summonses against P&O European Ferries (Dover) and seven staff of the former Townsend Thoresen company, owners of the 1980-built, 7,951 grt, ro-ro passenger/cargo ferry *Herald of Free Enterprise* which capsized off Zeebrugge on 6 March 1987.

The decision to prosecute P&O European Ferries was taken after a 15 month investigation by Kent Police. Three former directors named in the summonses, returnable at Bow Street Magistrates Court, have left the company. Two of the crew members were disciplined by the public enquiry and two others heavily criticised. The proceedings relate to the deaths of two passengers and two crew members.

INMARSAT

The International Maritime Satellite Organisation, Inmarsat, operates a system of satellites to provide a range of high quality mobile telecommunications services for commercial and distress and safety applicatons, at sea, in the air and on land, worldwide.

The Services that the Inmarsat satellite system can support include direct-dial telephone, telex, facsimile and data connections for maritime applications; flight-deck voice and data, automatic position and status reporting and direct-dial passenger telephone for aircraft; and two-way data communcations, position reporting and fleet managment for land transport.

Headquartered in London, Inmarsat began operations on 1 February 1982.

Current maritime users of its system include oil tankers, liquid natural gas carriers, offshore drilling rigs, seismic survey ships, fishing boats, cargo and container vessels, passenger liners, ice-breakers, tugs, cable-laying ships and luxury yachts, among others. The system is also used for some land-based applications, including the provision of emergency transportable communications at time of human disaster and natural catastrophe. As of January 1989 over 8,400 ship earth stations or transportable versions were commissioned for use with the Inmarsat system.

Inmarsat is now introducing its range of satellite communciations services for the aeronautical community and the first satellite-equipped aircraft began service in February 1989. Because it can provide high quality, reliable communications links almost anywhere in the world, many of the world's airline corporate and general aviation operators are planning to fit satellite equipment over the next few years.

THE ORGANISATION

Fifty five countries have joined by becoming party to the Inmarsat Convention. These countries have either signed the Operating agreement themselves, or (in most cases) have designated a telecommunications entity, public or private as their representative to Inmarsat. This representative is known as the Inmarsat Signatory.

Inmarsat has a three-tier organisational structure. **The Assembly:** Composed of representatives of all member-countries, each of which has one vote. It meets once every two years to review the activities and objectives of Inmarsat and to make recommendations to the Council. **The Council:** This is the main decision making body of Inmarsat. It consists of representatives of the 18 Signatories with the largest investment in the organisation, together with four other representatives which are elected on the basis of geographical representation, and with due regard for the interests of developing countries. It meets at least three times a year and each member has a voting power equal to its investment share. **The Directorate:** Headed by the Director General as Chief executive and legal representative. He is responsible to the Council, and has charge of the day to day running of the organisation and system.

The organisation is financed by the Signatories of the member countries, each of which has an investment share based on its country's actual usage of the system. The 55 member countries are:- Algeria; Argentina; Australia; Bahrain; Belgium; Brazil; Bulgaria; Canada; Chile; China, People's Republic of; Colombia; Czechoslovakia; Denmark; Egypt; Finland; France; Gabon; German Democratic Republic; Germany, Federal Republic of; Greece; India; Indonesia; Iran; Iraq; Israel; Italy; Japan; Korea, Republic of; Kuwait; Liberia; Malaysia; Netherlands; New Zealand; Nigeria; Norway; Oman; Pakistan; Panama; Peru; Philippines; Poland; Portugal; Qatar; Saudi Arabia;

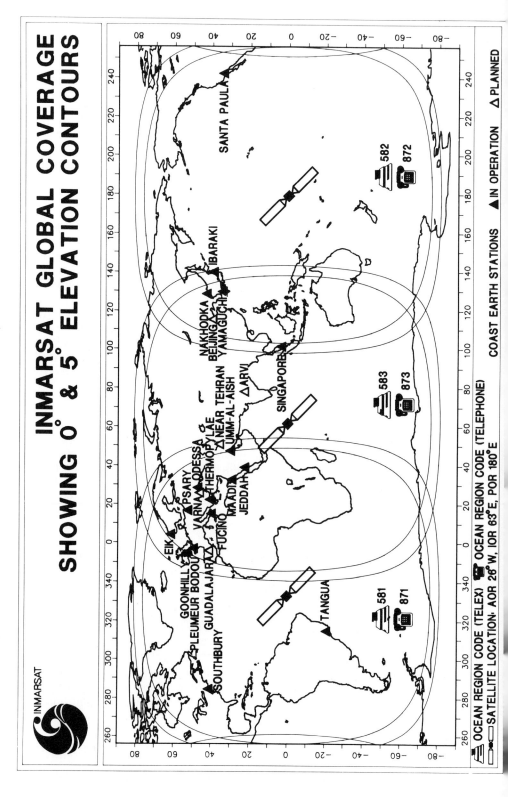

Singapore; Spain; Sri Lanka; Sweden; Tunisia; United Arab Emirates; United Kingdom; USA; USSR (includes the Byelorussion and Ukranian SSRs.)

THE SYSTEM

In order to operate its system, Inmarsat leases the Marecs A and B2 satellites from the European Space Agency, maritime communications subsystems (MCS) on three Intelsat V satellites from the International Telecommunications Satellite Organisation and capacity on three Marisat satellites from Comsat General of the United States. The system is currently configured as follows:

OCEAN REGION	ATLANTIC	INDIAN	PACIFIC
Operational Location:	Marecs B2 26W	Intelsat MCS-A 63E	Intelsat MCS-D 180E
Spare Location:	Intelsat MCS-B 18.5W		Marecs A 178E
Spare Location:	Marisat-F1 15W	Marisat-F2 72.5E	Marisat-F3 176.5E

Inmarsat is now in the process of procuring a second generation of satellites. The Inmarsat-2 spacecraft, the first of which is expected to become operational in early 1990, will have a capacity about triple that of the most powerful satellite in the present system.

Coast Earth Stations

The coast earth stations provide the link between the satellites and the telecommunications networks ashore. Coast earth stations are generally owned and operated by the Signatories of the countries in which they are located. There are now 20 coast earth stations: Thermopylae (Greece), Tangua (Brazil), Pleumeur Bodou (France), Fuicino (Italy), Ibaraki and Yamaguchi (Japan), Umm-al- Aish (Kuwait), Eik (Norway), Singapore, Goonhilly (UK), Jeddah (Saudi Arabia), Southbury and Santa Paula (USA), two stations at Odessa, two stations and Nakhodka (USSR), two stations at Psary (Poland) and one at Maadi (Egypt).

Ship Earth Stations

The ship earth station puts the shipboard user in instant contact with the rest of the world and consists of two parts, the above-deck and below-deck hardware.

Inmarsat has two designated ship earth station types, Standard-A and Standard-C. **Standard-A** has a parabolic dish antenna typically between 0.8m and 12m in diameter, and housed in a protective fibre glass radome. The antenna is mounted on a stabilised platform, enabling the antenna beam to remain pointed at the satellite regardless of ship course or movement. Signals are transmitted to the satellite at 1.6 GHz and received at 1.5 GHz.

Below-deck equipment consists of telex and telephone and a variety of optional equipment for facsimile, data ad slow-scan television. Low and medium speed data transmission is available via a voice channel at up to 9600 bits per second in both directions. With a specially prepared satellite channel in the ship-to-shore direction, high speed data transmission at up to 56 kilobits per second is also available. **Standard-C** is a new type of light weight, low-cost satellite communications terminal, capable of receiving and/or transmitting data or text.

Network co-ordination stations (NCS) contracts have been placed for each ocean

egion. Standard-C pre-operational services are available in the Atlantic Ocean Region and global commercial service will commence in early 1990.

Standard-C Ship Earth Stations are currently being developed by a number of manufacturers. In November, 1988, the Conference of Contracting Governments to the Safety of Life at Sea (SOLAS) Convention adopted satellite communications including standard-C as a means of satisfying maritime safety requirements. In addition, they will also find numerous applications in non-convention vessels, including fishing and leisure craft which require dependable communications at low cost.

As well as receiving and transmitting text or data messages, the terminals may be used as Enhanced Group Call (EGC) receivers for the receipt of Maritime Safety Information and other group or area broadcast information, global message paging and news bulletins. It will make a significant contribution to the International Maritime Organization's Global Maritime Distress and Safety System (GMDSS).

Communications originating from a Standard-C terminal will be transmitted in bursts, via satellite, to a coast earth station. At the coast earth station, the messages will be stored and automatically retransmitted to their destination — in the form that has been nominated by the sender: telex, electronic mail, etc — via the normal national and international telecommunications networks. Standard-C transmissions will be digital with data being transmitted and received at an information rate of 600 bits/sec. The terminal will operate at low power through its omnidirectional antenna anywhere with the coverage of Inmarsat's satellites.

On land, and subject to national and international regulations, Standard-C could also be used for remote monitoring and control applications, such as unmanned weather stations or oil and gas well-heads.

GMDSS

The International Maritime Organization (IMO) has developed a "Global Maritime Distress and Safety System" (GMDSS) to replace the present martime distress and safety system. The GMDSS will rely heavily on automation and will use Inmarsat's satellites for rapid annd reliable communcations. It was included in new amendments to the SOLAS Convention by a Conference of Contracting Governments in November 1988, which will come into force 1 February 1992.

The same Conference also agreed that an Inmarsat enhanced Group Call (EGC) receiving facility should be included in the ship carriage requirements, making it possible for anyone with appropriate satellite communications receiving capability including Standard-C class 2 Ship Earth Station), to obtain vital Maritime Safety information applying to any specified geographical area.

A distress capability for alerting by satellite EPIRB may be provided by Inmarsat geostationary satellites as well as polar orbiting satellites.

The L-band satellite EPIRB (the acronym for Emergency Position-Indicating Radio Beacon) is capable of sending a message via satellite giving the ship's ID number and its position, time, nature of distance, course and speed. IMO prepared the operational requirements, while the International Radio Consultative Committee (CCIR) developed technical provisions for a geostationary satellite EPIRB system. Inmarsat made available satellite capacity for a series of extensive demonstrations of L- Band EPIRBs.

The COSPAS-SARSAT search and rescue satellite system has been developed by Canada, the United States, France and the Soviet Union. These detect EPIRB signals transmitted on 121.5 and 243 megahertz, as well as on 406 megahertz, which was

THE SYSTEM

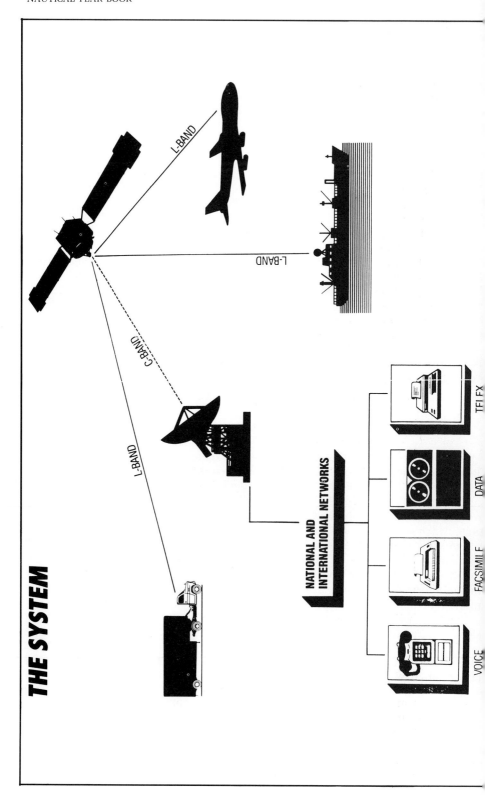

recently allocated specifically for low power emergency beacons. By measuring the Doppler effect in the received signals, the system is able to locate the position of the EPIRB.

(Full details of the procedures, requirements and equipment involved are contained in IMO Publication, Global Maritime Distress and Safety System, sales number: 970 86.20.E.)

NEW SERVICES

The Enhanced Group Call system (EGC) enables Inmarsat to provide a unique global service capable of addressing messages to predetermined groups of ships or all vessels in both fixed and variable geographical areas.

The system is able to meet the requirements of authorities and adminstrations for the broadcasting anywhere in the world of global, regional or local navigation warnings, meteorological warnings and forecasts and shore-to-ship distress alerts (SafetyNet™ service). In addition to covering the mid-ocean areas, the EGC system could also provide an automated service in coastal areas where shipping density is low or areas where it may not be economical to install a 518 KHz Navtex transmitter. Commercial users can address any national or commercial fleets of ships in a single group call (FleetNet ™ service). It is possible to offer subscription type services (e.g. news) to any mixed group of vessels.

A particularly useful feature is the ability to direct a call to a given geographical area. The area may be fixed, as in the case of a NAVAREA or weather forecast area, or it may be uniquely defined. this will be useful for messages, such as a local storm warning or a shore-to-ship distress alert, for which it is inappropriate to alert all ships in an ocean.

Aboard ship, EGC messages will be received either via a stand-alone device or via a Standard-C Ship Earth Station (SES). Standard-C has been included in the amendments to the SOLAS Convention.

Intelligent receivers will enable a ship's officer to determine which area and group messages the ship should receive according to the planned sailing route. The receiver would suppress the printing of repetitions of previously received error-free messages. The receiver will not, however, be able to bar "ALL SHIP" messages.

Aeronautical Satellite Communications: Inmarsat is intending to offer a wide range of satellite communications services to the world's aviation community. Some of these services are already in operation, on a trial and demonstration basis and others are expected to follow within the next 12 months.

Two types of services are under development. The first will provide low-speed data links for air traffic control centre automatic dependent surveillance, aeronautical operational control, system performance monitoring and other safety related communications. The equipment required on board an aircraft in order to access this service will be compact and simple, probably using low-gain conformal patch or blade antennas.

The second service will require more sophisticated electronically-steerable, higher-gain antennas. This service will be capable of providing higher-speed data and voice communications including payphone facilities for airline passengers.

Inmarsat has worked in close co-operation with industry specialists to ensure that its system architecture and specifications meet industry requirements. It assisted the Airlines Electronics Engineering Committee (AEEC), related sub-committees and with the continuing ICAO work in the AMSS Panel.

ADVANTAGES AND APPLICATIONS

Present airlines communications, which are dependent upon HF and VHF radio, are limited in range, capacity and reliability. They are also adversely affected by propagation conditions. As a result, there are large areas of the world where aircraft can have difficulty communicating. Inmarsat satellite communications, on the other hand, are highly reliable and are unaffected by ionospheric propagation conditions. The Inmarsat satellite system provides virtual global coverage so that aircraft can be assured of high-quality, reliable communications links using equipment built to agreed aviation industry international standards.

Voice services are expected to be popular with airline passengers, placing telephone calls, through in-cabin handsets activated by credit cards and switched through the receiving earth stations into the international telecommunications network. Voice facilities services are also being planned for the flight deck to provide ATC and airline company safety communications services. Voice may also be a requirement for certain airline management and air traffic services communications. Business flyers may also wish to send and receive facsimile messages and some may send data using portable micro computer terminals.

A number of airlines have already, or have advanced plans, to fit satellite communications data and voice equipment. Th world's major aircraft manufacturer, Boeing, is already offering satellite communications equipment as an option on its major passenger aircraft lines. Several of Inmarsat's member countries have indicated firm plans to build and bring into operation ground stations to operate with the aeronautical services. The United Kingdom (BTI), Norway, Singapore and the United States, all expect to be in operation in 1989; Australia, France and Canada, in 1990; followed by the USSR, Japan and the Federal Republic of Germany.

Some of these have formed into consortia in order to provide full global service. For instance, BTI has teamed with the Norwegian Telecommunications Administration, Telecom Singapore and British Airways to form the Skyphone consortium, and Australia, France and Canada are teaming with SITA (Societe Internationale de Telecommunications Aeronautiques), the inter-airline communications cooperative.

Inmarsat expects that, within the next few years, use of satellite communciations will become routine throughout aircraft operators and general aviation. This will lead to improved operating efficiency and economy.

Inmarsat, 40 Melton Street, London NW1 2EQ, England. Telephone (01) 387 9089 . Telex 29701 INMARSAT G. Facsimile (01) 387 2115.

HYUNDAI MARINE SERVICE CO., LTD.

HEAD OFFICE: 183-2 Jang Saeng PO Dong, Ulsan, Korea
Tel: (0522) 72-7371, 8331, 5587, 7004
Launch Service Office: 72-7021

CABLE ADDRESS: HMSC ULSAN PO Box 74, Ulsan, Korea
Telex: HYSERV K-52262   Fax: (0522) 76-0067

BUSAN OFFICE: Tel: (051) 257-4024   Fax: (051) 244-6831

**Ship Chandler – Launch Service
– Line Handling – Ship Guard –
Laundry Service – Lashing & Shoring
– Cleaning – Bonded Stores –**

ACCURATE, EXPEDITIOUS AND RELIABLE SERVICES
ARE OUR REPUTATION

President: Captain Oh, Jeong Ki

'STORING SHIPS IS TEAMWORK'

by Salvatore Ciuoffo, President, International Ship Suppliers Association

The work of promoting and developing the International Ship Suppliers ssociation has continued during the past year, so that it can increasingly be garded as truly representative of the ship supply trade throughout the world. ISSA's licy has always been to encourage the establishment of national associations, hich it is hoped will then become members of the international body. Last year we ere able to announce the inclusion of Cyprus and Yugoslavia in our membership aking a total of 29 national association members. This year, although they have not t applied for membership of ISSA, we are glad to announce the establishment of tional associations in Malta and Venezuela.

Throughout the year the campaign has continued to ensure that ship suppliers are t disadvantaged by any new regulations relating to the maritime lien and the arrest ships. The joint UNCTAD/IMO committee of experts on this complex subject has et in both Geneva and London, when the President was able to represent ISSA as a n-governmental consultative body. This committee will now meet only one more ne, when it is expected to complete its work on the maritime lien section of its enda.

The ISSA convention in 1988 was held in Montreal, Canada, when, as might be pected, among attendants from many different countries, there was a substantial legation from the USA, whose association, the National Association of Marine rvices (NAMS), held its own meetings during the conference. In 1989 the nvention will be held in Rome, in 1990 in Singapore and in 1991, Oslo, monstrating the extent to which ISSA has become a world-wide organisation.

ISSA was founded in 1955 by the national ship supplier associations of four ropean countries, Belgium, Finland, the Federal Republic of Germany and the etherlands, and has grown steadily to its present size with nearly 2,000 members orldwide. Its aims are to promote the economic interests of ship suppliers and courage contact between them and their national associations. Also of importance the establishment of contact on an international level with shipowners and their ganisations, particularly on a purchasing and storing level. The promotion of a tter understanding of international laws relating to the storing of ships is also an portant part of the association's work, hence its concern over the revision of the aritime lien conventions.

ISSA's publications are distributed to shipowners, chambers of commerce and her related organisations, maritime schools and the press, as well as to member and n-member suppliers. They include a quarterly newsletter, known as Storing Ships ews, a Register of members, a coded ship stores catalogue, and the annual report of convention, published under the title Storing Ships is Teamwork. This phrase is e slogan of the Association, emphasising, as it does, the importance of close operation and understanding between supplier and the shipowner and his vessels, thout which the important task of storing international shipping would be possible to achieve.

SHIP CHANDLERS
(Provisions and Deck/Engine/Cabin Stores)

ANTWERP

Gylstorff & Co	**Gylstorff Engineering**
Gen. Shipchandlers.	Technical Supplier & Agencies.

Paardenmarkt 64 – B-2000 Antwerpen – Belguim.
Tel: 225.16.16 (5 lines), Telex: 33833, Telefax: 231.18.14.

HAIFA

תברת לים בעמ **LAYAM CO. LTD.**

**SUPPLIERS TO
SHIPS • DIPLOMATIC CORPS
U.N. INSTITUTIONS • DUTY FREE TRADE
HEAD OFFICE:**
Haifa — 9 Pal Yam Avenue: Phone: (04) 652111
Telex: 46688 LAYAM IL
Fax: 4-652 118

BRANCHES

Ashdod/Port of Ashdod — Phone: (08)531981-521530
Eilat — P.O.B. 65 — Phone: (059) 73159-73150
Jerusalem — 3 Yannai St. — Phone: (02) 225852—227749
Tel Aviv — 17 Saadia Gaon St. — Phone: (03) 5613720-5613721

HONG KONG

FORTUNE SHIP-CHANDLERS CO. LTD.

15B Mercer Street,
Ground Floor, Central,
Hong Kong

Telephone: 5-443429, 5-436417
Telex: 84086 FORSC HX

LAS PALMAS

GENERAL SHIP SUPPLIER

CASANOVA

MANUEL DIAZ CASANOVA, S.A.

PROVISIONS
CABIN STORES
DECK-ENGINE
OPERATING OWN TRUCKS AND BARGES
DELIVERY OUTSIDE HARBOUR LIMITS
SUPPLIES ARE PALLETIZED WITH
SHRINK-WRAP POLYTHILENE COVERS
DELIVERY F.A.S.

FOR WEEK-END DELIVERIES PLEASE
LET US HAVE YOUR REQUISITONS
BEFORE 12 HRS. ON FRIDAY.

WE OFFER A RELIABLE 24 HOURS
A DAY SERVICE 7 DAYS A WEEK.

MAIL ADDRESS:
P.O. BOX 2186
35008 LAS PALMAS DE G C
CANARY ISLANDS SPAIN
OFFICES AND WAREHOUSES:
URBANIZACION «EL CEBADAL»
VIAL I
C/ DOCTOR JUAN DOMINGUEZ PEREZ, 14
PUERTO DE LA LUZ
PHONES: 34 - 28 - 265432/267213/263959
TELEX: 96296 MDCL - E
FAX: 34 - 28 - 260681
ESTABL. YEAR 1900
STORAGE AREA 4.000 sqm
REEFER STORAGE 500 cbm
COLD STORAGE 700 cbm
BONDED STORES AVAILABLE
ENGLISH - FRENCH - KOREAN
AND ITALIAN SPOKEN

158

CANARY ISLANDS

PANAMA CANAL

159

PIRAEUS

PORTUGAL

TAMPA

TRIESTE

MAJOR WATERWAYS OF THE WORLD

DARDANELLES AND BOSPORUS

European Turkey is separated from Asian Turkey by the Bosporus at Istanbul and by the Dardanelles.

The Bosporus Straits, running roughly north-south, is a winding natural waterway 17 miles in length varying in width from just over half a mile to two miles, these factors together with strong currents make the Bosporus difficult to negotiate for larger vessels. At the northern end the straits open into the Black Sea and at the southern end into the Sea of Marmara.

The Dardanelles, about 40 miles in length with a width varying from 1 to 14 miles, forms the approach to the Sea of Marmara, the Bosporus and the Black Sea for vessels entering from the Mediterranean.

Passage Formalities

Vessels may pass through the Dardanelles and Bosporus at any time of the day. They must announce, by international signals, their nationality, tonnage and destination; must fly their national flag and the signal flags for 'Q' and 'T' and hoist the Turkish flag at the foremast.

Northbound vessels on arrival at Canakkale must stop to allow officials and agents to come alongside. The Bill of Health must be produced to the Sanitary Officer and they also obtain a sanitary voucher.Thereafter they may cross the Sea of Marmara, pass the Bosporus northbound and proceed to their destination in the Black Sea.

Southbound vessels proceeding in transit from Black Sea Ports to the Mediterranean must stop at Quarantine Station before Buyukdere to allow Quarantine and agents vessels to come alongisde. The sanitary voucher which had been received on the Northbound voyage must be submitted.

Vessels proceeding to Turkish ports in the Black Sea or from Turkish Black Sea Ports to the Mediterranean are subject to inward and outward Customs and Immigration controls at Ahirkapi Anchorage. At Istanbul, vessels may slow or anchor in order to communicate with agents, take on supplies, etc. Such a stop must not exceed 48 hours. Thereafter full clearance is imposed and appropriate dues must be paid.

Pilot Stations (See numbered positions on map)
1. Dardanelles Pilot: Optional, boards vessels off Mehmetcik Point (Cape Helles). Pilots are available on all ports in the Sea of Marmara.
2. Bosporus Pilot Northbound: Optional, boards vessels off southern entrance to Bosporus.
3. Bosporus Pilot Southbound: Optional, boards vessels off Kavak Point.
4. Izmit Bay Pilotage: Compulsory. Pilots board vessels off Darica Point.

All stations are equipped with 'VHF' and can be contacted on channel 16, round the clock.

Foreign vessels of all tonnages entering the Bosporus on voyage to a port in the Sea of Marmara or leaving a port in the Sea of Marmara on voyage through the Bosporus are compelled to take a pilot between the Black Sea entrance of the Bosporus and ports in the Sea of Marmara.

Anchorage for Transitting Vessels
5. Ahirkapi Anchorage: Southwest of Seraglio Point. Mainly for large vessels and tankers.
6. Buyukdere Anchorage: On the northern section of the Bosporus, Short stay for medium size vessels up to 40000 DWT.

Crew repatriation and replacement are not allowed in transitting. Vessels should anchor at Akirkapi and obtain Customs and Immigration clearance to embark or disembark crew members. In this case appropriate dues must be paid. Sick and injured crew members are not subject to this rule.

DARDANELLES AND BOSPORUS

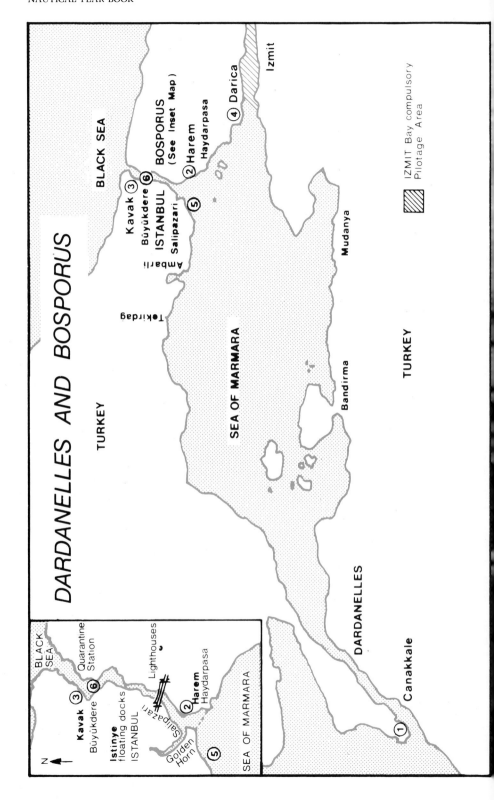

IZMIT Bay compulsory
Pilotage Area

INNER ROUTE OF THE GREAT BARRIER REEF
including Torres Strait, Great North East Channel
and Hydrographers Passage

Australia is separated from Papua New Guinea by Torres Strait. Use of the Torres Strait route, as a handy and economic short cut between East Australian ports and Asia, began with early sailing ship traffic bringing passengers and cargo to the colony at Port Jackson (Sydney) and then heading off to the East in search of a profitable return cargo. As a recognised safe shipping channel it did not gain prominence until the arrival of the steamship on the world's oceans in the mid 1800s.

Hydrographers Passage is arguably the world's newest shipping channel, being discovered as recently as 1981. Over the next three years it was surveyed, charted and equipped with navigational aids and was ready for use in late 1984.

But for the profuse growth of coral reefs the Torres Strait route would be relatively simple to navigate. Unfortunately, the warm sea conditions provide an ideal habitat for many different species of coral polyp. The result has been the slow erection, over perhaps millions of years, of what is now called the Great Barrier Reef.

About 80,000 square miles in area, the Reef stretches from the Tropic of Capricorn northwards to the gulf of Papua, some 1,250 miles in length. Its width and density vary. Reef waters, while navigationally tricky, are nevertheless safely navigable with the assistance of a licensed pilot.

The main shipping channels that exist through this region are:

Inner Route — the principal NW/SE channel through the Reef, hugging the Australian coastline all the way to Torres Strait. The Inner Route can be likened to a river estuary; broad and open in the south, narrowing further north.

Great North East Channel — a route from Torres Strait in a northeasterly direction following the course of the Gulf of Papua, and skirting the northern extremity of the Reef.

Hydrographers Passage — a NE/SW deepwater channel through the Reef that connects central Queensland's coal export terminal at Hay Point with the clear waters of the Coral Sea.

Palm Passage — a deepwater exit connecting the ports of Townsville and Lucinda with the Coral Sea.

Grafton Passage — a deepwater channel across the Reef near Cairns and Mourilyan.

Economic Benefits
Depending on departure and destination points, the Torres Strait route can reduce passage lengths by considerable amounts. The weather conditions are favourable most times of the year and the route should be considered a better alternative to the Great Australian Bight (especially during the winter months; April to November) even when actual voyage distances are greater. Australian bulk carriers in the 150,000 tonne range engaged on the Port Hedland, W.A. to Port Kembla, N.S.W. iron ore trade proceed via Torres Strait when lightship, even though the voyage is some 600 miles longer.

Vessels loading at Queensland ports north of the Tropic of Capricorn and proceeding northwards to their destination have the added advantage between 1 April and the end of November of being able to load to the Tropical Load Line.

Hydrographers Passage reduces the length of the voyage from Hay Point to Japan (as compared to the track south of the Reef) by about 240 miles. Deepy laden vessels (those exceeding the 12.2m draft restriction in Torres Strait) bound for Europe via Suez find the route via Hydrographers Passage and north of Papua New Guinea to be some 125 miles shorter than the Great Australian Bight track. Europe-bound vessels too deep for Suez have also found this a more expedient alternative to the Cape of Good Hope, even though it is about 850 miles longer.

Restrictions
International shipping can pass freely through the whole Great Barrier Reef region at any time of the night or day. Pilotage, while not compulsory, is covered by an International Maritime Organization declaration (Resolution 619, passed at IMO's 15th General Assembly in November 1987) which recommends that vessels employ a pilot of the Queensland Coast and Torres Strait Pilot Service for the Inner Route north of Cairns, the Great North East Channel, and Hydrographers Passage. In addition, the Australian Government recommends that shipmasters unfamiliar with the southern section of the Inner Route employ a pilot in those waters.

Draft restrictions:
Inner Route, Torres Strait and Great North East Channel — 12.2m.

Speed restrictions:
Normally none, except as required to maintain a safe under keel clearance.

THE QUEENSLAND COAST AND TORRES STRAIT PILOT SERVICE

THE SERVICE — All Pilots, appointed from Command, are Licensed by the Marine Board of Queensland under the Authority of the Queensland Marine Acts, 1958/1975. Controlled by the Joint Secretaries, appointed by similar authority. Over 100 million tons of shipping piloted annually. (Established 106 years).

LICENSED PILOTAGE SERVICES

(1) Between Booby Island or Goods Island and all Australian East Coast Ports and New Zealand via the Torres Strait and Great Barrier Reef Inner route. *Note:* (Vessels bound to or from New Zealand Ports board pilots off Gladstone North Point Lat. 23° 44′S., Long. 151° 21′E.)

(2) Between Booby Island or Goods Island and Pacific Ports via Torres Strait, Great North-East Channel and pilot landing/boarding area off Basilisk Beacon at entrance to Port Moresby.

(3) Between the Grafton Passage (Euston Reef, Lat. 16° 39′S., Long. 146° 14′E.) Palm Passage Pith Reef Lat. 18° 13′S., Long 147° 07′E., Hydrographers Passage Blossom Bank Lat. 19° 47′S., Long. 150° 24′E., and all Queensland Ports, including Hay Point (*see* 'Deep Draught Shipping below) and Cape Flattery.

(4) Between all Queensland Ports.

SUPPLEMENTARY PILOTAGE SERVICES

(1) Between Darwin, via the Clarence and Dundas Straits; Gove, Groote Eylandt, Weipa and all Australian East Coast Ports and New Zealand via the Torres Strait and Great Barrier Reef Inner Route.

(2) Between Darwin; via the Clarence and Dundas Straits; Gove, Groote Eylandt, Weipa and Pacific Ports via the Torres Strait, Great North East Channel and Pilot landing/boarding area off Basilisk Beacon at Entrance to Port Moresby.

(3) Between Main Ports in Papua/New Guinea, Solomon Islands (Kieta) and the Australian Mainland. Pilotage through the China Strait is subject to Draught (12.2m. or 40ft.).

THE INNER ROUTE — Ensures sheltered water for over a thousand miles of its length and lies within the natural breakwater of the Great Barrier Reef. It is the shortest, safest and most economical route from New Zealand, Australia East Coast and South Pacific Ocean to Indonesia and Asia. It lies in the permanent tropical loading zone.

RECOMMENDATION ON PILOTAGE — Attention is drawn to the Recommendation on the use of Pilots approved by the 15th General Assembly of the International Maritime Organisation.

The recommendation is that: "Vessels 100 m. in length and over and all loaded oil tankers, chemical carriers or liquefied gas carriers irrespective of size, use the pilotage services provided by The Queensland Coast & Torres Strait Pilot Service when navigating in Torres Strait and inner route of the Great Barrier Reef between Booby Island and Cairns, or through the Great North East Channel, or Hydrographers Passage."

The Australian Department of Transport also recommends that Masters unfamiliar with the area south of Cairns, Grafton or Palm Passages, also use the service of a Pilot (Resolution A619[15]).

DEEP DRAUGHT SHIPPING

TORRES STRAIT — As at March 1989 the maximum recommended draught is 12.2m. The two tidally-restricted and therefore, controlling areas for traversing the Torres Strait are Gannet Passage (Booby Island) and Prince of Wales Channel. The latest surveys show a channel, marked by light buoys, as having 10.10 m. (33.1 ft.) at datum in Gannet Passage. Minimum underkeel clearances acceptable to the Service are 1.0 m. in Gannet Passage and 10% of draught in Prince of Wales Channel, where draughts exceed 11.89 m. and 1.0 m. where draughts are 11.89 m. or less. Draught limitations apply from Booby Island through the Prince of Wales Channel details of which can be obtained from "2S TORRES SYDNEY".

In mid 1989 VARZIN PASSAGE, 4.5 miles north of Booby Island, will be opened for navigation with a minimum datum of 10.50 metres (34.40ft.).

HAY POINT-DALRYMPLE BAY-ABBOT POINT — The maximum draught between these ports and Grafton Passage, Palm Passage, Hydrographers Passage or Point Cartwright is only limited by the departure draught from these ports. Hydrographers passage is the shortest safe route from Hay Point/Dalrymple Bay to the N.W. Pacific and Suez. From 1st April to 30th November the seaward approaches to the Barrier Reef North of 22° 30′S., are in the tropical loading zone.

PILOT BOARDING/LANDING PLACES

AUSTRALIA EAST COAST — Port Kembla, Botany Bay, Sydney or 1½ miles off Sydney Heads. Newcastle, Brisbane or Brisbane Pilot Vessel off Cartwright Point, all Queensland Ports and Fairways, Grafton Passage (off Euston Reef Beacon). Palm Passage off Pith Reef, Hydrographers Passage off Blossom Bank and off Edward Island (Whitsunday Islands).

TORRES STRAIT — Booby Island (4.4 miles west of Booby Island Light): Goods Island (2.5 miles west of Goods Island Light).

GULF PORTS — Weipa, Groote Eylandt, Grove.

NORTHERN TERRITORY — Darwin.

PAPUA/NEW GUINEA — Off Basilisk Light Beacon (Entrance to Port Moresby) and all main ports.

OTHER PLACES — By arrangement with 2S 'TORRES' SYDNEY.

TO ORDER A PILOT

SOUTH OR EAST BOUND — Masters are requested to advise about five days beforehand 2S 'TORRES' SYDNEY their eta, maximum draught, where bound and which pilot boarding station is required. Masters should also radio 4I 'TORIND' THURSDAY ISLAND 24 hours and 6 hours before arrival, confirming or adjusting the eta, stating local time (K). Messages to TORIND should be sent to Thursday Island Radio, V.I.I.

NORTH OR WEST BOUND — If an Australian port instruct agent to arrange giving as much notice as possible. If from an overseas or intermediate port and requiring a pilot to board outside a port radio 2S 'TORRES' SYDNEY about five days prior to arrival at embarkation point, advising eta, maximum draught and where bound. Radio 2S 'TORRES' SYDNEY of any material change to eta, 24 hours before arrival and confirm 6 hours before arrival. All messages to 2S 'TORRES SYDNEY' will be acknowledged. Radion messages are delivered 24 hours a day seven days a week, holidays included.

V.H.F. RADIO CONTACT

(1) **Thursday Is. Call "REEF PILOTS", Channel 16. Pilot Launches watch Channel 16.**

(2) **Cairns Fairway. Call "TORRES PILOTS", Channel 20 (long range).**

(3) **Hydrographer's Passage. Call "TORRES PILOTS", Channel 16, work Channel 09.**

NAVIGATIONAL (LOADLINES) REGULATION ZONES — *See* elsewhere this publication for Areas and Seasonal periods Australian coast and adjacent areas. From 1st April to the 30th November vessels proceeding to the Coral Sea may load to tropical marks and proceed via Grafton Passage, Palm Passage or Hydrographers Passage, always in the tropical zone.

Joint Secretaries: **N. R. ROGERS, S. D. RADFORD, P. SUTTON**
c/o BANKS BROS & STREET, 66 King Street, SYDNEY, Box 1573 G.P.O. 2001
Telephone: **(02) 292125, International +61 2 292125** *Code Address:* **'TORRES' SYDNEY** *Telex:* **AA20269, SYDNEY**
Telephones (after hours): **349-1402, 816-1603, 960-3950**

Pilot Stations

Inner Route:
At or outside any Queensland or N.S.W. port. Also off Edward Island in the Whitsunday Group.

Torres Strait:
Just west of of Booby Island or Goods Island, as desired.

Great North East channel:
At or outside Port Moresby.

Hydrographers Passage:
Inbound, at Blossom Bank outside the Reef. Outbound, at the Hay Point or Abbot Point berths.

Palm Passage:
At Pith Reef on the outer edge of the Reef or at the loading berth.

Grafton Passage:
At Euston Reef on the outer edge of the Reef or at the loading berth.

The normal boarding method at sea is by means of a pilot launch. However, at Hydrographers Passage and at Edward Island a land-on helicopter only is used; at Palm Passage a land-on helicopter is used for suitable vessels; in other places land-on helicopters are occasionally available when requested.

Queensland Coast and Torres Strait Pilot Service, GPO Box 1573, Sydney, NSW, 2001, Australia.

KIEL CANAL

The Kiel Canal, or in German Nord-Oostee Kanal, cuts across the base of Schleswig-Holstein, linking the North Sea with the Baltic Sea thus avoiding the dangerous route via the Skaw and through the Danish Sound and Belts.

The canal starts from near the mouth of the River Elbe at Brunsbuttel and reaches the Baltic at Kiel-Holtenau near the port of Kiel.

From Brunsbuttel the width of the canal for the first 67 km. is 162m. There follows a short stretch of 3 km. where the width increases to 214 m. before returning to 162m. for the following 8 km. The final 19 km. to the exit at Kiel has a width of 102 m. Along the length of the canal there are thirteen 'Sidings' where the canal banks widen out and vessels can lay by. Average transit time is seven to eight hours, including lock time at Brunsbuttel and Kiel. Maximum speed allowed on the waterway is 8 knots. There are four locks at each end of the canal: the New Locks have a usable length of 310 m., usable width of 42 m. and a permitted depth of 9.5 m and the Old Locks a usable length of 125 m., usable width of 22 m. and a maximum permitted depth at Brunsbuttel of 6 m. and at Kiel-Holtenau of 7 m.

At Brunsbuttel 10.40 m. depth is permitted in the fairway to the canal up to 6 km. in the Binnenhafen. At Kiel-Holtenau 9.70 m. depth is permitted for vessels up to 15,000 grt and 160 m. loa in the fairway up to the ferry line (97.42 km.) in the Binnenhafen to enable vessels to reach the coal discharge berth at the Kiel power station.

The Kiel Canal near Albersdorf   (Photo H. Arnold)

The harbours at Brunsbuttel and Holtenau, also at Rendsburg, on the canal, offer good mooring berths for large vessels. Along the canal banks are loading and discharging berths for coasting vessels.

Pilotage is compulsory on the canal. The pilot is taken on at either Brunsbuttel or Holtenau and is responsible for steering the vessel throughout the canal transit. Administration dues and pilotage fees are charged.

There are several high level bridges crossing the canal under which vessels with 40 m. maximum above water level can pass. The canal has lamps on both banks along its length and can be used day and night. Dry-docks and large shiprepair yards are found at Kiel and Rendsburg and vessels can take coal or oil bunkers, fresh water, provisions and stores at either end of the canal.

In 1988, 46,825 vessels transitted the canal, a 3.3% rise over 1987.

Authority: Wasser und Schiffahrtsamt, Kiel-Holtenau, Postfach 80 68, 2300 Kiel 17 and Wasser und Schiffahrtsamt, Brunsbuttel, 2212 Brunsbuttel.

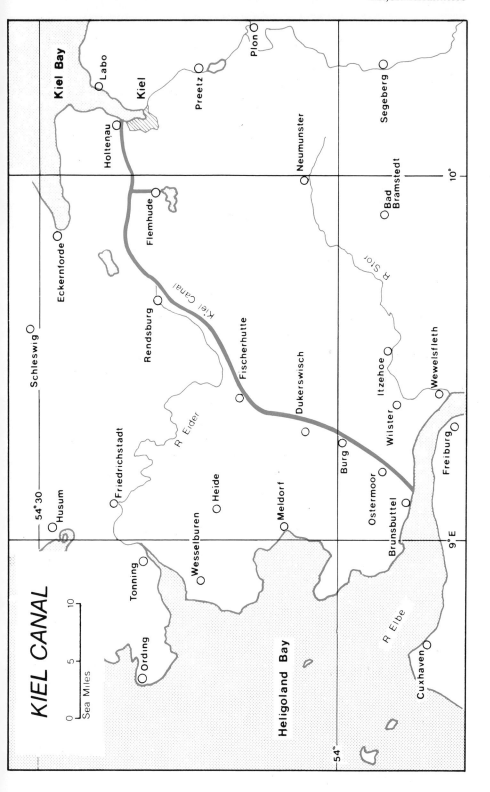

KIEL CANAL

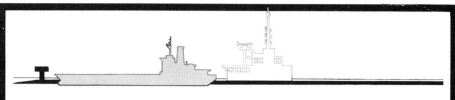

NEW WATERWAY AND APPROACHES

The ports in the delta of the Meuse and Rhine rivers have throughout the ages fought against silt to remain open to shipping. When dredging no longer sufficed, the port of Rotterdam had a canal cut through the Isle of Voorne in 1827. During the age of steam, vessels grew in size and engineer Pieter Caland devised a new outlet to the sea, the New Waterway, which today is still Rotterdam's link with the North Sea.

The Netherlands situated at the mouths of the Rivers Rhine, Meuse and Scheldt, has a large transit trade with the hinterland of Europe with Rotterdam, incorporating the separate harbour of Dordrecht, Schiedam, Vlaardingen, Maassuluis and Hook of Holland, located on both sides of the New Waterway and the New Meuse giving open connections both to the River Rhine and the North Sea, It is a port of call for over 400 overseas shipping lines which between them account for some 11,000 regular sailings a year and is the largest bulk cargo port in the world. The port is fully mechanised and organised as a storage distribution centre for ore, grain, coal, fertilisers and other dry bulk cargoes. It is also one of the world's largest container ports and crude oil has turned the port into Western Europe's discharging centre for large tankers. Other tankers and pipeleines carry the crude oil and oil products to refineries in the Netherlands and abroad. Each year more than 30,000 seagoing vessels call and inland waterway barges handle shipments to and from the continental hinterland. The gigantic scaling-up which occurred in the 1960s in transport as in other things necessitated constant deepening of the New Waterway and the adjoining basins. To accommodate fully-laden vessels up to 200,000 dwt drawing up to 62ft., a 12 km. trench was dug in the seabed off the Hook of Holland in 1969. By opening this Euro-Channel in 1978 to vessels drawing 68ft. Rotterdam handled over 300 million tonnes of cargo in 1979. The large carriers were allowed to use the channels only subject to certain conditions — when the tide was high enough and there was not too strong a swell running. To ensure that vessels were not surprised by falling tides a hydrometeorological information system was set up and strict rules imposed.

A number of projects that will considerably improve access to the European continent are currently in hand. In 1985 Rotterdam became accessible to fully laden bulk carriers and tankers of up 350,000 dwt drawing 72 feet.

The first stage of this project was completed in August, 1983, when vessels drawing 70 feet were able to enter the Waterway. Discussions have also been held regarding a further deepening of the port and approach channel to 75 feet so that 400,000 dwt carriers can enter. The current project covers the most densely navigated region in the world, extending over some   350 kms. from Rotterdam-Europoort to the Strait of Dover. The Meuse and Euro-Channels cover 12 and 46 kms. respectively of this distance, as measured from the Hook of Holland. Alongside these channels several anchoring and turning areas have been deepened.

Deepening of the Euro-Channels was a Dutch project with international angles involving all the states bordering on the southern reaches of the North Sea. The Dutch State Waterways Department and Hydrographic Survey also made a close study, involving fresh soundings, where necessary, of the southern North Sea and the Strait of Dover to find the best route and dredging was carried out where needed. Because of the narrow width of the shipping channel in the southern North Sea, a Decca location-finding system has been reinforced by a new transmitter on the east coast of England at Thorpeness and a number of buoys have been installed. This permits deep-draught vessels to fix their positions more easily and navigate in greater safety, while the improved system also benefits other shipping.

At the beginning of the Euro-Channel an unmanned measuring post with a helicopter platform has been built at sea to gather data on water level, wave lengths and wave drift — information which is needed to decide whether a vessel can proceed up the channel. New navigation rules have been discussed with the coastal states and the Dutch Directorate-General for Shipping and Maritime Affairs has prepared a new shipping plan, permitting adequate responses to any eventuality. When approaching the Strait of Dover Masters can ask for a North Sea Pilot who is put on board by helicopter from France.

Vessel Traffic Management

A new, highly advanced Vessel Traffic Management System, replacing the chain of shore-based radar stations, came into operation during 1986 to watch over every shipping movement in and around the port. Computer predictions of vessels' movements before they take place will guarantee maximum safety.

The system covers the Euro-Channel and Hook of Holland Roadstead, the Rotterdam Waterway and Nieuwe Maas River up to 3 kms. upstream from Van Brienenoord Bridge, Koningshaven, the Oude Maas River up to 5 kms. upstream from the Spijkenisse Bridge, the Beer Canal, Caland Canal and Hartel Canal including the dock basins bordering these.

Authority: Port of Rotterdam, P.O Box 6622, 3002 AP Rotterdam, Netherlands.
Telephone (10)-4896911. Telex 23077 EUROT NL.

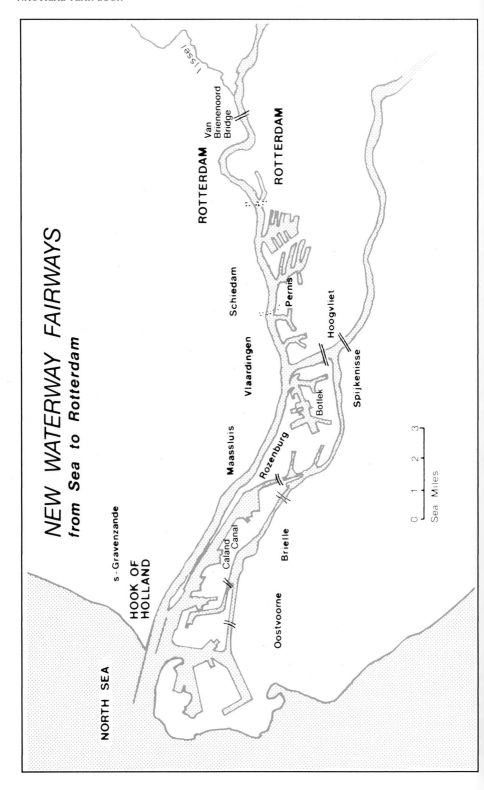

NEW WATERWAY FAIRWAYS
from Sea to Rotterdam

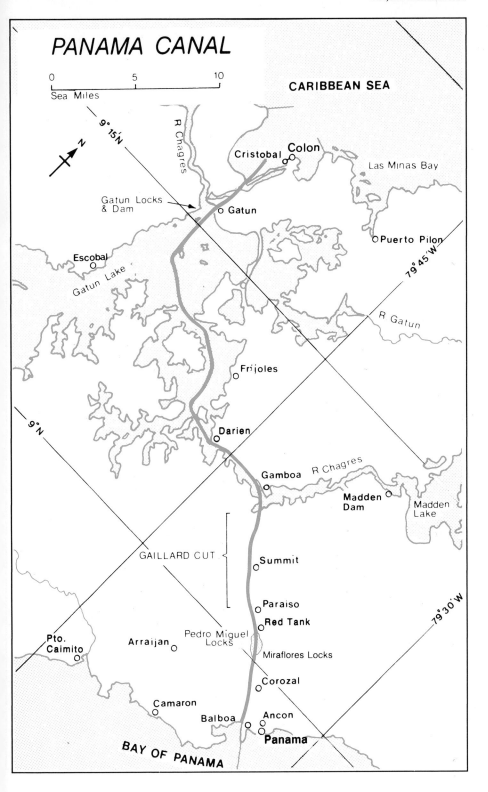

PANAMA CANAL

0   5   10
Sea Miles

CARIBBEAN SEA

9° 15'N

R Chagres

Cristobal   Colon

Las Minas Bay

Gatun Locks & Dam →   o Gatun

O Puerto Pilon

79°45'W

Escobal
o

Gatun Lake

R Gatun

Frijoles
o

9° N

Darien
o

Gamboa   R Chagres
o

Madden o
Dam

Madden Lake

GAILLARD CUT {   Summit
o

Paraiso
o

Red Tank
o

Pedro Miguel
Locks

Pto. Caimito
o

Arraijan
o

Miraflores Locks

79°30'W

Corozal
o

Camaron
o

Balboa

Ancon
o

Panama

BAY OF PANAMA

173

PANAMA CANAL

In 1524, Charles V of Spain ordered the first survey of a proposed canal route through the Isthmus of Panama. More than three centuries passed before the first construction was started. The French laboured 20 years, beginning in 1880, but disease and financial problems defeated them.

In 1903 Panama and the United States signed a treaty by which the United States undertook to construct an interoceanic ship canal across the Isthmus of Panama and the following year the United States purchased from the French Canal Company its rights and properties for $40 million and began construction. The project was completed in ten years at a cost of about $387 million.

The building of the Canal involved three main problems, engineering, sanitation, and organisation. Its successful completion was due principally to the engineering and administrative skills of such men as John F. Stevens and Col. George W.L Goethals, and to the solution of extensive health problems by Col. William C. Gorgas.

The engineering problems involved digging through the Continental Divide, constructing the largest earth dam ever built up to that time, designing and building the most massive canal locks ever envisaged, constructing the largest gates ever swung and solving environmental problems of enormous proportions.

Long range plans have been developed for a variety of improvements to the Canal, which include such things as widening and deepening selected portions of the channel, straightening some pronounced curves by removing portions of islands or peninsulas, and continuous dredging throughout the waterway.

Today more than 70 years after the first official ocean-to-ocean transit of the waterway, the United States and Panama have embarked on a partnership for the management, operation and defence of the Canal. Under two new treaties signed in a ceremony in Washington, D.C., on September 7, 1977, the Canal will be operated until the turn of the century under arrangements designed to strengthen the bonds of friendship and co-operation between the two countries. The treaties were approved by Panama in a plebiscite on October 23, 1977, and the U.S. Senate gave its advice and consent to their ratification in March and April 1978. The new treaties went into effect on October 1, 1979.

The Panama Canal Commission

The Panama Canal Commission, a U.S. Government agency, operates the Canal. The Commission has a binational supervisory board of nine members and about 8,000 employees. The Commission replaced the former Panama Canal Company on October 1, 1979; also on that date the Canal Zone and its Government were disestablished. The United States will transfer the Canal to Panama on December 31, 1999.

Trade

A large share of world trade passes through the Canal over many of the world's principal trade routes. In 1987 there were 13,444 transits involving 148.9m tons of cargo. The approximate mileage saved between the East Coast of Colombia and Hong Kong via the Canal versus the shortest alternative route is 3,000 miles; between Japan and New York, 3,300 miles; between Chile and Western Europe, 1,450 miles; and between Ecuador and New York, 7,400 miles.

During its years of operation more than 625,000 vessels have transitted the waterway, carrying nearly 4 billion long tons of cargo from one ocean to the other. Average Canal Waters Time (total time spent at the Panama Canal, including waiting time and in-transit time) is about 20 hours. Transit time is about nine hours. Tugs, towing, locomotives, and locks transit personnel ensure the rapid transit of vessels through the Canal. Of the thousands of vessels transitting the Canal each year, more than 2,000 of them, about 20 per cent of total oceangoing transits, are PANAMAX size, the largest vessels the waterway can accommodate. To facilitate the passage a reservation system is available to provide a guaranteed priority transit upon request. The Panama Canal Commission believes the trend is firmly set towards larger ships using the canal and in 1986 completed a dredging project to allow a year-round draught of 39.5 feet.

Physical Features

The Canal is 50 miles long from deep water in the Atlantic to deep water in the Pacific and was cut through one of the narrowest saddles of the long, mountainous isthmus and joins the North and South American continents. The original elevation was 312 feet above sea level where it crosses the Continental Divide in the rugged mountain range.

The Canal runs from northwest to southeast with the Atlantic entrance being 33.5 miles north and 27 miles west of the Pacific entrance. The straight line distance between the two entrances is 43 miles.

Its principal physical features are the two terminal ports, short sections of the channel at either end at sea level, the three sets of twin locks, Gatun Lake and Gaillard Cut.

A vessel entering the Canal from the Atlantic enters the channel from Limon Bay at the Cristobal breakwater. This sea-level section of the Canal channel on the Atlantic side is $6\frac{1}{2}$ miles long and 500 feet wide and runs through a mangrove swamp that is only a few feet above sea level in most places.

Whenever a ship passes through the Canal some 52 million gallons of water are pumped into the locks, water which is ultimately lost to the sea. Much of the water comes from Gatun Lake and the nearby Madden Lake, formed by damming in 1935 to provide additional water during the dry season.

A vessel is raised or lowered 85 feet in a continuous flight of three steps at Gatun Locks. Each lock chamber is 110 feet wide and 1,000 feet long, the length of the docks, including the two approach walls, being 1 1/5 miles.

Gatun Lake and Dam

Gatun Lake, through which the vessels travel for $23\frac{1}{2}$ miles from Gatun Locks to the north end of Gaillard Cut, is one of the largest artificial bodies of water in the world. It covers an area of 163.38 square miles and was formed by an earthen dam across the Chagres River adjacent to Gatun Locks. The two wings of the dam, and the spillway have an aggregate length of about $1\frac{1}{2}$ miles. The dam is nearly half a mile wide at the base, sloping to a width of 100 feet at the crest, which is 105 feet above sea level, or 20 feet above the normal level of Gatun Lake.

Gaillard Cut

During construction the Gaillard Cut was called Culebra Cut, but was renamed for Col. David Dubose Gaillard, the engineer who was in charge of this section of the Canal work.

This portion of the channel is nine miles long and was carved through rock and shale for most of the distance. It was here that the principal excavation was required and here that devastating slides occurred during construction and soon after the Canal was opened.

A vessel enters the Cut where the Chagres River flows into the Canal channel at Gamboa. More than any other section of the Canal the Gaillard Cut gives the impression of the waterway as an enormous ditch. A short distance before the vessel reaches Pedro Miguel Locks it passes Gold Hill on the left, the highest promontory along the channel which rises to 662 feet above sea level.

Contractor's Hill, on the west bank opposite Gold Hill, originally had an altitude of 410 feet, but this was reduced to 370 feet to stabilise the hill in 1954. The channel in Gaillard Cut was originally excavated to a width of 300 feet. During the 1930's and 1940's, the straight section immediately north of Gold Hill was widened to 500 feet to provide a passing section for large vessels and during the period 1957-1971, the remaining portions of the Cut were also widened to 500 feet.

Authority: The Panama Canal Commission, APO Miami 34011 (Postal address). Telex 3034.

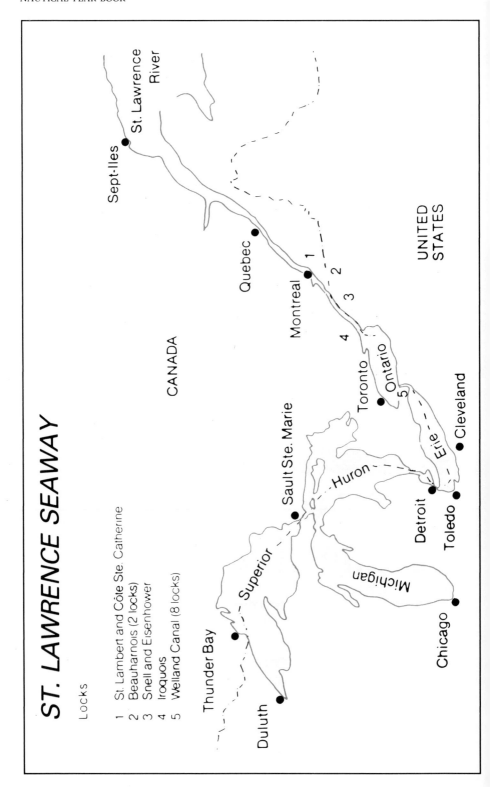

ST. LAWRENCE SEAWAY

Locks

1 St. Lambert and Côte Ste. Catherine
2 Beauharnois (2 locks)
3 Snell and Eisenhower
4 Iroquois
5 Welland Canal (8 locks)

We've opened the way to the heart of North America

The St. Lawrence Seaway Authority

Canada

THE ST. LAWRENCE SEAWAY

The natural waterway formed by the St. Lawrence River, the Great Lakes and their connecting channels stretches more than 2,300 miles (3,700 km) from the Atlantic Ocean to the heartland o North America. With the completion of the present Seaway system in 1959, the waterway has become an important international trade route.

When the St. Lawrence River was first explored by Frenchman Jacques Cartier on his second voyages of the New World in 1535, the Lachine Rapids, a few miles past Montreal, proved to be ar impassable barrier. Further up-river, even more tumultuous waters awaited later explorers. Between Lake Ontario and Lake Eire, the 326 ft (99.4 m) drop on the Niagara River ruled out any movement by natural waterway between the two lakes; and in the Upper Lakes, St. Mary's Falls blocked water transportation into Lake Superior.

The concept of canals on the St. Lawrence to improve upon nature originated as early as 1690. By the early 1700s, work had begun to provide a canal with an average 3 ft (0.9 m) depth between Lake St Louis and Montreal. In 1780, a series of small locks were put in operation between Lake St.Louis and Lake St. Francis.

The first major navigation works on the St. Lawrence made their appearance in 1825, with the completion of the Lachine Canal comprising seven locks to by-pass the Lachine Rapids. Some 1£ years later the Long Sault Rapids were circumvented with the building of the Cornwall Canal.

With the union of Upper and Lower Canada in 1841, a broader financial base permitted the Government to invest in larger scale transportation facilities and an active canal construction programme was embarked upon. Completed in 1845, the Beauharnois Canal, 200 feet (61 m) long and with a draught of 9 feet (2.7 m) made it possible for vessels to avoid the Soulanges Rapids. The navigational difficulties created by the series of rapids between Long Sault and Prescott were overcome by 1847 with the opening of the Williamsburg Canal system. During this period also, the original Lachine Canal was widened and deepened to match the Beauharnois Canal and, by the middle of the 19th century, the principal natural obstacles to transportation on the St. Lawrence had all been surmounted by man-made waterways.

Efforts to by-pass the falls at Niagara had gone on concurrently with the work on the St. Lawrence River and the first Welland Canal, begun by William Hamilton Merritt in 1824, was opened in 1829 The canal, $27\frac{1}{2}$ miles (44 km) in length, contained forty wooden locks 8 feet (2.4 m) in depth. The original depth was increased to 9 feet (2.7 m) by 1850 with the construction of the second Welland Canal and the number of locks reduced to 27, each built of cut stone. In 1855, when the State of Michigan completed a canal around the St. Mary's Falls at Sault St. Marie, a navigable waterway with a minimum depth of 9 feet (2.7 m) was available from the Atlantic Ocean to Lake Superior.

The report of the Royal Commission on Canals in 1871 recommended a deeper draught system with uniform dimensions for all locks on the St. Lawrence and Welland sections and prompted the Federal Government to embark once again on a canal building programme. The new locks opened in 1883 on the Lachine Canal were 270 feet (82.3 m) in length and 45 feet (13.7 m) in width and these dimensions became the standard for the waterway as a whole.

The third Welland Canal was begun in 1873 and finished in 1887. It consisted of 26 stone locks of the same size as those built on the Lachine Canal at about the same time and it had a depth of 14 feet (4.3 m). When the river section was completed in 1904, a second St. Lawrence-Great Lakes system had come into operation, providing a channel with a minimum depth of 14 feet (4.3 m) from Montreal to the Lakehead. Three large U.S. locks together with a single Canadian lock had been built at Sault Ste. Marie betwen 1887 and 1895.

The present Welland Canal is the fourth to be built across the Niagara escarpment. Construction began in 1913 and one lock was substantially complete by 1916, when activities were stopped by World War I. Building resumed shortly after the war but it was not until 1932 that the canal was completed. The number of locks had been reduced from 26 to eight, with minimum dimensions of 76 feet (233.5 m) in length, 80 feet (24.4 m) in width and with 30 feet (9.1 m) of water over the sills.

The opening of the fourth Welland canal produced a waterway system which was unbalanced in the sense that ships built to take full advantage of the new canal dimensions were cut off from the Atlantic by the smaller canals in the St.Lawrence section.

Interest in the construction of a deep waterway on the St. Lawrence was evident in both Canada and the United States before the turn of the century. Canada took the initiative in December 1951, when the Federal Government passed an act to establish The St. Lawrence Seaway Authority for constructing,maintaining and operating, either wholly in Canada or in conjunction with the United States, a deep draught waterway between the Port of Montreal and Lake Erie. Then, in May 1954, the United States Congress passed the Wiley-Dondero Act authorising an American agency to build the navigational Rapids section of the St.Lawrence River. The project was completed five years later and through transit of the Seaway began on April 25, 1959. Well over 1 billion tons of cargo have moved through the Seaway since then.

The locks built on the St. Lawrence during this period are almost identical in size to those that had been designed for the Welland Canal in the early 20th century. Five of the locks are located on the Canadian side of the river and two on the United States side. The minimum depth of the new section is 27 feet (8.2 m) and the rest of the system, including the Welland and the connecting channels, was brought to this standard. Thus, by the early 1960's, a depth of 27 feet (8.2 m) was available over the entire route from Montreal to Lake Superior and the St. Lawrence Seaway had come into existence. Once a vessel has reached Lake Superior it has climbed more than 600 feet (183 m) above sea level.

The St Lawrence Seway, which is currently in the midst of a $175 million seven-year modernisation, claims it offers a cheaper alternative to the industrial areas surrounding the Great Lakes than river and overland transport in North America.

Locks and Channels:

The seven locks in the St. Lawrence River are all similar in size. The specifications are:

Length, breast wall to gate fender	766 feet
(Ships may not exceed 730 feet in overall length and 76 feet extreme breadth)	
Width	80 feet
Depth over sills	30 feet
Locks:	Lift
St. Lambert	15 feet
Côte Ste. Catherine	30 feet
Lower Beauharnois and Upper Beauharnois	41 feet
Snell	45 feet
Eisenhower	38 feet
Iroquois	5 to 6 feet

The locks of the Welland Canal have the same controlling dimensions as those of the Montreal-Lake Ontario Section.

Locks 1-7 of the Welland Canal are lift locks. Lock 8 is essentially a guard lock. Locks 4, 5, 6 are twinned and in flight.

The Welland Canal is 26 miles long and overcomes a difference in level of 326 feet between Lake Ontario and Lake Erie.

The controlling channel dimmensions for the Seaway, Lake Erie to Montreal, are:

Depth to a minimum of 27 feet — to permit transit of vessels drawing 26 feet (fresh water draught).

Width of channel:	
(a) When flanked by two embankments	200 feet minimum
(b) When flanked by one embankment	300 feet minimum
(c) In open reaches	450 feet minimum

Locking Procedures:

All locks on the St. Lawrence Seaway are filled or emptied by gravity. To raise a vessel the upstream valves are opened and the water simply flows into the chamber through openings at the bottom of the walls.

To lower a vessel the above steps are reversed. It takes less than ten minutes to raise or lower the water level with more than 20 million gallons used for each lockage. Additional time, however, is required for the vessel to carefully manoeuvre in and out of the chambers. The average lockage requires approximately 33 minutes from the time the bow passes the approach wall until the stern is cleared of the outermost boom.

Tolls and lockage fees:

Tolls on the Seaway are assessed on the gross registered tonnage of the vessel and on classified cargo commodities. Vessels are also charged a fee for each of the locks of the Welland Canal they transit.

Authorities: The St. Lawrence Seaway Authority — Head Office, 360 Albert Street, Ottawa, Ontario, Canada, K1R 7X7.
Saint Lawrence Seaway Development Corporation — Operations Headquarters, 180 Andrews Street, Massena, N.Y., U.S.A. 13662.

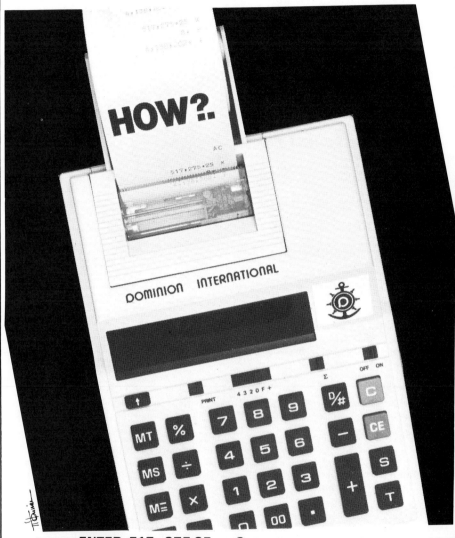

SUEZ CANAL

The idea of connecting the Mediterranean and the Red Sea by a direct navigable waterway facilitating trade between the East and West dates back forty centuries. Egypt was the first country in the world to create a man-made canal serving trade and connecting the two hemispheres.

The first Canal connecting the Mediterranean and the Red Sea indirectly via the River Nile and its branches was dug under the reign of Senausret III (1887 - 1849 B.C.). Vessels coming from the Greek Sea (Mediterranean), used to go through the eastern branch (the Pelusiac branch) of the Nile, which had then seven branches, to the town of Bubastis (Zagazig) whence they went through the canal eastward, passing by the town of Tekhou (Abou Sweir) to the Bitter Lakes. These Lakes were, at that time, an open gulf connected with the Red Sea.

By 910 B.C., in the reign of Pharaoh Necho II, sand silted in the Canal because it had been long neglected and a bar separated the Red Sea from the Bitter Lakes. Necho began to dig the Canal but later abandoned the idea.

When Darius Hystaspes, King of Persia, ruled Egypt in the year 510 B.C. the Canal was reopened. He succeeded only in connecting the Bitter Lakes with the Red Sea by minor Canals unfit for navigation except during the period of the Nile flood. This Canal was then neglected.

Under Ptolemy II (285 B.C.) and Ptolemy III (246 B.C.) the Canal, over its whole length, was once more made fit for navigation and the section between the Bitter Lakes and the Red Sea was redug to replace the minor canals. This Canal was again neglected by time.

In 98 B.C. the Roman Emperor Trajan ordered a new connection to be dug beginning at Babylon (Old Cairo) and ending at the village known as Abbassa, where it joined the old branch (Bubastis — Bitter Lakes) or (Zagazig — Bitter Lakes). Once again the Canal was not maintained and it was out of use by the end of the third century.

Following the Islamic conquest (640 A D) Amro Ibn El Ass had the idea of digging a direct Canal connecting the two seas and crossing the low flat plain extending south of Farma, a town which was situated near the present Port Said. However Caliph Omar Ibn El Khattab opposed the project for fear of exposing all Egypt to be flooded by the Red Sea. He ordered the restoration of the Canal of the Roman Emperor Trajan in order to allow vessels to sail to the Hedjaz (Saudi Arabia), the Yemen and India. This Canal was called the Canal of the Caliph and was used for about 150 years.

All the preceding Canals joined the Mediterranean and the Red Sea indirectly via the River Nile and its branches. However, in the 19th century, the idea of connecting the two seas by a direct Canal was put forward, with a view to facilitating trade between the East and West.

Excavation of the present day Canal began on April 25, 1859 and it was opened to navigation on November 17, 1869. By the Treaty of Constantinople of October 29, 1988, the Canal is open to vessels of all nations and free from blockade, except in time of war.

When the Canal was nationalised by President Nasser on 26 July 1956 the permissible draught was 35 feet, allowing the transit of 30,000 ton tankers. Following the six day war the Canal was closed for eight years but after the clearance of mines and sunken vessels it was reopened on 5 June, 1975 and development of the Canal was started and completed in 1980.

One of the targets achieved by the first phase of the development programme was the straightening of the curves of the Canal. The radius of the curves, which ranged from 2,000 metres to 3,000 metres is now 5,000 metres and the width of the Canal at the curves has been increased. This first phase included huge earth moving operations, the volume of earth removed amounting to about 107 million cubic metres and involved removing earth above the waterlevel eastward of the Canal along a distance varying from 150 metres deep in the north to 120 metres in the south. Revetments were constructed to protect the banks against caving and erosion caused by the transit vessels. These new revetments, built of steel piles and stones, cover a distance of 154 km. At the same time 131 km. of the old revetments were removed.

By the second half of 1990 the Canal will be able to accept fully laden tankers of around 200,000 tonnes deadweight. The widening programme has already been completed from Port Said to canal kilometre 122 and Suez Canal Authority dredgers are now working in the remaining southern part, widening the waterway by up to 50 metres.

Bollard posts are installed along the waterway, fixed in either huge concrete blocks on the banks or in caissons in the Bitter Lakes. Such posts can take a bollard pull of 100 tons and are used for the mooring of vessels in cases of emergency. To protect the entrance of the Port Said by-pass against high waves and strong currents two breakwaters have been constructed. The first extends 2.5km. east of the by-pass and the second 500 metres to the west.

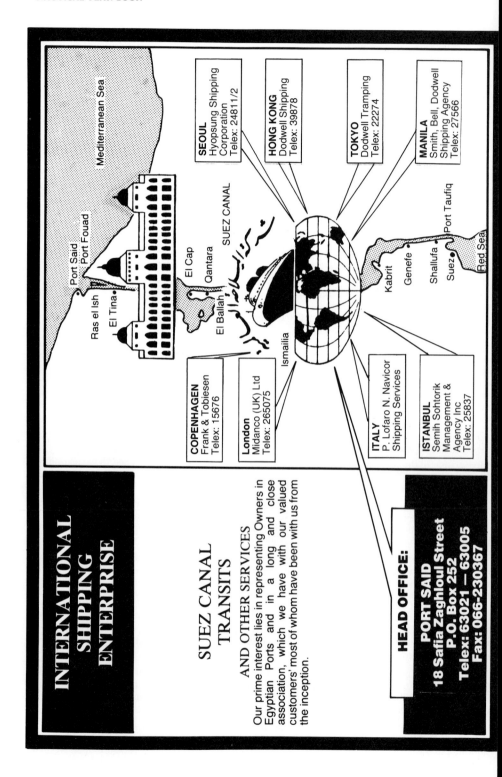

INTERNATIONAL SHIPPING ENTERPRISE

SUEZ CANAL TRANSITS

AND OTHER SERVICES

Our prime interest lies in representing Owners in Egyptian Ports and in a long and close association, which we have with our valued customers', most of whom have been with us from the inception.

HEAD OFFICE:

PORT SAID
18 Safia Zaghloul Street
P.O. Box 252
Telex: 63021 — 63005
Fax: 066-230367

COPENHAGEN
Frank & Tobiesen
Telex: 15676

London
Midanco (UK) Ltd
Telex: 265075

ITALY
P. Lofaro N. Navicor
Shipping Services

ISTANBUL
Semih Sohtorik
Management &
Agency Inc
Telex: 25837

SEOUL
Hyopsung Shipping
Corporation
Telex: 24811/2

HONG KONG
Dodwell Shipping
Telex: 39878

TOKYO
Dodwell Tramping
Telex: 22274

MANILA
Smith, Bell, Dodwell
Shipping Agency
Telex: 27566

Mediterranean Sea

Port Said
Port Fouad
Ras el Ish
El Tina
El Cap
Qantara
El Ballah
Ismailia
SUEZ CANAL

Kabrit
Genefe
Shallufa
Suez
Port Taufiq
Red Sea

The canal is 162.5 km long; including the approaches, it measures 193.5 km. At Port Said the Canal is entered at the southern end of Husein Basin. There is a second channel east of the main channel which rejoins about 2.5 km. south of the entrance. An additional channel used by supertankers has been created from km. 17 in the Canal to the Mediterranean giving access to vessels without passing Port Said harbour. The Canal runs south through Lake Manzala and into Lake Timsah, the midway point. On the northern shore of Lake Timsah is Ismailia where the headquarters of the Suez Canal Authority is situated. The waterway continues from the southern end of Lake Timsah through several lagoons and passes through the Great Bitter Lake and Little Bitter Lake before reaching the Red Sea at Port Tewfik.

Convoy System

Passage through the Canal is controlled by a convoy system; two southbound convoys leave Port Said and one northbound convoy leaves Suez daily. The First Southbound convoy starts at 0100 hours. Vessels can join this convoy provided they arrive by 1800 hours. The Second Southbound convoy starts 0700 hours and vessels can join this convoy provided they arrive by 0200 hours. The Northbound convoy starts at 0615 hours and ends at 1130 hours. To join this convoy a vessel must have arrived and be available: containerships, tankers and bulk carriers by 0000 hours; cargo and other vessels by 0200 hours. When the northbound convoy leaves Suez at 0615 hours first of the two southbound convoys, the N1, has already been travelling for five hours. It leaves Port Said at about 0100 hours with the last vessel entering the canal at Port Said at around 0500 hours, depending on the size of the convoy. The convoy takes a maximum of 40 ships from Port Said straight to the Bitter lakes. The normal speed is 14 km per hour and this may be increased to 15 or 16 km when strong winds prevail. In the western anchorages of the Bitter Lakes, the N1 convoy drops anchor and waits for the northbound convoy to pass.

The second southbound convoy (N2) — which has a maximum of 12 ships — leaves between 0700 and 0900 hours proceeding at 14km per hour to the Ballah Loop double-lane section of the canal, between the canal kilometres 51 and 61. The convoy stops in the canal's western branch, awaiting the passage of the last northbound ship through the eastern branch before it can continue south. The Canal does not operate a pre-booking system. However vessels that have booked to transit on a certain day do have priority on that day.

Navigation and Traffic Control

The Canal operates around the clock and vessels transitting during darkness must be fitted with a searchlight and overhead lights visible from all points. The distance between vessels in the canal is kept to at least one kilometre for cargo ships and three kilometres for tankers. As additional safety measures, the Canal Authority insists on one escorting tug for every tanker above 110,000 tonnes and two for ships above 150,000 tonnes, as well as for LPG carriers, chemical carriers and other vessels with dangerous cargoes.

Pilotage is compulsory for ships above 300 net tons and the Canal authority employs more than 250 pilots. Every vessel has four different pilots for a full transit. Going south, the first pilot takes her from the roadsteads into Port Said, the second from Port Said to Ismailia, the third from Ismailia to Suez and the fourth through the port of Suez into the open sea. A speed limit is imposed varying from 13 to 16 kms per hour according to the category and tonnage of vessel. In the Southern Sector it varies between 11 and 15 kms per hour depending on the velocity and direction of the tidal current. On average, a vessel takes 14 hours to transit the Canal.

Tonnage on which all dues and charges are paid is net tonnage resulting from a system of measurement laid down by the International Commission at Constantinople in 1873.

The Canal avoids the long haul around the Cape of Good Hope, and saves, for example, 10,090 sailing miles between Piraeus and Jeddah, 4,513 miles on a voyage from Rotterdam to Bombay and 2,261 miles between New York and Singapore. The canal has helped to bring several revolutions. Following its opening in 1869, long-haul steamships could carry one third more cargo, due to the fact that the shorter voyage and reduction in distance between bunkering stations meant that less fuel had to be carried. That helped steamships to win the competitive race against the clippers. Also when the canal was closed from 1967 to 1975, as a result of the Israeli-Arab war, the closure was one of the major reasons for shipowners ordering VLCCs and ULCCs.

Authority: Suez Canal Authority, Ismailia. Telephone 20001. Telex 92153 and 54168.

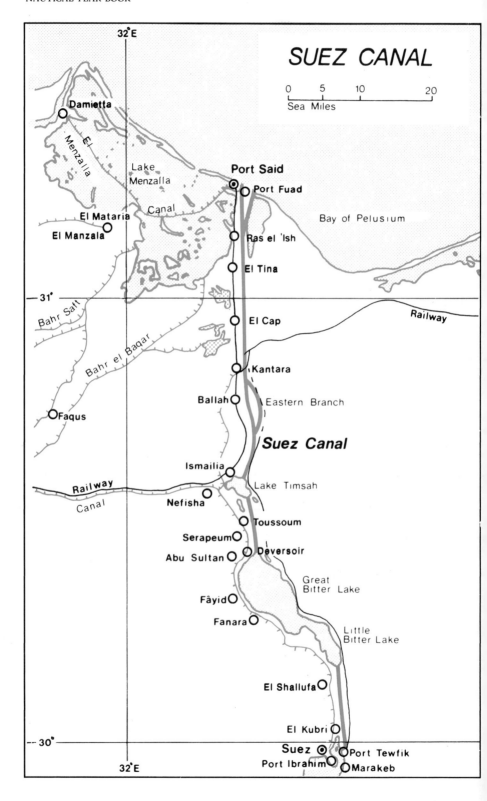

SUEZ CANAL

TENNESSEE-TOMBIGBEE WATERWAY

The canal link between the Tennessee and Tombigbee rivers in the United States began operations in June 1985 providing a second outlet to the Gulf of Mexico for the vast Mississippi Basin, creating a more direct link between the Ohio River, with its industrial centres of Pittsburgh, Cincinatti and Louisville, and the sea. The 234 mile waterway can save shippers up to 800 miles over the alternative Mississippi River.

The waterway extends northward from the junction of the Black Warrior and Tombigbee Rivers near Demopolis in west central Alabama to the Pickwick Reservoir on the Tennessee River in the northeast corner of Mississippi. The elevation drop between these two points is 341 feet and required the construction of five dams and 10 locks: the waterway is 300 feet wide, 9 feet deep. The locks are 110 feet wide and 600 feet long and capable of accommodating a tug and eight standard barges at a time. More than 14 million gallons of water are taken in and discharged through the average lock each time it is operated to provide a lift of 29-30 feet.

Above the river section for 44 miles the waterway becomes a canal which roughly parallels the river. Five locks and spillways control the water levels in this section. At the north end of the canal section the Bay Springs Lock and Dam northeast of Tupelo, Mississippi, the northernmost structure on the waterway with its 84 feet lift, is the highest on the Tenn-Tom. Above Bay Springs the northernmost Divide Section leads into the Tennessee River.

Principal commodities that travel the route are crushed rock, chemicals, wood, asphalt, iron ore, logs, grain, fuel, fertiliser, soya beans, salt and steel.

The waterway creates a chain of lakes with some 42,000 acres of water surface between Demopolis Lake and Pickwick Lake and at the same time furnishes land for recreational use.

There are some 49 public use areas along the route. Facilities include boat launching ramps, fishing piers, tent, trailer and rustic camping areas, and nature study and hiking areas, along with the usual beaches and picnic grounds. Visitors are welcome to visit the locks and dams to observe their operation.

Authority: Alabama State Docks, Department, P.O. Box 1588, Mobile, AL 36633. Tel: TWX 810 741-7748.

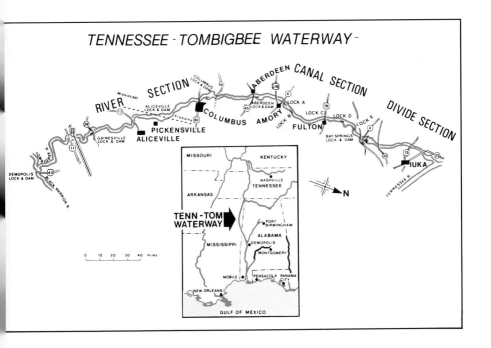

YANGTZE RIVER

Known to the Chinese as the Ch'ang Chiang — Long River, or the Ta Chiang — Great River, or simply the Chiang, the Yangtze River, the great artery of China, over 6,300 km. long and transversing six provinces, is one of the four largest rivers in the world.

The first mention of the river in history dates from the time of Emperor Yu (B.C. 2205-2197).

Its sources are on the eastern side of the mountains of Tibet and for the first 3,200 km. the river is confined to ravine or valley, the valley being seldom much wider than the river bed. In the last 1,600 km. to the sea the valley widens, and the river flows through an alluvial plain.

The drainage area is about 750,000 square miles in extent, comprising the greater part of nine provinces. The lower reaches are slow flowing and carry large amounts of silt in suspension to the Yellow Sea (hence its name).

During the last few years many river ports have been opened to foreign vessels but strictly for direct calls only. It is still not allowed for these foreign vessels to ship cargo between one river port and another. Navigable waters of the main stream capable of taking vessels over 1,000 dwt amount to 2,600 km., and the growth of freight and passenger traffic in the area has been given new impetus with the revitalised economy and thriving commerce of China.

Situated 7 km. south of the river mouth, which is 45/65 km. wide, is Shanghai, the major port of China, stretching along the banks of the Yangtze and Huangpu Rivers. Together with extensive wharf frontage the port has facilities for container and ro/ro, ore and bulk vessels and tankers.

Ninetysix km. up river from Wusong, situated at the river mouth, is the major port of Nantong, incorporating Langshan, capable of taking vessels up to 16,000 t. A new berth is under construction here and others are planned.

Further up-river, 144 km. from Wusong, on the south bank of the river is Zhangji Agang. Here vessels of up to 10,000 dwt can be accommodated. Container facilities are also available.

Zhenjiang, situated midway between Nantong and Nanjing, is a major inland transportation centre. There are berths for small vessels and inland river craft. At nearby Dagang a new port area is under construction.

Nanjing, handling mainly coal and oil, is subject to silting. A new port area about 15 km downstream is under construction. The port of Wuhu, with a water depth of up to 20m. at certain times of year handles vessels up to 10,000 t.

Near the borders of Hubei and Anhui Provinces, 400 miles from Shanghai, is the port of Jiujiang where vessels up to 5,000 t can be handled at the main pier. A new passenger terminal and a new wharf to accommodate vessels up to 5,000 t are under construction.

The tides in the upper reaches of the Yangtze fluctuate widely. They can rise to 25.3 m. at the port of Wuhan, in Hubei Province, during the spring and fall to 11.3 m. during the December to March dry season. At Yangluo, 30 km. from Wuhan, where the river is wide and has a minimum depth of 10m. even during the dry season, 12 berths are to be built to handle general, coal, grain and container cargoes.

At Chongqing, where the tidal range can be as much as 20 m. between summer and winter, there are facilities for acceptance of vessels up to 5,000 t. New berths are under construction for river/sea shipments.

In the first nine months of 1985, 1,950,000 t of imports and exports was handled at the various harbours on the river.

Authority: Yangtze River Navigation Administration.

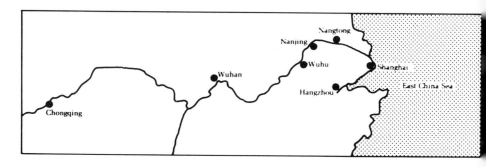

NATIONAL AND INTERNATIONAL ORGANISATIONS

Associated British Ports

150 Holborn, London EC1N 2LR, England.
Telephone (01) 430 1177. Telex 23923.
Established 1981.

Associated British Ports (ABP) is the United Kingdom's largest port operator. It controls 19 ports of varying sizes and locations which together handle around a quarter of the UK's seaborne trade.

ABP was set up under the Transport Act 1981 to take over the administration of the 19 ports from the British Transport Docks Board. ABP operates as a statutory corporation, with similar functions to those of the BTDB, but is a wholly-owned subsidiary of Associated British Ports Holdings PLC.

Their ports provide facilities for practically every sort of cargo currently handled and ABP has invested heavily in capital equipment at the 19 ports to ensure that its facilities match the requirements of today's shipping industry.

Baltic and International Maritime Council (BIMCO)

Kristianiagade 19, DK-2100 Copenhagen, Denmark.
Telephone (01) 263000. Telex 19086. Facsimile (01) 263335.
Established 1905.

BIMCO's membership comprises shipowners and managers, shipbrokers, port and chartering agents, and clubs, such as P&I, Freight, Demurrage and Defence Associations, shipping federations, shipowners' and shipbrokers' associations. Representing members from more than 100 countries, BIMCO is a focal point for shipping professionals where vital information is collected, collated and made available to all members for the good of the industry.

Activities:

BIMCO is an acknowledged centre for the development of modern and reasonable documents for the transportation of goods by sea. Gencon, Barecon, Conlinebill — these are just a few of the documents formulated over the years.

BIMCO represents its members within international organisations, especially UNCTAD (The United Nations Conference on Trade and Development) and the IMO (International Maritime Organization), and works in close rapport with other shipping bodies. The organisation is a permanent member of the Maritime Security Council's Ocean Carrier Committee, and one of the operating companies of the Maritime Advisory Exchange.

Members have free access to a range of services, including cross-checking of disbursements accounts, interpretation of charter party clauses, exposure to freight taxes, port conditions and port charges, ad hoc warnings on objectionable terms and much more.

Newsletters, Bulletins and specialised handbooks on shipping topics are published.

Courses on practical shipping arranged world-wide, and a cooperation with the Institute of Chartered Shipbrokers has been established in a bid to enhance opportunities for professional education and training.

Development of software applications for the shipping industry.

The Baltic Exchange

14-20 St. Mary Axe, London EC3A 8BU, England.
Telephone (01) 623 5501. Telex 8811373. Facsimile (01) 623 3645.
Established 18th Century.

The Baltic Exchange is the world's leading international shipping market and a major earner of foreign currency for Britain.

The membership is mostly corporate, each member company being represented on the Exchange by individual men and women with wide-ranging skills and expertise.

Shipping is the main activity. Baltic members act for owners seeking out cargo and merchants and traders seeking the right ship. Members handle at some stage most of the world's cargo business and global sales of second-hand tonnage.

Other important activities include air-broking and commodity trading. The Baltic Futures Exchange is the recognised investment exchange for several futures market, BIFFEX, trading a dry bulk cargo contract against the Baltic Freight Index. The other markets trade futures in grain, potatoes, soyabean meal and meat.

Hallmark of the Baltic membership has been its high standard of business conduct ever since the original Baltic Coffee House introduced rules for its members in 1823.

Institute of Chartered Shipbrokers (ICS)

Baltic Exchange Chambers, 24 St. Mary Axe, London EC3A 8DE, England.
Telephone (01) 283 1361. Telex 8812708.
Established 1911.

The Institute is the professional body for shipbrokers and was originally founded in London in 1911 but later gathered into it various district associations and was incorproated in 1920 by Royal Charter. It carries out the functions normal to any professional institute but high in its priorities is the setting, and maintenance of standards, and the examination, in both theory and practice, of those engaged as shipbrokers. Aside from local branches in the UK there are branches in Hong Kong, Singapore and Ireland.

Institute of Freight Forwarders

Redfern House, Browells Lane, Feltham, Middlesex TW13 7EP, England.
Telephone (01) 844 2266. Telex 8953060.
Established 1944.

During the war years the need for an organisation to raise the status of shipping and forwarding agents, as well as to represent their collective intrests, became apparent. This led to the establishment of the present institute.

As the only representative organisation of freight forwarders in this country the Institute became increasingly involved in negotiations with the representatives of carriers and of the users of international transport and also with Government Departments, HM Customs, Port Authorities and other organisations both domestic and international.

In order that this dual role could be performed more effectively the constitution was revised in April 1970 to provide for membership of both individuals engaged in international freight forwarding work and freight forwarding organisations and other allied interests.

The Institute seeks to promote the interests and welfare of forwarders, to improve and maintain their professional status, and to achieve and preserve high standards of professional conduct and skill. Its objects include the encouragement of initiative and enterprise. It is specifically intended that should watch over, promote and safeguard the interests of the general public by the maintenance of high professional standards, and it seeks to ensure that membership of the Institute shall denote integrity and a high quality of service.

The International Association of Independent Tanker Owners (INTERTANKO)

Lange-Rolvsgt. 5, N-0273 Oslo 2, Norway.
Telephone (02) 44 03 40. Telex 19751. Facsimile (02) 56 32 22.

The Association was originally established in the U.K. as the voice of independent, namely non-oil company, tanker owners, *vis a vis* the oil majors. It moved to Oslo in 1970 since when it has assumed broader base and today has members from over thirty countries representing some 140 million dwt tanker tonnage. Its aims and objectives are:

To promote the interests of the members internationally; to co-operate with other technical, commercial or industrial interests and to participate in the deliberations of other international bodies to the extent that it assists the general aims.

Membership is open to owners or managers of 'tank vessels' of more than 1,000 tons.

Its principal interest is to promote safety at sea and a free competitive tanker market. It also deals with commercially orientated issues like charter party problems, Worldscale and market research. It is funded on the basis of a certain fee per tanker per year.

International Chamber of Commerce — ICC Commission on Sea Transport

0 Cours Albert 1er, 75008 Paris, France.
Telephone (1) 49 53 28 28. Telex 650770. Facsimile (1) 42 25 86 63.

The International Chamber of Commerce, the world business organisation, has four principal functions:

to represent the business community at international levels, especially as business spokesman to the United Nations and specialised governmental agencies; to promote world trade and investment based on free and fair competition; to harmonise trade practices, and formulate guidelines for international trade services to business.

It works through a number of commissions, among them being trade policy, energy, environment, banking, insurance, taxation, and marketing.

The ICC Commission on Sea Transport brings together business interests in maritime affairs from developed and developing nations, including shipowners, shippers, insurers, forwarders, bankers, as well as observers from governmental and non-governmental international shipping organisations. This uniquely representative membership permits the ICC to speak with authority on behalf of commercial shipping interests worldwide.

International Chamber of Shipping

30-32 St Mary Axe, London EC3A 8ET, London.
Telephone (01) 282 2922. Telex 884008.
Established 1921.

The International Chamber is the oldest and most prestigious of the international associations c shipowners' in London.

Members comprise shipowners' associations from 34 countries. Its members represent some 50 pe cent of the world's merchant tonnage.

The scope of objectives of the chamber are:
To promote the interests of its members in matters of general policy; to frame policies and t develop these through intergovernmental organisations, governments in member countries or i other ways and to co-operate with other appropriate bodies on matters of mutual concern and a necessary to take part in the deliberations of other international bodies.

Lloyd's Register of Shipping

71 Fenchurch Street, London EC3M 4BS, England.
Telephone (01) 709 9166. Telex 888379 LR LON G. Facsimile (01) 488 4796.
Established 1760.

Lloyd's Register of Shipping is an independent classification society. It sets and maintain standards of safety and reliability by establishing requirements for design, construction an maintenance of ships.

There are two fundamental principles of ship classification. First, a ship should comply with standard of construction which ensures adequate strength and reliability; and second, it should b adquately maintained throughout its life to ensure a continuing standard of strength. Rules for shi construction are laid down by LR and are constantly updated in line with changes and technologic: statutory requirements if it is to be 'classed', that is built and maintained, under survey, by LR.

In addition to the classification services, LR offers numerous back-up and advisory services. Whei there is damage to a ship or failure of its machinery an LR surveryor can give on-the-spot technic: advice anywhere in the world.

LR is not just involved in the business of shipping, it also inspects offshore rigs and platforms an land-based installations such as power plants, refineries and pipelines. It has more than 240 exclusiv

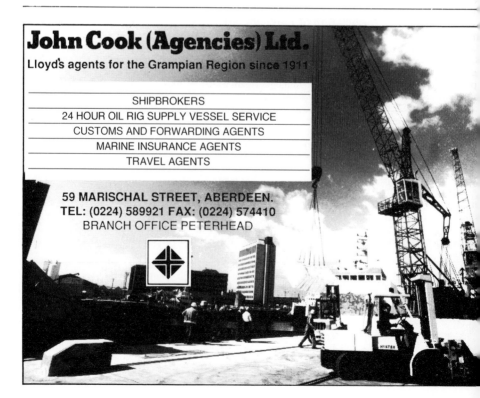

offices worldwide served by 3,000 technical and administrative staff and carries out statutory work on behalf of more than 125 governments.

LR is completely autonomous and financially independent with a governing body of shipowners, builders and underwriters. Income derived from fees and the sale of publications, such as the Register of Ships, is used for research and to improve services.

The London Maritime Arbitrators' Association (LMAA)

30-32 St. Mary Axe, London EC3A 8ET, England.
Telephone (01) 626 8131. Telex 884008. Facsimile (01) 626 8135.
Established 1960.

This association was formed by members of the Baltic Exchange and the Institute of Chartered Shipbrokers who were also practising arbitrators. It has, among its objectives, the advancement of standards in arbitration and the promotion of desirable changes in commercial law, the encouragement of arbitration in London as an effective and expeditious alternative to the courts for the resolution of commercial disputes; and generally to exchange views amongst its members and with others engaged in, or concerned with, maritime affairs.

National Union of Marine Aviation & Shipping Transport Officers (NUMAST)

Oceanair House, 750-760 High Road, Leytonstone, London E11 3BB, England.
Telephone (01) 989 6677. Telex 892648. Facsimile (01) 530 1015.
Established 1985.

NUMAST previously the Merchant Navy & Airline Officers Association (MNAOA) is the largest of the British seafarers organisations. Its change of name occurred with the merger of two former officers unions — the Mercantile Marine Services Association (MMSA), the Radio & Electronic Officers Union (REOU), with the MNAOA in 1985.

Shipmasters and officers serving on UK flag ships or rigs can belong to NUMAST, as well as those serving in foreign fleets. NUMAST membership includes cadets and officers of all ranks and within all departments as well as British airline crews and employees working ashore engaged in various fields associated with shipping, such as marine radio and electronics technicians.

NUMAST represents shipmasters and officers at national negotiations conducted annually at the National Maritime Board Joint Officers Panel, which continue to be conducted separately from those affecting ratings on the same ships. NUMAST remains federated to the NMB within the British Seafarers Joint Council (BSJC) a body concerned with the representation of matters of common interest to merchant navy personnel of all ranks.

It also negotiates at company level on behalf of ships' officers employed within General Council of British Shipping affiliated fleets and many non-federated fleets and also with various off-shore agencies and foreign employers. National Committees advise the governing Council of NUMAST on specialist interests involving such sections of the membership as airline employees, shipmasters, radio officers and offshore oil members.

National Union of Seamen (NUS)

Maritime House, Old Town, Clapham, London SW4 OJP, England.
Telephone (01) 622 5581. Telex 8814611.
Established 1887.

The National Union of Seamen is the trades union to which British merchant navy ratings and some non-British ratings belong. The union was founded by Havelock Wilson as 'The National Amalgamated Sailors and Firemens Union of Great Britain and Northern Ireland'.

The NUS is affiliated to the British Trades Union Congress and the Labour Party. Internationally it is affiliated to the International Transport Workers Federation (ITF) and its membership comprises ratings from all departments on board ship including the chief petty officer ranks. Union policy is formulated at a Biennial General Meeting attended by elected union delegates and by the elected executive council.

Trinity House, Corporation of

4th floor, Lloyd's Chambers, 1 Portsoken Street, London E1 8BT, England.
Telephone (01) 480 6601. Telex 987526 NAVAID G.
Established 1514.

Of the three statutory bodies known as General Lighthouse Authorities the oldest is the Corporation of Trinity House which can trace its origins back to a Charter granted by Henry VIII in 1514. Although its original reponsibilities were for pilotage and as a charity, the right to erect beacons and establish buoyage did not come until 1594 and it was not until 1836 that Trinity House was empowered to buy out owners of the remaining English and Welsh Lighthouses that were not already in its hands. Today, the Service is responsible for marine aids to general navigation around the coast of England, Wales and the Channel Islands. It is also responsible for light stations on each of Gibraltar Sombrero Island (near Anguilla) and for one in the Falkland Islands.

United Nations Bodies

The UN Convention on the Law of the Sea (ULCLOS) regularly meets and aims to set up the juridicial and administrative structure called for. It exists for the ordering of human relations at sea

The International Court of Justice in the Hague, copes with various maritime disputes and the General Agreement on Tariffs and Trade, based in Geneva, is concerned with the regulations of policies and the reconciliation of protective tariffs with measures that make for freer trade.

The Paris-based Organisation for Economic Co-operation and Development (OECD) embraces all aspects of shipping. It is made up of a group of western nations, plus the United States, Japan Australia and New Zealand.

The UN Conference on Trade and Development (UNCTAD) has close working relations with the International Labour Organisation (ILO) and the International Maritime Organization (IMO) technically the principal UN authority on shipping matters.

The International Tele-communications Union (ITU), in Geneva, works closely with the IMO UNCTAD and the ILO in the field of electronic communications and the allocation of frequencies and positions for geo-stationary satellites. These satellites affect weather forecasting services, navigation and emergency assistance.

The International Labour Organisation (ILO) was created by the Treaty of Versailles in 1919 to unite representatives of governments, employers and workers in a common effort to establish social justice as the foundation of universal peace. Originally an autonomous part of the League of Nations it became in 1946 the first specialised agency associated with the United Nations. Today it has a membership of 150 states.

UNESCO, the UN Educational Scientific and Cultural Organisation, in Paris, maintains an active Maritime Division and houses the Intergovernmental Oceanographic Commission (IOC). A wide variety of projects relating to ocean currents, marine biology and weather reporting are dealt with by global and regional groups that are embraced by UNESCO's programmes. Some of these are: GIPME A Global Investigation of Pollution in the Maritime Environment; GLOSS, A Global Sea Level Observing System; GEEP, Group of Experts on the Effects of Pollution; MEDPOL, A Mediterranean Pollution Monitoring and Research Programme; and collaboration with ICES, the International Council for the Exploration of the Sea.

IN 1969 ICSPRO, the Inter-Secretariat Committee on Scientific Programmes Relating to Oceanography was created, a collaboration agreement reached by the UN bureaucracies concerned

The World Meterological organisation, based in Geneva, has a Technical Commission for Marine Meteorology (CMM), which in an earlier form, in 1907, was the Technical Commission for Storm Warnings and Marine Meteorology.

The financial segments of the UN embrace the World Bank group and the International Monetary Fund. The World Bank, also officially the International Bank for Reconstruction and Development works through subdivisions, the International Finance Corporation which will deal with commercial interests given government guarantees and a new soft loan International Development Association (IDA).

The UN Development Programme, (UNDP), gives separate and supplementary support to technical assistance undertaken by the UN specialised agencies at sea as on land. This umbrella programme has Resident Representatives and offices in most Third World countries.

The use of nuclear power on ships and the transport of nuclear wastes from reactors have been a source of alarm and the International Atomic Energy Agency (IAEA) is the agency involved; it is empowered to pass judgement on the design of ships and of their use of harbour facilities.

The Commonwealth Secretariat, with its headquarters in London, provides a common ground for the old members of the British Empire and the present states that are, independently, still members of the Commonwealth.

NAUTICAL COLLEGES & SCHOOLS

Aberdeen Technical College
Gallowgate, Aberdeen AB9 1DN, Scotland.
Tel (0224) 640366.

Australian Maritime College
PO Box 986, Launceston 7250, Tasmania.
Tel (03) 260711.

Brunel Technical College
Ashley Down, Bristol BS7 9BU, England.
Tel (0272) 41241.

**City of London Polytechnic, Faculty of
Transport**
100 Minories, London EC3N 1JN, England.
Tel (01) 283 1030.

**Colegio de Oficiales de la Marina Mercante
Espanola (COMME)**
Calle Orense 39-3B, 28020 Madrid, Spain.
Tel (91) 4563757.

College of Maritime Studies
Warsash, Southampton SO3 6ZL, England.
Tel (04895) 6161. Tx 477632 WRSASH G.

College of Nautical Studies
21 Thistle Street, Glasgow G5 9XB.
Scotland. Tel (041) 429 3201.

Ecole Nationale de Marine Marchande
Routé du Cap, Ste-Andresse, F-76060 Le Havre,
France.

Escola Nautica
Rua do Arsenal H, Lisbon, Portugal.

Escuela Oficial de Nautica Barcelona
Plaza de Palacio, Barcelona, Spain.

Fachhochschule Hamburg
Fachbereich Seefahrt, Rainsvilleterrasse 4,D-
2000 Hamburg 50, FRG.

Hogere Zeevaartschool
Nieuwe Vaart 3, Amsterdam, Netherlands.

Hong Kong Polytechnic, Nautical Studies
Hung Hom, Kowloon, Hong Kong.
Tx 38964 POLYX HX.

**Indefatigable and Nautical Sea Training
School for Boys**
Plas Llanfair, Llanfairpwll, Anglesey, Wales
Registered Office: Room 22, 1st Floor, Oriel
Chambers, 14 Water Street, Liverpool L2 8TD,
England. Tel (051) 227 3417.

Kobenhavens Navigationsskole
Lerso Parkalle 2, DK-2100 Copenhagen,
Denmark.

Leith Nautical College
24 Milton Road, Leith, Edinburgh EH15 2PP,
Scotland. Tel (031) 699 8461.

Lowestoft College of Further Education
St. Peters Street, Lowestoft, Suffolk, England.
Tel (0502) 83521.

Manukan Polytechnic
Maritime Studies Dept., PO Box 61-066,
Auckland, New Zealand. Tel (09) 274 6009.
Fax (09) 274 4711.

Marine Society
202 Lambeth Road, London SE1 7JW, England.
Tel (01) 261 9535.

National Maritime Polytechnic
Tacloban City, Leyte, Philippines.

National Sea Training College
Denton, Gravesend, Kent DA12 2HR, England.
Tel (0474) 63656.

National Sea Training Schools
30-32 St. Mary Axe, London EC3A 8ET,
England. Tel (01) 283 2922. Tx 884008.

Nautical College
Broadwater, Fleetwood, Lancs FY7 8JZ, England.
Tel (03917) 79123. Tx 677348.

Plymouth Polytechnic
Institute of Marine Studies, Drake Circus,
Plymouth England.
Tel (0752) 264667. Tx 45423 PPLRC G.

Singapore Polytechnic, Maritime Department
Prince Edward Road, PO Box 2023, Singapore 2,
Republic of Singapore.

Sjobefalskolan
Stigbergsgatan 30, S-116 35 Stockholm, Sweden.

Sjomannsskolen Oslo
Karlsborgvei 4, Oslo 1, Norway.

**South Glamorgan Institute of Higher
Education, Maritime Studies**
Western Avenue, Cardiff CF5 2YB, Wales.
Tel (0222) 551111.

South Tyneside College
St. Georges Avenue, South Shields, Tyne & Wear
NE34 6ET, England.
Tel (091) 456 0403, Tx 537864.

**Sydney Technical College, School of
Navigation**
Broadway, Sydney, N.S.W. 2007, Australia.

University of Strathclyde
Centre for Advanced Maritime Studies, 16
Richmond Street, Glasgow G1 1XQ. Scotland.
Tel (041) 553 1103. Tx 77472.

**University of Wales, Institute of Science and
Technology (UWIST)**
Dept. of Maritime Studies, Aberconway Building,
Colum Drive, Cardiff CF1 3EU, Wales. Tel (0222)
42588. Tx 497368.

University of Ulster at Jordanstown
Dept. of Maritime Studies, Shore Road,
Newtownabbey, Co. Antrim BT37 0QB, Northern
Ireland. Tel Belfast 365131.

CAMERON MARKBY HEWITT

INSURANCE AND REINSURANCE SOLICITORS

Lloyd's Office:
Room 639, Floor 6
Lloyd's, 1 Lime Street
London EC3M 7DQ

Tel: 01-623 7100 (exts 4412/4437)
Fax: 01-929 4700

Sceptre Court
40 Tower Hill
London
EC3N 4BB

Tel: 01-702 2345
Fax: 01-702 2303
Telex: 925779 CAMLAW G

Sceptre Court

LLOYD'S AND INSURANCE

IMPÉRIO

THE LARGEST PORTUGUESE INSURANCE COMPANY
LEADER IN THE MARINE, AVIATION AND TRANSPORT MARKET

FRENCH BRANCH OFFICE
25, Rue d'Astorg, 75008 PARIS - FRANCE
Phone 42 68 18 11 - Telex 640976 IMP FRA

GREEK BRANCH OFFICE
125, Mixalakopoulou - Ambelokipi - ATHENS - GREECE
Phone 775 50 31/6 - Telex 221382 IMP GR

SPANISH BRANCH OFFICES
Zurbano, 25 - MADRID 4 - SPAIN
Phone 410 21 00 - Telex 48608 IMSE
Colon, 37 - 4.° - VIGO - SPAIN
Phone 86 22 36 71

LONDON CONTACT OFFICE
Plantation House, 23 - Road Lane - LONDON EC3M 8AP - ENGLAND
Phone 626 74 77 - Telex 884023 IMPRE

LISBOA HEAD OFFICE
62, Rua Garrett - 1200 LISBOA - PORTUGAL
Phones 346 29 21 - 346 55 85
Telex 12585 - 16644 SAGIMP P - Fac simile 347 53 08

LLOYD'S IN THE 1990's

by

Murray Lawrence — Chairman of Lloyd's

Challenges and difficulties of varying degrees have been a feature of Lloyd's long history. The ability of its underwriters and brokers to innovate and exploit opportunities has been a major factor in ensuring its continuing role as the world's premier insurance market. Lloyd's is also vitally important to the British and European economies, contributing in 1987 nearly £2.4 billion to the UK balance of payments, an increase over the previous year against the general trend. This represented more than a quarter of the City's total overseas earnings and was nearly twice as much as those of the entire UK banking sector.

Lloyd's has now embarked upon its fourth century of successful and continuous trading and I believe that the spirit of innovation and foresight which has always been the hallmark of the market's development will be tested to the full as we confront new opportunities, especially those offered by the opening up of European insurance markets.

As regards Europe, the buzz word is 1992 but, for the Lloyd's market and other non-life insurers, the important date is much closer, July 1990, when the services directive comes into force. As members, the UK transacts insurance in the EEC under three main directives. The first covers reinsurance and, basically, this busness has always been free to travel across frontiers.

The second is the establishment directive which has applied since the 1970s. Under this we have the right to transact business throughout the EEC by means of establishment — the ability to open a branch or agency in another EEC country and transact business there subject, of course, to local regulation. Lloyd's, not having a presence in any territory other than the UK, exercises this right through representative offices which are required of us by all territories in which we are licenced. Currently we have offices in Belgium, France, Ireland, Italy and the Netherlands. We have appointed a representative in West Germany and an office opened there eralier this year. Greece and Spain are under consideration. These offices play no direct part in broking or underwriting the business, but are legal entities.

Thirdly, the services directive, which has been a bone of contention for twenty years. The UK has been pressing throughout for this measure, which would enable citizens from any member state to buy insurance in any other member state with the ultimate insurer subject to the regulations of his own country and not those of the country of the policyholder.

In June 1988 this directive was finally approved and it is this directive which becomes operative next year. It applies to commercial and industrial businesses but then only to risks above a certain size as measured by their capital, revenue or number of employees. This is fine as far as it goes, and a vast improvement on where we started. We believe, however, that any commercial or industrial client should be free to place his business wherever he wishes and we will be working, therefore, to reduce and finally eliminate all thresholds for these classes.

Thus, it would appear, there are now great opportunities in Europe, especially as it has a population of 320 million but a per capita spend on insurance only 36 per cent of that in the USA, Lloyd's largest market. However, this needs putting in perspective. I believe that progress in Europe will be slow. We have a very small involvement there

(only eight per cent of our premium income excluding the UK) and we would hope fo
a meaningful improvement in this over the next few years.

But the freedoms we are looking forward to will provide threats as well a
opportunities. Why is it that freedom to trade in insurance in the EEC has lagged
twenty years behind freedom of trade in goods? The answer is simply that in the earl
1970s, the UK insurance industry was much stronger than its rivals in Europe and
they have secured a 20-year breathing space to get their act together. So 1990 wil
provide us with threats as well as opportunities.

However, while we should be on our guard, I do not believe that we should b
unduly alarmed. London has always been a free city for insurance. Any company can
open up in London if they can meet the Department of Trade and Industry's financia
requirements and its conditions of 'fitness and properness'. In fact from a total of 83
insurance companies operating in the UK, some 157 are already from overseas.

So, what are our concerns over 1990? Firstly, will the playing fields of Europe reall
be level? Will every country carry out the necessary administrative and legal change
and will they do this in time for 1990? Perhaps more important, will everyone abid
by the spirit as well as the letter of the law since, only then, can we be certain there wil
be true freedom in the marketplace. We are concerned that deeply ingrained nationa
attitudes may take time to change and that, while technically having feedom to trade
we may find ourselves frozen out for a number of years until the necessary thaw take
place.

Our last concern relates to what is often described as 'fortress Europe' and we hav
no intention now of becoming 'little Europeans'. We would find it totall
unacceptable to exchange the freedom of doing business round the world which w
currently enjoy, for the freedom of doing business merely within the EEC. This coul
happen if individual countries were only prepared to take down the protectiv
barriers they have built round their own economies in return for a tariff wel
surrounding the European community as a whole. This is something which certainl
everyone in the Government and in the financial services sector of the UK i
determined should not happen.

Two events in recent years, the storm of October 1987, which devastated parts o
Southern England and Western Europe, and the Piper Alpha disaster involving tragi
loss of life, were grim examples of the force and unpredictability of nature. They als
provide a graphic reminder of the pivotal role played by insurers — none more so tha
underwriters at Lloyd's — in providing the insurance and reinsurance cover withou
which progress and enterprise or even daily life is not possible.

Massive insurance losses such as these also highlight the two main areas where th
Lloyd's market faces its greatest challenge moving towards the 1990s, namel
solvency and business development.

The first relates directly to the structure of Lloyd's and the way in which th
market's capital base is organised. All of Lloyd's 31,300 underwriting members o
Names accept insurance risks for their personal profit or loss and are liable to the ful
extent of their personal wealth to meet their insurance obligations.

Escalating costs from the run-off of old underwriting years, particularly on the U
general liability account, are of great concern to the Names and have been one of th
reasons leading to pressure for the abandonment of unlimited liability. In January thi
year, the Council of Lloyd's re-affirmed that unlimited liability would remai
fundamental to the transactions of insurance at Lloyd's. It did so in the strong belie
that this is the unique feature which underlines policies written at Lloyd's and i
therefore critical to the market's continuing prosperity.

In addition, any individual commencing underwriting must now show means of a
least £250,000 and maintain funds at Lloyd's equivalent to 30% of the premium the

wish to accept in an underwriting year. Existing Names have until 1992 to come into line with these requirements.

Lloyd's is therefore determined to maintain the capacity it needs for underwriting the wide range of business coming to London from around the world, with an adequate margin to allow it to respond flexibly and quickly to cyclical changes in premium rates. Some Names with small capacity may be replaced by fewer Names with larger capacity and greater wealth to withstand the vicissitudes of long-term business. This is not an unhealthy development but rather a source of continuing reinforcement of security for Lloyd's policyholders.

The second challenge is the need to secure a sound commercial future for Lloyd's and its membership by consolidating its base in existing markets and seeking to develop its position in new areas, in particular the EEC, to which I have already referred.

The role of the Council of LLoyd's in planning the market's European strategy is to open and to keep open as many doors as possible. It is entirely up to underwriters and brokers whether, and to what extent, they walk through them. Many individual strategies are now being worked out in the market.

It is vital that the necessary infrastructure is in place before Lloyd's seeks to write a large volume of business in EEC countries, particularly in the area of claims processing and documentation, and to this end the Lloyd's market invested £125 million during last year alone in information technology and electronic networking through the London Insurance Market Network.

This will not only make possible much more efficient and cost effective service of business, it will also open up new classes of business to be underwritten which were previously uneconomic or inefficient under the old methods of transacting it.

Those of us who work in the Lloyd's community must always remember that insurance is a service business and that nobody owes us a living. So in addition to Lloyd's unrivalled security, so often taken for granted, we must offer the policyholder a product that he wants in a cost efficient manner. As the market place becomes more competitive each year we shall have to concentrate upon greater efficiency as well as flexibility of cover and the security of the market. Vigorous efforts will be needed to improve the cost effectiveness of the market for without real progress here the market will be unable to take full advantage of the opportunities which present themselves in the next year or two. The Council of Lloyd's is taking decisions to facilitate this process but it will only succeed if underwriters, managing agents and brokers work together to give these matters their wholehearted support.

LLoyd's looks forward to next year, to 1992 and indeed to the 21st century with confidence, but not with complacency. Traditionally, one of LLoyd's great strengths has been flexibility and this will be at a premium in commercial life in the future. In addition Lloyd's has the greatest collection of underwriting talent in the world, security second to none, a splendid marketing force in the brokers and a loyal and responsive capital base in the membership.

We at Lloyd's are heirs to a famous name but we are only life tenants and it is up to us to see that when we hand on our inheritance, it is more highly regarded even than today. The basic challenges which the Council faces is how to galvanise the separate entities which together make up Lloyd's in such a way that we can take the fullest advantage of our name.

With these objectives in mind I believe we can retain sound stewardship of this Society and pass it on to our successors, maybe changed, but still as the recognised "Insurers to the World".

LLOYD'S OF LONDON

The most famous insurance market in the world has many facets. It is at once a society of underwriters, a corporation, a world centre of marine intelligence and an important specialist publishing house for maritime and legal affairs.

No other market is so individual and yet so comprehensive. Dating back to the coffee house days of marine underwriting, Lloyd's is still made up of syndicates, or groups of underwriters, who specialise in various types of risk. Still pre-eminent in marine insurance, Lloyd's underwriters today insure oil rigs and submersibles along with cargo vessels and giant supertankers. Lloyd's aviation market insures space satellites as well as the world's leading airlines, while its non-marine underwriters deal in everything from petro-chemical plants to footballer's legs, and such complex and sophisticated types of business as bank insurance and political expropriation.

For three centuries, Lloyd's reputation has depended on both the integrity and the pioneering skill and inventiveness of its underwriters, who are in turn linked closely to the brokers who place the world's risks with them. One 19th century Lloyd's man, asked to define the nature of the market, is said to have replied simply, *"Individually we are underwriters. Collectively we are Lloyd's"*. As a description of one of the world's most remarkable business institutions, his words have not been bettered.

From Coffee House to Corporation

Coffee houses were an institution in 17th century London. Of the 300 said to have existed in Charles II's time, most had a specific clientele. For the poets and wits there was the Bedford in Covent Garden, for the doctors there was Child's near St. Pauls, and for the City merchants there were a score of coffee houses in the network of small alleys round the Royal Exchange.

After the Great Fire of London new centres of commerce began to develop further east, and in Tower Street — part of what is now Eastcheap — Edward Lloyd opened his coffee house in the 1680s. Partly because of its location near the river, it became a meeting place for merchants concerned with the insurance of ships and their cargoes.

At that time there were no insurance companies as we now know them. The practice was for underwriters — so-called because they signed their names underneath the wording of policies — to guarantee commercial ventures on an individual basis. Lloyd's coffee house became recognised as a likely place for shipowners to find underwriters and Edward Lloyd was quick to encourage the increased custom which thus came his way.

Over the next century the rough and ready arrangements of the coffee house became steadily more formal. Until then Lloyd's had had something of the atmosphere of a private club, but now this was to be altered by restrictions on membership, by the introduction of subscriptions and by extensions of the power of the Committee. These developments were reflected in an Act of Parliament granting Incorporation in 1871. This has been amended by further Acts in 1911, 1951 and 1982.

Lloyd's is a unique society, whose members transact insurance business on an individual basis, at the same time providing a market for worldwide insurance risks. The modern Corporation does not accept insurance — any more than Edward Lloyd did — nor does it assume liability for the business transacted by its members. Its role is to provide the premises, to see that the rules of the Council are kept and to administer the numerous and complex supporting services.

he Market

The heart of Lloyd's is a single room known as simply 'the Room'. What the visitor es, once he has taken in its size, splendour and high-tech design, is a vast number of eople sitting, mostly in groups of seven or eight at boxes.

Each box is the place of business — one might almost say the pitch in the market — f an underwriter, who may be writing business for a syndicate of several hundred eople. These, known as underwriting 'names' or members, provide through their ersonal resources the financial capacity the underwriter needs to take on business.

Lloyd's syndicates — they include marine, non-marine, aviation and motor — have ver 31,000 underwriting members between them. The marine market at Lloyd's mains the world's pre-eminent insurance centre for this class of business. Huge ams of cover are sought not only for conventional fleets but for the oil rigs, VLCCs d container ships which are the modern equivalent of the barques and schooners sured in the coffee house.

Most people associate the name of Lloyd's primarily with marine insurance, but owadays most of its premium income is derived from non-marine sources. This evelopment is above all due to Cuthbert Heath, who in the latter part of the 19th ntury wrote, among other pioneering risks, the first jewellers' block policy, the first urglary insurance and the first loss of profits cover.

The first aviation insurance was accepted at Lloyd's in 1911, and the aviation arket now has an annual premium income exceeding £540m., the insurances of the eets of most leading world airlines being placed at Lloyd's. Motor insurance, xcluding overseas business, accounts for over £480m. of the total premium income f Lloyd's underwriters.

Between them these various markets make not only a sizeable profit for Lloyd's ndicates but a massive contribution to the invisible exports so vital to the nation's onomy.

Lloyd's tradition is not observed merely for its own sake. The underwriters' boxes e not just quaint survivals; they are the modern means by which Lloyd's, bearing in ind the price of accommodation in the City of London, manages to be so cost-fective. Another useful conversion of tradition to modern use is the process by hich brokers in the Room may contact colleagues. Known as 'calling', this dates ack to the coffee house where a boy called 'the Kidney' read notices from a pulpit. oday the method consists of a waiter calling the name over a microphone; once a roker hears his name called, he will go to the nearest video screen in the Room where e will find a message telling him to contact a colleague or his office.

No description of the Room would be complete without a mention of its most mous symbol, the Lutine Bell, Originally belonging to the frigate HMS *Lutine*, hich was lost in 1799 with all hands and a valuable cargo, the bell hangs in the aller's rostrum. Traditionally the ringing of the bell meant that an announcement as to follow about the loss or safe arrival of a vessel known to be overdue — the aim eing to inform all underwriters simultaneously of important news, so that none had e advantage of special knowledge. Since the development of modern ommunications, however, the bell is now seldom rung except on ceremonial casions.

Of the innumerable number of people likely to be engaged in business at any oment in the Room, roughly half are brokers. Insurance may only be placed in the arket through one of the 263 firms accredited as Lloyd's brokers, who are an ssential link in the chain between the insured and the undewriter. The broker, in lacing a risk, represents his client, not the underwriter, and it is his task to obtain the est terms possible for him.

Good faith between broker and underwriter is essential. Their mutual confidence is

exemplified by the 'slip', a piece of paper bearing the basic details of the risk to ▌
placed. In the first instance this slip is the only paper evidence of their agreement, y
despite this simplicity, a broker knows that if a slip bears an underwriter's initials
bona fide claim will be honoured. The prompt payment of claims by Lloyd
underwriters following the San Francisco earthquake of 1906, while many oth
insurers defaulted, serves as a prime example of how the name of Lloyd's has come
be identified with that most vital requirement for the insurer — a reputation for payir
claims promptly.

The New Lloyd's

Through the years, and especially since its first Act of Incorporation, the mark
has grown many times over. In 1928 Lloyd's moved from the Royal Exchange to ne
quarters, designed by Sir Edwin Cooper on the site of the old East India House
Leadenhall Street. Thirty years later it moved to the Lime Street building, which wา
opened by HM The Queen Mother in November 1957.

In 1978 Lloyd's again faced the prospect of unacceptable overcrowding of tl
market, and a decision was taken to commission the eminent architect Richard Roge
to design a new home for Lloyd's which would enable the market to grow whi
maintaining the concept of a single Underwriting Room well into the next centur
Opened by HM The Queen in November 1986, the new Lloyd's has attracted hug
admiration and interest in architectural circles world-wide.

Rogers' design is dominated by the great atrium rising through twelve floors and ▌
by the arched window which makes it a landmark across the City. Communicatior
between the four floors which make up the Underwriting Room is by means
escalators. These, with the open galleries, ensure that the long established concept
a single Underwriting Room is retained. The 'calling' and broker's location syste:
provides effective communications in a room located on five different floors. By tl
same token intelligence and other information is posted on each gallery of the marke

Lloyd's has always been the home of innovation but has also derived its strength l
regard for its traditions. It is a happy circumstance, therefore, that the great rostrur
from the Edwin Cooper Room was found to be in excellent condition after nearly ะ
years in store. It now stands under the atrium and is yet again a natural centre to tl
Room, accommodating the Lutine Bell and the caller.

Membership

What are the conditions under which someone may become an underwritir
member of Lloyd's? In the past membership was restricted to British-born men, b
nowadays it has been widened to include men and women of any nationalit
Members must be prepared to transact business with unlimited personal liability, ar
are required to satisfy the Committee as to their integrity and financial standing. Eac
underwriting member or 'name' must also furnish security in an approved form, to l
held in trust by the Corporation of Lloyd's, the amount varying according to tl
volume of business to be transacted on his behalf.

Members must also agree to pay all premiums into Premium Trust Funds, fro
which only claims, expenses and ascertained profits may be paid. They must al:
contribute to a Central Fund, which is intended to meet a member's underwritir
liabilities in the unlikely event of his security and personal assets being insufficient
meet his losses. The Central Fund, now amounting to over £300m., is for tl
protection of the assured, not the underwriting member, who remains responsible f
his liabilities to the full extent of his personal fortune.

A further requirement is that all underwriting members must submit to the Annu
Solvency Audit — the first link in the chain of security around the Lloyd's policy. F

means of the Audit a member must show that the value of his underwriting assets is enough to meet his liabilities for all classes of business, estimated according to the Audit regulations.

The Audit is designed to detect any weakness in a member's position. Setting adequate reserves at a level to give margins of security, it is conducted by an auditor approved by the Council, whose certificate must also be approved by the Department of Trade.

Managing the Market

Lloyd's is governed by a Council of 28 people, made up of twelve members who are active in the market, eight non-working members, and another eight outsiders nominated by the Council and approved by the Governor of the Bank of England. Among the nominated members is a Chief Executive who has the status of a Deputy Chairman of Lloyd's.

The new Council of Lloyd's is an autonomous body unique in the government of financial institutions. Though it has considerable regulatory, and if need be, disciplinary powers, it follows the examples of its forerunners in intervening as little as possible in the day-to-day business of the market. It is responsible for the election of new underwriting members, and makes it its business to keep constant watch on the financial stability of both brokers and underwriters. As the governing body of Lloyd's, it is also concerned with putting the market's special viewpoint to the Department of Trade, to the EEC and to foreign governments in whose territories Lloyd's conducts its worldwide business.

In the past all insurance policies at Lloyd's were signed by the individual underwriters, who accepted a share of the risks. Today this function is performed by Lloyd's Policy Signing Office — LPSO — a group within the Corporation, under the control of a Board of Management responsible to the Committee of Lloyd's. LPSO provides a range of services to underwriters and brokers including the checking of policies, endorsements, etc., with brokers' slips, signing them on behalf of all subscribing syndicates and embossing them with the LPSO seal.

In 1961 a system of central accounting for the Lloyd's market was introduced, based on details provided by LPSO. Settlement is made centrally each month on the agreed figures issued by the Office. In 1978 LPSO moved out of London to Gun Wharf at Chatham, Kent, where a new Lloyd's building now stands close to the historic dockyard. Lloyd's Management Services Group is also based at Chatham, while Lloyd's of London Press, including Lloyd's Intelligence Department has its head office in Colchester.

Networking at the new Lloyd's

Lloyd's is currently engaged in a revolution in information technology which will enable it both to generate more business and to improve the quality of service to its clients. In 1988 — the tercentenary of the first recorded mention of Edward Lloyd's coffee house — the Lloyd's Community made an investment of £125m in technology which included the London Insurance Market Network, known as LIMNET. A key step in this major programme will be the introduction of a fully computerised claims service from mid-1990 onwards. By January 1991 it is planned that all claims will be handled by the new means.

The year 1989 saw the extension of electronic networking to LPSO. Premiums and policy advices, previously recorded on punched cards and magnetic tape, are now also transmitted direct to the market from the LPSO computers. Reducing paperwork, duplication and distribution costs, electronic networking will, over the next few years, set a high standard of streamlined communications for the new Lloyd's.

LLOYD'S OF LONDON PRESS PUBLICATIONS AND SERVICES

SHIPPING INTELLIGENCE FOR THE WORLD

The origins of Lloyd's of London Press as the world's foremost authority on maritime information began in a modest coffee house overst 300 years ago.

When Edward Lloyd opened his doors, ships' captains, merchants,shipowners and underwriters filed in from the taverns, inns and street to discuss transactions and snippets of news. Lloyd's coffee house quickly established itself as a trustworthy source of maritime news; Edward Lloyd sending runners to the docks for information and publishing their findings in **Lloyd's News** (the forerunner of **Lloyd's List International**), first produced in 1696.

With this unrivalled source of shipping information Edward Lloyd assured himself of immortality as the founder of an autonomous society of underwriters which developed into Lloyd's of London.

Over the ensuing three hundred years the need for reliable shipping information both within Lloyd's and amongst thousands of other shipping related companies throughout the world has grown steadily.

From sailing ships to space ships

To meet this ever growing need for information on all aspects of maritime activity the Corporation of Lloyd's centralised data collection into a wholly new company as the publishing and intelligence arm of the Corporation.

From those early days of billowing sail and manual printing to today's satellites and computers, Lloyd's of London Press have kept abreast of technological developments to offer a service second to none.

Order in a sea of information

To gain a full appreciation of the international scope of Lloyd's of London Press, one needs to comprehend the vast amount of raw information processed by the Company's computer operators 24 hours a day, 7 days a week, 52 weeks a year.

Cataloguing information on the movements of over 44,000 vessels, Lloyd's of London Press receive some 110,000 messages every year detailing 2 million shipping movements, forming a unique information service not only to marine underwriters but to the shipping community at large.

The intelligence network which makes all this possible consists of 1,800 agents, sub-agents and special correspondents in ports around the world.

The oracle of sea facts

The capacity of Lloyd's of London Press to not only collect and collate information but also to process the raw data into relevant publications depends to a large extent upon the capabilities of its computer systems. The Company is a forerunner in the development and implementation of the latest communications technology from satellite stations to viewdata.

Data to digest

As the need for accurate information on which to base future commercial policies has grown, LLP has diversified to meet the demands of thousands of companies and now offers information not only in print form but also on computer tapes, computer printout, on-line data bases and viewdata. The data can be made available on a regular or *ad hoc* basis either as raw information or with professional analysis from the Intelligence Department or Lloyd's Maritime Information Services.

Read all about it

Flagship of the LLP publications is **Lloyd's List International**, which followed the news-sheet **Lloyd's News** in 1734. Originally published twice a week, with shipping and business news collected for the benefit of Lloyd's coffee house clients, it is today a thriving international daily newspaper, with a circulation in excess of 15,000 and a readership of over 70,000. In two and a half centuries it has been joined by well over 160 other titles.

These range from the daily **Lloyd's Shipping Index**, the "bible" of current voyage information which logs positions of nearly 24,000 merchant vessels, and the weekly directory **Lloyd's Loading List**, "bible" of the UK freighting industry, to the analytical **Lloyd's Shipping Economist** and the learned **Lloyd's Law Reports**. In between are dozens of weekly and monthly magazines, directories and annuals, notably **Lloyd's Nautical Year Book** and the prestigious family of **Lloyd's Diaries**.

Today, with over 160 titles, LLP is the leading publisher of periodicals and books for the business, finance, insurance, shipping and transportation community worldwide — businesses whose activities are so closely linked by trade and intermodalism.

Step to the future

Most of the increase in hard copy publications has been made since LLP was formed as a Company in 1973 — when only 13 titles existed.

However in keeping with the Company's progressive policy of development, the greatest stride has been into electronic publishing.

Now on-line viewdata services such as **Ships Latest Position**, providing up-to-date movements of over 25,000 deepsea merchant vessels and **British Isles Port Data**, presenting a picture of ships berthed and expected at every significant port of Great Britain and Ireland are available.

The latest offering is **Lloyd's Transpotel**, a massive electronic freighting information system linking major European countries which, in a joint venture with Maritime Cargo Processing has launched an EDI service for the electronic transmission of standard international trade documents.

For further information of LLP publishing activities and services contact:
The Manager,
Sales & Marketing,
Lloyd's of London Press Limited,
Sheepen Place, Colchester,
Essex CO3 3LP, England.
Tel: 0206 772277
Telex: 987321 LLOYDS G
Facsimilie 0206 46273 Group 2/3

LLOYD'S INTELLIGENCE DEPARTMENT

The function of Lloyd's Intelligence Department is to gather and process information of interest to the insurance and shipping communities.

The vast majority of the messages received in the Department contain shippping movement information which is disseminated to the market at Lloyd's and through publications produced by Lloyd's of London Press Ltd. In the course of a year, the Department receives over two million movements of shipping, and maintains information on excess of 44,000 vessels. This data is also stored for historical purposes on a computer database and can be provided to subscribers in the form of magnetic tape or computer printout.

The developments and accessibility of communication systems worldwide now enables the Department to maintain almost instantaneous contact with the majority of Lloyd's Agents who maintain coverage of shipping activity at over 1800 ports.

The information received over the computerised telex installation in the Intelligence Department consists both of movements of ships and of casualties on a global scale. It is necessary therefore to maintain a staff throughout the day and night to ensure that messages reporting incidents of a serious or immediate nature are actioned without delay.

Much of the casualty information is gleaned from Lloyd's Agents who are often notified of vessels in distress by local radio stations, harbour officials, ships' agents, etc., while, around the shores of the British Isles, the coast radio stations and the worldwide station at Portishead telex direct to Lloyd's all news of vessels in need of assistance. Similarly, Coastguard Rescue Centres worldwide keep Lloyd's advised with news of casualties. It is immaterial whether a casualty is insured at Lloyd's, the information gathered is made available on a worldwide scale for the benefit of the insurance and shipping community.

Other sources of information are Lloyd's brokers who by tradition inform the Intelligence Department of any reports they might receive; also The Salvage Association who, together with the Intelligence Department, have a common interest in protecting Underwriters' interests.

Service to the Underwriting Room

During office hours edited casualty reports are transmitted by landline from the Department's Colchester offices to London, for display in the Underwriting Room at Lloyd's in order that the marine insurance market may be aware of vessels in casualty. In the course of a year, over 14,000 reports will be displayed. This same information is published in concise form daily in Lloyd's List.

If the incident is of a sufficiently serious nature which may result in either the loss of, or extensive damage to the vessel so that she may become a potential loss, an entry is made in the Casualty Book which stands at the centre of the Underwriting Room so that the market is aware of the seriousness of the case. There have been many historic entries made in the book like *Titanic, Flying Enterprise, Torrey Canyon, Amoco Cadiz* and *Salem*, to name but a few. Entries in the Book are still made using a quill pen. Also in the Underwriting room is the Lutine Bell, which is rung on the instructions of the Manager of the Intelligence Department when definite news of an overdue vessel is received, on which the reinsurance rate has reached a certain percentage. It is then necessary to notify every Member in the Underwriting Room at the same time regarding either the safety or loss of the vessel concerned. One ring is given for bad news and two for good news

As a result of arrangements made by the Department comprehensive aircraft casualty reports are received from Lloyd's Agents, Government Departments and other authoritative sources. A service is also provided to the non-marine market and includes reports of serious fires, strikes, robberies involving heavy losses and damage to industrial areas, crops, etc., by flood, storm or earthquake. Both these Aviation and non-marine reports are displayed in the Underwriting Room for the benefit of market underwriters. This information is also made available in the columns of the Casualty Page of Lloyd's List.

Search and Rescue

Owners and other interested parties who are concerned about the safety of a vessel because of non-arrival in port or absence of radio communication are advised to contact the Intelligence Department which has facilities for broadcasts to be made to shipping requesting later news.

Lloyd's Agents and search and rescue organisations can also be alerted. During search operations, the Department maintains a constant liaison with rescue authorities and owners.

Casualty Reporting Service

Since the Department is manned 24 hours a day, it is in a unique position to offer a continuous casualty reporting service to shipowners, tug and salvage companies, dock and repair yards and the world's press. Lloyd's is recognised by the authorities as being the organisation best equipped for informing tug companies of casualties and the Intelligence Department has arrangements with tug companies throughout the world for them to be notified in the event of a casualty occurring in areas in which their tugs are operating.

Further details of services provided by the Department are available from:

Lloyd's Intelligence Department,
Sheepen Place,
Colchester, Essex CO3 3LP, England.
Telephone: 0206 772277. Telex: 987321 LLOYDS G. Cables: LLOYDS LONDON EC3.
Facsimilie: 0206 46273 Group 2/3.

LLOYD'S MARITIME INFORMATION SERVICES

Lloyd's Maritime Information Services Ltd. is a joint venture company owned by Lloyd's Register of Shipping and Lloyd's of London Press Ltd., and was founded in 1986 to enable the maritime community to have access to what is probably the largest source of commercially available shipping information worldwide. The data gathering network encompases the Lloyd's Register Offices in over a hundred countries worldwide, together with the 1800 Lloyd's Agents and Sub-agents in principle ports throughout the world, government departments, ship owners, and other authorative sources.

Information is maintained on six large computer data bases, providing coverage of over 75,000 self-propelled sea-going merchant ships of 100 gross tonnage and above, comprising the world merchant fleet plus those that are on order or under construction, together with movements and ownership details, all referenced by the unique Lloyd's Register identity number:

- New Construction — 2800 vessels on file.
- Ship Particulars — Approximately 150 key data items for the merchant fleet of 75,000 vessels.
- Ship Movements — Reported current movements of 30,000 merchant vessels, plus voyage histories back to 1 January 1976.
- Charter Fixtures — Over 100,000 fixtures — cargoes, vessels, rates, charterers — since 1 January 1986.
- Ship Owners and Parent Companies — Over 40,000 Registered Owners, Managers, and Parent Companies with address details.
- Ship Casualties and Demolition — All reported tanker incidents, plus all reported serious casualties for other vessels.

Information can be provided on-line, by computer tape or diskette for input into the clients' own computer system and by hard copy. Special watch and tracker services are offered to monitor the movements of specific vessels. A telephone enquiry service is available for the latest information on ship owners, ship names, casualties, etc. Lloyd's Maritime also has access to vast amounts of historical and other Maritime information which is also made available to clients.

Lloyd's Maritime provides information services, high level consultancy, and multi-subscriber products to a very wide client base in shipping, transport, energy, law, finance, insurance, research and other business throughout the world. The services are utilised in the following ways:

Sales and marketing

Operations

Research & Development

Consultancy

On-line Services

Lloyd's Maritime offer three on-line services:

Seadata is an on-line retrieval system allowing access to all available Lloyd's Maritime files except charter fixtures, for look-up and ship-type search facilities. Once connected to the system, users may switch from file to file. Seadata is available to subscribers on-line at remote locations using terminals, micro-computers and teletypes capable of a variety of emulations, which are supported through protocol converters.

Mardata combines the benefits of on line retrieval with a power statistical and analytical capability. Mardata may be accessed by a wide variety of terminals including telex, personal computers or word processing systems equipped with communication modems from more than 750 metropolitan centres in 25 countries, using the General Electric Mark III Communications Network.

Viewdata Provides the latest report of movements of the Sea-going merchant fleet, which can be searched by vessel type, on either port or ship name. Information includes, flag, deadweight, voyage, and latest reported position.

The service also provides the complete picture of ships berthed and expected at every significant port in Great Britain and Ireland.

Shipping Economics Advisory Group

This Division within Lloyd's Maritime provides high level business consultancy services, specialising in the strategic, economic and commercial aspects of shipping and its related industries. Multi-subscriber services are also provided, including monthly tanker reports, tanker and dry bulk market forecasts, oil industry and liner trade analysis.

For further information on Lloyd's Maritime services please contact:

Steve Clayton or Peter Whyman, Lloyd's Maritime, One Singer Street, London EC2A 4LQ, England.
Telephone: (01)-490 1720. Telex: 987321 LLOYDS G. Facsimile: (01)-250 3142.

or

Roland Ellen, Lloyd's Maritime, Collwyn House, Sheepen Place, Colchester, Essex CO3 3LP, England.
Telephone: (0206) 772277. Fax: 0206 46273 (Group 111).
Telex 987321 LLOYDS G.

or

Kathleen O'Connell, Lloyd's Maritime, 1200 Summer Street, Stamford CT 06905, United States. Telephone (203)-359 8383. Fax: 203-358 0437.

or

our agencies in Hong Kong, telephone: (5)-854-1538; Japan, telephone: (03)-435-5477; Australia, telephone: (02) 262 1424; Finland, telephone: (921) 334133 or Greece, telephone: (01) 413 1098.

LLOYD'S INSURANCE BROKERS

All Lloyd's insurance brokers are members of the British Insurance & Investment Brokers' Association of which they form a separate Region. The Regional Committee which looks after matters affecting Lloyd's brokers is the Lloyd's Insurance Brokers' Committee. The BIIBA and the LIBC are at:

Biiba House, 14 Bevis Marks, London EC3A 7NT, England. Tel (01) 623 9043.

On 6 May 1990 the London area telephone code 01 will change. 071 for inner London; 081 for outer London. See pages 10 and 11.

A.A. Commercial Insurance Brokers Ltd
Prince Consort House, 27 Albert Embankment, London SE1 7TF. England. Tel (01) 582 5244. Tx 923006.

Adam Brothers Contingency Ltd
15 St. Helen's Place, London, EC3A 6AB, England. Tel (01) 638 3211. Tx 889209.

Aldgate Insurance Brokers (Marine) Ltd
Sedgwick Centre, London E1 8DX, England. Tel (01) 377 3456. Tx 882131.

Alexander & Alexander Ltd
22 Billiter Street, London EC3A 2SA, England. Tel (01) 488 0808. Tx 882171.

Alexander Stenhouse Ltd
PO Box 214, 10 Devonshire Square, London EC2M 4LE, England. Tel (01) 621 9990. Tx 920368.

Alsford Page & Gems Ltd
81 Fenchurch Street, London EC3M 4BT, England. Tel (01) 481 4411. Tx 8951937.

Alwen Hough Johnson Ltd
Latham House, 16 Minories, London EC3N 1AN, England. Tel (01) 480 5454. Tx 883730.

Anslow-Wilson & Amery Ltd
9-13 Fenchurch Buildings, London EC3M 5HR, England. Tel (01) 488 0622. Tx 8953680.

APS International Ltd
Walsingham House, 35 Seething Lane, London EC3N 4AH, England. Tel (01) 488 3288. Tx 929124.

B&C Aviation Insurance & Reinsurance Brokers Ltd
6 Alie Street, London E1 8DD, England. Tel (01) 488 9000. Tx 8811401.

B&C Insurance Brokers Ltd
32/38 Dukes Place, London EC3A 7LX, England. Tel (01) 626 4393. Tx 886191.

B&C Insurance Brokers (UK) Ltd
6 Alie Street, London E1 8DD, England. Tel (01) 488 9000. Tx 8811401.

B&C Marine Brokers Ltd
6 Alie Street, London E1 8DD, England. Tel (01) 488 9000. Tx 8811401.

B&C Non-Marine Brokers Ltd
6 Alie Street, London E1 8DD, England. Tel (01) 488 9000. Tx 8811401.

Babets Ltd
Brunning House, 100 Whitechapel Road, London E1 1JB, England. Tel (01) 377 9311.

Bain Clarkson Ltd
Bain Dawes House, 15 Minories, London EC3N 1NJ, England. Tel (01) 481 3232. Tx 8813411.

Ballantyne, McKean & Sullivan Ltd
Latham House, 16 Minories, London EC3N 1AN, England. Tel (01) 480 7288. Tx 8956198.

Bankamerica Insurance Brokers Ltd
25 Cannon Street, London EC4P 4HN, England. Tel (01) 634 4357. Tx 888412/5.

John Bannerman Ltd
35 Wellington Street, Covent Garden, London WC2E 7BP, England. Tel (01) 836 1023.

Barclays Insurance Brokers International Ltd
Capital House, 42 Weston Street, London SE1 3QA, England. Tel (01) 378 6410. Tx 883012.

Robert Barrow Ltd
24/26 Minories, London EC3N 1BY, England. Tel (01) 709 9611. Tx 885576.

Bell & Clements Ltd
2 London Wall Buildings, London Wall, London EC2M 5PP, England. Tel (01) 628 1414.

Bell Nicholson Henderson Ltd
12-14 Folgate Street, London E1 6BX, England. Tel (01) 377 1800. Tx 883516.

Benfield, Lovick & Rees Co Ltd
5th Floor, Chesterfield House, 26-28 Fenchurch Street, London EC3M 3DQ, England. Tel (01) 626 5432. Tx 884687.

Bennett Gould & Partners Ltd
4 London Wall Building, Blomfield Street,
London EC2M 5NT, England.
Tel (01) 588 8052. Tx 887800.

Berisford Mocatta & Co Ltd
47 Mark Lane, London EC3R 7QH,
England.
Tel (01) 481 9144. Tx 8814740.

Berry Palmer & Lyle Ltd
24/26 Minories, London EC3N 1BY,
England.
Tel (01) 265 1921. Tx 928459.

J Besso & Co
Besso House, 401 Mile End Road, London
E3 4PD, England.
Tel (01) 980 7290. Tx 938046.

Alfred Blackmore & Co Ltd
25 Eastcheap, London EC3M 1DE,
England.
Tel (01) 283 2525. Tx 884183.

Blackwell Green Ltd
4 Botolph Alley, London EC3R 8DR,
England.
Tel (01) 626 5161. Tx 888387.

Blake Marston Priest Ltd
52 Station Road, Egham, Surrey TW20
9LB, England.
Tel (0784) 31213.

E.W. Blanch (U.K.) Ltd
Bevis Marks House, 24-25 Bevis Marks,
London EC3A 7JB, England.
Tel (01) 621 9067. Tx 888906.

Bland Welch & Co Ltd
The Sedgwick Centre, 10 Whitechapel
High Street, London E1 8DX, England.
Tel (01) 377 3456. Tx 882131.

C.T. Bowring & Co (Insurance) Ltd
PO Box 145, The Bowring Building, Tower
Place, London EC3P 3BE, England.
Tel (01) 283 3100. Tx 888321.

C.T. Bowring Reinsurance Ltd
PO Box 145, The Bowring Building, Tower
Place, London EC3P 3BE, England.
Tel (01) 283 3100. Tx 888321.

Frank Bradford & Co Ltd
Artillery House, 35 Artillery Lane, London
E1 9LR, England.
Tel (01) 407 7144. Tx 88870

Robt. Bradford & Co Ltd
2 London Bridge, London SE1 9RB,
England.
Tel (01) 403 1234. Tx 884944.

Robt. Bradford Hobbs Savill Ltd
2 London Bridge, London SE1 9RB,
England.
Tel (01) 403 1234. Tx 884944.

Bradstock, Blunt & Crawley Ltd
58-59 Fenchurch Street, London EC3M
4AB, England.
Tel (01) 436 7878. Tx 884234.

Bradstock, Blunt & Thompson Ltd
52/53 Russell Square, London WC1B 4HP,
England.
Tel (01) 436 7878. Tx 881218.

**T.A. Braithwaite & Associates (Insurance
Brokers) Ltd**
107 Cannon Street, London EC4N 5AD,
England.
Tel (01) 283 3996. Tx 8955359.

Brown Shipley Insurance Brokers Ltd
4 Heron Quay, London E14 9XE, England.
Tel (01) 538 8810. Tx 883675.

Derek Bryant Insurance Brokers Ltd
39 Botolph Lane, London EC3R 8DE,
England.
Tel (01) 623 0011. Tx 884006.

J.K. Buckenham Ltd
Chesterfield House, 26/28 Fenchurch
Street, London EC3M 3DQ, England.
Tel (01) 929 1754. Tx 883920.

Norman Butcher & Jones Group Ltd
120-122 Southwark Street, London SE1
0SU, England.
Tel (01) 928 7654. Tx 919146.

Butcher Robinson & Staples Ltd
Collegiate House, St. Thomas Street,
London SE1 9RY, England.
Tel (01) 407 0626. Tx 8814885.

Butcher Robinson & Staples International Ltd
Collegiate House, St. Thomas Street,
London SE1 9RY.
England.
Tel (01) 929 7797.

Byas, Mosley & Co Ltd
William Byas House, 14-18 Clare Street,
London EC3N 1JX. England.
Tel (01) 481 0101. Tx 894266.

**Cameron Richard and Smith Insurance
Services Ltd**
Boundary House, 7-17 Jewry Street,
London EC3N 2HP, England.
Tel (01) 488 4554. Tx 923007.

Carritt & Partners Ltd
14 Fenchurch Avenue, London EC3N 5BS,
England.
Tel (01) 626 2641. Tx 8813423.

Carter, Wilkes & Fane Ltd
Bevis Marks House, 24-25 Bevis Marks,
London EC3A 7JB, England.
Tel (01) 621 9067. Tx 888906.

R.K. Carvill & Co Ltd
St. Helen's, 1 Undershaft, London EC3P
3DQ, England.
Tel (01) 929 2800. Tx 8952946.

Chandler Hargreaves Ltd
Chandler House, 5-7 Marshalsea Road,
London SE1 1EF, England.
Tel (01) 407 8000. Tx 883973.

Citicorp Insurance Brokers Ltd
St. Clare House, 30-33 Minories, London
EC3N 1DD, England.
Tel (01) 488 1388. Tx 883485.

Citicorp Insurance Brokers (Marine) Ltd
1 Seething Lane, London EC3N 4NH,
England.
Tel (01) 481 9090. Tx 883756.

Clarkson Puckle Ltd
Ibex House, Minories, London EC3N 1HQ,
England.
Tel (01) 709 0744. Tx 883808.

Denis M. Clayton & Co Ltd
Landmark House, 69 Leadenhall Street,
London EC3A 2AD England.
Tel (01) 480 6410. Tx 884600.

Colburn, French and Kneen
19/21 Great Tower Street, London EC3R
5AQ, England.
Tel (01) 626 5644. Tx 883289.

C.J. Coleman & Co Ltd
155-157 Minories, London EC3N 1BT,
England.
Tel (01) 488 2211. Tx 8811661.

Cooper, Gay & Co Ltd
Cereal House, Mark Lane, London EC3R
7NE, England.
Tel (01) 480 7322. Tx 885717.

Cork Bays & Fisher Ltd
10 Chaterhouse Square, London EC1M 6JS,
England.
Tel (01) 250 3456. Tx 22501.

Corrie Bauckham Batts Stickland Ltd
Portsoken House, 155 Minories, London
EC3N 1BT, England.
Tel (01) 480 6587. Tx 884326.

Craven Farmer Ltd
10 Lloyd's Avenue, London EC3N 3AX,
England.
Tel (01) 481 4941. Tx 8812186.

Crawley, Warren & Co Ltd
8 Lloyd's Avenue, London EC3N 3HD,
England.
Tel (01) 488 1414. Tx 8956151.

Credit Insurance Association Ltd
13 Grosvenor Place, London SW1X 7HH,
England.
Tel (01) 235 3550.

**Credit & Political Risks Reinsurance Brokers
Ltd**
13 Grosvenor Place, London SW1X 7HH,
England.
Tel (01) 235 3550.

Crowley Colosso Ltd
Ibex House, Minories, London EC3N 1JJ,
England.
Tel: (01) 782 9782. Tx 887441.

Cullis Raggett Ltd
Cityside, Adler Street, London E1 1EN,
England.
Tel (01) 375 1881. Tx 9413579.

Dashwood, Brewer & Phipps Ltd
Independent House, 7 Cutler Street,
London E1 7DJ, England.
Tel (01) 626 3711. Tx 885410.

R.L. Davison & Co.Ltd
5 Stone House Court, London, EC3A 7AX,
England.
Tel (01) 377 9876. Tx 893467.

SBJ Devitt Ltd
100 Whitechapel Road, London E1 1JP,
England.
Tel (01) 247 8888. Tx 886129.

Dewey Warren & Co Ltd
9-10 St. Mary at Hill, London EC3R 8EE,
England.
Tel (01) 626 0982.

D.G. Durham & Co Ltd
Black Lion House, 31-55 Whitechapel
Road, London E1 1DU, England.
Tel (01) 377 0220. Tx 884639.

D.G. Durham International Ltd
Black Lion House. 31-55 Whitechapel
Road, London E1 1DU, England.
Tel (01) 377 0220. Tx 884639.

Durtnell & Fowler Ltd
10 Trinity Square, London EC3P 3AX,
England.
Tel (01) 488 8111.

Egis (International) Ltd
Enterprise House, 59/65 Upper Ground,
London SE1 9PQ, England.
Tel (01) 401 2388. Tx 888485.

Ellinger, Heath, Western & Co
Plantation House, 23 Rood Lane, London
EC3M 3AN, England.
Tel (01) 626 3733. Tx 888697.

Anthony Endersby Ltd
Bankside House, 107/112 Leadenhall
Street, London EC3A 4AR, England.
Tel (01) 929 2899. Tx 887325.

Euings (London) Ltd
The Sedgwick Centre, 10 Whitechapel
High Street, London E1 8DX, England.
Tel (01) 377 3456. Tx 882131.

Evans-Lombe, Aston & Co Ltd
38 Borough High Street, London SE1,
England.
Tel (01) 403 3355. Tx 8813669.

Fenchurch Aviation Brokers Ltd
136 Minories, London EC3N 1QN,
England.
Tel (01) 488 2388. Tx 887004.

Fenchurch Insurance Brokers Ltd
89-111 High Road, South Woodford,
London E18 2RH, England.
Tel (01) 505 3333. Tx 897309.

Fenchurch International Ltd
136 Minories, London EC3N 1QN,
England.
Tel (01) 488 2388. Tx 887004.

Fenchurch International Reinsurance Brokers Ltd
136 Minories, London EC3N 1QN, England.
Tel (01) 488 2388. Tx 887004.

Fenchurch Marine Brokers Ltd
136 Minories, London EC3N 1QN, England.
Tel (01) 488 2388. Tx 887004.

Fenchurch North America Ltd
136 Minories, London EC3N 1QN, England.
Tel (01) 488 2388. Tx 887004.

Fenchurch Scott Reinsurance Brokers Ltd
142 Minories, London EC3N 1BH, England.
Tel (01) 488 4525. Tx 883712.

Fielding, Juggins, Money & Stewart Ltd
1 Pepys Street, London EC3N 2PL, England.
Tel (01) 488 1488. Tx 8812615/6.

Robert Bruce Fitzmaurice Ltd
Byward House, 16 Byward Street, London EC3R 5BA, England.
Tel (01) 480 5158. Tx 8955710.

Robert Fleming Insurance Brokers Ltd
Staple Hall, Stone House Court, London EC3A 7AX, England.
Tel (01) 621 1263. Tx 883735.

Robert Fraser Insurancce Brokers Ltd
Brooks House, Brooks Wharf, Upper Thames Street, London EC4V 3DE, England.
Tel (01) 248 6455. Tx 894262.

Frizzell Insurance annd Financial Services Ltd
Frizzell House, 14-22 Elder Street, London E1 6DF, England.
Tel (01) 247 6595. Tx 8811077.

Frizzell International Ltd
Frizzell House, 14-22 Elder Street, London E1 6DF, England.
Tel (01) 247 6595. Tx 8811077.

Frizzell Professional Indemnity Ltd
Frizzell House, 14-22 Elder Street, London E1 6DF, England.
Tel (01) 247 6595. Tx 8811077.

Frizzell UK Ltd
Frizzell House, 14-22 Elder Street, London E1 6DF, England.
Tel (01) 247 6595. Tx 8811077.

Furness-Houlder (Insurance) Ltd
Bankside House, 107-112 Leadenhall Street, London EC3A 4AA, England.
Tel (01) 621 1166. Tx 884494.

Furness-Houlder Ltd
52 Leadenhall Street, London EC3A 2BR, England.
Tel (01) 508 5533. Tx 884494.

Gallagher Plumer Ltd
9 Alie Street, London E1 8DE, England.
Tel (01) 623 5511. Tx 887355.

Garratt, Son & Flowerdew Ltd
7 Winckley Square, Preston, Lancashire, England.
Tel (0772) 51841. Tx 67648.

Gault, Armstrong & Kemble Ltd
Blomfield House, 85 London Wall, London EC2M 7AD, England.
Tel (01) 638 3191. Tx 8812097.

Genavco Insurance Ltd
Genavco House, 17 Waterloo Place, London SW1Y 4AR, England.
Tel (01) 930 5331. Tx 919861.

Gibbs Hartley Cooper Ltd
Bishops Court, 27-33 Artillery Lane, London E1 7LP, England.
Tel (01) 247 5433. Tx 8950791.

Greig Fester Ltd
Regis House, 43-46 King William Street, London EC4R 9AD, England.
Tel (01) 623 3177. Tx 883206.

Guest Kreiger Ltd
21 New Street, London EC2M 4HH, England.
Tel (01) 623 6622. Tx 8953582.

David Gyngell & Co Ltd
3rd Floor, 3 Lovat Lane, London EC3, England.
Tel (01) 621 9058 Tx 883563.

Hadley Cannon (International) Ltd
32-35 Botolph Lane, London EC3R 8DE, England.
Tel (01) 623 2411. Tx 884304.

Halford Shead & Co Ltd
8 Devonshire Square, London EC2M 4PL, England.
Tel (01) 623 5500. Tx 882171.

Hall Agencies Ltd
16 Byward Street, London EC3R 5HJ, London.
Tel (01) 480 5162. Tx 892374.

Hall Harford Jeffreys Ltd
16 Byward Street, London EC3R 5HJ, England.
Tel (01) 480 5162. Tx 892374.

Edgar Hamilton Ltd
69-71 Great Eastern Street, London EC2A 3HU, England.
Tel (01) 739 4300. Tx 25866.

Hargreaves, Reiss & Quinn Ltd
10 Crispin Street, London E1, England.
Tel (01) 247 8133. Tx 884180.

Harrington, Austin Ltd
Bishopsgate House, 5-7 Folgate Street, London E1 6BX, England.
Tel (01) 377 9900. Tx 884383.

Harris & Dixon (Insurance Brokers) Ltd
  21 New Street, Bishopsgate, London EC2M
  4HR, England.
  Tel (01) 623 6622. Tx 888161.

C.E. Heath & Co (Aviation) Ltd
  Cuthbert Heath House, 150 Minories,
  London EC3N 1NR, England.
  Tel (01) 488 2488. Tx 8813001.

C.E. Heath & Co (Insurance Broking) Ltd
  Cuthbert Heath House, 150 Minories,
  London EC3N 1NR, England.
  Tel (01) 488 2488. Tx 8813001.

C.E. Heath & Co (Marine) Ltd
  Cuthbert Heath House, 150 Minories,
  London EC3N 1NR, England.
  Tel (01) 488 2488. Tx 8813001.

C.E. Heath & Co (North America) Ltd
  Cuthbert Heath House, 150 Minories,
  London EC3N 1NR, England.
  Tel (01) 488 2488. Tx 8813001.

Heath Fielding Insurance Broking Ltd
  Cuthbert Heath House, 150 Minories,
  London EC3N 1NR, England.
  Tel (01) 488 2488. Tx 8813001.

Heath Fielding Reinsurance Broking Ltd
  Cuthbert Heath House, 150 Minories,
  London EC3N 1NR, England.
  Tel (01) 488 2488. Tx 8813001.

Heath Martens Horner
  Cuthbert Heath House, 150 Minories,
  London EC3N 1NR, England.
  Tel (01) 488 2488. Tx 8813001.

Hinton Hill & Philipps Ltd
  82-86 Fenchurch Street, London EC3M
  4BY, England.
  Tel (01) 480 5152. Tx 883422.

**Hogg Robinson & Gardner Mountain
Insurance Brokers Ltd**
  Lloyd's Chambers, 1 Portsoken Street,
  London E1 8DF, England.
  Tel (01) 480 4000. Tx 884633.

Horace Holman & Co Ltd
  12 Camomile Street, London EC3A 7BP,
  England.
  Tel (01) 283 7522. Tx 8814518.

Alexander Howden Ltd
  8 Devonshire Square, London EC2M 4PL,
  England.
  Tel (01) 283 3456. Tx 882171.

Alexander Howden Group Ltd
  8 Devonshire Square, London EC2M 4PL,
  England.
  Tel (01) 623 5500. Tx 882171.

Alexander Howden Insurance Brokers Ltd 8
  Devonshire Square, London EC2M 4PL,
  England.
  Tel (01) 623 5500. Tx 882171.

Alexander Howden Reinsurance Brokers Ltd
  8 Devonshire Square, London EC2M 4PL.
  England.
  Tel (01) 623 5500. Tx 882171.

HRGM Ltd
  Lloyd's Chambers, 1 Portsoken Street,
  London E1 8DF, England.
  Tel (01) 480 4000. Tx 884633.

Hughes-Gibb & Co Ltd
  10 Trinity Square, London EC3P 3AX,
  England.
  Tel (01) 488 8111. Tx 885311.

**Nelson Hurst & Marsh (International &
Reinsurance Brokers) Ltd**
  1 Seething Lane, London EC3N 4NH,
  England.
  Tel (01) 481 9090. Tx 883756.

Nelson Hurst & March Ltd
  1 Seething Lane, London EC3N 4NH,
  England.
  Tel (01) 481 9090. Tx 883756.

Hutchison & Craft (London) Ltd
  Durham House, 38 Eastcheap, London
  EC3M 1DY, England.
  Tel (01) 621 1710. Tx 8811515.

Insurance Brokers International Ltd
  Capital House, 42 Weston Street, London
  SE1 3QD, England.
  Tel (01) 403 2600. Tx 887037.

**Investment Insurance International
(Managers) Ltd**
  Lloyd's Chambers, 1 Portsoken Street,
  London E1 8DF, England.
  Tel (01) 480 4000. Tx 884633.

T.L. Ireland & Co (Insurance Brokers) Ltd
  15-16 America Square, London EC3N 2LA,
  England.
  Tel (01) 480 7961. Tx 885758.

James Hunt DIx (Insurance) Ltd
  Trade Indemnity House, 12-34 Great
  Eastern Street, London EC2A 3EB,
  England.
  Tel (01) 729 2525. Tx 887219.

Jardine Insurance Brokers International Ltd
  Jardine House, 6 Crutched Friars, London
  EC3N 2HT, England.
  Tel (01) 528 4444. Tx 9413847.

Jardine Insurance Brokers Ltd
  Jardine House, 6 Crutched Friars, London
  EC3N 2HT, England.
  Tel (01) 528 4444. Tx 924093.

Jardine Thompson Graham Ltd
  19 Eastcheap, London EC3M 1HJ, England.
  Tel (01) 623 4611. Tx 8814844.

Jenner Fenton Slade Ltd
  Knolly's House, 47 Mark Lane, London
  EC3R 7QH, England.
  Tel (01) 929 4500. Tx 894567.

**Jenner Fenton Slade Reinsurance Brokers
Ltd**
  Knolly's House, 47 Mark Lane, London
  EC3R 7QH, England.
  Tel (01) 929 4500. Tx 894567.

Johnson & Higgins Ltd
18 Mansell Street, London E1 8AA,
England.
Tel (01) 488 0111. Tx 893572.

Johnson, Puddifoot & Last Ltd
Bevis Marks House, 24/25 Bevis Marks,
London EC3A 7JB, England.
Tel (01) 623 4484. Tx 8814449.

Anthony Kidd Agencies Ltd
PO Box 30, Waltham Cross, Hertfordshire
EN8 7EE, England.
Tel (0992) 27944. Tx 268604.

Kingaby Simmons Ltd
Insurance House, 125/129, Vaughan Way,
Leicester LE1 4SB, England.
Tel (0533) 487000. Tx 34615.

Kininimonth Lambert Ltd
53 Eastcheap, London EC3P 3HL, England.
Tel (01) 282 2000. Tx 8814631.

Stafford Knight & Co Ltd
4-5 London Wall Buildings, London EC2M
5NR, England.
Tel (01) 628 3135.

Lander Eberli Shorter Ltd
Lyon House, 160-166 Borough High Street,
London SE1 1JR, England.
Tel (01) 407 7144. Tx 889360.

Lander Eberli Shorter (Aviation) Ltd
Lyon House, 160-166 Borough High Street,
London SE1 1JR, England.
Tel (01) 407 7144. Tx 889360.

Roger Lark & Sons
Astral House, Wakering Road, Barking,
Essex, England.
Tel (01) 594 9711.

Leslie & Godwin Ltd
Frank B. Hall House, PO Box 219,
6 Braham Street, London E1 8ED, England.
Tel (01) 480 7200. Tx 8950221.

Lloyd Thompson Ltd
14 Lovat Lane, London EC3R 8DT,
England.
Tel (01) 623 5616. Tx 885671.

Lochain Patrick Insurance Brokers Ltd
Prospect House, 87/95 Mansell Street,
London E1 8AU, England.
Tel (01) 480 7500. Tx 883794.

London Insurance Brokers Ltd
Hulton House, 161-166 Fleet Street,
London EC4A 4DY, England.
Tel (01) 353 0941.

London Special Risks Ltd
24/26 Minories, London EC3N 1BY,
England.
Tel (01) 709 9611. Tx 885576.

Lowndes Lambert Aviation Ltd
53 Eastcheap, London EC3P 3HL, England.
Tel (01) 283 2000. Tx 8814631.

Lowndes Lambert Cargo Ltd
53 Eastcheap, London EC3P 3HL, England.
Tel (01) 283 2000. Tx 8814631.

Lowndes Lambert Group Ltd
53 Eastcheap, London EC3P 3HL, England.
Tel (01) 283 2000. Tx 8814631.

Lowndes Lambert International Ltd
53 Eastcheap, London EC3P 3HL, England.
Tel (01) 283 2000. Tx 8814631.

Lowndes Lambert Marine Ltd
53 Eastcheap, London EC3P 3HL, England.
Tel (01) 283 2000. Tx 8814631.

Lowndes Lambert Oil & Energy Ltd
53 Eastcheap, London EC3P 3HL, England.
Tel (01) 283 2000. Tx 8814631.

Lowndes Lambert UK Ltd
53 Eastcheap, London EC3P 3HL, England.
Tel (01) 283 2000. Tx 8814631.

LPH Pitman Ltd
St. Michael's Rectory, St. Michael's Alley,
Cornhill, London EC3V 9DS, England.
Tel (01) 283 9831. Tx 8954698.

Lyon Jago Webb Ltd
Lyon House, 160-166 Borough High Street,
London SE1 1LB, England.
Tel (01) 407 7144. Tx 889360.

Ian McCall & Co Ltd
22-23 Widegate Street, London E1 7HX,
England.
Tel (01) 377 8585. Tx 884631.

Macey Williams Ltd
10 New Street, London EC2M 4TP,
England.
Tel (01) 623 4344. Tx 886618.

Manning Beard Ltd
Lutidine House, 3-5 Crutched Friars,
London EC3N 2HT, England.
Tel (01) 488 9881. Tx 885475.

Manson, Byng & Co Ltd
Hampden House, Great Hampden, Bucks,
HP16 9RD, England.
Tel (02406) 6555 or (01) 488 9576.
Tx 83688.

T.H. March & Co Ltd
Saint Dunstan's House, Carey Lane,
London EC2V 8AD, England.
Tel (01) 606 1282. Tx 29750.

Meacock, Samuelson & Devitt Ltd
100 Whitechapel Road, London E1 1JB,
England.
Tel (01) 247 8888. Tx 886129.

Meadows Tolley Insurance Brokers Ltd
70 Borough High Street, London SE1 1YF,
England.
Tel (01) 378 0702. Tx 896449.

R. Mears & Co Ltd
Latham House, 16 Minories, London EC3N
1AX, England.
Tel (01) 702 3571. Tx 923510 RMC G.

idland Hogg Robinson Ltd
Lloyd's Chambers, 1 Portsoken Street,
London E1 8DF, England.
Tel (01) 480 4000. Tx 884633.

iles Smith Anderson & Game Ltd
26 Bastwick Street, Goswell Road, London
EC1V 3PS, England.
Tel (01) 253 3434. Tx 261067.

iles Smith Reinsurance Ltd
26 Bastwick Street, Goswell Road, London
EC1V 3PS, England.
Tel (01) 253 3434. Tx 261067.

os. R. Miller (Aviation Brokers) Ltd
Dawson House, 5 Jewry Street, London
EC3N 2EX, England.
Tel (01) 488 2345. Tx 886535.

**os. R. Miller (Energy Insurance Services)
d**
Dawson House, 5 Jewry Street, London
EC3N 2EX, England.
Tel (01) 488 2345. Tx 888905.

os. R. Miller & Son (Home) Ltd
Dawson House, 5 Jewry Street, London
EC3N 2EX, England.
Tel (01) 488 2345. Tx 885597.

os. R. Miller & Son (Insurance)
Dawson House, 5 Jewry Street, London
EC3N 2EX, England.
Tel (01) 488 2345. Tx 888905.

os. R. Miller & Son (Insurance) Ltd
Dawson House, 5 Jewry Street, London
EC3N 2EX, England.
Tel (01) 488 2345. Tx 888905.

os. R. Miller & Son (Overseas) Ltd
Dawson House, 5 Jewry Street, London
EC3N 3EX, England.
Tel (01) 488 2345. Tx 886535.

**os. R. Miller & Son (Reinsurance Brokers)
Ltd**
Dawson House, 5 Jewry Street, London
EC3N 2EX, England.
Tel (01) 488 2345. Tx 885597.

H. Minet & Co Ltd
Minet House, 100 Leman Street, London
E1 8HG, England.
Tel (01) 481 0707. Tx 8813901.

ristopher Moran & Co Ltd
Moran House, 48 Gray's Inn Road, London
WC1X 8LT, England.
Tel (01) 404 0778. Tx 8813719.

orice Tozer & Beck (Aviation) Ltd
8 Devonshire Square, London EC2M 4PL,
England.
Tel (01) 623 5500. Tx 882171.

S. Mosse & Partners Ltd
4/5 Queen Victoria Terrace, Sovereign
Close, London, E1 9HA, England.
Tel (01) 488 4303. Tx 885996.

Nasco Insurance Brokers Ltd
18 Mansell Street, London E1 8AA,
England.
Tel (01) 481 4444. Tx 8814743.

Needler Heath Ltd
Top Floor, 8 St Peters Hill, Grantham,
Lincs., England.
Tel (0476) 75545.

Nicholson Chamberlain & Colls Ltd
PO Box 211, St. Helen's, 1 Undershaft,
London EC3A 8JD, England.
Tel (01) 929 4031. Tx 929464.

Nicolls Pointing Coulson Ltd
Lloyd's Avenue House, 6 Lloyd's Avenue,
London EC3N 3AX, England.
Tel (01) 488 2121. Tx 889101.

Noble & Wilkins Ltd
Union House, 117 High Street, Billericay,
Essex, England.
Tel (02774) 55111.

Norex Insurance Brokers Ltd
Norex House, Goodmans Yard, London E1
8BJ.
Tel (01) 481 1212. Tx 8958057.

Oakeley, Vaughan & Co Ltd
5 Old Mill Parade, Victoria Road, Romford,
Essex RM1 2HU, England.
Tel (0708) 768613. Tx 888903.

Onyl De Falbe International Ltd
1/7 Shand Street, London SE1 2ES,
England.
Tel (01) 962 9060.

Paul Bradford & Co Ltd
8 Montague Close, London Bridge, London
SE1 9RD, England.
Tel (01) 407 5555. Tx 884944.

E.W. Payne Ltd
Aldgate House, 33 Aldgate High Street,
London EC3N 1AJ, England.
Tel (01) 623 8080. Tx 8952031.

E.W. Payne (International) Ltd
Aldgate House, 33 Aldgate High Street,
London EC3N 1AJ, England.
Tel (01) 623 8080. Tx 8952031.

E.W. Payne & Co (Marine) Ltd
Sedgwick Centre, London E1 8DX,
England.
Tel (01) 377 3456. Tx 882131.

E.W. Payne (North America) Ltd
Aldgate House, 33 Aldgate High Street,
London EC3N 1AJ, England.
Tel (01) 623 8080. Tx 8952031.

E.W. Payne (U.K.) Ltd
Aldgate House, 33 Aldgate High Street,
London EC3N 1AJ, England.
Tel (01) 623 8080. Tx 8952031.

John Plumer & Partners Ltd
9 Alie Street, London E1 8DE, England.
Tel (01) 623 5511. Tx 887355.

Pointon York Vos Ltd
7 Cavendish Square, London W1A 1DJ,
England.
Tel (01) 631 3015. Tx 21215.

Price Forbes Ltd
Sackville House, 143-152 Fenchurch
Street, London EC3M 6BN, England.
Tel (01) 929 1717. Tx 945121.

Professional Liability Brokers Ltd
120/122 Southwark Street, London SE1
0SU.
Tel (01) 928 7654. Tx 919146.

Pulford Winstone & Tennant Ltd
37/39 Lime Street, London EC3M 7AY,
England.
Tel. (01) 283 3702. Tx 935113.

PWS Cross & Barnard Ltd
52-56 Minories, London EC3N 1JJ,
England.
Tel (01) 480 6622. Tx 887265/883244.

PWS International Ltd
52-56 Minories, London EC3N 1JJ,
England.
Tel (01) 480 6622. Tx 887265/883244.

PWS Marine Ltd
52-56 Minories, London EC3N 1JJ,
England.
Tel (01) 480 6622. Tx 887265/883244.

PWS North America
52-56 Minories, London EC3N 1JJ,
England.
Tel (01) 480 6622. Tx 887265/883244.

RAC Insurance Brokers Ltd
69 Hermitage Road, Hitchin, Herts
SG5 1DH, England.
Tel (0462) 421424. Tx 82380.

RTC Ltd
32-35 Botolph Lane, London EC3R 8DE,
England.
Tel (01) 623 2411. Tx 884304.

Rattner Mackenzie Ltd
Walsingham House, 35 Seething Lane,
London EC3N 4AH, England.
Tel (01) 480 5511. Tx 884527.

Richards, Longstaff (Insurance) Ltd
Battlebridge House, 97 Tooley Street,
London SE1 9RD, England.
Tel (01) 407 4466. Tx 888893.

Richardson Hosken Ltd
325-331 High Road, Ilford, Essex IG1 1UJ,
England.
Tel (01) 514 3333. Tx 8814328.

Roberts Morris Bray (Insurance Brokers)Ltd
12 Cleveland Row, St. James', London
SW1A 1DH, England.
Tel (01) 930 9914. Tx 918585.

Ropner Insurance Serives Ltd
Boundary House, 7-17 Jewry Street,
London EC3N 2HP, England.
Tel (01) 488 4533.

Rowbotham Baxter Ltd
Rowbotham House, 9 Clare Street, Lond‹
EC3N 1BE, England.
Tel (01) 480 6644. Tx 8954807.

SG Services Ltd
Sedgwick Centre, London E1 8DX,
England.
Tel (01) 377 3456. Tx 882131.

Sale Tilney Intersure Ltd
Walsingham House, 35 Seething Lane,
London EC3N 4DQ, England.
Tel (01) 480 6445. Tx 8814471/8811893.

Seascope Insurance Services Ltd
Walsingham House, 35 Seething Lane,
London EC3N 4AH, England.
Tel (01) 488 3288. Tx 929124.

Seascope Reinsurance Brokers Ltd
Walsingham House, Seething Lane,
London EC3N 3BY, England.
Tel (01) 488 3288. Tx 929124.

Sedgwick Ltd
Sedgwick Centre, London E1 8DX,
England.
Tel (01) 377 3456. Tx 882131.

Sedgwick Aviation Ltd
Sedgwick Centre, London E1 8DX,
England.
Tel (01) 377 3456. Tx 882131.

Sedgwick Cargo Ltd
Sedgwick Centre, London E1 8DX,
England.
Tel (01) 377 3456. Tx 882131.

Sedgwick Energy Ltd
Sedgwick Centre, London E1 8DX,
England.
Tel (01) 377 3456. Tx 882131.

Sedgwick International Ltd
Sedgwick Centre, London E1 8DX,
England.
Tel (01) 377 3456. Tx 882131.

Sedgwick Marine & Cargo Ltd
Sedgwick Centre, London E1 8DX,
England.
Tel (01) 377 3456. Tx 882131.

Sedgwick Non-Marine Risks Ltd
Sedgwick Centre, London E1 8DX,
England.
Tel (01) 377 3456. Tx 882131.

Sedgwick U.K. (London) Ltd
Sedgwick Centre, London E1 8DX,
England.
Tel (01) 377 3456. Tx 882131.

Sedgwick U.K. (National) Ltd
Sedgwick Centre, London E1 8DX,
England.
Tel (01) 377 3456. Tx 882131.

Smith, Bilbrough & Co
33-38 Dukes Place, London EC3A 7PS,
England.
Tel (01) 281 5801. Tx 888267.

alter F. Smith & Co Ltd
30 Elder Street, London E1 6BT, England.
Tel (01) 247 0381.

obert Sparrow & Co. Ltd.,
88/89 Gracechurch Street, London EC3V
0DN, England.
Tel (01) 623 4485. Tx 915039.

eel Burrill Jones Ltd
Bankside House, 107-112 Leadenhall
Street, London EC3A 4AP, England.
Tel (01) 623 4411. Tx 887830.

mes Steele (Insurance) Ltd
Yacht Centre, PO Box 1, Rayleigh, Essex
SS6 7RB, England.
Tel (0268) 771311. Tx 885717.

en-Re (U.K.) Ltd
PO Box 214, 2 South Place, London EC2P
2DX, England.
Tel (01) 628 6011. Tx 8813371.

erling Offices (London) Ltd
8 Devonshire Square, London EC2M 4PL,
England.
Tel (01) 623 5500. Tx 882171.

ewart Wrightson Ltd
1 Camomile Street, London EC3A 7HJ,
England.
Tel (01) 623 7511. Tx 8811181.

J. Symons & Co Ltd
Symons House, 22 Alie Street, London
E1 8DH, England.
Tel (01) 488 2131. Tx 888484.

M. Thompson & Co Ltd
6 Lloyd's Avenue, London EC3N 3AX,
England.
Tel (01) 481 2884. Tx 8956505.

ompson Heath & Bond Ltd
12 Poverest Street, Orpington, Kent BR5
2TP, England.
Tel (0689) 27044. Tx 869552.

ower Hill Insurance Brokers Ltd
St. Clare House, 30-33 Minories, London
EC3N 1DJ, England.
Tel (01) 488 9567. Tx 896625.

owry Law (General Insurance) Ltd
Godolphin House, Stoke Poges Lane,
Slough, Berkshire SL1 3PB, England.
Tel (0753) 821241.

orman Tremellen & Co
Tremellen House, Burrell Road, Haywards
Heath, West Sussex RH16 1TW, England.
Tel (0444) 453181.

Trevor, Mortleman & Poland Ltd
Wigham House, 16-30 Wakering Road,
Barking, Essex IG11 8PB, England.
Tel (01) 594 7222. Tx 887501.

P. Turner & Co Ltd
30-34 New Bridge Street, London EC4V
6BJ, England.
Tel (01) 236 4451. Tx 886786.

L.A. Tyer & Co Ltd
5-10 Bury Street, London EC3A 5HH,
England.
Tel (01) 621 1400. Tx 885330.

Tyser & Co
Ellerman House, 12-20 Camomile Street,
London EC3A 7PJ, England.
Tel (01) 623 6262. Tx 883907.

Tyser Low Ltd
Regis House, King William Street, London
EC4R 9BD, England.
Tel (01) 626 8171. Tx 893453.

United African Insurance Brokers Ltd
10 Trinity Square, London EC3P 3AX,
England.
Tel (01) 488 8111. Tx 882141.

United Insurance Brokers Ltd
Ibex House, 42-47 Minories, London EC3N
1DY, England.
Tel (01) 488 0551. Tx 8954250.

Wackerbarth, Hardman (Insurance Brokers)
Ltd
7th Fl, International House, Creechurch
Lane, London.
Tel (01) 283 0798. Tx 918530.

Walsham Brothers & Co Ltd
4 Fenchurch Avenue, London EC3M 5BS,
England.
Tel (01) 623 2711.

Watts, Watts Ltd
St. Olaf House, London Bridge, London
SE1 2PL, England.
Tel (01) 403 6060. Tx 886459.

Andrew Weir Insurance Brokers Ltd
17A-18 Bevis Marks, London EC3A 7BB,
England.
Tel (01) 283 1266. Tx 887392.

Well Marine Reinsurance Brokers Ltd
14 Trinity Square, London EC3N 4AA,
England.
Tel (01) 481 2935. Tx 883756.

E.J. Welton & Co Ltd
5 St. Helen's Place, London EC3A 6DP,
England.
Tel (01) 638 4601. Tx 8952022.

Willis, Faber & Dumas Ltd
10 Trinity Square, London EC3P 3AX,
England.
Tel (01) 488 8111. Tx 882141.

Willis, Faber & Willcox Ltd
10 Trinity Square, London EC3P 3AX,
England.
Tel (01) 488 8111. Tx 882141.

Willis Wrightson Ltd
1 Camomile Street, London EC3A 7HJ,
England.
Tel (01) 623 7511. Tx 8811181.

Winchester Bowring Ltd
Ambassador House, 2 White Kennett

Street, Houndsditch, London E1 7BT, England.
Tel (01) 247 7611. Tx 886915.

Winchester Insurance Brokers
Lyon House, 160/166 Borough High Street, London SE1 1JR, England.
Tel (01) 407 6144. Tx 889360.

Windsor Insurance Brokers Ltd
Lyon House, 160/166 Borough High Stre
London SE1 1JR, England.
Tel (01) 407 7144. Tx 889360.

F.E. Wright (U.K.) Ltd
109 Borough High Street, London SE1
1NL, England.
Tel (01) 407 4477.

LLOYD'S AGENCY SYSTEM

A Unique Organisation Spanning the World

The Lloyd's Agency system, as we know it today, was organised in 1811 when the subscribers to Lloyd's agreed to formalise the rather haphazard and cumbersome means previously employed to appoint representatives to gather information and care for their interests as insurers of ships and cargo in casualty.

The Committee of Lloyd's was invested with the responsibility of establishing the system and today Lloyd's Agents are asked to carry out specific duties for the Corporation of Lloyd's in addition to their normal business activities. When acting as agents of the Corporation, their duties are to collect and transmit to the Corporation information of likely interest to the Lloyd's Market and insurers worldwide.

The basic qualifications for a Lloyd's Agent have remained unchanged since 1811, namely that they should be resident and well established at the place concerned and be of high commercial status and integrity.

It became common practice for insurers, both Lloyd's and companies worldwide, to include in their policies and certificates a requirement that surveys to establish the extent and cause of loss or damage to ships, their cargo and goods in transit by land, sea and air be held by Lloyd's Agents or by surveyors appointed by them. It should be noted however that in carrying out surveys or other tasks, whether for Insurers or other Principals, the company would be employed directly by these parties and would not be acting as an agent of Lloyd's itself.

Where a Lloyd's Agent is asked to carry out a survey, the surveyor may be responsible not only for reporting the condition of the subject matter, the extent and cause of damage, but if requested, also recommend steps to minimise loss, alternative uses for damaged goods and even may suggest means to prevent recurrence of such losses. In agreeing with an applicant for survey a figure for depreciation endeavours would be made to see that justice is done to the insurers, the claimant, carriers and/or all other interested parties.

Knowledge of a wide range of commodities and long experience of various modes of transport greatly aids the surveyor who may be the Agent himself, an employee, or a non-staff expert commissioned to hold a specific survey. Agents may employ the services of such experts if they consider the nature of the survey requires it. From time to time they may also utilise the services of analysts and other specialists to investigate and establish the cause of damage.

The introduction of containers in recent decades has resulted not only in changes in the transport field but required Agents and surveyors to learn a completely new set of environmental conditions affecting the transport of goods and the losses and damage caused thereby.

In 1866 certain selected Lloyd's Agents were authorised by the Committee of Lloyd's to adjust, settle and purchase claims on Lloyd's policies and certificates which made special provisions for the settlement of claims abroad. This does not mean paying the claim on behalf of Underwriters but only that the Agent concerned may, at his discretion, purchase title to the claim on behalf of the Corporation of Lloyd's who thereafter become the claimants on Underwriters.

The twentieth century has seen an increase in the scope and complexity of insurance and has involved Lloyd's Agents in an ever widening field of activity including both Aviation and Non-Marine surveys and investigations.

Inevitably the Agency system has varied in size both to meet the needs of the time and in view of communications systems available. Originally the horse carriage and sailing ship limited the speed of communications and the ability of surveyors to respond rapidly to requests for their services. Lloyd's and Lloyd's Agents were early users of telegraphic facilities and strong backers of Marconi's early radio stations before a Post Office monopoly was established in the United Kingdom. Today the latest developments in public document transmission, computers and printing will be found employed in the gathering and distribution of information.

In the following pages will be found an alphabetical directory of Lloyd's Agents worldwide. Inquiries about the Agents and Sub-Agents should be addressed to the Controller of Agencies at Lloyd's from whom an official list giving full details of the Agencies can be obtained.

MADEIRA
PORT OF FUNCHAL

SHIPPING AGENCY SERVICES

BLANDY

BLANDY BROTHERS & CO. LDA.

LLOYD'S AGENTS

PHONE: 20161
TELEX: 72125 BLNDY P
CABLES: BLANDY FUNCHAL
FAX: (351)(91)27699

LONDON CORRESPONDENTS: **BLANDY BROTHERS & CO. LTD.**
7/8 HATHERLEY STREET, VINCENT SQUARE, LONDON SW1P 2QT.
TEL.: 01-821 9901 and 01-821 9902
TELEX: 291819 BLANDY G

INDEX OF LLOYD'S AGENCIES BY COUNTRY

AFGHANISTAN
  Kabul

ALGERIA
  El Djazair (Algiers)

ARGENTINA
  Buenos Aires
  Rosario

AUSTRALIA
  Adelaide
  Brisbane
  Darwin
  Fremantle
  Hobart
  Launceston
  Mackay
  Melbourne
  Sydney
  Townsville

AUSTRIA
  Vienna

AZORES
  St. Michael's
  Terceira

BAHAMAS
  Freeport
  Nassau

BAHRAIN

BANGLADESH
  Chittagong

BELGIUM
  Antwerp

BELIZE
  Belize City

BENIN, People's Republic of
  Cotonou

BERMUDA

BOLIVIA
  La Paz

BOTSWANA
  Gaborone

BRAZIL
  Belem
  Porto Alegre
  Recife
  Rio de Janeiro
  Rio Grande
  Salvador
  Santos

BULGARIA
  Sofia

BURMA
  Rangoon

BURUNDI
  Bujumbura

CAMEROON
  Douala

CANADA
  Calgary
  Charlottetown
  Halifax
  Montreal
  North Sydney
  St. John's
  Toronto
  Vancouver
  Winnipeg

CANARY ISLANDS
  Grand Canary
  Tenerife

CAPE VERDE ISLANDS
  St. Vincent

CAYMAN ISLANDS
  Grand Cayman

CENTRAL AFRICAN
REPUBLIC
  Bangui

CHILE
  Arica
  Iquique
  Punta Arenas
  Santiago
  Valdivia

CHINA
  Beijing
  Dalian
  Guangzhou
  Qingdao
  Shanghai
  Tianjin

CHRISTMAS ISLANDS

COLOMBIA
  Bogota

CONGO
  Pointe Noire

COOK ISLANDS
  Rarotonga

COSTA RICA
  San Jose

CUBA
  Havana

CYPRUS
  Limassol

CZECHOLSLOVAKIA
  Prague

DENMARK
  Aalborg
  Aarhus
  Copenhagen
  Esbjerg
  Odense

DJIBOUTI, Republic of
  Djibouti

DOMINICAN REPUBLIC
  Santo Domingo

ECUADOR
  Guayaquil

EGYPT
  Alexandria
  Cairo
  Port Said

EIRE
  Cork
  Dublin
  Galway
  Limerick
  Waterford

EL SALVADOR
  San Salvador

ETHIOPIA
  Addis Ababa

FALKLAND ISLANDS
  Port Stanley

FAROES
  Torshavn

FIJI
  Suva

FINLAND
  Helsinki
  Mariehamn
  Oulu
  Rauma
  Turku
  Vaasa

FRANCE
  Ajaccio
  Bordeaux
  Boulogne
  Brest
  Cherbourg
  Dunkirk
  La Rochelle
  Le Havre
  Lorient
  Marseilles
  Nantes
  Nice
  Pari
  St. Malo

FRENCH GUIANA
  Cayenne

FRENCH POLYNESIA
  Tahiti

GABON
  Libreville

GAMBIA
  Banjul

GERMANY
  Bremen
  Duisburg
  Hamburg
  Kiel
  Lubeck
  Mannheim
  Munich

GHANA
  Accra

GIBRALTAR

GREECE
  Mitylene
  Piraeus
  Rhodes
  Samos

GUATEMALA
  Guatemala City

GUINEA
  Conakry

GUINE—BISSAU
  Bissau

GUYANA
  Georgetown

HAITI
  Port au Prince

HAWAIIAN ISLANDS
  Honolulu

HOLLAND
  Amsterdam
  Rotterdam

HONDURAS
  Puerto Cortes

HONG KONG

HUNGARY
  Budapest

ICELAND
  Reykjavik

INDIA
  Bombay
  Calcutta
  Cochin
  Madras
  Mangalore
  New Delhi
  Visakhapatnam

INDONESIA
  Jakarta
  Medan
  Palembang
  Semarang
  Surabaya
  Ujung Pandang

IRAN
  Teheran

IRAQ
  Baghdad

ISRAEL
  Haifa

ITALY
  Ancona
  Bari
  Brindisi
  Genoa
  Leghorn
  Messina
  Naples
  Palermo
  Rome
  Taranto
  Trieste
  Venice

IVORY COAST
  Abidjan

JAMAICA
  Kingston

JAPAN
  Kobe
  Moji
  Okinawa
  Yokohama

JORDAN
  Amman

KENYA
  Mombassa
  Nairobi

KUWAIT

LEBANON
  Beirut

LIBERIA
  Monrovia

LIBYAN ARAB REPUBLIC
  Bengazi

MADAGASCAR
  Antananarivo (Tananarive)

MADEIRA

MALAWI
  Blantyre   continued

MALAYSIA
  Kota Kinabalu
  Kuala Lumpur
  Kuching
  Penang
  Port Kelang
  Sandakan

MALTA

MARIANA ISLANDS
  Guam

MAURITANIA
  Nouadhibou
  Nouakchott

MAURITIUS

MEXICO
  Acapulco
  Coatzacoalcos
  Ensenada
  Manzanillo
  Mazatlan
  Merida
  Mexico
  Salina Cruz
  Tampico
  Veracruz

MOROCCO
  Agadir
  Casablanca

MOZAMBIQUE
  Beira
  Maputo

NAURU

NEGARA BRUNEI
DARUSSALAM
  Bandar Seri Begawan

NETHERLANDS ANTILLES
  Curacao

NEW CALEDONIA

NEW ZEALAND
  Auckland
  Christchurch
  Dunedin
  Invercargill
  Wellington

NICARAGUA
  Managua

NIGERIA
  Lagos
  Port Harcourt

NORFOLK ISLAND

NORTHERN IRELAND
  Belfast
  Londonderry
  Warrenpoint

NORWAY
  Bergen
  Harstad
  Kirkenes
  Kristiansand S.
  Narvik
  Oslo
  Stavanger
  Tromso
  Trondhheim

PAKISTAN
  Karachi

PANAMA
  Balboa
  Cristobal
  Panama City

PAPUA NEW GUINEA
  Lae
  Port Moresby
  Rabaul

PARAGUAY
  Asuncion

PERU
  Lima
  Mollendo

PHILIPPINES
  Manila

POLAND
  Gdynia
  Szczecin

PORTUGAL
  Lisbon
  Oporto

PUERTO RICO
  San Juan

QATAR
  Doha

REUNION

ROMANIA
  Bucharest

RWANDA
  Kigali

SAMOA, AMERICAN
  Pago Pago

SAMOA, WESTERN
  Apia

SAO TOME AND PRINCIPE
  Sao Tome

SAUDI ARABIA
  Dammam
  Jeddah

SENEGAL
  Dakar

SEYCHELLES

SIERRA LEONE
  Freetown

SINGAPORE

SOLOMON ISLANDS
  Honiara

SOMALI REPUBLIC
  Mogadishu

SOUTH AFRICA
  Cape Town
  Durban
  Johannesburg
  Port Elizabeth

SOUTH KOREA
  Pusan

SPAIN
  Barcelona
  Bilbao
  Cadiz
  Corunna
  Ferrol
  Gijon
  Madrid
  Malaga
  Palma
  Tarragona
  Valencia
  Vigo

SPANISH TERRITORIES OF
NORTH AFRICA
  Ceuta

SRI LANKA
  Colombo
  Galle

ST. HELENA

SUDAN
  Khartoum
  Port Sudan

SULTANATE OF OMAN
  Muscat
  Salalah

SURINAME
  Paramaribo

SWEDEN
  Gelfe
  Gothenburg
  Halmstad
  Helsingborg
  Kalmar
  Karlshamn
  Lulea
  Malmo
  Ornskoldsvik
  Stockholm
  Sundsvall
  Umea
  Visby

SWITZERLAND
  Basle
  Neuchatel

SYRIA
  Lattakia

TAIWAN
  Taipei

TANZANIA
  Dar-es-Salaam
  Tanga

THAILAND
  Bangkok

TONGA
  Lome

TUNISIA
  Tunis

TURKEY
  Iskenderun
  Istanbul
  Ismir
  Mersin

TURKS AND CAICOS
ISLANDS
  Turks Island

UGANDA
  Kampala

U.S.S.R.
  Moscow

UNITED ARAB EMIRATES
  Abu Dhabi
  Dubai

UNITED KINGDOM
  Aberdeen
  Avonmouth
  Barrow-in-Furness
  Boston
  Cardiff
  Colchester
  Dover
  Dundee
  Falmouth
  Glasgow
  Guernsey
  Holyhead
  Hull
  Ipswich

Isle of Man
Jersey
Kirkwall
Leith
Lerwick
Liverpool
London
Lowestoft
Middlesbrough
Montrose
Newcastle-on-Tyne
Penzance
Plymouth
Southampton
Stornoway
Swansea
Whitehaven

UNITED STATES OF
AMERICA
  Anchorage
  Baltimore
  Boston
  Charleston
  Chicago
  Cleveland
  Detroit
  Houston
  Jacksonville
  Los Angeles
  Miami
  Mobile
  New Orleans
  New York
  Norfolk
  Portland (Maine)
  Portland (Oregon)
  San Francisco
  Savannah
  Seattle
  Tampa
  Wilmington

URUGUAY
  Montevideo

VANUATU

VENEZUELA
  Caracas
  Maracaibo

VIRGIN ISLANDS (BRITISH)
  Tortola

VIRGIN ISLANDS (U.S.A.)
  St. Croix
  St. Thomas

WEST INDIES
  Antigua
  Barbados
  Dominica
  Grenada
  Guadeloupe
  Martinique
  Montserrat
  St. Kitts
  St. Lucia
  St. Vincent
  Trinidad

YEMEN ARAB REPUBLIC
  Hodeidah

YEMEN, People's Democratic
Republic of
  Aden

YUGOSLAVIA
  Rijeka

ZIARE
  Kinshasa

ZAMBIA
  Lusaka

ZIMBABWE
  Bulawayo
  Harare

LLOYD'S AGENTS AND THEIR SUB-AGENCIES

This list of Lloyd's Agents and their Sub-Agents is arranged alphabetically by place name.

When writing to a Lloyd's Agent the name of the town/city and country must be included in their address.

The abbreviation a.o.h. stands for after office hours.

The place names immediately following an Agent are the Sub-Agencies to that Agent.

It is possible that some Agency details have changed since the time of going to press.

AALBORG, Denmark—Rechnitzer, Thomsen & Co. Ltd., 8 Strandvejen, (P.O. Box 1410), DK-9100.
Tel (8) 124422 (a.o.h. 182189). Tx 69738 RTHCO DK. Cables MARITIME.

AARHUS, Denmark—P.H. Hojgaard Jensen ApS., 8 Asmusvaenget, (P.O. Box 19), DK-8530 Hjortshoj.
Tel (06) 196500 (a.o.h. 222984). Tx 64448 PHHJ DK (Messages to commence: For Lloyd's Agent). Cables TELOSCOM.
Kolding, Fredericia, Vejle, Horsens, Grenaa, Randers.

ABERDEEN, United Kingdom—John Cook (Agencies) Ltd., Carleton Buildings, 59 Marischal Street, AB9 8AZ.
Tel (0224) 589921 (24 hours) (a.o.h. 322936). Tx 73134 COOKAB G. Cables COOK.

ABIDJAN, Ivory Coast—Societe Abidjanaise D'Expertises (SABEX), 25 Avenue Chardy, (P.O. Box 1033), 01.
Tel 322015, 323175 & 225188 (a.o.h. 321566 & 228668). Tx 23272 SABEXCI. Cables COMISAV.
San Pedro, Upper Volta (Haute-Volta), Bobo-Dioulasso.

ABU DHABI, United Arab Emirates—Abu Dhabi Maritime & Mercantile International, (P.O. Box 247).
Tel (2) 323131 & 331703 (a.o.h. 728321). Tx 22245 ADMMI EM. Cables ADMMI.

ACAPULCO, Mexico—Agencias Maritimas del Pacifico, S.A., Costera Miguel Aleman, 215, Edificio Manper, Desp. 104-105, (P.O. Box 51).
Tel (748) 22672, 21956 & 35654 (a.o.h. 27780 & 34515). Tx 16724 AMMSAME. Cables AMMSA.

ACCRA, Ghana—Ghana Inspections Limited, Tecnoa House, Derby Avenue, (P.O. Box 199).
Tel 65311 & 64331. Tx 2037 MAFRIC GHANA. Cables LLOYDAGENT.
Kumasi

ADDIS ABABA, Ethiopia—Gellatly, Hankey & o., (Ethiopia) S. C., Cunningham Street, (P.O. Box 482).
Tel 550570, 5519778 & 550622/4 (a.o.h. 184341 & 126192). Tx 21064 GELLATLY ADDIS. Cables GELLATLY.
Dire Dawa, Assab, Massawa.

ADELAIDE, Australia—Danzas Wills Pty. Ltd., 4-6 Santo Parade, Port Adelaide, S. Aust. 5015.
Tel (08) 475366 (a.o.h. 491411 & 43658). Tx 88134 DWADL AA. Cables WILLSANDCO.
Port Lincoln, Whyalla, Port Pirie, Wallaroo.

ADEN, People's Democratic Republic of Yemen—Yemen Insurance & Reinsurance Co., Saila Road, (P.O. Box 456), Crater.
Tel 51464/7 & 52327. Tx 2245 SHAMIN AD. Cables SHAMIN.
Mukalla.

AGADIR, Morocco—Ernest Corcos, M.B.E., 7 Avenue des F.A.R., (P.O. Box 54).
Tel (8) 41331 (a.o.h. 22219). Tx 81618 ERCOS AGDIR. Cables ERCOS.

AJACCIO, France—Walter Tschumi, 13 Rue Marechal Ornano, (P.O. Box 55), F-20176.
Tel 95214339 (24 hours). Tx 460627 CORSICA F. Cables BRITISHIPS.
Calvi & Ile Rousse, Bastia.

ALEXANDRIA, Arab Republic of Egypt—Marine Technical Services Company, 95 Ismail Mehana Street.
Tel 4918947 (24 hours). Tx 54568 SACOS UN. Cables DELANY.

AMMAN, Jordan—Spinney's 1948 Ltd., Sahaab Road, Queismeh, (P.O. Box 40).
Tel 779141/3 (a.o.h. (6) 821134 & 668441. Tx 21814 SPINEX JO. Cables SPINNEYS.
Aqaba.

AMSTERDAM, Holland—Messrs. Alfred Schroder, Building "De Walvis", Grote Bickerstraat 74, 1012 KS, (P.O. Box 357, 1000 AJ).
Tel (20) 5572933 (a.o.h. (2995) 3368, (70) 281366 & (2154) 17259). Tx 12016 SAFE NL (For

attention Alfred Schroder). Cables SCHRODERLLOYD'S.
  Delfzyl, Terschelling, Harlingen, Ymuiden (Ijmuiden).

ANCHORAGE, United States of America—B.J. Logan Associates, 405 East Fireweed Lane, Room 2, (2nd Floor), AK 99503, (P.O. Box 101853, AK 99510-1853).
  Tel (907) 272-7724 (a.o.h. 36082, 31387 & 930218). Cables LOGANSUR.

ANCONA, Italy—Adriano & Armando Montevecchi S.N.C., 18, Via 29 Settembre, (P.O. Box 145), I-60100.
  Tel (71) 200554 & 204147 (a.o.h. 31386/7 & 930218). Tx 560069 & 560047 AGBKANI. (Messages to commence: For Mont). Cables MONTEVECCHI.
  Pescara, Ravenna.

ANTANANARIVO (Tananarive), Madagascar—Roger Duponsel & Cie., 18 Avenue de l'Independance, (P.O. Box 405).
  Tel 22655 & 26331/3 (a.o.h. 40702). Tx 22244 ASSURBIEN TANA. Cables ASSURBIEN.
  Antsiranana (Diego Suarez), Taomasina (Tamatave), Tolagnaro (Fort Dauphin), Toliary (Tulear), Mahajanga (Majunga), Nosy Be (Nossi-Be), Sambava.

ANTIGUA, West Indies—George W. Bennett, Bryson & Co. Ltd., Long & Church Street, (P.O. Box 162), St. John's.
  Tel 4621200 (a.o.h. 4611346 & 4612337). Tx 2128 BRYSONS AK. Cables BENNETT.

ANTWERP, Belgium—Gellatly Hankey Marine Services (Belgium) N.V., Rubenscenter, Nationalestraat 5, B-2000.
  Tel (3) 2314946 (a.o.h. 2261080 & 665259). Tx 72338 GELHAN B.
  Zeebrugge, Ostend, Luxembourg.

APIA, Western Samoa—Morris Hedstrom Samoa Ltd., (P.O. Box 1857).
  Tel 22722 (a.o.h. 22597). Tx 224 MORRISHED SX. Cables MORRISHED.

ARICA, Chile—S. B. Dawson y Cia Ltda., Dpto 12, (P.O. Box 705).
  Tel 31098 (24 hours). Tx 223189 SBDAW CK. Cables DAWSON.

ASMARA, Ethiopia—Gellatly, Hankey & Co., (Ethiopia) S.C., Kebedesh Seium Street No. 30, (P.O. Box 906). Tel 110369 & 110598. Tx 42030 GELLATLY ASMARA. Cables GELLATLY.

ASUNCION, Paraguay—Gibson Brothers, S.A.C.I., Calle Presidente Franco, 775, (P.O. Box 233).
  Tel 602002 & 605054 (a.o.h. 65054 & 62002). Tx 278 GBS PY. Cables GIBSON.

AUCKLAND, New Zealand—Robins MBS Marine, Level 4, 130 Khyber Pass Road, (P.O. Box 335).
  Tel (9) 394377 (a.o.h. 581204 & 764210). Tx 60906 MARINER NZ.
  New Plymouth, Mount Maunganui & Tauranga.

AVONMOUTH, United Kingdom—Lovell Hodder Whitwill Ltd., Avonmouth Dock, BS11 9DG.
  Tel (0272) 823251 (a.o.h. (0272) 779137). Tx 44168 HODDER G.

BAGHDAD, Iraq—Burjony Bureau Khalid L. Alexander Iskender Building, Sa'adoon Street, (P.O. Box 3166).
  Tel (01) 8871099 (a.o.h. 7190094). Tx 214264 BURJ IK. (Messages to commence: For Lloyd's Agents Baghdad). Cables ALBURJONY.

BAHRAIN—Government Road, Manama, (P.O. Box 828).
  Tel 253535 (a.o.h. 661281, 714942 & 259073). Tx 8212 BMMI BN. Cables MARINT.

BALBOA, Panama—Associated Steamship Agents, S.A., Building No 49, Diablo road, (P.O. Box 2007).
  Tel (52) 521258/9, 326074 & 325639. (a.o.h. (60) 9452 & (42) 1579). Tx 3012 or 2709 SHIPAGT.
  Cables SHIPAGENT.

BALTIMORE, United States of America—Carman & Company Inc., Dundalk Marine Terminal, 2700 Broening Highway, 21222.
  Tel (301) 633-5940 (a.o.h 235-1132 & 736-7966). Tx 9102503975 ESL UQ. Cables CARMANCO.

BANDAR SERI BEGAWAN, Negara Brunei Darussalam—Jasra Harrisons Sdn. Bhd., Jl. Kianggeh/Jl. MacArthur, (P.O. Boxes 25 & 2255).
  Tel (02) 42361/3 & 43887 (a.o.h. 30990). Tx 2214 HNCBWN BU. Cables CROSFIELD.
  Kuala Beliat.

BANGKOK, Thailand—The Borneo Co. (Thailand) Ltd., 16th floor, Sathorn Thani 2, 92/44 Sathorn Nua Road 10500.
  Tel (2) 234 8480/1 (a.o.h. 278-0846 & 466-1435). Tx 84342 BCTL TH. Cables INSCBORN.
  Haadyai.

BANGUI, Central African Republic—Les Commissaires d'Avaries Reunis, Rond Point Barthelemy Boganda, (B.P. 513).

Tel 611023 (a.o.h. 612021). Tx 5217 PUBLIC A RC. (Messages to commence: For Lloyd's Agents B.P. 513). Cables COMISAV.

BANJUL, Gambia—S. Madi (Gambia) Ltd., 10c Cameron Street, (P.O. Box 255/256).
Tel 27372, 27487 & 27281 (a.o.h. 92713 & 92720). Tx 2209 MADI GV. Cables MADI.

BARBADOS, West Indies—Gardiner Austin & Co. Ltd., Knights Building, Fontabelle, St. Michael, (P.O. Box 67), Bridgetown.
Tel 426-2830 & 426-1623 (a.o.h. 4293207 & 4333366). Tx 2567 CAVAN WB. Cables CAVAN.

BARCELONA, Spain—McAndrews & Co. Ltd., Plaza del Duque de Medinaceli, 5, (P.O. Box 441), 08002. Tel (93) 3182050 & 3173558 (a.o.h. 3218333). Tx 54060 MCBAR E.
Palamos, Rosas.

BARI, Italy—P. Lorusso & Co., 133 Via Piccinni, (P.O. Box 258), 70122 Bari.
Tel (080) 212840 & 218229 (a.o.h. 218874 & 323096). Tx 810044 OSUROLI. Cables OSSUROL.
Barletta, Manfredonia, Monopoli, Molfetta.

BARROW-IN-FURNESS, United Kingdom—James Fisher & Sons, P.L.C., (P.O. Box 4). LA14 1HR.
Tel (0229) 22323 (a.o.h. 28996). Tx 65163 FISHER G. Cables FISHER.

BASLE, Switzerland—Keller Shipping Ltd., Holbeinstrasse, 68, (P.O. Box 3479) CH-4002.
Tel (61) 237940 (a.o.h. 472235 & 767210). Tx 963467 LINES CH & 962135 SHIP CH. Cables KELLERSHIP.

BASRAH, Iraq—Burjony Bureau Khalid L. Burjony, Thowrah Street, (P.O. Box 2), Ashar.
Tel (040) 218282 (a.o.h. 217593). Tx 217058 BURJONY IK. Cables BURJONY.

BEIJING, Peoples Republic of China—The People's Insurance Company of China, 410 Fue Cheng Men Nei Da Jie. Tel 6016688. Tx 22102 PICC CN. Cables 42001 BEIJING.

BEIRA, Mozambique—Manica Freight Services (Mocambique) S.A.R.L., Largo Joao Coutinho 148, (P.O. Boxes 44 & 258).
Tel 22916, 22572 & 25163 (a.o.h. 23465). Tx 7-345 MTCBA MO & 7-445 MMLBA MO. Cables MANICA or MARROJAR.
Quelimane, Pebane, Nacala.

BEIRUT, Lebanon—G. Sahyouni & Co. SARL, Hafiz El Hasem Building, (P.O. Box 175-452).
Quarantine Bridge, Tripoli Road.
Tel (01) 582601/2 & 894377 (a.o.h. (01) 412404, (04) 925058 or (04) 323782). Tx 44545 & 23438 ATON LE.

BELEM, Brazil — Agencias Mundiais Ltda., Edificio Booth, Avendida Presidente Vargas 121, (P.O. Box 190), 66000 PA.
Tel (091) 224-4822/4078/4267 (a.o.h. 222-4078 & 235-0359). Tx 911184 & 911799 AMUN BR.
Cables AMSANAV.
Fortaleza, Macapa, Manaus.

BELFAST, Northern Ireland—McCalla Freight Ltd., Prince's Dock Street, Donegall Quay, BT1 3AA.
Tel (0232) 746405/6 (a.o.h. 703237). Tx 74182 MCCFRT.
Bangor, Larne, Cushendall, Rathlin Island.

BELIZE CITY, Belize—The Belize Estate & Produce Co. Ltd., 81 North Front Street, (P.O. Box 151).
Tel (2) 77011/2, & 73213 (a.o.h. 77918). Tx 238 BESTATE BZ.

BENGHAZI, Libyan Arab Republic—Shahat Shipping Co., (P.O. Box 2973 or 1496).
Tel 93559, 92236, 92025 & 93970 (a.o.h. 94490). Tx 40076 & 40105 SHAHATLY.
Cables SHAHATSHIP.

BERGEN, Norway—Messrs. Jacob Christensen, O Nesttunvei 16, (P.O. Box 310), 5051 Nesttun.
Tel (05) 132780 (a.o.h. 134545 & 309381). Tx 42143 PREST N.
Odda.

BERMUDA— Harnett & Richardson Ltd., 75 Front Street, (P.O. Box 836), Hamilton 5.
Tel 27500 (a.o.h. 6-4356 & 5-4442). Tx 3233 HARNT BA. Cables HARNT.

BILBAO, Spain—Messrs. Sucesor de J. Innes, Barroeta Aldamar, 3, 48001.
Tel (94) 423061 & 4237648 (a.o.h. 4632160). Tx 31969 SJIN E.
Pasajes, Santona, Santander.

BISSAU, Guine-Bissau—H. P. Rosa, 14, Rua No. 7, (P.O. Box 41).
Tel (21) 2241 & 3737 (a.o.h. (21) 3229). Tx 258 HP ROSA. (Messages to commence: For HP Rosa). Cables ROSA.

BLANTYRE, Malawi—Mandala Limited, P.O. Box 49.
Tel 631011 (a.o.h. 630652). Tx 44128 ALCOR MI. Cables ALCOR.

BOGOTA, Colombia — Toplis and Harding Hudson Ltda., Calle 17, 12-45, Piso 5, (P.O. Box 093853).
Tel 2189261, 2189124, 2189103, 2189281, 21892224 & 2189203 (a.o.h. 2114814). Tx 43138 AJUS CO. Cables AJUSTADOR.
    Medellin, Pereira, Buenaventura, Cali, Tumaco, Pasto, Santa Marta, Barranquilla, Cartagena, San Andres Island, Turbo, Bucaramanga.

BOMBAY, India—Tata Tea Ltd., Chartered Bank Building, Mahatma Gandhi Road, (P.O. Box 73), 400001.
Tel (22) 2044344 & 2048355 (a.o.h. 8222571 & 521583). Tx 011-6983 TFIN IN.
Cables SALVAGE.
    Goa.

BORDEAUX, France—Jean-Francois Chevreau, Bourse Maritime, Place Laine, F-33075 Cedex.
Tel 56521687/8 (a.o.h. 56022694 & 802546). Tx 560943 ASSUMAR BORDX. (Messages to commence: For Lloyd's Agent). Cables COMITASSUR.

BOSTON, United Kingdom—Read & Sutcliffe Ltd., 22 Wide Bargate, Boston PE21 6HG.
Tel (0205) 310444 (a.o.h. 820937). Tx 37509 & 377423 RANDS G.
    Wisbech, King's Lynn.

BOSTON, United States of America—Frank Gair Macomber Claims Agency Inc., 400 Washington Street, Braintree, MA 02184.
Tel (617) 848-7576/7 (a.o.h. 0205-56355). Tx 940283 ELYSIUM BRAE. Cables ELYSIUM.

BOULOGNE-SUR-MER, France—Continex International (Fret) S.A., 40 Grande Rue, (P.O. Box 65), F-62201 Cedex.
Tel 21305404690 (a.o.h. 838983 & 830292). Tx 110930 CTX BGE. Cables GLYCONIC.
    Calais, St. Valery-sur-Somme.

BREMEN, Germany—F. Reck & Co., GmbH, Herrlichkeit 5, (P.O. Box 10 23 40), D-2800, 1.
Tel (421) 500601 (a.o.h. (421) 236002 & (4792) 7405). Tx 0245134 RECK D. Cables FREDERECK.
    Wilhelmshaven, Emden.

BREST, France—Societe de la Menardiere, 6 Cours d'Ajot, (P.O. Box 117) F-29268.
Tel 98803270 (24 hours). Tx 940270 MENARD F. Cables MENARDIERE.

BRINDISI, Italy—Ditta Teodoro Titi di Angelo Titi, Corso Garibaldi 73/75, (P.O. Box 149), I-72100.
Tel (831) 23514/5 (a.o.h. 23550 & 21036). Tx 813356 TITI I. Cables TITI.

BRISBANE, Australia—Macdonald Hamilton & Co. Pty. Ltd., Broadlands House, 8th Floor, 26 Wharf Street.
Tel (7) 2297594 (a.o.h. 379 4104). Tx 145668 DLSHIP AA. Cables NALDHAM.
    Bundaberg.

BUCHAREST, Romania—Administratia Asigurarilor de Stat (ADAS), Str. Smirdan 5, 79118.
Tel 150519. Tx 11209 ADAS R. Cables ADAS BUC.
    Constantza, Galatz.

BUDAPEST, Hungary—Hungaria Biztosito, 1 Disz Ter 4-5, 1014 Budapest.
Tel (1) 755736 (a.o.h. (1) 222728). Tx 223199 HIREC H.

BUENOS AIRES, Argentina—Cooper Brothers, Viamonte 464, 10th Floor, 1053.
Tel (1) 3113121/3 & 3132186 (a.o.h. 7481289 & 7483218). Tx 23141 COOBRAR.
Cables REPOOC.
    Puerto Deseado, Bahia Blanca, Necochea, Mar del Plata, La Plata, Campana, San Pedro, Ramallo, Puerto Madryn.

BUJUMBURA, Burundi—A Bauwen—L. Louis S.P.R.L., Avenue de la Poste 49A.
Tel 2032. Tx 82 BDI. (attention A. Bauwen/A Louis). Cables BAUWEN.

BULAWAYO, Zimbabwe—Gordon & Gordon (Private) Ltd., 13 Eighth Avenue, (P.O. Box 618).
Tel 60357 (a.o.h. 64567). Cables LLOYDAGENT.
    Gweru.

CADIZ, Spain—G. &. J. MacPherson Soc. Ltda., Fermin Salvochea 4, (P.O. Box 10, 11004).
Tel (956) 213329 & 212656 (a.o.h. 255036 & 832327). Tx 76044 MACE. Cables MACPHERSON.
    Algeciras.

CAIRO, Arab Republic of Egypt—Marine Technical Services Company, Flat 6B-28 Cherif Pasha Street.
Tel (2) 3935724. Tx 92222 or 92354 HILTLS UN. (Messages to commence: For Lloyd's Agents — Box No. 15). Cables DELANY.

CALCUTTA, India — Tata Tea Limited, 1 Bishop Lefroy Road, (P.O. Box 209) 700020.

Tel (33) 440747, 441891, 443977 & 443654 (a.o.h. 452916). Tx (021)-7225 & (021)-3168 TFIN IN. Cables MERCATOR.

CALGARY, Canada—Toole, Peet & Co. Ltd., 1135-17th Avenue S.W., (P.O. Box 4650, Station 'C'), Calgary T2T 5R5.
Tel (403) 245-1177 (24 hours). Tx 03 822781 TOOLE PEET CGY. Cables TOPECO.
Edmonton, Yukon, Whitehorse.

CAPE TOWN, South Africa—Rennie, Murray & Co. (Pty) Ltd., Suite 1900, Main Tower, Cape Town Centre, Heerengracht, 8001, (P.O. Box 2415, 8000).
Tel (21) 2141500 (a.o.h. 743339). Tx (9) 550037 RENMUR. (Prefix not required for teletex).
Cables CLARMUR.
Port Nolloth, Mossel Bay, Windhoek, Walvis Bay, Luderitz.

CARACAS, Venezuela—Frank B. Hill & Co. S.A., Centro Plaza, Torre 'D', Nivel 15, Oficina B. Los Palos Grandes 1062. (Address for letters: P.O. Box 69198 Altamira).
Tel (2) 2844775 & 2847242 (a.o.h. 2839168). Tx 24803 HILLC VC.
Porlamar, Island of Margarita, Puerto Ordaz, Puerto la Cruz.

CARDIFF, United Kingdom—Cory Brothers Shipping Ltd., Cory's Buildings, 57 Bute Street, CF1 1SZ.
Tel (0222) 481141/6 (a.o.h. 830362 & 513603). Tx 498300. Cables CORY.
Newport, Milford Haven.

CASABLANCA, Morocco—Marbar S.A., 81 Avenue Houmane Elfatouaki, (P.O. Box 13169), 01.
Tel 224190 (a.o.h. 364604, 360170 & 361571). Tx 21011, 21012 & 22072 BARIMER M. Cables BARIMER.
Nador, Safi, Tangier.

CAYENNE, French Guiana—Societe Sainte Claire, S.A.R.L., 8 Rue de Remire, (P.O. Box 216), F-97300. Tel 310023. Tx 910330 SOSAC FG. Cables SAINTCLAIRE.

CEUTA, Spanish Territories of North Africa—Imco S.L., Calle Queipo de Llano 2.2a, (P.O. Box 186).
Tel (956) 516933 (a.o.h. 521484). Tx 78089 FONCABE. (Messages to commence: For Britain).
Cables BRITAIN.
Melilla.

CHARLESTON, United States of America—Lucas & Brown Inc., Suite 101, 198 East Bay Street, Sc 29401, (P.O. Box 536, SC 29402).
Tel (803) 577-5782/3 (24 hours). Tx 5101009657 LUCASBROWN SC. Cables LUCAS.

CHARLOTTETOWN, Canada—Hyndman & co. Ltd., 57 Queen Street, (P.O. Box 790), C1A 7L9.
Tel (902) 566-4244 (24 hours) Tx 01444186 HYNDMAN CHTN.

CHERBOURG, France—Pierre-Yves Laplume, C/o Worms Services Maritimes, Quai de Normandie, (PO Box 434), 50104, Cherbourg, Cedex.
Tel 33433402 & 33432535 (a.o.h. 33931334 & 33528922). Tx 170725 WJCHERB F.
Cables WORMS.
Caen.

CHICAGO, United States of America—Toplis and Harding Inc., 222 South Riverside Plaza, IL 60606.
Tel (312) 648-1300 (24 hours). Tx 253047 TOPLIS CGO.

CHITTAGONG, Bangladesh—James Finlay P.L.C., Finlay House, Agrabad, (P.O. Box 118).
Tel 500631/5 (a.o.h. 204231 & 203992). Tx 66231 JFCO BJ. Cables LIZBIL.
Khulna, Dhaka.

CHRISTCHURCH, New Zealand—Seatrans New Zealand Ltd., Metropolitan Life Building, (2nd Floor), 7 Liverpool Street, (P.O. Box 1357), 1.
Tel (3) 797520 (a.o.h. 596911). Tx 4396 STRCHCH NZ. Cables SEATRAN.

CHRISTMAS ISLAND, Indian Ocean—Christmas Island Marine Department, PO Box MMM, Christmas Island, Indian Ocean 6798. Tel 6724-8434 (a.o.h 6724-8212). Fax 6724-8435.

CLEVELAND, United States of America—Champness and Associates Inc., 1138 W.9th Street, Ohio 44113.
Tel (216) 861-1004 (a.o.h. (313) 477-7335). Tx 231248 MARSERV RROU.

COATZACOALCOS, Mexico—Tomas Ruiz, S.A., Calle Juarez 207, (P.O. Box 18), 96400.
Tel (921) 20117, 29542 & 20400 (a.o.h. 22022 & 22637). Tx 78820 RUIZME. Cables LARRAURI.
Dos Bocas, Frontera, Ciudad del Carmen, Campeche.

COCHIN, India—Peirce Leslie India Ltd., Bristow Road, Willingdon Island (P.O. Box 565), 682003.

Tel 6868/9 & 26123 (a.o.h. 6376 & 69592). Tx 0885-6215 PLI IN & 0885-6473 PLTL IN. Cables PEIRCEWIL.

Calicut (Kozhikode), Quilon.

COLCHESTER, United Kingdom—W. Fieldgate & Son Ltd., Haven Quay, CO2 8JE.
Tel (0206) 865432 (a.o.h. 383931). Tx 98126 FLDGTE G. Cables TOWAGE.

COLOMBO, Sri Lanka—Aitken, Spence & Co Ltd.,315 Vauxhall Street, 2.
Tel (1) 548471/3 (a.o.h. 580778 or 553872). Tx 21788 AIRACE CE.
Jaffna, Kayts, Kankesanturai & Point Pedro, Trincomalee, Male.

CONAKRY, Republic of Guinea—Cie. des Experts Maritimes (CEM), P.O. Box 818, (all communicatons should be marked for Mr. J. M. Duconge).
Tel 443861 (24 hours). Tx 2107 SATAG GE. (Messages to commence: For A. Quedrue, CEM).

COPENHAGEN, Denmark—Messrs. A. Pruser, Forbindelsesvej, 12, DK-2100,0.
Tel (01) 262528 (a.o.h. (02) 991856 & (03) 694415). Tx 22316 ESTEPH DK. (Messages to commence: For Lloyd's Agents). Cables LLOYDSAGENT.
Holbaek, Kalundborg, Korsor, Gulfhavn, Naestved, Koge, Nykobing, Bandholm, Nakskov, Ronne.

CORK, Eire—Clyde Shipping Ireland Ltd., Mainport, Monahan Road.
Tel (021) 317900 (a.o.h. 021-811414 or 361547). Tx 76120 MAIN EI. Cables CUMBRAE.
Bantry.

CORUNNA, Spain—Henry Guyatt & Sons Ltd., Avenida Linares Rivas, 18-21, 2 Dcha, 15005.
Tel (981) 222824 & 222888 (a.o.h. 224615, 226277 & 228588). Tx 82174 GUYAT E.
Cables HENRYGUYATT.

COTONOU, People's Republic of Benin—Compagnie des Experts Maritime du Benin (CEM), P.O. Box 269.
Tel 315159 (a.o.h. 300887). Tx 5368 EXPER CTNOU. Cables EXPERMAR.
Niamey, Niger.

CRISTOBAL, Panama—Associated Steamship Agents, S.A., Masonic Temple Building, (P.O. Box 5027).
Tel (45) 0461/2 (a.o.h. (507) 421579 & 609452). Tx 8815 SHIPAGT PPG & 9229 SHIPAGT PA.
Cables SHIPSAGENT.

CURACAO, Netherlands Antilles — Maduro & Curiel's Insurance Services, N.V., Schottegatweg Oost No. 130, (P.O. Box 175 or 305) Netherlands Antilles.
Tel 615025/6, 612511 (a.o.h. (9) 79907). Tx 1288 MCINS. Cables MADUROBANKINS.
Bonaire, Aruba.

DAKAR, Senegal—SOEAM (Senegal) S.A., 53 Boulevard Pinet-Laprade, P.O. Box 835.
Tel 235743 & 233779, (a.o.h. 210478 & 220078). Tx 508 & 3193 MAFRIC SG. Cables MAFRIC.
Senegal, Mali.

DALIAN, People's Republic of China—The People's Insurance Company of China, 141 Zhong Chan Road. Tel 333447. Tx 86215 PICC CN. Cables 42001 DALIAN.

DAMMAM, Saudi Arabia—The Arabian Establishment for Trade, Shiek M Al-Ard Building 6th Floor, Street No. 1 , (P.O. Box 6850).
Tel (3) 8331620 & 8331260 (a.o.h. 842905). Tx 801750 LOYDAG SJ. Cables MEYASSER.

DAR-ES-SALAAM, Tanzania—Toplis & Harding (Tanzania) Ltd., 1st Floor DSM Bookshop Building, Indira Gandhi Street, P.O. Box 799.
Tel (51) 25508, 29077 & 33764. Tx 41512 ADJUST TZ.
Mtwara, Lindi, Iringa, Tabora, Dodoma, Shinyanga, Mwanza.

DARWIN, Australia—R.B. Halstead & Associates Pty. Ltd., 30 Stuart Highway, Stuart Park, N.T. 8020, (P.O. Box 4528, N.T. 0801). Tel (89) 819497 & 818625 (a.o.h. 271439). Fax (89) 813610.
Tel (89) 819497 & 818625 (a.o.h. 271439). Fax (89) 813610.

DETROIT, United States of America—Toplis and Harding Inc., 150 Griswold Avenue, Suite 1400 MI 48226-3485.
Tel (313) 965-3033 (a.o.h. 313 (8269746). Tx 230478 TOPLIS DET. Cables TOPHARD.

DJIBOUTI, Republic of Djibouti—Gellatly, Hankey et Cie (Djibouti) S.A., 9/11 Rue de Geneve, (P.O. Box 81).
Tel 353844, 351858 & 351960 (a.o.h. 350655 & 353820). Tx 5843 GELLATLY DJ.
Cables GELLATLY

DOHA, Qatar—ACE (Qatar) Limited, Al Maneh Building, Sheik Ali Street, (P.O. Box 2745).
Tel 324661 (a.o.h. 853251). Tx 4266 ACE DH. Cables ACE.

DOMINICA, West Indies—H.H.V. Whitchurch & Co. Ltd., Old Street, (P.O. Box 71), Roseau.
Tel 82181 (a.o.h. 82931 & 84082). Tx 8614 WHITDOM DO. Cables WHITCHURCH.

DOUALA, Cameroon—Societe Des Commissaires d'Avaries Reunis (SCAR), (P.O. Box 278).
Tel 427160 & 426260 (a.o.h. 424368 & 428903). Tx 6139 COMISAV KN. Cables COMISAV.

DOVER, United Kingdom—George Hammond (Shipping) Ltd., Limekiln Street, CT17 9EE.
Tel (0304) 201201 (a.o.h. 203333). Tx 96115 & 96213 HAM HO G. Cables HAMMOND.
Sheerness, Whitstable.

DUBAI, United Arab Emirates—Maritime and Mercantile International (Private) Ltd., P.O. Box 70.
Tel (4) 228181 (24 hours). Tx 45425 GRAY EM. Cables GRAY.

DUBLIN, Toplis and Harding Marine, 120 Lower Rathmines Road, 6.
Tel (0001) 965275 & 965003. Tx 92282 TAHM EI.
Arklow, Dundalk, Sligo.

DUISBURG. Germany—Peter Reschop, Havariekommissariat Peter Reschop G.m.b.H.,
Zieglerstrasse, 31, D-4100.
Tel (0203) 331061 (24 hours) (a.o.h. (208) 373871 & (2845) 8121). Tx (17) 203315 RESCHOP.
(Prefix not required for teletex). Cables RESOP.
Cologne (Koln).

DUNDEE, United Kingdom—Barrie & Nairn, 49 Meadowside, DD1 1EH.
Tel (0382) 23044/6 (a.o.h. 79964 & 77075). Tx 76177 NAIRN G. Cables CHARLES or NAIRN.

DUNEDIN, New Zealand—Tapley Swift Shipping Agencies Ltd., Trident House, 40 Jetty Street,
(P.O. Box 385).
Tel (24) 740810 (a.o.h. Port Chalmers 8609). Tx 5788 TRIDENT NZ. Cables TRIDENT.

DUNKIRK, France—P.A. Bourbonnaud, 3 Quai du Risban, (P.O. Box 1-034), 59375 Cedex 1.
Tel 28668614 (a.o.h. 28631714). Tx 820209 COMAVAR F. Cables BOURBONNAUD.

DURBAN, South Africa—Rennie, Murray & Co. (Pty) Ltd., Renfreight House (2nd Floor), 41
Victoria Embankment, 4001, (P.O. Box 2475, 4000).
Tel (31) 3280912 (a.o.h. 742545 & 447738). Tx 620805 SA.
East London, Richards Bay, Manzini.

EL DJAZAIR (Algiers), Algeria—Societe Algerienne des Etablissements Mory & Cie., 8 Boulevard
Colonel Amirouche, (P.O. Box 234 Alger Gare).
Tel 631962/65 (a.o.h. 600272 & 638468). Tx 67354 MORY ALGER. Cables MORY.
Annaba, Skikda, Oran.

ENSENDADA, Mexico—Agencias Maritmas del Pacifico, S.A., Virgilio Uribe 433/455,
(P.O. Box 329).
Tel (667) 82176/7 & 40935 (a.o.h. 82757 & 61243). Tx 56517 AMMSA ENS. Cables AMMSA.

ESBJERG, Denmark—C. Breinholt A/S, D. Lauritzensvej, 14, (P.O. Box 20), DK-6701.
Tel (75) 180411 (24 hours). Tx 54101 BREIN DK. Cables BREINHOLT.

FALMOUTH, United Kingdom—G.C. Fox & Co., 48 Arwenack Street, TR11 3SA.
Tel (0326) 311300 (a.o.h. 313857 & 311510). Tx 45237 FOX G. Cables FOX.
Fowey.

FERROL, Spain—Anton, Martin (Shipping) Ltd., San Francisco, 46, (P.O. Box 917), 15401.
Tel (81) 352102, 351480 & 352497. Tx 85512 ANMAR E.
Cables LLOYDSAGENT & AEGYPTO.

FREEPORT, Bahamas—E.H. Mundy & Co. (Bahamas) Ltd., New Building, The Harbour, (P.O. Box
F-2492).
Tel (809) 352-9691/5 (a.o.h. 373-3759). Tx 30008 MUNDICO FP. Cables MUNDICO.

FREETOWN, Sierra Leone—Mining and General Services Ltd., 2 Blackhall Road, (P.O. Box 68).
Tel 50922, 50906, 50920 & 51395 (a.o.h. 024469 & 024201). Tx 3226 MAGS SL. Cables MAGS.

FREMANTLE, Australia—Danzas Wills Pty. Ltd., 14 Phillimore Street, (P.O. Box 94), W. Aust.
6160.
Tel (09) 3351177 (a.o.h. 4571702). Tx 95522 SEAWIL AA. Cables WILLSINTER.
Geraldton, Bunbury.

GABORONE, Botswana—Manica Freight Services (Botswana) (Proprietary) Ltd., Botsalano House,
The Mall, P.O. Box 1372.
Tel 51485/6 & 53574/5 (a.o.h. 353894.) Tx 2334 MANFS BD.
Francistown, Lobatse, Kasane.

GALLE, Sri Lanka—Clark, Spence & Co. Ltd., Clan House, 24 Church Street, (P.O. Box 11), Fort.

Tel (9) 22083 (a.o.h. 22392). Tx 21142 AITKENCE. (Messages to commence: For Spence Galle). Cables SPENCE.

GALWAY, Eire—Thomas McDonogh & Sons Ltd., Merchants Road.
Tel (091) 66111 (a.o.h. 25527). Tx 50136 MCD EI. Cables MCDONOGH.

GDYNIA, Poland—Polska Izba Handlu Zagranicznego Komisariat Awaryjny (The Polish Chamber of Foreign Trade), Pulaskiego, 6, (P.O. Box 106), 81-368.
Tel (98) 202279 & 218746. Tx 54504 IHAZA PL.

GEFLE (Gavle), Sweden—Captain M.O.R. Bergland, Gavle Hamn, Fredriksskans, 5-805 95.
Tel (026) 178861 (a.o.h. 128472). Tx 47349 GAVPORT S. (Messages to commence: For Lloyd's Agents).
Norrsundet.

GENOA, Italy—Gastaldi International S.r.l., Via Cairoli, 1, I-16124. (P.O. Box 1855, I-16100).
Tel (10) 28591 (a.o.h. 307666, 367808 & 883461). Tx 271574 LLOYGE I. Cables DICKSURVEY.
Turin, Savona, La Spezia, Sardinia, Cagliari, Alghero Porto Torres, Olbia.

GEORGETOWN, Guyana—Guyana National Shipping Corporation Ltd., 5/9 Lombard Street, (P.O. Box 10447). Tel (01) 68896 (a.o.h. 64442 & 51204). Tx 2232 NATSHIP GY. Cables DEMINSCE.

GIBRALTAR—Smith, Imossi & Co. Ltd., 47 Irish Town, (P.O. Box 185).
Tel 78645/6 (a.o.h. 71076 & 78356). Tx 2220 JAVA GK. Cables JAVA.

GIJON, Spain—Casimiro Velasco S.A., Calle Corrida, 8, (P.O. Box 67).
Tel (85) 354643 & 354644 (a.o.h. 33045). Tx 87371 CVSAG E. Cables CASIMIRO.

GLASGOW, United Kingdom—MacLeod & McAllister Ltd., The Bowring Building, 151 West George Street, G2 2JL.
Tel (041) 226 4855 (a.o.h. (041) 9595443). Tx 77396 DIAL G. (Messages to commence: For Lloyd's Agent).
Stranraer, Irvine, Ardrossan, Kyle of Lochalsh, Wick, Invergordon, Inverness.

GOTHENBURG, Sweden—Lindahl & Collin A/B., Hulda Lindgrens gata 3 (P.O. Box 2118, S-421 02 V. Frolunda).
Tel (31) 490950 (a.o.h. 297839). Tx 20710 CARGO S. Cables LLOYDSAGENT.
Uddevalla, Lysekil, Varberg, Falkenberg.

GRAND CANARY, Canary Islands—Blandy Comisarios de Averias S.A., Simon Bolivar 12, (Ap. 2222), 35080 Las Palmas.
Tel (28) 260850 & 267750. Tx 95353 & 95153 MIDAT E. Cables BLANDY.
Lanzarote, Island of.

GRAND CAYMAN, Cayman Islands—H.O. Merren & Co. Ltd., North Church Street, (P.O. Box 63).
Tel 94866 & 94426 (a.o.h. 92653) Tx 4385 MERREN CP. Cables HOMCO.

GRENADA, West Indies—Jonas Browne & Hubbard (Grenada) Ltd., Young Street, St. George's.
Tel 2087, 2088, 2967 & 2887 (a.o.h. 5392). Tx 3443 JBANDH GA.

GUADELOUPE, West Indies—Robert Bonnet, 8 Quai Lardenoy, (P.O. Box 4) F-97151 Pointe-a-Pitre Cedex. Tel 820023. Cables ROBERT BONNET.
Basse-Terre.

GUAM, Mariana Islands (U.S.A.)—Atkins Kroll Inc., Suite 116, PAG Building, 1026 Cabras Highway, Piti, 96910.
Tel (671) 477 5921/2/3 (a.o.h. (671) 477 5924). Tx 721 6133. Cables ATOLIA.
Saipan.

GUANGZHOU, People's Republic of China—The People's Insurance Company of China, 137 Chang Di.
Tel 861227, 861226 & 861558. Tx 44462 PICCG CN. Cables 42001 GUANGZHOU.

GUATEMALA CITY, Guatemala—G.W.F. Franklin Ltd., 12th Calle A., 2-34, (P.O. Box 263), 01901.
Tel (2) 536826, 83233 & 84640 (a.o.h.691091). Tx 9282 FRANGU GU. Cables FRANKLIN.
Quezaltenango, Champerico, Puerto Barrios.

GUAYAQUIL, Ecuador—Anglo Sociedad Anonima Comercial e Industrial, Junin 105 y Malecon, 2° Piso, (P.O. Box 410).
Tel (4)305700 (a.o.h. 387196). Tx 43165 & 43043 SCAEL ED. Cables SCAEL.
Esmeraldas, Manta, Quito.

GUERNSEY, United Kingdom—Commodore Shipping Co. Ltd., Commodore House, Bulwer Avenue, St. Sampsons, (P.O.Box 10, St. Peter Port).
Tel (0481) 46841 (a.o.h. 36396). Tx 4191401 COMMGY.
Alderney.

HAIFA, Israel—Surdam (Agencies 1980) Ltd., 60 Hameginim Avenue, (P.O. Box 33024, 31330).
Tel (4) 523231 (a.o.h. 24210). Tx 46515 AMSUR IL.
Tel Aviv.

HALIFAX, Canada—Pickford & Black, Cogswell Tower, Suite 920, P.O. Box 1117, B3J 2X1.
Tel (902) 423-9191 (a.o.h. 435-6991). Tx 01921693 WARREMPB HFX. Cables PICKFORD.
Windsor, Yarmouth.

HALMSTAD, Sweden—A/B Th. Schele, Bredgatan 2, S-302 45. (P.O. Box 92, S-301 02).
Tel (35) 100440 (a.o.h. 36178). Tx 38100 SCHELE S. Cables SCHELE.

HAMBURG, Germany—OHG Gellatly, Hankey & Co., G.m.b.H. & Co., Ehrenbergstrasse, 59, D-2000,50.
Tel (040) 381891/6 (a.o.h. (40) 896543 & (4101) 46184). Tx 212951 GHCO D. Cables
GELLATLY.

HARARE, Zimbabwe—Garner & Whaley (Pvt.) Ltd., 8th Floor, Throgmorton House, 51 Samora
Machel Avenue, (cnr. Julius Nyerere Way). (P.O. Box 1216).
Tel (14) 720410 & 724010 (a.o.h. (14) 701401). Tx 24164 GDWOOD ZW. Cables AVERAGE.
Mutare (Umtali), Hwange.

HARSTAD, Norway—Polarkonsult A/S Verkstedveien 3A, (P.O. Box 877), N-94 Harstad.
Tel (82) 66611 (a.o.h. 73645, 77021 & 60206). Tx 64482 POKON N.

HAVANA, Cuba—Thomas Simon, Jr., 356 Obispo Street, (P.O. Box 1746).
Tel 80-6663 & 62-3760 (a.o.h. 3-8723). Tx 512422 LLOYD'S CU. Cables DONWHEEL.

HELSINGBORG, Sweden—Damco Survey AB., Gravorgatan 15, S-253 68.
Tel (42) 292290 (a.o.h. 237090 & 261808). Tx 72985.

HELSINKI, Finland—O.Y. Lars Krogius, A.B., Asemamiehenkatu 2, SF-00520.
Tel (0) 148911 (a.o.h. 6987734). Tx 124506 KROCO SF. Cables GROGIUSCO.
Hango, Lovisa, Kotka, Hamina.

HOBART, Australia—Associated Shipping Agency Pty. Ltd., 53 Salamanca Place, Tas. 7000. (P.O.
Box 924, G.P.O., Tas. 7001).
Tel (002) 344833 (a.o.h. 729788 & 293173). Tx 58086 ASSAP AA. Cables JOINTSHIPS.

HODEIDAH, Yemen Arab Republic—Hodeidah Shippiing & Transport Co. Ltd., P.O. Box 3337.
Tel 238130/2 & 238270 (a.o.h. 217314 & 217708).Tx 5510 HDSHIP YE. Cables HODSHIP.
Sana, Taiz, Mokha.

HOLYHEAD (Gwynedd), United Kingdom—Holyhead Shipping Agency Ltd., Newry Beach Yard,
LL65 1YB.
Tel (0407) 2117 & 50111 (a.o.h. 2568 & 741183). Tx 61179 SALTOW G. Cables SALVTOW.

HONG KONG—Gilman & Co. Ltd., 22nd Floor, Tai Yau Building, 181 Johnston Road, Wanchai,
(P.O. Box 56).
Tel (5) 8930322 (a.o.h. (5) 290312, 297232 & 290331). Tx 74607 GMINS HX. Cables
GILMANINS.
Macao.

HONIARA, Solomon Islands—Tradco Shipping Ltd., City Centre Building, Mendana Avenue, (P.O.
Box 114). Tel 22588/9 (a.o.h. 30363). Tx 66313 TRADCO HQ. Cables TRADCO HONIARA.

HONOLULU, Hawaiian Islands, U.S.A.—Theo. H. Davies & Co. Ltd., 608 Fort Street, HI 96813.
(P.O. Box 3020, HI 96802).
Tel (808) 531-8531 (a.o.h. 945-3876). Tx 7238305 DAVIS HJ & 7430018 STEAM. Cables
DRACOSTEAM.

HOUSTON, United States of America—J.R. Bencal & Associates Inc., 4815 F.M. 2351,
Friendswood, Tx 77546. (P.O. Box 58585, Tx 77258).
Tel (713) 482-3386 (24 hours). Tx 9108804177 BENTOM FROD.
Brownsville.

HULL, United Kingdom—Escombe Lambert Ltd., Europa House, 184 Ferensway, HU1 3UE.
Tel (0482) 224151 (a.o.h. 867920). Tx 592245 ELLHUL G. Cables ESCOMBE.
Goole, Guinness, Immingham, Grimsby.

INVERCARGILL, New Zealand—Bain Shipping Services Ltd., Main Road, (P.O. Box 5075),
Lorneville No. 6RD.
Tel (021) 59543 (24 hours). Tx 5480 BEESHIP NZ. Cables BEESHIP BLUFF.

IPSWICH, United Kingdom—Cory Brothers Shipping Ltd., Powell Duffryn House, Cliff Quay,
IP3 0BG.
Tel (0473) 217979 (a.o.h. (0449) 612112 & (0206) 395380). Tx 98282 & 98147

CB IPS G. Cables CORY.
Felixstowe.

IQUIQUE, Chile—S.B. Dawson y Cia Ltda, Zegers, 231 y 249, (P.O. Box 379).
Tel 21873 (24 hours). Tx 223189 SBDAW CK. Cables DAWSON.

ISKENDERUN, Turkey—Catoni Maritime Agencies S.A., Marechal Chakmak Caddesi 28, (P.O. Box 160), 3120.
Tel (881) 11227, 11208 & 11069 (a.o.h. (081) 12682 & 11899). Tx 68125 & 68057 CATI TR. Cables CATONMAR.

ISLE OF MAN, United Kingdom—G.T. Rowe, A.I.C.S., The Ramsey Steamship Co. Ltd., 13 North Quay, Douglas. Tel (0624) 73557 (a.o.h. 75628). Tx 627279 RSSIOM G. Cables KEEGAN.

ISTANBUL, Turkey—Vitsan Mumessillik ve Ticaret A.S., Bilezik Sokak No. 2, (P.O. Box 689, SISLI), 80225 Findikli.
Tel (1) 1520600 (a.o.h. 3568669 & 3555672). Tx 25272 WHIT TR, 22504 VITN TR & 24749 VTSN TR. Cables VITSAN.
Ankara, Trabzon, Samsun, Derince, Izmit, Bandirma.

IZMIR, Turkey—Isbirligi ve Ticaret Anonim Sirketi, Bozkurt Cadesi 32, (P.O. Box 205) Kahramanlar Izmir 35230.
Tel (51) 255221 (a.o.h. 159637). Tx 53045 ISB TR. Cables FOIGGER.

JACKSONVILLE, United States of America—Toplis & Harding Inc., 4110 Southpoint Boulevard, Suite 108, FL 32216.
Tel (904) 281-0304 (a.o.h. 641 7889). Tx 56568 TOPLIS JAX. Cables LLOYDAGENT or TOPLIS.

JAKARTA, Indonesia—Superintending Company of Indonesia Ltd., B Terminal Building, Perum Angkasa Pura Complex, Jalan Angkasa, Keymayoran, Jakarta Pusat 10610.
(PO Box 4032, Jakarta 10001).
Tel: (21) 410908 & 415227. Tx 49262 & 49245.

JEDDAH, Saudi Arabia—The Arabian Establishment for Trade, Al Jowhara Building, Medina Road, (P.O. Box 9963, 21423 S.A.).
Tel (2) 6435289 & 6442635 (a.o.h. 6822201 Ext. 622 & 6915759 Ext. 125). Tx 600583 AIS SJ.
Riyadh.

JERSEY, United Kingdom—F.B. Perry, Jersey Shipping Co. Ltd., 6 Caledonia Place, St. Helier, C.I.
Tel (0534) 20452 (a.o.h. 41531). Tx 4192195 JYSHIP G.

JOHANNESBURG, South Africa—Rennie, Murray & Co. (Pty) Ltd., 7th Floor, Safren House, 19 Ameshoff Street, Braamfontein 2001. (P.O. Box 11194, Johannesburg 2000).
Tel (11) 407 2597, 407 2577, 407 2111. (a.o.h. 787-7095 & 782-2248). Tx 428305 SA.
Cables CLARMUR.

KABUL, Afghanistan—Afghan National Insurance Co., Pamir Building, Taimoor Shahiwat, (P.O. Box 329). Tel 23856 & 22284. Tx 31 BANKMILLIE AF. Cables AFINSURE.

KALMAR, Sweden—A/B Broderna Hoglund, Skeppsbron 4, S-391 00, (P.O. Box 39, S-391 20).
Tel (480) 22330 (a.o.h. 14756 & 23020). Tx 43054 HOGLUND S. Cables HOGLUND.

KAMPALA, Uganda—Toplis & Harding (Uganda) Ltd., Crusader House, 3 Portal Avenue. (*All mail to be addressed to Lloyd's Agency, Nairobi, Kenya*).
Tel 245116 & 235025 (a.o.h. 268923). Tx 61448 AGNES. Cables MACDAL.

KARACHI, Pakistan—Mackinnon, Mackenzie & Co. of Pakistan (Private) Ltd., Mackinnons' Building, 1.1, Chungrigar Road, (P.O. Box 4679), 0225.
Tel 2413041/6 2412916 (a.o.h. 438634). Tx 24517, 2883 & 25607 MACK PK.
Cables MACKINNONS.
Lahore.

KARLSHAMN, Sweden—A/B Lundstrom & Nilsson, (P.O. Box 125). S374 22.
Tel (0454) 18060 (a.o.h. 11335 & 15985). Tx 4562 LUNDSTR S. Cables LUNDSTROMS.

KHARTOUM, Sudan—Gezira Trade & Services Co. Ltd., Gamaa Avenue, (P.O. Box 215).
Tel 81691 & 79060. Tx 22302 MAYO SD & 22315 GZRA SD. Cables MAYO.
El Obeid, Juba, Wad Medani.

KIEL, Germany—Sartori & Berger, Wall 49-51, (P.O. Box 3807), D-2300.
Tel (431) 9810 (a.o.h. 65356). Tx 292832 SBK D. Cables SARTORIBERG.

KIGALI, Rwanda—Magasins Generaux du Rwanda S.A.R.L., P.O. Box 51.
Tel 75543, 73548, 75212 & 72188 (a.o.h. 6722). Tx 516 TRANSIN RW.

KINGSTON, Jamaica—R.S. Gamble & Son Ltd., 134 Harbour Street, (P.O. Box 98).
Tel 92-21620/3 (a.o.h. 924-1113 & 925-9402). Tx 2262 GAMBLE JA. Cables GAMBLE.

KINSHASA, Zaire—Zaire Containers S.P.R.L., 4200 Avenue General Bobozo Adruma, (P.O. Box 10698).
Tel 28508, 26781, 27341 & 289504 (a.o.h. 80339). Tx 21585 & 21586 ZATAIN ZR. Cables ZATAINKIN.
Banana, Boma, Matadi, Lubumbashi.

KIRKENES, Norway—Kirkenes Skipsekspedisjon A/S., Lonboms Plass 5, (P.O. Box 53), N-9901.
Tel (85) 91251 (a.o.h. 92447). Tx 64191 ALMAR N. Cables ALMAR.

KIRKWALL, United Kingdom—Messrs. John Jolly, 21 Bridge Street, (P.O. Box 2), KW15 1HR.
Tel (0856) 2268 (24 hours). Tx 75253 JJOLLY G. Cables JOLLY KIRKWALL TELEX.
Stromness.

KOBE, Japan—Cornes & Co. Ltd., Towa Building, 2-3 Kaigan-dori 2 Chome, Chuo-Ku, 650. (P.O. Box 45, Kobe Port 651-01).
Tel (078) 332-3421, 332-1155 & 391-2833 (a.o.h. 842-5186). Tx 5622310 CORKOB J. Cables CORNES.

KOTA KINABALU, Malaysia—Harrisons and Crossfield (Sabah) Sdn., Bhd., 19 Jalan Haji Saman, (P.O Box 10022), 88800.
Tel (88) 52430 & 215011 (a.o.h. 221878). Tx 80652 HNCBKI MA & 80288 BAWAYS MA.
Cables CROSFIELD.
Labuan.

KRISTIANSAND S. (Christiansand), Norway—Kristiansand Shippping & Terminal Service A/S, Vestre Strandgate, 29, (P.O. Box 251), N-4601.
Tel (42) 26160 (a.o.h. 22412, 44680 & 47275). Tx 56 21063 KST N. Cables TERMINAL.
Mandal, Arendal.

KUALA LUMPUR, Malaysia—Harper Wira Insurance Surveyors and Adjusters Sdn. Bhd., 14 Jalan Bersatu 13/4, 46200 Petaling Jaya (P.O. Box 1094) (Jalan Semangat) (46870 Petaling Jaya) Selangor Darul Ehsan, Malaysia.
Tel (3) 7559884 (a.o.h. 7180997 & 6891330). Tx 37664 HARPJ MA. Cables ACHAN.
Johor Baru, Kuantan, Malacca.

KUCHING, Malaysia—Sebor (Sarawak) Trading Sdn. Bhd., Bangunan Sebor, Lot 2678 Lorong Sebor, Section 64 Ktld, Jalan Kwong Lee Bank 93450, Sarawak. (P.O. Box 2621, 93752).
Tel (082) 486094, 335677 & 333081 (a.o.h. 440899). Tx 70813 SEBOR MA.
Cables SEBORCO.
Sibu, Miri, Bintulu.

KUWAIT—Kuwait Maritime & Mercantile Co. K.S.C., Mackenzie Building, Arabian Gulf Street, (P.O. Box 78 SAFAT).
Tel 5635433, 9024148 & 2423987 (a.o.h. 5393988, 5655034 & 2423987). Tx 22005 GRAY KT & 23371 KMMC KT. Cables GRAY or KMMC.

LA PAZ, Bolivia—La Britanica S.A., Avenida Camacho 1372, (1er Piso), (P.O. Box 8584).
Tel 350822, 358652 & 364474 (a.o.h. 390183). Tx 3321 BRITAN BV. Cables BRITANNIA.
Cochabamba, Oruro, Santa Cruz.

LA ROCHELLE, France—Miss Martine Le Boutillier, 106 Boulevard Emile-Delmas, (P.O. Box 2038), F-17009 Cedex.
Tel 46421344 (a.o.h. 46438104). Tx 790742 SHIPS F. Cables DAYLIGHT.

LAE, Papua New Guinea—Burns Philp (PNG) Limited, Marsina Street, (P.O. Box 79).
Tel 433682, 433744 & 433681 (a.o.h. 424813). Tx 42510 BURPHIL NE. Cables BURPHIL.
Madang, Wewak.

LAGOS, Nigeria—Gellatly Hankey Marine Services, 13/15 Wharf Road, (P.O. Box 52), Apapa.
Tel (1) 871899 & 872396 (a.o.h. 874727). Tx 22225 BRETT NG. Cables BRETTCALCA LAGOS.
Kano, Ibadan.

LATTAKIA, Syria—Syrian Maritime & Transport Agencies S.A., Rue du Port, (P.O. Box 93).
Tel (041) 30210/1. Tx 451022 PRIMAR SY. Cables MARITIME.
Tartous, Banias, Aleppo, Damascus.

LAUNCESTON, Australia—William Holyman & Sons Pty Ltd., Remount Road, Mowbray, PO Box 70, Tas., 7250. Tel (03) 263388 (a.o.h. 442780). Tx 58517 HOLYMAN AA.

LE HAVRE, France—Jacques Durand-Viel, 73-75 Quai de Southampton, (P.O. Box 1395), F-76066 Cedex.
Tel 35412018 (a.o.h. 36461463). Tx 190693 AGENT. (Messages to commence: For Department Duravel). Cables DURAVAL.
Treport, Fecamp, Rouen, Honfleur.

LEGHORN, Italy—Ditta Vincenzo Capanna S.a.s., Via Cogorano 25, (P.O. Box 286), I-57123.
  Tel (586) 22032 & 22033 (a.o.h. 803464 & 804020). Tx 590055 VINCA I. Cables VINCA.
    Bologna, Florence (Firenze), Marina Di Carrara, Viareggio, Piombino, Elba, Island of,
    Follonica.

LEITH, United Kingdom—Brantford Internatioal Agencies Ltd., Atlantic Chambers, 55 Constitution
  Street, Edinburgh EH6 7AY.
  Tel (031) 554 0651/9 (a.o.h. 337 5975). Tx 72115 BRANFD G. Cables BRANTFORD.
    Burntisland, Grangemouth.

LERWICK, United Kingdom—Hay & Co. (Lerwick), 66 Commercial Road, ZE1 ONJ).
  Tel (0595) 2533 (24 hours). Tx 75295 HAYLWK G. Cables HAY.
    Unst, Island of.

LIBREVILLE, Gabon—Les Commissaires d'Avaries Reunis, Avenue du Marquis de Compiegne,
  (P.O. Box 187).
  Tel 720857, 701206 & 765742 (a.o.h. 720918). Tx 5706 COMISAV GO. Cables COMISAV.
    Port Gentil.

LIMA, Peru—International Inspection Services Ltd., Tungasuca 288, San Miguel, (P.O Box 5344,
  100).
  Tel (51) 641969. (a.o.h. 639076, 626307 & 455392). Tx 25490 LINWOOD PU.
  Cables LINWOOD.
    Paita and Bayovar, Pimentel, Salaverry, Iquitos, Pisco.

LIMASSOL, Cyprus—Orphanides & Murat, 140A Franklin Roosevelt Avenue, (P.O. Box 80).
  Tel (51) 62521 (a.o.h. 55074 & 53810). Tx 2468 ROTA CY. Cables ROTALLOYD'S.
    Nicosia, Larnaca, Paphos.

LIMERICK, Eire—Mullock & Sons (Shipbrokers) Ltd., Security House, 15 Lower Mallow Street.
  Tel (061) 315315 (a.o.h. 345439, 316248 & 347163). Tx. 70711 MULL EL. Cables MULLOCK &
  MULLPROMPT.

LISBON, Portugal—James Rawes & Ca. Lta., Street address: Praca Duque De Terceira, No. 4-2
  Andar, 1200. Postal address: 47 Rua Bernadino Costa, (P.O. Box 2122), 1103 Codex.
  Tel (1) 364337/9 (a.o.h. 560813 & 2850593). Tx 12341 & 18337 RAWES P. Cables RAWES.
    Sao Pedro de Muel, Nazare, Sao Martinho do Porto, Peniche, Setubal, Sines, Lagos,
    Faro, Vila Real de Santo Antonio.

LIVERPOOL, United Kingdom—The Liverpool & Glasgow Salvage Association, 179 Sefton House,
  Exchange Buildings, L2 3QR.
  Tel (051) 236 3821/7 (a.o.h. (0772) 812956 & (051) 639 3638). Tx 627388 SALVOR G.
  Cables SALVAGIUM.
    Birmingham, Llanddulas, Rhyl, Mostyn, Fleetwood, Heysham.

LOME, Togo—Compagnie des Experts Maritimes du Togo (CEM), Rue du Gabon, (P.O Box 31).
  Tel 212308, 215685 & 211562 (24 hours). Tx 5337 EXPERT TO. (Messages to commence: For
  CEM). Cables EXPERMARI.

LONDON, United Kingdom—Administration Branch, Agency Dept., Lloyd's, London House, (5th
  Floor), 6 London Street, EC3R 7AB.
  Tel (01) 623 7100 (Ext. 3500 or 3318). Tx 987321 LLOYDS G. Cables LLOYD'S LONDON EC3.

LONDONDERRY, Northern Ireland—John W. Corbett & Son Ltd., 15 Bay Road, BT48 7SH.
  Tel (0504) 360330 (a.o.h. 45884 & 41855). Tx 74516 LANES G. Cables CORBETT.
    Portrush, Letterkenny.

LORIENT, France—M.A. Jacquemin, 58 Avenue de la Perriere, F-56100, Cedex. (P.O. Box 133,
  F-56103, Cedex).
  Tel 97654545 (a.o.h. 97822573). Tx 950812 SHIPLOR F. Cables SHIPLOR.

LOS ANGELES, United States of America—Toplis & Harding Inc., 3580 Wilshire Boulevard, (Suite
  1130), CA 90010. (P.O. Box 76836, CA 90076).
  Tel (213) 382-8336 (24 hours) & 738-7755. Tx 6836831 TOPLIS UW & 798584 TOPLIS LA.
  Cables TOPLIS OR LLOYDAGENTS.
    San Diego.

LOWESTOFT, United Kingdom—Small & Co. (Shipping) Ltd., Waveney Chambers, Waveney
  Road, NR32 1BP.
  Tel (0502) 572301 (a.o.h. 565588). Tx 97319 SMALL G.
    Great Yarmouth.

LUBECK, Germany—Wolfgang Gaedertz & Co.—Friedrich Schneider GmbH, Gross Burgstrasse 55-
  57, (P.O. Box 1265), D-2400.

Tel (451) 71557/9 (a.o.h. 495446). Tx 0211646 HOMAN D. Cables WOLFGANG.

LULEA, Sweden—Lulea Shipping, A.B., Kyrkogatan 1, S-951 34.
Tel (920) 11801/2 (a.o.h. 40102 & 26633). Tx 68325 LULSHIP S. Cables LULEASHIP.
Skelleftehamn, Pitea.

LUSAKA, Zambia—Walford Meadows Ltd., Kachiza Road, Plot No. 7262/3, (P.O. Box 31280).
Tel (01) 218047 & 217804 (a.o.h. 281270). Tx 41610 LUWAL ZA. Cables WALFCA.
Ndola.

MACKAY, Australia—The Adelaide Steamship Co. Ltd., Pier Office, Outer Harbour, (P.O. Box 11),
Q'ld 4740.
Tel (079) 551244 (a.o.h. 421708, 547251 & 522359). Tx 48137 ADSTEAM AA. Cables
MADSTEAM.

MADEIRA—Blandy Brothers & Co. Lda., Avenida Zarco 2, (P.O Box 408) 9006 Funchal Codex.
Tel (91) 20161, 32065 & 32060 (a.o.h. 20274 & 27856). Tx 72125 BLNDY P. Cables BLANDY.

MADRAS, India—Wilson & Company Limited, Chordia Mansion, 739 Anna Salai, (P.O. Box 393),
600002.
Tel (44) 863276 & 860939 (a.o.h. 477122). Tx 417833 WILS IN. Cables WILSON.
Kakinada.

MADRID, Spain—MacAndrews & Co. Ltd., Plaza de las Cortes, 4-5th Floor, 28014.
Tel (91) 429-6987 (a.o.h. 4393749 & 2591504). Tx 27643 MCMAD E. Cables MACANDREWS.
Huelva, Seville.

MALAGA, Spain—Thomas Wilson S.A., Calle Vendeja 6, (P.O. Box 135), 29001.
Tel (52) 214272 & 212195 (a.o.h. 292137 & 225989). Tx 79090 TWI E. Cables WILSON.
Motril.

MALMO, Sweden—Frick & Frick Ltd., Baltzarsgatan, 25, (P.O. Bos 4300), S-203 14.
Tel (040) 73940 (a.o.h. 911186 & 974178). Tx 32126 FRICKO S. Cables FRICKO.
Trelleborg, Ystad.

MALTA—O.F. Gollcher & Sons Ltd., 19 Zachary Street, (P.O. Box 268), Valletta.
Tel (0356) 233758, 624373 & 231851 (a.o.h. 334742, 330537 & 2226930). Tx 1227 & 1283.
GOLCHR MW. Cables GOLLCHER VALLETTAMALTA.

MANAGUA, Nicaragua—E. Palazio & Co.Ltd., Km. 6.5. Carretera Norte, (P.O. Box 1329).
Tel (2) 44399 & 40590 (a.o.h. 58420). Tx 3752315 PALAZIO NK & 3752402 ALMAR NK.
Cables PALAZIO.
Corinto, San Juan Del Sur, Puerto Cabezas, Bluefields.

MANGALORE, India—Peirce Leslie India Ltd., 22/945 Jeppu Road, (P.O. Boxes 9 & 239), 575001.
Tel (824) 24694 & 23232 (a.o.h. 26069 & 25442). Tx 0832-205 PLI IN & 0832-255 PLI IN. Cables
PEIRCESHIP.

MANILA, Philippines—Smith, Bell & Co. Inc., Smith Bell Building, 2294 Pasong Tamo Extension,
Makati 3116, Metro Manila, (P.O. Box 311, Manila D-406).
Tel 888461/5 & 886795 (a.o.h. 993154). Tx 63335 BELLAD PN. Cables BELLOYDS.
Davao, Cebu.

MANNHEIM, Germany—Messrs. Friedrich Hartmann vorm. J. Kerschgens, 2 Beethovenstrasse,
D-6800.
Tel (621) 418065 (a.o.h. (0621) 794944 & (06203) 64841). Tx 462498 HARTM D.

MANZANILLO, Mexico—Agencias Maritimas del Pacifico, S.A., Avenida Morelos, 128,
(P.O. Box 42).
Tel 22126, 21007 & 20082 (a.o.h. 22759). Tx 62509 AMSAME. Cables AMMSA.
Guadalajara.

MAPUTO, Mozambique—Manica Freight Services (Mozambique) S.A.R.L., Praca Dos
Trabalhadores 51, P.O. Box 292 or 577.
Tel 29664, 31082, 25041/5, 23012/6 (a.o.h. 27298, 741915 & 27251). Tx 6221 or
6222 CONFA MO.

MARACAIBO, Venezuela—Frank B. Hill & Co. S.A., Edif Centro Profesional del Norte, Avda. 4
(Bella Vista) Piso 6, (P.O. Box 285), 4001.
Tel (61) 920770 (a.o.h. 917477). Tx 61149 HILL VC. Cables ROYALINCO.

MARIEHAMN, Finland—Stig H. Lundqvist, Lundqvist Rederierna A.B., Norra Esplanadgatan, 9,
SF-22100.
Tel (28) 16411 (a.o.h. 16400). Tx 63113 LUNDQ SF. Cables LUNDQVISTS.

MARSEILLES, France—Gellatly, Hankey & Cie., (France) S.A.R.L.,20 Quai Du Lazaret, 13217,
Cedex 2.

Tel 91905465. Tx 440541 GELATLY F. Cables GELATLY.
> Port la Nouvelle, Sete, Port St. Louis, Port de Brouc, Toulon, Mazamet.

MARTINIQUE, West Indies—Paul Porry, Immeuble du Port, 8 Avenue Maurice Bishop, F-97200 Fort de France.
Tel 637345 (a.o.h. 640062 & 625096). Tx 912463 PORRY MR. Cables POLPORY.

MAURITIUS—Ireland, Fraser & Co. Ltd., 10 Dr. Ferriere Street, (P.O. Box 58), Port Louis.
Tel (08) 2811 (9 lines) (a.o.h. 536604 & 541199). Tx 4696 INSPECT IW. Cables IRELAND.

MAZATLAN, Mexico—Agencias Maritimas del Pacifico, S.A., Av., Emilio Barragan y Vicente Guerrero, (P.O. Box 180), 82000 SIN.
Tel (678) 12634 & 15207 (a.o.h. 23320, 13553 & 14313). Tx 66861 AMMSA ME. Cables AMMSA.
> Guaymas.

MEDAN, Indonesia—Superintending Company of Indonesia Ltd., Jl Palang Merah, 114A.
Tel (61) 513880 & 331125. Tx 51509 SUCOF IA. Cables SUCOFINDO.

MELBOURNE, Australia—P & O Australia Ltd., (Fifth floor), 45 William Street, (P.O. Box 88A).
Tel (03) 621114 (a.o.h. 7873125). Tx 30129 BFORT AA & 32236 PANDOR AA. (Mesages to commence: For Lloyd's Agents). Cables LLOYDSAGNT.

MERIDA, Mexico—Manuel Mier y Teran, S.A. Calle 32 Num 198 X 17, Colonia Garcia Gineres, 97070, Yucatan.
Tel (992) 5-44-88, 5-45-77 & 5-45-99 (a.o.h. 7-02-72). Tx 753834 REIMME. Cables REIM.

MERSIN, Turkey—Catoni Maritime Agencies S.A., Cakmak Cad. Ortaokul Sk. No. 3/B (P.O. Box 273). Tel (741) 12728, 30604 & 34078 (a.o.h. 11160 & 60960). Tx 67188 CATM TR. Cables CATONMAR.
> Antalya, Turkish Administered Cyprus: Nicosia.

MESSINA, Italy—S.W. Garbutt & Son, S.A.S., Via Garibaldi 267a, I-98122.
Tel (90) 46977 (a.o.h. 51012 & 393034). Tx 980043 CARBOY I.
> Sicily, Siracusa, Priolo, Catania, Milazzo, Calabria, Reggio, Crotone.

MEXICO CITY, Mexico—Jaime Papworth e Hijos S.A. de C.V., Avenida Toluca 158, Alvaro Obregon 01780, Mexico D.F. (Address for letters, A. Postal No. 99082, Mexico D.F.).
Tel 595-42-21. Tx 1773003 WPCME. (Messages to commence: For Papworth). Cables PAPWORTH.
> Puebla City.

MIAMI, United States of America—Donald J. Mahoney & Co. Inc., The Tamiami Mall, 8776 S.W. 8th Street, FL 33174. (P.O. Box 140805, CORAL GABLES, FL 33114).
Tel (305) 553-7066/9 (a.o.h. 271-0854). Tx 522268 DONMAHONEY MIAMI FL. Cables DONMAHONEY.

MIDDLESBROUGH, United Kingdom—Constantine & Brantford Ltd., York House, Borough Road, TS1 2HP.
Tel (0642) 243231/8 (a.o.h. 815138). Tx 58502 NORCON G. Cables METEOR.
> Hartlepool, Whitby.

MITYLENE, Greece—D. Mousalas Borthers, P. Countourioti Street No. 73, (P.O. Box 10), 81100.
Tel (0251) 282427 (a.o.h. 27935). Tx 297104 ENS GR MITYLENE SOURLANGASSONS.
(Messages to commence: For Lloyd's Agents). Cables MOUSALAS BROS.
> Islands of Lemnos and Chios.

MOBILE, United States of America—Captain C.L. Hamilton, 156 State Street, AL 36602. (P.O. Box 302 AL 366301).
Tel (205) 433-9997 (24 hours). Tx 505401 MUR STEVE. (Messages to commence: Attention Hamilton). Cables CLHAMCO.

MOGADISHU, Somali Republic—Omer Ali Dualeh, P.O. Box 126.
Tel 22010. Tx 3668 O.A.D. SM. Cables OMERCO.

MOJI, Japan—Holme Ringer & Co. Ltd., 9-9 Minatomachi, Moji-ku, Kitakyushu City, 801, (P.O. Box 72, Moji Port, 801).
Tel (93) 331 1313 (a.o.h. 381 4810). Tx 713403 & 713413 RINGER J. Cables RINGER KITAKYUSHU.

MOLLENDO, Peru—Donnelly & Cia. S.A., 164 Calle Arequipa, (P.O. Box 4).
Tel 2928 & 2721 (a.o.h. 2068). Tx 59653 DONNELLY PE. Cables DONNELLY.

MOMBASA, Kenya—Toplis & Harding (Kenya) Ltd., Cannon Towers, Moi Avenue, (P.O. Box 82208).

Tel (11) 25247 & 312965. (a.o.h. 471008 & 495265). Tx 21205 & 21134 MACKENZIES. Cables MACKENZIES (Attn. Lloyd's Agent).

MONROVIA, Liberia—Denco Shipping Lines Inc., United Nations Drive, (P.O. Box 1587).
Tel 222085 & 221905 (a.o.h. 262819 & 261981). Tx 44258 & 44425 DENCO LI. Cables DENCO.
Buchanan, Cape Palmas.

MONTEVIDEO, Uruguay—Agencia Maritima Thomas J. Schandy, Calle Colon 1580.
Tel 950168 (a.o.h. 407890 & 506253). Tx 22029 SCHANDY UY. Cables SCHANDYS.

MONTREAL, Canada—Boyd, Phillips & Co. Ltd., Suite 1600, 507 Place D'Armes, H2Y 2W8.
Tel (514) 849-5277 (a.o.h. 465-8651). Tx 055 60550 BOYPHIL MONTREAL.
St. John, N.B., Magdalen Islands, Quebec City, Ottawa, Kingston.

MONTROSE, United Kingdon—Piggins & Rex, Meridan Street, DD10 8DS.
Tel (0674) 72827 (a.o.h. 73472). Tx 76251 MOSHIP G. Cables SHIPPING.

MONTSERRAT, West Indies—W. Llewellyn Wall & Co. Ltd., Empire House, Parliament Street, (P.O. Box 224), Plymouth.
Tel 2581/2 (a.o.h. 2306). Tx 5719 WLWALL MK. Cables LEWAL.

MOSCOW, Union of Soviet Socialist Republics—Insurance Company of the U.S.S.R. (Ingosstrakh) Ltd., Pjatnitskaja ul. 12, M-35, (P.O. Box 113805).
Tel 231-16-77. Tx 411144 INGS SU. Cables INGOSSTRAKH.

MUNICH, Germany—C. Gielisch GmbH, P.O. Box 1261, D-8011 Aschheim.
Tel (089) 906425 (24 hours). Tx 529478 CGIE D. Cables LLOYDSMUNICH.

MUSCAT, Sultanate of Oman—Oman United Agencies L.L.C., Ruwi, (P.O. Box 3985).
Tel 793395 & 701291 (a.o.h. 602978, 705763 & 600243). Tx 3215 OUA ON.
Cables OMANUNITED.

NAIROBI, Kenya—Toplis & Harding (Kenya) Ltd., Phoenix House, Kenyatta Avenue, (P.O. Box 10942).
Tel (2) 334273/4 (a.o.h. 582680 & 61837). Tx. 25366 ICEAL. Cables TOPLIS NAIROBI.

NANTES, France—Claude Vigneron, 70 Quai de la Fosse, (P.O. Box 779), F-44000 Cedex.
Tel 40738559 (a.o.h. 40474668 & 40893784). Tx 700578 GUIBAL F. Cables GUIBAL.
Sables d'Olonne.

NAPLES, Italy—Gastaldi International S.r.l., VIA A. Depretis, 102/110, I-80133.
Tel (081) 5525561 & 5523001 (a.o.h. 656674 & 467606). Tx 710152 & 710163 DICKNA I. Cables DICK (Attn: Lloyd's Agency).
Gaeta, Salerno.

NARVIK, Norway—Hans Jorgen Reinkjop, C/o Messrs. Luossavaara-Kiirunavaara A/B., (P.O. Box 310-312), N-5801.
Tel (82) 42625 & 41020 (a.o.h. 44382). Tx 64022 LKAB N (Messages to commence: For Lloyd's Agent). Cables LLOYDSAGENT.
Bodo.

NASSAU, Bahamas—Nassau Survey Agency Ltd., Star Plaza, Mackey Street, (P.O. Box N-8733).
Tel (393) 3403/7 (a.o.h. (393) 3380). Tx 20179 STARINS NS. Cables LLOYDSAGENT.

NAURU, Republic of Nauru—Nauru Phosphate Corporation, Aiwo.
Tel 4189/91 (a.o.h. 4439). Tx 33082 NRUPHOS ZV. Cables NAURUPHOS.

NEUCHATEL, Switzerland—Commisariat d'Aviares (Transport) S.A., 6 Rue des Beaux-Arts, (P.O. Box 1081), CH-2001.
Tel (38) 250533/4 (a.o.h. (38) 421217). Tx 952522 CASA CH. Cables CLAIMARINE.

NEW CALEDONIA—Thomas A. Hagen, Societe W.A. Johnston, S.A.R.L., 7 Rue Anatole, France, (P.O. Box 449), Noumea.
Tel 272083 (a.o.h. 277100). Tx 3070 JOHNSTON NM. Cables JOHNSTON.

NEW DELHI, India—Tata Tea Ltd., Hamilton House, A Block, Connaught Place (P.O. Box 25).
Tel (11) 3326527 & 3327528 (a.o.h. 611431). Tx 316262 TFIN IN. Cables MERCATOR.

NEW ORLEANS, United States of America—Matthews, Matson and Kelly Inc., 3525 N. Causeway Boulevard, Suite 601, Metairie, Louisiana 70002.
Tel (504) 831-2678, 831-2993 & 831-2844 (a.o.h. 845-8415 & 892-6034). Tx 754934 MMK NOLN.

NEW YORK, United States of America—Toplis & Harding Inc., 195 Broadway, New York, NY 10007.
Tel (212) 267-2700 (a.o.h. (201) 905-1241 & (718) 698-5821). Tx 233158 THNY UR & 645-440.
Cables LLOYDAGENT.

NEWCASTLE-UPON-TYNE, United Kingdom—Anthony & Bainbridge Ltd., 3-6 Exchange Buildings, Quayside, NE1 3AP.
Tel (091) 2326411 (a.o.h. (091) 2851991 & (091) 2741512). Tx 53242 ANBA G.
Berwick-upon-Tweed, Craster, Cresswell, Morpeth, Newbiggin, Blyth, Sunderland, Seahouses, Amble.

NICE, France—Etienne Ricci, 'Le Palace', 8 Rue Alphonse Karr, F-06000.
Tel 93872772 (a.o.h. 93814768). Tx 970703 COMAV F.
Cannes, Monace, Monte Carlo.

NORFOLK, United States of America—Henry Eagleton Company Inc., 765 W. Little Creek Road, Suite 1, 23509.
Tel (804) 451 0622. (a.o.h. 481 0991). Fax (804) 451 0684.

NORFOLK ISLAND—Norfolk Marine and Fire Agencies, Taylor's Road, (P.O. Box 28), 2899.
Tel 2181 (24 hours). Tx (766) 32006 NORMAFIRE NISA. Cables NORMAFIRE.

NORTH SYDNEY, Canada—Joseph Salter's Sons Ltd., 299 Commercial Street, (P.O. Box 188), B2A 3M3.
Tel (902) 794-4717 (a.o.h. 794-3639). Cables SALTER.

NOUADHIBOU, Mauritania—Societe d'Acconage et de Manutention en Mauritanie (SAMMA), P.O Box 258/278.
Tel 2263 & 2364 (a.o.h. 2900 & 2910). Tx 433 SAMMAR NDB. Cables SAMMAR.

NOUAKCHOTT, Mauritania—Societe Generale de Consignation et d'Enterprise Maritimes, Sogeco (P.O. Box 351).
Tel 527-40, 522-59 (a.o.h. 529-60 & 525-00). Tx. 557 MAFRIC & 502 MAFRIC. Cables OUESTARIMAR.

ODENSE, Denmark—Messrs. Chr. Clemmensen, Englandsgade 3, (P.O. Box 80), DK-5100.
Tel (09) 120033 (a.o.h. 965303). Tx 59828 CLEM DK. Cables CLEMMENSEN.
Kerteminde, Middelfart, Assens, Maarstal, Rudkobing, Svendborg, Nyborg.

OKINAWA, Japan—Southwest Adjustment Co., Tomari Port Building, 2nd Fl., 25-25-3-Chome, Maejima, Naha, 900.
Tel (988) 681341 & 637221. Cables OKISWAC NAHA OKINAWA.

OPORTO, Portugal—Rawes (Peritagens) Lta., Rua de Julio Dinis 891-2°E, 4000.
Tel (2) 694851 & 694921 (a.o.h. 681210 & 7112376). Tx 28537 RAWCO P. Cables RAWES.
Figueira da Foz.

ORNSKOLDSVIK, Sweden—Grundberg Shipping AB, Storgatan 6, (P.O. Box 30), S-891 01.
Tel (0660) 10235 (a.o.h. 50694 & 16144). Tx 6057 GRUSHIP S. Cables GRUNDBERG.

OSLO, Norway—Chr. Thorbjornsen A/S., Grev. Wedels Plass., 4, 0151.
Tel (2) 427095 (a.o.h. 509293 & 440602). Tx 72400 FOTEX N. (Messages to commence: Attention FIX). Cables FIX.
Skien, Larvik, Sandefjord, Tonsberg, Drammen, Moss, Fredrikstad, Halden.

OULU, Finland—O.Y. Herman Andersson, Jaasalontie, SF—90400. (P.O. Box 37, SF-90401).
Tel (981) 221144 (24 hours) (a.o.h. 552342). Tx 32146 ANSON SF. Cables ANDERSSON.
Kemi, Raahe (Brahestad), Kokkola (Yxpila).

PAGOPAGO, American Samoa—G.H.C. Reid & Co. Ltd., P.O. Box 1269, American Samoa 96799.
Tel (684) 699-1854 (a.o.h. 6999966). Tx (782)-515 REIDCO SB. Cables REIDCO.

PALEMBANG, Indonesia—Superintending Company of Indonesia., Jl. Veteran No. 35B.
Tel (711) 21377 & 23141 (a.o.h. 24149). Cables SUCOFINIDO.
Padang, Telukbetung, Kalimantan, Pontianak.

PALERMO, Italy—Placido Mancuso & Figli SNC, Via Roma, 386, I-90139.
Tel (91) 585102, 585155 & 588661 (a.o.h. 583463 & 309174). Tx 910039 MANCUS I. Cables MANCUSO.
Trapani, Marsala, Port Empedocle, Licata, Gela.

PALMA, Spain—Miguel Puigserver, S.A., Av. Antonio Maura 26, (P.O. Box 87).
Tel (971) 715303 (a.o.h. 261973). Tx 68589 PULET E. Cables PUIGMULET.

PANAMA CITY, Panama—Pacific Dodwell, S.A., Edificio Plaza Regency, (11th Floor—Off 'A'), Via Espana 177, (P.O. Box 8151).
Tel 692411 & 693718 (a.o.h. (507) 230315). Tx 2118 PACIFIC PA & 2693 PACIFIC PG. Cables PACIFIC.

PARAMARIBO, Suriname—Handelmij Van Romondt N.V., Waterkant, 40-42, (P.O. Box 1837).

Tel 72831 & 77684 (a.o.h. 51423). Tx 314 ROMONDT SN. Cables VANROMONDT.

PARIS, France—Toplis & Harding S.A., 80 Boulevard Haussmann, F-75008.
Tel (1) 43873730/1 (a.o.h. 39650187, 43544780 & 39732366). Tx 2902009 TOPLI.
Cables TOPLIS.
Strasbourg, Lyon.

PENANG, Malaysia—Sandilands Claims & Settlements Sdn., Bhd., 1-E Penang Street, 10200. (P.O. Box 699, 10790).
Tel (4) 615166 & 615375 (a.o.h. 361993). Tx MA 40093 SACSET. Cables SANCLASET.
Ipoh, Kota Baharu, Kemaman, Phuket, Thailand.

PENZANCE, United Kingdom—J.H. Bennetts Ltd., 72/73 Market Jew Street, TR18 2LF.
Tel (0736) 60666 & 60760 (a.o.h. 740942 & 61602). Tx 45530 JHB G. Cables PROGRESS.

PIRAEUS, Greece—Miller Limited E.P.E., 117 Notara Street, (P.O. Box 80071), 18535.
Tel (1) 4522655, 4522657 (a.o.h. 4612961 & 8980012). Tx 212903 MILA GR & 211309 MILA GR.
Cables THOSMILLER.
Corfu, Volos, Thessaloniki, Canea & Iraklion, Crete.

PLYMOUTH, United Kinghdom—W.D. Tamlyn & Co. Ltd., Victoria Wharves, Coxside, PL4 0RF.
Tel (0752) 663444 (a.o.h. 564843 & 492137). Tx. 45247 TAMLYN G. Cables FREIGHTS
PLYMOUTH TELEX.
Bideford.

POINTE NOIRE, Congo—Les Commissaires d'Avaries Reunis, Enciente Portuaire Immeuble
C.F.C.O., (P.O. Box 548).
Tel 94-02-31 (a.o.h. 94-02-32). Tx 8201 FREIGHT KG. (Messages to commence: For Lloyd's
Agents). Cables COMISAV.
Brazzaville.

PORT AU PRINCE, Haiti—Ets. J.B. Vital S.A., (P.O. Box 87).
Tel 2-2640, 2-2840 & 2-2446 (a.o.h. 71920/1 & 74030). Tx 2030402 & 2030012 VITAL. Cables
VITAL.
Jacmel, Aux Cayes, Miragoane, Cap Haitien.

PORT ELIZABETH, South Africa—Rennie, Murray & Co. (Pty) Ltd., Suite 407, Safmarine Centre,
9 Main Street, 6001. (P.O. Box 506,6000).
Tel (41) 558306/7 (a.o.h. 313336). Tx 24-3251 RENPI SA. Cables CLARMUR.

PORT HARCOURT, Nigeria—Fraser & Shepherd, Umarco Building, 11 Industry Road, (P.O. Box
525). Tel (084) 334727. Tx 61172 MAFRIC NG (Attention Lloyd's Agents). Cables HUFRAS.
Warri, Aba, Calabar.

PORT KELANG, Malaysia—Harper Wira Insurance Surveyors and Adjusters Sdn. Bhd., Insurance
Division, 26/28 Jalan Cunagh, (P.O. Box 32, 42000 Selangor).
Tel (3) 3687201/5, 3687698 & 3686600 (a.o.h. 3315644). Tx 39513 or 39672. Cables ACHAN.

PORT MORESBY, Papua New Guinea—Burns Philip (PNG) Limited, Champion Parade &
Musgrave Street, (P.O. Box 1403).
Tel 229207 & 229290 (a.o.h. 217872 & 211285). Tx 22116 BURPHIL NE. Cables BURSHIP.

PORT SAID, Arab Republic of Egypt—El Meina Shipping Agency, 40 El Goumhouria Street, (P.O.
Boxes 328 & 130).
Tel 220675/7, 237073 & 222883 (24 hours). Tx 63263 & 63034 MENIA UN. Cables MINSHIP.
Suez.

PORT STANLEY, Falkland Islands—Falkland Islands Co. Ltd., Crozier Place, (P.O. Box 202).
Tel 300 & 60 (a.o.h. 412 & 136). Tx 2418 FALKISCO FK. Cables FLEETWING.

PORT SUDAN, Sudan—Gezira Trade & Services Co. Ltd., (P.O. Box 17).
Tel 2029, 2534 (24 hours) & 2783. Tx 70003 MAYO SD. Cables MAYO.

PORTLAND (Maine), United States of America—Chase, Leavitt & Co., 10 Dana Street, (P.O. Box
589), 04112.
Tel (207) 772-3751 (a.o.h. 799-1932 & 797-2352). Tx 950027 SHIPAGENT POR. Cables
LEAVITT.

PORTLAND (Oregon), United States of America—Alexander Gow Inc., Suite 103, 1750 N.W. Front
Avenue, 97209. Tel (503) 224-4005. Tx 364006 GOWLLOYD PTLD.

PORTO ALEGRE, Brazil—Expresso Mercantil Agencia Maritima Ltda., Edificio Formac, Travessa
Francisco Leonardo Truda, 40, (P.O. Box 166), 90000.
Tel (0512) 246155 (a.o.h. (532) 323037). Tx 51-1214 EXME BR. Cables EMAM.

PRAGUE, Czechoslovakia—Ceska Statni Pojistovna, Nove Mesto,Spalena 16, (P.O. Box 841), 11400.
Tel (2) 298641 (a.o.h. 2148111). Tx 121112 CPOJ C. Cables STAPOJ.

PUERTO CORTES, Honduras, C.A.—Agencia Guzman y Cia., S. de R.L. de C.V., Apartado Postal 13.
Tel 550287, 550753 & 550129 (a.o.h. 550732, 550423 & 550050). Tx 8011 ANGELEVI HO. Cables GUZCO.
San Pedro Sula, San Lorenzo, La Ceiba, Tegucigalpa.

PUNTA ARENAS, Chile—King & Cia. Ltda., Calle Roca 817, (of. 54). (P.O. Box 22-D).
Tel (61) 223008 (a.o.h. (61) 221557, 227903, 221963). Tx 280039 BOOTH CL. (Messages to commence: "Para King Telephone 23008"). Cables OVINGDEAN.
Coyahique.

PUSAN, South Korea—Hyopsung Shipping Corporation, Yuchang Building (12 Floor), 25-2, 4-Ka, Chungang-Dong, Chung-Ku, (P.O. Box 75).
Tel 463-0041 & 6551/5 (a.o.h. 625 9880). Tx 53323 & 53374 HYOPSUNG K.
Seoul, Inchon.

QINGDAO, People's Republic of China—The People's Insurance Company of China, Zhong Shan Road. Tel 221011 & 224169. Tx 32142 PICC CN. Cables 42001 QINGDAO.

RABAUL, Papua New Guinea—Burns, Philip (PNG) Ltd., Mango Avenue, (P.O. Box 87).
Tel 922813 (a.o.h. 922504). Tx 92806 BURPHIL NE or 21219 HQTAC BM. Cables BURPHIL.
Kimbe, Kavieng, Bougainville, Island of.

RANGOON, Burma—Burma Ports Corporation, Traffic Department, Agency Division, No. 83/91. Bo Aung Gyaw Stret, (P.O. Box 146).
Tel 74628 & 71163 (a.o.h. 75733). Tx 21208 or 21210 HQTAC BM. Cables TRANSAGENT.
Akyab, Bassein.

RAROTONGA, Cook Islands—Cook Islands Trading Corporation Ltd.,Private Bag 1.
Tel (682) 22-000 (a.o.h. 27-006). Tx 62013 CITCO RG. Cables CITCO.

RAUMA, Finland—O.Y. Grundstrom & Heinrichs A.B., Satana, SF-26100,(P.O. Box 68 SF-26101).
Tel (9) 38 3121 (a.o.h. (38) 240040 & 80129). Tx 65113 GRUHE SF. Cables GRUNDRICHS.

RECIFE, Brazil—Eden Maurice Thom, Thom & Cia. Ltda., Rua da Moeda, 63, (P.O. Box 46), 50000.
Tel (081) 2241622 & 2241329 (a.o.h. 2684135 & 4312019). Tx 081 1234 & 081 2207 THOM BR.
Cables THOM.
Maceio.

REUNION—Harold J. Thomson, 23 Rue Marcel Carne.
Tel 422320 (a.o.h. 448383). Tx 916252 NOSHEX. Cables NOSHEX.

REYKJAVIK, Iceland—Konnun HF, Sudurlandsbraut 10, IS-108, (P.O. Box 8734, IS-128).
Tel (1) 688422 (a.o.h. 43941, 42974 & 14147). Tx 2051 INSURE IS. Cables KONNUN.
Akureyri.

RHODES, Greece—D.E. Demetriades & Co. Ltd., 25th Martiou St., 23 (P.O. Box 47), GR 851 00.
Tel (241) 27306, 27247 & 22615 (a.o.h. 24963 & 27419). Tx 292282 BPRO GR. Cables DAKIS.
Islands of Leros, Calymnos, Cos, Carpathos, Cassos.

RIJEKA, Yugoslavia—Jadroagent, Koblerov trg b.b., (P.O. Box 120), 51000.
Tel (051) 38759 (a.o.h. 615424). Tx 24153 JADRAG YU. Cables JADROAGENT.
Ljubljana, Koper, Pula, Novi Sad, Zadar, Sibenik, Split, Kardeljevo (Ploce), Dubrovnik, Bijela, Bar.

RIO DE JANEIRO, Brazil—Expresso Mercantil Agencia Maritima Ltda., Avenida Rio Branco, 25 (2nd Floor), (P.O. Box 969), 20.090.
Tel (021) 223-2126 (a.o.h. 2469392, 4471413 & 3252456). Tx 2123416 & 2132428 EMAM BR.
Cables CEMIL.
Vitoria.

RIO GRANDE, Brazil—Rex V. Wigg, (British Vice-Consul), Rua Francisco Marques, 163, (P.O. Box 52), 96200.
Tel (532) 327788, 327550 & 327650 (a.o.h. 321575). Tx. 532191 SIAS BR. Cables BRITAIN.
Itajai, Sao Francisco do Sul.

ROME, Italy—Gastaldi International S.r.l., Via S. Godenzo, 187, 1-00189.
Tel (6) 3668251 & 3653603 (a.o.h. 3664689). Tx 620313 IMS I. Cables DICKSURVEY.
Civitavecchia.

ROSARIO, Argentina—Platamar, S.A., Maipu, 648 (P.O. Box 248), 2000.

Tel (41) 216439, 213577 & 216511 (a.o.h. 384842 & 212933). Tx 41720 LLOYD AR.
Cables PLATAMAR.
    San Nicolas, Santa Fe.

ROTTERDAM, Holland—John Hudig & Son, B.V., Willemskade, 23 3016 DM. (P.O. Box 520,
3000 AM).
Tel (10) 4119002 (a.o.h. (1827) 2839, (10) 4224844). Tx 23292 JHSON NL.
Cables BLOKHUYZEN.
    Hook of Holland, Dordrecht, Flushing (Vlissingen), Terneuzen.

ST. CROIX, Virgin Islands (U.S.A.)—Rob't L. Merwin & Co. Inc., P.O. Box 427, Frederiksted,
00841-0427.
Tel (809) 7722264 (a.o.h. 7720519). Tx 3475046 SERVICE VN. (Messages to commence: For
Merwin Lloyd's Agents). Cables MERWIN.

ST. HELENA—Solomon & Co. (St. Helena) Plc., Main Street, Jamestown.
Tel 254. Tx 204 SOLO HL. Cables SOLOMON.

ST. JOHN'S, Canada—Reed Stenhouse Ltd., P.O. Box 12000, St. John's N.F. A1B 3T6.
Tel (709) 739-1000 (a.o.h. 726-1246). Tx 0164541 REEDSTEN SNF.
    Goose Bay, St. Pierre.

ST. KITTS, West Indies—Delisle, Walwyn & Co. Ltd., Liverpool Row, (P.O. Box 44), Basseterre.
Tel 2631/4 (a.o.h. 2221). Tx 6835 DELWAL KC. Cables DELWAL.
    St. Maarten, Netherlands Antilles.

ST. LUCIA, West Indies—Minvielle & Chastanet Ltd., Bridge Street, (P.O. Box 99 & 92), Castries.
Tel 23493 & 22811/9 (a.o.h. 28634 & 25626). Tx 6204 COMCHAST LC & 6336 CHASTANET LC.
Cables CHASTANET.

ST. MALO, France—Y. J. Delamaire & P. Y. Brochard, 2 Chaussee des Corsaires, (P.O. Box 179), F-
35409.
Tel 99560721 (a.o.h. 99818580 & 99817518). Tx 730926 NAVAL SMALO.
Cables NAVAL ST. MALO 35.

ST. MICHAEL'S, Azores—Albano de Oliviera, Sucr., Avenida Infante D. Henrique, 5, (1st Floor),
(P.O. Box 153), 9500 Ponta Delgada.
Tel Ponta Delgada 22638 (a.o.h. 32263). Tx 82117 LLOYDS P.
Cables LLOYDS PONTADELGADA.

ST. THOMAS, Virgin Islands (U.S.A.)—B.A. Johnson and Associates Inc., P.O. Box 4337, 00801.
Tel (809) 775 6140 (a.o.h. (809) 774 7603). Tx 347 4077 SURVEY STT.

ST. VINCENT, Cape Verde Islands—Agencia Nacional de Viagens, P.O. Box 142.
Tel 2418, 2420 & 311356 (a.o.h. 315386). Tx. 3083 ANVSV CV. Cables ANV-SV.

ST. VINCENT, West Indies—Hazells Ltd., Market Square, (P.O. Box 108).
Tel 61201 (a.o.h. 61105 & 84234). Tx 7512 HAZELLS VQ. Cables HAZEL.

SALALAH, Sultanate of Oman—Oman United Agencies (Dhofar) L.L.C., P.O. Box 18179.
Tel 294820, 290012 & 291132 (a.o.h. 463095, 291920 & 295505). Tx 7614 OUAD MB SLL.
Cables OMANUNITED

SALINA CRUZ, Mexico—Agencias Maritimas del Pacifico, S.A., Pacifico 13 Altos, (P.O. Box 36),
70600.
Tel 40233 & 41947 (a.o.h. 40212 & 40369). Tx 78300 OPERME. Cables AMMSA.

SALVADOR, Brazil—Expresso Mercantil Agencia Maritima Ltda., Avenida Estados Unidos 340
(6th Floor), (P.O. Box 959), 40000.
Tel (71) 242-7011 (a.o.h. 2403104, 3847833 & 2357449). Tx 711134 EXME BR. Cables EMAM.
    Ilheus.

SAMOS, Greece—Messrs G. & D.L. Marc, 15 Th. Sofoulis Str. (P.O. Box 10) 831 00.
Tel (273) 22641/5 (a.o.h. (256) 9018). Tx 294110 RHEN, 294154 HAGI & 294172 TONE. Cables
MARC.

SAN FRANCISCO, United States of America—Toplis & Harding Inc., 101 California Street, Suite
1750, 94111.
Tel (415) 392-6355 (a.o.h. 256 9018). Tx 34230. Cables TOPLIS.

SAN JOSE, Costa Rica—Lyon & Co. Ltd., Calle 2, Avenida Central 1a, (P.O. Box 10184), 1000.
Tel 212611, 2316453 & 231690 (a.o.h. 286164). Tx 2577 LYON CR.

SAN JUAN, Puerto Rico (U.S.A.)—Francis B. Crocco Inc., Puerto Rico Drydock Administration
Building, Pier 15, Santurce, (P.O. Box 1411), 00903.
Tel (809) 723-2103/4 & 732-2985 (a.o.h. 783-6992 & 780 4473). Tx 3252364 & 3857005 SURVEY
PT. Cables SURVEYOR.

SAN SALVADOR, El Salvador—Gibson y Cia. (Suc.), 17 Calle Poniente, 320, Centro de Gobierno, (P.O. Box 242), 01-107.
Tel 711050, 711081, 711668 & 226104 (a.o.h. 74-0875 & 26-1906). Tx 20174 GIBSON. Cables GIBSON.

SANDAKAN, Malaysia—Harrisons and Crosfield (Sabah) Sdn., Bhd., Third Avenue and North Road, (P.O. Box 1205), 90008.
Tel (89) 42141 ext. 37 & 42624 (a.o.h. (89) 271512). Tx 82006 HNCSDK MA. Cables CROSFIELD.
Tawau, Lahad Datu.

SANTIAGO, Chile—Gibbs & Cia., S.A.C., Avenida Providencia 1050, (Address for letters: P.O. Box 1-T Tajamar).
Tel 2253634 & 2231061 (a.o.h. 2251780). Tx 340309 GIBBS CK. Cables ANTIPODEAN.
Tocopilla, Coquimbo, Valparaiso, San Antonio, Talca, Concepcion, Antofagasta.

SANTO DOMINGO, Dominican Republic—Frederic Schad Inc., Jose Gabriel Garcia, 26 (P.O. Box 941).
Tel 689-4131 & 9377 (a.o.h. 685-4622). Tx 3460029, 3460403, 3264109 & 3264122 SCHAD. Cables SCHAD.
La Romana, Barahona.

SANTOS, Brazil—Norton, Megaw & Co. Ltd., Praca Republica 87 8°, cj, 86, (P.O. Box 10), 11013.
Tel (0132) 345908 & 345914 a.o.h. (0132) 315447 (APT. 1819). Tx 131001 & 131111. (Messagss to commence: For Norton). Cables NORTON.
Paranagua, Sao Paulo

SAN TOME, Democratic Republic of Sao Tome and Principe—Hull, Blyth (Angola) Ltd., Praca de Indepencia, (P.O. Box 15).
Tel 21372, 21027 & 21026 (a.o.h. 22449). Tx 220 HBALTD ST. Cables VAPOR.

SAVANNAH, United States of America—Charles T. Theus Inc., 126 Habersham Street, (P.O. Box 8644), 31412.
Tel (912) 233-3588 (a.o.h. 897-1787 & 897-0893). Tx 9102400612 CT THEUS SAV.

SEATTLE, United States of America—Alexander Gow Inc., Suite 115, 221 First Avenue West, 98119.
Tel (206) 285 7776 (a.o.h.285 0520). Tx 320359 GOWLLOYD. Cables GOWLLOYD.

SEMARANG, Indonesia—Superintending Company of Indonesia Ltd., Jl. Teuku Umar 33, (P.O. Box 69), Semarang 50401. Tel (24) 312586 & 319995. Cables SUCOFINDO.
Cilacap.

SEYCHELLES—H. Savy & Co. (Seychelles) Pty. Ltd., State House Avenue, (P.O. Box 20), Victoria, Mahe.
Tel 22129 & 22120 (a.o.h. 23435). Tx 2229 HARVY SZ. Cables HARVY SEYCHELLES.

SHANGHAI, People's Republic of China—The People's Insurance Company of China, Zhong Shan Road E.1.
Tel 234305 (a.o.h. 315770). Tx 33128 PICCS CN. Cables 42001 SHANGHAI.

SINGAPORE—Boustead Services Pte. Ltd., 15 Hoe Chiang Road, 13-03, Sanford Building 0208. (Robinson Road, P.O. Box 3050, Singapore 3050).
Tel 2247766 (a.o.h. 2588781). Tx 21233 SEAHOSS RS. Cables BOUSMARINE.

SOFIA, Bulgaria—Bulgarkontrola, 42 Partchevitch Street, (P.O. Box 106), 1080.
Tel 85151, 872239 & 874092 (a.o.h. 627766). Tx 23318 BSK BG & 23653 BSK BG. Cables BULGARKONTROLA.
Plovdiv, Bourgas, Varna, Rousse.

SOUTHAMPTON, United Kingdom—Escombe Lambert Ltd., 204-206 Berth, Prince Charles Container Port, SO9 4TD.
Tel (0703) 789122 (a.o.h. 692810 & 473018). Tx 477010 EELSOT G. Cables ESCOMBE LAMBERT.
Shoreham-by-Sea, Portsmouth, Cowes, Isle of Wight, Newhaven, Poole, Weymouth & Portland, Bridport.

STAVANGER, Norway—Bergesen D.Y. A/S., Erichstrupgst 14, (P.O. Box 187), N-4001.
Tel (4) 527000 (a.o.h. 530615, 588275 & 560413). Tx 33028 BERDY N. Cables BERDY.
Haugesund, Flekkefjord, Egersund, Farsund.

STOCKHOLM, Sweden—Lindahl & Collin A/B., Heliosvagen 10 (P.O. Box 81093) S-104, 81.
Tel (8) 743065 (a.o.h. 385445 & 7177322). Tx 10614 ASSURE S.
Norrkoping, Oxelosund.

STORNOWAY, United Kingdom—Duncan MacIver Ltd., 3 Maritime Buildings, King Edward's Wharf, PA87 2XU.
Tel (0851) 2012 (a.o.h. 2682). Tx 75363 DMISTY G. Cables DUNCAN.

SUNDSVALL, Sweden—Sundsvall Shipagent AB., Jarnvagsparken, (P.O. Box 79), S-851 02.
Tel (060) 129410 (a.o.h. 156242, 585290 & 116059). Tx 71371 SUAGENTS. Cables SHIPAGENT.

SURABAYA, Indonesia—Superintending Company of Indonesia Ltd., Jl. Taman Jayengrono No. 1, (P.O. Box 30).
Tel (31) 43856/7 (24 hours), 22284 & 20231. Tx 34233 SCI SB JA. Cables SUCOFINDO.
Banjarmasin, Balikpapan.

SUVA, Fiji—Carpenters Shipping, 100 Thomson Street, Private Bag.
Tel 312244 (a.o.h. 322671). Tx 2199 CARSHIP FJ. Cables CARSHIP.
Lautoka, Labasa, Tarawa (Republic of Kiribati).

SWANSEA, United Kingdom—Burgess & Co. Ltd., Queen's Buildings, Cambrian Place, SA1 1TT.
Tel (0792) 650021/8 (a.o.h. 369943 & 405274). Tx 48133 BURSEA G. Cables BURGESS.
Port Talbot, Briton Ferry.

SYDNEY, Australia—ACTA Pty. Limited, 447 Kent Street, 2000. (P.O. Box 4006).
Tel (02) 2660633 (a.o.h. 3371418 & 4671928). Tx 121369 ACTAUST AA.

SZCZECIN, Poland—Polska Izba Handlu Zagranicznego Komisariat Awaryjny (The Polish Chamber of Foreign Trade), Plac Batorego, 4, 70 207.
Tel (95) 39393 (a.o.h. 78724). Tx 422225 POLCH PL. Cables POLCHAMBER.

TAHITI, French Polynesia—Compagnie Francaise Maritime de Tahiti, S.A., Immueble Importex Fare Ute., (P.O. Box 368), Papeete.
Tel 426393 (a.o.h. 426098). Tx 258 TAPORO FP PAPEETE. Cables TAPORO.

TAIPEI, Taiwan—Jardine, Matheson & Co. Ltd., World Trade Building, 50 Hsin Sheng South Road, Section 1, (P.O. Box 81).
Tel (02) 3931177 & 3954510/1 (a.o.h. 8727874). Tx 21851 JARDINES. (Messages to commence: For Lloyd's). Cables LLOYDS TAIPEI.

TAMPA, United States of America—Toplis and Harding Inc., 3804 Coconut Palm Drive, (Suite 115), 33619.
Tel (813) 628 4441 (a.o.h. (645) 3777). Tx 808859 TOPLIS TPA. Cables TOPLIS.

TAMPICO, Mexico—Pulford, S.A., Aduana 203 Sur, Desp. 105/107, P.C. 89000. (P.O. Box 160).
Tel (121) 2-32-70 & 2-70-78 (a.o.h. 32468, 33827 & 28946). Tx 14734 PULFME.
Cables PULFORD.
Monterrey.

TANGA, Tanzania—National Shipping Agencies Co. Ltd., Independence Avenue, (P.O. Box 89).
Tel (53) 3073 & 2611/4 (a.o.h. 40943). Tx 45026 NASACO TGA. Cables NASACO.
Arusha.

TARANTO, Italy—Valentino Gennarini, S.r.l., 31 Corso Vittorio Emanuele, 1-74100.
Tel (099) 407484/6 (a.o.h. 371594 & 337323). Tx 860005 MARGEN I. Cables CARGEN.
Gallipoli.

TARRAGONA, Spain—MacAndrews & Co. Ltd., Apartado Rambla Nova 114, 2nd Floor, Room 5, 43001.
Tel (77) 23317 & 237149 (a.o.h. 211929 & 648054). Tx 56536 MCTAR E. Cables
MACANDREWS.
San Carlos de la Rapita.

TEHERAN, Iran—Irano-German Insurance Services (Pvt. Co. Ltd.), Ave. Sanaie, 20th Street No. 54, 15869.
Tel (21) 827299 & 827733 (a.o.h. 4884577 & 4885211). Tx 215310 EXAD IR. (Messages to commence: For Surveyor I.D. No. 108). Cables SURVEYOR.

TENERIFE, Canary Islands—Hermanos Hamilton, S.A., Edificio Hamilton, Marine 7, (P.O. Box 203), 38002 Santa Cruz.
Tel (22) 247280/3 (a.o.h. 226864 & 260993). Tx 92591 HALL E.
Orotava, Island of La Palma.

TERCEIRA, Azores—Jose de Castro Franco, C/o Oceanica Ltd., Oceanica Building, (P.O. Box 4), 9760 Praia da Vitoria.
Tel 52077/79 & 317855 (a.o.h. 32262). Tx 82156 ANOCEA P. Cables OCEANICA.
Angra do Heroismo, Terceira and the Islands of: Graciosa, Flores, Fayal, Pico, St.
George Velas, St. George Calheta.

TIANJIN, People's Republic of China—The People's Insurance Company of China, Jie Fang Bei Lu He Ping District. Tel 393886 & 391297. Tx 23262 PICC CN. Cables 42001 TIANJIN.

TONGA—Burns Philp (South Sea) Co. Ltd., Salote Road, (P.O. Box 55), Nuku'alofa.
Tel 23378 (a.o.h. 22067). Tx 66220 BURNSTH TS. Cables BURNSOUTH.
Tonga, Vava'u, Niue Island.

TORONTO, Canada—Boyd, Phillips & Co. Ltd., 1 Yonge Street, Suite 2206.
Tel (416) 368 8013 (a.o.h. 827-4823). Tx 06-218844 ADJUSTOR TOR.

TORSHAVN, Faroes—Axel Mortensen, O.B.E., (British Consul), c/o P/F Marr & Co., Yviri vid Strond, 17, (P.O. Box 49), D-3800.
Tel 13510 (a.o.h. 12140 & 15372). Tx 81259 MARRCO FA. Cables PESCADO.

TORTOLA, Virgin Islands (British)—O'Neal & Mundy Shipping Co. Ltd., P.O Box 250, Roadtown.
Tel (49) 42268 & 42674 (a.o.h. 42436 & 42223). Tx 7957 ISATCO VB. Cables MUNDICO.

TOWNSVILLE, Australia—Burns, Philp & Co. Ltd., 50 Tully Street, (P.O. Box 5021 MC), Q'ld 4810.
Tel (077)715029 (a.o.h. 756266 & 712302). Tx 47132 BURSHIP. Cables BURSHIP.

TRIESTE, Italy—Samer & Co. Shipping S.r.l., Via Luigi Einaudi, 3, (P.O. Box 1380), 1-34121.
Tel (40) 7354 (a.o.h. 576392 & 200754). Tx 460070 or 460504 EWL I. Cables ELLERMANS.

TRINIDAD, West Indies—Huggins Services Ltd., Colonial Building, 72/74 South Quay, (P.O. Box 179), Port of Spain.
Tel (623) 5260, 8881, 2166 & 7161 (a.o.h. 642-2595). Tx 22272 HUGCO WG. Cables HUGGINS.

TROMSO, Norway—Rolv Berg Drive A/S, Sondre Tollbugt 15, (P.O. Box 96), N-9001.
Tel (83) 86520. Tx 64315 BERGD N.
Hammerfest.

TRONDHEIM, Norway—H. & F. Bachke, Fjordgt. 11, (P.O. Box 2503), N-7002.
Tel (07) 520124 (a.o.h. 510539). Tx 55035 BACOS N. Cables BACHKES.
Sandnessjoen, Namsos, Kristiansund N., Aalesund.

TUNIS, Tunisia—Societe Commerciale Tunisienne (SOCOTU), 59 Rue du 18 Janvier 1952, (P.O. Box 162), 1015.
Tel (1) 343533, 350517 & 244239 (a.o.h. 893993). Tx 15028, 14843 or 15558 SOCOTU TN.
Cables SOCOTU.
Gabes, Sfax, Sousse (Susa), Bizerta.

TURKS ISLAND, Turks and Caicos Islands—Turks Islands Importers Ltd., Queen Street, (P.O. Box 72), Grand Turk. Tel 2480/2 (a.o.h. 2490 & 2493). Cables TIMCO.

TURKU, Finland—O.Y. Wikestrom & Krogius, A.B., Linnankatu 35, (P.O. Box 145), SF-20101.
Tel (21) 335333 (a.o.h. (21) 787787 & (26) 33144). Tx 62231 WEEKO SF. Cables WIKESTROMS.

UJUNG PANDANG, Indonesia—Superintending Company of Indonesia Ltd., Jln, Veteran Selatan 158, (P.O. Box 22).
Tel 81508, 84585 & 84558 (a.o.h. 82163). Cables SUCOFINDO.
Manado, Ambon, Sorong.

UMEA, Sweden—Iwan Lundstedts Eftr. A.B., P.O. box 32, S-913 00 Holmsund.
Tel (90) 40004 & 40154 (a.o.h. 40168). Tx 54063 LUNDSTET S. Cables LUNDSTEDT.

VAASA, Finland—O.Y. Backman-Trummer Ab, Teollisuuskatu 1, SF-65170.
Tel (61) 239111 (a.o.h. (61) 212623, 117535 & 291514). Tx 74228 BATRU SF.
Jacobstad (Pietarsaari), Kristinestad (Kristiina).

VALDIVIA, Chile—Alfredo Schuster B., 60 Maipu Street, (P.O. Box 507).
Tel (63) 213272 & 213273 (24 hours). Tx 271001 BOOTH CL & 231043 AUTO CLUB. (Messages to commence: For Schuster). Cables SCHUSTER.
Osorno, Puerto Montt, Chiloe Island, Castro.

VALENCIA, Spain—MacAndrews & Co. Ltd., Universidad, 4, 46003. (Address for letters: P.O. Box 12, 46080).
Tel (96) 3522487 & 3230769 (a.o.h. 3604547). Tx 62717 MCVAL E. Cables MACANDREWS.
Almeria, Cartagena, Torrevieja, Santa Pola, Alicante, Gandia, Burriana, Castellon de la Plana, Benicarlo.

VANCOUVER, Canada—Reed Stenhouse Companies Ltd., 7th Floor, 900 Howe Street, (P.O. Box 3228), V6B 3X6.
Tel (604) 688-4442 (a.o.h. 929-6418). Tx 0451381 REEDSTEN VCR. (Messages to commence: For Lloyd's Agents). Cables BELJAY.
Prince Rupert, Port Alberni, Nanaimo, Victoria.

VANUATU— Burns, Philp (Vanuatu) Ltd., Kumul Highway, (P.O. Box 27 or 28), Port Vila.
Tel 2456 (a.o.h. 2204). Tx 1011 BPVILA NH. Cables BURNSOUTH.
Espiritu Santo Island.

VENICE, Italy—G. Radonicich & C.s.a.s., 4150, (P.O. Box 718), 1-30100.
Tel (41) 5206755 (a.o.h. 615820). Tx 410029 RAMASI I. Cables RADONICICH.

VERACRUZ, Mexico—Castro Hermanos de Veracruz, S.C., Calle Emparam No. 149, 91700.
Tel (29) 314425 (a.o.h. 32-12-71 & 37-75-11). Tx Public Booth 151866 ME. (Messages to
comence: For Castro Hermanos). Cables CASTRO LLOYDSVERACRUZ.

VIENNA, Austria—Gellatly Hankey Marine Services (Austria) G.m.b.H., Grillpazerstrasse 5/13,
A1010.
Tel (1) 488831/2 (a.o.h. 5664243). Tx 133011 GHMS A. Cables MILLOYD.
Strasswalchen.

VIGO, Spain—Estanislao Duran e Hijos S.A., Avenida Canovas del Castillo, 22, (P.O. Box 75).
Tel (986) 431533, 432601 & 434127 (a.o.h. 416917, 490141 & 434251). Tx 83057 & 83308
DURAN E. Cables DURAN.
Villagarcia de Arosa, Marin.

VISAKHAPATNAM, India—Tata Tea Limited, Port Diagonal Road, (P.O. box 112), 530035.
Tel 62680 (a.o.h. 52857). Tx 0495510 TTLV. (Messages to commence: For Tata Tea Lloyd's
Agent). Cables MERCATOR.
Bheemunipatnam, Calingapatnam, Puri, Paradip Port.

VISBY, Sweden—A/B Carl E. Ekman, Hamngatan, 3, (P.O. Box 2067), S-621 02.
Tel (498) 49000 (a.o.h. 73133 & 76555). Tx 4134 EKMAN S. Cables EKMAN.

WARRENPOINT, Northern Ireland—Fisher Shipping Agency, The Docks, BT34 3JR.
Tel (06937) 73500 & 73875 (a.o.h. 72389). Tx 74930 FISHER G. Cables FISHER.

WATERFORD, Eire—Clyde Shipping Ireland Ltd., 15 Hillside Grove, Dunmore Road.
Tel (051) 75092 (24 hours). Tx 80120 WTC EI.
New Ross.

WELLINGTON, New Zealand—Dominion Adjusters (Wgtn) Ltd., 4th Floor, 203 Willis St. (P.O. Box
11-444).
Tel (4) 853-194 (a.o.h. (58) 88364). Tx 30047 ADJUST NZ.
Masterton, Napier, Nelson.

WHITEHAVEN, United Kingdom—J.G. Oldfield & Co., 44 Lowther Street, CA28 7JU.
Tel (0946) 692452/3 (a.o.h. (06576) 203 & (0900) 602461). Tx 64488 JASGER G.
Cables OLDFIELD.
Workington, Silloth.

WILMINGTON, United States of America—M.B. Ward & Son Inc., Unit 12, Downey Branch Office
Park, 3803 Wrightsville Avenue. (P.O. Box 3632, 28406).
Tel (919) 329-1425 (a.o.h. 762-9784). Tx 5109370312 WTRS SHPG. (Messages to commence:
For Lloyd's Agents). Cables WARDSON.

WINNIPEG, Canada—Morden & Helwig Ltd., Suite 412, 93 Lombard Avenue, R3B 3BI.
Tel (204) 944 9451. Tx 0757741 BRICKHOUSE. Cables M & H BROU WPG.

YOKOHAMA, Japan—Cornes & Co. Ltd., Yokohama Daiei Building, 10 Hon-cho 2-Chome,
Naka-ku, 231. (Address for letters: P.O. Box 288, Yokohama Port 231-91).
Tel (045) 201-8258, 201-8537 (Cargo), 201-8765 (Hull/Engine) & 201-3376 (Claims Settling)
(a.o.h. (3) 728 8155). Tx 3822242 CORNES J. Cables CORNES.

LLOYD'S AGENTS'
BUSINESS ANNOUNCEMENTS

255

FREETOWN, SIERRA LEONE

MINING AND GENERAL SERVICES, LIMITED
Lloyd's Agents

Ships' Agents, Cargo Surveyors & Superintendents.
Clearing & Forwarding Agents.
Travel Agents Courier Services.

---

2 Blackhall Road, Freetown, Sierra Leone
Address: P.O. Box 68   **Telephones:** 50906, 50922, 50920   **Telex:** 3226
Cables: "Mags".   Please contact Mr. R.R. Duncan, General Manager.

GIBRALTAR

SMITH IMOSSI & CO. LTD.

(Established 1837)

Agents for: Corporation of Lloyd's, Salvage Association, Lloyd's Register of Shipping, Institute of London Underwriters, Comite des Assureurs Maritimes, Sea-Land Containerships Ltd., Shaw Savill & Albion Co., Ltd., Royal Viking Line, Glen Lines Ltd., Chevron International Oil Co. Ltd., Lykes Lines, Naess Shipping Co., Alfred Holt & Co., Ocean Fleets Ltd., Wm. Thomson & Co. (Ben Line) Ltd., Compagnie Generale Maritime, Chargeurs Reunis, Worms & Co., Niarchos Ltd., N.Y.K. Lines, Polish Steamship Co., Polish Ocean Lines, Prudential Grace Lines Ltd., Kuwait Shipping Co.(S.A.K.), Claim Settling Agents for Insurance Underwriters, Correspondents for National Westminster Bank Ltd. **Telegraphic Address:** "Java Gibraltar". **Telephone:** 78645/78644. **Telex:** 2220 JAVA GK. **Fax:** 75959. Key individual contacts: P.L. Imossi (a.o.h. 78356) — A. J. Arias (a.o.h. 71076).

GUAM.

ATKINS KROLL, INC
LLOYD'S AGENTS
Correspondents:
American Institute Marine Underwriters
The Britannia Steamship Insurance Association Limited

SERVING GUAM, SAIPAN & MICRONESIA SINCE 1914

1026 Cabras Highway, Suite 116, P.A.G. Building, Piti, Guam 96910
Telephone: (671) 477-5921/2/3
Telex: 721-6133 AKSHIP GM
Fax: (671) 477-5924

 An Inchcape Pacific Company

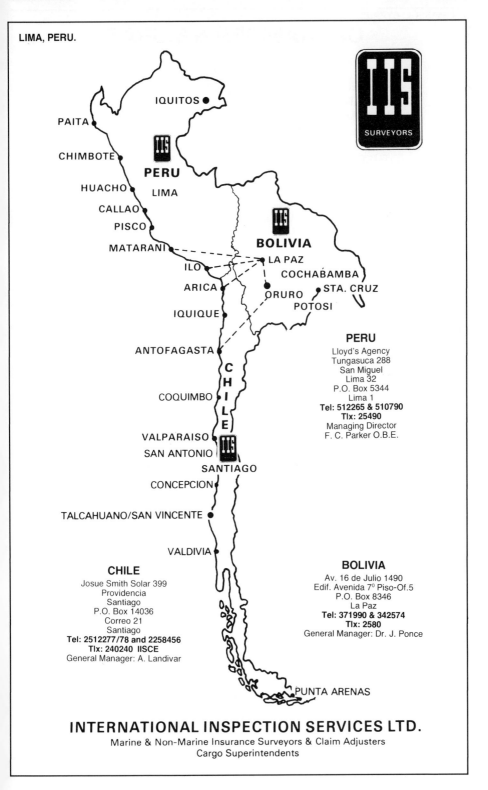

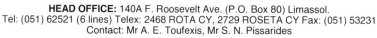

P & I CLUB ACTIVITIES IN THE PAST YEAR

by Mavis D'Souza
Editor Lloyd's Law Reports

The Liverpool and London P. & I. Insurance Association is considering the setting up of a new War Risks Association the aim of which would be to increase the choice given by the Club to shipowners in choosing war risk cover which the Club believes is limited for some shipowners at present. The Association is looking at a range of possible formats which a new Club or new class of war risks insurance should take. Should the new mutual get the go ahead from the executive committee of the Club, the new Club could have a similar structure to existing war risks mutual associations.

For many years the London Professional Indemnity market had been the major provider of E. & O. cover to Registered Insurance Brokers. Over the period the premiums had arisen alarmingly because of adverse experience and the cost of purchasing E. & O. cover now probably represents the second largest business item after salaries.

There was an increasing need for and dependence on professional indemnity cover caused by the escalating number of complaints from clients who were becoming even more aware of their legal rights.

Most other professionals such as accountants, architects, civil engineers, lawyers and the like are also facing the same problem and turning to the concept of mutuality so successfully pioneered by the P. & I. Clubs for shipowners.

Therefore the Indemnity Management Services the managers of the new P. & I. mutual for accountants have incorporated a new mutual, the London Insurance Brokers Mutual Co. Ltd. to offer cover for brokers' P. & I. risks. It is intended to offer cover to small to medium sized Registered Insurance Brokers.

The managers (IMS) will carry out day to day administration of the Club.

Cover for Port Authorities

The Through Transport Mutual Insurance Association has announced details of its new cover for Port Authorities. It will provide a single package encompassing all forms of cover required by port authorities, a skilled claims handling service, availability of advice based on the TT club's experience of the transport industry and discretionary cover. The cover will be marketed worldwide through brokers and indications are that demand will be strong attracting substantial reinsurance income to the London market. The cover is a logical extension of cover to existing terminal operators.

CISBACLUB, the Chartered and International Shipbrokers P. & I. Club Ltd. which currently provides professional and indemnity liability of 380 shipbrokers and agents in 47 countries worldwide, has extended the area of business for which the Club can accept new members. The Club is to seek new members from among ship managers, managing agents, custom brokers, forwarding agents and marine surveyors. The CISBACLUB board has agreed to alter the managers power to accommodate the new change. Up to now the position had been that any CISBACLUB member had to be substantially engaged in the business of ship agency or shipbroking to be eligible for entry.

The American Steamship Owners Mutual P. & I. Associaiton Inc. the leading P. & I. insurers of United States flag tonnage are to join the international group of P. & I. Clubs. This agreement is however subject to the agreement of the United States Justice Department. The attraction for the American club is the international group's reinsurance and pooling arrangements.

One of the major differences between the International Group and the American Club is that the International Group provides unlimited cover to its members while the American Club has a limit of about U.S. $460 million.

Dutch P. & I. Services B.V. which started its activities in June 1988 and is appointed by the P. & I. Clubs in all ports around the world acts as a P. & I. broker handling claims for and on behalf of members and Clubs on insurance contracts which have been concluded through their intermediary. They specialise in P. & I. insurance and will offer other insurance business. On P. & I. they cover all areas which include bluewater and coaster vessels, offshore vessels, inland craft and charterer's liabilities.

The plastic card

British Marine Mutual P. & I. Association which specialises in P. & I. insurance for small vessels has announced a complete rewrite of its Rule Book and has also introduced a rule Card as a handy reference to the rules themselves.

The major revision of the Club Rules is the first for about 50 years although there have been many minor changes during this period.

The Club which is now 112 years old and has some 16,000 vessels totalling approximately 1.3 million tons gross entered in its P. & I. class has introduced a single plastic card containing rules. The Card does not replace the rules but is a handy reference to the rules. When a problem arises members need instant guidance and occasionally there is not sufficient time to look up the rule book and try to decide what a particular rule means.

In response to demands from its membership the CISBACLUB is to revive its disbursement circular — the list of shipowners and charterers who are known to have defaulted on payment of disbursements commissions or fees. It will be available on a verbal confidential basis on request. The list will be compiled from information gathered from a number of industry sources and will be constantly updated by the Club's managers.

Iraq - Iran dispute

The Hellenic Mutual War Risks Association which is the largest war risk mutual has announced that it has cancelled its imposed exclusion cover for Iraqi and Iranian ports due to the continued success of the cease fire. This means that owners entered with the Club will now be covered for the ports of Bushire, Bandar Khomeni and Kharg Island. The direction does not affect the rest of the Persian Gulf and adjacent waters which include the Gulf of Oman north of 24 degrees north which are still additional premium areas.

The Gard Association has drawn the attention of its members to a situation in Korea where a number of banks and shipowners who operate liner services to Korea have become victims of a simple fraud operated by a local receiver. By using some convincing forgeries of bank guarantees the receiver managed to obtain the delivery of cargo worth millions of dollars without paying a cent to the banks holding the relevant bills of lading. Some of the banks involved have sued the shipowners alleging that the cargo was wrongfully delivered.

The Gard Association is strongly advising its members that in all cases involving delivery of cargo against a letter of indemnity backed by a bank guarantee their members should obtain confirmation of the validity of the guarantee from the bank prior to the releasing of the goods.

Small claims procedure under consideration

A small claims procedure providing for the swift and economical settlement of smaller disputes is being considered by London maritime arbitrators and views from the industry are being obtained to gauge the demand of such a service.

STRIKE COVER......DEFENCE COVER.....**P&I COVER**.....CONTAINER COVER.

Assuranceforeningen Gard
PO Box 1563 Myrene, N-4801 Arendal. Telephone 041 19100. International 47 41 19100.
Telex 21812 21813 CLUB N. Telecopier 47 41 24810 22187.

Gard (UK) Ltd.
51 Eastcheap, London EC3M 1JP. Telephone 01 283 5991. International 44 1 283 5991.
Telex 886891 883514 GARDUK G. Telecopier 44 1 623 8657.

This proposal follows the short form rules introduced by the London Maritime Arbitrators Association (LMAA) in 1984 which were superceded by the Third Schedule of the LMAA Terms 1987 but were directed to hearing on documents only.

The new proposal would provide a more simplified and less costly means of settlement of small claims. It would put a ceiling of U.S. $25,000 on claims with the parties to the arbitration agreeing to be bound by the decision of a sole arbitrator with no recourse to appeal.

Further there would be no hearing unless the arbitrator considered it essential while the procedure would be made less expensive and speedier by allowing no time for the discovery of documents which in conventional arbitration proceedings can greatly extend the time taken to conclude the case.

The demand for arbitration is growing and it is thought that the development of such a small claims service would encourage those who might otherwise not bother to seek a ruling on a dispute because of the apparent insignificant size of the sum of money involved.

It is apparent that arbitration cases have been increasing in London although in some areas the original concept of a cheap and efficient service has become complicated with both sides frequently being represented by Counsel, the gathering of written evidence and the arbitration often being treated as a preface to a full scale commercial court hearing.

Canadian Arctic waters

The Canadian Arctic Waters Pollution Prevention Act came into force on 2 August 1972 and members of P. & I. Clubs who propose trading to Canadian Arctic waters covered by the Act must be aware of the regulations relating to evidence of financial responsibility and the information to be included in the declaration to be sworn to the Canadian Ministry of Transport.

The provisions of the Act are restricted to Canadian Arctic waters north of the 60th parrallel. The Act provides *inter alia* that an owner of a ship will be liable for the deposit of waste in Canadian Arctic waters subject to the limits of liability provided in the 1969 International Convention Damage on Civil Liability for Oil Pollution Damage. Waste includes such persistent oils as crude oil, fuel oil and whale oil, whether carried on board a ship as cargo or bunkers. All owners who carry such waste in bulk must present a sworn declaration to the Ministry of Transport. However if the vessel carries as cargo more than 2000 tons of waste in bulk the owner must produce a duplicate original of a special policy together with the sworn declaration. Non compliance with the provisions of those regulations is punishable by a fine not exceeding Canadian $25,000.

LIVERPOOL AND LONDON SIGNALS SUCCESS

Liverpool and London's success is no secret. A combination of experience and flair has enabled the Association to sustain growth at an unprecedented rate, whilst maintaining the highest levels of service our members have come to expect, together with exceptional financial stability.

For further information, or a copy of our handbook, please contact

Hugh Bryant or **Russ Bradshaw**

Liverpool & London P&I Management Limited,
Royal Liver Building, Liverpool L3 1HU.

Telephone 051-236 3777, Telex 628431 LIVLON G, Facsimile 051-236 0053

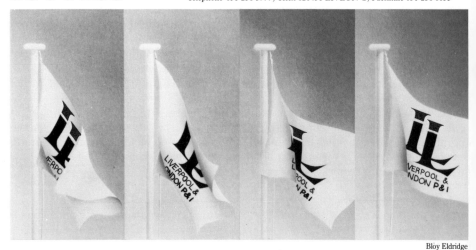

Bloy Eldridge

P. & I. CLUBS

Assuranceforeningen Gard
PO Box 1563, Myrene, N-4801 Arendal,
Norway. Tel (041) 25900. Tx 21812 CLUB N.
Fax (041) 24810. Cables GARD
U.K. Sudsidiary: Gard (U.K.) Ltd,
51 Eastcheap, London EC3, England.
Tel (01) 283 5991. Tx 886891 GARDUK G.
Fax (01) 623 8657.

Assuranceforeningen Skuld (Gjensidig)
Stortingsgaten 18, PO Box 1376, Oslo 1,
Norway. Tel (02) 420640. Tx 71091 SKULD N.
Fax (02) 424885. Cables SKULD.
Danish Office: Frederiksborggade 15,
DK-1360 Copenhagen, Denmark.
Tel (01) 116861. Tx 19561 SKULD DK.
Fax (01) 113341.
French Office: 30 Rue General Giraud,
Rouen, France. Tx 180712 SKULD F.
Swedish Office: Pontonjargatan 12, S-10226
Stockholm 12, Sweden. Tel (01) 541220.
Tx 10384 SKULD S.

**Britannia Steam Ship Insurance Association
Ltd, The**
Managers: Tindall, Riley & Co., New City
Court, St. Thomas St, London SE1 9RR
England. Tel (01) 407 3588.
Tx 883386 TRILEY G. Fax (01) 403 3942.
Cables SURENESS.

**British Marine Mutual Insurance Association
Ltd**
Walsingham House, 35 Seething Lane,
London EC3N 4DQ, England.
Tel (01) 488 1024. Tx 887795 BMM G.
Cables MUTUAL.

**Chartered & International Shipbrokers' P & I
Club Ltd**
Managers: Tindall, Riley & Co., New City
Court, St. Thomas Street, London SE1
9RR, England. Tel (01) 407 3588.
Tx 883386 TRILEY G. Fax (01) 403 3942.
Cables SURNESS.

**Charterers Mutual Assurance Association
Ltd**
Managers: Michael Else & Co. Ltd,
Plantation House, 10-15 Mincing Lane,
London EC3M 3DX, England.
Tel (01) 623 2391. Tx 8812501 ELAN G.
Cables ELAN.

**Japan Ship Owners' Mutual Protection &
Indemnity Association**
Head Office: 2-15-14 Nichonbashi,
Ningyocho, Chuoh-ku, Tokyo, Japan.
Tel (03) 662 7401. Tx 2225196 SHIPPI J.
Fax (03) 662 7400. Cables
PANDIMUTUAL.
U.K. Office: New City Court, St. Thomas
Street, London SE1 9RS, England.
Tel (01) 407 2865. Tx 918736 JPILDN G.
Hong Kong Office: c/o Sedgwick Chartered
Hong Kong Ltd, 2702 Admiralty Centre,
Tower 1, Harcourt Road, Hong Kong.
Tx 61687 SEDCH HX. Fax (5) 8610046.

**Liverpool & London Steamship Protection
and Indemnity Association Ltd**
Managers: Liverpool & London P & I
Management Ltd, 1st Floor, Royal Liver
Building, Pier Head, Liverpool L3 1HU,
England. Tel (051) 236 3777. Tx 628431
LIVLON G. Fax (051) 236 0053.

**London Steam-Ship Owner's Mutual
Insurance Association Ltd**
Managers: A. Bilbrough & Co. Ltd,
6th floor, 52 Leadenhall Street, London
EC3A 2BJ. England. Tel (01) 488 1444.
Tx 886394 BILBRO. Fax (01) 488 0012.
Cables BILBROUGH.
Greek Office: 67 Atki Miaouli, Piraeus,
Greece. Tel (01) 4812271/3. Tx 211809
BILB GR. Fax (01) 4517287.
Hong Kong Office: 1407 Guardian House,
32 Oi Kwan Road, Hong Kong.
Tel (5) 739293/4. Tx 85128 ABILB HX.
Fax (5) 2348022. Cables BILBROUGH.

**Newcastle Protection & Indemnity
Association**
Centro House, 3 Cloth Market,
Newcastle on Tyne NE1 1NT, England.
Tel (091) 232 4591. Tx 537389 NPANDI G.
Fax (091) 232 5361. Cables SCORFIELD.

**North of England Protection & Indemnity
Association Ltd**
Head Office: Douglas House, 4 Neville
Street, Newcastle on Tyne NE1 5DS,
England. Tel (091) 232 5221.
Tx 53634 NEPIA G. Fax (091) 261 0540.
Cables NORPRINDEM.

**Ocean Marine Mutual Protection &
Indemnity Association Ltd**
Managers: Ocean Management Ltd,
Gretton House, Duke Street, Grand Turk,
British West Indies.
U.K. Correspondents: Ocean P & I Services,
Waterloo Chambers, Waterloo Lane,
Chelmsford CM1 1BD, Essex, England.
Tel (0245) 350070.

Post & Co. (P & I)
Westersingel 94, PO Box 443, 3015 LC
Rotterdam, Netherlands.
Tel (010) 4362033. Tx 21320 POST NL.
Fax (010) 4366184.
U.K. Office: 23-24 Lovat Lane, London
EC3R 8EB, England. Tel (01) 929 4419.
Tx 929628 POSTUK G. Fax (01) 929 0505.

Shipowners' Mutual Strike Insurance Association (Bermuda) Ltd

Managers: John Laing Management (Bermuda) Ltd, Commerce Building, Front Street, PO Box 1732, Hamilton 5, Bermuda. Tel 50543. Tx 3334 LAING BA. Cables SEADEW.

U.K. Office: John Laing (Strike Club Correspondents) Ltd, Fountain House, 130 Fenchurch Street, London EC3M 5DJ, England. Tel (01) 626 3083. Tx 888259 STRIKE G. Cables STRIKE.

Monaco Office: 29 Boulevard Princesse Charlotte, MC 98000 Monte Carlo, Monaco. Tel 93500245. Tx 469266 LAING MC. Cables SEADEW.

Shipowners' Protection and Indemnity Association Ltd

Ibex House, 42-47 Minories, London EC3N 1BP, England. Tel (01) 488 0911. Tx 893744 SOPCLB G. Fax (01) 480 5606. Cables SOPCLUB. Managers for The Shipowners' Mutual Protection & Indemnity Association (Luxembourg).

Standard Steamship Owners' P&I Association (Bermuda) Ltd

Managers: Charles Taylor & Co. (Bermuda), Barnaby Building, Barnaby Street, PO Box 1743, Hamilton, Bermuda. Tel 27655. Tx 3343 BA. Cables ADNO.

U.K. Office: Charles Taylor & Co., International House, World Trade Centre, 1 St. Kathrine's Way, London E1 9UN, England. Tel (01) 488 3494. Tx 883555 ADNO G. Fax (01) 481 9545. Cables ADNO.

Steamship Mutual Underwriting Association (Bermuda) Ltd

Managers: Steamship Mutual Management (Bermuda) Ltd, Washington Mall, Church Street, PO Box 447, Hamilton, Bermuda. Tel 5-4502. Tx 3411 SMUAB BA. Fax 28787.

U.K. Office: Aquatical House, 39 Bell Lane, London E1 7LU, England. Tel (01) 247 5490. Tx 9413451/920120 SMUAL G. Fax (01) 377 2912. Cables AQUATICAL.

Sunderland Steamship Protection and Indemnity Association

Tavistock House, Borough Road, PO Box 5, Sunderland SR1 1PH, England. Tel (0783) 653321. Tx 53352 SUNDPI G. Fax (0783) 44998. Cables AVERAGE.

Sveriges Angfartyges Assurans Forening (The Swedish Club)

Amerikahuset Barlastgatan 2, PO Box 4094, S-400 40 Gothenburg, Sweden. Tel (031) 124620. Tx 2504 SWCLUB S. Fax (031) 142545. Cables SECURITAS.

Greek Office: Agio Nicolaou 3, 185 37 Piraeus, Greece. Tel (01) 4519067. Tx 213244 CONT GR.

Hong Kong Office: Suite 1502, Two Exchange Square, 8 Connaught Place, Hong Kong. Tel (5) 216373. Tx 85314 SCLUB HX. Fax (5) 297274.

Transmarine Mutual Loss of Hire Assurance Association Ltd

Managers: Else Allan Neil Ltd, Plantation House, 10-15 Mincing Lane, London EC3M 3DX, England. Tel (01) 623 2391. Tx 8812501 ELAN G. Cables ELAN.

Transport Intermediaries Mutual Insurance Association Ltd

Managers: Thos. R. Miller & Son (Bermuda), Mercury House, PO Box HM 665, Hamilton 5, Bermuda. Tel 24724. Tx 3317 MUTUAL BA. Fax 23694. Cables MUTUALITY.

U.K. Office: Transport Intermediaries Services, Creechurch House, 37-45 Creechurch Lane, London EC3A 5DJ England. Tel (01) 283 4646. Tx 8814516 TIM G. Fax (01) 283 5614.

United Kingdom Mutual Steam Ship Assurance Association (Bermuda) Ltd

Managers: Thos. R. Miller & Son (Bermuda), Mercury House, PO Box HM 665, Hamilton 5, Bermuda. Tel 24724. Tx 3317 MUTUAL BA. Fax 23694. Cables MUTUALITY.

U.K. Office: Thos. R. Miller & Son, International House, 26 Creechurch Lane, London EC3A 5BA, England. Tel (01) 283 4646. Tx 886271 MUTUAL G. Fax (01) 283 5614. Cables MUTUALITY.

West of England Ship Owners' Mutual Protection & Indemnity Association (Luxembourg)

33 Boulevard Prince Henri, Luxembourg. Tel 470067. Tx 2702 WESENG LU. Fax 25253. Cables WESTENG.

U.K. Office: International House, World Trade Centre, 1 St. Katherine's Way, London E1 9UE, England, Tel (01) 480 7272. Tx 8958951 WESTEN G Fax: (01) 480 7648. Cables WESTENG.

HULL CASUALTY STATISTICS

The figures shown in these tables are those which have been posted in the Loss Book of the Institute of London Underwriters, 49 Leadenhall Street, London, EC3A 2BE, England, to whom the Publisher extends his thanks for permission to reproduce the same.

They refer to vessels of 500 tons gross and over and include Constructive Total Losses.

During 1988, the Instutute recorded the loss of 147 ships, representing a total of 775,856 tons gross.

The total included a number of smaller vessels with very high values in relation to their size, so the total cost to insurers was probably no less than in previous years.

The largest loss of the year (other than war losses) was the Liberian tanker *Odyssey* 65,746 tons gross, which broke in two in the Atlantic in November with the loss of 27 lives.

Almost two thirds of all vessels totally lost during the year fell into the categories of weather, founderings, and abandonments and strandings, with losses from heavy weather increasing slightly.

There was a marked decline in the number of vessels totally lost as a result of collision. Their number dropped by half, from 16 to eight.

As in 1987, one vessel was lost as a result of contact.

The proportion of vessels lost following a fire or explosion remains at a similar level to previous years, although slightly up on the 1987 figure in terms of the number of vessels lost.

There was a significant increase in the number of vessels lost in the machinery, shafts and propeller category (two in 1987 and eight in 1988). Seven of the eight vessels lost were over 15 years old.

WORLD TOTAL LOSSES 1986–1988
(500 tons gross and over)

Nature of Casualty	1986		1987		1988		1983-1987 AVERAGE	
	No.	Gr. Tons.	No.	Gr. Tons.	No.	Gr. Tons.	No.	Gr. Tons.
Weather	40	458,205	46	408,406	49	260,862	43.0	281,428
Founderings & Abandonments	32	113,481	19	66,052	29	65,685	29.4	108,006
Strandings	23	166,547	19	245,501	17	150,193	30.0	262,115
Collisions	7	25,263	16	113,190	8	25,427	11.8	71,627
Contact	2	3,788	1	27,288	1	1,567	3.8	20,779
Fires & Explosions	38	339,470	28	246,876	34	233,897	47.6	408,847
Missing	2	2,198	5	51,944	1	9,909	2.0	19,778
Machinery Shafts & Props.	9	88,553	2	1,496	8	28,316	5.4	58,286
Other Casualties	3	9,917	3	18,147	—	—	8.2	29,644
TOTALS	156	1,207,422	139	1,178,900	147	775,856	181.2	1,260,510
World Tonnage		395,463,677		394,018,761		393,798,970		403,681,314
Loss Ratio %		.30		.30		.20		.31

ANNUAL LOSSES BY TONNAGE
1972-1987

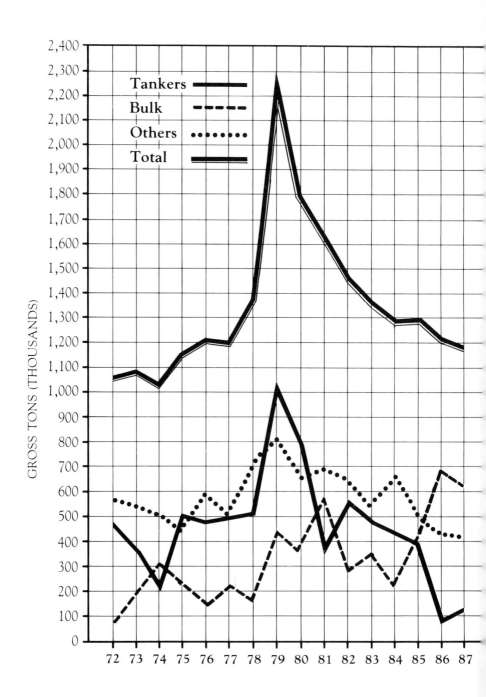

ANNUAL LOSSES BY NUMBER OF SHIPS
1972-1987

ESTIMATED COST OF TOTAL LOSSES
1975-1986

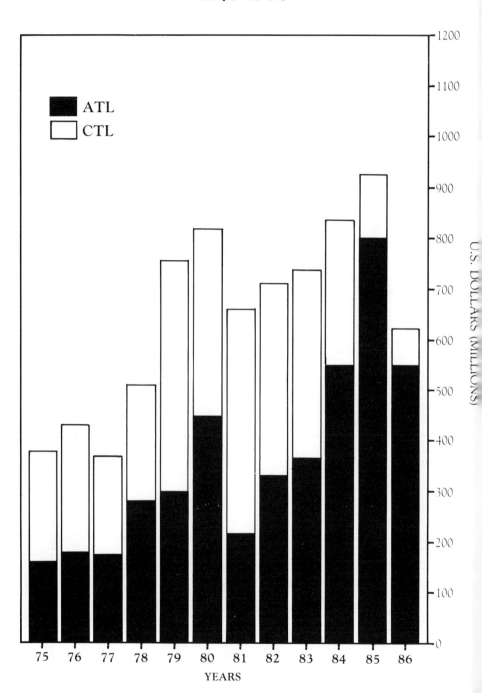

IMB INDEPENDENT MARITIME BUREAU N.V.

Member of the group van Ameyde International Marine Surveyors.

MARINE, CARGO and INDUSTRIAL SURVEYORS.

- Inspectors for Liberian Bureau of Maritime Affairs.
- Authorized surveyors for Panama Bureau of Shipping.
- Non-exclusive surveyors for Germanischer Lloyd, Korean Register of Shipping.
- China register of Shipping, Registro Italiano Navale, Hellenic Register of Shipping.
- Principal Representatives for: International Cargo Gear Bureau Inc. U.S.A.
- Marine consultants — Arbitrators — Owners representatives.
- Surveys of onshore installations, tanks, machinery.
- Cargo damage and condition surveys.

SERVING: OWNERS, CHARTERERS, INSURERS, P & I CLUBS, FINANCIERS, IN CO-OPERATION WITH THEIR LOCAL AGENTS AND REPRESENTATIVES.

REDWOOD ANTILLES

AFFILIATED:
- Quality and quanity inspection on oil products.
- Bunker survey.
- Cargo-Loss control.

SERVING: CARRIERS, INSURERS, SHIPPERS, CONSIGNEES, STEVEDORES

Maduro Plaza Building, P.O.Box 3030, Curaçao, Neth. Antilles,
Tel. office: (+599-9) 370733, Fax. (+599-9) 370743,
Telex: 1272 IMB NA / 1199 REDW NA

TOPLIS

SERVING

AND HARDING plc

Toplis and Harding plc, 2 Heron Quay, London E14 9XE
Telephone: (01) 538 3975   Telex: 887460   Fax: (01) 538 4163

SCHEDULE OF SERVICES

Agricultural Losses
Aquacultural Losses
Average Adjusting
Aviation
Bankers Losses
Bonds
Business Interruption
Burglary, Theft and All Risks
Commercial Fire
Computer Losses
Consequential Losses
Contract Guarantees
Construction Risks and Liabilities
Contingency
Employers Liability
Engineering and Petro-Chemicals
Equine
Fidelity Guarantee
Film Production
Fine Art, Jewellery & Ceramics
Financial Risks
Livestock
Marine & Marine Transit
Oil and Gas offshore platforms
Personal Accident & Sickness
Pluvius
Political Risks
Pollution and Toxic Waste
Prcducts Liability
Professional Indemnity
Road Haulage and Transit
Third Party Risks

TOPLIS INSURANCE SERVICES

Toplis Insurance Services has been established as a specialist Division within the Group to provide claims management and handling expertise to clients in the U.K. and throughout the World.

The Division is designed to provide a full claims service and is staffed and controlled by personnel trained in both insurance and legal disciplines.

The expertise of the Division extends to the provision of all supervisory functions including policy and reinsurance contract interpretation, investigation of cases in dispute up to settlement and the need to comply with regulartory or statutory requirements.

The spread of Group offices allows these services to be offered to clients worldwide.

TOPLIS INTERNATIONAL

Toplis International provide professional services to both local and international insurance markets in all aspects of claims handling arising from marine, fire, accident, contractors all risks, liability, and special risks policies outside the United Kingdom and North America.

Head Office:

15-17 Christopher Street, London EC2A 2BS
Tel: +441 623 1040
Fax: +441 626 7523
Telex: 927733

Africa	Latin America, Caribbean
Kenya	*Barbados*
	Chile
Tanzania	*Colombia*
Zambia	*Jamaica*
	Panama
Asia	*Trinidad*
Hong Kong	*Venezuela*
Malaysia	
	Middle East
Philippines	*Arabian Area*
	Yemen Arab Republic
Singapore	*Cyprus*
Brunei	*Gulf Area*
	United Arab Emirates
Australasia and Oceania	*Sultanate of Oman*
8 offices throughout the Area	

Europe	
France	Toplis Marine Overseas Offices
Greece	*Hong Kong*
Netherlands	*Kenya*
Spain	*Tanzania*
Switzerland	*Australia*
West Germany	
Republic of Ireland	

MAXSON YOUNG ASSOCIATES

Maxson Young Associates trades as the North American Division of The Toplis and Harding Group with specific responsibility for operations in the United States, Canada and Mexico.

Head Office:

San Francisco
Maxson Young Associates Inc
100 Spear Street, Suite 1125, San Francisco CA94105
Tel: +1 415 543 3655   Telex: 278283 MYA SF
Fax: +1 415 896 5713
And at Los Angeles, Miami, Minneapolis, New York, Portland, Seattle, Spokane

E NEEDS OF INSURERS
1790–1990

Toplis UK is a broadly based organisation operating out of some 50 strategically located offices all of which are under the day to day control of local Regional Directors.

Head Office:
2 Heron Quay, London E14 9XE
Tel: 01-538 3960 +441 538 3960 Telex: 887427
Fax: 01-538 4158 +441 538 4158

OFFICE TELEPHONE NUMBERS

EMERGENCY OUT-OF-HOURS FREEPHONE 0800 282 372

	Tel. Nos.	Fax. Nos
Aberdeen	0224 643454	0224 644639
Ashford	0233 610862	0233 610863
Banbury	0295 268388	0295 272104
Barnstaple	0271 78581	0271 79986
Barrow in Furness	0229 38060	0229 870299
Belfast	0232 246503/4/5	0232 245382
Birmingham	021 236 3584	021 233 2081
Blackpool	0253 20138	0253 752738
Brighton	0273 693527	0273 693545
Bristol	0272 273065	0272 292875
Cardiff	0222 490753	0222 490928
Carmarthen	0267 232929/ 234269	0267 232815
Cheltenham	0242 512180	0242 224434
Chester	0244 317416	0244 317934
Colchester	0206 41040	0206 762787
Edinburgh	031 557 2933	031 557 4401
Enfield	01 366 0986	01 367 7394
Exeter	0392 431281	0392 421507
Glasgow	041 332 1029/ 333 9182	041 332 2536
Harrogate	0423 501359	0423 531185
Haverfordwest	0437 763934	0437 760789
Kendal	0539 29568	0539 740547
Kidderminster	0562 742272	0562 753410
Kingston	01 541 5222	01 549 6237
Lancaster	0524 66151	0524 841944
Leamington Spa	0926 882271	0926 452149
Leeds	0532 438182	0532 424335
Leicester	0533 470543	0533 471793
Liverpool	051 227 2591	051 227 2717
Llandudno	0492 77578	0492 860692
London	01 538 3960	01 538 4158

Macclesfield	0625 619125	0625 615115
Manchester	061 236 8881	061 236 8801
Newcastle upon Tyne	091 232 4475	091 261 9224
Newport, Gwent	0633 246262	0633 244121
Northampton	0604 231055	0604 20637
Norwich	0603 665661	0603 761495
Orpington, Kent	0689 31345	0689 39339
Penzance	0736 69180	0736 51205
Peterborough	0733 555433	0733 555408
Plymouth	0752 793346	0752 793347
Preston	0772 54694	0772 204861
Reading	0734 410541	0734 431864
Scunthorpe	0724 848823	0724 280013
Sheffield	0742 753378	0742 723643
Shrewsbury	0743 231200	0743 271044
Southampton	0703 228223	0703 632318
Swansea	0792 649426	0792 468628
Torquay	0803 214353	0803 214355
Truro	0872 71391	0872 223427

TOPLIS CONSTRUCTION

Toplis Construction is a specialist Division within the Toplis and Harding Group providing claims handling services in those fields of industry and commerce that are directly or indirectly connected with construction both in the United Kingdom and abroad.

2 Heron Quay, London E14 9XE
Tel: 01 538 3975 +441 538 3975 Telex: 887427
Fax: 01 538 4158 +441 538 4158

TOPLIS ENGINEERING

This specialist Division of the Group provides engineering consultancy in all fields of industry and commerce

2 Heron Quay, London E14 9XE
Tel: 01 538 4869 +441 538 4869 Telex: 887427
Fax: 01-538 4158 +441 538 4158

and at Bristol, Manchester

International
Middle East
Hong Kong
Chile
Trinidad
Venezuela
Australasia
Africa

THE SALVAGE ASSOCIATION

The Salvage Association is the world's leading organisation of marine casualty and investigative surveyors with twentynine exclusive offices in the ship repair centres of the world. In addition the Association works with the Lloyd's Agency network ensuring that local advice is promptly available

The Association has been closely linked with the London Insurance Market since it was established in 1856, as a non- profit making organisation, by a group of underwriting members of Lloyd's and representatives of marine insurance companies in London. It was quickly successful in providing a service to underwriters, shipping and cargo interests and in recognition of this was incorporated by Royal Charter in 1867.

The Association maintains its link with Lloyd's and the Institute of London Underwriters, who together provide its Chairman, Deputy Chairman and Committee, who are responsible for policy However, the Association prides itself on its motto 'Quaerite Vera' 'Seek the Truth' and acts with objectivity no matter who the instructing principal. It accepts instructions from underwriters worldwide, as well as from shipowners, cargo owners, P. and I. Clubs, banks, government departments and the many other parties involved in maritime trade. Over 12,000 cases a year are handled by the Association and wherever there are marine casualties the Association is almost certain to be involved, whether casualties of the Arctic ice or of the latest tropical storm or hurricane.

The Association's offices throughout the world are staffed by qualified, highly experienced marine and nautical surveyors. The surveyors not only have seagoing experience but have had considerable commercial experience before joining the Association. Branch offices, through their regular contact with port authorities, ship repairers, towage and salvage companies, are able to provide local expertise which is shared with other branches for the benefit of instructing principals Complementing this expertise is that of the naval architects' department in London which has unrivalled experience in damage engineering developed as a result of regular involvement with marine casualties.

Casualty Investigation

The Association's principal activity is casualty investigation. The attending surveyor notes the extent of damage, agrees with the shipowners' representative the extent of repairs necessary, and, in major cases, liaises with the owners' representatives in the drawing up of a repair specification Assistance is also given in respect of the most efficient and economical method of effecting the repairs. The cause of damage as alleged by owners is discussed and, if appropriate, agreed. The surveyor later assists in negotiating accounts and, if he considers them fair and reasonable, approves the repair costs. His final report will include all the foregoing so that underwriters can consider the claim and average adjusters can apportion the costs involved to the appropriate interest.

Loss Prevention

Increasingly underwriters, P. and I. Clubs and mortgagee banks require the Association to conduct condition and pre-risk surveys. In the case of towage, load-outs of outside and valuable cargoes and voyages which pose more than the usual degree of risk. Underwriters, in order to minimise the risk often impose warranties that The Salvage Association shall approve the voyage arrangements. The Association considers pre-risk and loss prevention surveys to be valuable safeguards for underwriters and others who are on risk.

Cargo

From the very beginning cargo work has formed an important part of the Association's activities The Cargo Department in London and the Association's specialist staff cargo surveyors in North America are involved in hundreds of cases annually conducting General Average and cargo surveys and initiating, where appropriate, fraud and other investigations. One of the prime reasons for the establishment of the Association was to enable the many cargo interests affected by marine casualties to be represented by one central organisation and the Association's Cargo Department continues to fulfil this important role — particularly where general cargoes need to be salvaged and transhipped For instance in the 1970s the Association played a leading role in recovering and disposing of cargoes lying in ships trapped in the Suez Canal.

To instruct the Association, or for further information and a copy of the current International Office Directory, contact: Head Office London:

Bankside House, 107/112 Leadenhall Street, London EC3A 4AP, England.
Telephone: (01) 623 1299. Telex: Casualty advices: 940 17187. Miscellaneous: 940 17770.
Cables: Wreckage London EC3. Facsimile: (01) 626 4963.

New York Office: 29 Broadway, 21st floor, New York 10006, U.S.A. Telephone: (212) 785 1720 .
Telex: RCA 232067, WUI 620911.
Cables: Wreckage. Facsimile: (212) 785 1732.

or the offices at Glasgow, Southampton, Lisbon, Antwerp, Rotterdam, Hamburg, Genoa, Marseilles, Piraeus, Durban, Cape Town, Dubai, Singapore, Hong Kong, Yokohama, Kobe, Pusan, Norfolk (Va), Jacksonville, New Orleans, Houston, San Francisco, Seattle, Montreal, St Catharines (Ont.), Halifax (N.S.), Vancouver (B.C.)

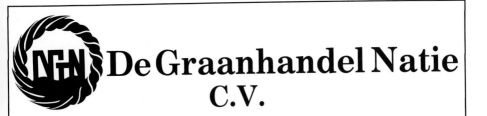

The Chartered Institute of Loss Adjusters

Council and Officers for the Year 1989-90

President:
P. A. GREGG, A.C.I.I., F.C.I.L.A.

Deputy President:
N. H. KELLY, A.C.I.I., F.C.I.L.A.

Vice Presidents:
B. J. REMBGES, F.C.I.I., F.C.I.L.A.
R. O. HARRIS, A.C.I.I., F.C.I.L.A.
L. PARKER, F.C.I.I., F.C.I.L.A.

Council:
J. R. M. BALL, F.C.I.I., F.C.I.L.A.
T. P. CRAWFORD, A.C.I.I., F.C.I.L.A., A.C.I.Arb. (Republic of Ireland)
W. CURRIE, A.C.I.I., F.C.I.L.A. (Scottish Area)
W. J. DUFFIELD, F.C.I.I., F.C.I.L.A. (Midlands Area)
M. J. FALLON, F.C.I.I., F.C.I.L.A., A.C.I.Arb (North West Area)
B. W. G. FITZGERALD, A.C.I.I., F.C.I.L.A. (London and Home Counties Area)
L. T. GILLIES, A.C.I.I., F.C.I.L.A. (London and Home Counties Area)
C. A. HART, F.C.I.L.A. (London and Home Counties Area)
G. M. HAYWARD, A.C.I.I., F.C.I.L.A. (Western Area)
R. D. KNIBB, A. C.I.I., F.C.I.L.A. (Western Area)
A. J. LUND, A.C.I.I., F.C.I.L.A. (North East Area)
G. J. MAHONEY, F.C.I.L.A., A.C.I.Arb. (London and Home Counties Area)
R. H. W. MITCHELL, B.Sc., C.Eng., F.I.Ch.E., F.C.I.Arb., F.C.I.L.A, F.Inst. Pet.
R. PREEDY, A.C.I.I., F.C.I.L.A. (Southern Area)
S. REID, F.C.I.I., F.C.I.L.A.
G. A. SCOTT, F.R.I.C.S., A.C.I.I., F.C.I.L.A. (Scottish Area)
I. R. SIMMONDS, F.C.I.I., F.C.I.L.A. (Midlands Area)
B. D. SIMPSON, A.C.I.I., F.C.I.L.A. (North West Area)
R. STERRITT, F.C.I.I., F.C.I.L.A. (Northern Ireland Area)
C. H. W. STORER, A.C.I.I., F.C.I.L.A.
M. E. TOMLINSON, A.C.I.I., F.C.I.L.A. (North East Area)

President — Australasian Division:
C. H. WRIGHT, F.A.I.I., F.C.I.L.A.

Hon Secretary:
T. R. TICKLE, F.C.I.L.A.

Hon. Treasurer:
J. A. SEVERN, F.C.I.L.A.

Chairman Examinations Committee:
N. C. WARDEN, B.A., A.C.M.A., F.C.I.L.A.

Hon. Solicitor:
A. C. FEAR, (Turner Kenneth Brown), 100 Fetter Lane, London EC4A 1DD

Hon. Auditors:
SOUTHWELL, TYRRELL & CO, 9 Newbury Street, London EC1A 7HU

Director:
A. F. CLACK, B.A., F.C.I.I.

Registered Office:
Manfield House, 376 Strand, London WC2R 0LR
(entrance Southampton Street)
Tel: 01-240 1496 & 01-836 6482
Fax: 01-836 0340

THE CHARTERED LOSS ADJUSTER

A chartered loss adjuster is appointed by an insurance underwriter to investigate and make recommendations for settlement of, generally, the larger non-marine claims. Insurers normally use their own officials to settle the smaller claims, and small claims can sometimes be settled by correspondence. Occasionally loss adjusters are given authority to settle, within wide limits, all claims of a particular type. Some firms of loss adjusters specialise in the adjustment of marine losses, particularly in the overseas market, but these are exceptional: chartered loss adjusters tended to specialise in the adjustment of fire losses (the original title of their profesional body was the Association of Fire Loss Adjusters) but they now generally deal with claims arising from fire, special perils, consequential loss, burglary and theft, goods in transit, contractor's all risks, and public products liability.

Chartered loss adjusters can offer much in the negotiation and settlement of claims, the two most important factors being expertise and impartiality. Dealing with a complex claim may require the efforts of a multi-disciplinary team which a firm of loss adjusters is in a unique position to provide. Many chartered loss adjusters are also qualified as chartered surveyors, chartered accountants and lawyers, and their skill in these disciplines is often involved in the settlement of claims.

It is not normally the task of the loss adjuster to effect settlement of claims (the circumstances in which they do have already been mentioned). Having investigated the claim thoroughly they make recommendations for payment and, in the normal course of events, the insurers will accept these recommendations. It is in this connection that the impartiality of the adjuster is important. He is normally, but not invariably, appointed by the insurers and paid by them and to this extent is their agent in the settlement of the claim. However, the chartered loss adjuster's code of conduct enjoins that he should act impartially. The adjuster is paid a fee by the insurer for his work, but there is no recognised scale of fees. All things being equal, the larger the claim, the greater the fee it will attract, but size is not the sole factor. The complexity of the claim can be equally important. A very large claim, particularly for a total loss of property, can be relatively easy to settle but a large partial loss, if it involves substantial rebuilding work and problems with stock and consequential loss, can be very complex and require much expertise to settle. Obviously he has a duty to the insurers in the event of an overstated and, a fortiori, a fraudulent claim, but he will also draw the attention of the insured to any item which he has inadvertently omitted from the claim, particularly if the insured does not have the benefit of professional representation. A person who acts professionally in the making of a claim on behalf of the insured is known as an assessor, and may be a member of the Institute of Public Loss Assessors: this is the distinction between the terms adjusters and assessor, although the term assessor is still sometimes applied, especially by the courts, to adjusters.

All chartered loss adjusters are governed by the Charter, Bye-laws and Recommended Code of Practice of the Chartered Institute of Loss Adjusters, which was honoured by the grant of its Charter in 1961. This was a quite remarkable achievement, as there had been no recognised association of adjusters until 1941 when, under government pressure in order to ensure the best use of resources in time of war, the Association of Fire Loss Adjusters was formed.

The Institute is concerned to promote the efficiency and usefulness of the profession by compelling the observance of strict rules of professional conduct by members. In particular, the Institute has very strict rules regarding soliciting business, which is completely forbidden, and advertising and entertaining which are allowed only subject to very stringent conditions.

There are rules to prevent conflict of interest in a loss adjuster's work, and in general the sharing of profits except with other loss adjusters or persons in cognate professions is forbidden except under certain strictly controlled conditions. In particular, the Institute's code of conduct provides specific guidance for members who are also Lloyd's underwriters, so that any possible conflict of interest between the two roles shall be avoided.

The Council of the Institute carries out its detailed work through the Examinations and Education Committees, the Technical Committee and the Publicity and Public Relations Committee.

LOSS ADJUSTERS

Members of the Chartered Institute of Loss Adjusters

UNITED KINGDOM AND IRISH REPUBLIC

LONDON

BROCKLEHURST GROUP,
Battlebridge House,
87/113 Tooley Street,
London SE1 2RA.
Telephone: 01-407 6361/6, 1827/8 & 1106.
Telex: 884780.
Fax: G2/3 01-407 3996.
Lloyd's PBX 4140.
Cables: Brocklehurst London SE1.

C. Brocklehurst & Son	6th Floor
Brocklehursts	6th Floor
Brocklehurst International Associates	5th Floor
Brocklehurst Aviation	6th Floor
Brocklehurst Fine Art	6th Floor
Brocklehurst Marine	6th Floor
Brocklehurst Contingency and C.A.R.	6th Floor

City Office
Suite 655, Lloyd's,
One Lime Street, London EC3M 7DQ.
Telephone: 01-623 7100 extensions 4895/6
& 01-626 5243.
Telex: 987321 (quote "Brocklehursts").
Fax: G2/3 01-626 4941.

DAVIES AND COMPANY
(INTERNATIONAL LOSS ADJUSTERS),
Creechurch House,
Creechurch Lane,
London EC3A 5DJ.
Telephone: 01-283 8497.
Telex: 8813100.
Fax: 01-623 3576.

DAVIES AND COMPANY,
Sinclair House,
The Avenue,
Ealing, London W13 8NT.
Telephone: 01-988 5664.
Fax: 01-997 3518.

DAVIES AND COMPANY,
Gilbert House,
207 Anerley Road,
London SE20.
Telephone: 01-778 9211.
Fax: 01-778 9401.

ELLIS & BUCKLE,
Centre Point,
103 New Oxford Street,
London WC1A 1QT.
Telephone: 01-379 7988.
Fax: 01-379 4504.

ELLIS & BUCKLE,
Hyde House,
The Hyde,
London NW9 6LH.
Telephone: 01-200 5678.
Fax: 01-200 3529.

ELLIS & BUCKLE,
8, The Office Village,
4 Romford Road,
Stratford,
London E15 4EA.
Telephone: 01-534 5534.
Telex: 262809 SOVIL G.
Fax: 01-519 8134.

THOMAS HOWELL KIEWIT
INTERNATIONAL GROUP LTD.,
Thomas Howell Kiewit (International) Ltd.,
60 Mark Lane,
London EC3R 7NE.
Telephone: 01-265 0611.
Telex: 8813641 THKIL.
Cables: Howkiet Ldn EC3.
Fax: 01-481 2856.

THOMAS HOWELL, SELFE
(SOUTHERN) LTD.,
6th Floor, A Block,
Plantation House,
31/35 Fenchurch Street,
London EC3M 3BQ.
Telephone: 01-626 9092/01-626 2626.
Telex: 893965 THSLON G.
Fax: 01-626 1640.

DOUGLAS JACKSON & CO.,
(ADJUSTERS) LTD.,
Insurance Loss Adjusters, Marine Surveyors.

DOUGLAS JACKSON & CO.,
(SURVEYS) LTD.,
Marine and General Cargo Surveyors.
Globe House,
Crucifix Lane,
London SE1 3XE.
Telephone: 01-407 5599
Telex: 884550 DJACLN G.
Fax: 01-357 7634
And at Liverpool

LONDON *(continued)*

MATTHEWS-DANIEL INTERNATIONAL (LONDON) LTD.,
Marlon House,
71-74 Mark Lane,
London EC3R 7HS.
Telephone: 01-702 9697.
Telex: 886856 MDLON G.
Fax: 01-481 2365.

GRAHAM MILLER & CO. LTD.,
229/230 Shoreditch High St., London E1 6PJ.
Telephone: 01-375 0471.
Telex: 884132 MILOVR G/938134 MILOVR G.
Fax: 01-375 2040.
R.J. Gent (01-504 2251).

RICH WHEELER & CO. LTD.
1 Cathedral Street,
London SE1 9DE.
Telephone: 01-407 3249.
Telex: 8814585.
Fax: 01-378 0299.

ROBINS DAVIES & LITTLE LTD.,
Davies House,
1/3 Sun Street, London EC2A 2BJ.
Telephone: 01-638 9481.
Telex: 888317.
Fax: 01-374 8298/01-588 9828.

ROBINS DAVIES & LITTLE LTD.,
Northway House,
High Road,
Whetstone, London N20 9NR.
Telephone: 01-446 8522.
Telex: 269000.
Fax: 01-446 7083.

ROBINS DAVIES (LONDON INTERNATIONAL) LTD.,
Davies House,
1-3 Sun Street,
London EC2A 2BJ.
Telephone: 01-638 9481
Telex: 888317
Fax: 01-623 5053

ABERDEEN

ROBINS McTEAR LTD.,
13 Albyn Terrace,
Aberdeen AB1 1YP.
Telephone: 0224-643388.
Fax: 0224-641688.

ABERYSTWYTH (CENTRAL WALES)

BROCKLEHURSTS,
32 North Parade,
Aberystwyth,
Dyfed SY23 2HL.
Telephone: 0970-624921.

ANGLESEY (NORTH WALES)

BROCKLEHURSTS,
Mulcair House,
Penmynydd Road,
Llanfair P.G.,
Bangor, Gwynedd.
Telephone: 0248-714730.
Fax: 0248-712750.

ASHFORD

ROBINS DAVIES & LITTLE (SOUTHERN)LTD.,
9 North Street,
Ashford,
Kent TN24 8LF.
Telephone: 0233 46516.
Fax: 0233 610265.

AYR

ROBINS McTEAR LTD.,
64 Kyle Street,
Ayr KA7 1RZ.
Telephone: 0292-268821/281433.
Fax: 0292-611187.

BANGOR

THOMAS HOWELL, SELFE (NORTHERN) LTD.,
210A High street,
Bangor,
Gwynedd LL57 1NY.
Telephone: 0248-370159.

BARNSTAPLE

ROBINS DAVIES & WARE LTD.,
4 Taw Vale,
Barnstaple,
Devon EX32 8NJ.
Telephone: 0271-78991.
Fax: 0392-413321.

BELFAST

BROCKLEHURSTS,
10-12 Lisburn Road,
Belfast BT9 6AA.
Telephone: 0232-327541 & 327545.
Fax: 0232-331296.

THOMAS HOWELL, SELFE (NORTHERN IRELAND) LTD.,
Stokes House,
25 College Square East,
Belfast BT1 6DE.
Chartered Loss Adjusters, Surveyors,
Telephone: 0232-324861.
Fax: 0232 326840.

ROBINS AHW LIMITED,
65-67 Chichester Street,
Belfast BT1 4JE.
Telephone: 0232-330090.
Fax: 0232-233756.

BIRMINGHAM

BROCKLEHURSTS,
65 Church Street,
Birmingham B3 2DP.
Telephone: 021-233 1566.
Telex: 338671.
Fax: 021-200 1176.

DAVIES & CO.,
Hagley House,
85 Hagley Road,
Edgbaston,
Birmingham B16 8QG.
Telephone: 021 456 1344.
Fax: 021 456 1109.

ELLIS & BUCKLE,
40 Great Charles Street,
Birmingham B3 2LX.
Telephone: 021-236 4411.
Fax: 021-233 2671.

**THOMAS HOWELL, SELFE
(MIDLANDS) LTD.,**
11th Floor,
Commercial Union House,
Martineau Square,
Birmingham B2 4UT.
Telephone: 021-200 3121.
Telex: 338593.
Fax: 021-236 2847.

**ROBINS DAVIES & LITTLE
(MIDLANDS) LTD.,**
Equity & Law House,
35/37 Great Charles Street,
Birmingham B3 3JY.
Telephone: 021-236 4811.
Fax: 021-200 1246.

BLACKPOOL

BROCKLEHURSTS,
257 Church Street,
Blackpool, Lancashire FY1 3PQ.
Telephone: 0253-20029.
Fax: 0253-751571.

BOLTON

BROCKLEHURSTS,
24 Mawdsley Street,
Bolton, Lancashire BL1 1LF.
Telephone: 0204-34928.
Fax: 0204-362505.

BOSTON, Lincs.

**THOMAS HOWELL, SELFE
(MIDLANDS) LTD.,**
9 Horncastle Road,
Boston PE21 9BN.
Telephone: 0205-311123.

BOURNEMOUTH

BROCKLEHURSTS,
Stirling House,
48-50 Poole Hill,
Bournemouth BH2 5PS.
Telephone: 0202-24961/294378.
Fax: 0202-299567.

ELLIS & BUCKLE,
7 Trinity,
161 Old Christchurch Road,
Bournemouth BH1 1JU.
Telephone: 0202-25361.
Fax: 0202-299315.

**THOMAS HOWELL, SELFE
(SOUTHERN) LTD.,**
12 Christchurch Road,
Bournemouth BH1 3LJ.
Telephone: 0202-295933.
Fax: 0202 299407

BRADFORD

ELLIS & BUCKLE,
Fourth Floor,
Arndale House,
Charles Street,
Bradford BD1 1EJ.
Telephone: 0274-309796.
Fax: 0274-306428.

**THOMAS HOWELL, SELFE
(NORTHERN) LTD.,**
Alliance House,
29/31 Kirkgate,
Bradford BD1 1QB.
Telephone: 0274-725232.
Fax: 0274-723251.

ROBINS FLETCHER LTD.,
Midland House,
2 Station Forecourt,
Bradford BD1 4HZ.
Telephone: 0274-723763.
Fax: 0274-393514.

BRIGHTON

BROCKLEHURSTS,
42 Bond Street,
Brighton BN1 1RD.
Telephone: 0273-206166.
Fax: 0273-21044.

ELLIS & BUCKLE
Equity and Law House,
102 Queens Road,
Brighton BN1 3XF.
Telephone: 0273-23471.
Fax: 0273-205912.

BRIGHTON *(continued)*

**THOMAS HOWELL, SELFE
(SOUTHERN) LTD.,**
33 Bond Street,
Brighton, Sussex BN1 1RD.
Telephone: 0273-203211.
Fax: 0273 206914

**ROBINS DAVIES & LITTLE
(SOUTHERN) LTD.,**
33 West Street,
Brighton,
Sussex BN1 2RE.
Telephone: 0273-23644/206511.
Fax: 0273-204454.

BRISTOL

BROCKLEHURSTS,
54 Baldwin Street,
Bristol BS1 1QW.
Telephone: 0272-290528
Fax: 0272-225091.

ELLIS & BUCKLE,
Southgate,
Whitefriars,
Lewins Mead,
Bristol BS1 2NT.
Telephone: 0272-299537.
Telex: 449731.
Fax: 0272-299393.

**THOMAS HOWELL, SELFE
(WESTERN) LTD.,**
Prudential Buildings,
Wine Street,
Bristol BS1 2PH.
Telephone: 0272-279106.
Fax: 0272-291452.

ROBINS DAVIES & WARE LTD.,
2 Berkeley Square,
Clifton,
Bristol BS8 1HL.
Telephone: 0272-279118.
Fax: 0272-272442.

BURNLEY

BROCKLEHURSTS,
84 St. James Street,
Burnley, BB11 1NJ.
Telephone: 0282-39347.
Fax: 0282-38038.

**THOMAS HOWELL, SELFE
(NORTHERN) LTD.,**
Prudential Buildings,
50 Manchester Road, Burnley BB11 1HJ.
Telephone: 0282-57636.

CAMBRIDGE

ELLIS & BUCKLE,
Sidney House,
Sussex Street,
Cambridge CB1 1PF.
Telephone: 0223-69711.
Fax: 0223-68763.

**THOMAS HOWELL, SELFE
(SOUTHERN) LTD.,**
Block 'B',
The Westbrook Centre,
Milton Road,
Cambridge CB4 1YQ.
Telephone: 0223-67841.
Fax: 0223 323183

**ROBINS DAVIES & LITTLE
(EAST ANGLIA) LTD.,**
Prudential Buildings,
59 St. Andrew's Street,
Cambridge CB2 2BZ.
Telephone: 0223-464774.
Fax: 0223-464727.

CANTERBURY

BROCKLEHURSTS,
1 Oaten Hill Court,
Oaten Hill,
Canterbury,
Kent CT1 3HS.
Telephone: 0277-458314.
Fax: 0227-762367.

ELLIS & BUCKLE,
17/19 St. George's Street,
Canterbury CT1 2JT.
Telephone: 0227-451566.
Fax: 0227-762147.

CARDIFF

BROCKLEHURSTS,
3rd Floor,
14 Cathedral Road,
Cardiff CF1 9LJ.
Telephone: 0222-24209/0.
Fax: 0222-377575.

ELLIS & BUCKLE,
Park House,
Greyfriars Road,
Cardiff CF1 3RE.
Telephone: 0222-378651.
Fax: 0222-373854.

**THOMAS HOWELL, SELFE,
(WESTERN) LTD.,**
Arlbee House,
Greyfriars Road,
Cardiff CF1 3AE.
Telephone: 0222-340512.
Fax: 0222-225572.

ROBINS DAVIES & LITTLE (WALES) LTD.,
4 Cathedral Road,
Cardiff CF1 9LJ.
Telephone: 0222-345061.
Fax: 0222-377356.

CARDIGAN

BROCKLEHURSTS,
Manchester House,
Grosvenor Hill,
Cardigan SA43 1HY.
Telephone: 0239-614562.

CARLISLE

BROCKLEHURSTS,
2 Currie Street,
Carlisle, Cumbria CA1 1HH.
Telephone: 0228 22757.
Fax: 0228-22796.

ROBINS DAVIES & LITTLE (NORTH EAST) LTD.,
11 Devonshire Street,
Carlisle CA3 8LL.
Telephone: 0228-48401.
Fax: 0228-515626.

CHELMSFORD

BROCKLEHURSTS,
Duke House,
Victoria Road South,
Chelmsford,
Essex CM1 1LN.
Telephone: 0245-267930.
Telex: 8953957.
Fax: G2/3 01-407 3996.

ELLIS & BUCKLE,
135 New London Road,
Chelmsford CM2 0QT.
Telephone: 0245-262107.
Fax: 0245-490729.

THOMAS HOWELL, SELFE (SOUTHERN) LTD.,
Nelson House, 23/27 Moulsham Street,
Chelmsford, Essex CM2 0XH.
Telephone: 0245-269695.
Fax: 0245-257869.

GRAHAM MILLER & CO. LTD.,
Friars House, 6/10 Parkway,
Chelmsford, Essex CM2 0NF.
Telephone: 0245-268447.
Fax: 0245-281228.
J. Benjamin: 01-508 4765.
I. Watt: 0702 470422.

CHESTER

BROCKLEHURSTS,
1 Kings Buildings,
King Street,
Chester CH1 2AJ.
Telephone: 0244-310123/6, 313766
Fax: 0244-328946.
Marine Tel: 0244-311275.
Telex: 61449.
Marine Fax: 0244-42464.

THOMAS HOWELL, SELFE (NORTHERN) LTD.,
Newgate House,
Newgate Street,
Chester CH1 1DE.
Telephone: 0244-328351.

CHIPPING NORTON

RICH, WHEELER & CO. LTD.,
2 West Street,
Chipping Norton,
Oxfordshire OX7 5AA.
Telephone: 0608-41351.
Fax: 0608-41176.

COLCHESTER

DAVIES AND COMPANY,
Balkerne House,
64/65 North Hill,
Colchester, Essex CO1 1PX.
Telephone: 0206-562949.
Fax: 0206-46111.

COLWYN BAY

BROCKLEHURSTS,
6 Wynnstay Road,
Colwyn Bay,
Clwyd, Wales LL29 8NB.
Telephone: 0492-532276.

CORK

THOMAS HOWELL, SELFE (IRELAND) LTD.,
112 Oliver Plunkett Street,
Cork, Eire.
Telephone: 01035321-271577.
Fax: 01035321-272853.

COVENTRY

BROCKLEHURSTS,
12th Floor,
Station Tower,
Station Square,
Coventry CV1 2GA.
Telephone: 0203-633777.
Telex: 338671.

ELLIS & BUCKLE,
4 Copthall House,
Station Square,
Coventry CV1 2PP.
Telephone: 0203-553881.
Fax: 0203-552331.

THOMAS HOWELL, SELFE (MIDLANDS) LTD.,
3 Station Tower,
Station Square, Coventry CV1 2GJ.
Telephone: 0203-553331.
Fax: 0203-632309

CROYDON (South London)

BROCKLEHURSTS,
6th Floor,
Wettern House,
Dingwall Road,
Croydon CR9 2TB.
Telephone: 01-681 6859.
Fax: 01-681 5919.

CROYDON SOUTH LONDON

ELLIS & BUCKLE,
Canterbury House,
Sydenham Road,
Croydon,
Surrey CR0 9XE.
Telephone: 01-686 9292.
Fax: 01-681 3429.

**THOMAS HOWELL, SELFE
(SOUTHERN) LTD.,**
Prudential House,
Wellesley Road, Croydon CR9 2EG.
Telephone: 01-680 5757.
Telex: 261862 THSCO G.
Fax: 01-680 0348.

GRAHAM MILLER & CO. LTD.,
Wettern House, Dingwall Road,
Croydon CR0 0XH.
Telephone: 01-681 5865.
Telex: 9413692 GRAMIL G.
Fax: 01-688 2275.
J. Pattullo 0689-58288.

ROBINS DAVIES & LITTLE LTD.,
9 Bedford Park,
Croydon CR9 2ND.
Telephone: 01-680 2797.
Telex: 922233.
Fax: 01-681 5165.

DARLINGTON

ELLIS & BUCKLE,
Crown Street Chambers,
Crown Street,
Darlington DL1 1RN.
Telephone: 0325-481141.
Fax: 0325-468168.

DERBY

**THOMAS HOWELL, SELFE
(MIDLANDS) LTD.,**
5th Floor,
Celtic House,
Heritage Gate,
Derby DE1 1QX.
Telephone: 0332-361424
Fax: 0332-292448.

DUBLIN

ROBIN DAVIES (IRELAND) LTD.,
32 Kildare Street,
Dublin 2, Eire.
Telephone: 0001-612102/616665/68208⸳
Fax: 0001-613736.

**THOMAS HOWELL, SELFE
(IRELAND) LTD.,**
2 Clare Street,
Dublin 2, Eire.
Telephone: 0001-765701 & 614650.
Telex: 91136.
Fax: 0001-766140.

**WALTER HUME & CO. LTD.,
"INTERNATIONAL ADJUSTERS",**
1-2 Suffolk Street,
Dublin 2, Republic of Ireland.
Telephone: 0001-710244.
Fax: 0001-710253.
Offices throughout Ireland.

DUMFRIES

ROBINS McTEAR LTD.,
11 Buccleuch Street,
Dumfries DG1 2AT.
Telephone: 0387-63956.
Fax: 0387-51836.

DUNDEE

**THOMAS HOWELL, SELFE
(SCOTLAND) LTD.,**
First Floor, Nethergate Centre,
35 Yeaman Shore,
Dundee DD1 4BU.
Telephone: 0382-27904.
Fax: 0382-200814

ROBINS McTEAR LTD.,
7 Ward Road,
Dundee DD1 1LP.
Telephone: 0382-24265/6.
Fax: 0382-202554.

EDINBURGH

ELLIS & BUCKLE,
9 South St. Andrew Street,
Edinburgh EH2 2AU.
Telephone: 031-556 6266.
Fax: 031-557 5470.

**THOMAS HOWELL, SELFE
(SCOTLAND) LTD.,**
1st Floor, 90A George Street,
Edinburgh EH2 3DF.
Telephone: 031-225 1388.
Fax: 031-220 2335

ROBINS McTEAR LTD.,
116 Dundas Street,
Edinburgh EH3 5DQ.
Telephone: 031-557 4088.
Fax: 031-557 5337.

EXETER

ELLIS & BUCKLE,
31/32 Southernhay East,
Exeter EX1 1NX.
Telephone: 0392-432621.
Fax: 0392-59634.

**THOMAS HOWELL, SELFE
(WESTERN) LTD.,**
Pearl Assurance House,
236 High Street,
Exeter EX4 3NE.
Telephone: 0392-211234.

ROBINS DAVIES & WARE LTD.,
Southernhay Court,
Southernhay East,
Exeter EX1 1NX.
Telephone: 0392-430001
Fax: 0392-413321.

GLASGOW

BROCKLEHURSTS,
135 Buchanan Street,
Glasgow G1 2JA.
Telephone: 041-221 8655.
Telex: 77664.
Fax: 041-221 1627.

CHRISTIE & CO (ADJUSTERS) LTD.,
Olympic House,
142 Queen Street,
Glasgow G1 3BU
Telephone: 041-248 4252.

ELLIS & BUCKLE,
144 West George Street,
Glasgow G2 2HG.
Telephone: 041-332 8161.
Fax: 041-332 7519.

**THOMAS HOWELL, SELFE
(SCOTLAND) LTD.,**
7th Floor,
90 St. Vincent Street,
Glasgow G2 5UB.
Telephone: 041-221 9121.
Fax: 041-221 5260

ROBINS McTEAR LTD.,
6 North Court,
St. Vincent Place, Glasgow G1 2DS.
Telephone: 041-248 6263.
Fax: 041-221 8057.

GLOUCESTER

**THOMAS HOWELL, SELFE
(MIDLANDS) LTD.,**
2nd Floor, Grosvenor House,
Station Road, Gloucester GL1 1SZ.
Telephone: 0452-502370.
Fax: 0452 307940

GREENOCK

ROBINS McTEAR LTD.,
18 Nicolson Street,
Greenock PA15 1JU.
Telephone: 0475-892253/4.
Fax: 0475-888013

GRIMSBY

**THOMAS HOWELL, SELFE
(NORTHERN) LTD.,**
Temple Chambers,
4 Abbey Road,
Grimsby, South Humberside DN32 0HF.
Telephone: 0472-41333.

ROBINS FLETCHER LTD.,
Yorkshire Bank Chambers,
Bethlehem Street,
Grimsby DN31 1LA.
Telephone: 0472-345136.
Fax: 0472-359100.

GUILDFORD

BROCKLEHURSTS,
77A, Woodbridge Road,
Guildford, Surrey GU1 4QH.
Telephone: 0483-37447 & 68811.
Fax: 0483-37943.

DAVIES AND COMPANY,
Ambersham House,
45 Woodbridge Road,
Guildford, Surrey GU1 4RN.
Telephone: 0483-577627.
Fax: 0483-35227.

ELLIS & BUCKLE,
32 High Street,
Guildford,
Surrey GU1 3EL.
Telephone: 0483-574117.
Fax: 0483-574247.

**THOMAS HOWELL, SELFE
(SOUTHERN) LTD.,**
Steward House,
Sydenham Road,
Guildford, Surrey GU1 3SR.
Telephone: 0483-63511.
Fax: 0483-300910.

ROBINS DAVIES & LITTLE LTD.,
67 Sydenham Road,
Guildford,
Surrey GU1 3RY.
Telephone: 0483-506888.
Fax: 0483-579653.

HAMILTON

ROBINS McTEAR LTD.,
P.O. Box 12,
42 Castle Street,
Hamilton ML3 6BX.
Telephone: 0698-429311.
Fax: 0698-891996.

HARTLEPOOL

ELLIS & BUCKLE,
Central Chambers,
161A York Road,
Hartlepool TS26 9EQ.
Telephone: 0429-862828.
Fax: 0429-862585.

HASTINGS

ELLIS & BUCKLE,
2nd floor, Queensbury House,
Havelock Road,
Hastings, East Sussex BN34 1BP.
Telephone: 0424-722155.
Fax: 0424-445741.

HEREFORD

BROCKLEHURSTS,
Wargrave House,
23 St. Owen Road,
Hereford HR1 2JB.
Telephone: 0432-59191.
Fax: 0432-353955.

HORLEY (For Gatwick)

BROCKLEHURSTS,
2 High Street,
Horley, Surrey RH6 7AY.
Telephone: 0293-786981.
Fax: G2/3 01-407 3996.
Aviation Telephone: 0293-772650 & 786981/2.
Telex: 884675.
Fax: 0293-775808.

HORSHAM

BROCKLEHURSTS,
31 Carfax,
Horsham,
Sussex RH12 1EE.
Telephone: 0403-41272/41283.
Telex: 878345.
Fax: 0403-41566.

HUDDERSFIELD

ROBINS FLETCHER LTD.,
142 Trinity Street,
Huddersfield HD1 4DT.
Telephone: 0484 28551.
Fax: 0484 435140.

HULL

BROCKLEHURSTS MARINE,
Suffolk House,
Silver Street, Hull, Yorkshire HU1 1JG.
Telephone: 0482-24756.
Telex: 597631.
Fax: 0482-20696.

**THOMAS HOWELL, SELFE
(NORTHERN) LTD.,**
Permanent House,
25 South Street,
Hull,
North Humberside HU1 3PB.
Telephone: 0482-223839.
Fax: 0482-219489.

ROBINS FLETCHER LTD.,
79 Beverley Road,
Hull HU3 1XR.
Telephone: 0482-26268.
Fax: 0482-217670.

ILFORD

ROBINS DAVIES & LITTLE LTD.,
Wentworth House,
350 Eastern Avenue,
Ilford, Essex IG2 6NY.
Telephone: 01-518 1321.
Telex: 894073.
Fax: 01-518 3742.

INVERNESS

ROBINS McTEAR LTD.,
19 Church Street,
Inverness IV1 1DY.
Telephone: 0463-233963.
Fax: 0463-710688.

IPSWICH

BROCKLEHURSTS,
Knapton Court,
Turret Lane,
Ipswich IP4 1DL.
Telephone: 0473-23211.
Fax: 0473-232148.

ELLIS & BUCKLE,
32 Queen Street,
Ipswich, Suffolk IP1 1SS.
Telephone: 0473-57287.
Fax: 0473-231277.

**THOMAS HOWELL, SELFE
(SOUTHERN) LTD,**
16/18 Princes Street,
Ipswich, Suffolk IP1 1PH.
Telephone: 0473-254455.
Fax: 0473-231252.

**ROBINS DAVIES & LITTLE
(EAST ANGLIA) LTD.,**
Archdeacon House,
Northgate Street,
Ipswich, Suffolk IP1 3BX.
Telephone: 0473-59601.
Fax: 0473-231287.

ISLE OF MAN

BROCKLEHURSTS (ISLE OF MAN) LTD.,
1 Church Street,
Douglas,
Isle of Man.
Telephone: 0624-72691.
Fax: 0624-661086.

**THOMAS HOWELL, SELFE
(ISLE OF MAN) LTD.,**
City Centre House,
18-20 Nelson Street,
Douglas,
Isle of Man.
Telephone: 0624-29557.

LANCASTER

ELLIS & BUCKLE,
King's Arcade,
King Street,
Lancaster LA1 1LE.
Telephone: 0524-841017.
Fax: 0524-841030.

LEEDS

BROCKLEHURSTS,
Coverdale House,
13/15 East Parade,
Leeds LS1 2BH.
Telephone: 0532-436353.
Fax: 0532-448152.

ELLIS & BUCKLE,
2nd Floor,
Abbey House,
11/12 Park Row,
Leeds LS1 5HD.
Telephone: 0532-422818.
Fax: 0532-422510.

**THOMAS HOWELL, SELFE
(NORTHERN) LTD.,**
Scottish Mutual House,
15/16 Park Row,
Leeds LS1 5HD.
Telephone: 0532-434949.
Telex: 557000.
Fax: 0532-423880.

ROBINS FLETCHER LTD.,
31/32 Park Row,
Leeds LS1 5JT.
Telephone: 0532-448711.
Telex: 557680.
Fax: 0532-420726.

LEICESTER

ELLIS & BUCKLE,
27 East Street,
Leicester LE1 6NB.
Telephone: 0533-549212.
Fax: 0533-540902.

**ROBINS DAVIES & LITTLE
(MIDLANDS) LTD.,**
Marlborough House,
38 Welford Road,
Leicester LE2 7AA.
Telephone: 0533-550323.
Fax: 0533-550706.

**THOMAS HOWELL, SELFE
(MIDLANDS) LTD.,**
2A New Walk,
Leicester LE1 6TF.
Telephone: 0533-553413.
Telex: 342566.
Fax: 0533-550838.

LINCOLN

**THOMAS HOWELL, SELFE
(MIDLANDS) LTD.,**
6th Floor, Wigford House,
Brayford Wharf East,
Lincoln LN5 7TN.
Telephone: 0522-540921.
Fax: 0522-536297

ROBINS FLETCHER LTD.,
Akrill House,
25 Clasketgate,
Lincoln LN2 1JJ.
Telephone: 0522-533125.
Fax: 0522-532940.

LISKEARD

GRAHAM MILLER & CO. LTD.,
Suite 1, South Phoenix, Minions,
Liskeard, Cornwall PL14 5LH.
Telephone: 0579-62003.
I. Williams 0579-62003.

LIVERPOOL

BROCKLEHURSTS,
1 Water Street,
Liverpool L1 0RD.
Telephone: 051-236 9621.
Fax: 051-236 3225.

ELLIS & BUCKLE,
Castle Chambers,
43 Castle Street,
Liverpool L2 9TG.
Telephone: 051-236 8001.
Fax: 051-236 1550.

**THOMAS HOWELL, SELFE
(NORTHERN) LTD.,**
Richmond House,
1 Rumford Place,
Liverpool L3 9RN.
Telephone: 051-236 7281.
Fax: 051-236 4544.

**ROBINS DAVIES & LITTLE
(NORTHERN) LTD.,**
Refuge Assurance House,
Lord Street,
Liverpool L2 1UD.
Telephone: 051-708 9477.
Telex: 627019.
Fax: 051-708 5783.

LONDONDERRY

**THOMAS HOWELL, SELFE
(NORTHERN IRELAND) LTD.,**
Anglia House,
3 The Diamond,
Londonderry BT48 6HN.
Telephone: 0504-261651.
Fax: 0504-269099.

ROBINS AHW LIMITED,
Northern Counties Building,
Custom House Street,
Londonderry BT48 6AE.
Telephone: 0504-267517/260580.
Fax: 0504-261199.

LUTON

BROCKLEHURSTS,
Halcyon House,
Percival Way,
Luton International Airport,
Luton, Bedfordshire LU2 9LU.
Telephone: 0582-414555.
Telex: 826736.
Fax: 0582-402602.

LUTON *(continued)*

ELLIS & BUCKLE,
Commerce House,
Stuart Street,
Luton, Beds LU1 5BY.
Telephone: 0582-455774.
Fax: 0582-416235.

MAIDSTONE

BROCKLEHURSTS
14 Tonbridge Road,
Maidstone,
Kent ME16 8RP.
Telephone: 0622-691474.
Fax: 0622-687876.

DAVIES AND COMPANY,
(Incorporating B.P. Regan & Co.)
75 College Road,
Maidstone, Kent ME15 6TF.
Telephone: 0622-673848.
Fax: 0622-687928.

ELLIS & BUCKLE,
3 Granada House,
Gabriels Hill,
Maidstone ME15 6JP.
Telephone: 0622-688466.
Fax: 0622-691389.

THOMAS HOWELL, SELFE
(SOUTHERN) LTD.,
1st Floor, Romney Court,
25 Romney Place,
Maidstone, Kent ME15 6LG.
Telephone: 0622-690969.
Fax: 0622-690271.

GRAHAM MILLER & CO. LTD.,
Rock House, 1 Bedford Place, London Road,
Maidstone, Kent ME16 8JQ.
Telephone: (0622) 671227/8.
Telex: 96171 GRAMIL G.
Fax: (0622) 59528.
Kevin Holt (0622) 813670.

ROBINS DAVIES & LITTLE
(SOUTHERN) LTD.
Fowden Hall,
51 London Road,
Maidstone Kent ME16 8JE.
Telephone: 0622-690080.
Telex: 965907.
Fax: 0622-687196.

MANCHESTER

BROCKLEHURSTS,
20 St. Ann's Square,
Manchester M2 7HU.
Telephone: 061-834 1631/5.
Telex: 667116.
Fax: 061-834 9260.

DAVIES & CO,
7 High Street,
Cheadle,
Manchester SK8 1AX.
Telephone: 061 428 0628.
Fax: 061-428 1237.

ELLIS & BUCKLE,
74 King Sreet,
Manchester M2 4NJ.
Telephone: 061-834 5075.
Fax: 061-832 1854.

THOMAS HOWELL, SELFE
(NORTHERN) LTD.,
Kings Court, Exchange Street,
Manchester M2 7AJ.
Telephone: 061-228 2911.
Telex: 666398.
Fax: 061-832 0591

ROBINS DAVIES & LITTLE
(NORTHERN) LTD.,
Peter House,
St. Peter's Square,
Manchester M1 5AS.
Telephone: 061-228 1661.
Telex: 668746.
Fax: 061-228 1701.

MIDDLESBROUGH

THOMAS HOWELL, SELFE
(NORTHERN) LTD.,
Prudential House,
31/33 Albert Road,
Middlesbrough, Cleveland TS1 1PE.
Telephone: 0642-224541 & 241071.

ROBINS DAVIES & LITTLE
(NORTH EAST) LTD.,
Pearl Assurance House,
44 Dundas Street,
Middlesbrough, Cleveland TS1 1HP.
Telephone: 0642-247734.
Fax: 0642-217308.

MILTON KEYNES

THOMAS HOWELL, SELFE
(MIDLANDS) LTD.,
4th Floor, Midsummer House,
Midsummer Boulevard,
Central Milton Keynes MK9 3BN.
Telephone: 0908-677776.
Fax: 0908-690485.

NEWCASTLE-UPON-TYNE

BROCKLEHURSTS,
15-17 Grey Street,
Newcastle-upon-Tyne,
NE1 6EE.
Telephone: 091-261 7151.
Fax: 091-222 0763.

NEWCASTLE UPON TYNE

ELLIS & BUCKLE,
Central Exchange Buildings,
93a Grey Street,
Newcastle-upon-Tyne NE1 6EG.
Telephone: 091-261 1337.
Fax: 091-232 8702.

**THOMAS HOWELL, SELFE
(NORTHERN) LTD.,**
"A" Floor, Milburn House,
Dean Street,
Newcastle-upon-Tyne NE1 1NN.
Telephone: 091-232 8691.
Fax: 091-222 0097.

**ROBINS DAVIES & LITTLE
(NORTH EAST) LTD.,**
Greys Building,
53 Grey Street,
Newcastle-upon-Tyne NE1 6QH.
Telephone: 091-232 2673.
Fax: 091-261 1631.

NORTHAMPTON

BROCKLEHURSTS,
33 Bridge Street,
Northampton NN1 1NS.
Telephone: 0604-259297.
Telex: 826736.

**THOMAS HOWELL, SELFE
(MIDLANDS) LTD.,**
Grosvenor Chambers,
Market Square,
Northampton NN1 2HE.
Telephone: 0604-230880.
Fax: 0604-234500.

NORWICH

BROCKLEHURST LOWTHER,
(Incorporating Lowther Associates Ltd.),
St. John's House,
25 St John Maddermarket,
Norwich NR2 1DN.
Telephone: 0603-630665.
Fax: 0603-760821.

ELLIS & BUCKLE,
20 Colegate,
Norwich NR3 1AP.
Telephone: 0603-660781.
Fax: 0603-630157.

**THOMAS HOWELL, SELFE
(MIDLANDS) LTD.,**
Britannia House,
45/53 Prince of Wales Road,
Norwich, Norfolk NR1 1BL.
Telephone: 0603-614326.
Fax: 0603-761280

NOTTINGHAM

BROCKLEHURSTS,
Gothic House, Barker Gate,
Nottingham NG1 1JS.
Telephone: 0602-504127.
Fax: 0602-586395.

ELLIS & BUCKLE,
1 East Circus Street,
Nottingham NG1 5LU.
Telephone: 0602-470021.
Fax: 0602-484107.

**THOMAS HOWELL, SELFE
(MIDLANDS) LTD.,**
Rodney House,
Castle Gate,
Nottingham NG1 7AW.
Telephone: 0602 583171.
Fax: 0602-483084.

OBAN

ROBINS McTEAR LTD,
Dunollie Halls,
Dunollie Road,
Oban PA34 5PH.
Telephone: 0631-64747.
Fax: 0631-62292.

OXFORD

DAVIES AND COMPANY,
Davies House, Oasis Park,
Eynsham, Oxford OX8 1TP.
Telephone: 0865-882979.
Fax: 0865-882961.

ELLIS & BUCKLE,
Clock Tower,
4 High Street,
Kidlington,
Oxford OX5 2YA.
Telephone: 0865-842211.
Fax: 0865-841555.

**THOMAS HOWELL, SELFE
(MIDLANDS) LTD.,**
87 London Road,
Headington,
Oxford OX3 9BE.
Telephone: 0865-751375.
Fax: 0865-741503.

PERTH

ROBINS McTEAR LTD.,
7 Atholl Crescent,
Perth PH1 5NG.
Telephone: 0738 36442.
Fax: 0382-202554.

304

PETERBOROUGH

BROCKLEHURSTS,
North Wing,
Broadway Court,
Broadway,
Peterborough PE1 1RS.
Telephone: 0733-555050.
Fax: 0733-557619.

THOMAS HOWELL, SELFE (MIDLANDS) LTD.,
5 Cathedral Square,
Peterborough PE1 1XH.
Telephone: 0733-42434.
Fax: 0733-557396.

PLYMOUTH

BROCKLEHURSTS,
36 Eastlake Street,
Plymouth,
Devon PL1 1VE.
Telephone: 0752-269252.
Fax: 0752-600331.

THOMAS HOWELL, SELFE (WESTERN) LTD.,
Pearl Assurance House,
50 Royal Parade,
Plymouth,
Devon PL1 1DZ.
Telephone: 0752-229555.

ROBINS DAVIES & WARE LTD,
Hyde Park House,
Mutley Plain,
Plymouth, Devon PL4 6LG.
Telephone: 0752-267331.
Fax: 0752-601343.

PORTSMOUTH

ELLIS & BUCKLE,
42 Arundel Street,
Portsmouth PO1 1TH.
Telephone: 0705 811304.
Fax: 0705 738180.

THOMAS HOWELL, SELFE (SOUTHERN) LTD.,
Prudential Buildings,
16 Guildhall Walk,
Portsmouth PO1 2DD.
Telephone: 0705-839641.
Fax: 0705 291883.

PRESTON

BROCKLEHURSTS,
30 Ribblesdale Place,
Preston,
Lancashire PR1 3NA.
Telephone: 0772-59641/2 & 53973.
Fax: 0772-203185.

THOMAS HOWELL, SELFE (NORTHERN) LTD.,
33 Ribblesdale Place,
Preston, Lancashire PR1 3NA.
Telephone: 0772-51343.
Fax: 0772-54050.

ROBINS DAVIES & LITTLE (NORTHERN) LTD.,
10 Winckley Square,
Preston, Lancashire PR1 3JJ.
Telephone: 0772-24826.
Fax: 0772-50457.

READING

BROCKLEHURSTS,
Holybrook House,
63 Castle Street,
Reading, Berkshire RG1 7SN.
Telephone: 0734 574222.
Fax: 0734 591627.

ELLIS & BUCKLE,
ARA House, 69 Honey End Lane,
Reading,
Berkshire RG3 4QL.
Telephone: 0734-597766.
Fax: 0734-391033.

THOMAS HOWELL, SELFE (SOUTHERN) LTD.,
Kings Point,
120 Kings Road,
Reading RG1 3BB.
Telephone: 0734-391779.
Fax: 0734-391763.

GRAHAM MILLER & CO. LTD.,
14B Norcot Road, Tilehurst,
Reading, Berkshire RG3 6BU.
Telephone: (0734) 451211.
Telex: 848322 MILOVR G.
Fax: (0734) 451216
M. Taylor.

ROBINS DAVIES & LITTLE LTD.,
Kennet House,
80 Kings Road,
Reading RG1 3BJ.
Telephone: 0734-594244.
Fax: 0734-505665.

ROMFORD

BROCKLEHURSTS,
1A Eastern Road,
Romford,
Essex RM1 3BU.
Telephone: 0708-24138/9.
Telex: 8953957.
Fax: 0708-42831.

DAVIES AND COMPANY,
Frankland Moore House,
185-187 High Road,
Chadwell Heath,
Romford,
Essex RM6 6NR.
Telephone: 01-597 2136.
Fax: 01-597 6853.

ST. HELENS

ELLIS & BUCKLE,
21-31 Barrow Street,
St. Helens WA10 1RX.
Telephone: 0744-613322.
Fax: 0744-26254.

SALE

BROCKLEHURSTS,
(CONTRACTORS CLAIMS UNIT)
2a Curzon Road,
Sale,
Cheshire M33 1DR.
Telephone: 061-905 1112.
Fax: 061-962 3830.

SALISBURY

BROCKLEHURSTS,
24 Catherine Street,
Salisbury SP1 2DA.
Telephone: 0722-20769.

SHEFFIELD

BROCKLEHURSTS,
Alliance House,
Leopold Street,
Sheffield S1 1RB.
Telephone: 0742-752906.
Fax: 0742-724088.

THOMAS HOWELL, SELFE
(NORTHERN) LTD.,
Alliance House,
Leopold Street,
Sheffield S1 2GY.
Telephone: 0742-750068.

ROBINS FLETCHER LTD.,
269 Glossop Road,
Sheffield S10 2JG.
Telephone: 0742 767131.
Fax: 0742 730419.

SHREWSBURY

BROCKLEHURSTS,
Claremont House,
Claremont Bank,
Shrewbury, Shropshire SY1 1RW.
Telephone: 0743-241216/7.
Fax: 0743-242301.

THOMAS HOWELL, SELFE
(MIDLANDS) LTD.,
Wightman Chambers,
14A The Square,
Shrewsbury,
Shropshire SY1 1LA.
Telephone: 0743-232411.
Fax: 0743 50041.

SOUTHAMPTON

BROCKLEHURSTS,
4th Floor, Brunswick House,
Brunswick Place,
Southampton,
Hampshire SO1 2AP.
Telephone: 0703-331622/3.
Fax: 0703-339389.

DAVIES AND COMPANY,
10 Cumberland Place,
Southampton,
Hampshire SO1 2BH.
Telephone: 0703-36922.
Fax: 0703-330701.

ELLIS & BUCKLE,
2 Carlton Crescent,
Southampton SO1 2EY.
Telephone: 0703-223477.
Fax: 0703-636590.

ROBINS DAVIES & LITTLE
(SOUTHERN) LTD,
Carlton House,
Carlton Place,
Southampton,
Hampshire SO1 2DZ.
Telephone: 0703 637744.
Fax: 0703-632069.

SOUTHEND-ON-SEA

ROBINS DAVIES & LITTLE LTD.,
Harcourt House,
5-15 Harcourt Avenue,
Southend-on-Sea, Essex SS2 6FG.
Telephone: 0702-349911.
Fax: 0702-433410.

SOUTHPORT

BROCKLEHURSTS,
Britannic Assurance House,
38 Hoghton Street,
Southport PR9 0PQ.
Telephone: 0704-43540.
Fax: 0704-500140.

STOKE-ON-TRENT

DAVIES AND COMPANY,
30 Gilman Place,
Hanley,
Stoke-on-Trent ST1 3PG.
Telephone: 0782-279216.
Fax: 0782-202237.

ROBINS DAVIES & LITTLE
(MIDLANDS) LTD.,
6 Gitana Street,
Hanley,
Stoke-on-Trent ST1 1RD.
Telephone: 0782 202056.
Fax: 0782-283837.

STOKE ON TRENT (continued)

THOMAS HOWELL, SELFE (MIDLANDS) LTD.,
48/56 Pall Mall,
Hanley, Stoke-on-Trent ST1 1EH.
Telephone: 0782-202707.
Fax: 0782-208044.

SUNDERLAND

ROBINS DAVIES & LITTLE (NORTH EAST) LTD.,
Maritime Buildings,
St. Thomas Street,
Sunderland SR1 1BL.
Telephone: 091-567 7267.
Fax: 091-510 0712.

SWANSEA

BROCKLEHURSTS,
Eagle Star House,
19 The Kingsway,
Swansea SA1 5JY.
Telephone: 0792-456070.
Fax: 0792-644487.

ELLIS & BUCKLE,
8th Floor,
Princess House,
Princes Way,
Swansea SA1 5LW.
Telephone: 0792-468524.
Fax: 0792-467412.

THOMAS HOWELL, SELFE (WESTERN) LTD.,
96/97 Mansel Street,
Swansea SA1 5UE.
Telephone: 0792-464634.

SWINDON

BROCKLEHURSTS,
Astoria House,
165/166 Victoria Road,
Swindon,
Wiltshire SN1 3BU.
Telephone: 0793 512400 & 485878.

THOMAS HOWELL, SELFE (WESTERN) LTD.,
103/104 Commercial Road,
Swindon,
Wiltsire SN1 5PL.
Telephone: 0793-618616.

TAUNTON

ROBINS DAVIES & WARE LTD.,
2 Middle Street,
Taunton,
Somerset TA1 1SH.
Telephone: 0823-333455.
Fax: 0392-413321.

TORQUAY

ROBINS DAVIES & WARE LTD.,
5-7 Abbey Road,
Torquay, Devon TQ2 5NF.
Telephone: 0803-295360/212304.
Fax: 0392-413321.

TRURO

ROBINS DAVIES & WARE LTD.,
Lower Terrace,
Newham,
Truro TR1 2ST.
Telephone: 0872-76029.
Fax: 0872-223771.

TWICKENHAM

ELLIS & BUCKLE,
Fourways House,
121 Nelson Road,
Twickenham,
Middx. TW2 7AZ.
Telephone: 01-755 1265.
Fax: 01-894 7706.

UXBRIDGE

ROBINS DAVIES & LITTLE LTD.,
1 Redford Way,
Uxbridge,
Middlesex UB8 1SZ.
Telephone: 0895-56731.
Telex: 888208.
Fax: 0895-57029.

WARRINGTON

THOMAS HOWELL, SELFE (NORTHERN) LTD.,
17 Palmyra Square,
Warrington WA1 1BS.
Telephone: 0925-50158.

WATFORD

BROCKLEHURSTS,
Woodford House,
25 Woodford Road,
Watford,
Hertfordshire WD1 1PB.
Telephone: 0923-34333.
Fax: 0923-228508.

THOMAS HOWELL, SELFE (SOUTHERN) LTD.,
1 Clarendon Road,
Watford,
Hertfordshire
WD1 1LH.
Telephone: 0923-248711.
Telex: 917248.
Fax: 0923-249821.

GRAHAM MILLER & CO. LTD.,
146 Queen's Rd, Watford, Herts WD1 2NX.
Telephone: (0923) 2401227.
Telex: 912014 GMWAT G.
Fax: (0923) 242843.
D. M. Symons.

WEMBLEY

CUNNINGHAM, HART & CO. LTD.,
Imperial Life House,
390/400 High Road,
Wembley,
Middlesex HA9 6UE.
Telephone: 01-903 7111.
Telex: 9419709.
Fax: 01-903 5269.

WINCHESTER

**THOMAS HOWELL, SELFE
(SOUTHERN) LTD.,**
Fountain House, Parchment Street,
Winchester,
Hampshire SO23 8AT.
Telephone: 0962-61624/5.
Telex: 477168.
Fax: 0962-840798.

WOLVERHAMPTON

ELLIS & BUCKLE,
16 Waterloo Road,
Wolverhampton WV1 4BL.
Telephone: 0902-771612.
Fax: 0902-713526.

**THOMAS HOWELL, SELFE
(MIDLANDS) LTD.,**
6 Waterloo Road,
Wolverhampton WV1 4ED.
Telephone: 0902-29921.
Fax: 0902-24816.

WORCESTER

ELLIS & BUCKLE,
Marmion House,
Copenhagen Street,
Worcester WR1 2HB.
Telephone: 0905-20578.
Fax: 0905-23805.

**THOMAS HOWELL, SELFE
(MIDLANDS) LTD.,**
14 Pierpoint Street,
Worcester WR1 1TA.
Telephone: 0905-28536 & 611711.
Fax: 0905 723528.

YORK

ROBINS FLETCHER LTD.,
51 Burton Stone Lane,
York YO3 6BT.
Telephone: 0904-642946.
Fax: 0904-624866.

OVERSEAS

AUSTRALIA

FULLARTON

**AVIATION & GENERAL INSURANCE
ADJUSTING CO. PTY. LTD.,**
246 Glen Osmond Road,
Fullarton, S.A. 5063.
Telephone: (08) 79-9971.
Fax: (08) 79-8884.

MELBOURNE

TOPLIS AND HARDING MARINE
throughout Australia call
Toll free no. 008 033 631.
P.O. Box 530, Ringwood, 3134.
Telephone: (03) 729 5590.
Telex: AA36041.
Fax: (03) 720 4104.

TOPLIS & HARDING (VICTORIA) PTY. LTD.,
521 Toorak Road, (P.O. Box 12),
Toorak, Vic. 3142.
Telephone: (03) 240 8522.
Telex: AA 32306.
Fax: (03) 241 8661.

PERTH

GRAHAM MILLER (W.A.),
220 St. George's Terrace,
Perth 6000,
Western Australia.
Telephone: 324 1625.
Telex: 197054.
Fax: 324 1596.

ST. LEONARDS

GIVENS EMERSON,
Suite 3B,
AMA House,
33-35 Atchison Street,
St. Leonard's N.S.W. 2065,
Australia.
Telephone: 612-438 2222.
Telegrams: LOSSADJU ST.
Telex: AA26541 GIVEM.
Fax: 612-438 4663.

AUSTRALIA (continued)
SYDNEY

BROCKLEHURSTS (AUSTRALIA) PTY. LTD.,
44 Bridge Street,
Sydney, N.S.W. 2000, Australia.
Telephone: 02-221-2822.
Telex: AA127606.
Fax: 02-221 2912.

ROBINS DAVIES AUSTRALIA (HOLDINGS) PTY. LTD.,
Australian Head Office:
Suite 302,
156 Pacific Highway,
Greenwich,
Sydney, N.S.W. 2065.
Telephone: (2) 906 1177
Fax: (2) 906 1171
Offices throughout Australia and Papua New Guinea.

AUSTRIA
VIENNA

GRAHAM MILLER EUROPE
Haus 129, A-3652 Leiben (Vienna).
Telephone: (2752) 7705.
Telex: 75311709.
Fax: (2752) 28664.
F. Fuchs.

BAHAMAS
NASSAU

PROFESSIONAL LOSS ADJUSTERS LTD.,/ THOMAS HOWELL KIEWIT
Tenwich Street West,
(Off Mt. Royal Avenue),
P.O. Box SS-6276, Nassau, Bahamas.
Telephone: 809-323 8210.
Telex: NS 520 ADJUSTERS.
Cables: ADJUSTERS NASSAU.

BAHRAIN

ROBINS DAVIES MIDDLE EAST S.A.R.L.,
P.O. Box 10125,
Diplomatic Area,
Manama,
Bahrain.
Telephone: 530577,
Telex: 9035 RDME BN.
Fax: 530917.

BARBADOS
BRIDGETOWN

GRAHAM MILLER LTD.,
1st Floor, Beckwith Mall, Nile Street,
Bridgetown.
Telephone: (809) 427-6521.
Fax: (809) 429 8255.
S. Convery (809) 429-8918.

BELGIUM
ANTWERP

TYLER & CO. (ANTWERP), S.P.R.L.,
67 Meir, 200 Antwerp,
Telephone: 03-231.87.50.
Telex: 34.152.
Fax: 03-231.87.60.

BRUSSELS

BROCKLEHURSTS (BENELUX) SA/NV,
Avenue des Arts 19/Bte 2,
1040 Brussels,
Belgium.
Telephone: (02) 217 2250.
Fax: (02) 218 3132.

GRAHAM MILLER & CO. (BENELUX) S.A.
Bd. Lambermont 426, 1030 Brussels.
Telephone: (02) 241 88 80.
Telex: 22434 Cables Millover.
Fax: (02) 2165217.
J.S. Horner (02) 354-8805.

ZEMST

ROBINS DAVIES PEETERMANS NV/SA,
Tervuren Sesteen Weg 724,
2959 Zemst,
Belgium.
Telephone: 15610418.
Telex: 2866.
Fax: 15616242.

BERMUDA
HAMILTON

BROCKLEHURST INTERNATIONAL ASSOCIATES LTD.,
P.O. Box HM 2267,
Sophia House,
Church Street,
Hamilton 5,
Bermuda.
Telephone: (809-29) 5-8495.
Telex: 3719 COURT BA.
Fax:809 292 1196.

BRUNEI
BANDAR SERI BEGAWAN

GRAHAM MILLER (SINGAPORE) PTE. LTD.,
No. 9 Block B, 2nd Floor,
Pap Jajjah Norain Complex,
Mile 1 1/2 Jalan Tutong,
Bandar Sesi Begawan 2600,
Brunei, Darussalam.
Telephone: 23409.
Telex: BU2549 BONDS.
Fax: (2) 23409.
S. Y. Heng.

CANADA
TORONTO

GRAHAM MILLER & CO. (CANADA) LTD.,
P.O. Box 36, Toronto M5G 2B7, Ontario.
Telephone: (416) 595 1822.
Fax: (416) 595 0788.
P. Bracken.

COLOMBIA
BOGOTA

GRAHAM MILLER & CO. (COLOMBIA) LTD.,
Carrera 12. 71-53 Oficina 102,
P.O. Box 94754, Bogota, D.E.
Telephone: (1) 235 0108/235 9620.
Fax: 235 0148.
R. Roa (1) 985 300 30.

EGYPT
CAIRO

MATTHEWS-DANIEL INTERNATIONAL (EGYPT) LTD.,
26 Asma Fahmy Street
Flat 15, 4th Floor,
Heliopolis, Cairo, Egypt.
Telephone: (02) 670232.
Telex: 21141 MDIE UN.
Fax: (02) 2907869.

FRANCE
MARSEILLE

GRAHAM MILLER (FRANCE) E.U.R.L.,
21 Rue de la Republique
P.O. Box 2459, 13002 Marseille Cedex.
Telephone: 9191 4643.
Telex: 402533 GMEMRS F.
Fax: 9190 1713.
G. Symonds 4228 8322.

PARIS

BROCKELHURST FRANCE,
27 rue Etienne Marcel,
75001 Paris.
Telephone: 4296 9226.
Telex: 240204 F.
Fax: 4286-0898.

GRAHAM MILLER (FRANCE) E.U.R.L.,
26 Rue de Mogador, 75009 Paris.
Telephone: (1) 4280 3781.
Telex: 650654 MILLOVER F.
Fax: (1) 4281 1665.
J. Beynon (4) 449 9486.

THOMAS HOWELL KIEWIT (FRANCE) Sarl.,
3 Rue Alfred Stevens,
75009 Paris.
Telephone: (1) 42 85 40 20.
Telex: 282090 SERI THK.
Fax: (1) 42 85 20 79

GERMANY
FRANKFURT

THOMAS HOWELL KIEWIT INTERNATIONAL GROUP LTD.,
Dietmar Jurgs/Thomas Howell Kiewit G.m.b.H.,
1 Eschersheimer Landstr,
6000, Frankfurt/Main.
Telephone: Frankfurt 590286.
Telex: 414055 THKFM.
Also offices in Hamburg & Nurnberg.

HAMBURG

THOMAS HOWELL KIEWIT GmbH,
Deichstrasse 50,
2000 Hamburg,
Germany.
Telephone: Hamburg 37 19 33.

NURNBERG

THOMAS HOWELL, KIEWIT GmbH,
Peterstrasse 30, 8500 Nurnberg 1,
Germany.
Telephone: Nurnberg 463028

GIBRALTAR

GRAHAM MILLER & CO. (GIBRALTAR) LTD.,
P.O. Box 620, International House,
Bell Lane, Gibraltar.
Telephone: 78003.
Fax: 79787

GREECE
ATHENS

GRAHAM MILLER (HELLAS) LTD.,
9a Apollonos Street, Athens 10557, Greece.
Telephone: (01) 3255560.
Fax: (01) 3252745.
St. G. Artopoulos (01) 9934061

GUERNSEY

BROCKLEHURSTS GUERNSEY LTD.,
Regency House,
Commercial Arcade,
St. Peter Port,
Guernsey, C.I.
Telephone: 0481-712295

HONG KONG

BROCKLEHURSTS (FAR EAST) LTD.,
Hoseinee House,
5th Floor,
69 Wyndham Street,
Central, Hong Kong.
Telephone: 5-265436/9.
Telex: 82069 BROCK HX.
Fax: 5-8106953

GRAHAM MILLER (HONG KONG) LTD.,
5th Floor, Printing House, 18 Ice House St.,
G.P.O. Box No. 6353, Hong Kong.
Telephone: (5) 265137.
Telex: 83626 MILOVR.
Fax: (5) 8450598.
Cables Millover.
N. Gale (5) 812 0993.

THOMAS HOWELL KIEWIT (HONG KONG) LTD.,
Room 1101 D'Aguilar Place,
No. 7 D'Aguilar Street, Central, Hong Kong.
Telephone: 5-212227.
Telex: 80989 THKHK.
Fax: 5-8100588

INDONESIA
JAKARTA

GRAHAM MILLER & CO.,
c/o P.T. Dharma Nilaitama
Wisma Dharmala Sakti
18th Floor, Jl. Jend Sudirman No.32,
Jakarta 10220.
Telephone: (21) 581116/581119.
Telex: 42790 DML JKT.
Fax: 584903.
Mr. Hardianto Setiobudi.

**P.T. SATRIA DHARMA PUSAKA/
THOMAS HOWELL KIEWIT,**
Prince Centre Building, 11/203,
JL Jend Sudirman 3-4,
Jakarta 10220, Indonesia.
Telephone: 581356, 588197, 588198 & 584189.
Telex: 44165 SDPTHKIA.

ISRAEL
TEL AVIV

SAGIV & CO.,
Loss Adjusters & Marine Surveyors Ltd.,
11 Sheinkin Street,
Tel Aviv 65231, Israel.
Telephone: 03-288204/5.
Telex: 342434 SAGIV.
Fax: 03-202802.

ITALY
AREZZO

BROCKLEHURST ITALIA S.r.l.,
Via Alessandro dal Borro, 86,
52100 Arezzo, Italy.
Telephone: 0575-357745.
Telex: 570400 (quote "Brocklehurst").
Fax: 0575-357746.

MILAN

BROCKLEHURST ITALIA S.r.l.,
Via Dei Carracci, 3,
20149 Milan, Italy.
Telephone: 010-392 435748 & 436606.
Telex: 340019 BROCKS I.
Fax: 02-4691228.

GRAHAM MILLER & CO. (ITALY) S.r.l.,
Via Olmetto 5, 20123 Milan.
Telephone: (02) 89010344, 8059430.
Telex: 335454 GME IT I.
Fax: (02) 72000019.
Cables Millover.
H. Page Taylor.

ROME

BROCKLEHURST ITALIA S.r.l.,
Via Tuscolana, 1675,
00044 Rome, Italy.
Telephone: 06-7970998.
Telex: 340019 BROCKS I.

GRAHAM MILLER & CO. (ITALY) S.r.l.,
Via Castelfranco Veneto 18. INT. 5A.
00191 Rome, Italy.
Telephone: (06) 328-8704.
Fax: 328-8652.
P. Litta (06) 528-4026.

JAMAICA
KINGSTON

GRAHAM MILLER & CO. (JAMAICA) LTD.,
Henderson House, 18 Ripon Road,
Kingston 5.
Telephone: (809) 926-4873.
Telex: 2194 MANCOM.
Fax: (809) 926 4369.
T. Dawson (809) 924-2235.

JERSEY

BROCKLEHURSTS (C.I.) LIMITED,
3 Mulcaster Street,
St. Helier, Jersey, C.I.
Telephone: 0534-33373.
Fax: 0534-59885.

GRAHAM MILLER & CO. (C.I.) LTD.,
Burlington House, St. Saviour's Road,
St. Helier, Jersey.
Telephone: (0534) 35845.
Fax: (0534) 32370.
R. Billington (0534) 54269.

JORDAN
AMMAN

SPINNEYS 1948 LIMITED,
P.O. Box 40,
Amman,
Jordan.
Telephone: 779141/2/3.
Telex: 21814 SPINEX JO.

KENYA
MOMBASA

W. J. BLAKEMAN LTD.,
Marine Division,
Ambalal House, P.O. Box 83975,
Mombasa Kenya.
Telephone: Mombasa 311358.
Telex: 21138 Adjusters.

NAIROBI

ROBINS BLAKEMAN LTD.,
International House,
P.O. Box 43675,
Nairobi,
Kenya.
Telephone: (2) 21420/(2) 21637.
Telex: 22618 ADUSTERS.
Fax: (2) 729792.
Office also in Mombasa.

KUWAIT

ROBINS DAVIES KUWAIT,
6th Floor,
Al Maidan Commercial Centre,
Ahmed Al-Jaber Street,
P.O. Box 268,
13129 Safat,
Kuwait.
Telephone: 2414131/2442150.
Telex: 30891 ADJUST KT.
Fax: 2414130.

MALAYSIA
IPOH

**THOMAS HOWELL KIEWIT
INTERNATIONAL GROUP LTD.,**
Thomas Howell Kiewit (Malaysia) Sdn. Bhd.,
Room 201, 2nd Floor,
Asia Life Building,
45 Hale Street,
3000 Ipoh, Perak.
Telephone: 05-541936, 543468.

JOHORE BAHRU

GRAHAM MILLER (MALAYSIA) SDN. BHD.
Room 1402, (Floor 14), Johor Tower,
Jalan Gereja, 80100 Johor Baru.
Telephone: 07-233715.
Telex: 32690 MILOVR.
F. Sim: 07-312976.

**THOMAS HOWELL KIEWIT
(MALAYSIA) SDN. BHD.,**
Suite 1002, 10th Floor, Johore Tower,
Jalan Gerja,
80100 Johore Bahru.
Telephone: 07-238977, 238876.

KOTA KINA BALU

**THOMAS HOWELL KIEWIT
INTERNATIONAL GROUP LTD.,**
Thomas Howell Kiewit (Malaysia) Sdn. Bhd.,
Rooms L, M, N,
3rd Floor, Central Building,
W.D.T. No. 248,
88999 Kota Kinabalu, Sabah.
Telephone: 088-216159, 216187.
Telex: MA80415 THKBKI.

KUALA LUMPUR

GRAHAM MILLER (MALAYSIA) SDN. BHD.,
11th Floor Plaza Atrium, Lorong P. Ramlee,
50250 Kuala Lumpur.
Telephone: 03-2382277.
Telex: 32690 MILOVR.
Fax: 03-238 5051.
J. McMahon: 03-255 5119.

ROBINS DAVIES (MALAYSIA) SDN. BHD.,
Chief Malaysian Office:
9th Floor, MUI Plaza,
Jalan P Ramlee,
50250 Kuala Lumpur,
Malaysia.
Telephone: (3) 2480288/2414280.
Telex: 32508 ROBINS MA.
Fax: (3) 2480832.
Offices also in Kota Kinabalu, Penang, Kuching.

**THOMAS HOWELL KIEWIT
INTERNATIONAL GROUP LTD.,**
Thomas Howell Kiewit (Malaysia) Sdn. Bhd.,
Lot 28.1, 28th Floor, West Wing,
Menara Maybank,
100 Jalan Tun Perak,
50050 Kuala Lumpur.
Telephone: 2321055.
Telex: MA 32200 THKIM.
Fax: 2321731.

KUANTAN

**THOMAS HOWELL KIEWIT
INTERNATIONAL GROUP LTD.,**
Thomas Howell Kiewit (Malaysia) Sdn. Bhd.,
No. 93, 1st Floor,
Bangunan, MBF, Jalan Haji Abdul Aziz,
25000 Kuantan, Pahang.
Telephone: 512511 & 512744.

KUCHING

**THOMAS HOWELL KIEWIT
(MALAYSIA) SDN. BHD.,**
Room 605, 6th Floor,
Wisma Bukit Mata Kuching.
Jalan Tunku Abdul Rahman,
P.O. Box 2706, 93754, Kuching, Sarawak.
Telephone: 082-411636, 428313.
Telex: MA 70460 THK KCH.

PENANG

**THOMAS HOWELL KIEWIT
INTERNATIONAL GROUP LTD.,**
Thomas Howell Kiewit (Malaysia) Sdn. Bhd.,
8.02, 8th Floor, Wisma Manilal,
3 Penang Street,
10200 Penang.
Telephone: 04-623779, 628164, 629210.
Telex: MA40347 THKIPG.

NETHERLANDS
AMSTERDAM

ROBINS DAVIES EXPERTISE B.V.,
Rembrandtgebouw,
Biesbosch 225.
1181 JC Amstelveen,
Holland.
Telephone: (20) 437701.
Telex: 14560 RODEX NL.
Fax: (20) 434860.

ROTTERDAM

THOMAS HOWELL KIEWIT INTERNATIONAL GROUP LTD.,
Thomas Howell Kiewit (International) B.V.,
166 Weena,
3012 CR Rotterdam, Holland.
Telephone: 10-414 9877.
Telex: 23131 KWTR.
Fax: 10-433 0306.

NETHERLANDS ANTILLES
CURACAO

INDEPENDENT MARITIME BUREAU INC.,
(Adjusters/Surveyors)
Dokweg 19,
Maduro Plaza,
Curacao,
Netherlands Antilles.
Telephone: +599 9 737033.
Fax: +599 9 737034.
Telex: 1272 IBM NA.
Affiliates: Bonaire, Aruba, St. Maarten and Surinam.

NEW ZEALAND
AUCKLAND

DUNSFORD MARINE LTD.,
Hull Cargo Surveyors & Assessors,
Adjusters Nautical Consultants.
Marina Control Building, Westhaven Drive.
Telephone: 09-781-254/7, Fax: 09-781-258.

ROBINS MBS MARINE,
LLOYD'S AGENTS,
130 Khyber Pass Road,
P.O. Box 335, Auckland 1.
Telephone: (09) 394-377
Telex: NZ60906 MARINER.
Fax: (09) 371-594.

CHRISTCHURCH

MACLEOD TAYLOR GORDON LIMITED,
Claims Assessors, Loss Adjusters
& Marine Surveyors.
22 Walker Street,
P.O. Box 4296, Christchurch.
Telephone: (03) 793-764.
Fax: (03) 793-757.

ROBINS MBS MARINE,
215 Gloucester Street,
P.O. Box 13-313, Christchurch.
Telephone: (03) 663-767
(03) 665-697.
Fax: (03) 663-231.

DUNEDIN

ROBINS MBS MARINE,
40 Manor Place,
P.O. Box 1402, Dunedin.
Telephone: (024) 771-011
(024) 773-030.
Fax: (024) 741-308.

GREYMOUTH

A.P. ORCHARD & ASSOCIATES LTD.,
P.O. Box 223, Greymouth, N.Z.
Telephone: 6420 & 5604 (027)
After hours Tel: 7448.
Telex: 4326.
Fax: 027-7592
Aviation and Marine.

WELLINGTON

GRAHAM MILLER & CO. NZ LTD.,
203 Willis Street, P.O. Box 11444, Wellington 1.
Telephone: 04-853193/326907.
Telex: NZ 30047 ADJUST.
Fax: 04-853190.
D. B. Denton.

ROBINS MBS MARINE,
44-52 The Terrace,
P.O. Box 1104, Wellington.
Telephone: (04) 726-586.
Fax: (04) 710-638.

NIGERIA
LAGOS

THOMAS HOWELL KIEWIT/ INTERNATIONAL LOSS ADJUSTERS (WEST AFRICA),
P.O. Box 3704, Lagos,
19 Eric Moore Close,
Iganmu, Lagos, Nigeria.
Telephone: 834167, 835087.
Cables: SOMAR LAGOS.
Telex: 27864 ILA NG.

NORWAY
BERGEN

BROCKLEHURST INTERNATIONAL ASS. (NORGE),
P.O. Box 513,
5001 Bergen, Norway.
Telephone: 010-475 295 583.
Telex: 72400.
Fax: 010 475 294 774.

STAVANGER

MATTHEWS-DANIEL INTERNATIONAL (NORGE) A.S.
P.O. Box 203,
N-4056 Tananger, Norway.
Telephone: (04) 696177.
Telex: 73770 PASCO N.
Fax: (04) 696774.

PHILIPPINES
MANILA

CONRADO R. MANGAHAS/THOMAS HOWELL KIEWIT,
Suite 400, 401, 406, EBA Building,
239 Juan Luna, Metro Manila, Philippines.
Telephone: 496-361, 496-332, 488-319.

**THOMAS HOWELL KIEWIT
INTERNATIONAL GROUP LTD.,**
Thomas Howell Kiewit, Saudi Arabia,
P.O. Box 481,
Dhahran Airport 31932,
Telephone: 03-8952166, 8950794.
Telex: 870875 THKALK SJ.
Fax: 03-895 3833.

**TOPLIS AND HARDING
(ARABIA) LIMITED, S.A.,**
P.O. Box 2795,
Al-Khobar 31952.
Telephone: 864 8226.
Telex: 872045 TOPLIS.
Fax: 864 8226.

**THOMAS HOWELL KIEWIT
INTERNATIONAL GROUP LTD.,**
Thomas Howell Kiewit, Saudi Arabia,
P.O. Box 6851,
Jeddah 21452.
Telephone: 6519492 & 6515172.
Telex: 603340 BANKHA SJ.
Fax: 6510058.

**TOPLIS AND HARDING
(ARABIA) LIMITED S.A,**
P.O. Box 9279,
Jeddah 21413.
Telephone: 665 0635.
Telex: 605263 TOPLIS.
Fax: 665 5011.
J. Gilfellon.
Home telephone: 6910828 x4222.

GRAHAM MILLER,
P.O. Box 996, Riyadh 11421.
Telephone: 1-4911312.
Telex: 404223 MILSA SJ.
Fax: 491 3254.
W. J. Morgan: 1-665 7031.

ROBINS DAVIES,
6th Floor,
Al Salem Centre,
Odiya,
P.O. Box 60231,
Riyadh 11545.
Telephone: (1) 4644986/(1) 4644989.
Telex: 401950 TANHAT SJ.
Fax: (1) 4656738.

**THOMAS HOWELL KIEWIT,
SAUDI ARABIA,**
P.O. Box 7974,
Riyadh 11472.
Telephone: 01-4647698, 4631984.
Telex: 405682 THKIR SJ.
Fax: 01-463 1796.

**TOPLIS AND HARDING
(ARABIA) LIMITED S.A.,**
P.O. Box 5176,
Riyadh 11553
Telephone: 479 0452.
Telex: 402409 TOPLIS.
Fax: 476 1331.
A. Henry
Home telephone: 241 1055 x6434.

BROCKLEHURSTS (FAR EAST) LTD.,
36 Robinson Road, 08-01,
City House,
Singapore 0106.
Telephone: 224 0160.
Telex: RS 22188 AVERAGE.
Fax: 2250428.

**MATTHEWS-DANIEL INTERNATIONAL
PTE. LTD.,**
140 Cecil Street, 12-02A,
PIL Building, Singapore 01065.
Telephone: 2258688/2247397 (24 hours).
Telex: 36356 MARINS.
Fax: 2247429 MATDAN.

**GRAHAM MILLER (SINGAPORE)
PTE. LTD.**
140 Cecil St., No. 12-01 PIL Building,
Singapore 0106.
Telephone: 2254211.
Telex: RS24568 MILOVER.
Cables: Millover.
Fax: 2253975.
H. S. Chan: 440 3115.

**ROBINS DAVIES HOLDINGS
(FAR EAST) LTD.,**
Regional Office:
10 Anson Road,
No. 27-14, International Plaza,
Singapore 0207.
Telephone: 224 8500/224 3347/224 8551.
Telex: RS29257 ROBINS.
Fax: 225 7936.

**THOMAS HOWELL KIEWIT
INTERNATIONAL GROUP LTD.,**
Thomas Howell Kiewit (Singapore) Pte. Ltd.,
156 Cecil Street, 05-02.
Far Eastern Bank Building,
Singapore 0106.
Telephone: 225 0111
Telex: RS42051 THKIS.
Fax: 225-4852.

DAVIES HONNET AND COMPANY,
P.O. Box 10767, Johannesburg 2000.
Telephone: 011-834 7241.

SOUTH AFRICA *(continued)*

**THOMAS HOWELL KIEWIT
(SA) (PTY) LTD.,**
P.O. Box 785665.
Sandton 2146, Republic of South Africa.
Telephone: Johannesburg 7834994/5.
Telex: 4-28276 SA.
Fax: Johannesburg 7830424.

SPAIN
MADRID

GRAHAM MILLER REVENGA S.A.,
c. Bristol 4, Bajo Izda, Madrid 28028.
Telephone: (1) 255-3626/255-3301
Telex: 49780 RRPE.
Fax: (1) 256-7219.
R. Revenga.

ROBINS DAVIES ESPANOLA S.L.,
Chief Spanish Office:
Avenida de Pio XII, 47,
28016 Madrid,
Spain.
Telephone: (1) 457 9093/(1) 458 1503 & 2011.
Telex: 46592 RDE E.
Fax: (1) 457 3080.
Offices also in Barcelona and Bilbao.

**THOMAS HOWELL KIEWIT
INTERNATIONAL GROUP LTD.,**
Thomas Howell Kiewit (Espana) Ltd.,
Edificio Iberia Mart I.
Pedro Teixeira 8-5, Madrid 28020.
Telephone: 456-3088/89 & 455-2599.
Telex: 45803 THKL E.
Fax: 456.5236.

SWITZERLAND
FRIBOURG

TOPLIS & HARDING LTD.,
3 impasse de la Ploetscha,
1700 Fribourg.
Telephone: 037-28 22 88.
Cables: Toplis Fribourg.
Telex: 942258 ADJR CH.
Fax: 037-282077.

ZURICH

BROCKLEHURSTS AG.,
Waffenplatzstrasse 64,
Postfach 8059,
8002 Zurich, Switzerland.
Telephone: 201-3673.
Telex: 815104.

GRAHAM MILLER & CO.,
C/o Adfida Trust A.G.
P.O. Box 577, CH8038 Zurich.
Telephone: 01-202 58 30.
Telex: 815639 ADFI CH
Fax: 01-202 5832
F. Birchmeier.

THAILAND
BANGKOK

GRAHAM MILLER (THAILAND) LTD.,
The Hong Kong & Shanghai Bank Building,
64 Silom Road, 3rd Floor, G.P.O. Box 2709,
Bangkok 10500.
Telephone: 2-236 1679/235 0894.
Telex: 81190 ATSERV TH.
Fax: 2-236 7749.
Cables: Millover Bangkok.
D. Sullivan: 2-258 9512.

UNITED ARAB EMIRATES
ABU DHABI

**MATTHEWS-DANIEL SERVICES
(BERMUDA) LTD.,**
P.O. Box 2472,
Abu Dhabi, United Arab Emirates.
Telephone: (02) 772055.
Telex: 23348 MDIAD EM.
Fax: (02) 782523.

DUBAI

GRAHAM MILLER (GULF) E.C.,
P.O. Box 2976, Dubai.
Telephone: 4-236370.
Telex: 47756 MILLOVER EM.
Cables Millover Dubai.
Fax: 4-224453.
D. Owen: 4-549481.

SHARJAH

MATTHEWS-DANIEL INTERNATIONAL,
P.O. Box 6461,
Sharjah,
United Arab Emirates.
Telephone: 352851.
Telex: 68603 MDILS EM.
Fax: 355829.

UNITED STATES OF AMERICA
HOUSTON

**BROCKLEHURST INTERNATIONAL
ASSOCIATES INC.,**
Allied-Northborough Building,
12941 North Freeway,
Suite 516, Houston, Texas 77060.
Telephone: 713-872 1621.
Telex: 910-8815786.
Fax: 010-1713 872 1707.

MATTHEWS-DANIEL COMPANY,
7135 Office City Drive,
Suite 100, P.O. Box 266836,
Houston, Texas 77207, USA.
Telephone: 713-644 1633.
Telex: 775237 MATDAN HOU.
Fax: 713-644 2107.

LONG BEACH

**INTERNATIONAL ADJUSTERS
(WESTERN) LTD.,**
100 Oceangate,
Long Beach,
California 90802, USA.
Telephone: 213-495 4422.
Telex: WU 194609 INKEYESLA, LSA.
Fax: 213-495 3232.
Home Office: New York, NY.

LOS ANGELES
THK PACIFIC/INTERNATIONAL SURPLUS ADJUSTING SERVICES INC.,
Suite 520,
3700 Wilshire Boulevard,
Los Angeles, California 90010 USA.
Telephone: 213-480 4639.
Telex: 3716071.
Fax: 213-480 4624.

NEW YORK
BROCKLEHURST INTERNATIONAL ASSOCIATES INC.,
18 John Street,
AKA 15,
Maiden Lane,
New York, NY 10038.
Telephone: 212-732 5834.
Telex: 640632.

INTERNATIONAL ADJUSTERS LTD.,
90 John Street,
New York, NY 10038.
Adjusters, Surveyors, Investigators, Cargo, Hull,
Air Cargo, Unusual and Special Risks, Non-
Marine, Loss Prevention and Recovery Problems.
Under Centralized Management Control.
All major ports and places United States and
Canada. Experienced World wide investigators
for National Marine Markets on Underwriting
and Claim Problems.
Telephone: 212-233 7060.
Telex: (ITT) 421909 (WU) 12-9136.
Cable Address: Intakeyes, New York.
Fax: 212-285 2380.
West Coast Office: Long Beach Calif.

GRAHAM MILLER INC.,
19 West 44th St. — Suite 1107
New York, NY 10036.
Telephone (212)719-3939.
Telex 497 6397 GM INC.
Fax (212) 719-4028.
Shaun Coyne.

OKLAHOMA CITY
BROCKLEHURST INTERNATIONAL ASSOCIATES INC.,
Suite 660, National Foundation West,
3555 N. W. 58th Street,
Oklahoma City, Oklahoma 73112.
Telephone: 405-947 3587.
Telex: 910-8313123.
Fax: 0101-405 947514.

URUGUAY
MONTEVIDEO
GRAHAM MILLER & CO. (SOUTH AMERICA),
c/o Mr. Roberto M. Pollero,
Costa Rica 6464, Montevideo.
Telephone: 598-2-50 04 50.
Telex: FRILANC UY 6208 FOR POLLERO.

VENEZUELA
CARACAS
GRAHAM MILLER VENEZUELA C.A.
Edificio Iasa. Piso 4, Oficina 404
Plaza La Castellana, Caracas 1060A.
Telephone: (02) 33 46 47, 33 51 65, 33 67 39.
Telex: 25296 COSMO VC.
Fax: (02) 325731.
L. J. Vicentini (02) 919151.

PERITAJES Y AJUSTES, C.A.,
Insurance Loss Adjusters,
P.O. Box 6348, Caracas 1010A.
Telephone: 02-817895 & 02-827934.
Telex: 26115/81301 PAYCA VC.
Cables: Ajustador Caracas.
Branch Offices: Puerto La Cruz, Puerto Ordaz,
Barquisimeto, Maracaibo, San Cristobal, Isla de
Margarita, Valencia, Ciudad Bolivar and Merida.
Member International Instututes of Loss
Adjusters.

WEST INDIES
JAMAICA — KINGSTON
THOMAS HOWELL KIEWIT INTERNATIONAL GROUP LTD.,
Thomas Howell Kiewit (Jamaica) Ltd.,
6 Trinidad Terrace,
Kingston 5.
Telephone: 926-4161, 4166, 4173 & 4187.
Telex: 2305 THKIL.
Cables: Howkiet Jamaica.
Fax: 929-7993.

TRINIDAD — PORT OF SPAIN
THOMAS HOWELL KIEWIT/ REES-WATKINS & ASSOCIATES LTD.,
40 Fitt Street,
Port of Spain,
Trinidad, West Indies.
Telephone: 628-2035/7 628 0200.
Telex: 22703 REEWAT WG.

ZAMBIA
LUSAKA
ROBINS DAVIES (AFRICA) LTD./ W. J. BLAKEMAN LTD.,
Premium House,
P.O. Box 33091,
Lusaka,
Zambia.
Telephone: (1) 215661/(1) 215407.
Telex: 45490 BLADJZA.
Office also in Ndola.

UNITED KINGDOM AND IRISH REPUBLIC
BOURNEMOUTH
FORWARD MARINE SERVICES LTD.,
Marine & Cargo Surveyors.
77 Corhampton Road,
Bournemouth BH6 5NX.
Telephone: 0202-421038.
Telex: 418297 Chacom G.
Fax: 0202-421038 Ext. 2.

GALWAY
SHANAHAN & ASSOCIATES,
Loss Adjusters,
Kiltartan House,
Forster Street, Galway.
Telephone: 091-67249, 67248, 67240.
Adjusters of all accident and fire losses to
Insurers.

WARRINGTON
PRIESTNER & COMPANY,
7 Bold Street,
Warrington, Cheshire WA1 1HY.
Telephone: 0925-34376 (8 lines).
Loss Adjusters, Valuers, Surveyors &
Agricultural Specialists.

Wm. Elmslie & Son
Danson Finlason Loftus & May

Average Adjusters professionally controlled by Members of the Association of Average Adjusters.

LONDON

2 Heron Quay
London, E14 9XE
Tel: 01-538 3955
Fax: 01-538 4160
Telex: 886383 (ELMBEN G)

MANCHESTER

St. James Buildings
89 Oxford Street, M1 6FQ
Tel: 061-236 7504
Fax: 061-236 7508
Telex: 668430

also

Elmslie Toplis Energy — Engery Claims Adjusters
Elmslie Services — Legal & Agency Services
Toplis Marine — Marine Surveyors

Divisions of Toplis Elmslie Marine
A subsidiary of Toplis and Harding plc

TOPLIS

ELMSLIE MARINE

Marine Claims Specialists

2 Heron Quay, London E14 9XE
Tel: 01-538 3955   Fax: 01-538 4160
Telex: 886383 (ELMBEN G)

We specialise in providing marine claims services including Average Adjusting, Energy Claims Adjusting, Marine Surveying and Legal and Agency Services. Our staff arc fully qualified in their respective fields and in particular our Average Adjusting divisions (Wm. Elmslie & Son and Danson Finlason Loftus & May) are professionally controlled by Full Members of the Association of Average Adjusters.

Manchester
Tel: (061) 236 0755   Fax: (061) 236 7508   Telex: 668430

Ipswich
Tel: (0473) 55711   Fax: (0473) 231265

Dublin (Lloyd's Agents)
Tel: (0001) 965275   Fax: (0001) 965598   Telex: 92282

Association of Average Adjusters

OFFICERS FOR THE YEAR 1989/90

Chairman:
C. S. HEBDITCH

Vice-Chairman:
G. W. MUNDAY

Joint Secretaries:
D. W. TAYLOR
H. R. P. SKINNER

Hon. Treasurer:
J. P. DUKE

Chairman, Examining Committee:
J. C. ALLEN

Panel of Referees (Arbitration Panel)
W. P. F. BENNETT
J. P. DUKE
H. G. HUDSON
G. S. HUGHES
W. RICHARDS
R. A. STACEY
D. J. WILSON

Registered Address:
Irongate House, Duke's Place, London EC3A 7LP
Telephone: 01-283 9033   Telex: 888470

Correspondence to:
HQS "Wellington", Temple Stairs, Victoria Embankment,
London WC2 2PN, England
Telephone: 01-240 5516

ASSOCIATION OF AVERAGE ADJUSTERS

The Association of Average Adjusters was founded in 1869 the role of the Average Adjuster and the aims of the Association being set out in the Preface to their rules.

Members of the Association are practising Average Adjusters who: being expert in the law and practice of general average and marine insurance, and having qualified by examination or other requirement of the Association of Average Adjusters apply their expertise for the benefit of the maritime and marine insurance communities.

Functions

The functions of the Average Adjuster are principally the following:

the adjustment of General Average: the adjustment of claims on policies of insurance on any interest directly or indirectly exposed to maritime perils: the preparation of statements of claim against third parties: the division of recoveries from third parties, or of proceeds of sale: the arbitration of disputes arising in relation to the above or associated matters.

In the discharge of these functions the Average Adjuster may be appointed by any member of the maritime or marine insurance communities having an interest in the matter concerned, and, irrespective of the identity of the party appointing him, the Average Adjuster shall act in an impartial and independent manner.

The Average Adjuster may advise any party seeking his opinion on any matter within the area of his expertise.

The Average Adjuster may assist in the collection of General Average, Salvage or other security.

The Average Adjuster may assist in effecting settlements under an average adjustment, or otherwise as required.

Aims

The aims of the Association are:

To promote professional standards and correct principles in the adjustment of marine claims by ensuring, through examination, that those entering into membership possess a high level of expertise.

To achieve uniformity of practice amongst Average Adjusters by provising a forum for discussion and by establishing rules of practice where necessary.

To ensure the independence and impartiality of its members by imposing a strict code of professional conduct.

To provide a service to the maritime community by establishing procedures by which advice on all aspects of marine claims may be obtained so as to facilitate their settlement.

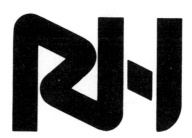

LEGAL/INTERNATIONAL REGULATIONS

ESSENTIAL BOOKS ON SHIPPING

REVIEW OF MARITIME CASES

by Mavis D'Souza

Barrister, Editor Lloyd's Law Reports

Once again the issue as to whether an arbitration had been abandoned by mutual consent came before the Courts. The House of Lords decided in the *Antclizo* that the issue would not be reconsidered and they refused to depart from their earlier decision in **Bremer Vulkan Schiffbau and Maschinenfabrik Corporation Ltd. v. South India Shipping Corporation (1981) 1 Lloyd's Rep. 253** holding that the arbitration was not so abandoned.

The House of Lords also considered the definition of the acronym "WIBON" i.e. "whether in berth or not" in the case of the *Kyzikos*. They concluded that the phrase was to be interpreted as being applicable only to cases where a berth was not available. The phrase did not apply to cases where a berth was available but the vessel was unable to reach it because of bad weather.

A case of whether a vessel had been scuttled with the consent of the owners came up for decision in the *Captain Panagos D.P.* before the Court of Appeal. They concluded that on the facts the vessel had been scuttled with the consent of the owners and the underwriters were not liable to indemnify the owners for the loss.

In the *Fanti* and *Padre Islands* the Court of Appeal concluded that the cargo-owners were entitled to bring their claim for damages to cargo directly against the Protection and Indemnity Clubs under the Third Parties (Rights against Insurers) Act 1930 as the shipowning companies had been wound up.

The Admiralty Court of the Queen's Bench had to decide in the *Powstaniec Wielkopolski* whether Gravesend Reach of the River Thames was to be regarded as a harbour so that the salvage services rendered to the defendants' vessel did not entitle the plaintiffs to claim remuneration. The Court concluded that no mariner would ordinarily describe Gravesend Reach as a harbour and in the circumstances the plaintiffs were entitled to a salvage reward.

FOOD CORPORATION OF INDIA v. ANTCLIZO SHIPPING CORPORATION (THE "ANTCLIZO") — (1988) 2 Lloyd's Rep. 93

Arbitration ⌐ Delay in prosecution — Whether arbitration abandoned by mutual consent.

By a charter-party dated 20 October 1973 the owners let their vessel *Antclizo* to the charterers for the carriage of wheat and similar commodities to various Indian ports.

The vessel reached Bombay at the end of 1973. In October 1974 the owners' agents sent to the charterers the owners' calculations showing discharging port demurrage of almost $187,000 to be due to the owners. Shortly afterwards the owners sought payment of the 10% balance of freight due on settlement of demurrage. No payment was made and the parties appointed their arbitrators.

In March 1975 the charterers made their own calculation. They calculated that the owners owed them a considerable amount of despatch. The charterers therefore deducted this despatch from the freight outstanding and paid the balance to the owners. The owners accepted this without comment.

Over the next 18 months no step was taken in the *Antclizo* arbitration but a series of letters were written concerning other charters on which the same demurrage dispute had arisen. The letters suggested that the owners wished the *Antclizo* arbitration to be treated as a test case but the charterers never agreed to this. In 1978 the arbitrators closed their files.

On 21 April 1983 the owners' solicitors sent a letter to the charterers requesting payment of the balance of freight and the demurrage and indicated their intention to proceed to an arbitration award if necessary.

The charterers applied for a declaration that the arbitration had been abandoned by mutual consent or alternatively that the owners were estopped from proceeding with the reference.

Mr. Justice Evans held that the charterers were not entitled to assume that the agreement to arbitrate had been abandoned. The Court of Appeal dismissed the appeal and the charterers appealed to the House of Lords.

Lord Goff of Chieveley delivered the main judgment with which all the other Law Lords agreed. He said that the Court of Appeal were right in affirming the decision of the learned Judge that no abandonment could be inferred from the facts of the present case.

The present case was not an appropriate case for the House of Lords to reconsider the principles upon which abandonment or estoppel could be inferred in cases such as the present.

In this case there was however expressed by all members of the Court of Appeal grave concern about the law as it now stood with regard to arbitrations which had been allowed to go to sleep for many years and it was plain the they were expressing a concern felt generally in the City of London.

Lord Goff said that it might be that the problem could be dealt with more expeditiously and most clearly by legislation conferring a power to dismiss claims in arbitration for want of prosecution similar to the power which now existed to dismiss similar actions for want of prosecution in the Courts. If that was right then in the interest of all concerned the sooner the matter was brought before the Legislature for consideration the better. The appeal would be dismissed.

SEACRYSTAL SHIPPING LTD. v. BULK TRANSPORT GROUP SHIPPING CO. LTD. (THE "KYZIKOS") — (1989) 1 Lloyd's Rep. 1

Charter-party (Voyage) — Demurrage — Whether laytime commenced when Notice of readiness given — Effect of "WIBON" provision

By a charter-party in the Gencon form dated 26 October 1984 the owners let their vessel *Kyzikos* to the charterers for the carriage of a cargo of steel and/or steel products from Italy to the U.S. Gulf. The ship was ordered to discharge at Houston. She arrived and anchored there at 0645 17 December 1984 and at some time before 1200 hours the master gave notice of readiness to discharge.

However although the berth at which the ship was to discharge was available for her use she was prevented from proceeding to it immediately because of fog which resulted in the pilot station being closed. Because of this the ship did not arrive in her berth until 1450 20 December 1984.

A dispute arose between the owners and the charterers with regard to the liability of the latter for demurrage at the port of discharge. The owners claimed U.S.$30,435.72 in respect of a balance of demurrage remaining unpaid. The charterers denied liability.

The essential question governing the validity of the claim was whether time for discharging counted during the period for which the vessel was prevented from proceeding to her berth by reason of fog.

The dispute was referred to arbitration and the arbitrator decided that the owners' claim succeeded in full. The charterers appealed against the award.

Mr. Justice Webster allowed the appeal and dismissed the owners' claim. The owners appealed and the Court of Appeal allowed the appeal restoring the arbitrator's award.

The charterers appealed to the House of Lords.

Lord Brandon said that the charter-party which was in the Gencon from provided *inter alia* by clause 5 that " . . . Time to count . . . Wipon/Wibon/Wifpon/Wccon and master to have to right to tender notice of readiness by cable . . ." Clause 6 provided that time lost in waiting for a berth to count as discharging time.

The acronyms used in clause 5 had the following meanings: Wipon — whether in port or not; wifpon — whether in free pratique or not; wibon — whether in berth or not; wccon — whether cleared customs or not.

The arbitrator concluded that the reference in clause 5 to wibon had the effect of making the charter into a port charter. The question of law was whether the provision "whether in berth or not" had the effect of converting a berth charter into a port charter in circumstances where a berth was available for the vessel.

The appeal raised two questions in relation to a voyage charter-party which it was common ground was a berth and not a port charter-party but contained a provision allowing the ship to give notice of readiness to discharge whether in berth or not. The first question was whether the ship could give a valid notice of readiness to discharge when on her arrival at her discharging port a berth for her was vacant but she was prevented from reaching it by bad weather, in this case fog. If that question was answered in the affirmative then the second question arose as to whether the ship could properly be said to be at the immediate and effective dispostion of the charterers as to qualify as an arrived ship under a port charter-party.

Mr. Justice Webster accepted that the phrase "Whether in berth or not" covered cases where the reason for the ship not being in berth was that no berth was available but did not cover cases where a berth was available but did not cover cases where a berth was available and the only reason why the ship was prevented from proceeding to her berth was bad weather. The Court of Appeal accepted that the phrase covered cases where a ship was unable to proceed to a berth either because none was available or because although a berth was available the ship was prevented by bad weather such as fog from proceeding to it.

The phrase has been interpreted in earlier cases as dealing with problems of congestion in ports and putting on the charterers rather than on the owners the risk of delay caused by such congestion. The phrase had over a very long period of time been treated as shorthand for what if set out in longhand would be "whether in berth (a berth being available) or not in berth (a berth not being available)".

The phrase "in berth or not" did not of itself indicate that being in berth or not was related to the availability of a berth. It was not possible however when interpreting a phrase which had been regularly included in berth charter-parties over a long period to disregard long established authority as to the purposes intended to be served by it. The authorities showed that since 1912 at least the purpose of the phrase was to deal with the problem of a ship chartered under a berth charter-party arriving at her destination and finding no berth available for her. There was no reported case prior to this one in which it had ever been suggested that the phrase was intended to deal with the problem of a ship chartered under a berth charter-party arriving at a port where a berth was available for her but being prevented by bad weather from proceeding to it.

The effect of the phrase was to convert a berth charter-party into a port-charter-party only in relation to a case where a berth was not available for the ship on her arrival and there was no good reason for applying that phrase to the wholly different kind of case where a berth was available for the ship on her arrival but she was prevented from proceeding to it by bad weather.

The phrase "wibon" was to be interpreted as applying only to cases where a berth was not available and not also to cases where a berth was available but was unreachable by reason of bad weather.

The appeal would be allowed.

Lords Bridge of Harwich, Lord Templeman Lord Ackner and Lord Oliver of Aylmerton agreed with Lord Brandon that the appeal should be allowed.

CONTINENTAL ILLINOIS NATIONAL BANK & TRUST CO. OF CHICAGO AND XENOFON MARITIME S.A. v. ALLIANCE ASSURANCE CO. LTD. (THE "CAPTAIN PANAGOS D.P.") — (1989) 1 Lloyd's Rep. 33

Insurance (Marine) — Vessel grounded on eastern shore of Red Sea — Whether loss of vessel procured or connived at by owners.

The second plaintiffs were the owners of the vessel *Captain Panagos D.P.* which was insured with the defendants. The vessel was mortgaged to the first plaintiffs who were the assignees of the insurance policy.

On 20 November 1982 the vessel grounded on the edge of the Farazan Sands on the eastern shore of the Red Sea in the course of a voyage from Canada to Bandar Abbas, Iran. On 23 November while still aground the vessel sustained a serious fire which caused extensive damage to the engineroom and to other parts of the vessel.

By a writ issued on 26 August the plaintiffs claimed against the defendants as the insurers with others of the risks covered by the policy for the constructive total loss of the vessel. Alternatively the plaintiffs claimed a partial loss in respect of each casualty.

The defendants denied liability contending that the losses were procured or connived at by the owners. They further contended that if one but not both of the casulties were was caused by the wilful misconduct of the owners so that the claim in respect of that casualty was fraudulent they were not liable for the other partial loss claim even if that claim was otherwise recoverable under the policy.

Mr. Justice Evans held that the vessel was deliberately run aground by the master Captain Lambros probably with the active co-operation of the second officer Mr. Dedes. The Judge concluded that the fire had been deliberately caused by the master and the second engineer and that Captain Pateras who at the material times was the managing director and the principal shareholder of the second plaintiffs had connived at both the grounding and the main fire. Mr Justice Evans rejected the plaintiffs' claims on the basis that they had failed to prove a loss by perils of the seas because the grounding was deliberate; that even if a barratry claim had been pleaded it would have been defeated because the owners had connived at the grounding; that the plaintiffs had proved a loss by fire because a barratrous fire was a fire within the meaning of the policy but that the claim for loss by fire was defeated by the owners' connivance.

In reaching his conclusion that Captain Pateras was privy to the grounding and to the fire the learned Judge had to rely on the circumstantial evidence and on the inferences which he felt able to draw from the evidence as there was no direct evidence against Captain Pateras who had died on 27

February 1983 some three months after the casualties. Captain Pateras never had the opportunity of defending himself against the serious allegations of wilful misconduct and fraud which were made against him in the action.

The plaintiffs appealed.

Lord Justice Neill said that it was now common ground that the stranding was the deliberate act of the master with the probable assistance of the second officer; that the main fire was the deliberate act of the master and the second engineer; that in the absence of proof the owners were privy to the stranding the owners could successfully claim under the policy for a loss by barratry; that in the absence of proof that the owners were privy to the fire the owners could successfully claim under the policy both for a loss by fire and if necessary for a loss by barratry; that the onus of proving the privity was on the owners; and that the burden of proof was a heavy burden commensurate with the gravity of the matter.

In a case such as the present the choice before the Court was a stark one. Either the vessel was cast away with the consent or the connivance of the owners or it was cast away by the master and some members of the crew for their own purposes. The task of the Court was to decide on which side the balance fell.

The evidence that Captain Pateras was concerned about his financial position and about the crisis in the charter market and in shipping generally was overwhelming. There was evidence that he wished to join some of his cousins in another business and to get away from the worries of his shipping company.

There was also evidence of the opportunity for communication between Captain Pateras and the master, and there was evidence that later communications took place between Captain Pateras and the master between October 7 and November 20.

The important factors were present i.e. a very strong motive and means of communication between the owner and the person responsible for the vessel.

There was no evidence whatever to show that Captain Lambros and Mr. Dedes had any motive of their own. Captain Lambros had been unemployed. He had no grudge against Captain Pateras or any reason to throw away a job which he had had only for some six weeks or so.

The case had to be decided on the balance of probabilities. Once it was accepted that the stranding and the fire were both deliberate the inference that Captain Pateras was privy to these acts and that they were not done for some private reason of Captain Lambros and Mr. Dedes was irresistible. The insurers had discharged the burden of proof and the appeal would be dismissed.

Sir Roger Ormrod and Lord Justice O'Connor agreed.

FIRMA C-TRADE S.A. v NEWCASTLE PROTECTION AND INDEMNITY ASSOCIATION (THE "FANTI"); SOCONY MOBIL OIL CO. INC. AND OTHERS v. WEST OF ENGLAND SHIP OWNERS MUTUAL INSURANCE ASSOCIATION LTD. (THE "PADRE ISLAND") (No.2) — (1989) 1 Lloyd's Rep. 239

Insurance (Marine) — P. and I. risks — Liabilities incurred by members towards third parties — Members wound up — Whether third parties could claim against Clubs.

The motor vessel *Fanti* was entered in the Newcastle Protection and Indemnity Association whose rules provided in rule 4 that the member shall be protected and indemnified against all or any claims and expenses (which were specified) which he shall become liable to pay and shall have in fact have paid in respect of a ship entered in this class of the association.

The stream tanker *Padre Island* was entered in the West of England Ship Owners Mutual Insurance Association Ltd. by rule 2 of whose rules the Club undertook to protect and indemnify the members in respect of losses or claims which they as owners of the entered vessel shall have become liable to pay and shall have in fact paid.

In both cases the claims and losses listed in the rules included *inter alia* claims for cargo damages.

Each vessel performed a voyage during which damage was caused to cargo and in each case the cargo-owners sued the shipowners to judgement; in each case an order was later made that the shipowning company would be wound up; in each case the cargo-owners then began arbitration proceedings against the club direct seeking recovery under the Third Parties (Rights against Insurers) Act 1930.

In the *Fanti* arbitration the umpire found for the Club. Mr. Justice Staughton disagreed with him and found for the cargo-owners on appeal. In the *Padre Island* arbitration the sole arbitrator found in favour of the Club. Mr. Justice Saville upheld his decision. The Newcastle Club appealed.

Lord Justice Bingham said that it was common ground that the contract made between the shipowner and the club was a contract of insurance and a contract of insurance was commonly said to be a contract of indemnity.

The members right to indemnity was subject to two conditions. The first was that the member should become or have become liable to pay a loss, a claim or expense under one of the listed heads and the second was that the member should have in fact paid the claim in question. The effect of that was that a member was to have no claim on the mutual funds provided by other members and himself unless he had become liable and had discharged the liability by payment. A member was to have no recourse to Club funds unless and until he was actually out of pocket.

The effect of rules 4 and 2 was to make prior payment by the members a conditions precedent of the members' right to be indemnified and the Clubs' duty to indemnify. Under the rules as framed the prior payment condition was not intended to apply if a member should become insolvent or be wound up, there being no right of indemnity in that situation at all.

It was common ground that those provisions were rendered ineffectual by the 1930 Act. Thus the contractual right to indemnity survived bankruptcy and winding up but unless the 1930 Act also rendered ineffectual the condition of prior payment the contractual right to indemnity must survive subject to that condition.

In was plain that upon the making of the winding up orders in these cases there was no transfer to the third party cargo-owners of an immediate right to payment by the respective Clubs because neither had such a right to be transferred. No cause of action against either club was transferred because neither member at the time of winding up had a cause of action, but such contingent right as the member had in respect of the specific liability was transferred pursuant to the 1930 Act.

Liability had been established against each member by judgment at the time when each member was wound up. *Prima facie* therefore the members' rights against the Clubs at that time were rights of indemnity against sums which they should respectively have paid in respect in respect of cargo damage within their Club cover. Since neither member had paid the rights were contingent and would only grow into effective rights of immediate indemnity upon payment. It was these contingent rights which were transferred pursuant to the 1930 Act.

Under the rules it was the same party (the member) who was subject to the burden of making payment and entitled to the benefit of enjoying the right to be indemnified. On the statutory transfer taking effect it was more natural to treat both the burden and benefit as being transferred to the third party.

The bundle of rights and duties which were transferred included the right to arbitrate. It also included the right of payment and the condition of prior payment. But the condition of prior payment was imposible to perform once the statutory transfer had taken effect and had to be denied effect.

The Club's obligation was to pay but to pay only a member who had suffered actual loss (by payment to a third party). Upon transfer the club's obligation would still be to pay and pay only a third party who had suffered actual loss (although not in this instance by payment out).

The condition as expressed in the insurance contract did not have the substantial effect of avoiding the contract upon the winding up of the member. Nor could it be said that the condition had the substantial effect of altering the rights of the parties on a winding up.

The rights of the members before winding up (assuming a third party claim within the policy cover to be established against them) were to be indemnified by the Clubs after paying the third party. Their rights after the winding up (on the same assumption) were the same.

The appeal in the *Fanti* would be dismissed.

THE "POWSTANIEC WIELKOPOLSKI" — (1989) 1 Lloyd's Rep. 58

Salvage — Remuneration — Plaintiffs rendered salvage assistance to defendants' vessel in Gravesend Reach of River Thames — Whether entitled to remuneration.

The *Powstaniec Weilkopolski* was a bulk carrier of 20,593 tons gross. At the material time she was laden with a cargo of 30,560 tonnes of wheat. The value of the ship her cargo bunkers and stores was nearly £7,000,000.

On 23 April 1985 the vessel was in Gravesend Reach within the port of London as defined by the Port of London Act 1968 lying moored fore and aft at buoys on the southern side of the river off Imperial Paper Mills while waiting for a berth at the Tilbury Grain Terminal. The bunkering barge *Varsseveld* was moored alongside the ship.

At about 1800 hours the wind was north-easterly about force 6 (strong breeze) and the tide was ebbing. Low water was predicted for 2207 hours. The ship's bow mooring began to part. At a later stage the stern moorings also parted. Thereafter the ship drifted to the north side of the river.

The plaintiffs tugs, *Sun London*, *Ionia* and *Hibernia* were lying further down Gravesend Reach, heard a report on VHF channel that the ship was breaking adrift and rendered salvage services to the ship. There was no call for assistance from the ship.

The plaintiffs claimed remuneration. The defendants denied that the services rendered by the plaintiffs were salvage services. They contended in their amended defence that the right to claim salvage was governed by the Merchant Shipping Act 1894 section 546 which as construed in accordance with section 742 excluded services performed within harbours; the plaintiffs' services were performed within a harbour i.e. the port of London and the plaintiffs were not entitiled to claim salvage in respect of those services.

Mr. Justice Sheen said that the question was whether by the enactment of the 1894 Act Parliament changed the substantive law of salvage by enacting indirectly that after the Act came into force salvage would not be payable for services rendered in certain tidal waters within the limits of the United Kingdon in which before the passing of the 1894 Act similar services would have attracted a salvage reward.

When construing an Act of Parliament it was to be presumed that Parliament intended to legislate in the public interest. One of the reasons for awarding salvage was to encourage mariners to voluntarily go to the assistance of vessels in distress and it was in the public interest that they should be so encouraged.

Section 742 of the 1894 Act defined harbour as including harbours properly so called whether natural or artificial estuaries navigable rivers piers jetties and other works in or at which vessels can get shelter or ship and unship goods or passengers; tidal water meant any part of a river or sea within the ebb and flow of the tide at ordinary spring tides and not being a harbour.

The only rivers up which vessels could proceed were navigable rivers and it would be absurd to enact that salvage was payable to the salvor of a vessel in distress in any part of a river within the ebb and flow of the tide within the limits of the United Kingdom so long as those waters were not an estuary or navigable river. Where else could a vessel be found on tidal water within the United Kingdom. For this reason the context did require that the word harbour in the definition of tidal water should not be given the meaning assigned to it by section 742.

The word harbour where it appeared in the definition of tidal water had to be given its natural and ordinary meaning. The vessel was in a reach of the River Thames. She was not in a harbour if that word was given its ordinary and natural meaning. Gravesend Reach might on occasion provide some shelter for vessels in weather conditions which would cause distress in the open seas but no mariner would ordinarily describe Gravesend reach as a harbour.

The place where the services of the plaintiffs were rendered was tidal and not a harbour. The Plaintiffs were entitiled to salvage remuneration.

Lloyd's Law Reports published monthly provide reports of important judicial decisions affecting the maritime and commercial spheres. It reports cases heard in the English, Scottish, Commonwealth and United States' courts. Each report contains a summary of the facts and legal issues raised, followed by the verbatim judgement of the court. In addition, each monthly issue has a table of cases previously reported and a comprehensive index by area of law.

MARITIME SOLICITORS

MEMBERS OF THE CITY OF LONDON ADMIRALTY SOLICITORS GROUP

BENTLEYS, STOKES & LOWLESS,

International House, 1 St. Katharine's Way,
London E1 9YL.
Telephone: 01-782 0990.
Telex: 888721 BENLAW G.
Fax: 01-782 0991.

CLIFFORD CHANCE,

Blackfriars House,
19 New Bridge Street,
London EC4V 6BY.
Telephone: 01-353 0211.
Telex: 8959997 CCSHIP G.
Fax: 01-489 0046.
Personnel/Shipping Dept. Partners:
A. G. Slater,
E. G. Patton,
A. A. Vlasto,
J. How,
M. G. Donithorn,
J. Bassindale,
C. C. Perrin.
Also at: Amsterdam, Brussels, Hong Kong, New
York, Paris, Singapore, United Arab Emirates.
Associated Offices at: Bahrain, Madrid, Saudi
Arabia, Tokyo.

CONSTANT & CONSTANT,

Sea Containers House,
20 Upper Ground,
Blackfriars Bridge,
London SE1 9DP.
Telephone: 01-261 0006 (IDD 441).
24 hour answering service: 01-638 3535.
Telex: 927766 TWOCTS G.
Fax: 01-401 2161/01-401 2731 (Groups 2/3).

WILLIAM A. CRUMP,

Rochester House,
42-44 Dolben Street,
London SE1 0UP.
Telephone: 01-620 0966.
Telex: 886806 LEGAL G.
Fax: 01-928 3330.
Also at Hong Kong.

ELBORNE MITCHELL,

Three Quays, Tower Hill,
London EC3R 6DS.
Telephone: 01-283 7281.
Telex: 885418 TACKLE G.
Fax: 01-283 5990.

CLIFFORD CHANCE

Blackfriars House, 19 New Bridge Street,
London EC4V 6BY
Telephone: 01-353 0211   Telex: 8959997 CCSHIP G
Fax: 01-489 0046

Personnel/Shipping Department Partners:

A. G. Slater   E. G. Patton
A. A. Vlasto   J. How
M. G. Donithorn   J. Bassindale
C. C. Perrin

SERVICES/ACTIVITIES: MARINE SOLICITORS

Also at:

U.A.E.

P.O. Box 13545
Dubai
Tel: 225203/281885
Telex: 46402 CALAW EM
Fax: 213397
Contact: James Whelon

P.O. Box 509
Sharjah
Tel: 356122
Telex: 68340 CCLAW EM
Fax: 3777430
Contact: James Whelan

SAUDIA ARABIA

Associated firm of: The Law firm of Salah Al.Hejailan

P.O. Box 1454
Riyadh 11431
Tel: 479 2200
Telex: 400486/401109 HEJLAN SJ
Fax: 479 1717
Contact: Richard Price, Partner

P.O. Box 15141
Jeddah 21444
Tel: 653 4422
Telex: 606766 HEJLAN SJ
Fax: 651 7241
Contact: Mohammed Amersi

HONG KONG

30th Floor, Connaught Centre
One Connaught Place, Hong Kong
Tel: 810 0229
Telex: 61770 CCLAW HX
Fax: 810 4858/4708/4743
Contact: Denis Brock

Offices also at: Amsterdam, Brussels, New York, Paris & Singapore.
Associated offices at: Bahrain, Madrid & Tokyo

HILL TAYLOR DICKINSON,
Irongate House, Duke's Place,
London EC3A 7LP.
Telephone: 01-283 9033, 01-895 0888.
Telex: 888470 HILDIC G.
Fax: 01-283 1144.

HOLMAN, FENWICK & WILLAN,
Marlow House,
Lloyds Avenue,
London EC3N 3AL.
Telephone: 01-488 2300.
Telex: 8812247 HFWLON.
Fax: 01-481 0316.
Also at: Hong Kong and Paris.

HORROCKS & CO.,
Clement House, 99 Aldwych,
London WC2B 4JF.
Telephone: 01-404 4645.
Telex: 886897 EQUITY G.
Fax: 01-831 6026.

INCE & CO.,
Knollys House, 11 Byward Street,
London EC3R 5EN.
Telephone: 01-623 2011.
Telex: 8955043 INCES G.
Fax: 01-623 3225.

INGLEDEW BROWN BENNISON & GARRETT,
International House,
26 Creechurch Lane,
London EC3A 5AL.
Telephone: 01-623 8899.
Telex: 885420 EIDENT G.
Fax: 01-626 3073.

MIDDLETON POTTS & CO.,
3 Cloth Street,
Long Lane,
London EC1A 7LD.
Telephone: 01-600 2333.
Telex: 928357/8/9 MIDLEX G.
Fax: 01-600 0108.

NORTON, ROSE,
P.O. Box 570,
Kempson House,
Camomile Street,
London EC3A 7AN.
Telephone: 01-283 2434.
Telex: 883652 NOROSE G.
Fax: 01-588 1181.

RICHARDS BUTLER,
Beaufort House,
St. Botolph Street,
London EC3A 7EE.
Telephone: 01-247 6555.
Telex: 949494 RBLAW G.
Fax: 01-247 5091.

MIDDLETON LEWIS LAWRENCE GRAHAM
1 Seething Lane
London EC3N 4AX

Telephone: 01-481 8361
Telex: 887133
Fax: 01-480 5156

SHAW AND CROFT,
30 St Mary Axe,
London EC3A 8DE.
Telephone: 01-283 6293.
Telex: 8956444 ASHORE G.
Fax: 01-626 3639.

SINCLAIR ROCHE & TEMPERLEY,
Stone House,
128-140 Bishopsgate,
London EC2M 4JP.
Telephone: 01-377 9044.
Telex: 889281 SINORD G.
Fax: 01-377 1528.
C.D.E.: 1075.

THOMAS COOPER & STIBBARD,
52 Leadenhall Street,
London EC3A 2DJ.
Telephone: 01-481 8851.
Telex: 886334 RECOUP G.
Fax: 01-480 6097.

WALTONS & MORSE,
Plantation House,
31-35 Fenchurch Street,
London EC3M 3NN.
Telephone: 01-623 4255.
Telex: 884209 WALTON G.
Fax: 01-626 4153.
Suit 642, Lloyd's.

UNITED KINGDOM AND IRISH REPUBLIC
LONDON

ALSOP WILKINSON,
Randall House,
6 Dowgate Hill,
London EC4R 2SS.
Telephone: 01 623-5141 and 01-248 4141.
Telex: 885593 Alsops G.
Fax: 01-623 8286.

HOLMES HARDINGHAM WALSER
JOHNSTON WINTER,
22-23 Great Tower Street,
London EC3R 5AQ.
Telephone: 01-283 0222.
Telex: 8812178 WINLAW.
Fax: 01-283 0768.

SIMMONS & SIMMONS,
14 Dominion Street,
London EC2M 2RJ.
Telephone: 01-628 2020.
Telex: 888562 SIMMON G.
Fax: 01-588 4129.
Also at: Brussels, Paris and Hong Kong.

WILDE SAPTE,
Queensbridge House,
60 Upper Thames Street,
London EC4V 3BD.
Telephone: 01-236 3050.
Telex: 887793.
Fax: 01-236 9624.

DUBLIN
McCANN FITZGERALD,
30 Upper Pembroke Street,
Dublin 2.
Telephone: Dublin 765881.
Telex: 93238.
Fax: 613409.

FELIXSTOWE
BIRKETT WESTHORP & LONG,
Suite 13a,
Orwell House,
Felixstowe,
Suffolk IP11 8QL.
Telephone: (0394) 67590.
Telex: 983242.
Fax: (0394) 673379.

LIVERPOOL
ALSOP WILKINSON,
India Buildings, Water Street,
Liverpool L2 0NH.
Telephone: 051-227 3060.
Telex: 627369 Alsops G.
Fax: 051-236 9208.

SUNDERLAND
HEDLEYS & CO.,
20A Fawcett Street,
Sunderland SR1 1RZ.
Telephone: 091-567 0101.
Telex: 537635 HEDLEX G.
Fax: 091-514 7212.
Document Exchange 60702 Sunderland.

Also as Hannay & Hannay
at South Shields.
We are members of a number of worldwide
networks of lawyers, debt collection agencies and
shipping correspondents.

WATERFORD
NOLAN FARRELL & GOFF,
Solicitors & Notaries,
Port Law Agents,
Newtown, Waterford, Ireland.
Telephone: 051 72934.
Telex: 80579.
Fax: 051-73804.
Dublin Agents:
27 Upper Ormond Quay.

OVERSEAS
AUSTRALIA
ADELAIDE
FINLAYSONS,
211 Victoria Square,
Adelaide, S. Australia 5000.
Telephone: 618 212 3901.
Telex: AA 82779.
Fax: 618 212 7608.

P&I Correspondents.
A.H. Ian Maitland 618 339 4329.

BRISBANE
MORRIS FLETCHER & CROSS,
Riverside Centre,
123 Eagle Street,
Brisbane, Queensland,
Australia.
Telephone: (07) 833 9666.
International: +61 7 833 9666.
Fax: (07) 832 4373.
DX: 102 Brisbane.
Telex: AA 41243.
Postal Address:
P.O. Box 7095,
Riverside Centre,
Brisbane 4001.
Refer: Mr David G. Thomas. Tel: (07) 833 9361.

DARWIN

MORRIS FLETCHER & CROSS,
National Mutual Centre,
9-11 Cavanagh Street,
Darwin, Northern Territory,
Australia.
Telephone: (089) 81 7333.
International: +61 89 81 7333.
Fax: (089) 81 4675.
DX: 134 Darwin.
Cables: FLETCROSS DARWIN.
Postal Address:
G.P.O. Box 612,
Darwin 0801,
Australia.
Refer: Mr David G. Thomas. Tel: (07) 833 9361
Ms Judith C. Kelly. Tel: (089) 81 7333.

MELBOURNE

WESTGARTH MIDDLETONS,
ACI House,
200 Queen Street,
Melbourne, Vic.,
3000 Australia.
Telephone: (03) 602 2000.
Telex: AA 31453.
Fax: (03) 602 5564.

PERTH

PARKER & PARKER,
Floor 23,
AMP Building,
140 St. George's Terrace,
Perth, Western Australia,
6000 Australia.
Telephone: (09) 322 0321.
Telex: AA 92636.
Fax: (09) 322 2243.
Contact: Oscar Shub.

SYDNEY

NORTON SMITH & CO.,
20 Martin Place,
Sydney, N.S.W. 2000,
Australia.
G.P.O. Box 1629,
Sydney, N.S.W. 2000,
Australia.
Telephone: (02) 232 8833.
Telex: 24633.
Fax: (02) 221 2949
(02) 232 3983.

WESTGARTH MIDDLETONS,
Prudential Building,
39 Martin Place,
Sydney, N.S.W.,
2000 Australia.
Telephone: (02) 233 6500.
Telex: AA 121733.
Fax: (02) 223 3022.

AUSTRIA
VIENNA

LAW OFFICES DR.F. SCHWANK,
Stock Exchange Building,
34 Wipplingerstrasse,
A-1010 Vienna.
Telephone: +43-1-553 57 04.
Telex: 136791 LEXEX A.
Fax: +43-1-533 57 06
+43-1-44 32 66.

BAHRAIN
MANAMA

NORTON ROSE,
Unitag House,
Manama,
P.O. Box 20437,
Bahrain.
Telephone: 232224.
Telex: 9276 BN.
Fax: 259810.

BANGLADESH
DHAKA

DOULAH & DOULAH,
Admiralty, Maritime & Shipping Lawyers,
G.P.O. Box 351, Dhaka-1000.
Telephone: 230525 & 383153.
Telex: 642401 SHER BJ & 642022 PCO BJ.
Fax: 880-2-41 29 72.

BELGIUM
BRUGGE

ASPEELE & BOUTEN,
Gistelse Steenweg 414,
B-8200 Brugge.
Telephone: Int. 50-38 69 71.
Telex: 81503.
Fax: Int. 50-38 93 97.

CAYMAN ISLANDS
GRAND CAYMAN

HUNTER & HUNTER,
Attorneys at Law,
Huntlaw Building, P.O. Box 190,
Grand Cayman, Cayman Islands,
British West Indies.
Telephone: (809) 949 4900.
Telex: CP 4250.
Fax: (809) 949 7876.

CYPRUS
LIMASSOL

CHRYSSES DEMETRIADES & CO.,
Fortuna Court, Block "B",
1st, 2nd & 3rd Floor,
284 Arch. Makarios III Ave.
Telephone: 51-62424 & 51-58003 (Accounts).
Telex: 2566 & 3780 DEMLAW CY.
Fax: 51-70055 & 51-77191.
Cables: DEMADVOCAT.

Also at: Nisosia and Piraeus (Greece).

NICOSIA

E.C. LEMONARIS LAW OFFICES,
Ayias Elenis Street No.6,
Third Floor, Office No. 34,
P.O. Box 2095,
Nicosia, Cyprus.
Telephone: (2) 454727, 454725.
Telex: 3294 KCL CY.
Fax: (2) 451987.

ECUADOR
QUITO

BERMEO & BERMEO LAW FIRM,
Edif. Banca de los Andes, Of. 201,
Amazonas 477 y Roca,
P.O. Box 545-C,
Quito, Ecuador.
Telex: 22065 BERMEO ED.
Fax: 593 2 564620

FRANCE
PARIS

HOLMAN, FENWICK & WILLAN,
3 Rue La Boëtie,
75008 Paris.
Telephone: 4265 5428.
Telex: HFWPAR 643657 F.
Telefax: 4265 4625.

GERMANY
HAMBURG

WESTPHAL & VOGES,
Esplanade 41,
D-2000 Hamburg 36.
Telephone: + 49-40-35 17 96.
Telex: 17 403 264.
Fax: 35 17 90.

GHANA
ACCRA

VIDAL L. BUCKLE & CO.,
Wuowoti Chambers,
10 Cantonments Road,
Accra,
Ghana.
Telephone: 775468 Accra.
Telex: 3033.
Attention: "WUOWOTI ACCRA"
Cable Address: "WUOWOTI ACCRA"
Mailing Address: P.O. Box 362, Accra, Ghana.

General Trail Appellate and Administrative
Practice in Corporate, Commercial, Revenue,
Maritime, Shipping, Transportation,
Aviation, Banking, Insurance,
Investment, Intellectual Property
and Property and Real Estate Law, Notaries
Public.

GIBRALTAR

J. A. HASSAN & PARTNERS,
57/63 Line Wall Road,
P.O. Box 199 & 612,
Gibraltar.
Telephone: 79000 (7 lines).
Telex: 2280 HASBAR GK.
Fax: 71966 (Group 3).
Telegrams: JUDICIUM.

ISOLA & ISOLA,
3 Bell Lane,
Gibraltar.
Telephone: (350) 78363.
Telex: 2255 ISOLA GK.
Fax: (350) 78890.

GREECE
ATHENS

P. J. ECONOMOU,
26 Asklipiou, 106 79 Athens.
Telephone: 360 3824.
Telex: 223306 ECO GR.
Fax: 363 9973.
Telegrams: LEXECON Athens.
Associated at: Limassol, Istanbul and UAE.

GUAM
AGANA

TIMOTHY A. STEWART,
162 Archbishop Flores Street,
Agana, Guam 96910.
Telephone: (671) 472 6978.
Telex: 650-299-5636 MCI UW.
Fax: (671) 472 8782.
Cables: LAWPAC GUAM.

HONG KONG

CLIFFORD CHANCE,
30th Floor,
Connaught Centre,
One Connaught Place,
Hong Kong.
Telephone: 810 0229.
Telex: 61770 CCLAW HX.
Fax: 810 4858/4708/4743.
Contact: Denis Brock.

CLYDE & CO.,
Admiralty Centre,
Tower 2, 19th Floor,
Harcourt Road,
Hong Kong.
Telephone: 5-290017.
Telex: 61972 CLYDE HX.
Fax: 5-865 4259.

CRUMP & CO.,
1208 International Building,
141 Des Voeux Road C, Hong Kong.

HOLMAN, FENWICK & WILLAN,
702 Tower 1,
Admiralty Centre,
18 Harcourt Road,
Hong Kong.
Telephone: 5-297021.
Telex: 63536 HFWHK HX.
Fax: 5-861 3007.

INCE & CO.,

Suite 1605, 16th Floor,
Tower 11, Admiralty Centre,
18 Harcourt Road, Hong Kong.
Telephone: 5-298010.
Telex: 65582 INCES HX.
Fax: 5-296206.

NORTON ROSE,

Alexandra House, 11th Floor,
16-20 Chater Road,
Hong Kong.
Telephone: 5-8432211.
Telex: 75107 HX.
Fax: 5-8459121.

RICHARDS BUTLER,

Alexandra House,
Nineteenth Floor,
16-20 Chater Road,
Hong Kong.
Telephone: 5-8108008.
Telex: 62554 RBLAW HX.
Fax: 5-8100664.

SINCLAIR ROCHE & TEMPERLEY,

10th Floor,
Bank of East Asia Building,
10 Des Voeux Road,
Central,
Hong Kong.
Telephone: 5232193/8.
Telex: 63646.
Fax: 5-8459244.

INDIA
BOMBAY

NARICHANIA AND NARICHANIA,

22 Sir P.M. Road, Fort,
Bombay 400 001, India.
Telephone: 286 12 27, 286 12 52.
Telex: 001-2928 VNCN IN.

MADRAS

NAGESHWARAN AND NARICHANIA,

157 Linghi Chetty Street,
Madras 600 001, India.
Telephone: 58 26 00, 58 99 19.
Telex: 41-8156 VNCN IN.

JAPAN
TOKYO

**THE BILLIS LAW OFFICE associated with
RICHARDS BUTLER,**

A full range of legal services to the maritime
community.
Sunbridge Ogawamachi Building,
2-3 Kanda - Ogawamachi,
2-Chome, Chiyoda-ku,
Tokyo 101, Japan.
Telephone: (03) 292 2500.
Telex: J33232 RBLAW.
Fax: (03) 292 2506.

MALTA
VALLETTA

CEFAI & ASSOCIATES,

28 Archbishop Street,
Valletta, Malta.
Telephone: 222097/338156.
Telex: 1806 TESSONS/808 INSURE.
Fax: 448273/316606.

Ship registration and mortgages, offshore
companies, debt collecting, general legal advice.

HUGH PERALTA & CO.,

3 Independence Square,
Valletta.
Telephone: 603025/621507.
Telex: 1536 LEXMAR.
Fax: 220222.

TONNA, CAMILLERI, VASSALLO & CO.,

52/2 Old Theatre Street,
Valletta, Malta.
Telephone: 223316/232271.
Telex: 891 TOCAVO.
Fax: 603291.

NEW ZEALAND
AUCKLAND

EARL KENT ALEXANDER BENNETT,

8th Floor, Downtown House,
Queen Elizabeth Square,
21-29 Queen Street,
Auckland, New Zealand.
P.O. Box 222, Auckland.
Telephone: (09) 303 2164.
DX 30.
Fax: (09) 393 797, Gp II & III.
Cable Address: HALSEARL.

NIGERIA
LAGOS

FRED AGBEYEGBE & CO.,

11th Floor, Stock Exchange House,
2/4 Customs Street,
P.O. Box 7755, Lagos.
Telephone: 667172/667069.
Telex: 22405 PLUSH NG.

PAKISTAN
KARACHI

ABRAHAM & SARWANA,

410 Press Center, Shahrah,
Kamal Ataturk, Karachi 01-18.
Telephone: 212378, 213128.
Telex: 28893 KSEL PK.

POLAND
GDANSK

MARCONSULT (POLAND) LTD.,

2 Ponczosnikow Street,
80-803 Gdansk.
Telephone: (48) 317429.
Telex: 512511 ZETG PL.

QATAR
DOHA

MAJDALANY & PARTNERS,

P.O. Box 4004,
Doha,
State of Qatar,
Arabian Gulf.
Telephone: (0974) 428899.
Telex: 4527 LEGAL DH.
Fax: (0974) 417 817.

SAUDI ARABIA
JEDDAH

CLIFFORD CHANCE,

Associated firm of:
THE LAW FIRM OF SALAH AL-HEJAILAN,
P.O. Box 15141,
Jeddah 21444, Saudi Arabia.
Telephone: 653 4422.
Telex: 606766 HEJLAN SJ.
Fax: 651 7241.
Contact: Mohammed Amersi.

RIYADH

CLIFFORD CHANCE,

Associated firm of:
THE LAW FIRM OF SALAH AL-HEJAILAN,
P.O Box 1454,
Riyadh 11431, Saudi Arabia.
Telephone: 479 2200.
Telex: 400486/401109 HEJLAN SJ.
Fax: 479 1717.
Contact: Richard Price — Partner.

SINGAPORE

NORTON ROSE,

5 Shenton Way, # 33-08,
UIC Building, 33rd Floor,
Singapore 0106.
Telephone: 2237311/1022.
Telex: 28880 RS.
Fax: 2245758.

SINCLAIR ROCHE & TEMPERLEY,

Raffles Place,
52-02 OUB Centre,
Singapore 0104.
Telephone: 5341444.
Telex: 20433.
Fax: 5325454.

UNITED ARAB EMIRATES
ABU DHABI

RICHARDS BUTLER,

P.O. Box 6904,
Saif Bin Ghobash Building,
Zayed the Second Street,
Abu Dhabi, U.A.E.
Telephone: 2-725561.
Telex: 22261 RBLAW EM.
Fax: 2-778630.

DUBAI

CLIFFORD CHANCE,

P.O. Box 13545,
Dubai, U.A.E.
Telephone: 225203/281885.
Telex: 46402 COLAW EM.
Fax: 213397.
Contact: James Whelan.

CLYDE & CO.,

British Bank of the Middle East Building,
Al Nasser Square,
P.O. Box 7001,
Dubai, U.A.E.

SHARJAH

CLIFFORD CHANCE,

P.O. Box 509,
Sharjah, U.A.E.
Telephone: 356122.
Telex: 68340 CCLAW EM.
Fax: 3777430.
Contact: James Whelan.

CLYDE & CO.,

National Bank of Abu Dhabi Building,
Al Boorj Avenue,
P.O. Box 6698,
Sharjah, U.A.E.

Since meeting for the first time in January 1959, the International Maritime Organization (IMO) has regarded itself as immune to the political and financial problems that have plagued so many other United Nations agencies over the years. The age of innocence ended in 1989 when the Organization found itself facing a major crisis for virtually the first time in its history.

The problem was caused by the failure of a large number of the Organization's 133 Member States to pay their annual contributions. In some cases arrears go back for many years, but until 1989 the Organization had always managed to cope because the non-contributors were relatively small countries in shipping terms (contributions to IMO are based primarily on the size of a country's merchant fleet). In 1988 Panama, the second biggest contributor, failed to pay, largely as a result of a political dispute with the United States. It became clear that the 1989 contribution could also be in doubt and the IMO Council meeting in November 1988 was forced to take drastic action to meet the anticipated budgetary deficit of over £900,000.

The programme of meetings for 1989 was cut from 24-1/2 weeks to 12-1/2, resulting in the cancellation of eight meetings of sub-committees of the Maritime Safety Committee (MSC).

This decision saved £488,000 and at the same time the Council increased the contribution payable by Members by £418,000. The Council considered a number of different options before agreeing on one that cut the meetings programme in half and also made savings of £150,000 during the year through staff turnover, reductions in temporary assistance and overtime, and cuts in supplies and travel. The savings reduced the total expenditure anticipated for 1989 from £11,053,100 to £10,564,700.

The only meetings of MSC sub-committees left were those on Safety of Navigation, Fire Protection and Bulk Chemicals.

The sub-committee meetings cancelled were Standards of Training and Watchkeeping; Radiocommunications; Containers and Cargoes; Life-saving, Search and Rescue; Stability, Load Lines and Fishing Vessels Safety; Ship Design and Equipment; Carriage of Dangerous Goods; and Safety of Navigation (December session). The Council noted that its decision should not be taken as a precedent for the future either in IMO or in other organizations of the United Nations system.

Although the immediate crisis was overcome in this way, the financial outlook remained gloomy and a special working group was established to consider both short-term and long-term measures. The Assembly, holding its 16th session in October 1989, was presented with a budget of around £26 million for the 1990-91 biennium — an increase of around 22 per cent, although this was caused largely by inflation and other factors outside IMO's control. This caused rumbles of discontent in some quarters and there was general agreement that sooner or later the method of raising contributions would have to be changed.

The fact is that several of the leading contributors to the IMO budget — such as Liberia, Panama and Cyprus — are developing countries, who are less able to pay than their richer fellow members. One scheme, which would have involved shipowners paying, was quickly dropped but something else could well be proposed in the near future.

Retirement of long-serving Secretary General

IMO's financial difficulties rather obscured the fact that 1988-89 was one of the most productive periods in the Organization's history — and at the same time an important turning point. This was largely because of the retirement, on 31 December

1989, of the Secretary-General, Mr C.P. Srivastava of India. He had been head of the organization since 1974 and during that period had established himself as one of the best-known figures in world shipping and IMO as an efficient and highly regarded Organization with a reputation for pragmatism.

Numerous tributes have been paid to Mr. Srivastava and his work with IMO and some of the most meaningful came from the IMO Member States themselves. The Canadian delegate to the Council, when Mr. Srivastava's retirement was announced in November 1988, said that his period of service "had been characterised by what Canada wished to see in all international organizations, namely talent, leadership, technical competence, universality of membership and a high degree of international co-operation."

Several delegates referred to Mr. Srivastava's personal and professional qualities which had done so much to foster the spirit of understanding and co-operation between IMO Member States.

His keenest interest in maritime education and the dissemination of maritime technology was mentioned and many delegates paid tribute to Mr. Srivastava's contribution to the establishment of the World Maritime University in Malmö, Sweden.

Mr. Srivastava will be succeeded by Mr. William A. O'Neil of Canada, who took up his post for a four-year term beginning on 1 January 1990.

Mr. O'Neil, who has been President of the St. Lawrence Seaway Authority since 1980, has been associated with IMO since 1972 when he was named as Canadian representative to the IMO Council, which normally meets twice a year and acts as IMO's governing body between biennial sessions of the Assembly. The Council consists of 32 Member States elected by the 133 Members of the Assembly.

In 1979 Mr. O'Neil was elected as chairman of the Council and was re-elected in 1981, 1983, 1985 and 1987.

CHANGES, AMENDMENTS AND ADDITIONS

The most important of all IMO technical conventions is the International Convention for the Safety of Life at Sea, 1974 (SOLAS). This was extensively amended in 1988 and 1989.

A number of changes dealing with the safety of roll-on/roll-off passenger ferries were adopted in October 1988 by the Maritime Safety Committee, IMO's senior technical body. The Committee met at the request of the United Kingdon Government to consider amendments proposed following the Herald of Free Enterprise disaster in which 193 people died. The amendments, which are expected to enter into force on 29 April 1990, affect Chapter II-1, which deals with construction, and apart from one item will apply to all passenger ships.

The first amendment, to Regulation 8, is designed to provide more information to the masters of ro-ro ships concerning their draught trim and stability after loading and before departure. Electronic loading and stability computers may be used for this purpose.

A new regulation (20-1) requires cargo loading doors to be closed and locked before departure. An appropriate entry in the ship's log must be made.

To ensure that the stability of ro-ro ships is not adversely affected by changes in weight, such as addition to the superstructure, a new Regulation 22 requires a lightweight survey to be carried out on all passenger ships at intervals not exceeding five years.

The Committee also agreed to a further change to Regulation 8 which is designed to improve the stability of passenger ships (including non ro-ro ships) in the damaged

condition. The amendment is intended to ensure that a ship that is damaged to a prescribed extent — as a result, for example, of a collison — will remain afloat and stable. The amendment, which represents a major advance in residual stability standards, takes into account such factors as the effect of the passengers crowding to one side of the ship, wind pressure, and the weight of survival craft being launched. This amendment will apply to passenger ships constructed on or after 29 April 1990.

The amendments were the second group of changes made to SOLAS since the *Herald of Free Enterprise* capsized off Zeebrugge in March 1987. The first group, also proposed by the United Kingdom, were adopted in April 1988 and entered into force on 22 October 1989. The SOLAS Convention covers 97% of the world's merchant fleet and this rapid response by IMO was made possible by the Convention's 'tacit acceptance' procedure which means that amendments automatically enter into force on a date selected by the MSC unless they are rejected in the meantime by a specific proportion of the Contracting Parties to the Convention.

Further measures to improve the safety of ro-ro ferries were adopted in April 1989. It is expected that the amendments will enter into force on 1 February 1992.

The main changes concern Chapter II-1 and II-2 of the Convention, which are respectively concerned with ships' construction and with fire protection, detection and extinction. Chapter II-1 covers subdivision and stability and machinery and electrical installations. One of the most important amendments is designed to reduce the number and size of openings in watertight bulkheads in passenger ships and to ensure that they are closed in the event of an emergency. There have been incidents in recent years in which ships have been lost because such openings have been left open, allowing water to pass rapidly from one compartment to another.

Chapter II-2 deals with fire protection, detection and extinction. Improvements have been introduced to fixed gas fire-extinguishing systems, smoke detection systems, arrangements for fuel and other oils, the location and separation of spaces and several other regulations.

Global Maritime Distress and Safety System

In November 1988 further changes were made to SOLAS when an IMO-convened conference adopted one of the biggest advances in maritime communications since the introduction of radio.

The conference, which was attended by representatives of 66 countries unanimously adopted amendments to SOLAS and its 1978 Protocol which will lead to the introduction of the Global Maritime Distress and Safety System (GMDSS).

The new system will be introduced in stages between 1993 and 1999. It will take into account technological advances such as satellite communications and result in the gradual phasing out of Morse radio-telegraphy, which has been the basis of the existing distress and safety system since the turn of the century.

The GMDSS is expected to enter into force on 1 February 1992 and is designed to overcome the shortcomings of the existing system which is a combination of radiotelephony and radiotelegraphy (using Morse). Maximum range is limited to around 250 nautical miles, and reception of messages can be affected by poor propagation conditions and other factors. Ships still sometime disappear without trace because a message cannot be sent in time or is not received.

The GMDSS will be a ship-to-shore, shore-to-ship and ship-to-ship system. The equipment required on board ships will depend not on their tonnage, as in the existing system, but on the sea areas in which they operate.

The new system will divide the oceans into four areas. Area A1 is within the range of VHF coastal radio (about 25 miles); Area A2 is with the range of coastal MF radio (up to 100 miles); Area A3 is within range of services provided by the International

t.t. Safina al Arab, 357.023 d.w.t., fully loaded, on fire in the Arabian Gulf. Salvaged by ITC's S-wind class tug Solano.

Worldwide seven oceangoing salvage tugs of 15.000 ihp available.

International Transport Contractors

Haarlem, The Netherlands
P.O. Box 21, 2000 AA Haarlem 5,
Kenaupark, 2011 MP Haarlem
The Netherlands
Telex 41865
Phone (023) 319197

Tokyo, Japan
Room 1103, 24 Mori Building
5-23, 3-Chome, Nishi-Shinbashi
Minato-ku, Tokyo, Japan
Telex 2426731
Phone (3) 433 3971/2

Houston, Texas, USA
Suite 224, 2nd Floor, 908
Town and Country Boulevard
Houston, Texas 77024 USA
Telex 762506
Phone (713) 932 6604/6605

Maritime Satellite Organisation (INMARSAT) which covers the whole globe excep
polar regions (e.g. up to 70°N); Area A4 means the remaining sea areas.

The GMDSS will be introduced in stages from 1993 to 1999.

Harmonisation of Survey and certification requirements

A number of IMO technical conventions require ships to be surveyed anc
certificates issued to show that they comply with requirements. In the case of the
SOLAS and Load Line Conventions and the International Convention for the
Prevention of Pollution from Ships, 1973 as modified by the Protocol of 1978 relatin;
thereto (MARPOL 73/78), these surveys have to be carried out when the ship is in por
or a repair yard. The ship is usually out of service for several days while this is bein;
done.

This results in delays and expense which are both compounded by the fact that th
survey dates and intervals between surveys required by various conventions do no
always coincide. As a result, a ship may have to go into port or a repair yard for
survey required by one convention shortly after doing the same thing in connectio
with another instrument.

A new system, adopted by a second conference, means the survey and certificatio
requirements of these three instruments will be harmonised, thus enabling delay
and costs to be kept to a minimum and at the same time making it easier fo
Administrations to ensure that convention requirements are being met.

The amendments to SOLAS and the Load Lines Conventions were adopted by th
diplomatic conference in the form of Protocols. The amendment procedure fo
MARPOL is different and a conference is not necessary.

The system adopted for the SOLAS and Load Lines Conventions does not involv
major changes to long-established procedures and practices currently used b
Administrations and Classification Societies.

The harmonised system will enter into force 12 months after both the SOLAS an
Load Lines Protocols have been accepted by at least 15 States whose combine
merchant fleets represent at least 50 per cent of world gross tonnage, but not before
February 1992.

International Convention on Salvage

Another major achievement came in April 1989 with the adoption of th
International Convention on Salvage, 1989 at a conference convened by IMO. Th
new Convention represents the biggest change to international law covering maritim
salvage for nearly 80 years. The new Convention is intended to replace a conventio
adopted in Brussels in 1910.

The 1910 Convention incorporates the principle 'no cure, no pay' under which
salvor is only rewarded for his services if the operation is successful. This concep
which has been in existence for many years, does not take pollution into account.
salvor who prevents a major pollution incident (for example, by towing a damage
tanker away from an environmentally sensitive area) but does not manage to save th
ship or the cargo gets nothing. There is therefore little incentive to a salvor
undertake an operation which has only a slim chance of success.

The new Convention seeks to remedy this deficiency by making provision, und
Article 14, for 'special compensation' to be paid to salvors when there is a threat
damage to the environment. Damage to the environment is defined as 'substanti
physical damage to human health or to marine life or resources in coastal or inlar
waters or areas adjacent thereto, caused by pollution, contamination, fire, explosic
or similar major incidents.'

The compensation will consist of the salvor's expenses, plus up to 30 per cent

these expenses if, thanks to the efforts of the salvor, environmental damage has bee minimised or prevented. The salvor's expenses are defined as 'out-of-pocke expenses reasonably incurred by the salvor in the salvage operation and a fair rate fc equipment and personnel actually and reasonably used.' The tribunal or arbitratc assessing the reward may increase the amount of compensation to a maximum of 10 per cent of the salvor's expenses 'if it deems it fair and just to do so.'

The Convention allows for special compensation to be paid under Article 14, if th salvor fails to earn a reward in the normal way (i.e. by salving the ship and cargo However, the compensation may only be paid if, and to the extent that, it exceeds th amount of a reward recoverable under Article 13 of the Convention, which establishe the criteria for fixing a reward. These factors include the salved value of the vessel an other property; the skill and efforts of the salvors in preventing or minimizing damag to the environment; the measure of success obtained; the nature and degree of th danger and a number of other factors.

If, on the other hand, the salvor is negligent and has consequently failed to prever or minimise environmental damage, special compensation may be denied or reducec

Payment of the reward is to be made by the vessel and other property interests i proportion to their respective salved values.

The Convention will enter into force one year after 15 States have consented to b bound by it.

The fight against marine pollution

An important stage in IMO's efforts to combat marine pollution came on 3 December 1988 with the entry into force of Annex V of the International Conventio for the Prevention of Pollution from Ships, 1973 as modified by the Protocol of 197 relating thereto.

The purpose of Annex V is to prevent pollution by the dumping of garbage, whic includes all kinds of victual, domestic and operational waste generated during th normal operation of the ship. It applies to all kinds of ships.

One of the most important provisions in the Annex is the ban on the dumping in the sea of all plastics, such as synthetic ropes, synthetic fishing nets and plast garbage bags.

Some other forms of garbage may be dumped under strictly controlled condition Dunnage, lining and packing materials can only be disposed of at sea more than 2 miles from land. Food wastes and all other garbage (including paper products, rag glass, metal, bottles and crockery) cannot be dumped within 12 miles of land, unles it has first been passed through a comminuter or grinder. Even so, the minimu distance from land when dumping is permitted is set at three miles.

Even stricter controls apply in what are termed 'Special Areas'. These are seas, suc as the Mediterranean, Baltic and Black Seas, together with some sea areas in th Middle East which are particularly at risk from pollution. Here dumping of all forms garbage except food wastes is completely banned, and even food wastes cannot t disposed of into the sea within 12 miles of land.

To enable ships to get rid of wastes, Contracting Parties to the Convention a obliged to provide facilities in ports for the reception of garbage.

DOCK EXPRESS

- Crane transports*
- Topside removal/installation*
- Module transports
- Floating cargoes
- Installation of subsea systems
- Jacket removal
- Project cargoes

* By means of the DOCK EXPRESS' unique forklift method

The Netherlands
Dock-Express Shipping B.V.
5, Veerkade
P.O. Box 23109
3001 KC Rotterdam
The Netherlands
Phone: (31) 10 - 4009100
Telex: 25289 dock nl
Telefax: (31) 10 - 4332040

Japan
Dock-Express Shipping B.V.
Japan Representative Office
Palace Royal Nagatacho
Room 406
9-8 Nagatacho, 2-chome
Chiyoda-Ku
Tokyo 100
Japan
Phone: (81) 3 - 5930814
Telex: 02228130 dockex j
Telefax: (81) 3 - 5932128

USA
Dock-Express Shipping B.V.
One Stamford Landing
62 Southfield Avenue
Stamford, Connecticut 06902
Phone: (1) 203 975 1010
Telex: 6718167 a/b vony
Telefax: (1) 203 325 1019

U.S.A.
Dock-Express Contractors Inc
3040 Post Oak Boulevard
Suite 1600
Houston, Texas 77056
U.S.A.
Phone: (1) 713 - 6260405
Telex: 4620418
Telefax: (1) 713 - 9613414

United Kingdom
Dock-Express Shipping B.V.
Baryta House
29, Victoria Avenue
Southend-On-Sea
Essex SS2 6AZ
U.K.
Phone: (44) 702 - 352458
Telex: 995177 dock g
Telefax: (44) 702 - 342517

IMO — A SUMMARY OF ADOPTED CONVENTIONS, PROTOCOLS, AMENDMENTS AND OTHER INSTRUMENTS

The industrial revolution of the eighteenth and nineteenth centuries and the upsurge in international commerce which resulted led to the adoption of a number of international treaties related to shipping, including safety. The subjects covered included tonnage measurement, the prevention of collisions, signalling and others.

By the end of the nineteenth century suggestions had even been made for the creation of a permanent international maritime body to deal with these and future measures. The plan was not put into effect, but international co-operation continued in the twentieth century, with the adoption of still more internationally developed treaties.

By the time the International Maritime Organization (IMO) came into existence in 1959 (until 1982 it was called the Inter-Governmental Maritime Consultative Organization — IMCO), several important international conventions had already been developed, including the International Convention for the Safety of Life at Sea of 1948, and the International Convention for the Prevention of Pollution of the Sea by Oil of 1954.

IMO became responsible for ensuring that the majority of these conventions were kept up to date. it was also given the task of developing new conventions as and when the need arose.

The creation of IMO coincided with a period of tremendous change in world shipping and the Organization was kept busy from the start developing new conventions and ensuring that existing instruments kept pace with changes in shipping technology. It is now responsible for 21 international conventions and agreements and has adopted no fewer than 32 different protocols or amendments.

Conventions and other multilateral instruments create international treaty obligations. Governments which ratify or accept them agree to bring their laws and measures into conformity with the provisions of such treaties. The purpose of IMO's instruments is to establish standards which are acceptable to as many countries as possible and can be implemented in the same way, thereby eliminating differences between national practices.

Since coming into existence the IMO has adopted multilateral treaties on a number of subjects concerned especially with the safety of shipping and the prevention of pollution from ships. Most of these are called conventions but a few are referred to as protocols or agreements. However, their legal status is the same.

Adoption

A proposal for developing an international treaty may be made in any of the organs of IMO. Formal approval is given either by the Assembly, the Organization's governing body which consists of all 131 Member States, or by the Council which performs the functions of the Assembly in between the biennial sessions of the latter.

A draft of the treaty is then prepared in one of the Organization's principal committees or sub-committees. When the draft is approved by the committee concerned (the Maritime Safety Committee, the Marine Environment Protection Committee or the Legal Committee) it is then submitted to an international diplomatic conference to which all Members of the United Nations and its specialised agencies are invited.

An IMO diplomatic conference usually lasts for between two and four weeks at the end of which a final convention or other treaty instrument is formally adopted.

Ratification

With the successful adoption of the convention, the onus for action moves to Governments. The speed with which the convention enters into force (that is, becomes binding on States which have agreed to be bound by it) depends upon the time taken by Governments to ratify or accept it. The consent to be bound may be expressed by signature, ratification, acceptance, approval or accession, depending on the wish of the States concerned. This procedure is generally referred to as "ratificatin". IMO treaties enter into force after a specific number of States have ratified them. Most IMO conventions require that a certain proportion of the world's total tonnage be covered before the conventions enter into force.

A Government ratifying a treaty has to ensure that its own national law conforms with its provisions. This usually involves some form of domestic legislative action.

After the requirements for entry into force of a treaty have been achieved, there is a "period of grace" before it actually comes into force. This period varies from a few months to a year or even two years, and is designed to enable the Governments concerned to take the necessary legislative or administrative measures for implementing the provisions of the convention.

Implementation

This is the third stage — and in many ways it is the most important. In many cases the main responsibility for the enforcement of an international treaty lies on the State under whose flag the ships concerned operate. Basically each Government is responsible for ensuring that ships which fly its flag conform to the requirements of treaties which it has ratified. However, many IMO treaties also contain provisions permitting or requiring other States, particularly port States, to enforce the requirements of the conventions concerned.

The effectiveness of a convention therefore depends to a considerable extent on the way in which it is enforced by the States entrusted with its implementation. IMO as an Organization has no authority or means to enforce or implement conventions against individual ships or States. The Organization's role is to encourage the Governments concerned to take the required measures. Where necessary, the Organization provides technical advice and assistance to Governments which may need such advice and assistance in taking the requisite action.

Amendment

All IMO's multilateral treaties contain provisions for amendment. This is especially important in the case of technical treaty instruments adopted under the auspices of IMO, which need to be updated and amended to take account of rapid changes in shipping and associated technology.

In some of the treaties, amendments duly adopted must be accepted by a specified proportion of Contracting Parties before they enter into force. This is known as the "express acceptance" procedure. In other cases a system called "tacit acceptance" has been adopted. This means that amendments adopted will enter into force on a specified date unless a stipulated number of Contracting Parties expressly indicate their objection to the amendments.

The "tacit acceptance" procedure was adopted by IMO in 1972 after it was realised that the procedure of "express acceptance" of amendments made it difficult, if not impossible, to get amendments into force. In some cases, some very important amendments could not be brought into force because the necessary numbers of express acceptances were not received.

To remedy that defect, all major technical conventions of IMO adopted since 1972 have incorporated the "tacit acceptance" of procedure for amendments.

Resolutions

Although the conventions and other international treaty instruments adopted by IMO are probably the best-known texts adopted by the Organization, a number of important international standards and regulations are in the form of recommendations adopted as resolutions by the IMO Assembly.

Since the first session in 1959, the Assembly has adopted nearly 600 resolutions. The majority of these contain recommendations on a wide range of matters, mostly technical, connected with safety at sea or the prevention of pollution from ships.

The chief difference between a recommendation adopted by the Assembly and a convention adopted at a diplomatic conference is that the recommendation is not a mandatory instrument. But recommendations may be equally effective in achieving the Organization's objectives, and in some cases even more so. Recommendations adopted by an Assembly resolution become effective immediately or within a short period. They do not have to wait for the completion of a lengthy entry-into-force procedure.

While not binding upon States in a legal sense, many of these guidelines form an essential component of the regulatory regimes envisaged in treaty instruments by acting as supplements to or reinforcements of their provisions.

Codes and recommendations adopted by means of an Assembly resolution, or sometimes a Committee resolution, are in fact implemented voluntarily by many States by means of national legislation. Thus practical effectiveness may not depend mainly on the legal character of the instrument but rather on the degree of acceptability of the contents. Most recommendations are observed by many countries and may, therefore, be more effective than a convention or other formal treaty which is not ratified or is ratified by only a few States.

Some of the important recommendations of IMO on technical matters are in the form of codes or guidelines.

Probably the best known and most important of the codes and recommendations adopted by the IMO Assembly is the International Maritime Dangerous Goods Code which was first adopted in 1965. It is designed as a guide to mariners, shippers, packers and others involved in the carriage of dangerous goods by sea and, since about 50% of all goods carried can be regarded as dangerous in some way or other, it is now widely accepted throughout the maritime community. The IMDG Code is a huge publication issued in five volumes totalling more than 10,000 pages. It is normally amended annually to reflect changes taking place in the industry, which involve modification to anything up to 500 pages at a time.

Other very important codes are:
(a) Code for the Construction and Equipment of Ships Carrying Dangerous Chemicals in bulk.
(b) Code for the Construction and Equipment of Ships Carrying Liquified Gases in Bulk.
(c) Code for Existing Ships carrying Liquified Gases in Bulk.

(d) Code of Safe Practice for Solid Bulk cargoes.

(e) Code for the Construction and Equipment of Mobile Offshore Drilling Units (MODU Code).

(f) Code of Safety for Dynamically Supported Craft.

(g) Code of Safety for Nuclear Merchant Ships.

(h) Code of Safe Practice for Ships Carrying Timber Deck Cargoes.

(i) Code of Safety for Special Purpose Ships.

(j) Code of Safety for Diving Systems.

(k) Code on Noise Levels on Board Ships

(l) Guidelines for the Design and Construction of Offshore Supply Vessels.

(m) International Code of Signals.

(n) Code of Practice for the Evaluation, Testing and Acceptance of Prototype Novel Life-saving Appliances and Arrangements.

(p) Code of safety for Fishermen and Fishing Vessels, which was developed by IMO, the Food and Agriculture Organisation of the United Nations (FAO) and the International Labour Organization (ILO), the provisions of which have been overtaken by the 1977 Torremolinos Convention.

Although the application of these Codes is generally voluntary, some require certification and are similar in character to conventions. That is why two new codes — the **International Bulk Chemical (IBC) Code** and **International Gas Carrier (IGC) Code**, which were adopted by the Maritime Safety Committee in 1983, have a different status. Their observance became mandatory for States Parties to the SOLAS Cnonvention when the 1983 amendments to the Convention entered into force on 1 July 1986. The amendments achieved this by requiring ships built on or after that date to comply with the requirements of the relevant code. The IBC Code has also been made mandatory under **MARPOL 73/78** as far as pollution aspects are concerned. Some other codes and recommendations such as the **Code of Safe Practice for the Evaluation, Testing and Acceptance of Prototype Novel Life-Saving Appliances and Arrangements**, are also mandatory in effect through providing detailed specifications in support of convention requirements.

Other important resolutions have been adopted to introduce new ideas and systems designed to improve maritime safety or prevent marine pollution from ships.

THE CONVENTIONS

The majority of conventions adopted under the auspices of IMO or for which the Organization is otherwise responsible falls into three main categories.

The first group is concerned with maritime safety; the second with the prevention of marine pollution; and the third with liability and compensation, especially in relation to damage caused by pollution. Outside these major groupings are two other conventions dealing with facilitation and tonnage measurement.

MARITIME SAFETY

International Convention for the Safety of Life at Sea, 1960 and 1974, as amended

Entry into force: 1960 Convention in 1965: 1974 version in 1980.
Amendments: 1981, 1983 (in force), 1988 (three times) and 1989.

The SOLAS Convention in its successive forms is generally regarded as the most important of all international treaties concerning the safety of merchant ships. The first version was adopted in 1914, the second in 1929 and the third in 1948.

The 1960 Convention was the first major task for IMO after its creation and it represented a considerable step forward in modernising regulations and in keeping pace with technical developments in the shipping industry.

The intention was to keep the Convention up to date by periodic amendments but in practice the amendments procedure incorporated proved to be very slow. It became clear that it would be impossible to secure the entry into force of amendments within a reasonable period of time.

As a result, a completely new convention was developed in 1974 which included not only the amendments agreed up until that date, but a new amendment procedure designed to ensure that changes could be made within a specified (and acceptably short) period of time.

357

The main objective of the SOLAS Convention is to establish minimum standards for the construction, equipment and operation of ships, compatible with their safety. Flag States are responsible for ensuring that ships under their flag comply with its requirements, and a number of certificates are prescribed in the Convention as proof that this has been done.

Control provisions also allow Contracting Governments to inspect ships of other Contracting States if there is reason for believing that the ship does not comply with the requirements of the Convention.

The contents of the eight chapters are:

Chapter 1: General requirements, such as regulations concerning surveys and the issuing of documents and provisions for the control of ships in ports of other Contracting Governments.

Chapter ll-1: Subdivision and stability. The most stringent requirements are those which apply to passenger ships, where the subdivision of the ship into watertight compartments must be such that after assumed damage to the hull the ship will remain afloat and stable. The degree of subdivision in ships generally varies according to length and the service in which the ship is engaged.

Requirements concerning machinery and electrical installations also appears in this chapter. The steering gear requirements are particularly important and were greatly changed by the 1981 amendments.

Chapter ll-2: Fire protection, detection and extinction. The provisions of this chapter are based on the following principles:

1. Division of the ship into main and vertical zones by thermal and structural boundaries.
2. Separation of accommodation spaces from the remainder of the ship by thermal and structural boundaries.
3. Restricted use of combustible materials.
4. Detection of any fire in the zone of origin.
5. Containment and extinction of any fire in the space of origin.
6. Protection of the means of escape or of access for fire fighting purposes.
7. Ready availability of fire-extinguishing appliances.
8. Minimisation of the possibility of ignition of flammable cargo vapour.

Requirments concerning fire protection of tankers were considerably strengthened in the 1981 amendments.

Chapter III: Life-saving appliances; the chapter was completely rewritten in the 1983 amendments. It not only takes into account technical changes, but also expedites the evaluation and introduction of further improvements.

Chapter IV: Radiotelegraphy and radiotelephony. Part A describes the type of facility to be carried. Operational requirements for watchkeeping and listening are given in part B, while technical provisions are detailed in part C. The radio officer's obligations regarding mandatory log-book entries are listed in part D.

The chapter is closely linked to the Radio Regulations of the International Telecommunication Union and was completely revised in November 1988.

Chapter V: Safety of Navigation: this chapter identifies certain navigation safety services which should be provided by Contracting Governments and sets forth provisions of an operational nature applicable in general to all ships. This is in contrast to the Convention as a whole, which only applies to certain classes of ship engaged on international voyages.

The subject covered include the maintenance of meteorological services for ships; the ice patrol service; routeing of ships; and the maintenance of search and rescue services. Additional requirements concerning shipborne navigational equipment were introduced in the 1981 amendments.

Chapter VI: Carriage of grain. Shifting is an inherent characteristic of grain, and its effect on a ship's stability can be disastrous. Consequently the SOLAS Convention contains provisions concerning the stowing, trimming and securing of grain cargoes.

Chapter VII: Carriage of dangerous goods. The chapter contains provisions for the classification, packing, marking, labelling and placarding, documentation and stowage of dangerous goods in packaged form, in solid form in bulk, and liquid chemicals and liquified gases in bulk. Under the 1983 amendments, chemical tankers and gas carriers built after 1 July 1986 are required to conform to the requirements of the International Bulk Chemical Code.

Chapter VIII: Nuclear ships. Only basic requirements are given and are particularly concerned with radiation hazards.

Further amendments were adopted in October 1988 and April 1989 while in November 1988 Chapter IV was completely revised and a new harmonised system of survey and certification introduced.

The Protocol of 1978, to the 1974 Convertion which entered into force in 1981 was adopted at an international conference on tanker safety and pollution prevention and made a number of important changes to chapter I, including the introduction of unscheduled inspection and/or mandatory annual surveys and the strengthening of Port State control requirements.

Chapter II-1, chapter II-2 and chapter V were also improved. In particular, the Protocol introduced requirements for the fitting of inert gas systems on tankers; for carriage of two radars on ships of 10,000 grt and above, and the duplication of steering gear on new tankers of 10,000 grt or above. **April 1988 amendments** affecting ro-ro ferries will enter into force October 1989.

International Convention on Load Lines, 1966.

Entry into force: 1968.

It has long been recognised that limitations on the draught to which a ship may be loaded make a significant contribution to her safety. These limits are given in the form of freeboards, which consitute, besides external weathertight and watertight integrity, the main objective of the Convention. It replaced a convention adopted in 1930.

The regulations take into account the potential hazards present in different zones and different seasons. The technical Annex contains several additional safety measures concerning doors, freeing ports, hatchways and other items. The main purpose of these measures is to ensure the watertight integrity of ships' hulls below the freeboard deck. **Amendments** were adopted to the Convention in 1971 (to make certain improvements to the text and to the chart of zones and seasonal areas); in 1975 (to introduce the principle of 'tacit acceptance' into the Convention); In 1979 (to make some alterations to zone boundaries off the coast of Australia), and in 1983 (to extend the summer and tropical zones southward off the coast of Chile).

None of these amendments has yet entered into force.

In November 1988 further amendments were adopted to harmonise survey and certificate requirements with those contained in SOLAS and MARPOL.

Special Trade Passenger Ships Agreement, 1971.

Entry into force: 1974.

The carriage of larger numbers of unberthed passengers in special trades such as the pilgrim trade — in a restricted sea area around the Indian Ocean — is of particular interest to countries in that area.

IMO convened an International Conference in 1971 to consider safety requirements for special trade passenger ships in relation to the 1960 SOLAS Convention.

Annexed to this Agreement are Special Trade Passenger Ships Rules, 1971, which provide modifications to the regulations of chapters II and III of the 1960 SOLAS Convention.

Protocol on Space Requirements for Special Trade Passenger Ships, 1973.

Entry into force: 1977.

Following a resolution of the International Conference on Special Trade Passenger Ships, 1971, IMO, in co-operation with other organizations, particularly the World Health Organization (WHO), drew up technical rules covering the safety aspects of the disposition of passengers on board such ships, which were adopted in 1973.

Convention on the International Regulations for Preventing Collisions at Sea, 1972, as amended.

Entry in force: 1977. Amended: 1981 (in force).

This Convention was designed to replace the Collision Regulations of 1960 which were annexed to the SOLAS Convention adopted in that year.

One of the most important innovations in the 1972 Regulations was the recognition given to the traffic separation schemes, observance of which is made mandatory under rule 10.

The Convention groups provisions into sections dealing with steering and sailing; lights and shapes and sound and light signals. There are also four annexes containing technical requirements concerning lights and shapes and their positioning; sound signalling appliances; additional signals for fishing vessels when operating in close proximity and international distress signals.

International Convention for Safe Containers, 1972, as amended.

Entry into force: 1977. Amended: 1981 and 1983 (in force).

The Convention has two goals. One is to maintain a high level of safety of human life in the transport and handling of containers by providing generally acceptable test procedures and related strength requirements which have proven adequate over the years.

The other is to facilitate the international transport of containers by providing uniform international safety regulation, equally applicable to all modes of surface transport. In this way, proliferation of divergent national safety regulations can be avoided.

The Convention sets out procedures whereby containers used in international transport will be safety-approved.

Convention on the International Maritime Satellite Organization, 1976 (plus Operating Agreement).

Entry into force: 1979.

For some years, maritime radiocommunications frequency bands have become increasingly congested and it was recognised that the use of space technology could help overcome that problem and many others which have arisen in recent years. The aim of the Convention was to establish an organisation (INMARSAT) which would improve maritime communications, thereby improving distress and safety of life at sea communications, the efficiency and management of ships, maritime public correspondence services, and radio-termination capabilities.

The Operating Agreement, adopted at the same time, set an initial capital ceiling for the organisation of US$ 200 million. Investment shares are determined on the basis of utilisation of the INMARSAT space segment. In 1985 the Operating Agreement was amended to permit INMARSAT to provide services for aircraft. The amendments is not yet in force.

INMARSAT began operations in 1981 and has its Headquarters in London.

Torremolinos International Convention for the Safety of Fishing Vessels, 1977.

This Convention is not yet in force.

The safety of fishing vessels has been a matter of great concern to IMO since it came into existence, but the great, differences in design and operation between fishing vessels and other types of ships had always proved a major obstacle to their inclusion in the SOLAS and Load Lines Conventions.

The Convention contains safety requirements for the construction and equipment of new, decked seagoing fishing vessels of 24 metres in length and over, including those vessels also processing their catch. Existing vessels are covered only in respect of radio requirements.

One of the most important features of the Convention is that it contains stability requirements for the first time in an international convention.

International Convention on Standards of Training, Certification and Watchkeeping for Seafarers, 1978.

Entry into force: 1984.

The Convention is the first to establish basic requirements on training, certification and watchkeeping for seafarers on an international level.

The technical provisions of the Convention are contained in an Annex, which is divided into six chapters. The first contains general provisions and the others deal with the master-deck department; special requirements for tankers; and proficiency in survival craft.

The requirements of the Convenion are augmented by 23 resolutions adopted by the Conference, many of which contain more detailed provisions on the subjects covered by the Convention itself.

International Convention on Maritime Search and Rescue, 1979.

Entry into force: 1985.

The main purpose of the Convention is to facilitate co-operation between Governments and between those participating in search and rescue (SAR) operations at sea by establishing an international SAR plan.

Parties to the Convention are required to ensure that arrangements are made for the provision of adequate SAR services in their coastal waters and encouraged to enter into SAR agreements with neighbouring States.

The Convention establishes preparatory measures which should be taken, including the establishment of rescue co-ordination centres and subcentres and the operating procedures to be followed in the event of emergencies or alerts and during SAR operations.

MARINE POLLUTION

International Convention for the Prevention of Pollution of the Sea by Oil, 1954, as amended.

Entry into force: 1958.

One of the earliest indications of marine pollution as a problem requiring international control was pollution of the sea by oil.

In 1954, the International Convention for the Prevention of Pollution of the Sea by Oil was agreed upon. The depository responsibilities for this Convention were passed to IMO when it was established in 1959. The Convention was amended three times (in 1962, 1969 and 1971).

The Convention has been effectively superseded by MARPOL 73/78 (which see).

International Convention Relating to Intervention on the High Seas in Cases of Oil Pollution Casualties, 1969.

Entry into force: 1975.

The Convention affirms the right of a coastal State to take such measures on the high seas as may be

necessary to prevent, mitigate or eliminate danger to its coastline or related interests from pollution by oil or the threat thereof, following upon a maritime casualty. The **Protocol of 1973** which entered into force in 1983 extends the Convention to pollutants other than oil (such as chemicals).

Convention on the Prevention of Marine Pollution by Dumping of Wastes and Other Matter, 1972 as amended.

Entry into force: 1975. Amended: 1978 and 1980.

The Convention (the "London Dumping Convention") has a global character, and represents a further step towards the international control and prevention of marine pollution. It prohibits the dumping of certain hazardous materials, requires a prior special permit for the dumping of a number of other identified materials and a prior general permit for other wastes or matter.

'Dumping' is defined as the deliberate disposal at sea of wastes or other matter from vessels, aircraft, platforms or other man-made structures, as well as the deliberate disposal of these vessels or platforms themselves.

Annexes list wastes which can not be dumped and others for which a special dumping permit is required.

In 1978, amendments were adopted to permit and control the incineration of wastes and other matter at sea. They entered into force the following year. In 1980, a list of substances requiring special care when being incinerated was added. The amendment entered into force in 1981. A new procedure for settling disputes was also adopted in 1978 but has not yet entered into force.

International Convention for the Prevention of Pollution from Ships, 1973, as modified by the Protocol of 1978 relating thereto (MARPOL 73/78).

Entry into force: 1983. Amended: 1984 and 1985 (in force).

The original 1973 Convention represented the most ambitious attempt made up until that time to combat pollution from ships. Five technical Annexes contained regulations to counter pollution by oil, noxious liquid substances carried in bulk, harmful substances carried in package form, sewage and garbage.

Progress towards entry into force was, however, slow and in **1978 a Protocol** was adopted which effectively absorbed the parent convention and at the same time made extensive modifications to Annex I (oil pollution). The Protocol entered into force in 1983 and Annex I became effective on that date; the entry into force of Annex II (chemicals) was deferred until 6 April 1987 to allow certain technical problems to be overcome. Acceptance of Annexes III, IV and V was not mandatory Annex V, which deals with the Prevention of pollution by sewage and garbage, entered into force on 31 December 1988.

The measures in Annex I are designed to eliminate operational pollution (such as that arising from tank cleaning) and to reduce accidental pollution by measures to protect the integrity of the cargo tanks as much as possible. Measures designed to make implementation of the Annex easier and more effective were introduced in the 1984 amendments. Annex II aims particularly at preventing pollution during discharges and was considerably amended in 1985. The changes are designed to make implementation easier and also to take into account technical developments. They also make mandatory the International Bulk Chemical Code which is concerned with carriage requirements.

LIABILITY AND COMPENSATION

International Convention on Civil Liability for Oil Pollution Damage, 1969.

Entry into force: 1979.

The aim of the Convention is to ensure that adequate compensation is available to persons who suffer oil pollution damage resulting from maritime casualties involving oil-carrying ships. It places the liability for such damage on the owner of the ship from which the pollution oil escaped or was discharged. Liability can be limited for each ton of the ship's gross tonnage, with a maximum liability for each incident.

The 1969 Civil Liabiliy Convention (CLC) used the 'Poincaré' franc, based on the 'official' value of gold, as the applicable unit of account, but the conversion of this into national currencies has become increasingly difficult. The **Protocol of 1976** which entered into force in 1981, provides for a new unit of account, based on the Special Drawing Rights (SDRs) as used by the International Monetary Fund (IMF).

Protocol of 1984 to the Convention: While the compensation system established by the 1969 CLC and 1971 Fund Convention has proved very useful, by the mid 1980s it was generally agreed that the limits of liability were too low to provide adequate compensation in the event of a major pollution incident and that compensation was often particularly unsatisfactory when caused by a small ship.

Under the CLC Protocol, all ships up to 5,000 gt will be exposed to a maximum liability of US$ 3.12

Classification Society
Established in 1960

Member of IACS

Services:
- Design Approval and Classification Survey of Hull, Machinery and Equipment
- Inspection of Offshore Structures
- Testing of Materials and Equipment
- Inspection of Industrial Plant
- Inspection of Apparatus for Marine Pollution
- Computer Service

KOREAN REGISTER OF SHIPPING

1465-10 Seocho-3 dong, Seocho-Ku, Seoul, Korea
C.P.O. Box 3229 Seoul, Cable Add: "KRSHEADOFFICE", Seoul
Tel: (02) 582-6001   Fax: (02) 584-8813
Telex: KRSHO K27358

Chairman and President:	Choi Byung-Soo
Vice President:	Kim Jae-Seung
Managing Director:	Koh Hong-Seok Park Yong-Chol,
	Cho Man-Jo Kim Yong-Cho

Overseas Branch Offices:

- Antwerp: (02) 541-2327
- Kobe: (078) 221-7693/4
- Los Angeles: (714) 865-7203
- Rotterdam: (010) 421-4797
- Tokyo: (03) 246-1971/3
- Buenos Aires: 392-8206
- Las Palmas: 26-3767
- New York: (203) 661 7771
- Samoa: 633-1409
- Houston: (713) 665-0440
- London: (01) 222-2840
- Paramaribo: 82511
- Singapore: 221-3319

million while for ships above 5,000 gt the limit will increase in proportion to their tonnage, up to a maximum of US$ 62 million for ships of 140,000 gt and above.

The 1984 Protocol provides for a new and simplified procedure for amending the liability limits in the Protocol.

International Convention on the Establishment of an International Fund for Compensation for Oil Pollution Damage, 1971.
Entry into force: 1978.

The Convention is supplementary to the Civil Liability Convention and enables additional compensation to be paid once the limits in the 1969 instrument have been reached. It established an International Oil Pollution Compensation Fund, contributions to which are made by all persons who receive oil by sea in Contracting States. The **Protocol of 1976** enables the Special Drawing Rights (SDRs) of the International Monetary Fund to be used as the unit of account instead of the 'Poincaré' franc. The **Protocol of 1984** is designed to raise the maximum amount of compensation available under the Convention and thereby enable greater compensation to be paid to victims of pollution incidents. Initially, total compensation available (including that under the CLC) will be raised to a maximum of US$ 140 million. However, when the total quantities of contributing oil received in three contracting states equals 600 million tons or more, the limit of compensation will be increased to a maximum of US$208 million.

Convention relating to Civil Liability in the Field of Maritime Carriage of Nuclear Materials, 1971.
Entry into force: 1975

The purpose of this Convention is to solve difficulties and conflicts which arise from the simultaneous application to nuclear damage of certain maritime conventions dealing with shipowners' liability, as well as other conventions which place liability arising from nuclear incidents on the operators of the nuclear installations from which, or to which, the material in question was being transported.

Athens Conventions relating to the Carriage of Passengers and their Luggage by Sea, 1974.
Entry into force: 1987.

The Convention is designed to consolidate and harmonise two earlier Brussels conventions dealing with passengers and luggage and adopted in 1961 and 1967, respectively. It establishes a regime of liability of the carrier for damage suffered by passengers carried on a seagoing vessel. For the death of, or personal injury to, a passenger the limit of liability is set at US$ 55,000 per carriage.

As far as loss or damage to luggage is concerned, the carrier's limit of liability varies, depending on whether the loss or damage occured in respect of cabin luggage, or a vehicle and/or luggage carried in or on it, or in respect of other luggage.

Protocol to the Convention enables the Special Drawing Rights of the International Monetary Fund to be used as the unit of account instead of the 'Poincaré' franc.

Convention on Limitation of Liability for Maritime Claims, 1976.
Entry into force: 1986.

The Convention replaces an earlier instrument and considerably raises the limit of liability for claims covered, in some cases by up to 250% to 300%. Limits are specified for two types of claims — claims for loss of life or personal injury, and property claims (such as damage to other ships, property or harbour works).

The Convention provides for a virtually unbreakable system of limiting liability. It declares that a person will not be able to limit liability only if "it is proved that the loss, resulted from his personal act or omission, committed with the intent to cause such a loss, or recklessly and with knowledge that such a loss would probably result".

OTHER SUBJECTS

Convention on Facilitation of International Maritime Traffic, 1965, as amended.
Entry into force 1967. Amended 1969, 1973, 1977 and 1986.

The Convention's main objectives are to prevent unnecessary delays in maritime traffic, to aid co-operation between Governments, and to secure the highest practicable degree of uniformity in formalities and other procedures.

The Annex to the Convention contains provisions relating to the arrival, stay and departure of ships

agemar

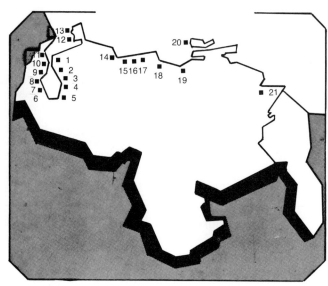

and persons, health and quarantine, and sanitary measures for plants and animals. The 1973 amendments, which entered into force in 1984, introduced the 'tacit acceptance' amendment procedure. The 1986 amendments enabled automatic data processing techniques to be taken into account.

International Convention on Tonnage Measurement of Ships, 1969.

Entry into force: 1982.

The Convention, which was adopted by IMO in 1969, is the first successful attempt to introduce a universal tonnage measurement system. It provides for gross and net tonnages, both of which are calculated independently. The entry into force of the Convention will result in the eventual elimination of the shelter-deck type vessel.

Existing ships, if not converted, are enabled to retain their existing tonnage for 12 years after entry into force. This is intended to ensure that ships are given reasonable safeguards in the interests of the economic welfare of the shipping industry.

The Convention was drafted to ensure that, as far as possible, gross and net tonnages calculated under the new system did not differ too greatly from those calculated under existing methods.

Convention for the Suppression of Unlawful Acts Against the Safety of Maritime Navigation, 1988.

The Convention is designed to ensure that appropriate action is taken against any person committing various acts against shipping, including seizure of a ship by force, acts of violence against persons on board ships and the placing of devices on board ship which are likely to damage or destroy it.

A Protocol adopted at the same time extends the provisions of the Convention to fixed platforms located on the Continental Shelf.

Neither instrument is yet in force.

International Convention on Salvage, 1989.

The Convention is intended to replace one adopted as long ago as 1910. One of the main purposes of the Convention is to take pollution into account. The existing 'no cure, no pay' system means that a salvor is only rewarded if a ship is salvaged. There is no compensation for actions which minimize or prevent pollution. The new Convention attempts to remedy this by providing compensation for actions which minimize or prevent pollution, even if the salvage operation is otherwise unsuccessful.

The Convention will enter into force a year after being ratified by 15 States.

Copies of all IMO Conventions, Protocols, Amendments, etc., may be obtained from: IMO, 4 Albert Embankment, London SE1 7SR, England. Telephone: 01-735 7611. Telex: 23588.

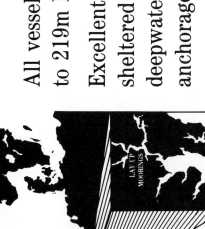

LLOYD'S STANDARD FORM
OF SALVAGE AGREEMENT

"NO-CURE, NO-PAY"

Initially introduced in the Dardanelles during 1890 an agreement between Henry Hozier, the Secretary of Lloyd's and, Vincent Grech, a local salvor, Lloyd's Standard Form of Salvage Agreement (or Lloyd's Open Form as it is frequently called) was rapidly adopted as a suitable vehicle for any salvage services to ships in casualty. The conditions surrounding groundings, collisions and other maritime emergencies do not usually permit the normal commercial procedures of inspection, estimate and quotation to be carried out before work starts. Agreements were drawn up specifically for each salvor until replaced, in 1892, by a combined general form.

The first fifteen years saw steady change as experience identified aspects needing revision and development until, in 1908, a standard form appeared that closely resembles that current today. Revision did continue with, in 1926, the introduction of an appeal procedure and the latest (1980) special provision to pay salvors expenses for work carried out on laden tankers to prevent oil pollution where salvage was not successful or failed because of official intervention.

The first case, the stranding and refloating by Vincent Grech of the Tyne-owned steamer Helen Otto in the Dardanelles on 12 October 1890, was referred to the Committee of Lloyd's who appointed two of their Members, George Hardy and Herbert de Rougemont, to arbitrate. The hearing took place on 19 November and the sum agreed between salvors and the Helen Otto's master, £950, was confirmed.

The second concerned the loss of the P.& O. steamer Hong Kong, wrecked at the entrance of the Red Sea on passage from the Far East to London on 1 December 1890. The Perim Coal Co. failed to refloat her due to bad weather and heavy seas but over a two month period were able to save most of her valuable cargo. When approached the Committee of Lloyd's appointed William Walton of Waltons & Co., Solicitors to the Corporation of Lloyd's as Arbitrator and he awarded £12,000 to the Perim Coal Co. for their services.

The Colina and Tamise were also handled in 1891, seven cases in 1892 and ten the following year. By the end of 1895 the total number of cases had risen to 49. Apart from the Helen Otto three were decided by the Secretary of Lloyd's, eight were referred to Sir Charles Hall, Q.C., who, however, was heavily engaged with other duties as the Recorder of the City of London and Member of Parliament for the Holborn Division of Finsbury. Most were handled by William Walton. In 1900 Mr. Butler Aspinall, Q.C., was appointed Arbitrator, a position held until his retirement in 1930. The widespread adoption of Lloyd's Form increased the workload so a panel was introduced in 1905 with the appointment of Mr. Frederick Laing, K.C., and Mr. William Pickford. By 1914 this panel had grown to six, a level that has been virtually maintained since as today there are eight Arbitrators and one Appeal Arbitrator.

The original provision for a lump sum agreement between master and salvor fell into disuse and it is now normal for all discussion on the level of the award to be left until completion of the salvage services. Of the cases that come to the attention of the Salvage Arbitration Branch of Lloyd's some 45 per cent are settled amicably and never come to arbitration. The others are the subject of private hearings with the parties involved represented by Counsel instructed by Admiralty solicitors making submissions to the Arbitrator appointed by the Committee of Lloyd's. Should either part be dissatisfied there is provision for an appeal which will be heard by the Appeal Arbitrator.

Salvors were deeply involved in the original drafting of Lloyd's Form and this is reflected today in the standing Working Party, chaired by the Appeal Arbitrator, which regularly reviews the working of the Form and makes any necessary submissions to the Committee of Lloyd's for revision. Together with salvors other interested parties represented include Lloyd's and company underwriters, P&I clubs, Admiralty Solicitors, Average Adjusters, shipowners and oil companies.

Copies of Lloyd's Standard Form of Salvage Agreement and information on the working of the Arbitrator service is available from The Manager, Salvage Arbitration Branch, Agency Department, Lloyd's, 1, Lime Street, London EC3M 7HA, England.

LLOYD'S STANDARD FORM OF SALVAGE
AGREEMENT

On board the   Dated   19

IT IS HEREBY AGREED between Captain   for and on behalf of the Owners
of the "   " her cargo freight bunkers and stores and   for and on behalf
of   (hereinafter called "the Contractor"):—
1.(a) The Contractor agrees to use his best endeavours to salve the   and/or her
cargo bunkers and stores and take them to   or other place to be hereafter agreed or if no
place is named or agreed to a place of safety. The Contractor further agrees to use his best endeavours
to prevent the escape of oil from the vessel while performing the services of salving the subject vessel
and/or her cargo bunkers and stores. The services shall be rendered and accepted as salvage services
upon the principle of "no cure — no pay" except that where the property being salved is a tanker laden
or partly laden with a cargo of oil and without negligence on the part of the Contractor and/or his
Servants and/or Agents (1) the services are not successful or (2) are only partially successful or (3) the
Contractor is prevented from completing the services the Contractor shall nevertheless be awarded
solely against the Owners of such tanker his reasonably incurred expenses and an increment not
exceeding 15 per cent of such expenses but only if and to the extent that such expenses together with
the increment are greater than any amount otherwise recoverable under this Agreement. Within the
meaning of the said exception to the principle of "no cure — no pay" expenses shall in addition to
actual out of pocket expenses include a fair rate for all tugs craft personnel and other equipment used
by the Contractor in the services and oil shall mean crude oil fuel oil heavy diesel oil and lubricating
oil.
(b) The Contractor's remuneration shall be fixed by arbitration in London in the manner herein
prescribed and any other difference arising out of this Agreement or the operations thereunder shall
be referred to arbitration in the same way. In the event of the services referred to in this Agreement or
any part of such services having been already rendered at the date of this Agreement by the
Contractor to the said vessel and/or her cargo bunkers and stores the provisions of this Agreement
shall apply to such services.
(c) It is hereby further agreed that the security to be provided to the Committee of Lloyd's the
Salved Values the Award and/or Interim Award and/or Award on Appeal of the Arbitrator and/or
Arbitrator(s) on Appeal shall be in   currency. If the Clause is not completed then the
security to be provided and the Salved Values the Award and/or Interim Award and/or Award on
Appeal of the Arbitrator and/or Arbitrator(s) on Appeal shall be in Pounds Sterling.
(d) This Agreement shall be governed by and arbitration thereunder shall be in accordance with
English law.
2. The Owners their Servants and Agents shall co-operate fully with the Contractor in and about the
salvage including obtaining entry to the place named in Clause 1 of this Agreement or such other
place as may be agreed or if applicable the place of safety to which the salved property is taken. The
Owners shall promptly accept redelivery of the salved property at such place. The Contractor may
make reasonable use of the vessel's machinery gear equipment anchors chains stores and other
appurtenances during and for the purpose of the operations free of expense but shall not
unnecessarily damage abandon or sacrifice the same or any property the subject of this Agreement.
3. The Master or other person signing this Agreement on behalf of the property to be salved is not
authorised to make or give and the Contractor shall not demand or take any payment draft or order as
inducement to or remuneration for entering into this Agreement.

PROVISIONS AS TO SECURITY

4. The Contractor shall immediately after the termination of the services or sooner in appropriate
cases notify the Committee of Lloyd's and where practicable the Owners of the amount for which he
requires security (inclusive of costs expenses and interest). Unless otherwise agreed by the parties
such security shall be given to the Committee of Lloyd's and security so given shall be in a form
approved by the Committee and shall be given by persons firms or corporations resident in the United
Kingdom either satisfactory to the Committee of Lloyd's or agreed by the Contractor. The Committee
of Lloyd's shall not be responsible for the sufficiency (whether in amount or otherwise) of any
security which shall be given nor for the default or insolvency of any person firm or corporation
giving the same.
5. Pending the completion of the security as aforesaid the Contractor shall have a maritime lien on
the property salved for his remuneration. Where the aforementioned exception to the principle of "no
cure — no pay" becomes likely to be applicable the Owners of the vessel shall on demand of the

Contractor provide security for the Contractor's remuneration under the aforementioned exception in accordance with Clause 4 hereof. The salved property shall not without the consent in writing of the Contractor be removed from the place (within the terms of Clause 1) to which the property is taken by the Contractor on the completion of the salvage services until security has been given as aforesaid. The Owners of the vessel their Servants and Agents shall use their best endeavours to ensure that the Cargo Owners provide security in accordance with the provisions of Clause 4 of this Agreement before the cargo is released. The Contractor agrees not to arrest or detain the property salved unless (a) the security be not given with 14 days (exclusive of Saturdays and Sundays or other days observed as general holidays at Lloyd's) after the date of the termination of the services (the Committee of Lloyd's not being responsible for the failure of the parties concerned to provide the required security within the said 14 days) or (b) the Contractor has reason to believe that the removal of the property is contemplated contrary to the above agreement. In the event of security not being provided or in the event of (1) any attempt being made to remove the property salved contrary to this agreement or (2) the Contractor having reasonable grounds to suppose that such an attempt will be made the Contractor may take steps to enforce his aforesaid lien. The Arbitrator appointed under Clause 6 or the person(s) appointed under Clause 13 hereof shall have the power in their absolute discretion to include in the amount awarded to the Contractor the whole or such part of the expense incurred by the Contractor in enforcing or protecting by insurance or otherwise or in taking reasonable steps to enforce or protect his lien as they shall think fit.

PROVISIONS AS TO ARBITRATION

6.(a) Where security within the provisions of this Agreement is given to the Committee of Lloyd's in whole or in part the said Committee shall appoint an Arbitrator in respect of the interests covered by such security.

(b) Whether security has been given or not the Committee of Lloyd's shall appoint an Arbitrator upon receipt of a written or telex or telegraphic notice of a claim for arbitration from any of the parties entitled or authorised to make such a claim.

7. Where an Arbitrator has been appointed by the Committee of Lloyd's and the parties do not wish to proceed to arbitration the parties shall jointly notify the said Committee in writing or by telex or by telegram and the said Committee may thereupon terminate the appointment of such Arbitrator as it may have appointed in accordance with Clause 6 of this Agreement.

8. Any of the following parties may make a claim for arbitration viz:- (1) The Owners of the ship. (2) The Owners of the cargo or any part thereof. (3) The Owners of any freight separately at risk or any part thereof (4) The Contractor. (5) The Owners of the bunkers and/or stores. (6) Any other person who is a party to this Agreement.

9. If the parties to any such Arbitration or any of them desire to be heard or to adduce evidence at the Arbitration they shall give notice to that effect to the Committee of Lloyd's and shall respectively nominate a person in the United Kingdom to represent them for all the purposes of the Arbitration and failing such notice and nomination being given the Arbitrator or Arbitrator(s) on Appeal may proceed as if the parties failing to give the same had renounced their right to be heard or adduce evidence.

10. The remuneration for the services within the meaning of this Agreement shall be fixed by an Arbitrator to be appointed by the Committee of Lloyd's and he shall have power to make an Interim Award ordering such payment on account as may seem fair and just and on such terms as may be fair and just.

CONDUCT OF THE ARBITRATION

11. The Arbitrator shall have power to obtain call for receive and act upon any such oral or documentary evidence or information (whether the same be strictly admissable as evidence or not) as he may think fit and to conduct the Arbitration in such manner in all respects as he may think fit and shall if in his opinion the amount of the security demanded is excessive have power in his absolute discretion to condemn the Contractor in the whole or part of the expense of providing such security and to deduct the amount in which the Contractor is so condemned from the salvage remuneration. Unless the Arbitrator shall otherwise direct the parties shall be at liberty to adduce expert evidence at the Arbitration. Any Award of the Arbitrator shall (subject to appeal as provided in this Agreement) be final and binding on all the parties concerned. The Arbitrator and the Committee of Lloyd's may charge reasonable fees and expenses for their services in connection with the Arbitration whether it proceeds to a hearing or not and all such fees and expenses shall be treated as part of the costs of the Arbitration. Save as aforesaid the statutory provisions as to Arbitration for the time being in force in England shall apply.

12. Interest at a rate per annum to be fixed by the Arbitrator from the expiration of 21 days

(exclusive of Saturdays and Sundays or other days observed as general holidays at Lloyd's) after the date of publication of the Award and/or Interim Award by the Committee of Lloyd's until the date payment is received by the Committee of Lloyd's both dates inclusive shall (subject to appeal as provided in this Agreement) be payable upon any sum awarded after deduction of any sums paid on account.

PROVISIONS AS TO APPEAL

13. Any of the persons named under Clause 8 may appeal from the Award but not without leave of the Arbitrator(s) on Appeal from an Interim Award made pursuant to the provisions of Clause 10 hereof by giving written or telegraphic or telex Notice of Appeal to the Committee of Lloyd's within 14 days (exclusive of Saturdays and Sundays or other days observed as general holidays at Lloyd's) after the date of the publication by the Committee of Lloyd's of the Award and may (without prejudice to their right of appeal under the first part of this Clause) within 14 days (exclusive of Saturdays and Sundays or other days observed as general holidays at Lloyd's) after receipt by them from the Committee of Lloyd's of notice of such appeal (such notice if sent by post to be deemed to be received on the day following that on which the said notice was posted) give written or telegraphic or telex Notice of Cross-Appeal to the Committee of Lloyd's. As soon as practicable after receipt of such notice or notices the Committee of Lloyd's shall refer the Appeal to the hearing and determination of a person or persons selected by it. In the event of an Appellant or Cross-Appellant withdrawing his Notice of Appeal or Cross-Appeal the hearing shall neverthless proceed in respect of such Notice of Appeal or Cross-Appeal as may remain. Any Award on Appeal shall be final and binding on all the parties concerned whether such parties were represented or not at either the Arbitration or at the Arbitration on Appeal.

CONDUCT OF APPEAL

14. No evidence other than the documents put in on the Arbitration and the Arbitrator's notes of the proceedings and oral evidence if any at the Arbitration and the Arbitrator's Reasons for his Award and Interim Award if any and the transcript if any of any evidence given at the Arbitration shall be used on the Appeal unless the Arbitrator(s) on the Appeal shall in his or their discretion call for or allow other evidence. The Arbitrator(s) on Appeal may conduct the Arbitration on Appeal in such manner in all respects as he or they may think fit and may act upon any such evidence or information (whether the same be strictly admissable as evidence or not) as he or they may think fit and may maintain increase or reduce the sum awarded by the Arbitrator with the like power as is conferred by Clause 11 on the Arbitrator to condemn the Contractor in the whole or part of the expense of providing security and to deduct the amount disallowed from the salvage remuneration. And he or they shall also make such order as he or they shall think fit as to the payment of interest on the sum awarded to the Contractor. The Arbitrator(s) on the Appeal may direct in what manner the costs of the Arbitration and of the Arbitration on Appeal shall be borne and paid and he or they and the Committee of Lloyd's may charge reasonable fees and expenses for their services in connection with the Arbitration on Appeal whether it proceeds to a hearing or not and all such fees and expenses shall be treated as part of the costs of the Arbitration on Appeal. Save as aforesaid the statutory provisions as to Arbitration for the time being in force in England shall apply.

PROVISIONS AS TO PAYMENT

15. (a) In case of Arbitration if no Notice of Appeal be received by the Committee of Lloyd's within 14 days (exclusive of Saturdays and Sundays or other days observed as general holidays at Lloyd's) after the date of the publication by the Committee of the Award and/or Interim Award the Committee shall call upon the party or parties concerned to pay the amount awarded and in the event of non-payment shall realize or enforce the security and pay therefrom to the Contractor (whose receipt shall be a good discharge to it) the amount awarded to him together with interest as hereinbefore provided but the Contractor shall reimburse the parties concerned to such extent as the final Award is less than the Interim Award.

(b) If Notice of Appeal be received by the Committee of Lloyd's in accordance with the provisions of Clause 13 hereof it shall as soon as but not until the Award on Appeal has been published by it call upon the party or parties concerned to pay the amount awarded and in the event of non-payment shall realize or enforce the security and pay therefrom to the Contractor (whose receipt shall be a good discharge to it) the amount awarded to him together with interest if any in such manner as shall comply with the provisions of the Award on Appeal.

(c) If the Award and/or Interim Award and/or Award on Appeal provides or provide that the costs of the Arbitration and/or of the Arbitration on Appeal or any part of such costs shall be borne by the

Contractor such costs may be deducted from the amount awarded before payment is made to the Contractor by the Committee of Lloyd's unless satisfactory security is provided by the Contractor for the payment of such costs.

(d) If any sum shall become payable to the Contractor as remuneration for his services and/or interest and/or costs as the result of an agreement made between the Contractor and the parties interested in the property salved or any of them the Committee of Lloyd's in the event of non-payment shall realize or enforce the security and pay therefrom to the Contractor (whose receipt shall be good discharge to it) the amount agreed upon between the parties.

(e) Without prejudice to the provisions of Clause 4 hereof the liability of the Committee of Lloyd's shall be limited in any event to the amount of security held by it.

GENERAL PROVISIONS

16. Notwithstanding anything hereinbefore contained should the operations be only partially successful without any negligence or want or ordinary skill and care on the part of the Contractor his Servants or Agents and any portion of the vessel her appurtenances bunkers stores and cargo be salved by the Contractor he shall be entitled to reasonable remuneration and such reasonable remuneration shall be fixed in case of difference by Arbitration in the manner hereinbefore prescribed.

17. The Master or other person signing this Agreement on behalf of the property to be salved enters into this Agreement as Agent for the vessel her cargo freight bunkers and stores and the respective owners thereof and binds each (but not the one for the other or himself personally) to the due performance thereof.

18. In considering what sums of money have been expended by the Contractor in rendering the services and/or in fixing the amount of the Award and/or Interim Award and/or Award on Appeal the Arbitrator or Arbitrator(s) on Appeal shall to such an extent and in so far as it may be fair and just in all the circumstances give effect to the consequences of any change or changes in the value of money or rates of exchange which may have occurred between the completion of the services and the date on which the Award and/or Interim Award and/or Award on Appeal is made.

19. Any Award notice authority order or other document signed by the Chairman of Lloyd's or any person authorised by the Committee of Lloyd's for the purpose shall be deemed to have in all respects as if it had been signed by every member of the Committee of Lloyd's.

20. The Contractor may claim salvage and enforce any Award or agreement made between the Contractor and the parties interested in the property salved against security provided under this Agreement if any in the name and on behalf of any Sub-Contractors Servants or Agents including Masters and members of the Crews of vessels employed by him in the services rendered hereunder provided that he first indemnifies and holds harmless the Owners of the property salved against all claims by or liabilities incurred to the said persons. Any such indemnity shall be provided in a form satisfactory to such Owners.

21. The Contractor shall be entitled to limit any liability to the Owners of the subject vessel and/or her cargo bunkers and stores which he and/or his Servants and/or Agents may incur in and about the services in the manner and to the extent provided by English law and as if the provisions of the Convention on Limitation of Liability for Maritime Claims 1976 were part of the law of English.

For and on behalf of the Contractor

....

(To be signed either by the Contractor personally or by the Master of the salving vessel or other person whose name is inserted in line 3 of this Agreement.)

For and on behalf of the Owners of property to be salved.

....

(To be signed by the Master or other person whose name is inserted in line 1 of this Agreement.)

GENERAL AVERAGE AND SALVAGE

Any extraordinary expenditure or sacrifice of ship, freight or cargo, intentionally and reasonably incurred or made in time of peril, in order to secure the common or general safety of the property involved in a maritime adventure may lead to a claim for General Average.

Those who incur such expenditure as well as the owners of any property sacrificed are entitled, subject to the conditions imposed by maritime law and contract, to a rateable contribution from the other parties interested. The apportionment is made by a Statement or Adjustment of General Average which is usually prepared by an Average Adjuster whose appointment rests primarily with the shipowners.

The shipowners are entitled to refuse delivery of cargo until adequate security has been provided by the receivers or cargo owners for the payment which shall eventually be found due from each. The security often takes the form of an Average Bond and, in addition, shipowners may demand a cash payment as a deposit in advance, or a Guarantee of the Corporation of Lloyd's or other approved security.

It is usual for underwriters (although not legally liable to do so) to refund to their assured any amounts thus deposited if Lloyd's Form of General Average Deposit Receipt is used and the funds have been deposited in a special account in a Bank. On completion of the General Average Statement the underwriters then claim any sum by which the amount deposited may be found to exceed the actual liability. The Deposit Receipts are carefully safeguarded as the issue of duplicates is undesirable. Lloyd's Form of General Average Deposit Receipt is a bearer document and does not require endorsement.

In cases where, owing to the nature of the average expenditure or sacrifice as, for example where a ship is towed or assisted and a salvage award or settlement has yet to be arrived at, or where damage to a probably serious extent has been caused by flooding the hold to extinguish a fire, but the extent of the damage cannot yet be ascertained — it is sometimes necessary for the shipowners to collect as a deposit from the cargo interests who have benefited from the expenditure or sacrifice a sum which may eventually prove to have been over-estimated. In order to avoid such collections, and as a convenience generally. Lloyd's has a system, applicable to insured cargo, under which the Guarantee of the Corporation of Lloyd's may be given in a form acceptable to shipowners in lieu of a cash deposit.

The Guarantees of the Corporation of Lloyd's are issued in London by the General Average, Salvage and Collision Section of Lloyd's, which, together with the Recoveries against Carriers Section, also acts for insurers in the exercise of their subrogation rights, and in General Average and Salvage cases investigates their rights and liabilities, on receipt of Deposit Receipts, documents of title, or details of any undertaking or security which has been provided to shipowners or to salvors by cargo interests.

Lloyd's Average Bond was completely revised in 1977 and the code title LAB 77 is incorporated to facilitate reference in telegraphic messages and computerised documents. The form produced at Lloyd's consists of two pages. The top page is the Average Bond part and the bottom page is for recording the value of the goods received. The particulars common to both pages coincide so that by the use of a sheet of carbon only one typing is necessary. The completion and return of the Average Bond part of the form may result in the early release of the goods and when their condition has been ascertained the information asked for in the bottom page (the Valuation Form) should be provided together with a copy of the commercial invoice to assist the Average Adjuster to draw up his Statement of Adjustment promptly.

Lloyd's Form of General Average Deposit Receipt and Lloyd's Average Bond Forms (LAB 77) with a detachable Valuation Form can be obtained from the General Average Section of Lloyd's Underwriters' Claims and Recoveries Office.

GENERAL AVERAGE
AND THE YORK-ANTWERP RULES

Contributed by Ernest Robert Lindley & Sons

The Origin of General Average

Historical records tell us that systems of general average, involving a contribution from the interests involved in a common maritime adventure, have been in existence since the earliest days of seaborne traffic. The object of the system was to encourage ship masters and others who sailed with them to make exertions to attain safety whenever a peril threatened the joint adventure. The prime example concerns the consent given by the owners of cargo to the ship master to make a judicious and timely sacrifice of their property, in the knowledge that their loss would be made good to them by rateable contribution from the other interests on the completion of the voyage.

Legal recognition of this consent, accorded the status of custom, appears in Justinian's Digest, and reads as follows:

"The Rhodian Law provides that if in order to lighten a ship merchandise is thrown overboard, that which has been given for all shall be replaced by the contribution of all."

Time has proved the wisdom and equity of the custom, which has been extended by practice over many years and is now recognised as part of the law of the sea in all maritime countries and is in many of them embodied in the form of a General Average Code.

General Average in English Law

In England no code of general average exists. Law and practice developed hand in hand. The records of decisions in the courts of law combined with the Rules of Practice of the Association of Average Adjusters (which in many instances are derived from the Customs of Lloyd's) provide in themselves an adequate working system, based upon knowledge acquired by actual experience.

Now, since the Marine Insurance Act, 1906, the legal authorities and the practice of average adjusters have been supplemented by a statutory definition of general average which appears in Section 66 of the Act, reading as follows:

"(1) A general average loss is a loss caused by or directly consequential on a general average act. It includes a general average expenditure as well as a general average sacrifice.

(2) There is a general average act where any extraordinary sacrifice or expenditure is voluntarily and reasonably made or incurred in time of peril for the purpose of preserving the property imperilled in the common adventure.

(3) Where there is a general average loss, the party on whom it falls is entitled, subject to the conditions imposed by maritime law, to a rateable contribution from the other parties interested, and such contribution is called a general average contribution.

Examples of General Average Sacrifices and Expenditure under English Law

According to Section 66 sub-section (1), a general average loss may be in the nature of a sacrifice or an expenditure. The following are examples of sacrifices and expenditure which may be admitted in general average under English law and practice:

Sacrifices

Cargo and Freight

1. Jettison from under deck.
2. Jettison from on deck, provided that on-deck stowage is in accordance with the recognised custom of the trade in which the ship is engaged.
3. Damage caused by water or other means used to extinguish a fire on board ship.
4. Discharge and re-shipment for the purpose of floating a stranded ship when in a position of peril.

Ship's Materials

5. Parts of the ship cut away for the common safety.
6. Chains and anchors slipped to avert a threatening peril.
7. Damage to a vessel's machinery, ropes, winches, windlass and other gear sustained in endeavours to float a stranded ship when in a position of peril.
8. Damage done in the efforts to extinguish a fire on board or in the process of jettisoning cargo.

Expenditure

9. Expenses incurred in floating a stranded ship if in peril.

10. Inward expenses entering a port of refuge for the purpose of repairing damage to ship.
11. Cost of discharging cargo at a port of refuge for the purpose of repairing damage to ship.
12. Cost of warehousing, warehouse rent on cargo, re-shipment of cargo and outward expenses leaving the port of refuge, but only when the cause of the vessel putting into port has been to repair damage which is itself the consequences of a general average act.

Variance of the Laws and Practices in different Countries

The examples of general average sacrifices and expenditure set out above are typical, and most of them would be the subject of allowance in general average according to the law and usages of all maritime nations. However, as the laws of different countries have developed in different directions, there are variations. In examples 10 and 12 it will be seen that allowance is made for the inward expenses entering a port of refuge to repair particular average damage or damage caused by general average sacrifice, whereas the outward expenses of leaving the port of refuge are only allowed in general average when the ship has put into the port in order to repair damage caused by general average sacrifice. In all other jurisdictions, both inward and outward port charges are allowed when a ship enters a port of refuge, even to repair particular average damage.

The process of adjustment is determined according to the law of the country in which the adventure ends, unless the contract of affreightment otherwise provides. It will therefore be seen that difficulties would arise if a general average had to be adjusted differently, according to whether the adventure ended in one country or another. For these reasons it has been recognised for a hundred years or more that it is in the interest of the maritime coummunity to regulate the adjustment of general average and so far as possible to obtain uniformity of practice by the express agreement of ship and cargo interests, in derogation of any law and practice inconsistent therewith.

This uniformity has been achieved by the almost universal practice of incorporating into the contract of affreightment a provision that general average shall be adjusted according to the York-Antwerp Rules.

The York-Antwerp Rules

The York-Antwerp Rules occupy a unique position in international maritime law. Unlike the Hague or Hague/Visby Rules regulating the law as to the carriage of goods by sea and the various Conventions relating to the limitation of Shipowners' liability (to name but two examples), they depend not upon Convention, still less upon Statute, but upon their voluntary acceptance by the maritime community. Although in a small number of instances, they have been imported into domestic legislation, the all but universal application of the York-Antwerp Rules in cases of general average has come about by their being incorporated by reference into bills of lading, contracts of affreightment and maritime insurance policies. Yet in spite of the purely consensual nature of their application, they have succeeded where other attempts to achieve international uniformity have failed.

The first steps towards international agreement on General Average were taken in 1860, and the first edition of the Rules, known as the York Rules, was drawn up in 1864. As a result of subsequent international conferences, the York Rules were extended and became the York-Antwerp Rules. The Rules were revised by subsequent conferences in 1890, 1924 and 1949 and the present version, known as the York-Antwerp Rules 1974, was approved at a conference of the Comité Maritime International held in Hamburg in March 1974.

The York-Antwerp Rules do not comprise a 'code' covering all aspects of general average; rather they provide a framework to fit or modify, as may be most desirable in the interests of uniformity, the laws and practices respecting general average in the various maritime countries of the world. This is recognised by the 'Rule of Interpretation', which, as an overture to the Rules proper, states in its first paragraph:

'In the adjustment of general average the following lettered and numbered Rules shall apply to the exclusion of any Law and Practice inconsistent therewith."

The reference to lettered and numbered Rules is explained by the desirability of setting forth a series of general principles, which are embodied in the lettered Rules, followed by a number of propositions, in rather greater detail, which deal with specific situations where, prior to the existence of the York-Antwerp Rules, the practice of different countries was at variance. The relationship between the lettered and numbered Rules is regulated by the second paragraph of the Rule of Interpretation, which reads:

"Except as provided by the numbered Rules, general average shall be adjusted according to the lettered Rules."

Adjustment

Upon the termination of the adventure the losses admissible in general average are assessed and apportioned over the net arrived values of the property saved plus the value of the sacrificed property which has been admitted in general average. It is this feature, namely the addition to the arrived value of the property saved of the amount "made good in general average" for property which has been sacrificed that preserves the equity of the apportionment by ensuring that the property sacrificed none the less makes its contribution to the general average losses, in the same way as does the property which is saved. The loss admitted in general average for the account of each of the parties to the adventure is compared with the contribution due from him, and a balance, either to be paid or to receive is arrived at. This, then, is the process of general average "adjustment".

How rights in General Average are secured

Under the laws of all maritime nations, a shipowner has a right of lien over the cargo at destination until the owner of it has paid his contribution in General Average, or the net balance due from him under the adjustment. This was no doubt the system which prevailed in the olden days, when the shipmaster and merchants arranged their own adjustment of the General Average on arrival of the ship. Subsequently, with the sophistication of maritime commerce, it became usual to entrust these calculations to an independent person, who became known as an adjuster of average, and the shipowners' right to hold the cargo was met by the owner of the cargo providing security for his eventual contribution, either by way of a cash deposit or a form of undertaking.

Under English law, a shipowner is bound to exercise his right to obtain General Average security whenever there has been a General Average sacrifice of some of the cargo interest giving rise to claims for contribution by the other interests saved. On the other hand, if the admissions in General Average concern only the sacrifices or expenditures of the shipowner, he is not bound to exercise his rights of General Average security, this is a matter for his own decision.

Nowadays General Average security is most usually provided by means of Lloyd's form of Average bond (LAB 77). This is an undertaking given by the owner of the cargo in consideration of its release from the shipwoner's right of lien, and in practice the undertaking contained in the bond is generally backed by the lodging of a General Average deposit or the provision of a guarantee from the cargo underwriters.

EEC DIRECTIVES —
TANKER CHECK LIST AND PILOTAGE

Following the grounding of the Liberian oil tanker *Amoco Cadiz* in March, 1978, resulting in heavy pollution of much of the coast of Brittany, the European Council declared at its meeting in Copenhagen or 7-8 April, 1978, that the Community should make the prevention and combating of marine pollution particularly from hydrocarbons, a major objective and invited the Council of Ministers, acting on proposals from the Commission and Member States, to take immediate and appropriate measures within the Community or within the competent international bodies. Subsequently, the Council of Environmen Ministers at its meeting on 26-27 June, 1978, adopted a Resolution setting up an Action Programme of the European Communities on the Control and Reduction of Pollution Caused by Oil Spills at Sea. The European Council at its meeting in Bremen on 6-7 July, 1978, declared that it deemed it necessary to take furthe measures to increase the safety of maritime traffic, taking into account the proposals of individual Membe States and the Commission, and re-affirmed the necessity to intensify their efforts to prevent and contro pollution of the sea, especially by hydrocarbons.

As a result of the Bremen meeting the West Germans, who at that time held the Presidency of the European Council, submitted proposals for Council Directives concerning Minimum Requirements for certair Tankers entering or leaving Community Ports, and concerning Pilotage of Vessels by Deep-Sea Pilots in the North Sea and English Channel. After negotiations, the Directives were adopted by the Council on 2 December, 1978, as Council Directives 79/116/EEC and 79/115/EEC respectively.

MINIMUM REQUIREMENT FOR CERTAIN TANKERS
ENTERING OR LEAVING COMMUNITY PORTS

Council Directive 79/116/EEC which was amended on 6 December, 1979, by Council Directive 79/1034 EEC, is commonly known as the "Tanker Check List" Directive. Its chief aim is to reduce the risk of incident involving tankers entering or leaving Member States' ports. It applies to all oil, gas and chemical tankers, c whatever flag, of 1,600 tons gross and over — whether fully or partly laden — and including those empty bu not yet "degassed or purged of vapour given off by hazardous residues". Such vessels are required to notify the competent authority of certain information before entering or leaving a seaport of a Member State.

In particular, the Directive places an obligation on the master, in advance of entering a port, to notify the (harbour) authority of any deficiencies which may decrease the normal safe manoeuvrability of the vessel affect the safety and easy flow of traffic or constitute a hazard to the marine environment or adjacent areas The master is also required to report any change which occurs in the information regarding deficiencies both before the tanker enters port and while she is within or leaving port. The other main provision of th Directive is a requirement that the master shall complete "truly and accurately" a tanker check lis concerning the status of the ship, her equipment and personnel for the information of the pilot and, i required, of the "competent authority". The check list should, inter alia, provide confirmation of deficiencie already reported.

The Directive also requires the tanker master to take certain other safety precautions, "while traversing th territorial waters adjacent to the port of entry or departure". Firstly he must, as soon as possible, establish radiotelephony communication with the coastal radio stations designated for that purpose, preferably o VHF — in particular, with the nearerst radar station, if available — and maintain such communicatior Secondly, he must make use, as far as possible, especially in conditions of restricted visibility, of the service provided by radar stations. And thirdly, he must make use of (district) pilots, in accordance with practice an with the regulations determined by the competent authoritites.

The Directive then goes on to impose a specific obligation on the pilot, requiring that if he learns that ther are any deficiencies which may prejudice the safe navigation of the vessel, he shall immediately report thes to the competent authority.

Having laid down all the foregoing requirements, the Directive then allows Member States to derogat from them where the state of navigational aids, the local situation or the traffic conditions so require c permit.

Finally, the Directive requires that any Member State, the competent authorities of which have bee informed of facts which involve or increase the risk for another Member State of a hazard being posed t certain maritime and coastal zones, shall take whatever measures are appropriate to inform the Member Sta concerned thereof as soon as possible.

Although the original "Tanker Check List" Directive was due to come into force by the end of 1979 and th amending Directive (which introduced some minor technical amendments concerned with tankers carryin chemicals or liquefied gas in bulk) by the end of 1980, they have yet to be fully implemented by all Membe

States. However, the British Government have introduced a number of measures to enable the United Kingdom to implement the Directives in full and without derogation. The obligations on the master to report certain information about his ship in advance of entering a port and to complete a tanker check list, and the obligation on the pilot to report, in certain circumstances, deficiencies in a ship under his pilotage, have been set out in the Merchant Shipping (Tankers) (EEC Requirements) Regulations 1981 (SI 1981 No. 1077), as amended by SI 1982 No. 1637. The Regulations designate the harbour authority as the "competent authority" referred to in the Directive for these purposes and provide for suitable penalties in the event of non-compliance. Authorities responsible for pilotage already determine and can enforce, regulations governing the use of pilots. The remaining requirements of the Directive have been implemented administratively and the measures impinging on shipowners and masters are described in Merchant Shipping Notice No. M 988.

PILOTAGE OF VESSELS BY DEEP SEA PILOTS IN THE NORTH SEA AND ENGLISH CHANNEL

The EEC Directive requires Member States which have coasts bordering on the North Sea or English Channel to take all necessary and appropriate measures to ensure that vessels availing themselves of the services of a deep sea pilot for pilotage in the North Sea or the English Channel be provided with adequately qualified deep sea pilots in possession of a certificate delivered by a competent authority of one of the Member States certifying that such pilots are qualified to pilot vessels in the North Sea and English Channel.

Each Member State is asked to take all necessary and appropriate measures to encourage vessels flying its national flag to avail themselves, in the English Channel and the North Sea, of the services of only those deep sea pilots who are in possession of a certificate as referred to above, or of an equivalent certificate delivered by another North Sea coastal State, when seeking the assistance of deep sea pilots.

The Directive arises from the fact that (by the nature of their operations mainly outside territorial waters) there is no statutory restriction on anyone offering their services as a deep sea pilot, whether qualified to do so or not. However, under UK legislation (Pilotage Act 1987), these authorities deemed competent, and duly authorised to do so, may grant deep sea certificates to persons who they consider qualified to act as pilots for areas of the sea outside the harbour of any authority which is a competent harbour authority within the meaning of the 1987 Act (though having no right to supersede any other person as pilot of a ship). The limits of the area or areas covered would be specified in the certificate. This does not preclude district (or harbour) pilots from also being certified as deep sea pilots.

In the United Kingdom there are four authorities which are deemed competent to grant deep sea certificates. These authorities follow the "Rules and Regulations for the Good Government of Deep-Sea Pilotage in the North Sea and English Channel" promulgated by the North Sea Pilotage Commission. This ensures that those who hold certificates granted by such authorities are adequately qualified in terms of the Council Directive.

In view of this, the UK Government decided to implement the EEC Directive by administrative means without further legislation. The Department of Trade issued a Merchant Shipping Notice ('M' Notice) M. 1001 in January 1982 for the attention of Masters and Shipowners, drawing attention to the Directive and to the means by which Masters can acquire the services of pilots in possession of deep sea certificates granted by the competent authorities in the UK and other Member States bordering on the North Sea and English Channel. The Notice includes specified information about whom to contact and where deep sea pilots usually board and disembark. By the time of publication a further M Notice, to supersede M. 1001, will have been issued. This Notice reflects the changes which took place in pilotage organisation during 1988 and in particular provides updated information concerning competent authorities in the UK.

The EEC Directive does not introduce compulsory deep sea pilotage. Whatever may be its merits, such a step presents considerable legal and practical problems, and could not be operated at this stage.

CARRIAGE OF GOODS BY SEA ACT, 1971

This Act came into force on the appointed day, 23 June 1977, pursuant to the issue of The Carriage of Goods by Sea Act 1971 (Commencement) Order 1977 made on 8 June 1977. The 1971 Act was enacted to enable effect to be given to the Rules known as the Hague-Visby Rules, the 1968 Protocol to the International Convention for the Unification of certain Rules of Law relating to Bills of lading 1924 (Cmnd. 3743) ("the Hague Rules"), which was ratified by the United Kingdom and came into force on the same day as the appointed day. The 1971 Act containing the Hague-Visby Rules repeals the Carriage of Goods by Sea Act 1924 containing the Hague Rules before amendment by the Protocol.

An Act to amend the law with respect to the carriage of goods by sea.   (8th April 1971).

Be it enacted by the Queen's most Excellent Majesty, by and with the advice and consent of the Lords Spiritual and Temporal, and Commons, in this present Parliament assembled, and by the authority of the same, as follows:-

Section 1 — Application of Hague Rules as amended

(1) In this Act, "the Rules" means the International Convention for the unification of certain rules of law relating to bills of lading signed at Brussels on 25 August 1924, as amended by the Protocol signed at Brussels on 23 February 1968 (and by the Protocol signed at Brussels on 21 December 1979).

(2) The provisions of the Rules, as set out in the Schedule to this Act, shall have the force of law.

(3) Without prejudice to subsection (2) above, the said provisions shall have effect (and have the force of law) in relation to and in connection with the carriage of goods by sea in ships where the port of shipment is a port in the United Kingdom, whether or not the carriage is between ports in two different States within the meaning of Article X of the Rules.

(4) Subject to subsection (6) below, nothing in this section shall be taken as applying anything in the Rules to any contract for the carriage of goods by sea, unless the contract expressly or by implication provides for the issue of a bill of lading or any similar document of title.

(5) (Repealed).

(6) Without prejudice to Article X(c) of the Rules, the Rules shall have the force of law in relation to—

  (a) any bill of lading if the contract gained in or evidenced by it expressly provides that the Rules shall govern the contract, and

  (b) any receipt which is a non-negotiable document marked as such if the contract contained in, or evidenced by it is a contract for the carriage of goods by sea which expressly provides that the Rules are to govern the contract as if the receipt were a bill of lading.

but subject, where paragraph (b) applies, to any necessary modifications and in particular with the ommision in Article III of the Rules of the second sentence of paragraph 4 and of paragraph 7.

(7) If and so far as the contract contained in or evidence by a bill of lading or receipt within paragraph (a) or (b) or sub-section (6) above applies to deck cargo or live animals, the Rule as given the force of law by that subsection shall have effect as if Article I(c) did not exclude deck cargo and live animals.

In this subsection "deck cargo" means cargo which by the contract of carriage is stated as being carried on deck and is so carried.

Section 2 — Contracting States, etc.

(1) If Her Majesty by Order in Council certifies to the following effect, that is to say, that for the purposes of the Rules —

  (a) A State specified in the Order is a contracting State, or is a contracting State in respect of any place or territory so specified;

  or

  (b) any place or territory specified in the Order forms part of a State so specified (whether a contracting State or not),

the Order shall, except so far as it has been superseded by a subsequent Order, be conclusive evidence of the matters so certified.

(2) An Order in Council under this section may be varied or revoked by a subsequent Order in Council.

Section 3 — Absolute warranty of seaworthiness not to be implied in contracts to which Rules apply.

There shall not be implied in any contract for the carriage of goods by sea to which the Rules apply by virtue of this Act any absolute undertaking by the carrier of the goods to provide a seaworthy ship.

Section 4 — Application of Act to British possessions, etc.

(1) Her Majesty may by Order in Council direct that this Act shall extend, subject to such exceptions, adaptations and modifications as may be specified in the Order, to all or any of the following territories, that is —

(a) any colony (not being a colony for whose external relations a country other than the United Kingdom is responsible).

(b) any country outside her Majesty's dominions in which Her Majesty has jurisdiction in right of Her Majesty's Government of the United Kingdom.

(2) An Order in Council under this section may contain such transitional and other consequential and incidental provisions as appear to Her Majesty to be expedient, including provisions amending or repealing any legislation about the carriage of goods by sea forming part of the law of any of the territories mentioned in paragraphs (a) and (b) above.

(3) An Order in Council under this section may be varied or revoked by a subsequent Order in Council.

Section 5 — Extension of application of Rules to carriage from ports in British possessions, etc.

(1) Her Majesty may by Order in Council provide that section 1(3) of this Act shall have effect as if the reference therein to the United Kingdom included a reference to all or any of the following territories, that is —

(a) the Isle of Man;

(b) any of the Channel Islands specified in the Order;

(c) any colony specified in the order (not being a colony for whose external relations a country other than the United Kingdom is responsible);

d) any associated state (as defined by section 1(3) of the West Indies Act 1967) specified in the Order;

(e) any country specified in the Order, being a country outside Her Majesty's dominions in which Her Majesty has jurisdiction in right of Her Majesty's Government of the United Kingdom.

(2) An Order in Council under this section may be varied or revoked by a subsequent Order in Council.

Section 6 — Supplemental

(1) This Act may be cited as the Carriage of Goods by Sea Act 1971.

(2) It is hereby declared that this Act extends to Northern Ireland.

(3) The following enactments shall be repealed, that is —

(a) the Carriage of goods by Sea Act 1924,

(b) section 12(4)(a) of the Nuclear Installations Act 1965,

and without prejudice to section 38(1) of the interpretation Act 1889 the reference to the said Act of 1924 in section 1(1)(i)(ii) of the Hovercraft Act 1968 shall include a reference to this Act.

(4) It is hereby declared that for the purposes of Article VIII of the Rules (section 18 of the Merchant Shipping Act 1979 (which) entirely exempts shipowners and others in certain circumstances from liability for loss of, or damage to, goods) is a provision relating to limitation of liability.

(5) This Act shall come into force on such day as Her Majesty may by Order in Council appoint and, for the purpose of the transition from the law in force immediately before the day appointed under this subsection to the provisions of this Act, the Order appointing the day may provide that those provisions shall have effect subject to such transitional provisions as may be contained in the order.

SCHEDULE

THE HAGUE RULES AS AMENDED BY THE BRUSSELS PROTOCOL 1968
ARTICLE 1

In these Rules the following words are employed, with the meanings set out below:-

    (a) "Carrier" includes the owner or the charterer who enters into a contract of carriage with a shipper.

    (b) "Contract of carriage" applies only to contracts of carriage covered by a bill of lading or any similar document of title, in so far as such document relates to the carriage of goods by sea, including any bill of lading-or any similar document as aforesaid issued under or pursuant to a charter party from the moment at which such bill of lading or similar document of title regulates the relations between a carrier and a holder of the same.

    (c) "Goods" includes goods, wares, merchandise, and articles of every kind whatsoever except live animals and cargo which by the contract of carriage is stated as being carried on deck and is so carried.

    (d) "Ship" means any vessel used for the carriage of goods by sea.

    (e) "Carriage of goods" covers the period from the time when the goods are loaded on to the time they are discharged from the ship.

ARTICLE II

Subject to the provisions of Article VI, under every contract of carriage of goods by sea the carrier, in relation to the loading, handling, stowage, carriage, custody, care and discharge of such goods, shall be subject to the responsibilities and liabilities, and entitled to the rights and immunities hereinafter set forth.

ARTICLE III

1. The carrier shall be bound before and at the beginning of the voyage to exercise due diligence to—

    (a) Make the ship seaworthy.

    (b) Properly man, equip and supply the ship.

    (c) Make the holds, refrigerating and cool chambers, and all other parts of the ship in which goods are carried, fit and safe for their reception, carriage and preservation.

2. Subject to the provisions of Article IV, the carrier shall properly and carefully load, handle, stow, carry, keep, care for, and discharge the goods carried.

3. After receiving the goods into his charge the carrier shall, on demand of the shipper, issue to the shipper a bill of lading showing among other things —

    (a) The leading marks necessary for identification of the goods as the same as furnished in writing by the shipper before the loading of such goods starts, provided such marks are stamped or otherwise shown clearly upon the goods if uncovered, or on the cases or coverings in which such goods are contained, in such a manner as should ordinarily remain legible until the end of the voyage.

    (b) Either the number of packages or pieces, or the quantity, or weight, as the case may be, as furnished in writing by the shipper.

    (c) The apparent order and condition of the goods.

Provided that no carrier, master or agent of the carrier shall be bound to state or show in the bill of lading any marks, number, quantity, or weight he has reasonable ground for suspecting not accurately to represent the goods actually received, or which he has had no reasonable means of checking.

4. Such a bill of lading shall be *prima facie* evidence of the receipt by the carrier of the goods as therein described in accordance with paragraph 3(a), (b) and (c). However, proof to the contrary shall not be admissible when the bill of lading has been transferred to a third party acting in good faith.

5. The shipper shall be deemed to have guaranteed to the carrier the accuracy at the time of shipment of the marks, number, quantity and weight, as furnished by him, and the shipper shall indemnify the carrier against all loss, damages and expenses arising or resulting from inaccuracies in such particulars. The right of the carrier to such indemnity shall in no way limit his responsibility and liability under the contract of carriage to any person other than the shipper.

6. Unless notice of loss or damage and the general nature of such loss or damage be given in writing to the carrier or his agent at the port of discharge before or at the time of the removal of the goods into

the custody of the person entitled to delivery thereof under the contract of carriage, or, if the loss or damage be not apparent, within three days, such removal shall be *prima facie* evidence of the delivery by the carrier of the goods as described in the bill of lading.

The notice in writing need not be given if the state of the goods has, at the time of their receipt, been the subject of joint survey or inspection.

Subject to paragraph 6 *bis* the carrier and the ship in any event be discharged from all liability whatsoever in respect of the goods, unless suit is brought within one year of their delivery or of the date when they should have been delivered. This period may, however, be extended if the parties so agree after the cause of action has arisen.

In the case of any actual or apprehended loss or damage the carrier and the receiver shall give all responsible facilities to each other for inspecting and tallying the goods.

6 *bis*. An action for indemnity against a third person may be brought even after the expiration of the year provided for in the preceding paragraph if brought within the time allowed by the law of the Court seized of the case. However, the time allowed shall be not less than three months, commencing from the day when the person bringing such action for indemnity has settled the claim or had been served with process in the action against himself.

7. After the goods are loaded the bill of lading to be issued by the carrier, master, or agent of the carrier, to the shipper shall, if the shipper so demands, be a "shipped" bill of lading, provided that if the shipper shall have previously taken up any document of title to such goods, he shall surrender the same as against the issue of the "shipped" bill of lading, but at the option of the carrier such document of title may be noted at the port of shipment by the carrier, master or agent with the name or names of the ship or ships upon which the goods have been shipped and the date or dates of shipment, and when so noted, if it shows the particulars mentioned in paragraph 3 of Article III, shall for the purpose of this article be deemed to consitute a "shipped" bill of lading.

8. Any clause, covenant, or agreement in a contract of carriage relieving the carrier or the ship from liability for loss or damage to, or in connection with, goods arising from negligence, fault, or failure in the duties and obligations provided in this article or lessening such liability otherwise than as provided in these Rules, shall be null and void and of no effect. A benefit of insurance in favour of the carrier or similar clause shall be deemed to be a clause relieving the carrier from liability.

2. Neither the carrier nor the ship shall be responsible for loss or damage arising or resulting from —

   (a) Act, neglect, or default of the master, mariner, pilot, or the servants of the carrier in the navigation or in the management of the ship.

(b) Fire, unless caused by the actual fault or privity of the carrier.

(c) Perils, dangers and accidents of the sea or other navigable waters.

(d) Act of God.

(e) Act of war.

(f) Act of public enemies.

(g) Arrest or restraint of princes, rulers or people, or seizure under legal process.

(h) Quarantine restrictions.

(i) Act or omission of the shipper or owner of the goods, his agent or representative.

(j) Strikes or lock-outs or stoppage or restraint of labour from whatever cause whether partial or general.

(k) Riots and civil commotions.

(l) Saving or attempting to save life or property at sea.

(m) Wastage in bulk or weight or any other loss or damage arising from inherent defects, quality or vice of the goods.

(n) Insufficiency of packing.

(o) Insufficiency or inadequacy of marks.

(p) Latent defects not discoverable by due diligence.

(q) Any other cause arising without the actual fault or privity of the carrier, or without the fault or neglect of the agents or servants of the carrier, but the burden of proof shall be on the person claiming the benefit of this exception to show that neither the actual fault or privity of the carrier nor the fault or neglect of the agents or servants of the carrier contributed to the loss or damage.

3. The shipper shall not be responsible for loss or damage sustained by the carrier or the ship arising or resulting from any cause without the act, fault or neglect of the shipper, his agents or his servants.

4. Any deviation in saving or attempting to save life or property at sea or any reasonable deviation shall not be deemed to be an infringement or breach of these Rules or of the contract of carriage, and the carrier shall not be liable for any loss or damage resulting therefrom.

5. (a) Unless the nature and value of such goods have been declared by the shipper before shipment and inserted in the bill of lading, neither the carrier nor the ship shall in any event be or become liable for any loss or damage to or in connection with the goods in an amount exceeding (666.67 units of account) per package or unit or (2 units of account per kilogramme) of gross weight of the goods lost or damaged, whichever is the higher.

(b) The total amount recoverable shall be calculated by reference to the value of such goods at the place and time at which goods are discharged from the ship in accordance with the contract or should have been so discharged.

The value of the goods shall be fixed according to the commodity exchange price or, if there be no such price, according to the current market price, or, if there be no commodity exchange price or current market price, by reference to the normal value of goods of the same kind and quality.

(c) Where a container, pallet or similar article of transport is used to consolidate goods, the number of packages or units enumerated in the bill of lading as packed in such article of transport shall be deemed the number of packages or units for the purpose of this paragraph as far as these packages or units are concerned. Except as aforesaid such article of transport shall be considered the package or unit.

(d) The unit of account mentioned in this Article is the special drawing right as defined by the International Monetary Fund. The amounts mentioned in sub-paragraph (a) of this paragraph shall be converted into national currency on the basis of the value of that currency on a date to be determined by the law of the Court seized of the case.

(e) Neither the carrier nor the ship be entitled to the benefit of the limitation of liability provided for in this paragraph if it is proved that the damage resulted from an act or omission of the carrier done with intent to cause damage, or recklessly and with knowledge that damage would probably result.

ARTICLE IV

1. Neither the carrier nor the ship shall be liable for loss or damage arising or resulting from

unseaworthiness unless caused by want of due diligence on the part of the carrier to make the ship seaworthy, and to secure that the ship is properly manned, equipped and supplied, and to make the holds, refrigerating and cool chambers and all other parts of the ship in which goods are carried fit and safe for their reception, carriage and preservation in accordance with the provisions of paragraph 1 of Article III. Whenever loss or damage has resulted from unseaworthiness the burden of providing the exercise of due diligence shall be on the carrier or other person claiming exemption under this article.

(f) The declaration mentioned in sub-paragraph (a) of this paragraph, if embodied in the bill of lading, shall be *prima facie* evidence, but shall not be binding or conclusive on the carrier.

(g) By agreement between the carrier, master or agent of the carrier and the shipper other maximum amounts than those mentioned in sub-paragraph (a) of this paragraph may be fixed, provided that no maximum amount so fixed shall be less than the appropriate maximum mentioned in that sub-paragraph.

(h) Neither the carrier nor the ship shall be responsible in any event for loss or damage to, or in connection with, goods if the nature or value thereof has been knowingly mis-stated by the shipper in the bill of lading.

6. Goods of an inflammable, explosive or dangerous nature to the shipment whereof the carrier, master or agent of the carrier has not consented with knowledge of their nature and character, may at any time before discharge be landed at any place, or destroyed or rendered innocuous by the carrier without compensation and the shipper of such goods shall be liable for all damages and expenses directly or indirectly arising out of or resulting from such shipment. If any such goods shipped with such knowledge and consent shall become a danger to the ship or cargo, they may in like manner be landed at any place, or destroyed or rendered innocuous by the carrier except to general average, if any.

ARTICLE IV BIS

1. The defences and limits of liability provided for in these Rules shall apply in any action against the carrier in respect of loss or damage to goods covered by a contract of carriage whether the action be founded in contract or in tort.

2. If such an action is brought against a servant or agent of the carrier (such servant or agent not being an independent contractor), such servant or agent shall be entitled to avail himself of the defences and limits of liability which the carrier is entitled to invoke under these Rules.

3. The aggregate of the amounts recoverable from the carrier, and such servants and agents, shall in no case exceed the limit provided for in these Rules.

4. Nevertheless, a servant or agent of the carrier shall not be entitled to avail himself of the provisions of this article, if it is proved that the damage resulted from an act or omission of the servant or agent done with intent to cause damage or recklessly and with knowledge that damage would probably result.

ARTICLE V

A carrier shall be at liberty to surrender in whole or in part all or any of his rights and immunities or to increase any of his responsibilities and obligations under these Rules, provided such surrender or increase shall be embodied in the bill of lading issued to the shipper. The provisions of these Rules shall not be applicable to charter parties, but if bills of lading are issued in the case of a ship under a charter party they shall comply with the terms of these Rules. Nothing in these Rules shall be held to prevent the insertion in a bill of lading of any lawful provision regarding general average.

ARTICLE VI

Notwithstanding the provisions of preceding articles, a carrier, master or agent of the carrier and a shipper shall in regard to any particular goods be at liberty to enter into any agreement in any terms as to the responsibility and liability of the carrier for such goods, and as to the rights and immunities of the carrier in respect of such goods, or his obligations as to seaworthiness, so far as this stipulation is not contrary to public policy, or the care or diligence of his servants or agents in regard to the loading, handling, stowage, carriage, custody, care and discharge of the goods carried by sea, provided that in this case no bill of lading has been or shall be issued and that the terms agreed shall be embodied in a receipt which shall be a non-negotiable document and shall be marked as such.

Any agreement so entered into shall have full legal effect.

Provided that this Article shall not apply to ordinary commercial shipments made in the ordinary course of trade, but only to order shipments where the character of condition of the property to be carried or the circumstances, terms and conditions under which the carriage is to be performed are such as reasonably to justify a special agreement.

ARTICLE VII

Nothing herein contained shall prevent a carrier or a shipper from entering into any agreement, stipulation, condition, reservation or exemption as to the responsibility and liability of the carrier or the ship for loss or damage to, or in connection with, the custody and care and handling of goods prior to the loading on, and subsequent to the discharge from the ship on which the goods are carried by sea.

ARTICLE VIII

The provisions of these Rules shall not affect the rights and obligations of the carrier under any atue for the time being in force relating to the limitation of the liability of owners of sea-going ssels.

ARTICLE IX

These Rules shall not affect the provisions of any international Convention or national law governing liability for nuclear damage.

ARTICLE X

The provisions of these Rules shall apply to every bill of lading relating to the carriage of goods between ports in two differrent States if:

(a) the bill of lading is issued in a contracting State,

or

(b) the carriage is from a port in a contracting State,

or

(c) the contract contained in or evidenced by the bill of lading provides that these Rules or legislation of any State giving effect to them are to govern the contract.

whatever may be the nationality of a ship, the carrier, the shipper, the consignee, or any other interested person.

(The last two paragraphs of this article are not reproduced. They require contracting States to apply the Rules to bills of lading mentioned in the article and authorised them to apply the Rules to other bills of lading.)

(Articles 11 to 16 of the International Convention for the unification of certain rules of law relating to bills of lading signed at Brussels on 25 August 1924 are not reproduced. They deal with the coming into force of the Convention, procedure for ratification, accession and denunciation, and the right to call for a fresh conference to consider amendments to the Rules contained in the Convention.)

Note:- Conversion of special drawing rights into sterling

(1) For the purposes of Article IV of the Rules set out in the Schedule to the Carriage of Goods by Sea Act 1971 as amended, the value on a particular day of one special drawing right shall be treated as equal to such a sum in sterling as the International Monetary Fund have fixed as being the equivalent of one special drawing right

    (a) for that day; or

    (b) if no sum has been fixed for that day, for the last day before that day for which a sum has been so fixed.

(2) A certificate given by or on behalf of the Treasury stating

    (a) that a particular sum in sterling has been fixed as aforesaid for a particular day; or

    (b) that no sum has been so fixed for a particular day and that a particular sum in sterling has been so fixed for a day which is the last day for which a sum has been so fixed before the particular day,

shall be conclusive evidence of those matters for the purposes of subsection (1) above; and a document purporting to be such a certificate shall in any proceedings be received in evidence and, unless the contrary is proved, be deemed to be such a certificate.

(3) The Treasury may charge a reasonable fee for any certificate given in pursuance of subsection (2) above, and any fee received by the Treasury by virtue of this subsection shall be paid into the Consolidated Fund.

MERCHANT SHIPPING NOTICES AND PRINCIPAL ACTS AND REGULATIONS ON MERCHANT SHIPPING

DEPARTMENT OF TRANSPORT

A review has been made of all notices isued in the Merchant Shipping Notices series and the following list shows the notices which were current at 30 April 1988, with amendments to January 1989. Two Appendices follow the main list. The M Notices marked with an asterisk are referred to in Appendix I to the numerical list; those marked † have a subsequent amendment. Appendix II lists Merchant Shipping Notices taken out of circulation since the publication of M.1287.

The list has been reproduced with permission, from Merchant Shiping Notice No M.1342 which supersedes that contained in Notice No M.1287.

A three volume set of M Notices consolidated to April 1987 is published by Her Majesty's Stationery Office, price £55, ISBN 0 11 550849 X. With over 300 Notices in force it is hoped that the production of this bound set will enable the information contained in M Notices to be disseminated more efficiently. The set will be kept up to date with annual supplements.

Notice No.	Subject	Date of Issue/Reprint
443	Fire in engine rooms	July 1975
474	Explosions in diesel engined vessels	September 1973
588	Engine room gantry cranes	July 1970
590	Dredger safety. Exclusion of water from void spaces	August 1970
620	Adjustment of boiler safety valves	October 1971
622	Miscellaneous opening in freeboard and super-structure decks, spurling pipes	October 1971
627	Simplified stability information for small ships	November 1971
631	Corrosion of copper pipes in the engine cooling system of inshore fishing vessels	February 1971
646	Toxic substances in electronic devices	October 1972
651	Fires involving lubricating oil	December 1972
662	Lists of crew	July 1973
673	Petrol in the fuel tanks of motor vehicles carried in roll-on/roll-off ferries.	January 1974
677	Amendment to M.673	February 1974
681	Fixed fire smothering gas installations: siting precautions for CO_2 cylinders	May 1974
686	Employment of Pakistani nationals as Masters or Ships' Officers	June 1974
687	Ships engaged in the carriage of timber	July 1974
699	Safety of beam trawlers and other fishing vessels	November 1974
700	Oil pollution prevention on tankers, separation of cargo oil piping system from the sea	November 1974
704	Radio aerial lead-ins	November 1974
705	The Merchant Shipping (Radio) (Fishing Vessels) Rules 1974	January 1975
709	Fire fighting on small cargo ships	April 1975
712	Shattering of windows in heavy weather	May 1975
718	Mooring, towing, hauling equipment on all ships	May 1975
719	Guide to the fishing industry on documents required by law to be maintained: vessels of 40 feet (12 metres) or more in length but less than 55 feet (16.8 metres)	July 1975
748	Safety of tugs while towing	February 1976
752	Safety: electric shock hazard in the use of electric arc welding plant	March 1976
757	Employer's Liability (Compulsory Insurance) Act 1969	August 1976
760	Tinted glass for wheel-house and bridge front wwindows	June 1976
764	Dispensations: fire-fighting training	June 1976
765	Maintenance and ready availability of fire appliances	June 1976
776	Inspection of ships' provisions under the Merchant Shipping Acts	September 1976
780	Issue of AB and efficient deck hand certificates	October 1976
781	Manning of oil rig supply vessels	October 1976
782	Polyurethane foam and other organic foam materials	November 1976
787	Disposal of out-of-date pyrotechnics	November 1976

As can be seen, from time to time Merchant Shipping Notices are issued out of sequence. Please do not contact the Department if this happens; the missing numbers will be issued in due course.

APPENDIX I TO MERCHANT SHIPPING NOTICE NO. M. 1287

Merchant Shipping Notices which are marked with an asterisk in the Main List are those directly related to regulations made under Section 21 of the Merchant Shipping Act 1979, and should be read in association with the regulations shown below:

Notice No.	Regulation Title	Statutory Instrument
898	Merchant Shipping (Pilot Ladders and Hoists) Regulations 1980 — Regs. 5(4), 6(2)(b) and 7(5)	1980/543
928	Merchant Shipping (Radio Installations) Regulations 1980 — Regs. 3(4)(a) and (b)	1980/529
(as amended by 948)		
932	Merchant Shipping (Passenger Ship Construction) Regulations 1980 — Reg. 41(2)	1980/535
(as amended by 945)		
963	Merchant Shipping (Cargo Ship Safety Equipment Survey) Regulations 1981 — Reg. 4(4)	1981/573
965	Merchant Shipping (Cargo Ship Construction and Survey) Regulations 1981 — Reg. 5	1981/572
981	Merchant Shipping (Certification of Ships' Cooks) Regulations 1984 — Reg. 2	1981/1076
1091	Merchant Shipping (Tankers — Officers and Ratings) Regulations 1984 — Reg. 2	1984/94
1092	Merchant Shipping (Certificates of Proficiency in Survival Craft) Regulations 1984 — Reg. 1(3)	1984/97
1095	Merchant Shipping (Engine Room Watch Ratings) Regulations 1984 — Reg. 2	1984/95
1096	Merchant Shipping (Navigational Watch Ratings) Regulations 1984 — Reg.2	1984/96
1102	Merchant Shipping (Certification and Watchkeeping) Regulations 1982 — Reg. 2(1)	1982/1699
1103	Merchant Shipping (Certification and Watchkeeping) Regulations 1982 — Regs. 2(1) and 5	1982/1699
1104	Merchant Shipping (Certification and Watchkeeping) Regulations 1982 — Schedule 2	1982/1699
1119	Merchant Shipping (Radio Installations) Regulations 1980	1980/529
1123	Merchant Shipping (Radio Installations) (Amendment) Regulations 1984	1984/346
1124	Merchant Shipping (Dangerous Goods) Regulations 1981 — Reg. 1(3)	1981/1747
1125	Merchant Shipping (Certification of Marine Engineer Officers) Regulations 1980 — Reg. 9(2)	1980/2025
	and Merchant Shipping (Certification of Deck Officers) Regulations 1980 — Reg. 9(2)	1980/2026

APPENDIX II TO MERCHANT SHIPPING NOTICE NO. M.1342

The following Merchant Shipping Notices which appeared in M.1287 have been taken out of circulation:

Notice Numbers: 524, 654, 659, 694, 720, 721, 739, 830, 831, 834, 878, 929, 935, 942, 952, 977, 986, 990, 998, 1000, 1002, 1003, 1009, 1029, 1043, 1046, 1049, 1062, 1063, 1064, 1065, 1066, 1071, 1081, 1087, 1106, 1107, 1183, 1222, 1223, 1224, 1225, 1230, 1241 and 1265.

PRINCIPAL ACTS AND REGULATIONS ON MERCHANT SHIPPING

The list of Principal Acts and Regulations on Merchant Shipping has been revised. The new list, covering crew matters, navigation, ship construction and equipment in UK ships has been updated to February 1989.

This material has been reproduced, with permission, from Merchant Shipping Notice No. M.1370 and supersedes previous Notices.

All Acts and Statutory Instruments in force can be purchased from Her Majesty's Stationery Office (HMSO) in London, Belfast, Birmingham, Bristol, Edinburgh or Manchester.

Statutory Instruments concerning offshore installations are issued by the Department of Energy and are not listed in this notice. The Continental Shelf Act (1964, C.29) and ensuing Statutory Instruments and Orders are available from HMSO under the headings:

Offshore Installations

The Continental Shelf (Protection of Installations) Orders.

Inquiries concerning Merchant Shipping Notices and further information about Merchant Shipping Publications should be addressed to Marine Library, Department of Transport, Sunley House, 90 High Holborn, London WC1V 6LP, England, the Department's Marine Offices at various ports throughout the United Kingdom or HMSO bookshops in Belfast, Birmingham, Bristol, Edinburgh or Manchester.

PRINCIPAL MERCHANT SHIPPING ACTS

1894 ch 60	Merchant Shipping Act
1906 ch 48	Merchant Shipping Act
1921 ch 28	Merchant Shipping Act
1932 ch 9	Merchant Shipping (Safety and Load Line Conventions) Act
1949 ch 43	Merchant Shipping (Safety Convention) Act
1950 ch 9	Merchant Shipping Act
1964 ch 47	Merchant Shipping Act
1965 ch 47	Merchant Shipping Act
1967 ch 27	Merchant Shipping (Load Lines) Act
1967 ch 64	Anchors and Chain Cables Act
1968 ch 59	Hovercraft Act
1970 ch 27	Fishing Vessels (Safety Provisions) Act
1970 ch 36	Merchant Shipping Act
1971 ch 59	Merchant Shipping (Oil Pollution) Act
1971 ch 60	Preventions of Oil Pollution Act
1974 ch 20	Dumping at Sea Act
1974 ch 43	Merchant Shipping Act
1977 ch 24	Merchant Shipping (Safety Convention) Act
1979 ch 39	Merchant Shipping Act
1981 ch 10	Merchant Shipping Act
1982 ch 37	Merchant Shipping (Liner Conferences) Act
1982 ch 13	Merchant Shipping Act
1983 ch 21	Pilotage Act
1984 ch 5	Merchant Shipping Act
1985 ch 22	Dangerous Vessels Act
1986 ch 6	Prevention of Oil Pollution Act
1986 ch 23	Safety at Sea Act
1988 ch 12	Merchant Shipping Act

(1) Commencement Orders

1971 No. 1423	(C.36) MS (Oil Pollution) Act 1971 (Commencement) Order
1972 No. 979	(C.15) Hovercraft Act 1968 (Commencement) Order
1972 No. 1977	C.44) MS Act 1970 (Commencement No. 1) Order
1973 No. 203	(C.60) Prevention of Oil Pollution Act 1971 (Commencement) Order
1974 No. 1194	(C.23) MS Act 1970 (Commencement No. 2) Order
1974 No. 1792	(C.31) MS Act 1974 (Commencement No. 1) Order
1974 No. 1908	(C.32) MS Act 1970 (Commencement No. 3) Order
1975 No. 866	(C.25) MS Act 1974 (Commencement No. 2) Order

1975 No. 867	(C.26) MS (Oil Pollution) Act 1971 (Commencement No.2) Order
1975 No. 2156	MS Act 1970 (Commencement No. 4) Order
1978 No. 797	(C.19) MS Act 1970 (Commencement No. 5) Order
1978 No. 1466	(C.41) MS Act 1974 (Commencement No. 3) Order
1979 No. 807	(C.19) MS Act 1979 (Commencement No. 1) Order
1979 No. 808	(C.20) MS Act 1974 (Commencement No. 4) Order
1979 No. 809	(C.21) MS Act 1970 (Commencement No. 6) Order
1979 No. 1578	(C.37) MS Act 1979 (Commencement No. 2) Order
1980 No. 354	(C.13) MS Act 1979 (Commencement No. 3) Order
1980 No. 528	(C.21) MS Safety Convention Act 1977 (Commencement) Order
1980 No. 923	(C.37) MS Act 1979 (Commencement No. 4) Order
1981 No. 405	(C.10) MS Act 1979 (Commencement No. 5) Order
1981 No. 1186	(C.23) MS Act 1970 (Commencement No. 7) Order
1982 No. 840	(C.21) MS Act 1970 (Commencement No. 8) Order
1982 No. 1616	(C.49) MS Act 1979 (Commencement No. 6) Order
1982 No. 1617	(C.50) MS Act 1970 (Commencement No. 9) Order
1983 No. 440	(C.15) MS Act 1979 (Commencement No. 7) Order
1983 No. 1312	(C.37) MS Act 1979 (Commencement No. 8) Order
1983 No. 1435	(C.40) MS Act 1983 (Commencement No. 1) Order
1983 No. 1601	(C.46) MS Act 1983 (Commencement No. 2) Order
1983 No. 1906	(C.52) MS Act 1981 (Commencement No. 2) Order
1985 No. 182	(C.4) MS Liner Conferences Act 1982 (Commencement) Order
1985 No. 1827	(C.42) MS Act 1979 (Commencement No. 9) Order
1986 No. 1052	(C.28) MS Act 1979 (Commencement No. 10) Order
1986 No. 1759	(C.61) MS The Safety at Sea Act 1986 (Commencement No. 1) Order
1986 No. 2066	(C.79) MS Act 1970 (Commencement No. 10) Order
1987 No. 635	(C.16) MS Act 1979 (Commencement No. 11) Order
1987 No. 719	(C.18) MS Act 1979 (Commencement No. 12) Order
1988 No. 1010	(C.32) MS The Merchant Shipping Act 1988 (Commencement No. 1) Order
1988 No. 1907	(C.71) MS The Merchant Shipping Act 1988 (Commencement No.2) Order

(2) **General**

1960 No. 1477	MS (Passenger Returns) Regulations
1972 No. 1876	MS (Unregistered Ships) Regulations
1973 No. 1979	MS (Metrication) Regulations
1979 No. 341	MS (Ships' Names) Regulations
1979 No. 1519	MS (Increased Penalties) Regulations
1979 No. 1577	MS (Returns of Births and Deaths) Regulations
1980 No. 531	MS (Safety Convention) (Transitional Provisions) Regulations
1980 No. 539	MS (Modification of Merchant Shipping (Safety Convention) Act 1949 and Merchant Shipping Act 1964) Regulations
1981 No. 237	MS (Safety Convention 1974) (Countries) Order
1981 No. 354	MS (Light Dues) Regulations
1981 No. 568	MS (Modification of Enactments) Regulations
1981 No. 584	MS (Safety Convention) (Transitional Provisions) Regulations
1982 No. 1752	MS (Section 52 Inquiries) Rules
1983 No. 1470	MS (Small Ships Register) Regulations
1985 No. 212	MS (Modification of Enactments) Regulations
1985 No. 405	MS (Liner Conferences) (Conditions for Recognition) Regulations
1985 No. 406	MS (Liner Conferences) (Mandatory Provisions) Regulations
1985 No. 1001	MS (Formal Investigations) Rules
1986 No. 1777	MS (Sterling Equivalent) (Various Enactments) Order
1986 No. 1932	MS (Liability of Shipowners and Others) (Rate of Interest) Order
1986 No. 2038	MS (Sterling Equivalents) (Various Enactments) (Amendment) Order
1986 No. 2224	MS (Limitations of Liability for Maritime Claims) (Parties to Convention) Order
1987 No. 670	MS Carriage of Passengers and Their Luggage by Sea (Domestic Carriage) Order
1987 No. 703	MS Carriage of Passengers and Their Luggage by Sea (Notice) Order
1987 No. 746	MS (Light Dues) (Amendment No. 2) Regulations
1987 No. 855	MS Carriage of Passengers and Their Luggage by Sea (United Kingdom Carriers) Order
1988 No. 191	MS (Passenger Boarding Cards) Regulations
1988 No. 297	MS The Pilotage Commission Provision of Funds Scheme 1988 (Confirmation) Order
1988 No. 330	MS (Light Dues) (Amendment) Regulations

1988 No. 641	MS (Passenger Boarding Cards) (Application to non-United Kingdom Ships) Regulations
1988 No. 1899	MS (Protection of Shipping and Trading Interests) USSR (Revocation) Order
1988 No. 2001	MS (Ships' Names) (Amendment) Regulations
1988 No. 2251	MS (Categorisation of Registries of Overseas Territories) Order
1989 No. 84	MS (Section 52 Inquiries) Rules (Amendment) Rules

(3) **Crew**

1970 No. 294	MS (Certificate of Competency as AB) Regulations
1972 No. 918	MS (Crew Agreements, Lists of Crew and Discharge of Seamen) Regulations
1972 No. 1304	Seamen's Savings Bank Regulations
1972 No. 1635	MS (Maintenance of Seamen's Dependants) Regulations
1972 No. 1698	MS (Seamen's Allotments) Regulations
1972 No. 1699	MS (Seamen's Wages) (Contributions) Regulations
1972 No. 1700	MS (Seamen's Wages and Accounts) Regulations
1972 No. 1871	MS (Provisions and Water) Regulations
1972 No. 1875	MS (Maintenance of Seamen's Dependants) (No. 2) Regulations
1978 No. 36	MS (Provisions and Water) (Amendment) Regulations
1978 No.1756	MS (Crew Agreements, Lists of Crew and Discharge of Seamen) (Amendment) Regulations
1978 No. 1757	MS (Seamen's Wages and Accounts) (Amendment) Regulations
1979 No. 97	MS (Repatriation) Regulations
1979 No. 1577	MS (Returns of Births and Deaths) Regulations
1981 No. 569	MS (Official Log Books) Regulations
1981 No. 1065	MS (Ships' Doctors) Regulations
1981 No. 1076	MS (Certification of Ships' Cooks) Regulations
1981 No. 1789	MS (Crew Agreements, List of Crew and Discharge of Seamen) (Amendment) Regulations
1982 No. 1023	MS (Compensation to Seamen — War Damage to Effects) Scheme
1982 No. 1525	MS (Foreign Deserters) (Disapplication) Order
1982 No. 1699	MS (Certification and Watchkeeping) Regulations
1983 No. 1801	MS (Property of Deceased Seamen and Official Logbooks) (Amendment) Regulations
1984 No. 94	MS (Tankers — Officers and Ratings) Regulations
1984 No. 95	MS (Engine Room Watch Ratings) Regulations
1984 No. 96	MS (Navigation Watch Ratings) Regulations
1984 No. 97	MS (Certificates of Proficiency in Survival Craft) Regulations
1985 No. 174	MS (Foreign Deserters) (Disapplication) Order
1985 No. 340	MS (Seamen's Wages and Accounts) Amendment) Regulations
1985 No. 1306	MS (Certification of Deck Officers) Regulations
1985 Mo. 1828	MS (Official Log Books) (Amendment) Regulations
1986 No. 1935	MS (Certification of Marine Engineers Officers and Licensing of Marine Engine Operators) Regulations
1986 No. 2220	MS (Certificates of Competency as AB) (Isle of Man) Order
1987 No. 408	MS (Seamen's Documents) Regulations
1987 No. 884	MS (Certification of Deck and Marine Engineer Officers and Licensing of Marine Engine Operators) (Amendment) Regulations
1988 No. 479	MS (Maintenance of Seamen's Dependants) (Amendment) Regulations
1988 No. 1716	MS (Operations Book) Regulations

(4) **Crew Accommodation**

1978 No. 795	MS (Crew Accommodation) Regulations
1979 No. 491	MS (Crew Accommodation) (Amendment) Regulations
1984 No. 41	MS (Crew Accommodation) (Amendment) Regulations

(5) **Dangerous Goods**

1981 No. 1077	MS (Tankers) (EEC Requirements) Regulations
1981 No. 1747	MS (Dangerous Goods) Regulations
1982 No. 1637	MS (Tankers) (EEC Requirements) (Amendment) Regulations
1986 No. 1069	MS (Dangerous Goods (Amendment) Regulations

(6) **Diving and Submersibles**

| 1975 No. 116 | MS (Diving Operations) Regulations |
| 1975 No. 2062 | MS (Diving Operations) (Amendment) Regulations |

1976 No. 940	MS (Registration of Submersible Craft) Regulations
1981 No. 1098	MS (Submersible Craft Construction and Survey) Regulations
1987 No. 306	MS (Submersible Craft) (Amendment) Regulations
1987 No. 311	MS (Submersible Craft Operations) Regulations
1987 No. 1603	MS (Submersible Craft Operations) (Amendment) Regulations

(7) Fees

1987 No. 2113	MS (Fees) (Amendment) (No 3) Regulations
1988 No. 478	MS (Fees) (Amendment) Regulations
1988 No. 1485	MS The Merchant Shipping (Fees) Regulations
1988 No. 1929	MS (Fees) (Amendment) Regulations

(8) Fire

1980 No. 544	MS (Fire Appliances) Regulations
1981 No. 574	MS (Fire Appliances) (Amendment) Regulations
1984 No. 1218	MS (Fire Protection) Regulations
1985 No. 1193	MS (Fire Protection) (Amendment) Regulations
1985 No. 1194	MS (Fire Appliances) (Amendment) Regulations
1985 No. 1218	MS (Fire Protection) (Ships Built Before 25 May 1980) Regulations
1986 No. 1070	MS (Fire Protection and Fire Appliances) (Amendment) Regulations
1986 No. 1248	MS (Fire Protection) (Non United Kingdom Ships) (Non-SOLAS) Rules

(9) Fishing Vessels

1970 No. 1453	Anchors and Chain Cables Rules
1972 No. 919	MS (Crew Agreements, Lists of Crew and Discharge of Seamen) (Fishing Vessels) Regulations
1972 No. 1701	MS (Seamen's Wages and Accounts) (Fishing Vessels) Regulations
1972 No. 1872	MS (Provisions and Water) (Fishing Vessels) Regulations
1972 No. 1877	MS (Unregistered Fishing Vessels) Regulations
1973 No. 1979	MS (Metrication) Regulations
1974 No. 1919	MS (Radio) (Fishing Vessels) Rules
1975 No. 330	Fishing Vessels (Safety Provisions) Rules
1975 No. 337	(C.8) Fishing Vessels (Safety Provisions) Act 1970 (Commencement) Order
1975 No. 471	Fishing Vessels (Safety Provisions) (Amendment) Rules
1975 No. 733	MS (Provisions and Water) (Fishing and Other Vessels) (Amendment) Regulations
1975 No. 2220	MS (Crew Accommodation) (Fishing Vessels) Regulations
1976 No. 432	Fishing Vessels (Safety Provisions) (Amendment) Rules
1977 No. 45	MS (Crew Agreements, Lists of Crew and Discharge of Seamen) (Merchant Ships and Other Vessels) Regulations
1977 No. 313	Fishing Vessels (Safety Provisions) (Amendment) Rules
1977 No. 498	Fishing Vessels (Safety Provisions) (Amendment No. 2) Rules
1978 No. 1598	Fishing Vessels (Safety Provisions) (Amendment) Rules
1978 No. 1873	Fishing Vessels (Safety Provisions) (Amendment No. 2) Rules
1981 No. 567	Fishing Vessels (Safety Provisions) (Amendment) Rules
1981 No. 570	MS (Official Log Books) (Fishing Vessels) Regulations
1981 No. 740	MS (Fishing Boats Registry) Order
1982 No. 1292	MS (Radio) (Fishing Vessels) (Amendment) Rule
1983 No. 478	MS Master and Seamen (Crew Agreements, Lists of Crew and Discharge of Seamen) (Fishing Vessels) (Amendments) Regulations
1984 No. 1115	Fishing Vessels (Certification of Deck Officers and Engineer Officers) Regulations
1985 No. 855	Fishing Vessels (Reporting of Accidents) Regulations
1986 No. 680	MS (Fishing Vessels) (Radios) (Fees) Regulations
1987 No. 1284	MS (Fishing Boats Registry) (Amendment) Order
1988 No. 38	MS The Fishing Vessels (Life-Saving Appliances) Regulations
1988 No. 252	MS (Fishing Boats Registry) (Amendment) Order
1988 No. 1547	MS The Merchant Shipping (Medical Stores) (Fishing Vessels) Regulations
1988 No. 1911	MS (Transitional Provisions — Fishing Vessels) Order
1988 No. 1926	MS (Registration of Fishing Vessels) Regulations
1988 No. 1909	MS (Fishing Vessels — Tonnage) Regulations
1988 No. 2003	MS (Fishing Vessels' Names) Regulations
1988 No. 2064	MS (Seamens' Wages and Accounts) (Fishing Vessels) (Amendment) Regulations

(10) Hovercraft

1972 No. 674	Hovercraft (General) Order
1972 No. 862	Civil Aviation Authority (Hovercraft) Regulations
1972 No. 971	Hovercraft (Application of Enactments) Order
1972 No. 979	(C.15) Hovercraft Act 1968 (Commencement) Order
1972 No. 1513	Hovercraft (Births, Deaths and Missing Persons) Regulations
1978 No. 1913	Hovercraft (Application of Enactments) (Amendment) Order
1979 No. 1309	Hovercraft (Application of Enactments) (Amendment) Order
1982 No. 715	Hovercraft (Application of Enactments) (Amendment) Order
1983 No. 769	Hovercraft (Application of Enactments) (Amendment) Order
1985 No. 1605	Hovercraft (Fees) Regulations
1986 No. 1305	Hovercraft (Civil Liability) Order
1987 No. 136	Hovercraft (Fees) (Amendment) Regulations

(11) Life Saving

1980 No. 538	MS (Life-saving Appliances) Regulations
1981 No. 577	MS (Life-saving Appliances) (Amendment) Regulations
1981 No. 1472	MS (Passenger Ship Classification) Regulations
1986 No. 1066	MS (Life-saving Appliances) Regulations
1986 No. 1071	MS (Musters and Training) Regulations
1986 No. 1072	MS (Life-saving Appliances Regulations 1980) (Amendment) Regulations

(12) Load Line

1968 No. 1053	MS (Load Line) Rules
1968 No. 1072	MS (Load Lines) (Length of Ship) Regulations
1968 No. 1089	MS (Load Lines) (Deck Cargo) Regulations
1968 No. 1116	MS (Load Lines) (Exemption) Order
1970 No. 1003	MS (Load Lines) (Amendment) Rules
1972 No. 1841	MS (Load Lines) (Particulars of Depth of Loading) Regulations
1973 No. 1979	MS (Metrication) Regulations
1977 No. 1875	MS (Load Line Convention) (Various Countries) Order
1979 No. 1267	MS (Load Line) (Amendment) Rules
1980 No. 641	MS (Load Line) (Amendment) Rules
1981 No. 236	MS (Load Line Convention) (Countries) Order
1985 No. 1217	MS (Grain) Regulations

(13) Marine Pollution

1957 No. 358	Oil in Navigable Waters (Transfer Records) Regulations
1967 No. 710	Oil in Navigable Waters (Heavy Diesel Oil) Regulations
1971 No. 1423	(C.36) MS (Oil Pollution) Act 1971 (Commencement) Order
1972 No. 1929	Oil in Navigable Waters (Records) Regulations
1973 No. 203	(C.60) Prevention of Oil Pollution Act 1971 (Commencement) Order
1975 No. 867	(C.26) MS (Oil Pollution) Act 1971 (Commencement No. 2) Order
1980 No. 1093	MS (Prevention of Pollution) (Intervention) Order
1981 No. 612	Prevention of Oil Pollution (Convention Countries) Order
1981 No. 912	MS (Oil Pollution) (Compulsory Insurance) Regulations
1982 No. 257	MS Oil Pollution (Compulsory Insurance) (Amendment) Regulations
1983 No. 1106	MS (Prevention of Oil Pollution) Order
1983 No. 1398	MS (Prevention of Oil Pollution) Regulations
1984 No. 862	MS Prevention of Pollution (Reception Facilities) Order
1985 No. 2002	MS (Prevention of Oil Pollution) (Amendment) Order
1985 No. 2040	MS (Prevention of Oil Pollution) (Amendment) Regulations
1986 No. 2223	MS International Oil Pollution Compensation Fund (Parties to Convention) Order
1986 No. 2225	MS (Oil Pollution) (Parties to Convention) Order
1987 No. 220	MS (Indemnification of Shipowners) Order
1987 No. 470	MS (Prevention and Control of Pollution) Order
1987 No. 549	MS (IBC Code) Regulations
1987 No. 550	MS (BCH Code) Regulations
1987 No. 551	MS (Control of Pollution of Noxious Liquid Substances in Bulk) Regulations
1987 No. 586	MS (Reporting of Pollution Incidents) Regulations
1988 No. 2252	MS (Prevention of Pollution by Garbage) Order
1988 No. 2292	MS (Prevention of Pollution by Garbage) Regulations
1988 No. 2293	MS (Reception Facilities for Garbage) Regulations

(14) Navigation and Collision Regulations

1975 No. 700	MS (Carriage of Nautical Publications) Rules
1977 No. 1010	MS (Signals of Distress) Rules
1981 No. 571	MS (Automatic Pilot and Testing of Steering Gear) Regulations
1983 No. 708	MS (Distress Signals and Prevention of Collisions) Regulations
1983 No. 762	MS (Distress Signals and Prevention of Collisions) (Overseas Territories) Order
1983 No. 768	Collision Rules (Seaplanes) Order
1986 No. 2285	General Lighthouse Authorities (Beacons, Hyperbolic Systems) Order
1987 No. 1591	MS (Smooth and Partially Smooth Waters) Regulations

(15) Occupational Health and Safety

1980 No. 686	MS (Code of Safe Working Practices Regulations)
1982 No. 876	MS (Safety Officials and Reporting of Accident and Dangerous Occurrences) Regulations
1983 No. 808	MS (Medical Examination) Regulations
1984 No. 93	MS (Safety Officials and Reporting of Accident and Dangerous Occurences) (Amendment) Regulations
1984 No. 408	MS (Health and Safety: General Duties) Regulations
1985 No. 512	MS (Medical Examination) (Amendment) Regulations
1985 No. 1664	MS (Protective Clothing and Equipment) Regulations
1986 No. 144	MS (Medical Stores) Regulations
1988 No. 1116	MS The Merchant Shipping (Medical Stores) (Amendment) Regulations
1988 No. 1396	MS (Health and Safety: General Duties) (Amendment) Regulations
1988 No. 1636	MS (Guarding of Machinery and Safety of Electrical Equipment) Regulations
1988 No. 1637	MS (Means of Access) Regulations
1988 No. 1638	MS (Entry into Dangerous Spaces) Regulations
1988 No. 1639	MS (Hatches and Lifting Plant) Regulations
1988 No. 1641	MS (Safe Movement on Board Ship) Regulations
1988 No. 2274	MS (Safety at Work Regulations) (Non-UK Ships) Regulations

(16) Radio and Navigational Equipment

1974 No. 1919	MS (Radio) (Fishing Vessels) Rules
1980 No. 529	MS Radio Installations Regulations
1980 No. 534	MS (Navigational Warnings) Regulations
1981 No. 406	MS (Navigational Warnings) (Amendment) Regulations
1991 No. 582	MS (Radio Installations) (Amendment) Regulations
1981 No. 583	MS (Radio Installations Surveys) Regulations
1982 No. 1292	MS (Radio) (Fishing Vessels) (Amendment) Rules
1984 No. 346	MS (Radio Installations) (Amendment) Regulation
1984 No. 1203	MS (Navigational Equipment) Regulations
1984 No. 1223	MS (Radio Installations) (Amendment No.2) Regulations
1985 No. 659	MS (Navigational Equipment) (Amendment) Regulations
1985 No. 1216	MS (Radio Installations) (Amendment) Regulations
1986 No. 1075	MS (Radio Installations) (Amendment) Regulations

(17) Ships — Construction and Equipment

1970 No. 1453	Anchors and Chain Cables Rules
1980 No. 535	MS (Passenger Ship Construction) Regulations
1981 No. 571	MS (Automatic Pilot and Testing of Steering Gear) Regulations
1981 No. 572	MS (Cargo Ship Construction and Survey) Regulations
1981 No. 573	MS (Cargo Ship Safety Equipment Survey) Regulations
1981 No. 580	MS (Passenger Ship Construction) (Amendment) Regulations
1981 No. 1472	MS (Passenger Ship Classification) Regulations
1984 No. 1216	MS (Passenger Ship Construction and Survey) Regulations
1984 No. 1217	MS (Cargo Ship Construction and Survey) Regulations
1984 No. 1219	MS (Cargo Ship Construction and Survey) Regulations 1981 (Amendment) Regulations
1985 No. 211	MS (Cargo Ship Safety Equipment Survey) (Amendment) Regulations
1985 No. 660	MS (Passenger Ship Construction) (Amendment) Regulations
1985 No. 661	MS (Application of Construction and Survey Regulations to Other Ships) Regulations

1985 No. 663	MS (Cargo Ship Construction and Survey) Regulations 1981 (Amendment) Regulations
1986 No. 1067	MS (Cargo Ship Construction and Survey) Regulations 1984 (Amendment) Regulations
1986 No. 1073	MS (Gas Carriers) Regulations
1986 No. 1074	MS (Passenger Ship Construction) (New and Existing Ships) (Amendment) Regulations
1987 No. 1298	MS (Closing of Openings in Hulls and in Watertight Bulkheads) Regulations
1987 No. 1886	MS (Passenger Ship Construction) (Amendment) Regulations
1987 No. 1961	MS (Pilot Ladders and Hoists) Regulations
1987 No. 2238	MS (Passenger Ship Construction) (Amendment No. 2) Regulations
1988 No 317	MS (Closing of Openings in Enclosed Superstructures and in Bulkhead above the Bulkhead Deck) Regulations
1988 No 642	MS (Closing of Openings in Enclosed Superstructures and in Bulkhead above the Bulkhead Deck) (Application to non-United Kingdom Ships) Regulations
1988 No 1275	MS (Weighing of Goods Vehicles and other Cargo) Regulations
1988 No 1693	MS (Stability of Passenger Ships) Regulations
1988 No 2272	MS (Emergency Equipment Lockers for Ro/Ro Passenger Ships) Regulations
1989 No 100	MS (Loading and Stability assessment of Ro/Ro Passenger Ships) Regulations

(18) Tonnage

1982 No. 841	MS (Tonnage Regulations)
1982 No. 1085	Tonnage (Various Countries) Order
1983 No. 439	MS (Deck Cargo Tonnage) Regulations
1986 No. 1040	MS (Liability of Shipowners and Others) (Calculations of Tonnage) Order
1988 No 1910	MS (Tonnage) (Amendment) Regulations

GENERAL INFORMATION

CALENDAR 1990

January

Mon	1	8	15	22	29
Tue	2	9	16	23	30
Wed	3	10	17	24	31
Thu	4	11	18	25	
Fri	5	12	19	26	
Sat	6	13	20	27	
Sun	7	14	21	28	

February

Mon		5	12	19	26
Tue		6	13	20	27
Wed		7	14	21	28
Thu	1	8	15	22	
Fri	2	9	16	23	
Sat	3	10	17	24	
Sun	4	11	18	25	

March

Mon		5	12	19	26
Tue		6	13	20	27
Wed		7	14	21	28
Thu	1	8	15	22	29
Fri	2	9	16	23	30
Sat	3	10	17	24	31
Sun	4	11	18	25	

April

Mon		2	9	16	23	30
Tue		3	10	17	24	
Wed		4	11	18	25	
Thu		5	12	19	26	
Fri		6	13	20	27	
Sat		7	14	21	28	
Sun	1	8	15	22	29	

May

Mon		7	14	21	28
Tue	1	8	15	22	29
Wed	2	9	16	23	30
Thu	3	10	17	24	31
Fri	4	11	18	25	
Sat	5	12	19	26	
Sun	6	13	20	27	

June

Mon		4	11	18	25
Tue		5	12	19	26
Wed		6	13	20	27
Thu		7	14	21	28
Fri	1	8	15	22	29
Sat	2	9	16	23	30
Sun	3	10	17	24	

July

Mon		2	9	16	23	30
Tue		3	10	17	24	31
Wed		4	11	18	25	
Thu		5	12	19	26	
Fri		6	13	20	27	
Sat		7	14	21	28	
Sun	1	8	15	22	29	

August

Mon		6	13	20	27
Tue		7	14	21	28
Wed	1	8	15	22	29
Thu	2	9	16	23	30
Fri	3	10	17	24	31
Sat	4	11	18	25	
Sun	5	12	19	26	

September

Mon		3	10	17	24
Tue		4	11	18	25
Wed		5	12	19	26
Thu		6	13	20	27
Fri		7	14	21	28
Sat	1	8	15	22	29
Sun	2	9	16	23	30

October

Mon	1	8	15	22	29
Tue	2	9	16	23	30
Wed	3	10	17	24	31
Thu	4	11	18	25	
Fri	5	12	19	26	
Sat	6	13	20	27	
Sun	7	14	21	28	

November

Mon		5	12	19	26
Tue		6	13	20	27
Wed		7	14	21	28
Thu	1	8	15	22	29
Fri	2	9	16	23	30
Sat	3	10	17	24	
Sun	4	11	18	25	

December

Mon		3	10	17	24
Tue		4	11	18	25
Wed		5	12	19	26
Thu		6	13	20	27
Fri		7	14	21	28
Sat	1	8	15	22	29
Sun	2	9	16	23	30

Ash Wednesday - February 28   Easter Day - April 15   Pentecost-June 3

NOTABLE DATES 1990

New Year's Day (Monday)	Jan 1
Bank Holiday (Scotland)	2
Epiphany	6
Foundation Day (Australia 1788)	26
Chinese New Year	27,28,29
Lincoln's Birthday (U.S.A.)	Feb 12
St. Valentine's Day	14
Ash Wednesday	28
St. David's Day	Mar 1
St. Patrick's Day (N. Ireland & Eire)	17
Mothering Sunday	25
British Summer Time Begins	25
Palm Sunday	Apr 8
Good Friday	13
Easter Day	15
Easter Monday Bank Holiday (except Scotland)	16
St. George's Day	23
May Day Bank Holiday (U.K.)	May 7
Ascension Day	24
Bank Holiday (U.K.)	28
Whit Sunday — Pentecost	June 3
Bank Holiday (Eire)	4
Trinity Sunday	10
Corpus Christi	14
Father's Day	17
National Day (Canada)	July 1
Independence Day U.S.A. (1776)	4
Bank Holiday (N. Ireland)	12
Bank Holiday (Scotland and Eire)	Aug 6
Bank Holiday (England, Wales and N. Ireland)	27
United Nations Day	Oct 24
British Summer Time Ends	28
Bank Holiday (Eire)	29
All Saints	Nov 1
Remembrance Sunday	11
Thanksgiving Day U.S.A.	22
St. Andrew's Day	30
Advent Sunday	Dec 2
Christmas Day (Tuesday)	25
Boxing Day	26
Hogmanay	31

WORLD HOLIDAYS 1989

Country	JANUARY	FEBRUARY	MARCH	APRIL	MAY	JUNE	JULY	AUGUST	SEPTEMBER	OCTOBER	NOVEMBER	DECEMBER
Australia	1,29			13,16 25								25,26
Austria	1,6			16	1,24	4,14		15		26	1	8,25 26
Belgium	1			16	1,24	4	21	15			1,11	25
Brazil	1	25,26 27		13,21	1	14			7	12	1,2 15	8,25
Canada	1			13,16	21		2*		3	8	12	25,26
China	1,27 28,29				1					1,2		
Denmark	1			12,13 16	11,24	4,5						25,26
England/Wales	1			13,16	7,28			27				25,26
Finland	1,6			13,15 16	1,19	2,3 23					3	6,25 26
France	1			16	1,8 24	4	14	15			1,11	25
East Germany	1			13,14 15	1	3,4				7		25,26
West Germany	1			13,16	1,24	4,17					21	25,26
Greece	1,6	26	25	13,16	1	4		15		28		25,26
Hong Kong	1,27 28,29			13,14 16		9* 11*		25,27				25,26
Ireland	1		17 19*	13,16		4		6		29		25,26
Israel				10,16 30	30				20,21 29	4,11		
Italy	1,6			15,16 25	1	2		15			1,4	8,25 26
Japan	1,15	11,12	21	29,30	3,4 5				15,23 24	10	3,23	

* Subject to confirmation.

Country	JANUARY	FEBRUARY	MARCH	APRIL	MAY	JUNE	JULY	AUGUST	SEPTEMBER	OCTOBER	NOVEMBER	DECEMBER
Luxembourg	1	26		16	1,24	4,23		15			1,2	25,26
Malta	1	10	19	13	1	29		15	8,21			8,13 25
Mexico	1	5,24	21	12,13	1,5 10				1,15 16	12	20	25
Netherlands	1			13,16 30	5,24	4						25,26
New Zealand	1	6		13,16 25		4				22		25,26
N. Ireland	1		17 19*	13,16	7,28		12	27				25,26
Norway	1			12,13 16	1,17 24	4						25,26
Poland	1			15,16	1	14	22				1	25,26
Portugal	1	27		13,25	1	10,14		15		5	1	1,8 25
Scotland	1,2			13	7,28			6				25,26
South Africa	1			6,13 16	7,24 31					10		16,25 26
Spain	1,6		19	12,13	1	14	25	15		12	1	8,25
Sweden	1,6			13,16	1,24	4,23					3	25,26
Switzerland	1			13,16	24	4						25
Turkey	1			23,26 27,28	19		3,4 5,6	30		29		
USA	1,15	12,19		13	28		4		3	8	11,12 22	25
USSR	1		8		1,2 9					7	7,8	
Venezuela	1	26,27		12,13 19	1	24	5,24			12		25

THE SHIPBROKERS' REGISTER

*Every Shipbroker and Shipping/Chartering Agent in the countries covered by
The Shipbrokers' Register is entitled to have his name, address, telegraphic address,
telex and telephone recorded in the Register free of all charge and without
any implied obligation whatsoever.*

The Register records some 12,500 shipbrokers and shipping/chartering agents in:

Europe	The Caribbean
Africa	The Middle East
North America	Asia
Central America	Australasia
South America	The Pacific Islands

Maritex and Inmarsat telex numbers.
There is also a special section for Ship Sale Brokers

Now published yearly

For orders and enquiries, please contact:

THE SHIPBROKERS' REGISTER

P.O. Box 2
261 22 LANDSKRONA
Telex: 72525   Wram S
Telephone: +46-418 25090
Fax: +46-418 233 32

COUNTRY INFORMATION

This section contains basic information of interest to those planning to visit or do business with a listed country. Data provided for each country — where applicable or available is:-(a)Capital city, (b)Total area of country, including inland water, in square miles and square kilometres, (c)Total population at last census, or latest available estimate, (d)Standard time, indicated in hours plus or minus GMT. No account is taken of any daylight saving time, (e)Language — official language or languages plus, where available, any other used regularly in business, (f)Unit of currency in use, (g)IDD code — international telephone direct dialling code when dialling into that country. It may not be possible to dial internationally from every country to every other country although an IDD code is shown, (h)Principal ports indicating the availability of facilities for the handling of particular types of cargo, provision of bunkers and shiprepair. Full details of facilities available at ports throughout the world is contained in "Lloyd's Ports of the World", available from Lloyd's of London Press, (i)Principal airports, giving distance from city centre in miles and kilometres.

ALGERIA
Capital: *Algiers.* **Area:** 919,595 sq.mls/2,318,741 sq.km. **Population:** 22,971,500. **Standard Time:** GMT + 1 hr. **Language:** Arabic, French. **Currency:** Algerian dinar of 100 centimes. **Weights & measures:** Metric system. **IDD Code:** dialling-in 213. **Principal ports:** *Algiers* — general cargo, containers, ro/ro, oil bunkers; *Annaba* — general cargo, bulk, oil, bunkers; *Arzew* — general cargo, oil, liquefied gas, bunkers; *Bejaia* — general cargo, oil, liquefied gas, bunkers; *Oran* — general cargo, containers, ro/ro, bunkers; *Skikda* — general cargo, oil, liquefied gas. **Principal airports:** *Algiers (Houari Boumendienne)* 12.5mls/20km, *Annaba (Les Salines)* 7.5mls/12km, *Constantine (Ain-el-Bey)* 5.5.mls/9km, *Oran (Tafaraoui)* 15.5mls/25km.

ARGENTINA
Capital: *Buenos Aires.* **Area:** 1,068,302 sq.mls/2,766,889 sq.km. **Population:** 30,564,000. **Standard Time:** GMT — 3 hrs. **Language:** Spanish. English widely understood. **Currency:** Austral of 100 centavos. **Weights & Measures:** Metric system. **IDD code:** Dialling-in 54. **Principal ports:** *Bahia Blanca* — general cargo, bulk grain, oil, bunkers; *Buenos Aires* — general cargo. containers, bulk grain, oil, liquefied gas, bunkers, shiprepair; *Rosario* — general cargo, bulk grain, oil, bunkers. **Principal airport:** *Buenos Aires (Ezeiza)* 31.5mls/50km.

AUSTRALIA
Capital: *Canberra.* **Area:** 2,966,151 sq.mls./7,682,300sq.km. **Population:** 16,262,120. **Standard Times:** W. Australia GMT + 8 hrs. N. Territory & S. Australia + 9.5 hrs. Capital Territory,New South Wales, Queensland, Tasmania & Victoria + 10 hrs. **Language:** English. **Currency:** Australian dollar of 100 cents. **Weights and measures:** Metric system. **IDD code:** dialling-in 61. **Principal ports:** *Adelaide* — general cargo, dry and liquid bulk, containers, ro/ro, oil, bunkers; *Brisbane* — general cargo, containers, ro/ro, dry and liquid bulk, oil, bunkers, shiprepair; *Burnie* — general cargo, containers, ro/ro, oil, bunkers; *Cairns* — general cargo, containers, ro/ro, bulk, oil, bunkers, shiprepair; *Devonport* — bulk, tanker terminal at *Kwinana*, bunkers; *Geelong* — general cargo, containers, ro/ro, bulk, oil, bunkers, shiprepair; *Gladstone* — general cargo, bulk, oil, liquefied gas, bunkers; *Hobart* — general cargo, bulk, containers, ro/ro, oil, liquefied gas, bunkers, shiprepair; *Launceston* — general cargo, containers, ro/ro, oil, bunkers, shiprepair; *Melbourne* — general cargo, containers, ro/ro, bulk, oil bunkers, shiprepair; *Newcastle* — general cargo, containers, ro/ro, bulk, oil, bunkers, shiprepair; *Port Kembla* — general cargo, containers, ro/ro, bulk, oil, bunkers; *Sydney* — general cargo, containers, ro/ro, bulk, oil, bunkers, shiprepair; *Townsville* — general cargo, containers, ro/ro, bulk, oil, liquefied gas, bunkers. **Principal airports:** *Adelaide* 5mls/8km, *Brisbane International* 4mls/6.5km, *Darwin* 5mls/8km, *Melbourne (Tullamarine)* 13.5mls/21km, *Perth* 6mls/10km, *Sydney (Kingsford Smith)* 7mls/11km.

AUSTRIA
Capital: *Vienna.* **Area:** 32,376 sq.mls/83,854 sq.km. **Population:** 7,566,000. **Standard Time:** GMT + 1 hr. **Language:** German. **Currency:** Austrian schilling of 100 groschen. **Weights & Measures:** Metric system. **IDD code:** dialling-in 43. **Principal airports:** *Klagenfurt (Worthersee)* 2mls/3km, *Salzburg* 3mls/5km, *Vienna (Schwechat)* 11mls/18km.

THE BAHAMAS
Capital: *Nassau*. **Area:** 5,382 sq.mls/13,939 sq.km. **Population:** 237,090. **Standard Time:** GMT − 5 hrs. **Language:** English. **Currency:** Bahamas dollar of 100 cents.**Weights & measures:** Imperial and metric system. **IDD code:** dialling-in 1809. **Principal ports:** *Freeport* − general cargo ro/ro, oil bunkers; *Nassau* − general cargo. **Principal airports:** *Freeport International* 3mls/5km, *Nassau International* 10mls/16km.

BAHRAIN
Capital: *Manama*. **Area:** 262 sq.mls/678 sq.km. **Population:** 417,210. **Standard Time:** GMT + 3 hrs. **Language:** Arabic, English. **Currency:** Bahrain dinar of 1,000 fils. **Weights & measures:** Metric system. **IDD code:** dialling-in 973. **Principal ports:** *Mina Sulman* − general cargo, containers, shiprepair; *Sitra* − oil bunkers. **Airport:** *Bahrain International*

BANGLADESH
Capital: *Dhaka*. **Area:** 55,598 sq.mls/143,998 sq.km. **Population:** 100,000,000. **Standard Time:** GMT + 6 hrs. **Language:** Bangla. English used in government and commercial circles. **Currency:** Taka of 100 paisa. **Weight & measures:** Gradual conversion from Imperial to metric, also local units. **IDD code:** dialling-in 880. **Principal ports:** *Chalna* − general cargo; *Chittagong* − general cargo, containers, bulk, oil, bunkers, shiprepair. **Principal airport:** *Dhaka (Zia International)* 12mls/20km.

BARBADOS
Capital: *Bridgetown*. **Area:** 166 sq.mls/429 sq km. **Population:** 253,000. **Standard Time:** GMT − 4 hrs. **Language:** English. **Currency:** Barbados dollar of 100 cents. **Weights & measures:** Metric, Imperial also in common use. **IDD code:** dialling-in 1 809. **Port:** *Bridgetown* − general cargo, containers, bulk, oil, bunkers. **Airport:** *Bridgetown (Grantley Adams International)* 11mls/128km.

BELGIUM
Capital: *Brussels*. **Area:** 11,783 sq.mls/30,519 sq. km. **Population:** 9,858,900. **Standard Time:** GMT + 1 hr. **Language:** Dutch, French, also German and English. **Currency:** Belgian franc of 100 centimes. **Weights & measures:** Metric system. **IDD code:** dialling-in 32. **Principal ports:** *Antwerp* − general cargo, containers, ro/ro, bulk, oil, liquefied gas, bunkers, shiprepair; *Brussels* − general cargo, bunkers; *Ghent* − general cargo, containers, ro/ro, bulk, oil, bunkers; shiprepair; *Ostend* − general cargo, containers, ro/ro, bunkers; *Zeebrugge* − general cargo, containers, ro/ro, bulk, oil, liquefied gas, bunkers. **Principal airports:** *Antwerp(Deurne)* 2mls/3km, *Brussels National* 7.5mls/12km, *Ostend* 3mls/5km.

BELIZE
Capital: *Belmopan*. **Area:** 8,867 sq.mls/22,964 sq.km. **Population:** 166,000. **Standard Time:** GMT − 6 hrs. **Language:** English, Spanish. **Currency:** Belize dollar of 100 cents. **Weights & measures;** Imperial and metric systems in use. **IDD code:** dialling-in 501 (not available from UK). **Principal port:** *Belize City* − general cargo, containers, ro/ro, oil, bunkers. **Principal airport:** *Belize City (Stanley International)* 10mls/16km.

BENIN
Capital: *Porto Novo*. **Area:** 43,484 sq.mls/112,622 sq.km. **Population:** 3,932,000. **Standard Time:** GMT + 1 hr. **Language:** French. Currency: CFA franc of 100 centimes. **Weights & measures:** Metric system. **IDD code:** dialling-in 229. **Principal port:** *Cotonou* − general cargo, containers, ro/ro, oil, bunkers. **Airport:** *Cotonou* 3mls/5km.

BERMUDA
Capital: *Hamilton*. **Area:** 20.5 sq.mls/53 sq.km. **Population:** 56,000. **Standard Time:** GMT − 4 hrs. **Language:** English. **Currency:** Bermuda dollar of 100 cents. **Weights & measures:** Metric, Imperial and U.S. systems. **IDD code:** dialling-in 1 809 29. **Principal ports:** *Hamilton* − general cargo, containers, ro/ro; *St. Georges* − general cargo, oil, bunkers. **Airport:** *Hamilton (Kindley Field International)* 12mls/19km.

BOLIVIA
Capital: *La Paz*. **Area:** 424,164 sq.mls/1,084,391 sq.km. **Population:** 6,429,000. **Standard Time:** GMT − 4 hrs. **Language:** Spanish, also English in business. **Currency:** Peso Boliviano of 100 centavos. **Weight & measures:** Metric system, also local units. **IDD code:** dialling-in 591 (not available from UK). **Principal airports:** *La Paz (El Alto)* 8.5mls/14km, *Santa Cruz (Viru Viru International)* 9.5mls/15km.

BRAZIL
Capital: *Brasilia*. **Area:** 3,286,488 sq.mls/8,511,965 sq.km. **Population:** 135,564,000. **Standard Time:** GMT − 3 hrs. **Language:** Portuguese, also English in business. **Currency:** Cruzado of 100 centavos. **Weights & measures:** Metric system. **IDD code:** dialling-in 55. **Principal ports:** *Belem* − general cargo,containers, bulk, oil, bunkers, shiprepair; *Fortaleza* − general cargo, bulk, oil, liquefied gas, bunkers; *Manaus* − general cargo, containers, ro/ro, bulk, oil, bunkers; *Paranagua* − general cargo, containers, ro/ro, bulk, oil, liquefied gas, bunkers; *Recife* − general cargo, containers,

bulk, oil, bunkers; *Rio de Janeiro* — general cargo, containers, bulk,, oil, bunkers, shiprepair; *Rio Grande* — general cargo, containers, bulk, oil, bunkers; *Salvador* — general cargo, ro/ro, bulk, oil, bunkers; *Santos* — general cargo, containers, ro/ro, bulk, oil, bunkers, shiprepair; *Vitoria* — general cargo, bulk, oil, bunkers. **Principal airports:** *Belem (Val de Cans)* 7.5mls/12km, *Brasilia International* 7mls/11km, *Recife (Guarapes)* 7mls/11km, *Rio de Janeiro International* 12.5mls/20km, *Sao Paulo (Guarulhos International)* 15.5mls/25km, *Sao Paulo (Viracopos)* 60mls/96.5km.

BRUNEI
Capital: *Bandar Seri Begawan.* **Area:** 2,226 sq.mls/5,765 sq.km. **Population:** 226,000. **Standard Time:** GMT + 8 hrs. **Business Language:** English. **Currency:** Brunei dollar of 100 cents. **Weights & measures:** Imperial, also local units. **IDD code:** dialling-in 673. **Principal port:** *Muara Harbour* — general cargo, containers, oil. **Principal airport:** *Bandar Seri Begawan (Brunei International)* 3mls/5km.

BULGARIA
Capital: *Sofia.* **Area:** 42,823 sq.mls/110,912 sq.km. **Population:** 8,948,390. **Standard Time:** GMT + 2 hrs. **Language:** Bulgarian, also English, French and German in business. **Currency:** Lev of 100 stotinki. **Weights & measures:** Metric system. **IDD code:** dialling-in 359. **Principal ports:** *Bourgas* — general cargo, bulk, oil, bunkers; *Varna* — general cargo, containers, bulk, oil, bunkers, shiprepair. **Principal airports:** *Bourgas International* 7.5mls/12km, *Sofia International* 6mls/10km, *Varna International* 5.5mls/9km.

BURMA
Capital: *Rangoon.* **Area:** 261,218 sq.mls/676,552 sq.km. **Population:** 37,153,000. **Standard Time:** GMT + 6.5 hrs. **Language:** Burmese, also English. **Currency:** Kyat of 100 pyas. **Weights & measures:** Imperial. **IDD code:** dialling-in 95. **Principal ports:** *Akyab* — general cargo; *Moulmein* — general cargo; *Rangoon* — general cargo, oil, bunkers. **Principal airport:** *Rangoon* 12mls/19km.

CANADA
Capital: *Ottawa.* **Area:** 3,849,674 sq.mls/9,970,610 sq.km. **Population:** 25,309,330. **Standard Times:** Newfoundland GMT − 3 hrs; Labrador, New Brunswick, Nova Scotia, Prince Edward Is., Quebec (East)− 4 hrs; Ontario (East), Quebec (West) − 5 hrs; Manitoba, Ontario (West), Saskatchewan (East) − 6 hrs; Alberta, Saskatchewan (West) − 7 hrs; British Columbia, Yukon − 8 hrs. **Language:** English, French. **Currency:** Canadian dollar of 100 cents. **Weights & measures:** metric system, also Imperial and U.S. systems. **IDD code:** dialling-in 1. **Principal ports:** *Corner Brook, Newfoundland general cargo, containers, bulk, oil, bunkers; Halifax* — general cargo, containers, ro/ro, bulk, oil, bunkers, shiprepair; *Hamilton* — general cargo, containers, ro/ro, bulk, oil, bunkers; *Kitimat* — general cargo, bulk; *Montreal* — general cargo, containers, ro/ro, bulk, oil, bunkers, shiprepair; *New Westminster* — general cargo, containers, ro/ro, bulk, bunkers; *Prince Rupert* — general cargo, ro/ro, bulk; *Quebec* — general cargo, containers, ro/ro, bulk, oil, bunkers, shiprepair; *St. John NB* — general cargo, containers, bulk, oil, bunkers, shiprepair; *St. John's, Newfoundland* — general cargo, containers, bulk, oil, bunkers, shiprepair; *Sorel* — bulk, bunkers, shiprepair; *Sydney NS* — general cargo, containers, ro/ro, bulk, oil, bunkers, shiprepair; *Three Rivers* — general cargo, containers, ro/ro, bulk, oil, bunkers; *Toronto* — general cargo, containers, ro/ro, bulk, oil, bunkers; *Vancouver* — general cargo, containers, ro/ro, bulk, oil, LPG, bunkers, shiprepair; *Victoria* — general cargo, containers, bunkers. **Principal airports:** *Calgary International* 7mls/11km, *Edmonton International* 17.5mls/28km, *Gander International* 2mls/3km, *Halifax International* 23mls/37km, *Montreal (Dorval International)* 14.5mls/23.5km, *Montreal (Mirabel)* 33mls/53km, *Ottawa (Uplands International)* 11mls/17.5km, *Toronto (Lester B. Pearson International)* 18mls/29km, *Vancouver International* 9mls/15km, *Victoria International* 17mls/27km, *Winnipeg International* 4mls/6.5km.

CHILE
Capital: *Santiago.* **Area:** 292,258 sq.mls/756,945 sq.km. **Population:** 12,074,000. **Standard Time:** GMT − 4 hrs. **Language:** Spanish. **Currency:** Chilean peso of 100 centavos. **Weights & measures:** Metric system. **IDD code:** dialling-in 56. **Principal ports:** *Antofagasta* — general cargo, containers, ro/ro, oil, bunkers; *Arica* — general cargo, containers, oil; *Coquimbo* — general cargo, containers, bulk; *Iquique* — general cargo, oil; *Punta Arenas* — general cargo, containers, oil, LPG, shiprepair; *San Antonio* — general cargo, containers, bulk, oil; *Talcahuano* — general cargo, bulk, shiprepair; *Tocopilla* — general cargo, bulk, oil; *Valparaiso* — general cargo, containers, bulk, oil, bunkers, shiprepair. **Principal airport:** *Santiago (Comodoro Arturo Merino Benitez)* 13mls/21km.

CHINA
Capital: *Beijing (Peking).* **Area:** 3,705,400 Sq.mls/9,596,900sq.km. **Population:** 1,080,000,000. **Standard Time:** GMT + 8 hrs. **Language:** Chinese (Mandarin). **Currency:** Yuan of 10 jiao or 100 fen. **Weights & measures:** Metric system, also local units. **IDD code:** dialling-in 86. **Principal ports:** *Dalian* — general cargo, containers, bulk, oil, bunkers, shiprepair; *Fuzhou* — general cargo, containers; *Huangpu* — general cargo, containers, bulk, oil, bunkers; *Qingdao* — general cargo, containers, bulk, oil, shiprepair; *Qinhuangdao* — general cargo, bulk, oil, bunkers; *Shanghai* —

general cargo, containers, ro/ro, bulk, oil, bunkers, shiprepair; *Xingang* — general cargo, containers, bulk, oil, bunkers, shiprepair; *Zhanjiang* — general cargo, containers, bulk, oil. **Principal airports:** *Beijing (Peking)* 16mls/26km, *Shanghai* 7.5mls/12km.

COLOMBIA

Capital: *Bogota.* **Area:** 439,737 sq.mls/1,138,914 sq.km. **Population:** 26,525,270. **Standard Time:** GMT — 5 hrs. **Language:**Spanish, also English for business transactions. **Currency:** Colombian peso of 100 centavos. **Weights & measures:** Metric systems. **IDD code:** dialling-in 57. **Principal ports:** *Barranquilla* — general cargo, containers, bulk, oil, bunkers; *Buenaventura* — general cargo, containers, bulk, oil, bunkers; *Cartagena* — general cargo, containers, oil; *Santa Marta* — general cargo, containers, oil. **Principal airports:** *Bogota (El Dorada)* 7.5mls/12km, *Cali (Palmaseca)* 12mls/19km, *Cartagena (Crespo)* 1ml/1.5km.

PEOPLES REPUBLIC OF THE CONGO

Capital: *Brazzaville.* **Area:** 132,047 sq.mls/342,000 sq.km. **Population:** 1,740,000. **Standard Time:** GMT + 1 hr. **Language:** French. **Currency:** CFA franc of 100 centimes. **Weights & measures:** Metric system. **IDD code:** dialling-in 242 (not available from the UK). **Principal port:** *Pointe Noire* — general cargo, containers, bulk, oil, bunkers. **Principal airport** *Brazzaville (Maya Maya)* 2mls/4km.

COSTA RICA

Capital: *San Jose:* **Area:** 19,730 sq.mls/51,110 sq.km. **Population:** 2,816,558. **Standard Time:** GMT —6 hrs. **Language:** Spanish. **Currency:** Colon of 100 centimos. **Weights & measures:** Metric system. **IDD code:** dialling-in 506. **Principal ports:** *Caldera* — general cargo, containers, ro/ro, bulk,oil; *Golfito* — general cargo; *Port Limon* — general cargo, containers, ro/ro, oil; *Puntarenas* — general cargo, oil. **Principal airport:** *San Jose (Juan Santamaria International)* 11mls/18km.

CUBA

Capital: *Havana.* **Area:** 42,803 sq.mls/110,860 sq.km. **Population:** 10,356,400. **Standard Time:** GMT — 5 hrs. **Language:** Spanish, English. **Currency:** Cuban pesos of 100 centavos. **Weights & measures:** Metric system. **IDD code:** dialling-in 53. **Principal ports:** *Cienfuegos* — general cargo, bulk, oil, bunkers; *Havana* — general cargo, containers, bulk, oil, bunkers, shiprepair; *Manzanillo* — bulk, oil; *Matanzas* — general cargo, bulk, oil; *Nuevitas* — general cargo, bulk; *Santiago de Cuba* — general cargo, bulk, oil. **Principal airport:** *Havana (Jose Marti International)* 11mls/18km.

CYPRUS

Capital: *Nicosia.* **Area:** 3,572 sq.mls/9,251 sq.km. **Population:** 673,100. **Standard Time:** GMT + 2 hrs. **Language:** Greek, Turkish, English. **Currency:** Cyprus pound of 100 cents. **Weights & measures:** Metric. **IDD code:** dialling-in 357. **Principal ports:** *Larnaca* — general cargo, containers, ro/ro, oil, liquefied gas, bunkers; *Limassol* — general cargo, containers, ro/ro, bulk, oil, bunkers. **Principal airport:** *Larnaca* 5mls/8km.

CZECHOSLOVAKIA

Capital: *Prague.* **Area:** 49,381 sq.mls/127,896 sq.km. **Population:** 15,500,000. **Standard Time:** GMT + 1 hr. **Language:** Czech, Slovak, also German and English in business. **Currency:** Koruna of 100 haler. **Weights & measures:** Metric system. **IDD code:** dialling-in 42. **Principal airport:** *Prague (Ruzyne)* 11mls/17km.

DENMARK

Capital: *Copenhagen.* **Area:** 16,633 sq.mls/43,080 sq.km. **Population:** 5,124,790. **Standard Time:** GMT + 1 hr. **Language:** Danish, also English and German in business. **Currency:** Krone of 100 øre. **Weights & measures:**Metric system. **IDD code:** dialling-in 45. **Principal ports:** *Aalborg* — general cargo,ro/ro, bulk, oil, liquefied gas, bunkers, shiprepair; *Aarhus* — general cargo, containers, ro/ro, oil, liquefied gas, bunkers, shiprepair; *Copenhagen* — general cargo, containers, ro/ro, bulk, oil, bunkers; *Esbjerg* — general cargo, containers, ro/ro bulk, oil, liquefied gas, bunkers; *Fredericia* — general cargo, containers, ro/ro, bulk, oil, liquefied gas, bunkers, shiprepair; *Odense* — general cargo, containers, ro/ro, bulk, oil, bunkers; *Vejle* — general cargo, ro/ro, bulk, oil, bunkers. **Principal airports:** *Aarhus (Tirstrup)* 25mls/38km, *Copenhagen* 6mls/10km.

DOMINICAN REPUBLIC

Capital: *Santo Domingo.* **Area:** 18,816 sq.mls/48,734 sq.km. **Population:** 6,416,000. **Standard Time:** GMT — 4 hrs. **Language:** Spanish. **Currency:** Peso of 100 centavos. **Weights & measures:** Metric system, Imperial units also in use. **IDD code:** dialling-in 1 809. **Principal ports:** *Puerto Plata* — general cargo,ro/ro, bunkers; *Rio Haina* — general cargo, containers, ro/ro, bulk, bunkers; *Santo Domingo* — general cargo, bunkers. **Principal airports:** *Puerto Plata (La Union), Santo Domingo (Las Americas)* 18.5mls/30km.

ECUADOR

Capital: *Quito.* **Area:** 109,484 sq.mls/283,560 sq.km. **Population:** 9,379,000. **Standard Time:** GMT — 5 hrs. **Language:** Spanish. **Currency:** Sucre of 100 centavos. **Weights & measures:** Metric system. **IDD code:** dialling-in 593. **Principal ports:** *Esmeraldas* — general cargo, ro/ro, oil loading at *Balao*

Terminal; Guauaquil — general cargo, containers, bulk, liquefied gas, bunkers; *Manta* — general cargo, containers, ro/ro, bulk. **Principal airports:** *Guayaquil (Simon Bolivar)* 3mls/5km, *Quito (Mariscal Sucre)* 5mls/8km.

EGYPT
Capital: *Cairo.* **Area:** 386,662 sq.mls/1,001,450 sq.km. **Population:** 52,000,000. **Standard Time:** GMT + 2 hrs. **Language:** Arabic, also English and French in business. **Currency:** Egyptian pound of 100 piastres. **Weights & measures:** Metric system, also local units in use. **IDD code:** dialling-in 20. **Principal ports:** *Alexandria* — general cargo, containers, ro/ro, bulk, oil, liquefied gas, bunkers, shiprepair; *Port Said* — general cargo, containers, ro/ro, bunkers, shiprepair; *Suez* — general cargo, oil, bulk, bunkers. **Principal airport:** *Cairo International* 14mls/22.5km.

ETHIOPIA
Capital: *Addis Ababa.* **Area:** 471,778 sq.mls/1,221,900 sq.km. **Population:** 43,350,000. **Standard Time:** GMT + 3 hrs. **Language:** Amharic, English. **Currency:** Birr of 100 cents. **Weights & measures:** Metric system, also local units in use. **IDD code:** dialling-in 251. **Principal ports:** *Assab* — general cargo, bulk, oil, bunkers; *Massawa* — general cargo, oil, bunkers. **Principal airport:** *Addis Ababa (Bole)* 5mls/8km.

FIJI
Capital: *Suva.* **Area:** 7,055 sq.mls/18,274 sq.km. **Population:** 715,373. **Standard Time:** GMT + 12 hrs. **Language:** English. **Currency:** Fiji dollar of 100 cents. **Weights & measures:** Metric system. **IDD code:** dialling-in 679. **Principal ports:** *Lautoka* — general cargo, ro/ro, oil, liquefied gas; *Levuka* — general cargo; *Suva* — general cargo, containers, ro/ro, bulk, oil, liquefied gas, bunkers, shiprepair. **Principal airport:** *Nandi International* 3mls/5km.

FINLAND
Capital: *Helsinki.* **Area:** 137,851 sq.mls/337,032 sq.km. **Population:** 4,908,000. **Standard Time:** GMT + 2 hrs. **Language:** Finnish, Swedish, also English and German in business. **Currency:** Markka of 100 pennia. **Weights & measures:** Metric system. **IDD code:** dialling-in 358. **Principal ports:** *Hamina* — general cargo, containers, ro/ro, bulk, oil, bunkers; *Hanko* — general cargo, containers, ro/ro, bulk, bunkers; *Helsinki* — general cargo, containers, ro/ro, bulk, oil, bunkers, shiprepair; *Kemi* — general cargo, ro/ro, oil, bunkers; *Kotka* — general cargo, containers, ro/ro, bulk, oil, bunkers, shiprepair; *Loviisa* — general cargo, containers, ro/ro, bulk; *Mariehamn* — general cargo, ro/ro, bulk, oil, bunkers; *Oulu* — general cargo, containers, ro/ro, bulk, oil, bunkers; *Rauma* — general cargo, containers, ro/ro, bulk, oil, bunkers, shiprepair; *Turku* — general cargo, containers, ro/ro, bulk, oil, bunkers, shiprepair; *Vaasa* — general cargo, bulk, oil, bunkers; *Ykspihlaja* — general cargo, ro/ro, bulk, oil. **Principal airport:** *Helsinki* 12mls/19km.

FRANCE
Capital: *Paris.* **Area:** 211,208 sq.mls/547,026 sq.km. **Population:** 55,279,000. **Standard Time:** GMT + 1 hr. **Language:** French. **Currency:** Franc of 100 centimes. **Weights & measures:** Metric system. **IDD code:** dialling-in 33. **Principal ports:** *Bayonne* — general cargo, bulk, oil, bunkers; *Bordeaux* — general cargo, ro/ro, bulk, oil, bunkers, shiprepair; *Boulogne* — general cargo, ro/ro, bulk, oil, bunkers; *Brest* — general cargo, oil, bunkers, shiprepair; *Calais* — general cargo, containers. ro/ro, bulk, oil, shiprepair; *Cherbourg* general cargo, containers, ro/ro, oil, bunkers, shiprepair; *Dieppe* — general cargo, containers, ro/ro, bulk, shiprepair; *Donges* — oil, liquefied gas, bunkers; *Dunkirk* — general cargo, containers, ro/ro, bulk, oil, bunkers, shiprepair; *Fos* — general cargo, containers, ro/ro, bulk, oil, liquefied gas, bunkers, shiprepair; *La Pallice* — general cargo, ro/ro, bulk, oil, bunkers, shiprepair; *Lavera* — oil, liquefied gas; *Le Havre* — general cargo, containers, ro/ro, dry and liquid bulk, oil, liquefied gas, bunkers, shiprepair; *Le Verdon* — containers, ro/ro, bulk, oil, bunkers; *Marseilles* — general cargo, containers, ro/ro, dry and liquid bulk, oil, liquefied gas, bunkers, shiprepair; *Nantes* — general cargo, containers, dry and liquid bulk, shiprepair; *Paris* — general cargo, containers, ro/ro; *Rouen* — general cargo, containers, ro/ro, dry and liquid bulk, oil, bunkers, shiprepair; *St. Louis du Rhone* — general cargo, containiers, ro/ro, dry and liquid bulk, oil, liquefied gas; *St. Malo* — general cargo, ro/ro, bulk; *St. Nazaire* — general cargo, bulk, shiprepair; *Sete* — general cargo, containers, ro/ro, bulk, oil, bunkers; *Toulon* — general cargo, containers, dry and liquid bulk, oil, shiprepair; *Ajaccio, Corsica* — general cargo, ro/ro, oil, liquefied gas; *Bastia, Corsica* — general cargo, ro/ro, oil, liquefied gas. **Principal airports:** *Bordeaux (Merignac)* 7.5mls/12km, *Lille (Lesquin)* 9mls/15km, *Lyon (Satolas)* 15.5mls/25km, *Marseilles (Marignane)* 15mls/24km, *Nantes (Chateau-Bougon)* 6 mls/9.5 km, *Nice (Cote d'Azur)* 4mls/7km, *Paris (Charles de Gaulle)* 14.5mls/23km, *Paris (Orly)* 9mls/14km, *Strasbourg (Entzheim)* 7mls/12km, *Toulouse (Blagnac)* 6mls/10kn.

GERMAN DEMOCRATIC REPUBLIC
Capital: *East Berlin.* **Area:** 41,828 sq.mls/108,333 sq.km. **Population:** 16,644,000. **Standard Time:** GMT + 1 hr. **Language:** German. **Currency:** Mark (Ostmark) of 100 pfennig. **Weights & measures:** Metric system. **IDD code:** dialling-in 37. **Principal ports:** *Rostock* — general cargo, containers, ro/ro, dry and liquid bulk, oil, liquefied gas, bunkers, shiprepair; *Stralsund* — general cargo, bulk; *Wismar*

— general cargo, dry and liquid bulk, oil, bunkers. **Principal airports:** *Berlin East (Schonefeld)* 12mls/19km, *Leipzig* 7.5mls/12km.

GERMAN FEDERAL REPUBLIC

Capital: *Bonn.* **Area:** 96,019 sq.mls/248,687 sq.km. **Population:** 61,149,000. **Standard Time:** GMT + 1 hr. **Language:** German. **Currency:** Deutsche Mark of 100 pfennig. **Weights & measures:** Metric system. **IDD code:** dialling-in 49. **Principal ports:** *Bremen* — general cargo, containers, ro/ro, dry and liquid bulk,oil, bunkers, shiprepair; *Bremerhaven* — general cargo, containers, ro/ro, bulk, bunkers, shiprepair; *Emden* — general cargo, ro/ro, bulk, oil, liquefied gas, bunkers, shiprepair; *Hamburg* — general cargo, containers, ro/ro, dry and liquid bulk, oil, bunkers, shiprepair; *Kiel* — general cargo, containers, ro/ro, bulk, bunkers, shiprepair; *Lubeck* — general cargo, containers, ro/ro, bulk, shiprepair; *Nordenham* — general cargo, dry and liquid bulk, bunkers. **Principal airports:** *Berlin West (Tegel)* 5mls/8km, *Bremen (Neuenland)* 2mls/3km, *Cologne/Bonn* 9mls/15km from Cologne, 12mls/20km from Bonn, *Dusseldorf* 5mls/8km, *Frankfurt International* 6mls/10km, *Hamburg (Fuhlsbutte)* 7.5mls/12km, *Hanover* 7mls/11km, *Munich (Riem)* 7mls/11km, *Nuremberg* 4mls/7.5km, *Stuttgart* 9mls/14km.

GHANA

Capital: *Accra.* **Area:** 92,100 sq.mls/238,539 sq.km. **Population:** 13,588,000. **Standard Time:** GMT. **Language:** English. **Currency:** New Cedi of 100 pesewas. **Weights & measures:** Metric system. **IDD code:** dialling-in 233. **Principal ports:** *Takoradi* — general cargo, bulk, oil, bunkers; *Tema* — general cargo, oil, bunkers. **Principal airport:** *Accra (Kotoka)* 6mls/10km.

GREECE

Capital: *Athens.* **Area:** 50,949 sq.mls/131,957 sq.km. **Population:** 9,935,000. **Standard Time:** GMT + 2 hrs. **Language:** Greek, also English and French in business. **Currency:** Drachma of 100 leptae. **Weights & measures:** Metric system. **IDD code:** dialling-in 30. **Principal ports:** *Patras* — general cargo, containers, oil, bunkers; *Piraeus* — general cargo, containers, bulk, oil, bunkers, shiprepair; *Thessaloniki* — general cargo, containers, bulk, oil, liquefied gas, bunkers; *Volos* — general cargo, ro/ro, bulk, oil, bunkers. **Principal airports:** *Athens (Hellinikon)* 6mls/10km, *Thessaloniki* 10mls/16km.

GUATEMALA

Capital: *Guatemala City.* **Area:** 42,042 sq.mls/108,80sq.km. **Population:** 7,963,000. **Standard Time:** GMT — 6 hrs. **Language:** Spanish. **Currency:** Quetzal of 100 centavos. **Weights & measures:** Metric system, also U.S. system and local units. **IDD code:** dialling-in 502. **Principal ports:** *Champerico* — general cargo; *Puerto Barrios* — general cargo, bulk, oil; *Puerto Quetzal* — general cargo, containers, bulk. **Principal airport:** *Guatemala City (La Aurora)* 4mls/6.5km.

GUYANA

Capital: *Georgetown.* **Area:** 83,000 sq.mls/214,970 sq.km. **Population:** 750,000. **Standard Time:** GMT — 3 hrs. **Language:** English. **Currency:** Guyana dollar of 100 cents. **Weights & measures:** Metric & Imperial systems. **IDD code:** dialling-in 592. **Principal port:** *Georgetown* — general cargo, containers, bulk, oil. **Principal airport:** *Georgetown (Timehri)* 25mls/40km.

HAITI

Capital: *Port au Prince.* **Area:** 10,714 sq.mls/27,750 sq.km. **Population:** 6,585,000. **Standard Time:** GMT — 5 hrs. **Language:** French, Creole. **Currency:** Gourde of 100 centimes. **Weights & measures:** Metric & U.S. systems. **IDD code:** dialling-in 509. **Principal ports:** *Cap Haitien* — general cargo, containers, ro/ro; *Port au Prince* — general cargo, containers, ro/ro, bulk, oil, liquefied gas. **Principal airport:** *Port au Prince International* 8mls/13km.

HONDURAS

Capital: *Tegucigalpa.* **Area:** 43,278 sq.mls/112,088 sq.km- **Population:** 4,372,000. **Standard Time:** GMT — 6 hrs. **Language:** Spanish. **Currency:** Lempira of 100 centavos. **Weights & measures:** Metric system, also U.S. system and local units. **IDD code:** dialling-in 504. **Principal ports:** *Puerto Cortes* — general cargo, containers, ro/ro, bulk, oil; *San Lorenzo* — general cargo, bulk; *Tela* — general cargo. **Principal airport:** *Tegucigalpa (Toncontin)* 3mls/5km.

HONG KONG

Capital: *Victoria.* **Area:** 412 sq.mls/1,067 sq.km. **Population:** 5,600,000. **Standard Time:** GMT + 8 hrs. **Language:** English, Chinese (Cantonese). **Currency:** Hong Kong dollar of 100 cents. **Weights & measures:** Metric and Imperial systems, also local units. **IDD code:** dialling-in 852. **Port** — general cargo, containers, ro/ro, bulk, bunkers, shiprepair. **Airport:** *Kai Tak* 4.5mls/7.5km from Victoria.

HUNGARY

Capital: *Budapest.* **Area:** 35,921 sq.mls/93,036 sq.km. **Population:** 10,658,000. **Standard Time:** GMT + 1 hrs. **Language:** Magyar, also English and German in business. **Currency:** Forint of 100 filler. **Weights & measures:** Metric system. **IDD code:** dialling-in 36. **Principal airport:** *Budapest (Ferihegy)* 10mls/16km.

ICELAND
Capital: *Reykjavik.* **Area:** 39,769 sq.mls/103,000 sq.km. **Population:** 247,000. **Standard Time:** GMT. **Language:** Icelandic, also English, German and Danish in business. **Currency:** Icelandic Krona of 100 aurar. **Weights & measures:** Metric system. **IDD code:** dialling-in 354. **Principal ports:** *Akureyri* — general cargo, oil; *Hafnafordur* — general cargo, oil, bunkers; *Reykjavik* — general cargo, ro/ro, bulk, oil, bunkers. **Principal airports:** *Keflavik* 32mls/51km from *Reykjavik, Reykjavik* 2.5mls/4km.

INDIA
Capital: *New Delhi.* **Area:** 1,269,219 sq.mls/3,287,263 sq.km. **Population:** 750,900,000. **Standard Time:** GMT + 5.5.hrs. **Language:** Hindi, English in official and business circles. **Currency:** Rupee of 100 paisa. **Weights & measures:** Metric and Imperial systems, also local units. **IDD code:** dialling-in 91. **Principal ports:** *Bombay* — general cargo, containers, bulk, oil, bunkers, shiprepair; *Calcutta* — general cargo, containers, bulk, oil, bunkers, shiprepair; *Cochin* — general cargo, containers, ro/ro, dry and liquid bulk, oil, liquefied gas, bunkers; *Haldia* — general cargo, containers, bulk oil, bunkers; *Kakinada* — general cargo, containers, bulk; *Kandla* — general cargo, containers, bulk, oil, liquefied gas, bunkers, shiprepair; *Madras* — general cargo, containers, bulk, oil, bunkers; *New Mangalore* — general cargo, containers, ro/ro, bulk, oil, bunkers; *Mormugao* — general cargo, dry and liquid bulk, oil, bunkers, shiprepair; *Tuticorin* — general cargo, containers, bulk, oil, bunkers; *Visakhapatnam* — general cargo, containers, bulk, oil, bunkers,shiprepair. **Principal airports:** *Bombay* 18mls/29km, *Calcutta* 8mls/13km, *Madras* 10ml/16km, *New Delhi* 9mls/14.5km.

INDONESIA
Capital: *Jakarta.* **Area:** 735,358 sq.mls/1,904,569 sq.km.. **Population:** 165,030,000. **Standard Time:** GMT + 7-9 hrs. **Language:** Bahasa Indonesia, also English and Dutch in business. **Currency:** Rupiah of 100 sen. **Weights & measures:** Metric system. **IDD code:** dialling-in 62. **Principal ports:** *Balikpapan* — general cargo, oil, bunkers; *Belawan* — general cargo, bunkers; *Jakarta* — general cargo, containers, bulk, oil, bunkers, shiprepair; *Palembang* — general cargo, containers, oil, bunkers; *Surabaya* — general cargo, containers, oil, bunkers, shiprepair. **Principal airports:** *Denpasar* 8mls/13km, *Jakarta International* 12.5mls/20km.

IRAN
Capital: *Tehran.* **Area:** 636,296 sq.mls/1,648,000 sq.km. **Population:** 49,765,000. **Standard Time:** GMT + 3.5 hrs. **Language:** Farsi, French and English in business. **Currency:** Rial of 100 dinars. **Weights & measures:** Metric system. **IDD code:** dialling-in 98. **Principal ports:** *Abadan* — oil, bunkers; *Bandar Khomeini* — general cargo, bulk; *Bandar Mahshahr* — general cargo, bulk, oil, bunkers; *Kharg Island* — oil, liquefied gas, bunkers; *Khorramshahr* — general cargo. **Principal airport:** *Tehran (Mehrabad)* 7mls/11km.

IRAQ
Capital: *Baghdad.* **Area:** 167,925 sq.mls/434,924 sq.km. **Population:** 16,278,320. **Standard Time:** GMT + 3 hrs. **Language:** Arabic, Kurdish, English. **Currency:** Iraqi dinar of 1,000 fils. **Weights & meausres:** Metric system. **IDD code:** dialling-in 964. **Principal ports:** *Basrah* — general cargo, bulk, oil, bunkers; *Umm Qasr* — general cargo, containers. Oil terminals at *Fao* and *Khor al Amaya.* **Principal airport:** *Baghdad (Saddam International)* 11mls/17km.

REPUBLIC OF IRELAND
Capital: *Dublin.* **Area:** 27,136 sq.mls/70,283 sq.km. **Population:** 3,540,650. **Standard Time:** GMT. **Language:** Irish and English. **Currency:** Punt of 100 pighne (Irish pound of 100 pence). **Weights & measures:** Metric and Imperial systems. **IDD code:** dialling-in 353. **Principal ports:** *Cork* — general cargo, containers, ro/ro, dry and liquid bulk, oil, liquefied gas, bunkers, shiprepair; *Dundalk* — general cargo, bulk; *Galway* — general cargo, containers, bulk, oil, bunkers; *Limerick* — general cargo, containers, bulk, oil, bunkers; *Waterford* — general cargo, containers. **Principal airports:** *Cork* 3.5mls/5.5km, *Dublin* 5.5mls/9km, *Shannon* 16mls/26km from Limerick.

ISRAEL
Capital: *Jerusalem.* **Area:** 8,019 sq.mls/20,770 sq.km. **Population:** 4,404,000. **Standard Time:** GMT + 2 hrs. **Language:** Hebrew, Arabic, also English and French. **Currency:** Shekel of 100 agorot. **Weights & measures:** Metric system. **IDD code:** dialling-in 972. **Principal ports:** *Ashdod* — general cargo, containers, ro/ro, bulk, bunkers; *Eliat* — general cargo, containers, bulk, oil, bunkers; *Haifa* — general cargo, containers, dry and liquid bulk, oil, bunkers, shiprepair. **Principal airport:** *Tel-Aviv Ben Gurion International)* 12mls/19km.

ITALY
Capital: *Rome.* **Area:** 116,324 sq.mls/301,278 sq.km. **Population:** 57,193,000. **Standard Time:** GMT + 1 hr. **Language:** Italian, also English in business. **Currency:** Lira. **Weights & measures:** Metric system. **IDD code:** dialling-in 39. **Principal ports:** *Ancona* — general cargo, containers, ro/ro, bulk, oil, bunkers, shiprepair; *Cagliari* — general cargo, containers, bulk, oil, bunkers;*Catania* — general cargo, containers, ro/ro, bulk,oil, bunkers; *Civitavecchia* — general cargo, bulk, oil, bunkers; *Genoa* — general cargo,containers, ro/ro, dry and liquid bulk, oil, bunkers, shiprepair; *La Spezia* — general

cargo, containers, bulk, oil, liquefied gas, bunkers, shiprepair; *Leghorn* — general cargo, containers, bulk, oil, bunkers, shiprepair; *Naples* — general cargo, containers, ro/ro, dry and liquid bulk, liquefied gas, bunkers, shiprepair; *Palermo* — general cargo, containers, dry and liquid bulk, oil, bunkers, shiprepair; *Ravenna* — general cargo, containers, ro/ro, dry and liquid bulk, oil, bunkers; *Savona* — general cargo, containers, ro/ro, dry and liquid bulk, oil, shiprepair; *Trieste* — general cargo, containers, ro/ro, dry and liquid bulk, oil, shiprepair; *Venice* — general cargo, containers, ro/ro, oil, liquefied gas, bunkers, shiprepair. **Principal airports:** *Bologna (G. Marconi)* 4mls/6.5km, *Genoa (Cristoforo Colombo)* 4.5mls/7km, *Milan (Linate)* 6mls/10km, *Naples (Capodichino)* 4.5mls/ 7km, *Pisa* 1.5mls/2km, *Rome (Leonardo de Vinci)* 22mls/35.5km, *Turin* 10mls/16km, *Venice* 8mls/ 13km.

IVORY COAST
Capital: *Abidjan.* **Area:** 124,503 sq.mls/322,462 sq.km. **Population:** 10,056,000. **Standard Time:** GMT. **Language:** French. **Currency:** CFA franc of 100 centimes. **Weights & measures:** Metric system. **IDD code:** dialling-in 225. **Principal port:** *Abidjan* — general cargo, containers, ro/ro, bulk, oil, bunkers. **Principal airport:** *Abidjan (Port Bouet)* 10mls/16km.

JAMAICA
Capital: *Kingston.* **Area:** 4,244 sq.mls/10,992 sq.km. **Population:** 2,355,000. **Standard Time:** GMT — 5 hrs. **Language:** English. **Currency:** Jamaican Dollar of 100 cents. **Weights & measures:** Imperial and metric systems. **IDD code:** dialling-in 1 809. **Principal ports:** *Kingston* — general cargo, containers, ro/ro, bulk, oil, bunkers; *Montego Bay* — general cargo, containers, oil, bunkers. **Principal airports:** *Kingston International* 11mls/17.5km, *Montego Bay (Sangster International)* 2mls/3.5km.

JAPAN
Capital: *Tokyo.* **Area:** 145,849sq.mls/337,748 sq.km. **Population:** 121,740,000.. **Standard Time:** GMT + 9 hrs. **Language:** Japanese, also English in business. **Currency:** Yen of 100 sen. **Weights & measures:**Metric system. **IDD code:** dialling-in 81. **Principal ports:** *Chiba* — general cargo, ro/ro, bulk, oil, liquefied gas, bunkers, shiprepair; *Hakodate* — general cargo, containers, ro/ro, bulk, oil; *Kawasaki* — general cargo, bulk, oil, liquefied gas, bunkers, shiprepair; *Kobe* — general cargo, containers, ro/ro, bulk, oil, liquefied gas, bunkers, shiprepair; *Moji* — general cargo, containers, bulk, oil, shiprepair; *Muroran* — general cargo, bulk, oil, shiprepair; *Nagoya* — general cargo, containers, ro/ro, bulk, oil, liquefied gas, bunkers, shiprepair; *Osaka* — general cargo, containers, ro/ro, bulk, oil, liquefied gas, bunkers, shiprepair; *Shimizu* — general cargo containers, bulk, oil; *Tokyo* — general cargo, containers, ro/ro, bulk, oil, bunkers; *Yokkaichi* — general cargo, containers, ro/ro, bulk, oil, bunkers; *Yokohama* — general cargo, containers, dry and liquid bulk,, oil, bunkers, shiprepair. **Principal airports:** *Nagoya (Komaki)* 11.5mls/18km, *Osaka International* 10mls/16km, *Tokyo (Narita)* 40mls/65 km.

JORDAN
Capital: *Amman.* **Area:** 37,738 sq.mls/97,740 sq.km. **Population:** 2,670,000. **Standard Time:** GMT + 2 hrs. **Language:** Arabic, English. **Currency:** Jordan dinar of 1,000 fils. **Weights & measures:** Metric system. **IDD code:** dialling-in 962. **Port:** *Aqaba* — general cargo, containers, ro/ro, dry and liquid bulk, oil, bunkers. **Principal airport:** *Amman (Queen Alia International)* 20mls/32km.

KENYA
Capital: *Nairobi.* **Area:** 224,961 sq.mls/582,646 sq.km. **Population:** 20,333,000. **Standard Time:** GMT + 3 hrs. **Language:** Kiswahili, English. **Currency:** Kenya shilling of 100 cents. **Weights & measures:** Metric system. **IDD code:** dialling-in 254. **Principal port:** *Mombasa* — general cargo, containers, ro/ro, dry and liquid bulk, oil, bunkers, shiprepair. **Principal airports:** *Mombasa (Moi International)* 8mls/13km, *Nairobi (Jomo Kenyatta International)* 4.5.mls/7km.

KOREA, NORTH
Capital: *Pyongyang.* **Area:** 46,540 sq.mls/120,538 sq.km. **Population:**20,385,000. **Standard Time:** GMT + 9 hrs. **Language:** Korean, also English in business. **Currency:** Won of 100 chen. **Weights & measures:** Metric system. **IDD code:** Not available. **Principal ports:** *Chogjin, Hungnam, Nampo.*

KOREA, REPUBLIC OF (SOUTH)
Capital: *Seoul.* **Area:** 38,025 sq.mls/98,484 sq.km. **Population:** 41,209,000. **Standard Time:** GMT + 9hrs. **Language:** Korean, also English in business. **Currency:** S. Korean Won of 100 jeon. **Weights & measures:** Metric system, also local units. **IDD code:** dialling-in 82. **Principal ports:** *Busan* — general cargo, containers, bulk, bunkers, shiprepair; *Inchon* — general cargo, containers, ro/ro, bulk, oil, liquefied gas, bunkers, shiprepair; *Ulsan* — general cargo, bulk, oil, liquefied gas, shiprepair. **Principal airport:***Seoul International (Kimpo)* 16mls/26km.

KUWAIT
Capital: *Kuwait.* **Area:** 6,877sq.mls/17,818 sq.km. **Population:** 1,695,000. **Standard Time:** GMT + 3 hrs. **Language:** Arabic, English. **Currency:** Kuwait dinar of 1,000 fils. **Weights & measures:** Metric

system. **IDD code:** dialling-in 965. **Principal ports:** *Kuwait* — general cargo, containers, bulk, bunkers, shiprepair; *Mina al Ahmadi* — oil, liquefied gas, bunkers; *Shuaiba* — general cargo, containers, ro/ro, bulk, oil, bunkers. **Principal airport:** *Kuwait International* 10 ml/16km.

LEBANON
Capital: *Beirut.* **Area:** 4,015 sq.mls/10,400 sq.km. **Population:** 2,668,000. **Standard Time:** GMT + 2 hrs. **Language:** Arabic, French. **Currency:** Lebanese poound of 100 piastres. **Weights & measures:** Metric system, also local units. **IDD code:** dialling-in 96. **Principal ports:** *Beirut* — general cargo, containers, ro/ro, bulk, oil, bunkers; *Tripoli* — general cargo, oil, bunkers. **Principal airport:** *Beirut International* 10mls/16km.

LIBERIA
Capital: *Monrovia.* **Area:** 43,000 sq.mls/111,369 sq.km. **Population:** 2,189,000. **Standard Time:** GMT. **Language:** English. **Currency:** Liberian dollar of 100 cents. **Weights & measures:** U.S. system. **IDD code:** dialling-in 231. **Principal ports:** *Buchanan* — general cargo, oil; *Monrovia* — general cargo, containers, bulk,oil, bunkers. **Principal airport:** *Monrovia (Roberts International)* 38mls/60km.

LIBYA
Capital: *Tripoli.* **Area:** 679,363 sq.mls/1,759,540 sq.km. **Population:** 3,800,000. **Standard Time:** GMT + 2 hrs. **Language:** Arabic, Italian, also English. **Currency:** Libyan dollar of 1,000 dirhams. **Weights & measures:** Metric system, also local units. **IDD code:** dialling-in 218. **Principal ports:** *Benghazi* — general cargo, containers, oil; *Marsa el Brega* — general cargo, oil, liquefied gas; *Tobruk* — general cargo, oil; *Tripoli* — general cargo, containers, ro/ro, bunkers. **Principal airports:** *Benghazi (Benina International)* 18mls/29km, *Tripoli International* 21mls/35km.

MADAGASCAR
Capital: *Antananarivo.* **Area:** 226,658 sq.mls/587,041 sq.km. **Population:** 11,000,000. **Standard Time:** GMT + 3 hrs. **Language:** Malagasy, French. **Currency:** Malagasy franc of 100 centimes. **Weights & measures:** Metric system. **IDD code:** dialling-in 261. **Principal ports:** *Antsiranana* — general cargo, containers, oil; *Mahajanga* — general cargo by lighter; *Toamasina* — general cargo, oil. **Principal airport:** *Antananarivo(Ivato)* 11mls/17km.

MALAYSIA (including Sabah and Sarawak)
Capital: *Kuala Lumpur.* **Area:** 127,581 sq.mls/330,434 sq.km. **Population:** 16,544,000. **Standard Time:** GMT + 8 hrs. **Language:** Bahasia Malaysia (Malay), English. **Currency:** Malaysian dollar of 100 cents. **Weights & measures:** Metric system, also local units. **IDD code:** dialling-in 60. **Principal ports:** *Johore Port* — general cargo, containers, dry and liquid bulk, oil, bunkers, shiprepair; *Kota Kinabalu* — general cargo, containers; *Kuching* — general cargo, containers, ro/ro, oil, bunkers; *Labuan* — general cargo, bulk, oil, shiprepair; *Miri* — general cargo, liquid bulk, oil; *Penang* — general cargo, containers, ro/ro bulk, oil, bunkers, shiprepair; *Port Kelang* — general cargo, containers, ro/ro, dry and liquid bulk, oil, shiprepair; *Sandakan* — general cargo, containers, liquid bulk, oil; *Tanjong Kidurong* — general cargo, containers, ro/ro, bulk, liquefied gas; *Tawau* — general cargo, containers, liquid bulk, oil. **Principal airports:** *Kota Kinabalu* 4mls/6.5km, *Kuala Lumpur (Subang International)* 14mls/22.5km, *Penang (Bayan Lepas International)* 10mls/16km.

MALTA
Capital: *Valletta.* **Area:** 122 sq.mls/316 sq.km. **Population:** 383,000. **Standard Time:** GMT + 1 hr. **Language:** Maltese, English. **Currency:** Maltese lira of 100 cents. **Weights & measures:** Metric system. **IDD code:** dialling-in 356. **Principal ports:** *Marsaxlokk* — general cargo, containers, ro/ro, bulk, oil, liquefied gas; *Valletta* — general cargo, containers, ro/ro, bunkers, shiprepair. **Principal airport:** *Luqa* 3mls/5km from Valletta.

MAURITANIA
Capital: *Nouakchott.* **Area:** 397,950 sq.mls/1,030,700 sq.km. **Population:** 1,888,000. **Standard Time:** GMT. **Language:** Arabic, French. **Currency:** Ouguiya of 5 khoums. **Weights & measures:** Metric system. **IDD code:** dialling-in 222 (not available from the UK). **Principal ports:** *Nouadhibou* — general cargo, bulk, oil, liquefied gas, bunkers; *Nouakchott* — general cargo. **Principal airport:** *Nouakchott* 2.5mls/4km.

MAURITIUS
Capital: *Port Louis.* **Area:** 788 sq.mls/2,040 sq.km. **Population:** 1,054,200. **Standard Time:** GMT + 4 hrs. **Language:** English, Creole, French. **Currency:** Mauritius rupee of 100 cents. **Weights & measures:** Metric system. **IDD code:** dialling-in 230. **Principal port:** *Port Louis* — general cargo, containers, dry and liquid bulk, liquefied gas, bunkers, shiprepair. **Principal airport:** *Port Louis (Plaisance)* 18mls/29km.

MEXICO
Capital: *Mexico City.* **Area:** 761,605 sq.mls/1,972,547 sq.km. **Population:** 78,524,000. **Standard Time:** GMT — 6 hrs. **Language:** Spanish, also English in business. **Currency:** Mexican peso of 100

centavos. **Weights & measures;** Metric system. **IDD code:** dialling-in 52. **Principal ports;** *Acapulco —* general cargo, oil; *Coatzacoalcos —* general cargo, containers, dry and liquid bulk, oil, liquefied gas, bunkers; *Guaymas —* general cargo, oil, bunkers; *Lazaro Cardenas —* general cargo, containers, bulk; *Mazatlan —* general cargo, containers, ro/ro, bulk, oil, shiprepair; *Progreso —* general cargo; *Tampico —* general cargo, containers, bulk, oil, bunkers, shiprepair; *Veracruz —* general cargo, containers, bulk, oil, liquefied gas, bunkers, shiprepair. **Principal airports:** *Acapulco International* 16mls/ 26km, *Mexico City International* 8mls/13km.

MOROCCO
Capital: *Rabat.* **Area:** 172,414 sq.mls/446,550 sq.km. **Population:** 23,602,000. **Standard TIme:** GMT + 1 hr. **Language:** Arabic, French, Spanish, also limited English. **Currency:** Moroccan dirham of 100 centimes. **Weights & measures:** Metric system. **IDD code:** dialling-in 212. **Principal ports:** *Agadir —* general cargo, ro/ro, oil, liquefied gas, bunkers; *Casablanca —* general cargo,containers, ro/ro, bulk, oil, bunkers, shiprepair; *Kenitra —* general cargo, bulk; *Safi —* general cargo, containers, dry and liquid bulk; *Tangier —* general cargo, bulk, ro/ro. **Principal airports:** *Agadir(Inezgane)* 5mls/8km, *Casablanca (Mohamed V)* 19mls/30km, *Marrakech (Menara)* 4mls/6km, *Rabat (Sale)* 6mls/10km, *Tangier (Boukhalef Souahel)* 9mls/15km.

MOZAMBIQUE
Capital: *Maputo.* **Area:** 309,495 sq.mls/801,590 sq.km. **Population:** 14,000,000. **Standard Time:** GMT + 2 hrs. **Language:** Portuguese. **Currency:** Metical of 100 centavos. **Weights & measures;** Metric system. **IDD code:** dialling-in 258. **Principal ports:** *Beira —* general cargo, containers, ro/ro, dry and liquid bulk, oil, bunkers; *Maputo —* general cargo, containers, ro/ro, bulk, oil, bunkers, shiprepair; *Nacala —* general cargo, containers, oil. **Principal airport:** *Maputo International* 5mls/ 8km.

NETHERLANDS
Capital: *Amsterdam.* **Seat of Government:** *The Hague.* **Area:** 15,770 sq.mls/40,844 sq.km. **Population:** 14,615,000. **Standard Time:** GMT + 1 hr. **Language:** Dutch, also, English, German and French in business. **Currency:** Guilder (florin) of 100 cents. **Weights & measures:** Metric system. **IDD code:** dialling-in 31. **Principal ports:** *Amsterdam —* general cargo, containers, ro/ro, dry and liquid bulk, oil, bunkers, shiprepair; *Delfzijl —* general cargo, containers, dry and liquid bulk, bunkers, shiprepair; *Dordrecht —* general cargo, containers ro/ro, bulk; *Harlingen —* general cargo, ro/ro, oil, liquefied gas, bunkers, shiprepair; *Terneuzen —* general cargo, ro/ro, bulk, liquefied gas; *Vlissingen (Flushing) —* general cargo, containers, ro/ro, dry and liquid bulk, oil, liquefied gas, bunkers, shiprepair; *Vlaardingen —* general cargo, dry and liquid bulk, bunkers, shiprepair; *Ymuiden —* general cargo, bulk, *Zaandam —* general cargo, containers, ro/ro, oil, bunkers. **Principal airports:** *Amsterdam (Schipol International)* 9.5mls/15km, *Maastricht* 4.5mls/7km, *Rotterdam* 5.5mls/9km.

NETHERLANDS ANTILLES
Capital: *Willemstad.* **Area:** 394 sq.mls/993 sq.km. **Population:** 183,000. **Standard Time:** GMT — 4 hrs. **Language:** Dutch. **Currency:** N.A. guilder of 100 cents. **Weights & measures:** Metric system. **IDD code:** dialling-in 599. **Principal ports:** *Kralendijk —* general cargo, ro/ro, oil; *Oranjestad —* general cargo, containers, bunkers, shiprepair; *Willemstad —* general cargo, containers, oil, bunkers, shiprepair. Oil terminals at *Bullen Bay, Caracas Bay, San Nicolas.* **Principal airports** *Curacao (Hato),* St. *Maarten (Juliana).*

NEW ZEALAND
Capital: *Wellington.* **Area:** 103,736 sq.mls/269,676 sq.km. **Population:** 3,307,000. **Standard Time:** GMT + 12 hrs. **Language:** English. **Currency:** New Zealand dollar of 100 cents. **Weights & measures:** Metric system. **IDD code:** dialling-in 64. **Principal ports:** *Auckland —* general cargo, containers, ro/ ro, bulk, oil, bunkers, shiprepair; *Bluff —* general cargo, containers, ro/ro, bulk, oil, shiprepair; *Dunedin —* general cargo, containers, ro/ro, oil, liquefied gas; *Lyttelton —* general cargo, containers, ro/ro, bulk, oil,liquefied gas,. bunkers, shiprepair; *Napier —* general cargo, containers, ro/ro, dry and liquid bulk, oil, bunkers; *New Plymouth —* general cargo, containers, bulk, oil, liquefied gas; *Timaru —* general cargo, containers, ro/ro, bulk, oil; *Wellington —* general cargo, containers, ro/ro, oil, bunkers, shiprepair. **Principal airports:** *Auckland International (Mangere)* 14mls/22.5km, *Christchurch International* 7mls/11km, *Wellington International* 5mls/8km.

NICARAGUA
Capital: *Managua.* **Area:** 50,193 sq.mls/130,000 sq.km. **Population:** 3,272,000. **Standard Time:** GMT — 6 hrs. **Language:** Spanish. **Currency:** Cordoba of 100 centavos. **Weights & measures:** Metric system, also local units. **IDD code:** dialling-in 505. **Principal ports:** *Corinto —* general cargo, oil; *Puerto Cabezas —* general cargo, bunkers, *San Juan del Sur —* general cargo. **Principal airports** *Managua International* 5mls/9km.

NIGERIA
Capital: *Lagos.* **Area:** 356,669 sq.mls/923,701 sq.km. **Population:** 100,000,000. **Standard Time:** GMT + 1 hr. **Language:** English. **Currency:** Naira of 100 kobo. **Weights & measures:** Metric system. **IDD**

code: dialling-in 234. **Principal ports:** *Calabar* — general cargo, bulk, oil, bunkers; *Lagos (including Apapa wharves)* — general cargo, containers, ro/ro, bulk, oil, bunkers, shiprepair; *Port Harcourt* — general cargo, ro/ro, bulk, oil, bunkers; *Sapele* — general cargo, containers, ro/ro, bulk, bunkers; *Warri* — general cargo, ro/ro, bunkers. **Principal airports:** *Kano (Melam-Amimi) International* 5mls/8km, *Lagos (Murtala Muhammed)* 13.5mls/22km, *Port Harcourt* 15mls/24km.

NORWAY
Capital: *Oslo.* **Area:** 125,181 sq.mls/324,219 sq.km. **Population:** 4,198,000. **Standard Time:** GMT + 1 hr. **Language:** Norwegian, also Danish, Swedish and English in business. **Currency:** Krone of 100 øre. **Weights & measures:** Metric system. **IDD code:** dialling-in 47. **Principal ports:** *Bergen* — general cargo, containers, ro/ro, bulk, oil, bunkers, shiprepair; *Drammen* — general cargo, containers, ro/ro, bulk, oil, liquefied gas, bunkers, shiprepair; *Haugesund* — general cargo, ro/ro, bulk, oil, bunkers, shiprepair; *Kristiansand S* — general cargo, containers, ro/ro, bulk, bunkers, shiprepair; *Oslo* — general cargo, containers, ro/ro, bulk, oil, bunkers; *Porsgrunn* — bulk oil, liquefied gas, bunkers, shiprepair; *Stavanger* — general cargo, containers, ro/ro, bulk, oil, bunkers, shiprepair; *Trondheim* — general cargo, containers, ro/ro, bulk, oil, bunkers, shiprepair. **Principal airports:** *Bergen (Flesland)* 12mls/19km, *Oslo (Fornebu)* 5mls/8km, *Stavanger (Sola)* 9mls/14.5km.

OMAN
Capital: *Muscat.* **Area:** 82,030 sq.mls/212,457 sq.km. **Population:** 1,500,000. **Standard Time:** GMT + 4 hrs. **Language:** Arabic, English. **Currency:** Omani rial of 1,000 baiza. **Weights & measures:** Metric system. **IDD code:** dialling-in 968. **Principal ports:** *Mina-al-Fahal* — oil, bunkers; *Mina Qaboos* — general cargo, containers, ro/ro, bulk, bunkers; *Mina Raysut* — general cargo, containers, bulk. **Principal airport:** *Muscat (Seeb)* 25mls/40km.

PAKISTAN
Capital: *Islamabad.* **Area:** 307,374 sq.mls/746,045 sq.km. **Population:** 96,180,000. **Standard Time:** GMT + 5 hrs. **Language:** Urdu, English. **Currency:** Rupee of 100 paisa. **Weights & measures:** Metric system, also local units. **IDD code:** dialling-in 92. **Principal port:** *Karachi* — general cargo, bulk, oil, bunkers, shiprepair. **Principal airports:** *Islamabad International* 5mls/8km, *Karachi (Civil)* 12mls/19km.

PANAMA
Capital: *Panama City.* **Area:** 29,762 sq.mls/77,082 sq.km. **Population:** 2,227,250. **Standard Time:** GMT − 5 hrs. **Language:** Spanish, English. **Currency:** Balboa of 100 centesimos. **Weights & measures:** Metric system. **IDD code:** dialling-in 507. **Principal ports:** *Almirante* — general cargo, oil; *Balboa* — general cargo, containers, oil, bunkers, shiprepair; *Cristobal* — general cargo, containers, oil, bunkers, shiprepair. **Principal airport:** *Panama City* 17mls/27km.

PAPUA NEW GUINEA
Capital: *Port Moresby.* **Area:** 178,704 sq.mls/462,840 sq.km. **Population:** 3,329,000. **Standard Time:** GMT + 10 hrs. **Language:** English, Pidgin. **Currency:** Kina of 100 toea. **Weights & measures:** Metric system. **IDD code:** dialling in-675. **Principal ports:** *Anewa Bay* — general cargo, containers, bulk, oil, liquefied gas; *Kaveieng* — general cargo, containers; *Lae* — general cargo, oil, liquefied gas; *Madang* — general cargo, containers, oil; *Port Moresby* — general cargo, containers, oil; *Rabaul* — general cargo, containers, oil, bunkers. **Principal airport:** *Port Moresby (Jackson Field)* 5mls/8km.

PARAGUAY
Capital: *Asuncion.* **Area:** 157,048 sq.mls/406,752 sq.kmm. **Population:** 3,930,000. **Standard Time:** GMT − 3 hrs. **Language:** English. **Currency:** Guarani of 100 centimos. **Weights & measures:** Metric system, also local units. **IDD code:** dialling-in 595. **Principal port:** *Asuncion* — general cargo, containers, dry and liquid bulk, oil. **Principal airport:** *Asuncion (Presidente Gen. Stroessner)* 9mls/15km.

PERU
Capital: *Lima.* **Area:** 496,225 sq.mls/1,285,216 sq.km. **Population:** 19,700,000. **Standard Time:** GMT − 5 hrs. **Language:** Spanish, Quecha, also English in business. **Currency:** Sol of 100 centavos. **Weights & measures:** Metric system, also local units. **IDD code:** dialling-in 51. **Principal ports:** *Callao* — general cargo, containers, bulk, oil, bunkers, shiprepair; *Matarani* — general cargo, containers, ro/ro, dry and liquid bulk; *Salaverry* — general cargo, dry and liquid bulk, oil; *San Juan* — general cargo; *San Nicolas* — general cargo, bulk, oil; *Takara* — general cargo, oil, bunkers. **Principal airport:** *Lima (Jorge Chavez International)* 10mls/16km

PHILIPPINES
Capital: *Manila.* **Area:** 115,831 sq.mls/300,000 sq.km. **Population:** 57,000,000. **Standard Time:** GMT + 8 hrs. **Language:** Filipino, English. **Currency:** Philippine peso of 100 centavos. **Weights & measures:** Metric system. **IDD code:** dialling-in 63. **Principal ports:** *Batangas* — general cargo, oil, bunkers; *Cebu* — general cargo, containers, bulk,oil, liquefied gas, bunkers; *Davao* — general cargo, containers, bulk, oil, liquefied gas, bunkers; *Iloilo* — general cargo, containers, bunkers; *Manila* —

general cargo, containers, ro/ro, oil, bunkers, shiprepair. **Principal airport:** *Manila International* 7.5mls/12km.

POLAND
Capital: *Warsaw.* **Area:** 120,727 sq.mls/312,683 sq.km. **Population:** 37,203,000. **Standard Time:** GMT + 1 hr. **Language:** Polish, also Russian, German and English in business. **Currency:** Zloty of 100 groszy. **Weights & measures:** Metric system. **IDD code:** dialling-in 48. **Principal ports:** *Gdansk —* general cargo, containers, ro/ro, bulk, oil, bunkers, shiprepair; *Gdynia —* general cargo, containers, ro/ro, bulk, oil, bunkers, shiprepair; *Szczecin —* general cargo, containers, bulk, bunkers, shiprepair. **Principal airport:** *Warsaw (Okecie)* 6mls/10km.

PORTUGAL
Capital: *Lisbon.* **Area:** 35,500 sq.mls/92,082 sq.km. **Population:** 10,229,000. **Standard Time:** GMT. **Language:** Portuguese, also Spanish, English and French in business. **Currency:** Escudo of 100 centavos. **Weights & measures:** Metric system. **IDD code:** dialling-in 351. **Principal ports:** *Leixoes —* general cargo, containers, ro/ro, oil, liquefied gas, bunkers, shiprepair; *Lisbon —* general cargo, containers, dry and liquid bulk, oil, liquefied gas, bunkers, shiprepair; *Setubal —* general cargo, bulk, bunkers, shiprepair. **Principal airports:** *Faro* 4.5mls/7km, *Lisbon* 4.5mls/7km, *Oporto (Porto)* 10.5mls/17km.

PUERTO RICO
Capital: *San Juan.* **Area:** 3,421 sq.mls/8,860 sq.km. **Population:** 3,279,000. **Standard Time:** GMT — 4 hrs. **Language:** Spanish, English. **Currency:** U.S. dollar of 100 cents. **Weights & measures:** U.S. system. **IDD code:** dialling-in 1 809 (not available from the UK). **Principal ports:** *Ponce —* general cargo, containers, ro/ro, bunkers; *San Juan —* general cargo, containers, ro/ro, oil, bunkers, shiprepair. **Principal airport:** *San Juan (Luis Munoz Marin International)* 9mls/14.5km.

QATAR
Capital: *Doha.* **Area:** 4,247 sq.mls/11,000 sq.km. **Population:** 315,000. **Standard Time:** GMT + 3 hrs. **Language:** Arabic, English. **Currency:** Qatar riyal of 100 dirhams. **Weights & measures:** Metric system. **IDD code:** dialling-in 9974. **Principal ports:** *Doha —* general cargo, containers; *Umm Said —* general cargo, dry and liquid bulk, oil, liquefied gas. **Principal airport:** *Doha* 5mls/8km.

ROMANIA
Capital: *Bucharest.* **Area:** 91,705 sq.mls/237,500 sq.km. **Population:** 22,823,500. **Standard Time:** GMT + 2 hrs. **Language:** Romanian, Hungarian, German. **Currency:** Leu of 100 bani. **Weights & measures:** Metric system. **IDD code:** dialling-in 40. **Principal ports:** *Constantza —* general cargo, containers, ro/ro, bulk, oil, bunkers, shiprepair; *Galatz —* general cargo, bulk, bunkers, shiprepair. **Principal airport:** *Bucharest (Otopeni)* 10mls/16km.

ST. CHRISTOPHER & NEVIS
Capital: *Basseterre.* **Area:** 101 sq.mls/261 sq.km. **Population:** 45,100. **Standard Time:** GMT — 4 hrs. **Language:** English. **Currency:** East Caribbean dollar of 100 cents. **Weights & measures:** Metric and Imperial systems. **IDD code:** dialling-in 1 809 469. **Principal port:** *Basseterre —* general, containers, ro/ro, bulk. **Principal airport:** *Basseterre (Golden Rock)* 2mls/3km.

ST. LUCIA
Capital: *Castries.* **Area:** 238 sq.mls/616 sq.km. **Population:** 138,000. **Standard Time:** GMT — 4 hrs. **Language:** English. **Currency:** East Caribbean dollar of 100 cents. **Weights & measures:** Metric and Imperial systems. **IDD code:** dialling-in 809 45. **Principal port:** *Castries —* general cargo, containers, ro/ro, bulk, oil, liquefied gas. **Principal airport:** *Castries (Vigie)* 2mls/3km.

SAUDI ARABIA
Capital: *Riyadh.* **Area:** 830,000 sq.mls/2,149,000 sq.km. **Population:** 12,400,000. **Standard Time:** GMT + 3 hrs. **Language:** Arabic, also English in business. **Currency:** Saudi riyal of 100 halalah. **Weights & measures:** Metric system. **IDD code:** dialling-in 966. **Principal ports:** *Dammam —* general cargo, containers, ro/ro, bulk, bunkers, shiprepair; *Gizan —* general cargo, containers, ro/ro, bunkers; *Jeddah —* general cargo, containers, ro/ro, bulk, oil, bunkers, shiprepair; *Jubail —* general cargo, containers, ro/ro, bulk, oil, bunkers; *Yanbu (Yenbo) —* general cargo, containers, ro/ro, bulk, oil, liquefied gas, bunkers. **Principal airports:** *Dhahran* 5mls/8km, *Jeddah (King Abdulaziz International)* 22mls/35km.

SENEGAL
Capital: *Dakar.* **Area:** 75,750 sq.mls/196,192 sq.km. **Population:** 6,540,000. **Standard Time:** GMT. **Language:** French. **Currency:** CFA franc of 100 centimes. **Weights & measures:** Metric system, **IDD code:** dialling-in 221. **Principal port:** *Dakar —* general cargo, containers, ro/ro, oil, liquefied gas, bunkers, shiprepair. **Principal airport:** *Dakar (Yoff)* 10.5mls/17km.

SIERRA LEONE
Capital: *Freetown.* **Area:** 27,699 sq.mls/71,740 sq.km. **Population:** 3,700,000. **Standard Time:** GMT. **Language:** English. **Currency:** CFA franc of 100 cents. **Weights & measures:** Metric system. **IDD**

code: dialling-in 232. **Principal port:** *Freetown* — general cargo, containers, bulk, oil, bunkers. **Principal airport:** *Freetown (Lungi International)* 18mls/29km.

SINGAPORE
Capital: *Singapore City.* **Area:** 224.5 sq.mls/581 sq.km. **Population:** 2,612,800. **Standard Time:** GMT + 8 hrs. **Language:** Malay, English, Mandarin, Tamil. **Currency:** Singapore dollar of 100 cents. **Weights & measures:** Metric system. **IDD code:** dialling-in 65. **Port:** *Singapore* — general cargo, containers, ro/ro, dry and liquid bulk, oil, liquefied gas, bunkers, shiprepair. **Airport:** *Singapore (Changi)* 12.5mls/20km.

SOMALIA
Capital: *Mogadiscio.* **Area:** 246,210 sq.mls/637,657 sq.km. **Population:** 5,800,000. **Standard Time:** GMT + 3 hrs. **Language:** Arabic, Italian, English. **Currency:** Somali shilling of 100 centesimi. **Weights & measures:** Metric system, also local units. **IDD code:** dialling-in 252. **Principal ports:** *Kismayu* — general cargo, containers; *Mogadiscio* — general cargo, containers, oil. **Principal airport:** *Mogadiscio International* 4mls/6km.

SOUTH AFRICA
Capital: *Pretoria.* **Area:** 471,445 sq.mls/1,221,037 sq.km. **Population:** 32,392,000. **Standard Time:** GMT + 2 hrs. **Language:** Afrikaans, English. **Currency:** Rand of 100 cents. **Weights & measures:** Metric system. **IDD code:** dialling-in 27. **Principal ports:** *Cape Town* — general cargo, containers, ro/ro, bulk, oil, bunkers, shiprepair; *Durban* — general cargo, containers, ro/ro, bulk, oil, bunkers, shiprepair; *East London* — general cargo, containers, ro/ro, bulk, bunkers, shiprepair; *Port Elizabeth* — general cargo, containers, ro/ro, bulk, bunkers. **Principal airports:** *Cape Town (D.F. Malan)* 9mls/14km, *Durban (Louis Botha)* 12mls/19.5km, *Johannesburg (Jan Smuts)* 15mls/24km.

SPAIN
Capital: *Madrid.* **Area:** 194,897 sq.mls/504,782 sq.km. **Population:** 38,818,350. **Standard Time:** GMT + 1 hr. **Language:** Spanish, also English in business. **Currency:** Peseta of 100 centimos. **Weights & measures:** Metric system. **IDD code:** dialling-in 34. **Principal ports:** *Algeciras* — general cargo, containers, ro/ro, bulk, oil, liquefied gas, bunkers; *Alicante* — general cargo, containers, ro/ro, oil, bunkers, shiprepair; *Aviles* — general cargo, containers, dry and liquid bulk, bunkers; *Barcelona* — general cargo, containers, ro/ro, bulk, oil, bunkers, shiprepair; *Bilbao* — general cargo, containers, ro/ro, bulk, oil; *Cadiz* — general cargo, containers, ro/ro, bulk, oil, bunkers, shiprepair; *Carthagena* — general cargo, containers, bulk oil, liquefied gas, bunkers, shiprepair; *Corunna* — general cargo, containers, ro/ro, bulk, oil, liquefied gas, bunkers, shiprepair; *Gijon* — general cargo, containers, ro/ro, bulk, oil, liquefied gas, bunkers, shiprepair; *Huelva* — general cargo, bulk, oil, liquefied gas, bunkers; *Malaga* — general cargo, containers, oil, liquefied gas, bunkers, shiprepair; *Palma de Mallorca* — general cargo, containers, ro/ro, oil, bunkers; *Pasajes* — general cargo, containers, ro/ro, bulk, oil, bunkers, shiprepair; *Santander* — general cargo, containers, ro/ro, dry and liquid bulk, oil, bunkers, shiprepair; *Seville* — general cargo, containers, ro/ro, bunkers; *Tarragona* — general cargo, containers, ro/ro, bulk, oil, bunkers, shiprepair; *Valencia* — general cargo, containers, ro/ro, dry and liquid bulk, oil, bunkers, shiprepair; *Vigo* — general cargo, containers, ro/ro, bulk, oil, liquefied gas, bunkers, shiprepair. **Principal airports:** *Alicante* 7.5mls/12km, *Barcelona* 9mls/15km, *Bilbao* 6mls/9km, *Las Palmas (Canary Islands)* 14mls/22km, *Madrid (Barajas)* 10mls/16km, *Palma de Mallorca* 5.5mls/9km, *Seville* 7.5mls/12km, *Valencia* 7mls/11km.

SRI LANKA
Capital: *Colombo.* **Area:** 25,332 sq.mls/65,610 sq.km. **Population:** 15,837,000. **Standard Time:** GMT + 5.5. hrs. **Language:** Sinhalese, English, Tamil. **Currency:** Sri Lanka rupee of 100 cents. **Weights & measures:** Metric system. **IDD code:** dialling-in 94. **Principal ports:** *Colombo* — general cargo, containers, bulk, oil, bunkers, shiprepair; *Trincomalee* — general cargo, bulk, oil, bunkers, shiprepair. **Principal airport:** *Colombo (Katunayake)* 20mls/32km.

SUDAN
Capital: *Khartoum.* **Area:** 967,500 sq.mls/2,505,631 sq.km. **Population:** 21,550,000. **Standard Time:** GMT + 2 hrs. **Language:** Arabic, English. **Currency:** Sudanese pound of 100 piastres. **Weights & measures:** Metric system, also Imperial and local units. **IDD code:** dialling-in 249. **Principal port:** *Port Sudan* — general cargo, containers, bulk, oil, liquefied gas, bunkers. **Principal airport:** *Khartoum* 2.5mls/4km.

SURINAME
Capital: *Paramaribo.* **Area:** 63,037 sq.mls/163,265 sq.km. **Population:** 375,000. **Standard Time:** GMT − 3 hrs. **Language:** Dutch, English. **Currency:** Suriname guilder of 100 cents. **Weights & measures:** Metric system. **IDD code:** dialling-in 597. **Principal port:** *Paramaribo* — general cargo, containers, bulk, oil, liquefied gas. **Principal airport:** *Paramaribo (Zanderij)* 28mls/45km.

SWEDEN
Capital: *Stockholm.* **Area:** 173,732 sq.mls/449,964 sq.km. **Population:** 8,358,000. **Standard Time:**

GMT + 1 hr. **Language:** Swedish, also English and German in business. **Currency:** Krone of 100 øre. **Weights & measures:** Metric system. **IDD code:** dialling-in 46. **Principal ports:** *Gavle (Gefle)* — general cargo, containers, ro/ro, bulk, oil, bunkers, shiprepair; *Gothenburg* — general cargo, containers, ro/ro, dry and liquid bulk, oil, bunkers, shiprepair; *Halmstad* — general cargo, containers, ro/ro, bulk, oil, bunkers; *Hernosand* — general cargo, bulk, oil, bunkers; *Helsingborg* — general cargo, containers, ro/ro, bulk, oil, bunkers, shiprepair; *Hudiksvall* — general cargo, containers, ro/ro, oil, bunkers; *Landskrona* — bulk, liquefied gas, bunkers, shiprepair; *Malmo* — general cargo, containers, ro/ro, bulk, oill, bunkers, shiprepair; *Norrkoping* — general cargo, containers, ro/ro, bulk, oil, bunkers; *Oxelosund* — general cargo, ro/ro, bulk, oil; *Stockholm* — general cargo, containers, ro/ro, bulk, oil, bunkers, shiprepair; *Sundsvall* — general cargo, containers, ro/ro, bulk, oil; *Wallhamm* — general cargo, containers, ro/ro, bunkers. **Principal airports:** *Gothenburg (Landvetter)* 15mls/25km, *Stockholm (Arlanda)* 25mls/41km.

SWITZERLAND
Capital: *Berne.* **Area:** 15,950 sq.mls/41,307 sq.km. **Population:** 6,532,400. **Standard Time:** GMT + 1 hr. **Language:** French, German, Italian. **Currency:** Swiss franc of 100 cents. **Weights & measures:** Metric system. **IDD code:** dialling-in 41. **Principal airports:** *Basle/Mulhouse* 7mls/12km, *Berne (Belp)* 5.5mls/9km, *Geneva* 2.5mls/4km, *Zurich* 7.5mls/12km.

SYRIA
Capital: *Damascus.* **Area:** 71,498 sq.mls/184,050 sq.km. **Population:** 10,267,000. **Standard Time:** GMT + 2 hrs. **Language:** Arabic, also French and English in business. **Currency:** Syrian pound of 100 piastres. **Weights & measures:** Metric system, also local units. **IDD code:** dialling-in 963. **Principal ports:** *Lattakia* — general cargo, containers, ro/ro, bulk, oil, bunkers; *Tartous* — general cargo, containers, ro/ro, bulk, oil, bunkers. **Principal airports:** *Aleppo (Nerjab)* 6.5.mls/10km.

TAIWAN
Capital: *Taipei.* **Area:** 13,800 sq.mls/35,739 sq.km. **Population:** 19,135,200. **Standard Time:** GMT + 8 hrs. **Language:** Chinese,also Japanese and Enlgish. **Currency:** New Taiwan dollar of 100 cents. **Weights & measures:** Metric system, also local units. **IDD code:** dialling-in 886. **Principal ports:** *Hualien* — general cargo, bulk, bunkers; *Kaohsiung* — general cargo, containers, ro/ro, dry and liquid bulk, oil, liquefied gas, bunkers, shiprepair; *Keelung* — general cargo, containers, bulk, oil, bunkers, shiprepair; *Taichung* — general cargo, containers, dry and liquid bulk, bunkers. **Principal airport:** *Taipei (Chiang Kai Shek International)* 25mls/40km.

THAILAND
Capital: *Bangkok.* **Area:**198,115 sq.mls/513,115 sq.km. **Population:** 52,970,000. **Standard Time:** GMT + 7 hrs. **Language:** Thai, Chinese, also English. **Currency:** Baht of 100 satang. **Weights & measures:** Metric system, also local units. **IDD code:** dialling-in 66. **Principal port:** *Bangkok* — general cargo, containers, ro/ro, bulk, oil, bunkers, shiprepair. **Principal airport:** *Bangkok International* 15.5mls/25km.

TRINIDAD & TOBAGO
Capital: *Port of Spain.* **Area:** 1,980 sq.mls/5,127 sq.km. **Population:** 1,185,000. **Standard Time:** GMT − 4 hrs. **Language:** English. **Currency:** Trinidad & Tobago dollar of 100 cents. **Weights & measures:** Metric and Imperial systems. **IDD code:** dialling-in 1 809. **Principal port:** *Port of Spain* — general cargo, containers, bunkers, shiprepair. **Principal airport:** *Port of Spain (Piarco International)* 16mls/25.2km.

TUNISIA
Capital: *Tunis.* **Area:** 63,170 sq.mls/163,610 sq.km. **Population:** 7,205,100. **Standard Time:** GMT + 1 hr. **Language:** Arabic, French. **Currency:** Tunisian dinar of 1,000 millimes. **Weights & measures:** Metric system, also local units. **IDD code:** dialling-in 216. **Principal ports:** *Bizerta* — general cargo, containers, dry and liquid bulk, oil; *Sfax* — general cargo, containers, bulk, oil, liquefied gas, bunkers; *Sousse* — general cargo, bulk; *Tunis* — general cargo, containers, ro/ro, liquid bulk, bunkers. **Principal airports:** *Djerba (Melita)* 3.5mls/6km, *Tunis (Carthage)* 5mls/8km.

TURKEY
Capital: *Ankara.* **Area:** 301,380 sq.mls/783,576 sq.km. **Population:** 51,428,510. **Standard Time:** GMT + 3 hrs. **Language:** Turkish, also German, French and English in business. **Currency:** Turkish lira of 100 kurus. **eights & measures:** Metric system. **IDD code:** dialling-in 90. **Principal ports:** *Iskenderun* — general cargo, containers, bulk, oil, bunkers; *Istanbul* — general cargo, oil, bunkers, shiprepair; *Izmir* — general cargo, containers, ro/ro, bulk, oil, bunkers, shiprepair; *Mersin* — general cargo, containers, ro/ro, bulk, oil, bunkers. **Principal airports:** *Ankara (Esenboga)* 22mls/35km, *Istanbul (Ataturk)* 15mls/24km.

U.S.S.R.
Capital: *Moscow.* **Area:** 8,649,460 sq.mls/22,402,000 sq.km. **Population:** 281,700,000. **Standard Time:** GMT + 3-11 hrs. **Language:** Russian, also English and German in business. **Currency:** Rouble

of 100 kopeks. **Weights & measures:** Metric system. **IDD code:** dialling-in 7. **Principal ports:** *Archanagel, Batum, Klaipeda, Leningrad, Murmansk, Nakhodka, Novorossisk, Odessa, Poti, Riga, Tallinn, Tuapse, Ventspils, Zhdanov.* **Principal airports:** *Leningrad (Pulkovo)* 10.5mls/17km, *Moscow (Sheremetyevo)* 18mls/29km.

UNITED ARAB EMIRATES
Composed of seven Emirates — *Abu Dhabi, Ajman, Dubai, Fujairah, Ras al Khaimah, Sharjah and Umm al Qaiwain.* **Area:** 32,278 sq.mls/83,000 sq.km. **Population:**1,600,000. **Standard Time:** GMT + 4 hrs. **Language:** Arabic, English. **Currency:** UAE dirham of 100 fils. **Weights & measures:** Metric and Imperial systems, also local units. **IDD code:** dialling-in 971. **Principal ports:** *Abu Dhabi* — general cargo, containers, ro/ro, bulk, bunkers; *Dubai* — general cargo, containers, ro/ro, oil, bunkers, shiprepair; *Fujairah* — general cargo, containers, bulk; *Jebel Ali* — general cargo, containers, ro/ro, oil, bunkers; *Jebel Dhanna* — general cargo, oil; *Khor Fakkan* — general cargo, containers, ro/ro, bulk, bunkers; *Mina Saqr* — general cargo, containers, ro/ro, bulk, bunkers; *Sharjah* — general cargo, containers, ro/ro, bulk, oil, bunkers; *Umm al Qaiwain* — general cargo, containers. **Principal airports.** *Abu Dhabi International* 23mls/37km, *Dubai* 2.5mls/4km, *Sharjah* 6mls/10km.

UNITED KINGDOM
Capital: *London.* **Area:** 94,227 sq.mls/244,046 sq.km. **Population:** 56,972,700. **Standard Time:** GMT. **Language:** English. **Currency:** Pound sterling of 100 pence. **Weights & measures:** Metric and Imperial systems. **IDD code:** dialling-in 44. **Principal ports:** *Aberdeen* — general cargo, containers, ro/ro, bulk, oil, offshore, bunkers, shiprepair; *Belfast* — general cargo, containers, ro/ro, dry and liquid bulk, oil, liquefied gas, bunkers, shiprepair; *Bristol/Avonmouth* — general cargo, containers, ro/ro, dry and liquid bulk, oil, liquefied gas, bunkers, shiprepair; *Cardiff* — general cargo, bulk, oil, bunkers, shiprepair; *Dover* — general cargo, containers, ro/ro, bulk, oil; *Dundee* — general cargo, containers, ro/ro, bulk, oil, offshore, bunkers; *Felixstowe* — general cargo, containers, ro/ro, oil, bunkers; *Glasgow* — general cargo, containers, bulk, bunkers, shiprepair; *Grangemouth* — general cargo, containers, ro/ro, bulk, oil, liquefied gas, bunkers, shiprepair; *Greenock* — general cargo, containers, ro/ro, bulk, bunkers, shiprepair; *Goole* — general cargo, containers, ro/ro, bulk, bunkers, shiprepair; *Hull* — general cargo, containers, ro/ro, dry and liquid bulk, oil, bunkers, shiprepair; *Immingham* — general cargo, containers, ro/ro, dry and liquid bulk, oil, bunkers, shiprepair; *Leith* — general cargo, containers, ro/ro, bulk, oil, bunkers, shiprepair; *Liverpool* — general cargo, containers, ro/ro, dry and liquid bulk, oil, bunkers, shiprepair; *London (including Tilbury)* — general cargo, containers, ro/ro, dry and liquid bulk, oil, bunkers, shiprepair; *Manchester* — general cargo, containers, ro/ro, dry and liquid bulk, oil, bunkers, shiprepair; *Middlesbrough* — general cargo, containers, ro/ro, dry and liquid bulk, oil, liquefied gas, bunkers, shiprepair; *Plymouth* — general cargo, ro/ro, bulk, bunkers; *Ridham Dock* — bulk; *Rochester* — general cargo, containers, bulk; *Sheerness* — general cargo,containers, ro/ro, dry and liquid bulk; *Shoreham* — general cargo, containers, ro/ro, bulk, oil, bunkers; *Southampton* — general cargo, containers, ro/ro, bulk, oil, liquefied gas, bunkers, shiprepair; *Sunderland* — general cargo, containers, ro/ro, bulk, oil, bunkers, shiprepair; *Tyne* — general cargo, containers, ro/ro, dry and liquid bulk, oil, bunkers, shiprepair. **Principal airports:** *Belfast International* 13mls/21km, *Birmingham International* 8mls/13km, *East Midlands International* 15mls/24km from Derby and Nottingham, *Edinburgh* 7mls/11km, *Glasgow* 9mls/14km, *Glasgow (Prestwick)* 32mls/51.5km, *Leeds/Bradford* 9mls/14.5km from Leeds, 7mls/ 11km from Bradford, *Liverpool International* 6mls/10km, *London (Heathrow)* 15mls/24km, *London (Gatwick)* 28mls/46km, *London (Stansted)* 34mls/55km, *London (Luton)* 32mls/51km, *Manchester International* 10mls/16km, *Newcastle International* 5mls/8km, *Tees-side* 13mls/21km from Middlesbrough.

UNITED STATES OF AMERICA
Capital: *Washington D.C.* **Area:** 3,618,787 sq.mls/9,372,614 sq.km. **Population:** 239,283,000. **Standard Time:** GMT — 5 hrs in Connecticut, Delaware, District of Columbia, Florida, Georgia, Indiana, Kentucky, Maine, Maryland, Massachusetts, Michigan, New Hampshire, New Jersey, New York, N. Carolina, Ohio, Pennsylvannia, Rhode Island, S. Carolina, Vermont, Virginia, West Virginia; GMT — 6 hrs in Alabama, Arkansas, Illinois, Iowa, Kansas, Louisiana, Minnesota, Mississippi, Missouri, Nebraska, N. Dakota, Oklahoma, S. Dakota (East), Tennessee, Texas, Wisconsin; GMT — 7 hrs in Arizona, Colorado,Idaho, Montana, New Mexico, S. Dakota (West), Utah, Wyoming; GMT — 8 hrs in California, Nevada, Oregon, Washington; GMT — 9 hrs in Alaska; GMT — 10 hrs in Hawaii. **Language:** English. **Currency:** U.S. dollar of 100 cents. **Weights & measures:** U.S. system. **IDD code:** dialling-in 1. **Principal ports:** *Anchorage, Alaska* — general cargo, containers, ro/ro, bulk, oil, bunkers; *Baltimore* — general cargo, containers, ro/ro, dry and liquid bulk, oil, liquefied gas, bunkers, shiprepair; *Boston* — general cargo, containers, bulk, oil, liquefied gas, bunkers, shiprepair; *Brownsville* — general cargo, dry and liquid bulk, oil, bunkers; *Charleston* — general cargo, containers, ro/ro, oil, bunkers, shiprepair; *Chicago* — general cargo, containers, dry and liquid bulk, bunkers; *Cleveland* — general cargo, containers, ro/ro, dry and liquid bulk, bunkers; *Corpus Christi*

— general cargo, containers, dry and liquid bulk, oil, liquefied gas, bunkers; *Detroit* — general cargo, containers, dry and liquid bulk, bunkers, shiprepair; *Duluth* — general cargo, containers, ro/ro, dry and liquid bulk, oil, bunkers, shiprepair; *Galveston* — general cargo, containers, bulk, oil, bunkers, shiprepair; *Hampton Roads (including Newport News, Norfolk, Portsmouth)* — general cargo, containers, ro/ro, dry and liquid bulk, oil, bunkers, shiprepair; *Houston* — general cargo, containers, ro/ro, dry and liquid bulk, oil, liquefied gas, bunkers, shiprepair; *Jacksonville* — general cargo, containers, ro/ro, dry and liquid bulk, oil, bunkers, shiprepair; *Lake Charles* — general cargo, containers, ro/ro, dry and liquid bulk, oil, liquefied gas, bunkers; *Long Beach* — general cargo, containers, ro/ro, dry and liquid bulk, oil, bunkers, shiprepair; *Los Angeles* — general cargo, containers, ro/ro, dry and liquid bulk, oil, bunkers, shiprepair; *Miami* — general cargo, containers, ro/ro, bunkers; *Mobile* — general cargo, containers, ro/ro, bulk, bunkers, shiprepair; *New Orleans* — general cargo, containers, ro/ro, bulk, oil, bunkers, shiprepair; *New York* — general cargo, containers, ro/ro, dry and liquid bulk, oil, liquefied gas, bunkers, shiprepair; *Oakland* general cargo, containers, ro/ro, bunkers; *Philadelphia* — general cargo, containers, ro/ro, dry and liquid bulk, oil, bunkers, shiprepair; *Portland, Oregon* — general cargo, containers, ro/ro, dry and liquid bulk, oil, bunkers, shiprepair; *San Diego* — general cargo, containers, bulk, bunkers; *San Francisco* — general cargo, containers, ro/ro, dry and liquid bulk, oil, bunkers, shiprepair; *Savannah* — general cargo, containers, ro/ro, dry and liquid bulk, oil, bunkers; *Seattle* — general cargo, containers, ro/ro, dry and liquid bulk, oil, bunkers, shiprepair; *Tacoma* — general cargo, containers, ro/ro, bulk, oil, bunkers, shiprepair. **Principal airports:** *Anchorage International* 7.5mls/11km, *Baltimore (Washington International)* 10mls/16km, *Boston (Logan International)* 4mls/6.5km, *Chicago (O'Hare International)* 21mls/35km, *Dallas/Fort Worth International* 14mls/22.5km from Dallas, *Honolulu International* 6mls/10km, *Los Angeles International* 15mls/24km, *Miami International* 7mls/11km, *New Orleans International* 13mls/21km, *New York (J.F. Kennedy International)* 14mls/22.5km, *San Francisco International* 13mls/21km, *Tampa International* 5mls/8km, *Washington (Dulles International)* 27mls/43km.

URUGUAY
Capital: *Montevideo*. **Area:** 68,037 sq.mls/176,215 sq.km. **Population:** 3,012,000. **Standard Time:** GMT − 3 hrs. **Language:** Spanish. **Currency:** Peso of 100 centesimos. **Weights & measures:** Metric system, also local units. **IDD code:** dialling-in 598. **Principal port:** *Montevideo* — general cargo, bulk, oil, liquefied gas, bunkers, shiprepair. **Principal airport:** *Montevideo (Carrasco)* 12.5mls/19km.

VENEZUELA
Capital: *Caracas*. **Area:** 352,144 sq.mls/912,050 sq.km. **Population:** 17,323,000. **Standard Time:** GMT − 4 hrs. **Language:** Spanish. **Currency:** Bolivar of 100 centimos. **Weights & measures:** Metric system, also local units. **IDD code:** dialling-in 58. **Principal ports:** *La Guaira* — general cargo, containers; *Maracaibo* — general cargo; *Puerto Cabello* — general cargo, bunkers. **Principal airports:** *Caracas (Simon Bolivar)* 13.5mls/22km, *Maracaibo (La Chinito)* 10.5mls/17km.

YEMEN, NORTH (Yemen Arab Republic)
Capital: *Sana'a*. **Area:** 75,000 sq.mls/194,235 sq.km. **Population:** 9,250,000. **Standard Time:** GMT + 3 hrs. **Language:** Arabic. **Currency:** Yemeni riyal of 100 fils. **Weights & measures:** Metric system, also local units. **IDD code:** dialling-in 967. **Principal ports:** *Hodeidah* — general cargo, containers, oil; *Mokha* — general cargo, oil. **Principal airport:** *Sana'a International* 8mls/13km.

YEMEN, SOUTH (Peoples Democratic Republic)
Capital: *Aden*. **Area:** 128,560 sq.mls/332,968 sq.km. **Population:** 2,500,000. **Standard Time:** GMT + 3 hrs. **Language:** Arabic, also English. **Currency:** South Yemen dinar of 1,000 fils. **Weights & measures:** Imperial system, also local units. **IDD code:** Not available. **Principal port:** *Aden* — general cargo, containers, ro/ro, oil, bunkers, shiprepair. **Principal airport:** *Aden (Khormaksar)* 6mls/9.5km.

YUGOSLAVIA
Capital: *Belgrade*. **Area:** 96,766 sq.mls/255,804 sq.km. **Population:** 23,123,000. **Standard Time:** GMT + 1 hr. **Language:** Serbo-Croat, also German and English in business. **Currency:** Yugoslav dinar of 100 para. **Weights & measures:** Metric system. **IDD code:** dialling-in 38. **Principal ports:** *Dubrovnik* — general cargo, containers, ro/ro; *Kardeljevo* — general cargo, containers, bulk, oil; *Koper* — general cargo, containers, ro/ro, bulk, oil; *Rijeka* — general cargo, containers, ro/ro, dry and liquid bulk, liquefied gas, bunkers, shiprepair; *Sibenik* — general cargo, dry and liquid bulk; *Split* — general cargo, bulk, oil, shiprepair. **Principal airports:** *Belgrade* 12mls/20km, *Dubrovnik* 13.5mls/22km, *Ljubljana (Brnik)* 22mls/35km, *Zagreb (Pleso)* 10mls/16km.

INFORMATION SOURCES

Associations and Organisations, Classification Societies, Government Departments, Maritime Services, Port Authorities, etc.

On 6 May 1990 the London area telephone code 01 will change. 071 for inner London, 081 for outer London. See pages 10 and 11.

Advisory Committee on Pollution of the Sea
3 Endsleigh Street, London, WC1H 0DD.
England. Tel (01) 388 2117. Tx 261681.

American Association of Port Authorities
1010 Duke Street, Alexandria, VA 22314,
USA. Tel (703) 684 5700. Tx 710 832 9823.

American Bureau of Shipping
45 Eisenhower Drive, Paramus, New Jersey
07652, USA. Tel (201) 368 9100.
Tx 421996.
London Office:
ABS House, Frying Pan Alley, London. E1
7HR, England. Tel (01) 247 3255.
Tx 885621.

American Institute of Marine Underwriters
14 Wall Street, New York, NY 10005, USA.
Tel (212) 233 0550. Fax (212) 227 5102.

American Institute of Merchant Shipping
Suite 511. 1000 16th Street NW.
Washington DC 20036, USA.
Tel (202) 775 4399. Fax (202) 659 3795.

American Society of Mechanical Engineers
United Engineering Center, 345 East 47th
Street, New York, NY 10017, USA.
Tel (212) 705 7722. Tx. 710 581 5267.

American Society of Naval Engineers Inc.
1452 Duke Street, Alexandria, VA 22314,
USA. Tel (703) 836 6727.

American Waterways Operators Inc (AWO)
Suite 1000, 1600 Wilson Boulevard,
Arlington, VA 22209, USA.
Tel (703) 841 9300.

Antwerpse Scheepvaartvereniging V.Z.W.
Korte Gathuisstraat 18, B-200 Antwerp,
Belgium. Tel (03) 233 5960. Tx 35359.

Asociacion de Navieros Españoles (ANAVE)
Pl de las Lealtad 4 5, Madrid 14, Spain.
Tel.(91) 2322109. Tx 43137 OFIC E.

Associated British Ports
150 High Holborn, London EC1N 2LR,
England. Tel (01) 430 1177. Tx 23913
ABPHQ G.

Association of Average Adjusters
Irongate House, Dukes Place, London
EC3A 7LP, England. Tel (01) 283 9033.

Association of British Chambers of Commerce
Sovereign House, 212A Shaftesbury
Avenue, London WC2H 8EW, England.
Tel (01) 240 5831. Tx 265871.

Association of British Insurers
Aldermary House, 10/15 Queen Street,
London EC4N 1TT, England.
Tel (01) 248 2477. Tx 937035.

Association of Consulting Engineers
Alliance House, 12 Caxton Street, London
SW1H 0QL, England. Tel (01) 226 6557.
Tx 265871.

Association of Insurance and Risk Managers in Industry & Commerce
Secretariat: 6 Lloyd's Avenue, London
EC3N 3AX, England. Tel (01) 480 7610.

Association of Norwegian Marine Yards
Oscargst. 20, P.O. Box 7072-H, Oslo 3,
Norway. Tel (02) 465820. Tx 76625.

Association of Ship Brokers & Agents (USA) Inc.
17 Battery Place, Room 711, New York, NY
10004, USA. Tel (212) 943 1340.

Association of West European Shipbuilders (AWES)
An der Alster 1, D-2000 Hamburg 1, West
Germany. Tel (040) 246305. Tx 2162496.

Auckland Harbour Board
Princes Wharf, Quay Street, Private Bag,
Auckland, New Zealand. Tel 795950.
Tx 2705 NZ.

Australasian National Maritime Association
500 Collins Street, Melbourne, (Box 365F
G.P.O.) Victoria 3000, Australia.
Tel (02) 621631. Tx. 32120.

Australian Sea Transport Policy Division
Department of Transport, PO Box 594,
Civic Square, A.C.T. 2617 Australia.
Tel (062) 687111. Tx 62018.

Baltic Exchange
14-20 St. Mary Axe, London EC3A 8BU,
England. Tel (01) 623 5501. Tx 8811373.

Baltic and International Maritime Council
19 Kristianiagade, DK-2100 Copenhagen,
Denmark. Tel (01) 263000. Tx 19086.

**Baltic International Freight Futures
Exchange Ltd (BIFFEX)**
Baltic Exchange Chambers, 24/28 St. Mary
Axe, London 3A 8EP, England.
Tel (01) 626 7985. Tx 916434.

**The Baltic Marine Environoment Protection
Commission**
Mannerheimintie 12A, SF-00100 Helsinki
10, Finland.

**BEAMA (The Federation of British
Electrotechnical and Allied Manufacturers'
Associations)**
Leicester House, 8 Leicester Street, London
WC2H 7BN, England. Tel (01) 437 0678.
Tx 263536 ELECT G.

Belfast Harbour Commissioners
Harbour Office, Belfast BT1 3AL, Northern
Ireland. Tel (0232) 234422. Tx 74204.

**Belgische Redersvereniginig Union des
Armateurs Belges (Belgium Shipowners'
Association)**
Lijnwaadmarkt 9, B-2000 Antwerp,
Belgium. Tel (03) 2327232.

**Belgium Ministry of Shipping
(Administration de la Marine et de la
Navigation Intérieure)**
Rue de'Arlon 104, B-1000 Brussels,
Belgium. Tel (02) 2331211. Tx 61880
VERTRA B.

**BIFFEX — See Baltic International Freight
Futures Exchange**

**BIMCO (The Baltic & International Maritime
Council)**
Kristiangade 19, DK-2100 Copenhagen,
Denmark. Tel (01) 263000. Tx 19086.

Bombay Port Trust
Administrative Offices Building, Shoorji,
Vallabhbas Marg., Bombay 400 038, India.
Tel 264354. Tx 112345.

Brazilian Ministry of Shipping
Esplanada dos Ministerios, Bloco 9,
Brasilia (DF) Brazil. Tel (061)226225.
Tx 611096 MNTR BR.

Bremen Port Authority
Uberseehafen, D-2800 Bremen 1, West
Germany.
Tel (0421) 397 8504. Tx 246089.

Brisbane Port Authority
PO Box 1818, Brisbane, Queensland 4001,
Australia. Tel (07) 833 0833. Tx 42780.

Bristol Port Authority
St Andrews Road, Avonmouth, Bristol
BS11 9DQ, England. Tel (0272) 823681.
Tx 44240 PBAAM.

**British Insurance and Investment Brokers'
Association**
Biiba House, 14 Bevis Marks, London
EC3A 7NT, England. Tel (01) 623 9043.

British Insurance Law Association
14/22 Elder Street, London E1 6DF,
England. Tel (01) 247 6595. Tx 8811077.

British Insurers' International Committee
Aldermary House, Queen Street, London
EC4N 1TT, England. Tel (01) 248 4477.
Tx 937035

British Marine Equipment Council
32-38 Leman Street, London E1 8EW,
England. Tel (01) 488 0171. Tx 886593.

British Marine Industries Federation
Boating Industry House, Vale Road,
Oatlands, Weybridge, Surrey KT13 9NS,
England. Tel (0932) 85411. Tx 885471
BOATIN G.

British Maritime Law Association
3rd Floor, 78 Fenchurch Street, London
EC3M 4BT, England. Tel (01) 702 9869.
Tx 884444.

British Ports Federation Ltd
7th Floor, Victoria House, Vernon Place,
London WC1B 4LL, England.
Tel (01) 242 1200. Tx 295741 BRITPA G.

British Sailors' Society
406-410 Eastern Avenue, Ilford, Essex IG2
6NG, England. Tel (01) 554 6285.

British Ship Research Association
Wallsend Research Station, Wallsend,
Tyne & Wear NE28 6UY, England.
Tel (0632) 625424. Tx 53476 BSRA G.

British Shipowners' Association
Milburn House, Dean Street, Newcastle-
Upon-Tyne NE1 1NP, England.
Tel (0632) 611661. Tx 53115 ROCHE G.

British Shippers' Council
Hermes House, St John's Road, Tunbridge
Wells, Kent TN4 9UZ, England.
Tel (0892) 26171. Tx 957158.

BSI (British Standards Institution)
2 Park Street, London W1A 2BS, England.
Tel (01) 629 9000. Tx BSILON G.

British Tugowners' Association
Central House, 32-36 High Street,
Stratford, London E15 2PS, England.
Tel (01) 519 4872. Tx 8814115

British Waterways Board
Melbury House, Melbury Terrace, London NW1 6JX, England. Tel (01) 262 6711. Tx 263605.

Buenos Aires Port Authority
Av. julio A. Roca, 734/4Z Buenos Aires, Argentina. Tel 345744. Tx 21879.

Bureau of Marine Transportation
1-3 Do-Dong, Choong-ku, Seoul, South Korea. Tel 230809.

Bureau Veritas
Head Office: 17 bis, Pl. des Reflets, La Defense 2, F92400 Courbevoie, France. Tel (1) 42915292. Tx 615370.
London Office: Capital House, 42 Weston Street, London EC1 3QL, England. Tel (01) 403 6266. Tx886201 BV LOND G.

Canadian Department of Industry, Trade & Commerce
Ottawa, Canada. Tel 992-9386.

Canadian Maritime Industries Association
PO Box 1429, Station B,Suite 801, 100 Sparks Street, Ottawa, Ontario K1P 5B7, Canada.
Tel (613) 232 7127. Tx 534848 CSSRA.

Canadian Shipowners' Association
Suite 705, 350 Sparks Street, Ottawa, Ontario K1R 7S8, Canada.
Tel (613) 232 3539. Tx 533522 DOMAR.

Caribbean Community
3rd Floor, Bank of Guyana Building, Avenue of the Republic, Georgetown, Guyana.

Central Office for International Railway Transport
Gryphenhubeliweg 30, CH-3006 Berne, Switzerland.

Chartered Institute of Arbitrators
75 Cannon Street, London EC4N 5BH, England. Tel (01) 236 8761. Tx 893466.

Chartered Institute of Loss Adjusters
Manfield House, 376 Strand, London WC2R OLR, England. Tel (01) 240 1496.

Chartered Institute of Transport
80 Portland Place, London W1N 4DP, England. Tel (01) 636 9952.

Chartered Insurance Institute
The Hall, 20 Aldermanbury, London EC2V 7HY, England. Tel (01) 606 3835.

Chemical Carriers Association Inc
45 Eisenhower Drive, Paramus, NJ, USA. 07652-1401.

Chicago Regional Port District
12800 Butler Drive, Lake Calumet Harbour Drive, Chicago, IL 60633, USA. Tel (312) 646 4400.

Chilean Department of Maritime Transport
Ministry of Transport, Amuntagui 139, Santiago de Chile, Chile. Tel 717363.

Chittagong Port Authority
Bandar Bhaban, PO Box 2013, Chittagong, Bangladesh. Tel 505021. Tx 66264 PORT BJ.

China, Peoples Republic, Register of Shipping
3 Wai Guam Xie Jie, An Ding Men Mei, Beijing, China. Tel (01) 4218354.Tx 210407.

China Corporation Register of Shipping
Head Office: 8th Floor, 103 Namking E Road, Section 3, Taipei 104, Taiwan. Tel (02) 506 2711. Tx 21534 CHISUR.

Clyde Port Authority
16 Robertson Street, Glasgow G2 8DS, Scotland. Tel (041) 221 8733. Tx 778446.

Comité Central des Armateurs de France
73 Boulevard Haussmann, 75008 Paris, France. Tel (1) 42653604. Tx 660532.

Comité Maritime International
Administrative Officer: Henry Voet-Genicot, 17 Borzestraat, B-200 Antwerp, Belgium. Tel 03/232 2471. Tx 31653 VOET.

Commission of the European Communities
Rue de la Loi 200, B-1049 Brussels, Belgium.

Commonwealth Secretariat
Marlborough House, Pall Mall, London SW1Y 5HX, England.Tel (01) 839 3411.

Confederation of British Industry
Centre Point, 103 New Oxford Street, London WC1A 1DU, England. Tel (01) 379 7400. Tx 21332 CBI G.

Confederation of Shipbuilding & Engineering Unions
140 Walworth Road, London SE17, England. Tel (01) 703 2215.

Confederazione Italiana degli Armatori Liberi (Italian Confederation of Free Shipowners)
Via dei Sabini 7, Rome Italy. Tel (06) 6787541. Tx 626135 ITARMA.

Conseil International Pour L'Exploration de la Mer
Palegade 2-4, DK-1261, Copenhagen K, Denmark. Tel (01) 154225. Tx 22498.

Cork Harbour Commissioners
Harbour Office, Custom House Street, PO Box 53, Cork, Co Cork, Irish Republic. Tel (021) 273125. Tx 75848.

Council of European & Japanese National Shipowners' Associations
30-32 St Mary Axe, London EC3A 8ET, England. Tel (01) 623 3281. Tx 8951282.

Crown Agents for Oversea Governments & Administrations
St Nicholas House, St Nicholas Road, Sutton, Surrey SM1 1EL, England. Tel (01) 643 3311. Tx 916205.

Customs Co-operation Council
28-38 Rue de l'Industrie, B-1040 Brussels, Belgium.

Customs & Excise, H.M., Headquarters
New King's Beam House, 22 Upper Ground, London SE1 9PJ, England. Tel (01) 620 1313. Tx 886321.

Cyprus Shipowners' Association
20 Arnalda Street, PO Box 1341, Nicosia 110, Cyprus. Tel (021) 44455. Tx 2137.

DSRK, DDR-Schiffs-Revision und Klassifikation
Eichenallee 12, DDR-1615 Zeuthen, East Germany. Tel 2633 and 2748/9. Tx 158721 DSRK DD. Berlin Tel 168 58 013.

Danish International Ship Register
Vermundsgade 38c, DK-2100 Copenhagen, Denmark.
Tel (01) 271515. Tx 31141.

Danish Ministry of Shipping
Slotsholmsgade 12, DK 1216 Copenhagen K, Denmark. Tel (01) 121197.

Danmarks Rederiforening (Danish Shipowners' Association)
Amaliegade 33, DK-1256 Copenhagen K, Denmark. Tel (01) 114088. Tx 16492.

Danube Commission
Benczur Utca 25, H-1068 Budapest, Hungary.

Doha Port Authority
Department of Ports, Ministry of Communications and Transport, PO Box 313, Doha, Qatar. Tel 414626. Tx 4373DH.

Dover Harbour Board
Harbour House, Dover CT17 9BU, England. Tel (0304) 240400. Tx 965924.

Dubai Port Authority
Port Rashid Authority, PO Box 2149, Dubai, United Arab Emirates. Tel 451545. Tx 47530 PRA.

Dublin Port & Docks Board
Port Centre, Alexandra Road, Dublin 1, Irish Republic. Tel (01) 722777. Tx 32508.

Durban Port Authority
PO Box 38006, Durban, South Africa. Tel 310 3555. Tx 621567.

Engineering Committee on Oceanic Resources
1 Birdcage Walk, London W1H 9JJ, England.

European Council of Chemical Manufacturers Federations
250 Avenue Louise (Bte 71), B-1050 Brussels, Belgium.

European Tugowners' Association
Central House, 32-66 High Street Stratford, London E15 2PS, England. Tel (01) 519 4872. Tx 8814115.

Export Council of Norway
Drammensveien 40, N-0255, Oslo 2, Norway. Tel (02) 437700. Tx 78532.

Export Credits Guarantee Department (ECGD)
50 Ludgate Hill, London EC4, England. Tel (01) 382 7000. Tx 883601 ECGDHQ G.

Felixstowe Port Authority
The Felixstowe Dock and Railway Co, European House, The Dock, Felixstowe, Suffolk IP11 8TB, England. Tel (0394) 604500. Tx 98277.

Finnish Ministry of Shippping
Aleksanterinkatu 10, S-00170 Helsinki 17, Finland. Tel (90) 1601. Tx 12645.

Finnish Port Association (Suomen Satamaliito)
Toinen linja 14, 00530 Helsinki 17, Finland. Tel (90) 7711.

Finnish Shipowners' Association
POB 155, Satamakatu 4, SF-00161 Helsinki, Finland. Tel (90) 170401. Tx 122751.

Food & Agriculture Organisation of the United Nations (FAO)
Via de Terme dei Carcalla, 00100 Rome, Italy. Tel 57971. Tx 611127 FAO I.

Fremantle Port Authority
1 Cliff Street, Fremantle 6160, Western Australia. Tel (09) 335 3981. Tx 92951, 95919 (shipping information only).

French Ministry of Shipping
Secretariat d'Etat de Mer, 3 Place de Fontenoy, F-75007 Paris, France. Tel (1) 4273 5505. Tx 250823.

Funchal Port Authority
Direccao do Portos da Madeira, Avenida Arriaga 50-1, Funchal, Madeira. Tel 21041. Tx 72290.

Galveston Port Authority
PO Box 328, Galveston, Tx 77553, USA. Tel (409) 765 9321. Tx 765436.

Gdynia Port Authority
Ul Rotterdamsk 9, 81-337 Gdynia, Poland. Tel 201001. Tx 54221.

General Council of British Shipping
(M.N.E. Headquarters): 30-32 St Mary Axe, London EC3A 8ET, England. Tel (01) 283 2922 and 626 8131. Tx 884008.

Genoa Port Authority
Consorzio Autonomo del Porto de Genova, Palazzo San Giorgio, 16100 Genoa, Italy. Tel (010) 26901. Tx 216579.

German East, Ministerium für Verkehrswesen
(Hauptverwaltung des Seeverkehrs) Vostrasse 33, 1086 Berlin, East Germany. Tel (02) 490. Tx 112661 MFVWS DD.

German West, Ministry of Transport
Kennedyalle 72, D-5300 Bonn, West
Germany. Tel (0228) 3001. Tx 885700.

Germanischer Lloyd
Head Office: Vorsetzen 32, Postfach
111606, D-2000 Hamburg 11, West
Germany. Tel (040) 361490.
Tx 212828 GLHH D.
UK Representative: A. Robertson, 4th
Floor, Riverdale House, 68 Molesworth
Street, London SE13 7EY, England.
Tel (01) 318 1319. Tx 28744.

**German Machinery Manufacturers &
Plantmakers Association (VDMA)**
Marine and Offshore Equipment Industries
Division, Sportallee 79, D-2000 Hamburg
63, West Germany.
Tel (040) 501092. Tx 2162523.

**German Shipbuilding & Ocean Industries
Association**
An der Alster 1, D-2000 Hamburg 1, West
Germany. Tel (040) 246205. Tx 2152496.

Gibraltar Port Authority
Port Office, Northmole, Gibraltar.
Tel 77254. Tx 2130.

Gothenburg Harbour Board
S-403 38, Gothenburg, Sweden.
Tel (031) 632000. Tx 20957 SCANPRT.

Greek Ministry of Shipping
Ministry of Mercantile Marine, 152 Gr.
Lambrakis Avenue, 185 18, Piraeus,
Greece.Tel (01) 4121211. Tx 211232.

Halifax Port Corporation
PO Box 336, Halifax B3J 2P6, Nova Scotia,
Canada. Tel 426 3643. Tx 1923591.

Hamburg Harbour Management
Alter Steinweg 4, D-2000 Hamburg 11,
West Germany. Tel (040) 349121.
Tx 211100 BWVLD.

Hampton Roads Port Authority
(Virginia Port Authority) 600 World Trade
Center, Norfolk, VA 23510, USA.
Tel (804) 623 8000. Tx 710 881 1231 TWX.

Hellenic Register of Shippping
23 Akti Miaouli, 185 35 Piraeus, Greece.
Tel (01) 4177632. Tx 211564.

Hodeidah Ports & Marine Affairs Corporation
PO Box 3183, Hodeidah, Yemen Arab
Republic. Tel 75057. Tx 5565 MAWANI.

Hong Kong Registry of Shipping
2 Harbour Building, 38 Pier Road, PO Box
4155, Hong Kong. Tel (5) 8524387.
Tx 64553.

Hong Kong Shipowners' Association Ltd
12th Floor, Queen's Centre, 58-64 Queens
Road East, Hong Kong. Tel (5) 200206.
Tx 89157 HKSOA HK.
Facsimilie 5-298246.

Honourable Company of Master Mariners
HQS "Wellington", Temple Stairs, Victoria
Embankment, London WC2H 2PN,
England. Tel (01) 836 8179.

Hungarian Ministry of Transport
Dobu 75/81, H-1400 Budapest V11,
Hungary. Tel Budapest 220-220.
Tx 225729.

Hydrographer of the Navy
Ministry of Defence, Taunton, Somerset
TA1 2DN, England. Tel (0823) 337900.
Tx 46274.

ICC Centre for Maritime Co-operation
Maritime House, 1 Linton Road, Barking,
Essex IG11 8HG, England.
Tel (01) 591 3000. Tx 8956492.

**Inchon District Maritime & Port
Administration**
No 1-17-7 Ga, Hang Dong, Chung-ku,
Inchon, South Korea. Tel (2) 0044.
Tx 23380 IDMAPA.

Indian Ministry of Transport & Tourism
New Delhi, India. Shipbuilding: Ministry
of Heavy Engineering, New Delhi.
Tx 312312.

Indian Register of Shipping
72 Maker Towers F, 7th Floor, Cuffe
Parade, Bombay 400 005, India.
Tel (22) 214588. Tx 113364.

Indian National Shipowners' Association
22 Maker Towers F, Cuffe Parade, Bombay,
India. Tel (22) 219111. Tx 113364 IRS.

INMARSAT
40 Melton Street, London NW1 2EQ,
England. Tel (01) 387 9089. Tx 297201.

Institute of Actuaries
Staple Inn Hall, High Holborn, London
WC1 7QJ, England. Tel (01) 242 0106.

Institute of Chartered Shipbrokers
Baltic Exchange Chambers, 24 St Mary
Axe, London EC3A 8DE, England.
Tel (01) 283 1361.
Tx 8812708 BROKER G.

Institute of Freight Forwarders Ltd
Redfern House, Browells Lane, Feltham,
Middlesex TW 13 7EP, England.
Tel (01) 844 2266. Tx 8953060.

Institute of Insurance Brokers
Barclays Bank Chambers, College Street,
Rushden, Northants NN10 ONW, England.
Tel (0933) 410003. Tx 311640.

Institute of International Container Lessors
P.O. Box 605, Bedford, New York 10506,
USA.
Tel (914) 234 3696. Fax (914) 234 3641.

Institute of London Underwriters
49 Leadenhall Street, London EC3A 2BE,
England. Tel (01) 488 2424. Tx 884165.

Institute of Marine Engineers
76 Mark Lane, London EC3R 7JN, England.
Tel (01) 481 8493. Tx 886841 IMARE G.

Institute of Maritime Law
Faculty of Law, The University,
Southampton, Hampshire SO9 5NH,
England. TEl (0703) 586182. Tx 47661
SOTONU G. Fax (0703) 671778.

Institute of Oceanographic Sciences
Wormley, Godalming, Surrey GU8 5UB,
England. Tel (042) 879 4141. Tx 858833.

Institute of Petroleum
61 New Cavendish Street, London W1M
8AR, England. Tel (01) 636 1004.

Insurance Adjusters' Association
152 Commercial Street, London E1 6NU,
England.

Insurance Ombudsman Bureau
31 Southampton Row, London WC1B 5JH,
England. Tel (01) 242 8613.

**Intergovernmental Oceanographic
Commission (IOC)**
Place de Fontenoy, Paris, France.

**Intergovernmental Standing Committee on
Shipping**
Bima Tower (9th floor), Digo Road, P.O.
Box 89112, Mombassa, Kenya.

**International Association of Classification
Societies**
Permanent Representative to IMO: 2nd
Floor, 37 Duke Street, St. James's, London
SW1V 6DH, England.

**International Association of Independent
Tanker Owners (INTERTANKO)**
Radhusgt 25, PO Box 1452, Vika 0116,
Oslo 1, Norway. Tel (02) 3352110.
Tx 19751.

**International Association of Lighthouse
Authorities**
13 Rue Yvon Villarceau, 75116 Paris,
France. Tel (1) 4500 3860. Tx 610480.

**International Association of Ports &
Harbours**
Head Office: Kotohira Kaikan Building, 2-8
Toranomon 1-chome, Minato-ku, Tokyo
105, Japan. Tel (03) 5914261. Tx 2222516.

**International Association of Producers of
Insurance and Reinsurance**
c/o Biiba House, 14 Bevis Marks, London
EC3A 7NT, England.

**International Cargo Handling Co-ordination
Association (ICHCA)**
Unit 4, Bondway Business Centre, 71
Bondway, London, SW8 1SH, England.
Tel (01) 793 1022. Tx 261106.

International Centre for Ocean Development
5670 Spring Garden Road, Halifax NS,
Canada B3J 1H6. Tel (902) 426 1512.
Tx 019-21670 ICOD HFX.

International Chamber of Shipping
30-32 St Mary Axe, London EC3A 8ET,
England. Tel (01) 282 2922. Tx 884008.

International Court of Justice (ICJ)
Peace Palace, The Hague, Netherlands.
Tel 924441. Tx 32323 ICJ NL.

**International Group of Protection and
Indemnity Associations**
78 Fenchurch Street, London EC3M 4BT,
England.

**International Hydrographic Bureau (IHB) &
International Hydrographic Organisation**
Avenue President J.F. Kennedy, BP 445,
Monte Carlo, Monaco. Tel 93-506587.
Tx 479164.

International Labour Office
Vincent House, Vincent Square, London
SW1P 2NB, England. Tel (01) 828 6401. Tx
886836.

International Labour Organisation (ILO)
Geneva, Switzerland. Tel 996111.
Tx 22271.

International Law Association
3 Paper Buildings, Temple, London EC4Y
7EU, England. Tel (01) 353 2904.

**International Life -saving Appliance
Manufacturers' Association**
P.O. Box 952, Shoreham, West Sussex
BN43 6AP, England.

International Maritime Committee
17 Borzestraat, B-2000 Antwerp, Belgium.

International Maritime Industries Forum
15a Hannover Street, London W1R 9HG,
England. Tel (01) 493 4599. Tx 28257.

International Maritime Organization (IMO)
4 Albert Embankment, London SE1 7SR,
England. Tel (01) 735 7611. Tx 23588.

**International Oil Pollution Compensation
Fund**
4 Albert Embankment, London SE1 7SR,
England. Tel (01) 582 2606.

International Road Transport Union
8 (IRU) Centre International, BP 44, 1211
Geneva 20, Switzerland.

International Salvage Union
Zalmstraat 1, NL-3016 DS Rotterdam,
Netherlands.

**International Shipowners' Association
(INSA)**
Sieroszowskiego 7, 81 376 Gydnia, Poland.
Tel (898) 210974. Tx 54250 INSA PL.

**International Ship Reporting Association
(ISRA)**
P.O. Box 504, 1970 AM Ijmuiden, Holland.
Tel (31) 2550 62223. Tx 41240 NL.

International Ship Suppliers Association
235 The Broadway, Wimbledon, London
SW19 1SD, England. Tel (01) 543 9161.
Tx 935741.

International Shipping Federation
30-32 St Mary Axe, London EC3A 8ET, England. Tel (01) 283 2922. Tx 884008.

International Tanker Owners's Pollution Federation Ltd
Staple Hall, Stonehouse Court, 87-90 Houndsditch, London EC3A 7AX, England. Tel (01) 621 1255. Tx 887514 TOVLOP B.

International Telecommunications Satellite Organization
3400 International Drive N.W., Washington, D.C. 20008-3098, USA.

International Telecommunications Union (ITU)
Place des Nations, Geneva, Switzerland. Tel 995111. Tx 421000 UIT CH.

International Transport Workers'Federation (ITF)
133-135 Great Suffolk Street, London SE1 1PD, England. Tel (01) 403 2733. Tx 8811397 ITF LDN.

International Union of Marine Insurance
c/o The Baloise Insurance Company Limited, CH-4002 Basle, Aeschengraben 21, Switzerland. Tel 061 55 7178. Tx 962182 BVG CH.

Irish Department of Transport
Kildare Street, Dublin 2, Irish Republic. Tel 789522. Tx 24651.

Isle of Man Ship Registry
Marine Administration, Sea Terminal Building, P.O. Box 11, Douglas, Isle of Man. Tel (0624) 23813. Tx 629335.

Israel Ministry of Shipping
30 Argon Street, Jerusalem, Israel. Tel 210111.

Italian Ministry of Merchant Marine
Viale dell' Arte 16, 00144 Rome, Italy. Tel (06) 5908. Tx 612153 MIMERC.

Japan Ship Centre (Jetro)
St Clare House, 30-33 London EC3, England. Tel (01) 488 0311. Tx 883877.

Japan Ship Exporters' Association
1-15-16 Toranomon, Minato-ku, Tokyo, Japan. Tel (03) 508 9661. Tx 32777 (Mark: Attention TK 00079 JSEA).

Japan Ship Machinery Export Association
1-15-16 Toranomon, Minato-ku, Tokyo 105, Japan. Tel (03) 504 0391. Tx 0222 2458.

Japanese Ministry of Shipping
(Unyo Sho), 1-3 Kasumigaseki 2-chome, Chiyoda-ku, Tokyo, Japan. Tel (03) 580 3111.

Japanese Shipowners' Association
Kaiun Building, 6-4 Hitakawa-cho 2-chome, Chiyoda-ku, Tokyo 102, Japan. Tel (03) 2647171. Tx 2322148 JSAJ.

Joint Maritime Congress
Suite 801, 444 North Capitol Street, Washington DC 20001, USA. Tel (202) 638 2405. Tx 88479.

Jugoslavenska Registrar Brodova
Marasovica 67, PO Box 257, Split, Yugoslavia. Tel 48955. Tx 26129.

Karachi Port Trust
PO Box 4725, Karachi, Pakistan. Tel 201319. Tx 2739-KR.

King George's Fund for Sailors
1 Chesham Street, London SE1X 8NF, England. Tel (01) 235 2884.

Kobe Port & Harbour Bureau
Kobe City Government, 5-1 Kano-cho, 6-chome, Chuo-ku, Kobe, Japan. Tel (78) 331 8181. Tx 78548.

Koninklijk Instituut van Ingenieurs (Royal Institution of Engineers in the Netherlands)
Prinssessegracht 23, PO Box 30424, 2514 AP, The Hague, Netherlands. Tel (070) 919900. Tx 33641 KIVI NL.

Koninklijke Nederlandse Redersvereniging (Royal Netherlands Shipowners' Association)
Van Vollenhovenstraat 3, PO Box 23454, 3016 BE Rotterdam, Netherlands. Tel (010) 4360400.

Korea Maritime Research Institute
Room 902, Boseung Building, 163-3, 2-Ga, Eurjira, Jung-Gu. Seoul, Korea. Tel 776 9153.

Korean Register of Shipping
1465-10 Seocho dong, Kangnam ku, Seoul, Korea. Tel (02) 582 6001. Tx 27358.

Kuwait Ministry of Shipping
Chambers Building, Ali Salem Street, PO Box 775, Kuwait. Tel 433864.

Kuwait Port & Public Authority
PO Box 3874, Safat, Kuwait. Tel 4833709. Tx 22740 HMSHP.

Lake Carriers' Association
915 Rockefeller Building, Cleveland, OH 44113, USA. Tel (216) 621 1107.

Liberian Registry of Shipping
551 Fifth Avenue, New York, NY 10176, USA. Tel (212) 286 0700. Tx 234347. Administration: 11800 Sunrise Valley Drive, Reston International Centre, Reston, VA 22901, USA. Tel (703) 620 4880. Tx 248736.

Liberian Shipowners Council Ltd.
Suite 2656, The Grayban Building, 420 Lexington Avenue, New York, NY 10170, USA. Tel (212) 867 8145. Tx 427540 LSC UI.

Liverpool & Glasgow Salvage Association
179 Sefton House, Exchange Buildings, Liverpool L2 3QR, England. Tel (051) 236 3821. Tx 627388 SALVOR G.

Liverpool Underwriters' Association
179 Sefton House, Exchange Buildings,
Liverpool L2 3QR, England.
Tel (051) 236 3821. Tx 627388.

Lloyd's Insurance Brokers' Committee
Biiba House, 14 Bevis Marks, London
EC3A 7NT, England. Tel (01) 623 9043.

Lloyd's Maritime Inc
1200 Summer Street, Stamford, CT 06905,
USA. Tel (203) 359 8363. Tx 509788. Fax
(203) 358 0437.

Lloyd's Maritime Information Services
One Singer Street, London, EC2A 4LQ,
England. Tel (01) 490 1720.
Tx 987321 LLOYDS G.
Fax (01) 250 3142.
Sheepen Place, Colchester, Essex CO3
3LP,England. Tel (0206) 772277.
Tx 987321 LLOYDS G.
Fax (0206) 46273.

Lloyd's of London
Lime Street, London EC3M 7HA, England.
Tel (01) 623 7100. Tx 987321 LLOYDS G.
Fax (01) 626 2389.

Lloyd's of London Press Ltd
Sheepen Place, Colchester, Essex CO3 3LP,
England. Tel (0206) 772277.
Tx 987321 LLOYDS G.
Fax (0206) 46273.

Far East
Lloyd's of London Press (Far East) Ltd
Room 1101, Hollywood Centre, Hollywood
Road, Hong Kong. Tel (5) 8543222.
Tx 66224 LLPFE HX. Fax (5) 8541538.

West Germany:
Lloyd's of London Press GmbH,
59 Ehrenbergstrasse, 2000 Hamburg 11,
West Germany. Tel (40) 389723.
Tx 212951.
Fax (40) 386883.

North America:
Lloyd's of London Press Inc.,
Suite 523, 611 Broadway, New York, NY
10002, USA.
Tel (211) 529 9500.
Tx 710 581 2659 LLP PUBLISH NY.
Fax (212) 529 9826.

Lloyd's Register of Shipping
Head Office; 71 Fenchurch Street, London
EC3M 4BS, England. Tel (01) 709 9166.
Tx 888379 LR LON G.
United States: 17 Battery Place, New York,
NY 10004, USA. Tel (212) 425 8050.
Tx 129240.
Japan: 5th Floor, Mori Building 32, 4-30,
3-chome Shiba Koen, Minato-Ku, Tokyo
105. Tel (01) 438 0481. Tx 2422289.

London Authority, Port of (PLA)
Europe House, World Trade Centre,
London E1 9AA, England.
Tel (01) 481 8484. Tx 9413062 POLA.

London General Shipowners' Society
30-32 St Mary Axe, London EC3A 8ET,
England. Tel (01) 283 2922.

London Maritime Arbitrators' Association
30-32 St Mary Axe, London EC3A 8ET,
England. Tel (01) 626 8131. Tx 884888.

Maltese Director of Ports
Ports Department, Pinto Wharf, Valletta,
Malta. Tel 22679. Tx 1110.

Manama Customs & Ports Directorate
PO Box 15, Manama, Bahrain. Tel 243533.
Tx 8642 MINA BN.

**Marine Information & Advisory Service
(MIAS)**
Institute of Oceanographic Sciences, Brook
Road, Wormley, Godalming, Surrey GU8
5UB, England. Tel (042) 879 4141.
Tx 858833 OCEANS G.

**Marine Society (Incorporates Seafarers'
Libraries, College of Sea, & Ship Adoption)**
202 Lambeth Road, London SE1 7JW,
England. Tel (01) 261 9535. Tx 934089.

**Maritime Association of the Port of New
York**
Suite 1006, 17 Battery Place, New York,
NY 10004, USA. Tel (212) 425 5704.
Tx 960301.

Maritime Institute of Ireland
Haigh Terrace, Dun Laoghaire, Co. Dublin,
Irish Republic. Tel (01) 800969.

**Marine Safety Council of the United States
Coast Guard**
Commandant (G-CMC/21) US Coast Guard,
Washington DC 20593, USA. Tx 892427.

Marseilles Port Authority
23 Place de la Joliette, PO Box 1965,
Marseilles-Cedex 02, France.
Tel (1) 91 919066. Tx 440746.

Medway Ports Authority
Dockyard House, Sheerness Docks,
Sheerness, Kent ME12 1RX, England.
Tel (0795) 580003. Tx 96233.

Merchant Navy Training Board
30-32 St Mary Axe, London EC3A 8ET,
England. Tel (01) 282 2922. Tx 884008.

Merchant Navy Welfare Board
19-21 Lancaster Gate, London W2 3LN,
England. Tel (01) 723 3642-3.

Meterological Office (UK)
Eastern Road, Bracknell, Berks RG11 1BZ,
England. Tel (0344) 420242. Tx 849801.

Missions to Seamen
St Michael Paternoster Royal, College Hill,
London EC4R 2RL, England.
Tel (01) 248 5202.

Montevideo Port Authority
Administracion National de Puertos,
Rambla 25 de Agosto de 1825, No 160,
Montevideo, Uruguay.
Cables PORTBOARD.

Montreal Port Authority
Port of Montreal Building, Cite du Havre,
Montreal PQ H3C 3RS, Canada.
Tel (514) 283 7011. Tx 5267699.

National Association of Marine Surveyors Inc.
305 Springhouse Lane, Moorestown, NJ
08057, USA.

National Association of Port Employers
7th Floor, Victoria House, Vernon Place,
London WC1B 4LL, England.
Tel (01) 242 1200. Tx 295741 BRITPA G.

National Corrosion Service,
National Physical Laboratory, Teddington,
Middlesex, England. Tel (01) 977 3222.

National Foundation for the Co-ordination of Maritime Research
Blaak 16, PO 21873, 3001 AW Rotterdam,
Netherlands. Tel (010) 4130960. Tx 26585.

National Maritime Board
30-32 St Mary Axe, London EC3A 8ET,
England. Tel (01) 283 9610.

National Maritime Museum
Greenwich, London SE10 9NF, England.
Tel (01) 858 4422.

National Physical Laboratory
Teddington, Middlesex TW11 0LW,
England. Tel (01) 977 3222. Tx 262344.

National Union of Marine, Aviation & Shipping Transport Officers (NUMAST)
Oceanair House, 750-760 High Road,
Leytonstone, London E11 3BB, England.
Tel (01) 989 6677. Tx 892648.

National Union of Seamen
Maritime House, Old Town, Clapham,
London SW4 0JP, England.
Tel (01) 622 5581/7. Tx 8814611.

Nautical Institute
202 Lambeth Road, London SE1 7LQ,
England. Tel (01) 928 1351.

Netherlands Maritime Information Centre
Blaak 16, PO Box 21873, 3001 AW
Rotterdam, Netherlands.
Tel (010) 4130960. Tx 26585.

Netherlands Ministry of Transport & Public Works
Directorate-General Shipping and Maritime
Affairs, Bordewijkstraat 4, PO Box 5817,
HV Risjwijk, Netherlands.
Tel (070) 949420. Tx 31040 DGSM NL.

New Orleans Board of Commissioners, Port of
PO Box 60046, New Orleans, LA 70160,
USA. Tel (504) 522 2551. Tx 587496.

New York & New Jersey, Port Authority of
1 World Trade Center, New York, NY
10048, USA. Tel (212) 466 8848.

New Zealand Ministry of Transport
Maritime Transport Division, PO Box 7006,
Wellington, New Zealand.Tel 04-828-198.
Fax 04-829-065.

Nippon Kaiji Koyokai
Head Office: 4-7 Kioi-cho, Chiyoda-ku,
Tokyo 102, Japan. Tel (03) 230 1201.
Tx 22975 CLASSNK.
Europe and Africa:
10th Floor, P & O Building, 122/138
Leadenhall Street, London EC3V 4PB,
England. Tel (01) 621 0963.
Tx 884019 NKLDN G.
North and South America:
17 Battery Place, Room 210, New York, NY
10004, USA. Tel (212) 425 3799/3834. Tx
232628 CLSNK UR.

Norske Veritas, Det.
Head Office: Veritasveien 1, PO Box 300,
N-1322 Hovik, Norway. Tel (02) 479911.
Tx 76192 VERIT.
United Kingdom, Northern Ireland & Eire:
Veritas House, Station Road, Sidcup, Kent
DA15 7BU, England. Tel (01) 309 7477.

Northern Lighthouse Board
84 George Street, Edinburgh EH2 3DA,
Scotland. Tel (031) 226 7051. Tx 72551.

Norwegian Ministry of Trade & Shipping
Victoria Terrasse 7, Oslo 1, Norway.
Tel (02) 314050. Tx 18670.
Building Division: Ministry of Industry,
Akersgt 42, Oslo 1, Norway.
Tel (02) 119090.

Oil Companies International Marine Forum (OCIMF)
6th Floor, Portland House, Stag Place,
London SW1E 5BH, England.
Tel (01) 828 7696. Tx 24942.

Organization for Arab Petroleum Exporting Countries
P.O. Box 20501, Kuwait.

Organisation for Economic Co-operation & Development (OECD)
2 Rue André Pascal, 75775 Paris Cedex 16,
France. Tel (1) 45248200. Tx 620160.

Organization of American States
17th Street and Constitution Avenue N.W.,
Washington, D.C. 20006, USA.

Oslo Port Authority
Vippetangen N-0150 Oslo 1, Norway.
Tel (02) 416860.

Pakistan Ministry of Shipping
(Ports and Shipping Wing), Somerset
House, Somerset Street, Karachi, Pakistan.
Tel 515732.

Panama Registry of Shipping
PO Box 5245, Panama 5. Tel 27166,
259277. Tx 368718, 368737.

Passenger Shipping Association (PSA)
93 Newman Street, London W1P 3LE,
England. Tel (01) 491 7693. Tx 298983.

Penang Port Commission
PO Box 143, Penang, Malaysia.
Tel (04) 612211. Tx 40157 PELPIN.

Polish Ministry of Shipping
ul Hoza 20, Warsaw, Poland. Tel 280471.
Tx 3407.

Polski Rejestr Statkow (Polish Register of Shipping)
ul Waly Piastowskie 24, 80-855 Gdansk,
Poland. Tel 317223. Tx 51273 PRSG PL.

Polish Shipping Mission in London
238 City Road, London EC1 2QL, England.
Tel (01) 253 8998. Tx 23256.

Port Kelang Port Authority
Jalan Pelabuhan, Port Kelang, Malaysia.
Tel 3688211. Tx 39524.

Portland (Oregon) Port Commission
700 N.E. Multnomah, PO Box 3529,
Portland, OR 97208, USA.
Tel (503) 231 5000. Tx 910 464 5105.

Portuguese Ministry of Shipping
Praca de Luis de Camos, 22-20-D, 1200
Lisbon, Portugal.

Quebec Port
150 Dalhousie Street,PO Box 2268, Quebec
G1K 7P7, Canada.
Tel (418) 648 3640. Tx 512297.

Regional Organization for the Protectin of the Marine Environment
P.O. Box 26388, Safat, Kuwait.

Registrar-General of Shipping & Seamen
Block 2, Government Buildings, Agnes
Road, Gabalfa, Cardiff CF4 4YA, Wales.
Tel (0222) 693131. Tx 498266.

Registro Italiano Navale (RINA)
Via Corsica 12, PO Box 1195, 16128 Genoa,
Italy. Tel (10) 53851. Tx 270022 RINAV.
London Office: 62 Aberdour Road,
Goodmayes, Ilford, Essex, England.
Tel (01) 590 6543. Tx 893466 CIARB.

Rotterdam Port Authority
PO Box 6622, 3002 AP, Rotterdam,
Netherlands. Tel (010) 4896911. Tx 23077.

Rotterdam Chamber of Commerce
Beursplein 37, 3011 AE Rotterdam,
Netherlands. Tel (010) 4145022 Tx. 23760.

Royal Alfred Seafarers' Society
Head Office: Weston Acres,
Woodmansterne Lane, Banstead, Surrey
SM7 3HB, England. Tel (0737) 352231.

Royal Institute of Navigation
Royal Geographical Society, 1 Kensington
Gore, London SW7 2AT, England.
Tel (01) 589 5021.

Royal Institution of Naval Architects, The
10 Upper Belgrave Street, London SW1X
8BQ, England. Tel (01) 235 4622.

Royal Meterological Society
James Glaisher House, Grenville Place,
Bracknell, Berks., RG 12 1BX, England.
Tel (0344) 422957.

Royal National Life-Boat Institution (RNLI)
West Quay, Poole, Dorset BH15 1HZ,
England. Tel (0202) 67133. Tx 41328.

Russian Ministry of Shipping
1/4 Ul Zhandova, Moscow K-12, USSR.

Russian Register of Shipping
8 Dvortsovaya Naberezhnaya, Leningrad
191041, USSR. Tel 312 8878. Tx 121515.

Sailors' Childrens Society
Newland House, Cottingham Road, Hull,
N. Humberside, England.
Tel (0482) 42312/2.

Saint John Port Authority
PO Box 6429, Station A, St John NBE2L
4R8, Canada. Tel (506) 648 4869.
Tx 1447281.

Salvage Association
Head Office: Bankside House, 107-112
Leadenhall Street, London EC3A 4AP,
England. Tel (01) 623 1299. Tx 888137.
Europe: Tavernier Building, Tavernierkaai
2, 2000 Antwerp 1, Belgium.
Tel (3) 2328682. Tx 3144.
Via Ravasco 10, Torre Nuova Carignano,
16128 Genoa, Italy. Tel (10) 540848.
Tx 270656.
Far East: Towa Building, 2-3 Kaigan-dori,
2-chome, Chuo-ku, Kobe , Japan.
Tel (078) 3913477.
Middle East: PO Box 9222, Dubai, United
Arab Emirates. Tel (04) 373100. Tx 47014.
North America: Suite 9251, Five World
Trade Center, New York, NY 10048-0939,
USA. Tel (212) 432 1970/5. Tx 232067.
South Africa: Albany House West, 13th
Floor, 65 Victoria Embankment, PO Box
55, Durban 4000, South Africa.
Tel (031) 305 3856. Tx 620269.

San Francisco Port Commission
Ferry Building, San Francisco, CA 949111,
USA. Tel (415) 391 8000. Tx 275940.

Scandinavian Tugowners' Association
PO Box 2235, S-403 14 Gothenburg,
Sweden. Tel (031) 177410. Tx 2591.

Seamen's Hospital Society
29 King William Walk, Greenwich,
London SE10 9HX, England.
Tel (01) 858 3696.

Shanghai Port Affairs Bureau
13 Zhongshan Dong Yi Ly, Shanghai,
China. Tel 211720.
Cables 3966 SHANGHAI.

Sharjah Port Authority
PO Box 510, Sharjah, United Arab
Emirates. Tel 541666. Tx 68138 SEAGUL.

Shipbuilders Council of America
Suite 1250, 1110 Vermont Avenue, NW
Washington, DC 20005, USA.
Tel (202) 775 9060. Tx 719 822 9524
SHIPBUILD WSH.

Shipowners' Refrigerated Cargo Research Association
Beagle House, 4 Braham Street, London E1
8EP, England.Tel (01) 488 1313.
Tx 883947.

Shipping Federation of Canada
Suite 326, 300 St Sacrament Street,
Montreal H2Y 1X4, Quebec, Canada.
Tel (514) 849 2325.

Shiprepairers & Shipbuilders Independent Association
33 Catherine Place, London SW1E 6DY,
England. Tel (01) 828 0933.

Singapore Authority, Port of (PSA)
PSA Building, 460 Alexandria Road,
Singapore 0511. Tel 274711. Tx. 21507.

Singapore Registry of Shipping
Marine Department, 1 Maritime Square 09-
66, World Trade Center, Singapore 0409.
Tel 2790217. Tx 50287.

Society for Nautical Research, The
National Maritime Museum, Greenwich,
London SE10, England. Tel (01) 858 4422

Society of Naval Architects & Marine Engineers
601 Pavonia Avenue, New Jersey, NJ
07306, USA. Tel (201) 798 4800.
Tx 126394.

Society for Underwater Technology
1 Birdcage Walk, London SW1H 9JJ,
England. Tel (01) 222 8658. Tx 917944.

South Korean Ministry of Transportation
1-3 Do-Dong, Choong-ku, Seoul, South
Korea. Tel 230809.

Spanish Ministry of Transport, Tourism & Communications
Dirección General de la Marina Mercante,
Ruiz de Alarcón 1, Madrid 14, Spain.
Tel (1) 2328420. Tx 43579 MAMER E.

Sri Lanka Register of Shipping
Queen Elizabeth Quay, Port of Colombo,
Colombo 1, Sri Lanka.
Tel 29613/4. Tx 21165.

St Lawrence Seaway Authority
360 Albert Street, Ottawa, Ontario, K1R
7X7, Canada

St. Vincent & Grenadines Registry of Shipping
Commisioner for Maritime Affairs, 74 Bvld
d'Italie E/F, Mc 98000, Monaco.
Tel 93 30 89 57. Tx 489171.
Also at: Av. Fontenex, CH-1207, Geneva,
Switzerland.
Tel (022) 356369. Tx 421925.

Sullom Voe Harbour Authority
Port Administration Building, Sella Ness,
Graven, Mossbank, Shetland ZE2 9QR, UK. Tel
(0806) 242551. Tx 75142 SULVOE.

Sunaman National Superintendency of Merchant Marine
Avenue Rio Branco 115, 14th Floor, 20 040
Rio de Janeiro, Brazil. Tel (021) 291 6655.

Sveriges Redareforening (Swedish Shipowners' Association)
Kungsportsavenyen 1, PO Box 53046,
40014 Gothenburg, Sweden.
Tel (031) 171830. Tx 27022 SWESHIP S.

Sveriges Skeppsklarare-och Skeppsmaklarforening (Swedish Shipbrokers' Association)
Sveavägen 28-30. PO Box 3193, S 103 63
Stockholm, Sweden. Tel (08) 219001.

Swedish Ministry of Shipping
Vasag 8-10, 10333 Stockholm, Sweden,
Tel (08) 7631000. Tx 17328 MINCOM S.

Swedish Shipbuilders' Association
Eriksberg, Box 8008, S-402 77,
Gothenburg, Sweden. Tel (031) 658549.
Tx 21454.

Sydney (NSW) Port Authority
The Maritime Services Board of New South
Wales, Circular Quay West, Sydney,
N.S.W. 2000, Australia. Tel 240 2111.
Tx 24944.

Taiwan Ministry of Shipping
Navigation and Aviation Department, 2
Changsha Street, Section 1, Taipei,
Taiwan. Tel 3112674.

Tees & Hartlepool Port Authority
Queen's Square, Middlesborough,
Hartlepool, Cleveland, England.
Tel (0642) 241121. Tx 58675 THPAG.

Thames Ship Society
18 Mead Way, Bromley, Kent, England.
Tel (01) 462 8333.

Ticaret Bakanligi (Ministry of Commerce)
Ankara, Turkey. Tel 255130/304200.
Tx 42204 DIST TR.

Toledo Port Authority
1 Maritime Plaza, Toledo, OH 43604, USA.
Tel (419) 243 8251.

Toronto Harbour Commissioners
60 Harbour Street, Toronto M5J 1B7,
Canada. Tel (416) 863 2000. Tx 6219666.

Trades Union Congress
Congress House, 23/28 Great Russell
Street, London WC1B 3LS, England.
Tel (01) 636 4030.

Transport & General Workers' Union
Transport House, Smith Square,
Westminster, London SW1P 3JB, England.
Tel (01) 828 7788. Tx 919009 TGWUMQ G.

Trinity House, Corporation of, London
4th Floor, Lloyd's Chambers, 1 Portsoken
Street, London E1 8BT. England.
Tel (01) 480 6601. Tx 987526.
Tx 884300 NAVAID G.

**United Kingdom Department of Trade &
Industry**
Shipbuilding & Electrical Engineering
Division, Ashdown House, 123 Victoria
Street, London SW1E 6RB, England.
Tel (01) 212 7676. Tx 8813148.

United Kingdom Department of Transport
Headquarters: 2 Marsham Street, London
SW1P 3EB, England. Tel (01) 212 3434.
Tx 22221 DOEMAR.

Shipping Policy Directorate: 2 Marsham
Street, London SW1P 3EB, England.
Tel (01) 276 3000.
Shipping Enquiries (01) 276 5942.

Marine Directorate: Sunley House, 90-93
High Holborn, London WC1V 6LP,
England. Tel (01) 405 6911. Tx 264084
MARBOT.

United Kingdoms Pilots' Association
Transport House, Smith Square, London
SW1P 3JB, England. Tel (01) 828 7788.

U.N. High Commission for Refuges
Palais des Nations, Geneva, Switzerland.
Tel 310261. Tx 28741 HCR CH.

U.N. Industrial Development Organisation
PO Box A 1400 Vienna, Austria. Tel 2631.
Tx 135612 UNOA.

United States Coast Guard
2100 2nd Street SW, Washington, DC
20593, USA. Tel (202) 367 1483.
Tx 892427.

Federal Maritime Commission: 1100 L
Street, N.W. Washington, DC20573, USA.
Tel (202) 655 4000. Tx 89473.

Vancouver Port Corporation
1900 Granville Street, Vancouver, BC V6C
2P9, Canada. Tel (604) 666 3226.
Tx 453310.

Virginia Port Authority
600 World Trade Centre, Norfolk, VA
23510, USA. Tel (804) 623 8000.
Tx 710 8811 1231.

Wellington Harbour Board
PO Box 893, Wellington, New Zealand.
Tel (04) 728899. Tx 30504.

World Bank Group
1818 H Street, N.W. Washington, DC,
USA. Tel (202)477 1234.

World Maritime University
Citadellsv 29, S 21120 Malmo, Sweden.

World Meterorological Organisation (WMO)
41 Guiseppe Motta, Geneva 20,
Switzerland.

Worldscale Association (NYC) Inc.
17 Battery Place, New York, NY 10004,
USA. Tel (212) 422 2786. Tx 62351.

London Affiliate: Worldscale Association
(London) Ltd., Prince Rupert House,
Queen Street, London EC4R 1AD, England.
Tel (01) 248 4747. Tx 885118.

Worshipful Company of Shipwrights
Ironmongers' Hall, Barbican, London
EC3Y 8AA, England. Tel (01) 606 2376.

Yokohama Port & Harbour Bureau
5F Sangyo Boeki Centre Building, 2
Yamashita-cho, Naka-ku, Yokohama,
Japan. Tel (045) 671 2880. Tx 3822844.

Zeebrugge Port Authority
Louis Coiseaukaai 2, B-8000 Bruges,
Belgium. Tel (050) 444211. Tx 81201.

Zhanjiang Port Affiars Bureau
1 Ren Min Road, Zhanjiang, China.
Cables 9054 ZHANJIANG.

Zhdanov Port Authority
Admirala Lunina 99, Zhdanov 341010,
Russia. Tel 59234. Cables MORPORT.

SOME GENERAL SHIPPING, INSURANCE
AND LEGAL TERMS

Abandonment: The right a marine assured has to abandon property in order to establish a constructive total loss. An underwriter is not obliged to accept abandonment, but if he does he accepts responsibility for the property and for any legal liabilities attaching thereto, in addition to being liable for the full sum assured.

Act of God: An inevitable event occuring without the intervention of man — such as flood, tempest, or death — operating in case of certain contracts, such as those of insurers or carriers.

Actual Total Loss: This relates to an insurance policy and can occur in any of four ways: (1) The property is completely destroyed; (2) The owner is irretrievably deprived of the property; (3) Goods change their character to such a degree that they can be said to be no longer the thing insured by the policy; (4) The subject matter of the insurance, be it ship or goods on board the ship that is recorded as "missing" at Lloyds.

Advance Note: A draft on a shipowner for wages, given to a seaman on signing Articles of Agreement and redeemable after the ship has sailed with the seaman on board.

Affidavit: A written declaration on oath.

Affreightment: A contract to carry goods by ship. Charter-parties and bills of lading are contracts of affreightment.

Agency Commission Clause: A clause in the standard hull clauses (1983) whereby no claim will be admitted under the policy to remunerate the assured for expense incurred, or time expended, in obtaining information or providing documents to support his claim.

All risks: An insurance term used in cargo insurance which means that the policy covers the insured property for loss caused by any fortuity. The policy does not cover inevitable loss. In practice, such a policy always specifies certain risks that are excluded from cover.

Arbitration: The submitting of matters of controversy to judgment by persons selected by all parties to the dispute.

Arrest: The detention of a vessel and/or other property until the purpose of the arrest has been fulfilled.

Arrival notification form: A document which advises a consignee or a container operator that goods or containers have arrived at the port of discharge.

Assessor: A person who officially estimates the value of goods for the purpose of apportioning the sum payable in the settlement of claims.

Assignment: The passing of beneficial rights from one party to another. A policy or certificate of insurance cannot be assigned after interest has passed, unless an agreement to assign was made, or implied, prior to the passing of interest. An assignee acquires no greater rights than were held by the assignor, and a breach of good faith by the assignor is deemed to be a breach on the part of the assignee. The Institute Time Clauses (Hulls) incorporate a clause which terminates the policy automatically if, amongst other things, the ship changes ownership or management unless the underwriters agree in writing to continue the insurance. This effectively restricts free assignment of a hull time policy. If underwriters do agree to the assignment an endorsement signed by the assignor, showing the date of assignment must be attached to the policy. The assignment is still subject to the restrictions above.

Assignee: One who receives rights from an assignor.

Assignor: One who assigns his rights to another.

Average: A partial loss.

Average (General): Partial loss of the whole adventure deliberately made to prevent total loss of the whole adventure. It may be sacrifice of property or expenditure incurred to save the adventure. Parties who benefit from a general average loss are required to make good that loss by contributing in the proportion that the saved value of the party's property bears to the saved value of all interests involved in the adventure. General average is a rule of the sea and is implied in all contracts of carriage by sea. Parties to the contract are liable to contribute in GA whether or not their property is insured.

Average (Particular): A fortuitous partial loss of insured property proximately caused by an insured peril, but which is not a general average loss.

Average Adjuster: A person appointed by a shipowner to collect data, guarantees, etc., in relation to general average, and to calculate contributions due from the parties concerned to make good general average losses. The adjuster may also adjust claims on hull insurance policies for submission to underwriters.

Average Bond: An agreement signed by all interested parties acknowledging their liability to pay a share of the loss under general average. A "general average guarantee" is sometimes referred to (particularly in the USA) as an "average bond".

Average Disbursements: Expenditure incurred by the shipowner in connection with a general average act or an act of salvage. Such expenditure, when properly incurred, is recoverable from the GA or salvage fund created by the adjuster. Hull underwriters are not liable directly for GA expenditure. The assured must recover his expenditure from the GA fund. Underwriters' liability for GA contribution, if any, will incorporate their proportion of the GA expenditure that is included in the contribution paid by the insured.

Avoidance: The right of an underwriter to avoid a contract of marine insurance from inception. This can occur in the event of a breach of good faith by the assured or by his broker or, in the case of a voyage policy, where the voyage does not commence within a reasonable time after acceptance of the risk by the underwriter.

Award: A decision given by a court of law or by an arbitrator to conclude a dispute. The term can be used also to define the amount of damages allowed, if any, in the award. A judge in court will often state the reasoning for the decision, whereas this is not the case, usually, with an arbitrator's award.

Back Freight: Payment due to the shipowner for the carriage of goods beyond the contract port owing to circumstances beyond the control of the shipowner.

Bare Boat Charter: Charterer hires a vessel for a long period, appoints the master and crew, and pays all running expenses.

Barratry: Any wrongful act, wilfully, committed, by the master, officers or crew to the detriment of the shipowner or charterer. The Institute hull clauses cover loss of or damage to the ship when it is proximately caused by barratry; except when it is excluded by the paramount exclusions in the clauses. For example, the latter would exclude barratry involving the use of an explosive or weapon of war; also barratry carried out by a seaman on strike.

Beaufort Scale: A windscale and sea disturbance table by which mariners grade the force of wind and height of waves, thus communicating the general condition of the sea to others by use of a wind force number.

Benefit of Insurance Clause: A clause in a contract between the assured and a bailee by which the bailee of goods claims the benefit of any insurance policy effected by the cargo owner on the goods in care of the bailee. Such a clause in a contract of carriage, issued in accordance with the Carriage of Goods by Sea Act, is void at law.

Bill of Exchange: An order in writing from one person or firm to another requiring them to pay a certain sum to a person named therein.

Bill of Lading: A document issued by an overseas carrier which is a receipt for cargo received on board and is evidence of the contract between shipper and shipowner. It is also evidence of title to the goods described on it.

Blue Peter: A rectangular flag, blue with a white square in the centre, which is displayed to indicate that a ship is ready to proceed.

Bonded Goods: Imported goods deposited in a Government warehouse until duty is paid.

Bonding Company: An organisation that is prepared to undertake an agreement to make good a financial guarantee on behalf of another responsible for such guarantee. Owners of "arrested" vessels may obtain such a bond to satisfy a court and to obtain release of the vessel.

Boot Topping: A protective composition painted round the hull of a ship to prevent corrosion between the load and light waterlines.

Bottom Treatment Clause: A clause in the standard hull clauses, whereby underwriters specify the extent to which they shall be liable for surface preparation and primer painting of plates in repairing the bottom of a ship damaged by an insured peril.

Bottomry Bill or Bond: The pledge of a ship, or of her cargo, as security for repayment of money advanced to the master in an emergency, and of no avail if the ship be lost.

Bow Thruster: A propeller used to provide a transverse thrust to the bow of the ship and to assist movement in confined spaces.

Breach of Warranty: The Marine Insurance Act (1906) demands that the assured comply literally with any warranty in the policy, whether it be an express warranty or an implied warranty. Non compliance, where not excused, is termed "breach of warranty", and discharges the underwriter from all liability under the policy, whether or not it relates to the breach, as from the date of the breach; but without prejudice to any valid claims arising from accidents occurring prior to the date of the breach. Breach of warranty is excused where circumstances have changed so that the warranty has become unnecessary; where it would be illegal to comply with the warranty; or where the policy conditions waive breach of warranty.

Breach of Warranty Clause: A clause in a policy whereby underwriters waive breach of certain specified warranties. In hull policies, the clause relates only to warranties as to cargo, trade, locality, towage, salvage services or date of sailing, and requires prompt notice, and amended conditions and an additional premium if underwriters so desire. There is no similar clause in cargo policies as a standard, but cargo underwriters usually waive breach of the implied warranties of seaworthiness and cargoworthiness of the overseas carrying vessel, provided the assured are not privy thereto.

Break Bulk: Applies to goods that have been stripped from containers (or other form of bulk carriage) for forwarding to final destination.

Break-up Voyage: A voyage where the ship's final destination is a break-up yard, for the purpose of breaking up the ship. The 1983 I.T.C. provide that where the insured ship undertakes such a voyage during the currency of the policy, any claim occurring subsequent to sailing on the break up voyage shall be limited to the scrap value of the ship. This does not apply if prior arrangements have been made with the underwriters regarding the break up voyage. The break-up voyage clause does not affect claims recoverable under the three fourths collision clause, nor under the GA and salvage charges clause.

Breaking Bulk: The initial opening of hatches on entering port and the commencement of discharge of cargo.

Breasthook: A place bracket joining the starboard and port stringers at the bow of a ship.

Broker: An agent representing a principal to buy or sell goods, merchandise or marketable securities, or to negotiate insurance, freight rates or other matters, for a principal; the sales or transactions being negotiated not in his own name but in that of the principal.

Carrier's Lien: The right to retain possession of goods pending payment of overdue freight charges. The term may refer, also, to the right of a carrier to retain cargo pending payment of a GA contribution; but may be discharged in such cases by the payment of a GA deposit or provision of an acceptable GA guarantee.

Causa Causans: The cause of a cause of loss.

Causa Proxima: Proximate cause.

Change of Voyage: This applies only to "voyage" policies (hull or cargo). A change of voyage occurs when the destination of the ship is voluntarily changed after commencement of the voyage. Unless arrangements have been made with the underwriters to continue cover, prior to the change, underwriters are discharged from all liability as from the time the decision to change the voyage is manifested; but without prejudice to any valid loss occuring prior to such time. Underwiters hold covered change of voyage; subject to prompt notice to underwriters, payment of an additional premium and change of conditions, if required.

Charter-party: An agreement whereby the shipowner hires his vessel to the charterer subject to certain conditions.

Classification Clause: An Insitute clause used in cargo open cover contracts to indicate the age and class of overseas carrying vessels acceptable at the premium rates specified in the contract. Basically, the ship must be iron or steel and mechanically self propelled. She must be fully classed with any of the listed classification societies. She must be no more than 15 years of age. The age limit is raised to 25 years for liners, provided they are over 1000grt and are not chartered. Goods carried by ships not attaining the required standard are held covered subject to payment of an additional premium.

Clean Bill of Lading: One in which there is nothing to qualify the admission that the goods are shipped in good order and condition.

Clearance Label: Denotes that a vessel has complied with all the regulations for clearance outward. It is attached to the Victualling Bill by the Customs officer who clears the vessel, and is then known as the Outward Clearance.

Cofferdam: Transverse double bulkheads at least three feet apart, extending from the keel to the upperdeck, to separate one part of the ship from another. Cofferdams are located either side of the engine-room space and are used as part of the collision bulkhead.

Co-Insurance: The sharing of an insurance risk between two or more parties, other than a contract of reinsurance.

Collision Clause: A clause in a hull policy, covering collision liability incurred by the assured (may be termed 'Collision Liability Clause').

Combi Ship: A ship designed to carry both conventional and containerised cargo.

Commixture: A mixture of two or more cargoes which cannot be separated into the relevant consignments.

Common Carrier: One who carries any type of goods, other than a carrier of special goods.

Compromised Total Loss: This term is used where hull underwriters agree to a compromised settlement for total loss of ship, in circumstances where neither an actual loss, nor a constructive total loss may be claimed, but the value of the ship when repaired does not justify the cost of repairs. This type of settlement is not subject to any basic rules, but usually applies to policies where the insured value of the ship is higher than her market value.

Conference Ship: A ship operated by a signatory to a shipping conference.

Consignee: The firm or persons authorised to receive the cargo and to whom it is consigned.

Constructive Total Loss: A right of a marine assured to claim a total loss on the policy because either (1) the property has been lost and recovery is unlikely; or (2) an actual loss appears to be unavoidable; or (3) to prevent an actual total loss it would be necessary to incur an expenditure which would exceed the saved value of the property or, in the case of a hull policy, the "insured" value expressed in the policy. To establish a claim for constructive total loss the assured must abandon what remains of the property to underwriters and give notice of his intention so to do.

Contact Damage: Damage to the ship caused by its striking any object other than another ship or vessel (the latter being termed "collision" damage). Damage to the ship caused by it being grounded or by striking rocks or submerged objects, other than in circumstances which constitute "standing". Damage to the ship cargo caused by any of the above circumstances or by physical touch with other cargoes or the ship's hull etc.

Continuation Clause: A clause providing for the continuation of a hull policy beyond the natural expiry date. The clause can be used at the option of a hull assured, whose ship is on a voyage at the time the policy is due to expire, but who does not wish to renew the hull policy for a further period of time. The assured, by giving notice to the underwriters before the expiry date of the policy, can continue cover until the ship arrives at her planned destination port. An additional premium is payable on a pro rata monthly basis for the time the policy is continued.

Contributory Value: The value of property saved by a general average or salvage act, on which the contribution by each interest to the loss is calculated.

Convertible Currency: A London market term for any currency other than Sterling, US dollars or Canadian dollars.

Counter Guarantee: An undertaking given by a cargo assured to an underwriter agreeing to reimburse the underwriter in the event that the issue of the underwriter's guarantee to pay a general average contribution results in payment in excess of the amount properly due under the policy.

Courts Martial: Courts constituted of naval or military officers for the trial of offences against discipline.

Customary Deductions: New for old deductions made by an average adjuster from the cost of repairs for general average damage to a ship over 15 years old. Hull underwriters do not make new for old deductions from claims for repairing damage to the ship, whether they be for GA sacrifice or particular average.

Dead Freight: Freight rate which is paid on empty space in a vessel when the charterer is responsible for the freight rate of a full cargo. It should be paid before sailing.

Deadweight Tonnage: Technically, the term refers to the actual weight of cargo, fuel and stores required to bring the ship down to her loadline marks. In marine insurance practice the term refers to the dimensions of a ship for the purpose of calculating the premium for a hull & machinery policy on full conditions.

Deals: Lengths of timber between 5ft. and 3ft. in length and between 2 inches and 9 inches thick.

Deck Log: Ship's log recording general details concerning the running of the ship, including accidents concerned with ship or cargo.

Declivity: The angle of the launching ways at a shipyard.

Deductible: An amount or percentage, expressed in a policy, that is deducted from partial loss claims.

Most commonly seen in policies covering hull and machinery, where the policy deductible is applied to all claims arising out of any accident or series of accidents comprising one occurrence, other than a total loss claim or sue and labour charges relating to a total loss. The cost of sighting the bottom for stranding damage is exempt from the deductible in the Institute hull clauses.

Defeasible Interest: A cargo insurable interest that ceases during the transit of goods.

Deferred Account: A system allowing the shipowner to pay his annual premium by instalments.

Demise Charterparty: An agreement whereby the charterer takes over control costs and responsibilities of the vessel for an agreed period.

Demurrage: The sum agreed by charter to be paid as damages for delay beyond the stipulated time for loading or discharging. It should be collected daily by the master or agent. The term is sometimes used in hull insurance practice to refer to loss of hire money.

Deposit Receipt: A receipt given in respect of a general average deposit payment.

Derelict: A vessel that has been abandoned by the crew but has not sunk.

Detention: Where demurrage is paid for an agreed number of days, any further delay is termed "detention", in respect of which the shipowner can claim unlimited damages.

Deviation: A deviation occurs when a ship is on a voyage and departs from the customary or designated route with the intention of returning to that route to complete the voyage. A hull time policy is not affected by deviation, nor is a cargo policy that is subject to the Institute Cargo Clauses. In the case of a hull voyage policy deviation discharges the underwriter from all liability as from the time the vessel leaves the stated or customary course, unless the assured gives the underwriter immediate notice of the deviation upon receipt of advices, agrees to any amended terms of cover required and pays an additional premium, if required.

Disbursements: Expenses incurred by the shipowner in connection with running a ship.

Disbursements Clause: A clause in a policy covering hull and machinery of a ship, which incorporates a warranty prohibiting the assured from effecting additional insurances to include total loss of the ship, other than those listed in the clause. Breach of this warranty is not held covered, and discharges the underwriter from all liability under the hull and machinery policy, as from the date of breach of warranty. The clause permits a maximum amount that may be insured in respect of 'disbursements', 'increased value', 'anticipated freight', etc. without breach of warranty taking place.

Dispatch Money: When so agreed in the charter-party, this is paid by the shipowner to the charterer as a result of the vessel completing loading or discharging before the stipulated time.

Displacement Tonnage: This term is chiefly used when referring to warships and is the actual weight of water displaced by the vessel when floating at her loaded draught.

Documents of Title: Documents produced by a consignee as evidence of right to take delivery of goods (eg Bill of Lading).

Drawback: A repayment of duty on the exportation of goods previously imported.

Drill Ship: A type of drilling rig used in oil exploration at sea.

Dumb Barge: A barge that has no means of propulsion.

Duty of Assured Clause: A clause, incorporated in the standard cargo and hull clauses that are attached to a MAR form of policy. The purpose of the clause is to direct the attention of the assured to the need to care for the insured property as though it were uninsured, taking all reasonable measures to prevent loss for which underwriters might be liable, and preserving underwriters' subrogation rights in respect of recoveries from other parties. The clause replaces the sue & labour clause that was incorporated in the SG policy, and provides that underwriters will pay expenses incurred by the assured, in the same manner that sue and labour charges were recoverable. The wording of the hull clause is different from that in the cargo clause, although the same principle pertains. The clause in the hull policy also incorporates the 'waiver clause' which comes into effect in cases of constructive total loss. Further, sue & labour charges recoverable under the hull clause are subject to the policy deductible (except when associated with a total loss) and are subject to reduction in event of underinsurance.

English Jurisdiction Clause: This clause appears in the MAR policy form, and applies to all claims except where a foreign jurisdiction clause is attached, by agreement with the underwriters, to the policy. The clause provides that claims under the policy are subject to English Jurisdiction, in the event that action is taken in a court of law against the underwriters.

English Law and Practice Clause: This clause appears in all Institute clauses published for attachment to the MAR form of policy. It provides that when one applies law and practice to the interpretation of the policy conditions, decisions must be based on English law and practice, irrespective of the country of jurisdiction.

Entering Inwards: The reporting of the vessel's arrival in port by the master at the Custom House. Permission to commence discharging is obtained.

Entreport: A place of transhipment.

Entry Outwards: The reporting of the intention to commence a new voyage by the master at the Custom House. Permission to commence loading is obtained.

Escalator Clause: A clause allowing for adjustment of the insured value in certain non-marine material damage insurances. A similar clause can be found in builders risks policies covering ships under construction.

Excess: The term 'excess' was used for many years in the marine market to denote an amount that had to be exceeded before a partial loss claim attached to the policy. Once the excess was passed the amount of the claim above the amount of the excess was paid. The term has gradually disappeared in the marine market, to be replaced by the term 'deductible', which has the same effect on partial loss claims.

Excess Point: Term used in excess of loss reinsurance to determine the point at which the reinsurer comes on risk.

Excess Value Insurance: This term was commonly used in the marine market in reference to insurances effected additionally to the policy covering the hull and machinery of a ship. These could apply to insurable interest in respect of ship-owners' liabilities, or additional insurances covering hull interests (eg disbursements). Today, the term 'excess liabilities' is used for the former, and 'increased value' for the latter.

Express Warranty: A warranty that is specified in the policy document, or is attached thereto. A warranty that applies to the policy, but is not expressed therein (eg warranty of legality), is termed an 'implied warranty'.

Extended Protest: Detailed statement made by the master of a vessel concerning an accident which has become the subject of a court case.

Extra Charges: Expenses incurred in connection with a claim under a policy.

Factor: An agent employed to sell in his own name (at the agreed commission) goods or merchandise belonging to his principal; his acts being binding in the principal at the instance of third parties. Compare with **Broker.**

Fac/oblig: Facultative/obligatory. A reinsurance term for a contract where the reassured can select which risks he cedes to the reinsurer, but the reinsurer is obliged to accept all cessions made.

First Three: A term on a slip requiring that subsequent amendments be subject to the three leader agreement.

Fixed Objects: Harbours, piers, etc., with which a ship might come into contact.

Floating Policy: A form of cargo policy to cover many individual voyages. Seldom used today, having been replaced in practice by the open cover and open policy.

Flotsam: Cargo cast or lost overboard and recoverable by reason of its remaining afloat.

Force Majeure: An occurrence outside human control (eg earthquake), a superior power.

Forebody: That part of a ship which is forward of midships.

Forecastle: Raised part at the bow of the ship.

Forefoot: The lower part in the stem of a ship that curves to meet the keel.

Foreign Jurisdiction Clause: A clause agreed by underwriters and attached to the policy, that provides for the policy to be subject to legal jurisdiction of the country named in the clause. This will, normally, take precedence over the English jurisdiction clause in the MAR policy form; but it is customary for the latter to be deleted in such cases to avoid confusion. It does not take precedence over the English law & practice clause in the Institute clauses.

Forestay: A wire support to the foreside of a mast.

Foul Bill: A bill of lading that has been claused to show that the goods were not received in a sound condition.

Franchise: In an English policy the term 'franchise' has been used to define a percentage expressed in the policy (the 'memorandum' in the SG policy form) which was applied to particular average losses. If the loss fell below this percentage of the amount insured, no claim attached to the policy. If the loss attained the franchise percentage, the claim was paid in full. Franchises have fallen into disuse in recent years for hull and cargo insurance, and do not appear in any of the new clauses for ships and cargoes. Nevertheless, a franchise has remained in policies covering the ship operator's interest in freight, and a franchise clause appears in the 1983 freight insurance clauses.

Freeboard: This is the height between the deck line and the Plimsoll (or Load) line.

Free in and out: Cargo to be loaded and discharged free to the vessel.

Freeing Port: An opening to allow water from the deck of a ship to flow over the side.

Free of Capture and Seizure: Commonly abbreviated to F.C.&.S., this term was used until 1982 in all marine insurance contracts to refer to the war exclusion clause. Its use was discontinued in the UK cargo insurance market in 1982 and in the hull insurance market in 1983.

Free on board: Goods delivered on board the vessel free of extra charge to the purchaser.

Freight: For insurance purposes, the term 'freight' relates to the remuneration received or receivable by a carrier for the carriage of goods, and can include the profit he derives from the carriage of his own goods. Where freight is paid in advance by the shipper, on a non returnable basis, the insurable interest is vested in the shipper, and is normally embraced within the insured value of the goods. Where freight is paid on 'outturn' of the goods at the destination port, the insurable interest is vested in the carrier (shipowner or charterer). In practice, most shipowners insure their freight on a time policy to reimburse them for loss of anticipated freight resulting from total loss of the ship. In shipping practice, the term freight may be used to define the goods carried in transit. Thus, personnel involved in arrangements for such transit may be termed 'freight forwarders'. It is commonplace to hear goods referred to as 'freight' in regard to rail carriage, air carriage, etc.

Freight Contingency: The insurable interest of a consignee who has paid freight on goods when delivered over the ship's side, but where the goods are still subject to peril until they arrive at the final destination.

Freight Forwarder: One who arranges the shipping of goods overseas.

Freight Rate: The charge for transporting goods by water.

Freight Waiver Clause: The underwriter insuring hull and machinery of a ship is entitled, on payment of a constructive total loss, to take over the ship, arrange to deliver the cargo and retain any freight earned thereby. The 'freight waiver clause' in the hull policy conditions waives this right. Prior to publication of the 1983 hull clauses, this clause was commonly termed the 'freight abandonment' clause.

Frustration of Adventure: A circumstance whereby a ship or goods cannot reach the contemplated destination but remain undamaged and are not lost to the owner. This peril is normally exluded from policies covering war risks and strike risks.

G.A. in Full Clause: A clause in a cargo policy whereby the underwriter agrees to pay general average contributions in full even though the contributory value may be greater than the insured value.

Garboard Strake: The shell plating of a ship that is next to the keelplate.

General Average: An internationally accepted rule of the sea. When a ship is in danger of total loss the master has the right to sacrifice property and/or incur reasonable expenditure to prevent the total loss. Measures taken for the sole benefit of any particular interest are not general average. On successful completion of the adventure, or if it is abandoned in a place of safety, on successful attainment of such place the ship is declared as entering "under average". Security in the shape of deposits or guarantees is taken from each cargo interest and an average adjuster is appointed. The adjuster calculates the value of the saved interest and each interest is required to contribute a rateable proportion to make good the general average loss. The MIA (1906) provides that underwriters are liable for general average contribution only where the circumstances causing the GA act constitute the operation of an insured peril. Hull underwriters have continued to maintain this rule in the 1983 types of insurance; but cargo underwriters no longer apply the rule in the 1982 standard cargo clauses. However, all marine policies on standard conditions, comply with the MIA provision that underwriters' liability is reduced by any underinsurance indicated by a comparison between the insured value and the contributory value in the GA adjustment.

General Average Bond: An agreement signed by all parties involved in a general average act.

General Average Contribution: The proportion payable by one of the parties involved in a general average act to make good the loss suffered in that act.

General Average Deposit: A deposit paid by a consignee in return for delivery of the goods where such goods are subject to general average contribution.

General Average Disbursements: Expenses paid by the shipowner as part of a general average act. Such expenses are recovered by the shipowner from the general average fund. Unlike GA sacrifice, there is no direct liability on hull underwriters to reimburse the assured for GA disbursement. The disbursements will be included in the final GA adjustment, and incorporated in the GA contribution, underwriters paying this insofar as it is recoverable under the policy.

General Average Fund: The total arrived at by adding together general average expenditure and the value of property sacrificed in a general act, plus costs of its adjustment.

General Average Guarantee: An undertaking by a financial house or an underwriter to pay the contribution due towards a general average fund.

General Exclusions Clause: A clause in the Institute Cargo Clauses 1982, which specifies risks that are excluded, irrespective of the risks covered elsewhere in the wording.

Grain Certificate: A certificate to show that the regulations have been complied with when carrying a grain cargo.

Gross Tonnage: This is the volume of the interior of the vessel including all spaces which are permanantly closed in (but excluding the double bottom), expressed in tons of 100 cubic tons.

Heavy Lift: A unit of cargo which cannot be lifted by the normal ship's lifting gear.

Held Covered: An agreement by underwriters to provide cover in certain circumstances. Where this is a policy provision, cover is subject to prompt advice to the underwriters that the circumstances have taken place, and payment of an additional premium, if required. The held covered provision may allow underwriters to amend the policy conditions. A 'held covered' provision in broker's slip is not legally binding on the subscribing underwriters until it is embodied in a legally valid policy, but underwriters should still ensure that they understand what is intended when initialling such slip agreements. Where it is agreed in the London market to hold covered a renewal, pending receipt of confirmation from the assured, such agreement is valid for no more than 14 days unless agreed otherwise.

High seas: Maritime areas that are outside the jurisdiction of any State.

Hogged: A hogged ship is one that is held amidships with both ends sagging lower than the centre.

Implied Warranty: A warranty that is not expressed in a policy, but which is implied to be therein by law (eg warranty of seaworthiness in a voyage policy, warranty of legality in all policies).

Incoterms: A set of ICC (International Chamber of Commerce) terms offered for optional use in trading contracts and intended to reduce misunderstandings in the meaning of international trading terms.

Increased Value Clause (Cargo): A clause in a cargo policy which provides that the insured value expressed in the policy be added to the insured value of any other policy effected on the same goods for the same voyage to indicate underinsurance. Liability under the policy with the clause is then applied in the proportion that the sum insured thereunder bears to the value of both policies. Recoveries are shared between the unnderwriters subscribing both policies in like proportions.

Indemnity: Liability of an insurer for loss under a policy.

Indirect Damage: Damage caused by an insured peril but not proximately caused thereby.

Inherent Vice or Nature: Inherent vice is a quality in a cargo which, if certain circumstances occur, will inevitably result in loss of or damage to the cargo. An example occurs in connection with soft coal. If the coal is loaded in a wet condition it is liable to spontaneous combustion if carried in an airless humid hold. Cargo policies, even those covering 'all risks', exclude claims for loss or damage suffered by insured goods when it is caused by inherent vice therein. Inherent nature is a natural quality in a cargo which will cause loss or damage eventually, irrespective of the circumstances. An example of inherent nature is deterioration in fruit, which is inevitable in due course if the fruit is not consumed before it occurs. Cargo policies exclude inherent nature in the insured goods.

In Personam: Legal action against a person.

In Rem: Legal action against an object or the owner thereof (eg action naming the ship).

Institute Cargo Clauses: Standard insurance conditions, published by the Institute of London Underwriters, for policies covering goods in transit overseas.

Institute Clause: A standard clause published by the Institute of London Underwriters.

Institute of London Underwriters: An organisation representing the interests of member insurance companies. Although the majority of members are British companies, membership is available to foreign companies. The Institute maintains a close liason with Lloyd's marine market, and provides facilities for a number of joint committees to operate.

Institute Time Clauses: Standard insurance conditions, published by the Institute of London Underwriters, for policies covering ships for a period of time.

Institute Warranties: A set of express warranties, published by the Institute of London Underwriters, for use in hull & machinery policies. The set comprises five locality warranties and one trade warranty; the latter relating to the carriage of Indian coal as cargo. In event of breach of any of the warranties, the assured is held covered by the breach of warranty clause in the Institute hull clauses (see "Breach of Warranty Clause").

Insurable Interest: The interest one has in relation to property exposed to peril whereby one may lose financially by the loss of, or damage to, such property or may incur a liability in respect thereof. A person who effects a marine insurance contract without an insurable interest or a reasonable expectation of acquiring such interest is guilty of an offence under English law. In order to claim under a policy, one must have an insurable interest in the subject matter insured at the time the loss occurs.

Insured Value: The value of property as expressed in a policy of insurance.

Invoice: A document setting out in detail the goods consigned, marks and numbers, cost, any charges, and name of consignee.

Inward Charges: Pilotage and other expenses incurred on entering port.

Irrespective of Percentage: This term was in common use in cargo insurance when the SG policy was in use. Its effect was to make claims payable without reference to the FPA warranty or the franchise expressed in the memorandum in the policy form. With the abrogation of the SG policy for cargo insurances, the term has fallen into disuse in the London market.

Jason Clause: A clause in a contract of affreightment relating to liability of the shipowner under the US Harter Act in disputes concerning general average.

Jerque Note: A document given to the master by the Customs after the inward cargo is discharged and the vessel has been rummaged.

Jetsam: Cargo or goods which sink when jettisoned. The term applies also to such goods when washed ashore.

Jettison: The act of throwing property (usually cargo or stores) overboard in order to save the vessel.

Joint Cargo Committee: A group of London company underwriters and Lloyd's underwriters who meet to discuss matters relating to cargo insurance and to make recommendations to the cargo insurance market.

Joint Hull Committee: A group of London company underwriters and Lloyd's underwriters who meet to discuss matters relating to hull insurance conditions and rating structures.

Jurisdiction Clause: A clause in a policy that specifies the country in which any court action relating to the policy must be pursued.

Jury Mast: A temporary mast.

Kingpost: A vertical mast that supports a derrick.

Knocked Down Condition: Goods (eg vehicles) dismantled for transit.

Lagan: Cargo thrown overboard, but buoyed so that it may be recovered.

Laker: A vessel specially constructed for navigation in the waterways of the Great Lakes and canal systems of North America.

Latent Defect: A defect in the construction of a ship or machinery that is not readily discernible to a competent person carrying out a normal inspection. Discovery of a latent defect does not give a rise to a claim on the ordinary hull policy, but damage caused thereby is usually covered.

Lay Days: Days allowed by charter for loading or discharging cargo.

Lay-up Return: A return of part of the annual premium on a ship time policy paid back to the assured by the underwriters because the ship has been laid up and not exposed to full navigational risks for a period of not less than 30 consecutive days. Such return is not paid until the natural expiry date of the policy, and is forfeit if the vessel becomes a total loss before such date.

Leadage: The cost of transporting coal from colliery to place of shipment.

Letter of Credit: A document authorising payment to the person named, subject to fulfilment of certain specified conditions on the part of the person authorised to receive money (eg evidence that goods have been shipped).

Lien: A legal right over goods, to hold them until the claim against the owner has been settled.

Light Bill: A Customers receipt for the payment of light dues.

Light Dues: Moneys collected by the U.K. Customs on behalf on Trinity House for the maintenance of lighthouses and buoys. Dues are levied on vessels according to their net registered tonnage,

Lighterage: The price paid for loading or unloading ships by lighters or barges.

Limber Hole: A drainage hole in a ship.

Limited Terms: An insurance expression meaning that the policy gives less cover than a policy on full conditions (eg total loss only).

Line Slip: A signing slip issued off a long term cover.

Liner: A ship on a regular schedule calling at specified ports.

Lloyd's Agents: Persons appointed by the Corporation of Lloyd's and stationed in most world ports. One of their many functions is to safeguard Lloyd's interests and report all movements and losses of ships.

Lloyd's Broker: An intermediary who negotiates insurance contracts with Lloyd's underwriters on behalf of his clients, the assured. For a broker to be admitted as a Lloyd's broker he must satisfy the Committee of Lloyd's that he is a suitable person to become a Lloyd's broker. Only Lloyd's brokers and their nominated substitutes (holding a valid Lloyd's ticket) are permitted to enter the underwriting room at Lloyd's to transact business with underwriters.

Lloyd's Register of Shipping: An independent non-profit-making Society. It undertakes surveys, classification of vessels, and produces various annual publications.

Load Line: The Load Line, sometimes called the Plimsoll Line, or "marks", indicates the depth in the water down to which a ship may be loaded; the position of these marks is governed by international convention.

Location Clause: A clause in a cargo insurance contract limiting insurance cover at any location during transit when the goods are not on the oversea vessel. The intention is to restrict accumulation of risk in one location, and normally applies to open cover conditions.

London Insurance Market Network: An electronic data transfer system embracing a network of computers. This system is designed to reduce the flow of paperwork and improve the flow of information within the London insurance market.

Loss of Specie: A change in the character of cargo which, in insurance terms, is effectively an actual total loss.

Lump Sum Freight: A fixed freight rate, regardless of how much cargo is loaded.

Machinery Damage Additional Deductible Clause: An Institute clause available for use in a policy covering hull & machinery that provides for an additional deductible to be applied to claims for damage to machinery which is attributable to negligence of master, officers or crew.

Made Good: The sums paid to general average fund to make good losses incurred by the general average act.

Malicious Damage Clause: A clause published by the Institute of London Underwriters for use in a cargo policy that is subject to the Institute Cargo Clauses (1982) B or C. It adds the risks of malicious acts, vandalism and sabotage to the cargo policy.

Manifest: A document containing the passenger list and details of all stores and cargo on board the vessel.

MAR Policy Form: A simplified form of marine insurance policy that was introduced in the Lloyd's marine insurance market to replace the SG policy form. A similar form of policy was introduced by the Institute of London Underwriters, for use by member companies, at the same time. The new policy form was introduced in 1982 for cargo insurance and in 1983 for hull insurances.

Maritime Lien: The claim a master and crew has on the vessel for the payment of wages due. The terms may be applied, also, to the rights of a salvor in regard to property that is subject to a salvage award; also, to the rights of a carrier in regard to cargo that is liable for a general average contribution.

Market Capacity: The maximum amount an insurance market can absorb as liability to its policy holders while maintaining a proper solvency margin.

Marks: A term used in shipping practice to refer to the loadline marks on the ship's hull. The term may be used also in regard to a bill of lading which shows the identification and destination markings on packages shipped.

Material Circumstances: Any circumstances that would affect a prudent underwriter in deciding whether or not to accept an insurance contract and in assessing the correct premium to charge.

Mate's Receipt: A receipt signed by the mate to say the cargo has been received on board in good order and condition.

Missing Ship: A ship is deemed to be "missing" when, following extensive inquiries, she is offically posted as "missing" at Lloyd's. She is then considered to be an "actual total loss" and policy claims for both hull and cargo are settled on that basis.

Name: An underwriting member at Lloyd's.

Nesting: Packing hollow-ware cargo (eg earthenware bowls) so that one item nests within another. Paper or straw may be used to separate each item and avoid damage.

Net Tonnage: This is the gross tonnage less the machinery, boiler and bunker, crew and stores spaces.

Network: See "London Insurance Market Network".

New for Old: When new material or parts replace damaged material or parts during repairs to a ship Underwriters are entitled to make a deduction from the claim as a result of betterment but they waive this right in practice. Average adjusters may apply the principle in general average for vessels over 15 years old.

No Cure — No Pay: The principle of pure salvage whereby the salvor who fails in his task receives no reward for his effort.

Not to Inure Clause: A clause in a cargo policy stating that the policy shall not inure to the benefit of a carrier or other bailee. The intention is to deny the right of carriers to benefit from the insurance when they claim such a right in the contracts of carriage.

Notary Public: An official certified to take affidavits and depositions from members of the public.

Notice of Abandonment: The initial action to be taken by an assured who wishes to claim a constructive total loss. Notice to underwriters must be given with reasonable diligence as soon as the assured is aware of the circumstance. Its purpose is to give the underwriter the opportunity to take action to prevent or minimise the loss.

Nuclear Exclusion Clause: A clause that is common to all insurance policies (though the wording may vary), whereby all loss of or damge to the subject matter insured arising from a nuclear weapon, or similar, is excluded from the policy cover.

Official Number: A registered number given to all merchant vessels and cut into the vessel's "main beam", together with the net registered tonnage.

Omnibus Clause: A clause in a hull policy extending liability cover to embrace, in addition to the assured's legal liability, the liability of other organisations who are connected with the ship. It usually excludes liability of shipyards, repair yards and others to whom underwriters do not wish to extend cover.

Open Charter: Where the charter-party specifies neither the kind of cargo nor the ports of destination.

Open Cover: A long term contract whereby the subscribing insurers agreed to accept declarations on the subject matter insured agreed as coming within the scope of the cover. It is customary for limits to be specified in the contract and for there to be a cancellation clause whereby either party may give notice to cancel the contract. Cargo contracts usually have a limit in respect of any one shipment or vessel or sending or other, as agreed in the contract, and may incorporate a location clause.

Open Policy: A cargo insurance policy designed to cover all consignments forwarded by the assured subject to a limit in any one vessel and, usually, a time limit during which declarations must attach. Unlike the floating policy it does not have an aggregate limit, but the underwriter can invoke a cancellation clause if he wishes to withdraw cover.

Ordinary Breakage: Breakage of fragile cargo which by its regularity has become accepted as inevitable loss during transit. It is not mentioned in the general exclusion clauses in the ICC (1982), and is one of the Statutory exclusions in the MIA, 1906.

Original Bill: Original Bill of Lading.

Orlop: Lowest deck of a ship.

Outturn: The quantity of cargo discharged from a ship.

Overage: A term used to define the addition premium paid under a cargo open cover in regard to the 'held covered' provision in the Institute classification clause.

Oxter Plate: A plate fitted to the top of a rudder post.

P & I Club: A mutual association formed by shipowners to provide protection from large financial loss suffered by one member by contribution towards that loss by all members. The P & I club covers liabilitity not insurable by the shipowner in the running of his ship. For example, collision liability not covered by the hull policy, contractual liability to cargo owners and others, defence costs, etc. Members pay an initial subscription which may be 'topped up' with calls on members if the fund held by the club is insufficient to meet demands upon it.

Particular Average: A fortuitous partial loss to the subject matter insured, proximately caused by an insured peril but which is not a general average loss.

Particular Charge: An expense incurred by an assured in relation to an insured loss. This can be a means of preventing further loss in transit (eg sue and labour charges), of assessing loss (eg a survey fee) or making good a loss at destination (eg repacking); sometimes referred to as an "extra charge" when it connected with a claim on the policy.

Percentage of Depreciation: The proportion of the total value of cargo that is the subject of loss from an insured peril. The percentage is applied to the sum insured by the policy to determine the amount of claim payable.

Perfecting the Sight: Adding necessary details of the bill of lading when such had been previously omitted.

Peril: A term used in the Marine Insurance Act (1906) to denote a hazard. The principle of proximate cause is applied to an insured peril to determine whether or not a loss is recoverable. In modern practice the terms 'risk' replace 'peril'.

Piracy: An assault on a vessel, cargo, crew or passengers at sea by persons owing no allegiance to a recognised flag and acting for personal gain. It also includes acts of rioters who attach a ship from the shore and of passengers who mutiny. This peril, along with war perils, was excluded from the SG policy by the F.C. & S. clause; to be reinstated if the cover conditions covered war risks. Thus, for many years piracy was related to war risks. The 1982 cargo war clauses do not cover piracy, and it is not embraced within the risks covered by the B or C cargo clauses. The 1983 hull clauses incorporate piracy among the risks covered by the standard marine clauses; piracy not being included in the war risks cover (1983).

Plimsoll Mark: The loading mark on the side of a vessel.

Policy: A contract of insurance.

Policy Proof of Interest: A policy wherein the underwriter agrees to waive proof that an insurable interest is enjoyed by the assured, at the time of loss, as a condition of claim payment. In other policies the underwriter is not liable for any claim where the assured is unable to prove that his interest in the subject matter of the insurance exists at the time of loss. P.P.I. policies are invalid in a court of law, but are not illegal except where no interest exists or where there was no reasonable expectation that it would exist at the time the policy was effected.

Pollution Hazard Clause: A clause in a hull policy, whereby underwriters cover deliberate damage or loss to the ship caused by Governmental authority in attempts to mitigate a threat of pollution hazard; where such relates to loss or damage to the ship and where it has not resulted from a want of due diligence on the part of the assured, owners or managers of the ship.

Portage Bill: A bill giving the statement of wages of each member of the crew at the end of a voyage.

Power of Attorney: A document which empowers one person to act for another.

Practique: Permission to land crew and cargo after the vessel has satisfied the port doctor as to the state of health on board.

Promissory Note: A note promising to pay a certain person a stated sum on a specified date.

Protest: A written declaration by the master and witnessed before a Notary Public.

Proximate Cause: The most effective cause of a loss in a chain of events leading to the loss. A basic principle of insurance in that, unless the policy provides otherwise, the underwriter is not liable for any loss that is not proximately caused by an insured peril.

Quayage: The charge for using a berth alongside a wharf.

Ranging Clause: A clause in a hull policy exempting underwriters from liability under the policy (for damage received as well as for damage done) in the event that the insured ship collides with another ship while the vessels are approaching or ranging alongside each other at sea for the purpose of transferring cargo. Cover may be obtained by arrangement with the underwriters, in practice, provided they are notified, of the intention to transfer cargo in this manner, in advance. The exemption does not apply to customary transhipment in port areas involving inshore harbour craft.

Receiver: The person appointed to "receive" and administer the rents and profits, or other moneys, accruing to an estate or business undertaking which is administered or wound-up under the supervision of the court. Official Receivers are officials permanantly employed to act in that capacity in bankruptcy proceedings or the winding-up of joint-stock companies.

Receiver of Wreck: An official who is responsible to the Dept. of Trade for all wreckage that is salved on the coastline, or found at sea and brought to a British port.

Reference: The submission of a matter in dispute to an arbitrator for his award.

Registry, Certificate of: A document giving all particulars of the vessel, including the names of the owner and the master.

Risk: A fortuity, it does not embrace inevitable loss. The term is used to define causes of loss covered by a policy.

Running Down Clause: A term sometimes used in market practice to define the collision liability clause in a hull policy.

Sailing cards: Cards issued by shipbrokers to their customers, giving particulars of the ship, or ships they are about to load, the loading berth, date of departure, etc.

Salvage: In maritime terms this relates to action carried out by a third party in the absence of contract whereby property in peril at sea is saved. The term is often used to define the money paid to a salvor as a reward for such service, but this should be termed a 'salvage award'. In marine insurance practice a salvage award, or a part thereof, which is recoverable under a marine insurance policy is termed a 'salvage charge'. The term 'salvage' may be used, in non-marine practice, to define property salved; as in the case of goods saved from a fire on land.

Salvage Association: An association, closely connected with the London insurance market, whose functions is to take instructions from interested parties (eg underwriters) to investigate casualties and to make recommendations for the preservation and protection of property; also to determine the extent and proximate cause of loss when required.

Salvage Award: An amount awarded to a salvor for services rendered in the salvage of property in peril at sea. The award may be made by a court or by arbitration, depending on the terms of the salvage contract. Underwriters contribute towards a salvage award insofar as the award is in respect of insured property in peril from an insured risk, subject to any restrictions imposed by the policy (eg a policy deductible) and, except where the policy provides otherwise, subject to reduction to reflect under-insurance, if any.

Salvage Loss: A compromised settlement on a cargo policy, usually when the adventure has been terminated short of destination and damaged goods are sold at the intermediate port. The underwriter pays the difference between the sum insured by the policy and the proceeds of the sale.

Scantling: The thickness of a steel plate in a ship.

Scraping the bottom: Removing weed and incrustation from the underside of a ship. Not covered by a hull policy; not even when necessary to repair damage recoverable under the policy.

Seaworthiness: The fitness of a ship to encounter the hazards of the sea with reasonable safety. In addition to having a sound hull the ship must be fully and competently crewed and sufficiently fuelled and provisioned for the next stage of voyage. All her equipment must be in proper working order and, if she carries cargo, she must be cargoworthy and properly trimmed and stowed. The MIA, 1906, incorporates an implied warranty in a hull voyage policy which requires the ship to be seaworthy at the commencement of the voyage and, if the voyage is in stages, at the commencement of each stage of the voyage. Breach of this warranty is not held covered, so in such case, the underwriters are discharged from all liability under the policy as from the date the ship sails in an unseaworthy condition. A similar implied warranty applies to seaworthiness of the carrying vessel in regard to a cargo policy; but underwriters waive breach of the warranty in this case, provided the assured and their servants are not privy thereto. The warranty in the MIA does not apply to a hull time policy, but if the ship sails in an unseaworthy condition, with the privity of the assured, the underwriter is not liable for any loss that is attributable to the unseaworthiness.

Security: A term used in marine insurance to define the insurers with whom a policy has been effected.

Sentimental Loss: A market loss to goods brought about by fear that goods may have suffered from a known casualty whereas no such loss exists in fact.

SG Policy: The policy form adopted by Lloyd's, in 1779, as a standard for all marine insurance business. The form covered both ship and goods on a specified voyage and required considerable adaptation to be used for modern hull and cargo business. The London company market adopted separate policy forms for hull and cargo business, but these were very similar to Lloyd's SG form and still required adaptation. In January, 1982, the London cargo insurance market replaced the SG form with the MAR form of policy. The London hull insurance market took the same measure in October 1983. The Institute clauses published for use with the SG form and its company counterpart have been withdrawn.

Ship's Articles: The agreement between the master and his crew, giving details of conditions and terms.

Ship's Husband: The shipowner's agent who superintends the vessel when in port.

Shipped Bill: A Bill of Lading that acknowledges the goods have been loaded on the ship.

Short Delivery: The quantity of cargo delivered is less than the bill of lading quantity.

Short Shipment: When the full amount intended to be shipped has not been shipped.

Short Term: A time policy effected for a period of less than 12 months.

Short Ton: Weight measurement of 2000lbs.

Shut Out: Cargo not loaded.

Sighting the Bottom: Examining the underside of a ship for damage following an accident. The Institute hull clauses provide that the underwriters will pay the cost of sighting the bottom, without applying the policy deductible and even if no damage is found, but only when the cost is incurred specially to examine the bottom following stranding.

Single Administrative Document: Produced by SITPRO (Simplication of International Trade Procedures), this document was introduced to the EEC in 1988. It is part of the 'aligned series' for the improvement of trade procedures and embraces, within a single document, the functions of some 70, previously used, Customs forms.

Sistership Clause: A clause in a hull policy whereby the underwriters agree to treat sisterships as if they were separately owned (and capable of legal liability, one to the other) in regard to collision liability claims and claims for salvage charges.

Slamming: Impact of water on the bows of the ship.

Sling Loss: Cargo lost by falling from ship's lifting tackle during loading or unloading.

Slip Registration: A procedure operating in the London insurance market whereby each risk placed by a broker's slip is registered at the time of placing. The registration is advised to the relevant policy signing and accounting office (ie LPSO, ILU, PSO or PSAC, as applicable), thereby enabling the relevant PSO to monitor the submission of premium documentation in time to meet the appropriate terms of trade settlement date.

Sparred: Describes a system of packing hollow-ware cargo whereby wooden supports hold the goods rigid during handling.

Special Drawing Rights: A term, introduced in 1984, to facilitate exchange rating regarding limitation of liability under international law. The SDR replaced the 'gold franc' in such calculations, from November 1984. The value of the SDR varies daily, and is obtainable from the customary financial sources of information.

Specie: Valuable cargo such as money, precious metal, jewellery, etc. (see also **Loss of Specie**).

Specific Performance: The remedy sought by a plaintiff who, instead of damages for a breach of contract, seeks the enforcement of the terms of the contract.

Spudding: Settling the legs of a submarine drilling rig in the seabed.

Statement of Claim: The first step in the pleadings to an action, in which the plaintiff particularises his claim, and the legal grounds on which it is based.

Statute-Barred: A debt the claim to which is barred by lapse of time under Statutes of Limitation.

Stemming: Arranging bunkers.

Stern Thruster: A propeller or water jet system set in the stern of the ship and positioned to give a sideways thrust to assist manoeuvring in a confined space.

Stoppage in Transitu: Right of a seller to give instruction to a carrier or other bailee to withold delivery to the buyer, usually due to non-payment for the goods.

Straddle Carrier: A vehicle specially constructed to lift and move containers in a dock area or container terminal area.

Strike Expenses: Expenses incurred as a result of a strike, such as forwarding costs for goods that cannot be discharged at the scheduled destination port or extra freight charged for overcarriage to another port when the scheduled discharge port is strikebound. These expenses are not covered by the marine policy with the standard strikes clauses attached thereto.

Stuffing: Placing goods into a container.

Subrogation: The right enjoyed by an underwriter to take over the rights and remedies available to an assured, following payment of a claim on the policy, in order to recover up to the amount of the claim from another party who was responsible for the loss.

Substituted Expenses: Expenses incurred in place of loss or expense which would be allowed as general average (eg cost of removal of a ship, with general average damage, to a place where repairs would cost less).

Sue and Labour Charges: Expenses incurred by a marine assured to prevent or minimise loss for which underwriters would have been liable. Expenditure incurred as part of a GA act is not allowed as sue and labour, nor are expenses incurred in a salvage operation involving a salvage award. Sue and Labour charges are recoverable under a marine insurance policy whether or not the purpose for which they were incurred was achieved. They are recoverable in addition to any other loss under the policy, even a total loss. Under a hull policy, except where they are associated with a total loss, S & L charges are subject to the policy deductible. Claims for S & L charges under a hull policy are subject to reduction to reflect underinsurance, if any.

Sue and Labour Clause: This clause formed part of the SG policy form and was the basis for applying to the policy expenses incurred by the assured to prevent loss for which underwriters would have been liable. The clause was not retained when the new MAR form of policy was introduced to replace the SG policy in 1982 (cargo) and 1983 (hull), and was, therefore, omitted from the new cargo and hull clauses drafted for attachment to the MAR form of policy. Nevertheless, the effect of the sue and labour clause is incorporated in the 'duty of the assured' clause in the new clauses.

Sweat Damage: Damage caused to cargo by condensation, usually due to lack of ventilation in a ship's hold.

Sympathetic Damage: Loss suffered by cargo following damage to other goods in the same ship. An example would be taint arising from odour given off by another cargo which has been damaged by seawater; where seawater damage is covered by the policy.

Syndicate: An association of two or more persons, constituted for carrying out a projected commercial or public undertaking.

Syndicate (Lloyd's): A group of underwriting members at Lloyd's whose acceptances and liabilities are handled jointly by an underwriting agency acting on their behalf, while each member remains legally liable solely for his/her own share of the syndicate's liability.

Tail Shaft: Extreme section at the aft end of a ship's propeller shaft.

Tanktainer: A cylindrically-shaped container intended for transport of liquid cargo.

Tank Top: Upper plating of the double bottom in a ship.

Tare: The weight of a container, box or other carrier of goods when empty.

Technical and Clauses Committee: A group Lloyd's and company underwriters who meet to discuss,, formulate and amend marine insurance clauses which are then recommended to the London market for general use.

Telemotor: Machinery which operates the steering system of a ship.

Tender Clause: A clause in a policy covering hull and machinery of a ship. It specifies the measures the assured must take in the event of an accident whereby a claim may arise under the policy, regarding advice to underwriters and Lloyd's agents and survey arrangements. The clause also gives underwriters rights regarding the taking of tenders for repairs, deciding the place and firm of repair and acceptance of the successful tender. It details the assured's rights in regard to delay experienced in awaiting further tenders requested by underwriters. A penalty is applied to the assured's claim for non compliance with the terms of the clause.

Third Party Liability: Legal liability to anyone other than another party to a contract (eg liability of one ship to another consequent upon a collision).

Three Leader Agreement: A condition in a slip or policy whereby the subscribing underwriters allow the leading underwriters to agree amendments etc., to the insurance on their behalf. Where both Lloyd's and ILU companies share the slip it is understood that the first two underwriters in each market subscribing the risk shall indicate their agreement to amendments, etc. It is, also, understood that the leaders' agreement relates only to changes which do not materially affect the cover (eg they cannot increase written lines).

Through Bill: A contract of affreightment that covers goods throughout the period of transit, including both overland and sea transit.

Time Charter: The charterer has the use of the vessel for a specified period. The shipowner supplies the crew and provisions.

Tomming Off: Using wedges between cargo and the ship's side or a bulkhead to prevent movement of the goods during transit.

Tonnage Deck: The uppermost continuous deck in ships having less than three decks, or the second continuous deck from below.

Tonne: Metric measurement of weight. 1000 kilograms.

Total Loss: This can be actual total loss or contructive total loss. In hull insurance it may include arranged or compromised total loss.

T.O.V.A.L.O.P.: Abbreviation for "Tanker Owners' Voluntary Agreement Concerning Liability for Oil Pollution". An agreement subscribed by most tanker owners world-wide, whereby owners agree to pay for clean-up costs incurred by Governments in respect of oil discharge from tankers belonging to such owners.

Tow: A ship being towed.

Towage Bill: An account rendered for towage expenses.

Tower's Liability: Liability incurred by any ship or vessel when she is towing another ship, vessel or other object.

Trade Ullage: An allowance for natural loss to cargo (eg evaporation).

Transhipment: The act of transferring goods from one vessel to another or from one conveyance to another, including periods at transhipping ports or places.

Transire: A Customs document used when a vessel is coasting, giving full cargo details. It serves as clearance from the port of issue.

Transit Clause: A clause in the Institute Cargo Clauses, specifying the attachment and termination of cover.

Transtainer: A vehicle used for carrying cargo containers during loading or discharge operations or within port of terminal areas (see **Straddle Carrier**).

Transverse: Across a ship at right angles to a line drawn from bow to stern.

Tween Decker: Any ship having one or more decks below the main deck.

Uberrimae Fidei: Utmost good faith.

Ullage: See **Trade Ullage.**

Unclean Bill: A bill of lading that has been claused by the carrier to show that the goods were not in sound condition when received.

Under Deck Tonnage: The capacity of the ship below the tonnage deck calculated in cubic tons.

Under Insurance: Insuring for less than the amount at risk.

Underwriter: One who agrees to compensate another person for loss from an insured peril in consideration of payment of a premium.

Underwriting Agency — LLoyd's: An organisation which is approved by the Council of Lloyd's to represent the interests of underwriting members at Lloyd's. The agency embraces the activities of both a members' agent and a managing agent. The members' agent looks after the financial and other relevant matters on behalf of the names in syndicates; but takes no part in the underwriting side of the business. The managing agent deals with all matters connected with the acceptance of business and appoints an active underwriter to whom is delegated the power to act as the syndicate's underwriting agent in concluding insurance contracts, through the medium of a Lloyd's broker, between the syndicate names and the assured.

Underwriting Agent — Company: One who is appointed by an insurance company to accept business on behalf of his principal; within the terms of the agency contract. An insurance broker's prinicpal is the assured, but an underwriting agent's principal is the insurer. An underwriting agent is not, normally, a salaried employee of the company; his services, customarily being rewarded by commission based on the amount of business he produces for the company.

Unearned Premium: Premium already paid to an underwriter which is in respect of a period when he was not at risk.

Unrepaired Damage: This term relates to damage to an insured ship, that has not been repaired at the time the policy expires. It applies to both time and voyage hull policies, and provides that underwriters are not liable for unrepaired damage if the ship becomes a total loss, from any cause (insured or not) before the expiry of the policy period. If the ship was not a total loss, the assured could normally claim a depreciation allowance for unrepaired damage, caused by an insured peril, on expiry of the policy.

Unseaworthy: The condition of a vessel where from any cause it is unsafe to send her to sea.

Unvalued Policy: A policy that does not express the insured value of the property insured, as distinct from the sum insured by the policy. A claim under an unvalued policy is limited to the insurable value of the subject matter insured at the time of loss, even though the sum insured may be more that the insurable value. Unvalued policies are normally used for policies covering such hull interest as 'excess liabilities' and 'anticipated freight'.

Valued Policy: A policy which specifies the insured value of the ship or goods insured, as the case may be. The value so expressed is conclusive of the insurable value of the ship or goods, as applicable, in the absence of fraud; but is not to be used to establish a constructive total loss, except where the policy so provides (as in hull policies). A policy that does not specify the insured value such as is an 'unvalued' policy.

Vice Propre: Inherent vice.

Victualling Bill: A document showing bonded stores for the vessel's use.

Void Policy: A policy which is not acceptable to a court of law as a valid legal document. Examples expressed in the MIA, 1906, are a gaming and wagering contract, a contract entered into where the assured had no insurable interest and no expectation of acquiring such interest, a policy which states 'interest or not interest', a PPI policy and a policy which contains terms whereby the underwriter waives any benefit of salvage to the insurer, or any similar terms.

Voidable Policy: A policy in respect of which the underwriter is entitled to avoid liability (see **Avoidance**).

Voyage Charter: The shipowner hires out his vessel, subject to various conditions, for the carriage of cargo for a single voyage.

Wagering Policy: A policy in respect of which the assured has no insurable interest.

Waiver Clause: A clause which entitles both underwriter and assured to take measures to prevent or reduce loss, without prejudice to the rights of either party.

Wale: A thick plate, on a ship, designed to withstand heavy impact.

Warehouse: Any building or structure used for the storage of goods.

Warehouseman: The person responsible for the care of goods while they are in store.

Warehousing Entry: A document required by Customs authorities when goods are placed in a bonded warehouse.

Warping: Using ropes or cables to manoeuvre a ship.

Warranty: A warranty in a marine insurance policy is an undertaking by the assured, whereby he promises that a certain thing shall be done or shall not be done, or that some condition will be fulfilled, or whereby he affirms or negatives the existence of a particular state of facts. A warranty may be express or implied, and must be complied with literally. Failure to comply with the warranty is termed 'breach of warranty', which, if not excused, discharges the underwriter from all liability under the policy as from the date of the breach.

Waterborne Agreement: An understanding in the British marine insurance market whereby underwriters will cover goods against war risks only while they are on board an overseas vessel. Limited cover is allowed while goods are in craft en route between ship and shore and, also, during transhipment.

Weather Working Day: A day of 24 hours on which work is not prevented by bad weather.

Wharfinger: The person in charge of a wharf.

Without Benefit of Salvage: A term in a marine insurance policy whereby the underwriter forgoes his subrogation rights. A marine insurance policy that incorporates such term is deemed by the Marine Insurance Act to be a gambling policy, and as such, is invalid in a court of law.

York/Antwerp Rules: A set of internationally accepted rules for application to general average circumstances. Most contracts of affreightment provide for general average to be adjusted in accordance with these rules. In the absence of such agreement adjustment is made in accordance with the law of the place where the adventure is terminated.

Many of the shipping and insurance terms and abbreviations have been contributed by Robert H. Brown, whose publication "Dictionary of Marine Insurance Terms and Clauses" should be consulted for further information.

SHIPPING, INSURANCE AND COMMERCIAL
ABBREVIATIONS

@ .... At (referring to price)
a.a. .... Always afloat, after arrival
A.A.D. .... Annual aggregate deductible
A.B. .... Able-bodied seaman
Abdnt. .... Abandonment
A.B.S. .... American Bureau of Shipping
Abt. .... About
A/C .... Account current
A.C.A.S. .... Advisory, Conciliation and
    Arbitration Service
Acc. .... Acceptance, Accepted
A.C.I.I. .... Associate of Chartered
    Insurance Institute
A. & C.P. .... Anchors and chains proved
Acct .... Account
A.C.V. .... Air cushion vehicle
    (hovercraft)
Ad. val. .... *Ad valorem* — according to
    value
A.F. .... Advanced Freight
a.f.a.a. .... as far as applicable
Agt. .... Agent, Against, Agreement
A.G.W.I. .... Atlantic, Gulf, West Indies
    Limits
a.h. .... After hatch
A.F.H. .... American hull form
    (insurance policy)
A.I.M.U. .... American Institute of
    Marine Underwriters
A.I.R.M.I.C. .... Association of Insurance and
    Risk Managers in Industry
    and Commerce
A.M.L. .... Absolute maximum loss
amt. .... Amount
A.M.V.E.R. .... Automated Mutual-
    Assistance Vessel Rescue
    System
ANF. .... Arrival notification form
A.O.B. .... Any one bottom
A.O.E. .... Any one event
A.O.L. .... Any one loss
a.o.loc. .... Any one location
A.O.O. .... Any one occurrence
A/or .... And/or
A.O.R. .... Any one risk
A.O.V. .... Any one vessel
A.O.Voy. .... Any one voyage
A.P. .... Additional premium
A.P.L. .... As per list
Appd. .... Approved
A.R. .... All risks
Arr. T.L. .... Arranged total loss
A/S .... After sight, Account sales,
    Alongside (chartering)
A.S.E.A.N. .... Association of South East
    Asian Nations
A.T.L. .... Actual total loss
Atl. .... Atlantic
At. wt. .... Atomic Weight
Aux. .... Auxiliary Vessel

Av. .... Average
A/v .... Average, *Ad valorem*
    (according to value)
Av. disbts. .... Average disbursements
B. or B/-. .... Bale, Bag
B & T cl .... Blocking & Trapping clause
Bar. .... Barrel
B.B. .... Bill Book, Below Bridges
B.B.cl. .... Both to blame collision clause
B/D .... Bank Draft, bar draft (grain
    trade)
Bd. .... Bound, bond
B.D.I. .... Both days inclusive
B.D.S. .... Broker's daily statement
Bdls .... Bundles
Bds. .... Boards
B/E .... Bill of Exchange, Bill of Entry
B/G .... Bondage goods
Bg. .... Bag
B/H .... Bill of Health, Bordeaux to
    Hamburg inclusive
Bk. .... Back, Backwardation, Book
B.H.P. .... Brake horse-power
B.I.A. .... British Insurance Association
B.I.I.B.A. .... British Insurance &
    Investment Brokers'
    Association
Bkge. .... Breakage, brokerage
B/L .... Bill of Lading
Bls. .... Bales, Barrels
b.m. .... Board measure (timber)
B/O .... Brought over
B.O. .... Buyer's option, Branch Office
B/P .... Bills payable
B.P.B. .... Bank Post Bill
B.R. .... Builders' Risks Insurance
B/R .... Bills receivable, Bordeaux or
    Rouen (grain trade)
B.R.C. .... Broker Regulatory
    Committee (Lloyds's),
    Brokers Registration
    Council
Brl. .... Barrel
B.S. .... Balance Sheet, Boiler Survey
B/S .... Bill of Sale, Bill of Store
B/s .... Bags, Bales
Bs/L .... Bill of Lading
B/St. .... Bill of Sight
B.S.T. .... British Summer Time
b.t. .... Berth terms
B.T.U. .... Bow Thrust Unit(s)
B.Th.U. .... British Thermal Unit
B.V. .... Bureau Veritas

C. .... Collected, Currency, Coupon,
    Coast
C/- .... Case
C.A.C.T.L.V.O. ... Compromised &/or arranged
    &/or constructive total loss
    of vessel only

C.A.D. .... Cash against documents
Canc. .... Cancelled
C. & D. .... Collected
          and delivered
c.& f. .... Cost and
          freight
C. & I. .... Cost and insurance
C. &/or J. .... China and/or Japan
CARICOM .... Caribbean Community
C.B. & H. .... Continent between Bordeaux
          and Hamburg
C.B.I. .... Confederation of British
          Industry
C.C. .... Civil commotions,
          Cancellation clause
C.C.I.S.G. .... Convention Contracts of
          International Sale
          of Goods
C.C.S.A. .... Collective company signing
          agreement
ccy .... Convertible currency
C.D. .... Country damage
C/D .... Commercial Dock, Consular
          Declaration
C.D.V. .... Current domestic value
c.f. .... Carried forward, Cubic feet
c.f.i. .... Cost, freight and insurance
C.f.o. .... Channel for orders, Calling
          for orders
C.F.R. .... Code of Federal Regulations
          (USA)
C.G.A. .... Cargo's proportion of General
          Average
C.G.S.A. .... Carriage of Goods by Sea Act
C.H. & H. .... Continent between Havre and
          Hamburg
chq. .... Cheque
C.I. .... Consular Invoice
C.I.E. .... Captain's imperfect entry
          (Customs)
c.i.f. .... Cost, insurance and freight
c.i.f.c.i. .... Cost, insurance, freight,
          commision and interest
C.I.I. .... Chartered Insurance Institute
C.K.D. .... Completely knocked down
C/L .... Craft loss
Cld. .... Cleared
Cmpl. .... Completed
C/N .... Credit Note, Consignment
          Note, Cover Note
C/O .... Certificate of Origin
C.O.B. .... Cargo on board
C.O.D. .... Cash on delivery
Com. .... Commission
Comp. T.L. .... Compromised total loss
Conds. .... Conditions
Consgt. .... Consignment
Cont. .... Continent of Europe
Cont. (A.H.) .... Continent, Antwerp-
          Hamburg range
Cont. (B.H.) .... Continent, Bordeaux-
          Hamburg range
Cont. (H.H.) .... Continent, Havre-Hamburg
          range

Conv. .... Conveyance
C/P .... Charter Party, Custom of Port
          (grain trade)
C.P.A. .... Claims payable abroad
Cpa. .... Closest point of approach
C.P.D. .... Charterers pay dues
C.P.P. .... Controllable Pitch Propellers
C.R. .... Current rate, Company's risk,
          Carrier's risk
Cr. .... Credit, Creditor
C.R.O. .... Cancelling returns only
c/s .... Cases
C.S.D. .... Closed shelter deck
C.S.T. .... Central standard time
C.T.L. .... Constructive total loss
Cts. .... Crates
cum. .... With, Cumulative
c.v. .... Chief value
C.W. .... Commercial weight
D. .... Delivery, Delivered
D/A .... Deposit account, Days after
          acceptance, Documents
          against acceptance,
          Discharge afloat,
          Deductable average
D.A.A. .... Documents against
          acceptance
D.B. .... Day Book, Deals and battens
          (timber trade)
D.B.B. .... Deals, battens and boards
Dbk. .... Drawback
D/C .... Deviation clause
D.D. .... Damage done
D/D .... Demand Draft, Delivered at
          Docks, Damage Done
D.D.C. .... Damage done in collision
D.D.E. .... Direct data entry
D/d .... Days after date, Days' date
dd. .... Delivered
dd/s. .... Delivered sound (grain trade)
Ded. .... Deductible
Def.a/c .... Deferred account
Det. .... Detained
D.F. .... Direction finder
d.f. .... Dead freight
Dft. .... Draft
DISH .... Data interchange in Shipping
Disbts. .... Disbursements
Displ. .... Displacement
DK. .... Deck
Dk. .... Dock
d.l.o. .... Dispatch loading only
D/N .... Debit note
D/O .... Delivery order
D/P .... Documents against payment
d.p. .... Direct port
d.p.r. .... Daily pro rata
D/R .... Deposit Receipt
Dr. .... Debit, Debtor, Drawer
D.R.C. .... Damaged received in
          collision
D/s .... Days after sight
D.T.B.A. .... Days to be agreed, date to be
          advised

D.T.I. .... Department of Trade and Industry
D/V .... Dual Valuation
D/W .... Dock Warrant
d.w.t. .... Deadweight tonnage
D.W.A.T. .... Deadweight all told
d.w.c. .... Deadweight capacity
Dy. .... Delivery
E. .... East
e. & e.a. .... Each and every accident
e. & e.l. .... Each and every loss
e. & e.o. .... Each and every occurrence
E.C.A. .... Economic Commission for Africa
E.C.E. .... Economic Commision for Europe
E.C.G.B. .... East Coast of Great Britain
E.C.G.D. .... Export Credit Guarantee Department
E.C.I. .... East Coast of Ireland
E.C.L.A. .... Economic Commission for Latin America
E.C.M.E. .... Economic Commission for the Middle East
E.C.U.K. .... East Coast of United Kingdom
E.C.V. .... Each cargo voyage
E.E. .... Errors excepted
E.C.C. .... European Economic Community
E.F.T.A. .... European Free Trade Association
E.I. .... Each incident
E.L. .... Employer's liability
E.M.L. .... Estimated maximum loss
E.M.P.L. .... Estimated maximum probable loss
E.M.S. .... European Monetary System
e.o.h.p. .... Excepted otherwise herein provided
E.P.I. .... Earned premium income
E.P.I.R.B. .... Emergency position indicator radio beacon
E.R.V. .... Each round voyage
E.S.D. .... Echo-sounding device
est. .... Estimated
EUROTOM .... European Atomic Energy Community
Exd. .... Examined
f.a. .... Free alongside
f.a.c. .... Fast as you can
Fac. .... Facultative
Fac./oblig. .... Facultative/obligatory
F.A.O. .... Food and Agriculture Organisation (U.N.)
F. & A.P. .... Fire and allied perils
f.a.q. .... Fair average quality
f.a.s. .... Free alongside ship, Firsts and seconds (American lumber)
F.C.A.R. .... Free of claim for accident reported
F.C.I.I. .... Fellow of the Chartered Insurance Institute

F.C.L. .... Full container loads
F.C.V. .... Full contract value, Full completed value
f.d. .... Free discharge, Free delivery, Free dispatch, Free docks
F.D.O. .... For declaration purposes only
F. & D. .... Freight and demurrage
f.f.a. .... Free from alongside, Free foreign agency
F.F.O. .... Fixed and floating objects
F.G.A. .... Foreign General Average
f.h. .... Fore hatch
f.i.a. .... Full interest admitted
f.i.b. .... Free into bunkers, Free into barge
F.I.C.S. .... Fellow of the Institute of Chartered Shipbrokers
F.I.L. .... Foreign insurance legislation
FIMBRA .... Financial Intermediaries, Managers and Brokers Regulatory Association
f.i.o. .... Free in and out
f.i.o.s. .... Free in and out stowed
f.i.o.s.t. .... Free in and out stowed and/or trimmed
f.i.o.t. .... Free in and out trimmed
f.i.t. .... Free of income tax
f.i.w. .... Free in wagon
F.L.E. .... Fire, lightning and explosion
f.o. .... For orders, Firm offer, Full out terms (grain trade)
f.o.b. .... Free on board
f.o.c. .... Free on car, Free of charge
F.O.C. .... Flag of convenience, Free of commission, Free of charge, Free of claims
F.O.M. .... Flag, ownership and management
F.O.N.A.S.B.A. ... Federation of National Association of Shipbrokers
f.o.q. .... Free on quay
f.o.r. .... Free on rail
F.O.S.F.A. .... Federation of Oils, Seeds & Fats Associations
f.o.t. .... Free on truck
f.o.w. .... Free on wagon, First open water
F.P. .... Floating Policy, Fully Paid
F.P.A. .... Free of Particular Average
F.P.T. .... Forepeak tank
F/R .... Freight release
F.R.C. .... Free of reported casualty
F.R.O. .... Fire risk only
f.r.o.f. .... Fire risk on Freight
Frt. .... Freight
f.s.l. .... Full signed line (insurance)
F.S.R. & C.C. ...... Free of strikes, riots and civil commotions
F.T.A. .... Freight Transport Association and Agents
f.t. .... Full terms
Fth. .... Fathom
f.t.r.r. & i. .... For their respective rights and interests

F.V.C. .... Fishing vessel clauses
fwd. .... Forward
f.w.d. .... Fresh water damage
f.w.l. .... Full written line (insurance)
F.W.P.C.A. .... Federal Water Pollution Control Act (USA)
F.W.T. & G.D. ..... Fair wear, tear and gradual deterioration
G.A. .... General Average
G/A con. .... General Average contribution
G/A dep. .... General Average deposit
G.A.D.V. .... Gross arrived damaged value
G.A.F.T.A. .... Grain & Feed Trade Assoc.
G.A.S.V. .... Gross arrived sound value
G.A.T.T. .... General Agreement on Tariffs and Trade
G.F. .... Government Form (chartering)
g.f.a. .... Good fair average
G.L. .... Germanischer Lloyd
g.m.b. .... Good merchantable brand
g.m.q. .... Good merchantable quality
G.M.T. .... Greenwich Mean Time
G.N.E.P.I. .... Gross net earned premium income
g.o.b. .... Good ordinary brand
G.O.P. .... Gross original premium
gr. .... Grain, Gross
G.R.T. .... Gross registered tonnage
Gr.t. .... Gross ton
G.S. .... Good safety
g.s.m. .... Good sound merchantable
guar. .... Guaranteed
Gy.C. .... Gyro Compass
H.A. or D. .... Havre, Antwerp or Dunkirk
Hbr. .... Harbour
h/c .... Held covered (insurance)
H.G.V. .... Heavy Goods Vehicle
H/H .... Havre to Hamburg
hk. .... Hook damage
H. & M. .... Hull and machinery
h. & o. .... Hook and oil damage
H.P.N. .... Horse-power nominal
H.S.S.C. .... Heating, sweating and spontaneous combustion
H.T. .... Half-time survey
H.W.D. .... Heavy weather damage
H.W.M. .... High water mark
H.W.O.S.T. .... High water ordinary spring tides
I.A.E.A. .... International Atomic Energy Agency
I.A.T.A. .... International Air Transport Association
I.B. .... Invoice Book, In Bond
I.B.C. .... Institute Builders' Clauses
I.B.N.R. .... Incurred but not reported
I.B.R.D. .... International Bank for Reconstruction and Development
I.C.A.O. .... International Civil Aviation Organisation
I.C.C. .... International Chamber of Commerce, Institute Cargo Clauses
I.C. & C. .... Invoice cost and charges
I.C.E.S. .... International Council for the Exploration of the sea
I.C.F.U. .... International Confederation of Free Trade Unions
I.C.S. .... Institute of Chartered Shipbrokers, International Chamber of Shipping
I.C.S.U. .... International Council of Scientific Unions
I.D.A. .... International Development Association
i.f. .... In full
I.F.C. .... Institute Freight Clauses, International Finance Corporation
I.F.F. .... Institute of Freight Forwarders
I.F.V.C. .... Institute Fishing Vessel Clauses
I.H.P. .... Indicated Horse-power
I.I.L. .... Insurance Institute of London
I.L.A. .... International Longshoremen's Association
I.L.O. .... International Labour Organisation
I.L.U. .... Insitute of London Underwriters
I.M.F. .... International Monetary Fund
I.M.I.F. .... International Maritime Industry Forum
I.M.O. .... International Maritime Organization
I.M.T.A. .... International Meat Trade Association
Inst. Wties .... Insurance warranties
Int. .... Interest
Inter Arr .... Internal arrangements
i/o .... In and/or overdeck
i. and/or o. .... In and/or overdeck
I.P.R.C. .... Institute Port Risks Clauses
I.R. .... Inland Revenue
i.r.o. .... In respect of
I.R.S. .... Indian Register of Shipping
I.S.F. .... International Shipping Federation
I.T.C. .... Institute Time Clauses (Hulls)
I.T.U. .... International Telecommunications Union
i.v. .... Invoice value, Increased value
I.V.C. .... Institute Voyage Clauses (Hulls)
I.Y.C. .... Institute Yacht Clauses
J/A .... Joint Account
J.C.C. .... Joint Cargo Committee
J.C.R.A. .... Joint Common Risks Agreement
Jett. .... Jettison
J.H.C. .... Joint Hull Committee
J.H.I.U. .... Japanese Hull Insurers'

Union

J.H.U.	Joint Hull Understandings
j. & w.o.	Jettison and washing overboard
K.D.	Knocked down
K.D.C.	Knocked down condition
kHz	Kilohertz
L/A	Letter of Authority, Landing Account, Lloyd's Agent
LANBY	Large automatic navigation buoy
L.A.S.H.	Lighter aboard ship
L.A.T.	Linseed Association Terms
L.A.T.F.	Lloyd's American Trust Fund
L.A.U.A.	Lloyd's Aviation Underwriters' Association
L.C.	London clause (chartering), Label clause
L/C	Letter of Credit
L.C.L.	Less than full container load
L.C.T.A.	London Corn Trade Association
L.d.d.	Loss during discharge
L. def.	Latent defect
ldg.	Loading
Ldg. & Dely	Landing and delivery
L.d.l.	Loss during loading
lds.	Loads
Leg. Chgs.	Legal charges
L.H.A.R.	London, Hull, Antwerp or Rotterdam
Liab	Liability
L.I.B.C.	Lloyd's Insurance Brokers' Committee
L.I.M.	London Insurance Market
L.I.M.D.S.M.	London Insurance Market Data Standards Manuel
L.I.M.N.	London Insurance Market Network
L.I.M.T.C.G.	London Insurance Market Technical Co-ordination Group
L.I.P.	Life Insurance Policy
Lkge & Bkge	Leakage and breakage
Ll. & Cos.	Lloyd's and Companies
L.L.T.	London landed terms
L.M.C.	Lloyd's machinery certificate
l.m.c.	Low middling clause (cotton trade)
L.M.C.C.	Lloyd's machinery certificate, continuous survey
L.N.G.	Liquified natural gas carrier
l.n.y.d.	Liability not yet determined
L.P.G.	Liquified petroleum gas carrier
L.P.S.O.	Lloyd's Policy Signing Office
L.R.	Lloyd's Register of Shipping
L.R.M.C.	Lloyd's refrigerating machinery certificate
l.s.	Lump sum
L.S. Cls	Livestock clauses
L.S.H.W. Liab	Longshoremen's and Harbour Workers' Liability

LTGE	Lighterage
L.S.T.	Local standard time
L.T.A.	Long term agreement
Ltr.	Lighter
Lt.-V.	Light-vessel
L/U	Leading Underwriter
l/u	Laid up, Letter of undertaking
L.U.A.	Lloyd's Underwriters' Association
L.U.A.A.	Lloyd's Underwriting Agents Association
L.U.A.M.C.	Leading underwriter agreement for marine cargo
L.U.A.M.H.	Leading underwriter agreement for marine hull
L.U.C.R.O.	Lloyd's Underwriters' Claims and Recoveries Office
L.W.	Low water
L.W.O.S.T.	Low water, ordinary spring tides
Machy	Machinery
Mal.d.	Malicious damage
MAR form	The standard form of marine insurance policy used in the London market by both Lloyd's and companies.
M.A.V.I.S.	Marine Audio-Visual Instruction Sytems
M. & D.P.	Minimum and deposit premium
M. & W.	Marine and war risks
M.B.D.	Machinery breakdown
M.C.	Machinery certificate
M/C	Metalling clause (marine insurance), Machinery certificate
M/D	Memorandum of deposit
M/d	Malicious damage
Mdse.	Merchandise
M.F.C.	Maximum foreseeable loss
M.H.	Main Hatch
M.H.W.S.	Mean High Water Springs
MHz	Megahertz
MIA	Marine Insurance Act
Min. B/L	Minimum Bill of Lading
MIN./DEP.	Minimum and deposit premium
M.I.P.	Marine Insurance Policy
M.L.W.S.	Mean Low Water Springs
M.M.	Mercantile Marine
m.m.	Made merchantable
M.M.A.	Merchandise Marks Act
M.N.S.C.	Managed Network Steering Committee
M.O.H.	Medical Officer of Health
Mort.	Mortality
m. pack	Missing package
M.P.L.	Maximum probable loss
M.R.	Mate's receipt
M.S.	Motor ship, Machinery survey
M/s	Months after sight
mst.	Measurement

M.T.	....	Mean Time
mt.	....	Empty
M.T.L.	....	Mean tidal level
N/a	....	No advice, No account, Not applicable
n.a.	....	Net absolutely
n.a.a.	....	Not always afloat
N.A.T.O.	....	North Atlantic Treaty Organisation
N/C	....	New charter, New crop
N.C.A.R.	....	No claim for accident reported
N.C.V.	....	No commercial value
n.d.w.	....	Net dead weight
N.E.	....	No effects
n.e.	....	Not exceeding
N.E.D.C.	....	National Economic Development Council
n.e.p.	....	Not elsewhere provided
n.e.s.	....	Not elsewhere specified
N/f.	....	No funds
N.H.P.	....	Nominal horse-power
N.K.K.	....	Nippon Kaiji Kyokai
N.K.O.R.L.	....	Not known or reported loss
N/m	....	No mark
N.M.A.	....	(Lloyd's) Underwriters Non-Marine Association
N/N	....	Not north of
N/o	....	No orders (banking)
N.O.C.	....	Notice of cancellation
nom. std.	....	Nominal standard
non.d.	....	Non delivery
n.o.p.	....	Not otherwise provided
n.p.	....	Net proceeds
n.r.	....	No risk, net register
n.r.a.d.	....	No risk after discharge
n/s	....	Not sufficient
n.s.p.f.	....	Not specifically provided for
N.V.	....	Norske Veritas
N.V.O.C.C.	....	Non vessel operating common carrier
o/a	....	On account of
o.a.	....	Over all
O.A.L.	....	Overall length
o/b	....	On or before
O/b	....	On board
O.B.O.	....	Oil/bulk/ore carrier
O/C	....	Open charter, Old charter, Old crop
o/c	....	Overcharge, open cover
Oc.B/L	....	Ocean bill of lading
Occ.	....	Occurrence
O.C.I.M.F.	....	Oil Companies International Marine Forum
O/D	....	Overdeck
o/d	....	On demand
O.E.C.D.	....	Organisation for Economic Co-operation and Development
O.G.P.I.	....	Original gross premium income (reinsurance)
O.N.P.I.	....	Original net premium income (reinsurance)
O.N.R.	....	Original net rate
O/o	....	Order of
O.P.	....	Open Policy
O.P.E.C.	....	Organisation of Petroleum Exporting Countries
O/R	....	Overriding commission
O.R.	....	Owner's risk, Original rate
O/S	....	On sample, Out of stock, On sale or return
O.S.D.	....	Open shelter deck
O/t	....	On truck
P	....	Package
P/A	....	Particular Average, Power of Attorney, Private Account
Pac.	....	Pacific coast ports
P.A.N.	....	Premium advice note
P. & I.	....	Protection and Indemnity
P. & L.	....	Profit and Loss
P.B.	....	Permanent Bunkers
P/C	....	Price Current, Petty Cash, Per cent, Particular charges, profit commission
P.D.	....	Port dues
P.D.O.	....	Property damage only
Pd.	....	Passed
Pers. Acc.	....	Personal Accident
Pfo.	....	Portfolio
P.I.	....	Personal injury
P.I.A.	....	Peril insured against
P.I.L.	....	Premium income limit
Pilf.	....	Pilferage
P.L.	....	Public liability
P/L	....	Partial loss
P.L.A.	....	Port of London Authority
pm	....	Premium
P.M.L.	....	Probable maximum loss
P/N	....	Promissory note
p.o.c.	....	Port of call
P.O.D.	....	Pay on delivery, Port of distress
p.p.	....	Picked ports, Per procurationem (on behalf of)
ppd.	....	Prepaid
p.p.i.	....	Policy proof of interest
ppt	....	Prompt loading
P.R.	....	Polski Rejestr. Port Risks, Pro rata
Prem. Red.	....	Premiums reducing
Prem. Res.	....	Premium reserve (reinsurance)
Pres.	....	Preserved
Prev.	....	Previous
Prof. Com.	....	Profit commission (reinsurance)
P/S	....	Public sale
P.S.A.C.	....	Policy Signing & Accounting Centre
P.S.T.	....	Pacific Standard Time
P.T.	....	Premium transfer
p.t.	....	Private terms
Ptg.Std.	....	Petrograd Standard (timber trade)
Qlty	....	Quality
qn	....	Quotation

Q.S. .... Quota share
R/A .... Refer to acceptor
R.A.T. .... Rapeseed Association Terms
R.& C.C. .... Riots and civil commotions
R.C.C. & S. .... Riots, civil commotions and strikes
R/D .... Refer to drawer
Rds. .... Roads
r.d. .... Running days
R.D.C. .... Running down clause
Ref. .... Refrigerating machinery
Reinst. .... Reinstatement
res. .... Residue, reserve
R.I. .... Registro Italiano
R.I.N.A. .... Registro Italiano Navale
R.N.L.I. .... Royal National Life-boat Institution
R.O.A. .... Reinsurance Offices Association
r.o.b. .... Remaining on board
R.O.D. .... Rust, oxidation and discolouration
Ro-ro .... Roll-on/Roll-off
Rotn. no. .... Rotation number
R/p .... Return of post for orders
R.P. .... Return premium
r.r.& i. .... Respective rights and interests
R.S. .... Revised Statutes (U.S.A.)
R.S. & C.C. .... Riots, Strikes and Civil Commotions
R.T. .... Rye terms
R.T.A. .... Rubber Trade Association
S.A. .... Salvage Association
S/A .... Subject to Acceptance (insurance)
s/a .... Subject to approval, Safe arrival
S. & A. .... Signing and accounting (procedure)
S. & F.A. .... Shippng and Forwarding Agent
S. & L. .... Sue & Labour (charges)
S.D.A. .... Single administrative document
s.a.n.r. .... Subject to approval no risk
S.B. .... Short Bill
S.B.M. .... Single buoy mooring
s.b.s. .... survey before shipment
s.c. .... Salvage charges
S.C.A. .... Settlement of claims abroad
Sch. .... Schooner
S.C.O.R. .... Scientific Commission on Oceanic Research
S.D.H.F. .... Standard Dutch Hull Form
S.d. .... Short delivery
Sd. .... Sailed
SDR .... Special drawing rights (limitation of liability)
S.E.P. .... Subject to endorsement on the policy
Sep. .... Separation procedure (signing and accounting)
S/Fee .... Survey Fee

SHinc. .... Sundays and Holidays included
SHex. .... Sundays and Holidays excepted
S.H.P. .... Shaft horse-power
S.I. .... Short Interest, Sum Insured International System of Units (Systeme International)
S.I.T.P.R.O. .... Simplification of Industrial Trade Procedures Board
S/I .... Sum insured
S.K.D. .... Semi knocked down
Sk. .... Sack
S.L. .... Salvage loss
S/L .... Sue and labour
s.l. .... Salvage loss
S/L.C. .... Sue and labour clause
S/L.Ch. .... Sue and labour charges
Sld. .... Sailed
S/N .... Shipping Note
S.O. .... Seller's option
S.O.L. .... Ship owner's liability
S.O.S. .... Service of suit
S.P. .... Supra Protest
s.p.d. .... Steamer pays dues
S.R. & C.C. .... Strikes, riots and civil commotions
S.R.L. .... Ship repairers' liability
S.S.C. .... Simultaneous settlements clause
S.S.N. .... Standard shipping notice
Std. .... Standard (timber trade)
Stev. Liab. .... Stevedores' liability
stg .... Sterling
stk .... Stock
Str. .... Steamer
Strd. .... Standard
S. to S. .... Station to station
S.W. .... Shipper's weights
S.W.D. .... Seawater damage
S.W.G. .... Standard wire gauge
Syn. .... Syndicate (Lloyd's)
T.B. .... Trial Balance
T.B.A. .... To be advised, To be agreed
T/C .... Till countermanded
T. & C.C. .... Technical and Clauses Committee
T. & G. .... Tongued and grooved (timber trade)
T.C.I. .... Time charterer's interest
Tcpa. .... Target closest point of approach
T.D.W. .... Tonnage deadweight
T.E. .... Trade expenses
T.E.E. .... Trans-Europe Express
T.F. .... Tropical freshwater
T.G.B. .... Tongued, grooved and beaded
T.I.B. .... Trimmed in bunkers
T.I.V. .... Total insured value
T.L. .... Total loss
T.L.O. .... Total loss only
T.L.V.O. .... Total loss of vessel only

T/O	Transfer order
T.O.C.	Terms of Credit (Lloyd's)
T.O.R.	Time on Risk
T.O.V.A.L.O.P. ...	Tanker Owners' Voluntary Agreement Concerning Liability for Oil Polution
T.P.I.	Tons per inch
T.P. Liab.	Third party liability
T.P.N.D.	Theft, pilferage and non-delivery
T.Q.	*Tale Quale* (as found)
Tr.	Trustee
Trlr.	Trawler
T/S	Transhipment
t. & s.	Touch and stay
T.S.I.	Total sum insured
T.T.	Telegraphic transfer
T.T.F.	Timber Trade Federation
TTY.	Treaty (reinsurance)
T.W.M.C.	Transport, wages, maintenance and care
U/A	Underwriting account
U/C	Under construction
u.c.b.	Unless caused by
U/D	Underdeck
U.K./Cont.	United Kingdom and Continent
U.K./Cont. (B.H) .	Bordeaux-Hamburg range
U.K./Cont. (H.H) .	Havre-Hamburg range
U.K./Cont. (G.H) .	Gibraltar-Hamburg range
U.K.f.o.	United Kingdom for orders
U.K.H.A.D.	United Kingdom, Havre, Antwerp or Dunkirk
U.L.C.C.	Ultra large crude carrier
U.N.	United Nations
U.N.C.L.O.S.	U.N. Conference on the Law of the Sea
U.N.C.T.A.D.	U.N. Conference on Trade and Development
U.N.D.P.	U.N. Development Programme
U.N.D.R.O.	U.N. Disaster Relief Co-ordinator
U.N.E.P.	U.N. Environment Programme
U.N.E.S.C.O.	U.N. Educational, Scientific and Cultural Organisation
U.N.L.	Ultimate net loss
u/o	Use and occupancy
u.p.	Under proof
U/R	Under repair
U.S.N.H.	United States North of Hatteras (Cape)
U.S.S.A.	United States Salvage Association

U.T.	Unlimited transhipment
uw.	Underwriter
V.C.	Valuation clause
Vd.	Valued
V.L.C.C.	Very large crude carrier
v.o.p.	Value as in original policy
V.T.S.	Vessel Traffic Systems
W.B.	Water ballast, Warehouse Book, Way Bill
W.B./E.I.	West Britain/East Ireland
w.b.s.	Without benefit of salvage
W.C.	West Coast
W.C.L.	World Confederation of Labour
W.C.S.A.	West Coast of South America
W/d.	Warranted
W.D.F.	Wireless direction finder
Wdg.	Wording
W.E.C.M.	Warranted existing class maintained
W.E.U.	Western European Union
W.F.T.U.	World Federation of Trade Unions
Wf.	Wharf
w.g.	Weight guaranteed
W.H.O.	World Health Organisation
W/M	Weight and/or Measurement
W.M.O.	World Meteorological Organisation
W.N.A.	Winter North Atlantic
w.o.b.	Washed overboard
W.O.L.	Wharfowners' liability
w.p.	Without prejudice, Weather permitting
w.p.p.	Waterproof paper packing
W.R.	Warehouse receipts
w.r.o.	War risk only
W.R.T.D.	Without reference to date
wt.	Weight
Wtd.	Warranted
Wties	Warranties
W.T.B.A.	Wording to be agreed
Wty	Warranty
W/W	Warehouse warrant
W.W.D.	Weather working days
x.c.	Ex coupon
x.d.	Ex dividend
x.in	Ex interest
x.new	Ex new
XS Loss	Excess loss reinsurance
XS pt.	Excess point
Y.A.R.	York-Antwerp Rules (General Average)
Yt	Yacht

Prepared with the assistance of R. H. Brown, author of
"Dictionary of Marine Insurance Terms and Clauses"

SEA DISTANCE TABLES
Distances in nautical miles.

From ANTWERP to

Aberdeen	458
Archangel	2,064
Bergen	608
Bishop Rock	452
Buenos Aires	6,336
Dover	135
Dundee	454
Glasgow	806
Grimsby	254
Hull	265
Leith	418
Sunderland	347
Tyne	335
Ushant	441
Ymuiden	132

From AUCKLAND to

Adelaide	2,035
Brisbane	1,358
Fremantle	3,202
Hobart	1,517
Honolulu	3,820
Los Angeles	5,659
Singapore	4,990
Sydney	1,274
Thursday Island	2,560
Valparaiso	5,247
Wellington	543

From BOMBAY to

Aden	1,640
Calcutta	2,120
Cape Town	4,600
Colombo	889
Copenhagen	6,732
Guayaquil	10,160
Karachi	465
Kuwait	1,537
London	6,260
Madras	1,450
Mauritius	2,518
Mina Qaboos	880
Rangoon	2,130
Singapore	2,460

From BUENOS AIRES to

Adelaide (via Cape Horn)	7,775
Antwerp	6,335
Bahia Blanca	509
Brisbane (via Cape Horn)	7,482
Cape Town	3,780
Cardiff	6,123
Copenhagen	6,761
Corunna	5,595
Fremantle	8,660
Glasgow	6,317
Guayaquil (via Magellan Strait)	4,443
Lisbon	5,300
Liverpool	6,258
Madeira	4,818

Melbourne (via Cape Horn)	7,384
Montevideo	115
New York	5,838
Recife	2,170
Rio de Janeiro	1,140
Santos	998
Southampton	6,125
Sydney (via Cape Horn)	7,269
Tyne	6,495
Vigo	5,545

From CALCUTTA to

Bombay	2,120
Cape Town	5,489
Colombo	1,230
Copenhagen	8,358
Guayaquil	12,015
Karachi	2,564
London	7,920
Madras	750
Mauritius	3,217
Singapore	1,630

From CALLAO to

Antofagasta	725
Coquimbo	1,100
Honolulu	5,130
London	6,135
Mazatlan	2,730
San Francisco	3,985
Tahiti	4,200
Valparaiso	1,290

From CAPE TOWN to

Adelaide	6,107
Aden	4,100
Ascension	2,380
Bermuda	6,180
Bombay	4,600
Brisbane	7,402
Buenos Aires	3,780
Calcutta	5,580
Colombo	4,350
Copenhagen	6,585
Dakar	3,590
Durban	798
Freetown	3,120
Fremantle	4,951
Karachi	4,665
Las Palmas	4,425
London	6,110
Madeira	4,675
Madras	4,960
Mauritius	2,280
Melbourne	6,445
Montevideo	3,660
New York	6,800
Rio de Janeiro	3,265
Singapore	5,630
Southampton	5,945
Sydney	6,904

From COLOMBO to

Adelaide	4,364
Aden	2,091
Brisbane	5,293
Calcutta	1,230
Cape Town	4,362
Copenhagen	7,168
Fremantle	3,126
Jakarta	1,830
Karachi	1,341
Kuwait	2,299
Madras	580
Mauritius	2099
Melbourne	4,675
Penang	1,284
Rangoon	1,257
Singapore	1,575
Suez	3394
Sydney	5,161

From COPENHAGEN to

Aden	5,077
Bombay	6,732
Buenos Aires	6,761
Calcutta	8,358
Cape Town	6,585
Colombo	7,168
Durban	7,355
Guayaquil	6,085
Liverpool	1,035
Melbourne	11,520
New York	3,550
Rangoon	8,370
Singapore	8,710

From DAKAR to

Cape Town	3,590
Cardiff	2,360
Freetown	501
Gibraltar	1,495
Liverpool	2,475
Madeira	1,082
Tenerife	840

From DOVER to

Amsterdam	165
Antwerp	135
Bishop Rock	314
Bordeaux	611
Calais	22
Dunkirk	38
Gibraltar	1,230
Hamburg	381
Le Havre	115
Liverpool	597
Plymouth	225
Rotterdam	137
Southampton	119
Ushant	310
Vigo	736

From DURBAN to

Aden	3,350
Beira	702
Cape Town	798
Fremantle	4,240
Karachi	3,885
Maputo	298
Mauritius	1,553
Port Elizabeth	384
Toamasina	1,360
Zanzibar	1,595

From FREETOWN to

Ascension	1,000
Cape Town	3,120
Dakar	470
Las Palmas	1,317
Bioko	1,500
Plymouth	2,700
St. Vincent, C.V.	850

From GIBRALTAR to

Azores	980
Barbados	3,250
Bermuda	2,930
Bombay	4,953
Brindisi	1,280
Dakar	1,500
Dover	1,230
Finisterre (Cape)	542
Genoa	860
Glasgow	1,373
Halifax, N.S.	2,675
Istanbul	1,820
Las Palmas	705
Liverpool	1,275
London	1,313
Madeira	610
Malta	990
Marseilles	690
Naples	975
New Orleans	4,550
New York	3,210
Plymouth	1,050
Port Said	1,905
St. Vincent, C.V.	1,560
Southampton	1,142
Tenerife	720
Ushant	920

From GLASGOW to

Adelaide	10,798
Antwerp	780
Archangel	2,035
Belfast	115
Brisbane (via Torres Strait)	12,022
Bristol	411
Buenos Aires	6,347
Cape Wrath	337
Cork	340
Colon	4,625
Dublin	198
Fremantle	9,600
Gibraltar	1,373
Hobart	11,261
Liverpool	212
Lizard	420
London	745
Londonderry	151
Melbourne	11,136
Nantes	669
Oslo	895
Takoradi	3,863
Southampton	570
Stranraer	87
Sydney	11,595
Tenerife	1,753
Ushant	1,005

From GUAYAQUIL to

Adelaide	8,130
Amsterdam	5,695
Bergen	6,122
Bombay	10,160
Bremen	5,908
Brisbane	7,346
Buenos Aires (via Magellan Strait)	4,443
Calcutta	12,015
Copenhagen	6,085
Fremantle (via Torres Strait)	8,922
Genoa	6,067
Hamburg	5,926
Le Havre	5,480
Liverpool	5,511
London	5,596
Melbourne	7,410
Montreal	4,020
New Orleans	2,258
New York	2,849
Rotterdam	5,670
Shanghai	8,882
Singapore	10,740
Wellington	6,020
Yokohama	7,996

From HALIFAX, N.S. to

Bermuda	750
Gibraltar	2,670
Havana	1,635
London	2,719
New York	590
Quebec	750
St. John's, N.F.	540

From HAMBURG to

Bahrain	6,682
Bombay	6,620
Buenos Aires	6,665
Gibraltar	1,607
Lagos	4,575
New Orleans	5,145
New York	3,535
Singapore	8,615
Suez	3,641
Sydney	11,865
Tokyo	11,588
Vancouver	9,182

From HAVANA to

Bermuda	1,145
Charleston	600
Halifax, N.S.	1,635
Hampton Roads	975
Key West	92
London	4,259
Montreal	2,528
New Orleans	585
Veracruz	860

From HONG KONG to

Adelaide	4,789
Brisbane (via Torres Strait)	4,046
Fremantle	3,505
Honolulu	4,860
Los Angeles	6,363
Manila	640
Melbourne (via Torres Strait)	5,014
Shanghai	850
Singapore	1,440
Sydney (via Torres Strait)	4,449
Vladivostok	1,640
Yokohama	1,585

From HONOLULU to

Auckland	3,815
Callao	5,130
Fiji Islands (Suva)	2,783
Hong Kong	4,860
San Francisco	2,090
Seattle	2,405
Sydney	4,420
Tahiti	2,360
Valparaiso	5,911
Vancouver	2,419
Yokohama	3,385

From ISTANBUL to

Batum	586
Constantza	194
Dardanelles	132
Gibraltar	1,810
Malta	850
Novorossisk	446
Odessa	344
Port Said	795

From JAKARTA to

Adelaide	3,047
Aden	3,885
Brisbane (via Torres Strait)	3,465
Colombo	1,842
Fremantle	1,761
Hobart	3,510
Melbourne	3,385
Padang	600
Shanghai	2,522
Sydney (via Torres Strait)	3,869
Thursday Island	2,165
Yokohama	3,220

From KARACHI to

Aden	1,470
Bombay	465
Calcutta	2,564
Cape Town	4,665
Colombo	1,341
Durban	3,885
Fremantle	4,438
Kuwait	1,107
Madras	1,910
Mombasa	2,359
Suez	2,772

From KINGSTON, Jamaica, to

Buenos Aires	5,224
Marseilles	4,655
Miami	747
New Orleans	1,155
New York	1,455
Rotterdam	4,320
Sydney	8,268
Tokyo	8,878

From KUWAIT to

Aden	1,939
Bombay	1,554
Cape Town	5,891
Colombo	2,500
Copenhagen	7,027
Guayaquil	10,460
Karachi	1,157
Mombasa	2,850
Rotterdam	6,675
Suez	3,219

From LAS PALMAS to

Cape Town	4,425
Freetown	1,320
Gibraltar	705
Lisbon	712
Liverpool	1,650
Plymouth	1,432
Recife	2,445
St. Vincent. C.V.	866
Tenerife	40
Ushant	1,306

From LISBON to

Buenos Aires	5,300
Finisterre (Cape)	264
Las Palmas	712
Liverpool	995
Madeira	530
Plymouth	770
Southampton	865
Ushant	655

From LIVERPOOL to

Adelaide	10,677
Bilbao	700
Bordeaux	670
Brisbane (via Torres Strait)	11,901
Buenos Aires	6,258
Copenhagen	1,035
Dakar	2,475
Fremantle	9,479
Gibraltar	1,275
Glasgow	212
Guayaquil	5,511
Las Palmas	1,650
Lisbon	995
Melbourne	11,015
New Orleans	4,530
New York	3,052
Oslo	958
Port Said	3,175
Santander	685
Sydney	11,474

From LONDON to

Adelaide	10,712
Antwerp	180
Bahrain	6,371
Bishop Rock	405
Bombay	6,260
Brisbane (via Torres Strait)	11,936
Copenhagen (via Kiel Canal)	587
Dover	90
Fremantle	9,514
Gothenburg	581
Guayaquil	5,596
Hamburg	427
Hobart	11,175
Leith	404
Leningrad (via Kiel Canal)	1,212
Melbourne	11,090
New York	3,270
Rotterdam	177
Sydney	11,509

From LOS ANGELES to

Fremantle	8,565
Manila	6,533
New York	4,928
Rotterdam	7,810
Singapore	7,669
Sydney	6,510
Tokyo	4,854

From MADRAS to

Aden	2,710
Bombay	1,450
Calcutta	750
Cape Town	4,960
Colombo	580
Karachi	1,910
Rangoon	980
Singapore	1,590

From MARSEILLES to

Adelaide	9,011
Brisbane (via Torres Strait)	10,235
Fremantle	7,813
Gibraltar	690
Hobart	9,474
London	2,005
Melbourne	9,439
Naples	455
Port Said	1,510
Southampton	1,833
Sydney	9,808

From MAURITIUS to

Aden	2,340
Bombay	2,540
Calcutta	3,240
Cape Town	2,280
Colombo	2,090
Durban	1,553
Melbourne	4,595
Rangoon	3,208

From MELBOURNE to

Adelaide	495
Aden	6,450
Colombo	4,675
Guayaquil	7,410
London	11,090
Mauritius	4,595
Shanghai	5,235
Sydney	575
Wellington	1,480

From MONTREAL to

Buenos Aires	6,474
Gibraltar	3,185
Lagos	5,217
New York	1,516
New Orleans	3,069
Rotterdam	3,205
Singapore	10,214
Suez	5,276
Sydney	10,971
Tokyo	10,997

From NEW ORLEANS to

Galveston	385
Gibraltar	4,550
Guayaquil	2,258
Hampton Roads	1,455
Havana	585
Kingston, Jamaica	1,115
Liverpool	4,530
London	4,782
New York	1,698
Plymouth	4,450
Veracruz	798

From NEW YORK to

Adelaide (via Panama)	10,323
Bermuda	695
Bishop Rock	2,903
Brisbane (via Panama)	9,727
Buenos Aires	5,838
Cape Town	6,800
Copenhagen	3,550
Fremantle	11,829
(via Panama and E. Aust.)	
Gibraltar	3,210
Guayaquil	2,849
Halifax, N.S.	590
Hobart (via Panama)	9,647
Kingston, Jamaica	1,455
Liverpool	3,073
London	3,270
Melbourne (via Panama)	9,932
Montevideo	5,722
New Orleans	1,698
Rio de Janeiro	4,750
Southampton	3,090
Sydney (via Panama)	9,689

From PANAMA CANAL to

Auckland	6,515
Callao	1,340
Gibraltar	4,329
Guayaquil	837
Hamburg	5,054
Havana	1,003
Hong Kong	9,196
Honolulu	4,688
Kingston, Jamaica	555
London	4,760
Los Angeles	2,912
Marseilles	5,019
Melbourne	7,916
Montreal	3,190
New Orleans	1,403
New York	1,972
Port Said	6,238
Rotterdam	4,801
San Francisco	3,245
Singapore	10,495
Sydney	7,673
Valparaiso	2,615
Vancouver	4,021
Yokohama	7,687

From PORT SAID to

Adelaide	7,500
Brisbane	8,811
Fremantle	6,301
Gibraltar	1,905
Hobart	7,962
Istanbul	795
Liverpool	3,175
London	3,213
Malta	935
Marseilles	1,510
Melbourne	7,837
Suez	87
Sydney	8,296

From RANGOON to

Bassein	248
Bombay	2,130
Calcutta	735
Colombo	1,257
Madras	980
Moulmein	149
Mauritius	3,208
Singapore	1,080

From RIO DE JANEIRO to

Adelaide (via Cape Horn)	8,579
Ascension	1,900
Brisbane (via Cape Horn)	8,286
Buenos Aires	1,140
Cape Horn	2,350
Cape Town	3,265
Fernando Noronha	1,384
Fremantle	8,177
Hobart (via Cape Horn)	7,899
London	5,205
Melbourne (via Cape Horn) ...	8,188
Montevideo	1,025
New York	4,750
Plymouth	4,900
Recife	1,080
St. Helena	2,110
St. Vincent, C.V.	2,688
Salvador	710
Southampton	5,035
Stanley (Falkland Is.)	1,860
Sydney (via Cape Horn)	8,073

From ROTTERDAM to

Aden	4,660
Buenos Aires	6,345
Cape Town	6,170
Colombo	6,752
Copenhgaen	485
Fremantle	9,590
Genoa	2,215
Guayaquil	5,670
Hamburg	325
Hong Kong	9,745
Lagos	4,192
Lisbon	1,085
London	177
Mombasa	6,260
New Orleans	4,814
New York	3,320
Piraeus	2,825
Port Said	3,265
San Francisco	8,110
Singapore	8,310
Sydney	11,595
Yokohama	11,200

From SAN FRANCISCO to

Acapulco	1,880
Adelaide	7,357
Auckland	6,680
Brisbane	6,193
Callao	3,990
Coquimbo	5,030
Fiji Islands (Suva)	4,760
Fremantle	8,524
Hobart	6,923
Honolulu	2,098
Magellan Strait	6,300
Mazatlan	1,350
Melbourne	6,966
Seattle	800
Sydney	6,456
Valparaiso	5,135
Vancouver	812
Yokohama	4,535

From SHANGHAI to

Guayaquil	8,882
Jakarta	2,522
Kobe	771
Manila	1,130
Melbourne	5,235
Singapore	2,183
Sydney	4,675
Yokohama	1,045

From SINGAPORE to

Adelaide	3,504
Aden	3,640
Bombay	2,460
Brisbane (via Torres Strait) ...	3,821
Calcutta	1,630
Cape Town	5,630
Colombo	1,575
Fremantle	2,220
Guayaquil	10,740
Hobart	3,967
Hong Kong	1,440
Jakarta	527
London	8,257
Los Angeles	7,669
Madras	1,590
Melbourne	3,842
Rangoon	1,080
Shanghai	2,183
Sydney	4,306
Vancouver	7,078
Yokohama	2,888

From SOUTHAMPTON to

Bermuda	2,956
Bishop Rock	219
Buenos Aires	6,125
Canary Islands	1,588
Cape Horn	7,258
Cape Town	5,945
Cherbourg	84
Dover	119
Finisterre (Cape)	596
Gibraltar	1,142
Le Havre	105
Lisbon	865
Madeira	1,325
Marseilles	1,833
New York	3,090
St. Malo	149
Singapore	8,078
Ushant	215

From SYDNEY to

Antwerp	11,569
Auckland	1,260
Brisbane	474
Cape Horn	5,750
Cape Town	6,287
Fiji Islands (Suva)	1,735
Glasgow	11,595
Hong Kong	4,470
Honolulu	4,415
Liverpool	11,474
London	11,558
Marseilles	9,808
Melbourne	575
Shanghai	4,675
Singapore	4,306
Southampton	11,368
Valparaiso	6,257
Wellington	1,233
Yokohama	4,379

From TAHITI to

Callao	4,200
Honolulu	2,260
Balboa	4,486
Sydney	3,060
Wellington	2,340

From VALPARAISO to

Adelaide	6,780
Antofagasta	576
Arica	879
Auckland	5,247
Brisbane	6,487
Callao	1,290
Coquimbo	190
Fremantle	7,827
Hobart	6,100
Honolulu	5,911
Iquique	769
London	7,419
Los Angeles	4,806
Magellan Strait	1,270
Mazatlan	4,100
Melbourne	6,389
Mollendo	960
San Francisco	5,135
Southampton	7,218
Sydney	6,257
Tahiti	4,210

From VANCOUVER to

Hamburg	9,182
Manila	5,976
New Orleans	5,468
New York	6,037
Sydney	6,820
Tokyo	4,280
Valparaiso	5,915

From YOKOHAMA to

Adelaide	5,353
Brisbane	3,980
Guangzhou	1,668
Cebu	1,762
Fremantle	4,460
Guayaquil	7,996
Hobart	5,014
Hong Kong	1,585
Honolulu	3,385
Inchon	1,033
Jakarta	3,220
Kaohsiung	1,337
Mazatlan	5,782
Melbourne	4,961
San Francisco	4,535
Seattle	4,244
Shanghai	1,045
Singapore	2,888
Suva	3,942
Sydney	4,379
Vancouver	4,260
Victoria, B.C.	4,194

PRINCIPAL CONFERENCES AND EXHIBITIONS
1990

Date	Event	Venue	Organiser
January			
February			
6-9	ONLINE '90	**Hamburg**	ONLINE GmbH Kongresse unde Messen fur Technische Kommunication,
	Technical Communications Exhibition & Conference		D-5620 Velbert 1, Postfach 10 08 66, Nevigeser Strasse 131, German Federal Republic. Tel 0205/23072. Fax 0205/21993. Tx 8597500 ONL D.
March			
6-9	Oceanology International 90	**Brighton**	Spearhead Exhibitions Ltd, Rowe House, Fife Road, Kingston-upon-Thames, Surrey KT1 1TA, England. Tel (01) 549 5831. Fax (01) 541 5657. Tx 928042 SPEARS G.
27-29	OAR 90. Offshore Abandonment & Removal 90	**Aberdeen**	Offshore Conferences & Exhibitions. (Address as for Spearhead Exhibitions — see above).
April			
3-6	PORTS TRANSPORT & EQUIPMENT 90	**Rotterdam**	AHOY', Zuiderparkweg 20-30, Postbus 5106, 3008 AC Rotterdam, Netherlands. Tel (010) 4104203. Tx 28977 AHOY' NL.
May			
15-17	RO-RO '90	Stazione Marittime **Trieste**	BML BUSINESS MEETINGS LTD 2 Station Road, Rickmansworth, Hertfordshire WD3 1QP, England. Tel (0923) 776363. Fax (0923) 777296. Tx 924312 GASTEC G.

Date	Event	Venue	Organiser
June 4-9	POSIDONIA	**Piraeus**	POSIDONIA EXHIBITIONS, P.O. Box 80, 162 St Nicholas House, 4-6 Efplias Street, 185 37 Piraeus, Greece. Tel (01) 451 7839, (01) 451 7868. Tx 241937 EXPO GR. Fax (01) 452 8976.
July			
August 6-11	NOR-FISHING '90 13th International Fisheries Fair	**Trondheim**	NORGES VAREMESSE, Sjølystentret, PO Box 130, Skøyen, N-0212 Oslo 2, Norway. Tel (02) 43 80 80. Fax (02) 43 19 14. Tx 78748 MESSE N.
September 19-23	ICELANDIC FISHERIES EXHIBITION	**Reykjavik**	INDUSTRIAL AND TRADE FAIRS INTERNATIONAL LTD, Oriel House, 26 The Quadrant, Richmond Surrey TW9 1DL, England. Tel (01) 940 6065. Fax: (01) 940 2171. Tx 8951389 ITFLON.
24-28	11TH INTERNATIONAL TUG CONVENTION	**Halifax, N.S.**	THOMAS REED PUBLICATIONS, 80 Combe Road, New Maldon, Surrey KT3 4QS. Tel: (01) 949 7033. Fax: (01) 949 0530. Tx: 883526.
25-29	SMM '90	**Hamburg**	HAMBURG MESSE UND CONGRESS GmbH Jungiusstrasse 13, Messehaus, Postfach 30 24 80, D-2000 Hamburg 36, German Federal Republic. Tel (040) 35 69-0. Tx Messe 212609, Congress Centrum 2162936. Fax 35 69 2180.
October 18-19	EMTEC Trade Days European Marine Trade Exhibition	**Hamburg**	HAMBURG MESSE UND CONGRESS GmbH (Address as for SMM '90 25-29 Sept)

Date	Event	Venue	Organiser
November			
6-9	IRM 90. Offshore Inspection, Repair & Maintenance Exhibition & Conference	**Aberdeen**	OFFSHORE CONFERENCES & EXHIBITIONS. (address as for Spearhead Exhibitions March 6-9).
14-16	MARINE EQUIPMENT TRADE SHOW (METS)	Rai Halls **Amsterdam**	RAI GEBOUW bv, Europaplein, 1078 GZ Amsterdam, Netherlands. Tel (020) 5 491 212. Tx 10613.
14-16	INTERNATIONAL MARITIME EXPOSITION (SNAME)	New York Hilton Hotel **New York**	REBER-FRIEL COMPANY, 221 King Manor Drive, King of Prussia, PA 19406. Tel (215) 272 4020.
December			
4-7	GASTECH '90	Rai Halls **Amsterdam**	BML BUSINESS MEETINGS LTD (Address as for RO-RO '90 15-17 May)

Conferences and Seminars.

The Legal Publishing and Conferences Division of Lloyd's of London Press regularly hold international Conferences and Seminars on shipping, insurance, legal and technical subjects.

The Conferences, generally of two days' duration, on topical matters, regularly attract over 200 decision makers worldwide.

The Seminars, spread over three or four days, are restricted to 35 delegates to enable maximum discussion and are used as a training ground.

Full details can be obtained from Legal Publishing & Conferences Division, Lloyd's of London Press Ltd, One Singer Street, London EC2A 4LQ. Telephone: (01) 250 1500. Telex 987321 LLOYDS G. Facsimile (01) 250 0660.

Our New York office, 611 Broadway also runs a programme of courses and conferences. Telephone: (212) 529 9500. Telex: 7105812659 LLP PUBLISH NY. Fax: (212) 529 9826.

WEIGHTS AND MEASURES

UNITED KINGDOM WEIGHTS AND MEASURES

The Imperial System of weights and measures was the main system of measurement in the United Kingdom until the late 1960s, although the use of metric units for most purposes was legalised by the Weights and Measures (Metric System) Act of 1897. The transition to the Metric System – The International System of Units (SI), recommended by the 1960 General Conference of Weights and Measures – is taking place gradually.

IMPERIAL SYSTEM

Length

12 inches (in)	= 1 foot (ft)
3 feet	= 1 yard (yd)
1760 yards	= 1 mile (mi)

Area

144 square inches (in²)	= 1 square foot (ft²)
9 square feet	= 1 square yard (yd²)
4840 square yards	= 1 acre

Capacity

5 fluid ounces (fl oz)	= 1 gill
4 gills	= 1 pint (pt)
2 pints	= 1 quart (qt)
4 quarts	= 1 gallon (gal)
8 gallons	= 1 bushel (bu)
8 bushels	= 1 quarter (qr)

Volume

1728 cubic inches (in³)	= 1 cubic foot (ft³)
27 cubic feet	= 1 cubic yard (yd³)

Weight (avoirdupois)

437.5 grains (gr)	= 1 ounce (oz)
16 drams (dr)	= 1 ounce
16 ounces	= 1 pound (lb)
28 pounds	= 1 quarter (qr)
4 quarters	= 1 hundredweight (cwt)
20 hundredweights	= 1 ton

METRIC SYSTEM

Length

10 millimetres (mm)	= 1 centimetre (cm)
10 centimetres	= 1 decimetre (dm)
100 centimetres	= 1 metre (m)
10 decimetres	= 1 metre
1000 metres	= 1 kilometre (km)

Area

100 square millimetres (mm²)	= 1 square centimetre (cm²)
100 square centimetres	= 1 square decimetre (dm²)
100 square decimetres	= 1 square metre (m²)
10000 square metres	= 1 hectare (ha)

Capacity

10 millilitres (ml)	= 1 centilitre (cl)
10 centilitres	= 1 decilitre (dl)
100 centilitres	= 1 litre (l)
100 litres	= 1 hectolitre (hl)

Volume

1000 cubic millimetres (mm³)	= 1 cubic centimetre (cm³)
1000 cubic centimetres	= 1 cubic decimetre (dm³)
1000 cubic decimetres	= 1 cubic metre (m³)

Weight (mass)

1000 milligrams (mg)	= 1 gram (g)
1000 grams	= 1 kilogram (kg)
1000 kilograms	= 1 tonne (t)

UNITED STATES SYSTEM

Units of measurement in the United States are the same as the Imperial System with certain exceptions, mainly for capacity and weight. Old Winchester measures are used instead of Imperial.

Capacity measurement is dependent on commodity being liquid or dry.

Dry measure

US dry bushel = 0.969 Imperial bushel

	= 0.3524 hectolitres.
2 pints	= 1 quart
4 quarts	= 1 gallon
2 gallons	= 1 peck
4 pecks	= 1 bushel

Liquid measure

US gallon = 0.83267 Imperial gallon

	= 3.785 litres.
8 drams	= 1 ounce
4 ounces	= 1 gill
4 gills	= 1 pint
2 pints	= 1 quart
4 quarts	= 1 gallon

Weight

16 drams	= 1 ounce
16 ounces	= 1 pound
100 pounds	= 1 short hundredweight
2000 pounds	= 1 short ton
20 short hundredweights	= 1 short ton

CONVERSION OF BAROMETRIC READINGS IN INCHES INTO MILLIBARS

Equivalents in Millibars of inches of Mercury at 32°F and Standard Gravity 980.665 cm/sec².

Mercury Inches	.00	.01	.02	.03	.04	.05	.06	.07	.08	.09
					Millibars					
27.0	914.3	914.7	915.0	915.3	915.7	916.0	916.4	916.7	917.0	917.4
27.1	917.7	918.1	918.4	918.7	919.1	919.4	919.7	920.1	920.4	920.7
27.2	921.1	921.4	921.8	922.1	922.5	922.8	923.1	923.5	923.8	924.1
27.3	924.5	924.8	925.2	925.5	925.8	926.2	926.5	926.9	927.2	927.5
27.4	927.9	928.2	928.5	928.9	929.2	929.6	929.9	930.2	930.6	930.9
27.5	931.3	931.6	931.9	932.3	932.6	933.0	933.3	933.6	934.0	934.3
27.6	934.6	935.0	935.3	935.7	936.0	936.3	936.7	937.0	937.4	937.7
27.7	938.0	938.4	938.7	939.0	939.4	939.7	940.1	940.4	940.7	941.1
27.8	941.4	941.8	942.1	942.4	942.8	943.1	943.4	943.8	944.1	944.5
27.9	944.8	945.1	945.5	945.8	946.2	946.5	946.8	947.2	947.5	947.9
28.0	948.2	948.5	948.9	949.2	949.5	949.9	950.2	950.6	950.9	951.2
28.1	951.6	951.9	952.3	952.6	952.9	953.3	953.6	953.9	954.3	954.6
28.2	955.0	955.3	955.6	956.0	956.3	956.7	957.0	957.3	957.7	958.0
28.3	958.3	958.7	959.0	959.4	959.7	960.0	960.4	960.7	961.1	961.4
28.4	961.7	962.1	962.4	962.8	963.1	963.4	963.8	964.1	964.4	964.8
28.5	965.1	965.5	965.8	966.1	966.5	966.8	967.2	967.5	967.8	968.2
28.6	968.5	968.8	969.2	969.5	969.9	970.2	970.5	970.9	971.2	971.6
28.7	971.9	972.2	972.6	972.9	973.2	973.6	973.9	974.3	974.6	974.9
28.8	975.3	975.6	976.0	976.3	976.6	977.0	977.3	977.7	978.0	978.3
28.9	978.7	979.0	979.3	979.7	980.0	980.4	980.7	981.0	981.4	981.7
29.0	982.1	982.4	982.7	983.1	983.4	983.7	984.1	984.4	984.8	985.1
29.1	985.4	985.8	986.1	986.5	986.8	987.1	987.5	987.8	988.1	988.5
29.2	988.8	989.2	989.5	989.8	990.2	990.5	990.9	991.2	991.5	991.9
29.3	992.2	992.6	992.9	993.2	993.6	993.9	994.2	994.6	994.9	995.3
29.4	995.6	995.9	996.3	996.6	997.0	997.3	997.6	998.0	998.3	998.6
29.5	999.0	999.3	999.7	1000.0	1000.3	1000.7	1001.0	1001.4	1001.7	1002.0
29.6	1002.4	1002.7	1003.0	1003.4	1003.7	1004.1	1004.4	1004.7	1005.1	1005.4
29.7	1005.8	1006.1	1006.4	1006.8	1007.1	1007.5	1007.8	1008.1	1008.5	1008.8
29.8	1009.1	1009.5	1009.8	1010.2	1010.5	1010.8	1011.2	1011.5	1011.9	1012.2
29.9	1012.5	1012.9	1013.2	1013.5	1013.9	1014.2	1014.6	1014.9	1015.2	1015.6
30.0	1015.9	1016.3	1016.6	1016.9	1017.3	1017.6	1017.9	1018.3	1018.6	1019.0
30.1	1019.3	1019.6	1020.0	1020.3	1020.7	1021.0	1021.3	1021.7	1022.0	1022.4
30.2	1022.7	1023.0	1023.4	1023.7	1024.0	1024.4	1024.7	1025.1	1025.4	1025.7
30.3	1026.1	1026.4	1026.8	1027.1	1027.4	1027.8	1028.1	1028.4	1028.8	1029.1
30.4	1029.5	1029.8	1030.1	1030.5	1030.8	1031.2	1031.5	1031.8	1032.2	1032.5
30.5	1032.8	1033.2	1033.5	1033.9	1034.2	1034.5	1034.9	1035.2	1035.6	1035.9
30.6	1036.2	1036.6	1036.9	1037.3	1037.6	1037.9	1038.3	1038.6	1038.9	1039.3
30.7	1039.6	1040.0	1040.3	1040.6	1041.0	1041.3	1041.7	1042.0	1042.3	1042.7
30.8	1043.0	1043.3	1043.7	1044.0	1044.4	1044.7	1045.0	1045.4	1045.7	1046.1
30.9	1046.4	1046.7	1047.1	1047.4	1047.7	1048.1	1048.4	1048.8	1049.1	1049.4

APPROXIMATE MULTIPLYING FACTORS FOR CRUDE OIL

Based on world average density, excluding natural gas liquids.

From \ To	Tonnes	Long Tons	Short Tons	Barrels	Kilolitres (m³)	1,000 Gallons (Imp.)	1,000 Gallons (U.S.)
				MULTIPLY BY			
Tonnes	1	0.984	1.102	7.33	1.16	0.256	0.308
Long Tons	1.016	1	1.120	7.45	1.18	0.261	0.313
Short Tons	0.907	0.893	1	6.65	1.05	0.233	0.279
Barrels	0.136	0.134	0.150	1	0.159	0.035	0.042
Kilolitres (m³)	0.863	0.849	0.951	6.29	1	0.220	0.264
1000 Galls (Imp.)	3.91	3.83	4.29	28.6	4.55	1	1.201
1000 Galls (U.S.)	3.25	3.19	3.58	23.8	3.79	0.833	1

APPROXIMATE MULTIPLYING FACTORS FOR CRUDE OIL AND PRODUCTS

	Barrels to Tonnes	Tonnes to Barrels	Barrels/Day to Tonnes/Year	Tonnes/Year to Barrels/Day
		MULTIPLY BY		
Crude Oil	0.136	7.33	49.8	0.0201
Motor Spirit	0.118	8.45	43.2	0.0232
Kerosine	0.128	7.80	46.8	0.0214
Gas/Diesel	0.133	7.50	48.7	0.0205
Fuel Oil	0.149	6.70	54.5	0.0184

POINTS OF THE COMPASS AND THEIR ANGLES WITH THE MERIDIAN

North		Points	°	′	″	Points	South	
		¼	2	48	45	¼		
		½	5	37	30	½		
		¾	8	26	15	¾		
N by E	N by W	1	11	15	0	1	S by E	S by W
		1¼	14	3	45	1¼		
		1½	16	52	30	1½		
		1¾	19	41	15	1¾		
NNE	NNW	2	22	30	0	2	SSE	SSW
		2¼	25	18	45	2¼		
		2½	28	7	30	2½		
		2¾	30	56	15	2¾		
NE by N	NW by N	3	33	45	0	3	SE by S	SW by S
		3¼	36	33	45	3¼		
		3½	39	22	30	3½		
		3¾	41	11	15	3¾		
NE	NW	4	45	0	0	4	SE	SW
		4¼	47	48	45	4¼		
		4½	50	37	30	4½		
		4¾	53	26	15	4¾		
NE by E	NW by W	5	56	15	0	5	SE by E	SW by W
		5¼	59	3	45	5¼		
		5½	61	52	30	5½		
		5¾	64	41	15	5¾		
ENE	WNW	6	67	30	0	6	ESE	WSW
		6¼	70	18	45	6¼		
		6½	73	7	30	6½		
		6¾	75	56	15	6¾		
E by N	W by N	7	78	45	0	7	E by S	W by S
		7¼	81	33	45	7¼		
		7½	84	22	30	7½		
		7¾	87	11	15	7¾		
East	West	8	90	0	0	8	East	West

CONTAINER DIMENSIONS AND CAPACITIES

General Cargo Containers

20ft x 8ft x 8ft (6.1m x 2.4m x 2.4m)

Minimum Interior Dimensions			Door Dimensions		Cubic Capacity (minimum)	Tare Weight (maximum)	Payload (ISO)
Length	Width	Height	Width	Height			
5905mm	2337mm	2235mm	2337mm	2138mm	30.8m³	2610kg	17710kg
232½in	92in	88in	92in	84½in	1090ft³	5752lb	39033lb

Tare weights vary between 1700kg and 2610kg. Gross weights between 20320kg and 22860kg.

20ft x 8ft x 8ft 6in (6.1m x 2.4m x 2.6m)

Minimum Interior Dimensions			Door Dimensions		Cubic Capacity (minimum)	Tare Weight (maximum)	Payload (ISO)
Length	Width	Height	Width	Height			
5893mm	2330mm	2381mm	2330mm	2273mm	32.7m³	2450kg	17870kg
232in	91¾in	93¾in	91¾in	89½in	1155ft³	5401lb	39396lb

Tare weights vary between 1854kg and 2450kg. Gross weights between 22860kg and 24000kg.

40ft x 8ft x 8ft 6in (12.2m x 2.4m x 2.6m)

Minimum Interior Dimensions			Door Dimensions		Cubic Capacity (minimum)	Tare Weight (maximum)	Payload (ISO)
Length	Width	Height	Width	Height			
12015mm	2337mm	2362mm	2337mm	2260mm	66.3m³	3900kg	26580kg
473in	92in	93in	92in	89in	2341ft³	8600lb	58582lb

Tare weights vary between 3450kg and 3900kg. Gross weight is 30480kg.

BEAUFORT WIND SCALE AND SEA DISTURBANCE TABLE

Wind Force*	Speed in knots†	Description	Wave Height in metres‡		Sea Conditions
			Avge	Max	
0	Less than 1	Calm	—	—	Sea like a mirror.
1	1-3	Light air	0.1	0.1	Ripples with the appearance of scales are formed but without foam crests.
2	4-6	Light breeze	0.2	0.3	Small wavelets, still short but more pronounced; crests have a glass appearance and do not break.
3	7-10	Gentle breeze	0.6	1.0	Large wavelets. Crests begin to break. Foam of glassy appearance. Perhaps scattered white horses.
4	11-16	Moderate breeze	1.0	1.5	Small waves, becoming longer; fairly frequent white horses.
5	17-21	Fresh breeze	2.0	2.5	Moderate waves, taking a more pronounced long form; many white horses are formed. (Chance of some spray.)
6	22-27	Strong breeze	3.0	4.0	Large waves begin to form; the white foam crests are more extensive everywhere. (Probably some spray.)
7	28-33	Near gale	4.0	5.5	Sea heaps up and white foam from breaking waves begins to be blown in streaks along the direction of the wind.
8	34-40	Gale	5.5	7.5	Moderately high waves of greater length; edges of crests begin to break in spindrift. The foam is blown in well-marked streaks along the direction of the wind.
9	41-47	Strong gale	7.0	10.0	High waves. Dense streaks of foam along the direction of the wind. Crests of waves begin to topple, tumble and roll over. Spray may affect visibility.
10	48-55	Storm	9.0	12.5	Very high waves with long overhanging crests. The resulting foam in great patches is blown in dense white streaks along the direction of the wind. On the whole the surface of the sea takes on a white appearance. The tumbling of the sea becomes heavy and shock-like. Visibility is affected.
11	56-63	Violent storm	11.5	16.0	Exceptionally high waves. (Small and medium-sized ships might for a time be lost to view behind the waves.) The sea is completely covered with long white patches of foam lying along the direction of the wind. Everywhere the edges of the wave crests are blown into froth. Visibility is affected.
12	64-71	Hurricane	14 or over		The air is filled with foam and spray. Sea completely white with driving spray; visibility is very seriously affected.

* The Beaufort wind force scale extends to Force 17 (up to 118 knots), but Force 12 is the highest which can be identified from the appearance of the sea.
† Determined at coast stations for a height of 10 metres above sea level. The Gale Warning Signal is hoisted in the British Isles for winds which may reach Force 8 or more.

‡ The approximate height of waves is shown indicating for each wind strength the average wave height and the likely maximum wave height. In enclosed waters or when near land with an offshore wind, wave heights will be smaller and the waves steeper.

BELLS AND WATCHES

The day of 24 hours is divided into seven watches and commences at noon.

Number of Bells	1200 to 1600 Afternoon watch	1600 to 1800 First Dog watch	1800 to 2000 Second or Last Dog watch	2000 to 2400 First watch	2400 to 0400 Middle watch	0400 to 0800 Morning watch	0800 to 1200 Forenoon watch
8	1200	1600	—	2000	2400	0400	0800
1	1230	1630	1830	2030	0030	0430	0830
2	1300	1700	1900	2100	0100	0500	0900
3	1330	1730	1930	2130	0130	0530	0930
4	1400	1800	—	2200	0200	0600	1000
5	1430	—	—	2230	0230	0630	1030
6	1500	—	—	2300	0300	0700	1100
7	1530	—	—	2330	0330	0730	1130
1	1545	—	1945	2345	0345	0745	1145
8	1600	—	2000	2400	0400	0800	1200

CONVERSION FACTORS AND TABLES

Length

Inches to millimetres	× 25·4	Millimetres to inches	× 0·0394
Inches to centimetres	× 2·54	Centimetres to inches	× 0·3937
Feet to centimetres	× 30·48	Centimetres to feet	× 0·0328
Feet to metres	× 0·3048	Metres to feet	× 3·2808
Yards to metres	× 0·9144	Metres to yards	× 1·0936
Miles to kilometres	× 1·6093	Kilometres to miles	× 0·6214

Weight (mass)

Pounds to kilograms	× 0·4536	Kilograms to pounds	× 2·2046
Tons to tonnes	× 1·016	Tonnes to tons	× 0·9842
Short tons to tonnes	× 0·90718	Tonnes to short tons	× 1·102

PHONETIC TABLES

For the pronunciation of letters and figures by radio-telephony or voice over a loud-hailer.

The syllables to be **emphasised** are in **bold type**.

Letter-Spelling Table

Letter	Code Word	Pronounced as
A	Alfa	**AL** FAH
B	Bravo	**BRAH** VOH
C	Charlie	**CHAR** LEE (or **SHAR** LEE)
D	Delta	**DELL** TAH
E	Echo	**ECK** OH
F	Foxtrot	**FOKS** TROT
G	Golf	**GOLF**
H	Hotel	HOH **TELL**
I	India	**IN** DEE AH
J	Juliette	**JEW** LEE **ETT**
K	Kilo	**KEY** LOH
L	Lima	**LEE** MAH
M	Mike	MIKE
N	November	NO **VEM** BER
O	Oscar	**OSS** CAH
P	Papa	PAH **PAH**
Q	Quebec	KEH **BEEK**
R	Romeo	**ROW** ME OH
S	Sierra	SEE **AIR** RAH
T	Tango	**TANG** GO
U	Uniform	YOU NEE FORM (or **OO** NEE FORM)
V	Victor	**VIK** TAH
W	Whiskey	**WISS** KEY
X	X-ray	**ECKS** RAY
Y	Yankee	**YANG** KEY
Z	Zulu	**ZOO** LOO

Figure-Spelling Table
Each syllable should be equally emphasised.

0	Nadazero	NAH-DAH-ZAY-ROH
1	Unaone	OO-NAH-WUN
2	Bissotwo	BEES-SOH-TOO
3	Terrathree	TAY-RAH-TREE
4	Kartefour	KAR-TAY-POWER
5	Pantafive	PAN-TAH-FIVE
6	Soxisix	SOK-SEE-SIX
7	Setteseven	SAY-TAY-SEVEN
8	Oktoeight	OK-TOH-AIT
9	Novenine	NO-VAY-NINER
Decimal point	Decimal	DAY-SEE-MAL
Full stop	STOP	STOP

SIGNAL STRENGTH

1. Scarcely Perceptible.
2. Weak.
3. Fairly Good.
4. Good.
5. Very Good.

LOAD LINE

The Load Line below which the vessel may not submerge, varies with the waters and areas through which she passes.

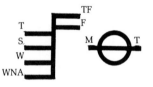

TF:	Tropical Fresh Water.
F:	Fresh Water.
T:	Tropical.
S,	together with horizontal line through circle: Summer Salt Water Load Line.
W:	Winter Salt Water Load Line.
WNA:	Winter loading for vessels crossing the North Atlantic that are less than 330 ft. in length.

VISIBILITY TABLE

Scale	Description	Limit of visibility
0	Dense fog	50 yards
1	Thick fog	300 yards
2	Fog	600 yards
3	Moderate fog	½ mile
4	Mist or thin fog	1 mile
5	Poor visibility	2 miles
6	Moderate visibility	5 miles
7	Good visibility	10 miles
8	Very good visibility	30 miles
9	Exceptional visibility	over 30 miles

INDEX TO ADVERTISERS